MOROCCO SINCE 1830

To Wong Mun Wei

C. R. PENNELL

Morocco since 1830

A History

NEW YORK UNIVERSITY PRESS
WASHINGTON SQUARE, NEW YORK

First published in the U.S.A. in 2000 by
NEW YORK UNIVERSITY PRESS
Washington Square
New York, NY 10003

Library of Congress Cataloging-in-Publication Data

Pennell, C.R.
Morocco since 1830: a history / C.R. Pennell.
p. cm.
Includes bibliographical references and index.
ISBN 0-8147-6676-5 (cloth) — ISBN 0-8147-6677-3 (pbk.)
1. Morocco—History—19th century. 2. Morocco—History—20th century. I. Title.
DT324P386 1999
964'. 03—dc21 99-33567
CIP

CONTENTS

Preface and Acknowledgements xv

Glossary xxiv

Abbreviations xxxiii

Transcription of Arabic xxxiii

Chapters

1. 1830 1

The face of Morocco 3
Tribes 7
Politics and religion 9
The Sultan 12
Jihad and the right to rule 14
The 'ulama 16
The Makhzan 18
The army 21
Finances 22
Trade and commerce 23
Commerce and the British 24
Rebellion 26
Bilad al-siba and bilad al-makhzan 28
Coercion and co-option 29
The towns 30
The slaves 32
The Jews 34
Morocco as mosaic 37

2. DEFEAT 40

The European challenge 40
The Algerian challenge 41
The Makhzan's commerce 43
Local commerce 45
Military weakness 46
Revolts 47
Defeat in Algeria 48

The call for reform 49
Military reform 51
The modernisers 52
Disorder 53
British and French rivalry 55
Opening Moroccan markets 58
The rise of John Drummond-Hay 60
The physical environment 62
Moroccan views of Europe 63
War with Spain 64
The moral of defeat 66

3. REFORM 68

The inheritance of the Spanish war 68
The aims of European diplomacy 70
Military reform 72
Economic reform 75
Technological innovation 76
Administration 78
Currency reform 79
Protégés 80
Jews 83
The Madrid conference 85
The Morocco question 87
Trade, protection, diplomacy and self-promotion 88
The rich and powerful 91
Rebels against the Sultan 94
Siba 96
The rise of the big qaids 98
Disorder and resistance 100
The Mahalla 103
Trade, treason and faith 105
The end of the old order 108
The failure of reforms? 109

4. COLLAPSE 111

Ba Ahmad's Morocco 111
The new Makhzan 111
Rebellion and repression 112
The big qaids 114

Economic problems 115
European diplomacy 117

Abdelaziz's Morocco 121

The new regime 121
Abdelaziz's reforms 122
Morocco and the European Entente 124
A generalised siba 125
The big qaids 126
The revolt of Abu Himara 127
The rise of the French 129
Resistance to French influence 130
The conference at Algeciras 132
The consequences of Algeciras 133
The origins of revolution 134
The revolution of Moulay Abdelhafid 136

Abdelhafid's Morocco 136

The bay'a compromised 138
Salafiyya 141
Constitutional nationalism 143
The Spanish and French advance in the east 145
The economic crisis 146
The French take-over 147
The revolt in the north and the French occupation of Fez 149
The de-internationalisation of the Morocco question 150
The imposition of the French Protectorate 151
The haemorrhaging Makhzan 152

5. CONQUEST 154

The Fez mutiny 155
Lyautey in Morocco 156
The abdication of Moulay Abdelhafid 157
El Hiba 157
The theory of Protectorate 158
Government in the French Protectorate 160
The big qaids 163
The origin of the Berber policy 164
The Spanish Protectorate 166
The international zone in Tangier 167
The beginnings of conquest 168
The Spanish zone 169

Land as a commodity 171
New cities 172
The legal façade 172
The First World War 174
The big qaids 175
Social policy of the French Protectorate 176
The wartime economy 178
The Spanish zone 180
Morocco After the First World War 182
Restructuring the administration 182
The end of the big qaids and the rise of Si Thami El Glaoui 183
Reform under colonialism 185
The Free School movement 186
'Useful' and 'Necessary' Morocco 186
The boundaries of Morocco 187
The Rif War 188
The attack on El Raisuni 188
The expectations of the Rifis and their leader 192
The international zone reborn 195
Divided economies 197
Taxation and land sales 198
The development of capitalist agriculture 200
Employment 201
The Jews and Zionism 203
The bases of nationalism 205
The Protectorate in question 207
A society of dualities 209

6. NATIONALISM 211

The final stages of conquest 216
The roots of future problems 218
The economic crisis 219
How the colons coped 224
Protest and nationalism 227
The Plan de Réformes 232
Politics in the Spanish zone 233
Sport and popular culture 236
The limits of economic growth 239
The strikes of 1936 241

General Noguès as Resident-General 242
Trade unions for the French 242
Economic reform 244
Nogués and the nationalists 245
The policies of the Hizb al-Watani 246
Campaigns and suppression 247
The Spanish Civil War and the Spanish zone 247
Privileged or underprivileged Jews? 250

7. WARS 254

The Second World War in Morocco 254
The war in the Spanish Zone 256
The third player: the United States 259
The Jews during the Second World War 261
The meeting at Casablanca 262
The Istiqlal manifesto 264
Morocco under the Free French 265

Morocco after the Second World War 268
The liberal experiment 268
The Spanish zone 271
The visit to Tangier, 1947 272
The Indian summer of settler colonialism 272
The broad nationalist coalition 274
The foreign policy of the nationalists 276
Morocco and Israel 277
The campaign against Sidi Mohammed 278
Guillaume as Resident-general 279
The protectorate's coup d'état 280
The ben Arafa interlude 283
The nationalists in the Spanish zone 285
War in the French zone 285
Aix-les-Bains 288
The Liberation Army 289
The return of the King 290
Independence from Spain 292
Independence undefined 294

8. INDEPENDENCE 297

The role of the King 299

The levers of coercive power 299
The entrenchment of Istiqlal 303
Rural rebellions 304
The economics of independence 305
Istiqlal undermined 307

Morocco's Place in the World 309

The Israeli-Palestinian conflict and the Moroccan Jews 309
The war in Algeria 311
The Cold War 312
The triumph of the palace 313

9. KINGSHIP 317

King Hassan's government 319
The politics of elites 319
The regime and its enemies 321
The first constitution 321
The economic crisis 324
The crisis in the rural world 327
The crisis in the cities 329
The second constitution 330
The Skhirat coup 331
The second coup 332
Morocco's expanding limits 333
The Spanish Sahara 334
The road to the International Court 337
The Green March 339

The New Morocco 340

The Saharan war 340
The diplomacy of the new Morocco 342
The Moroccan Jews 344
The economics of the new nationalism 345
A political opening in the new Morocco? 347

A New Society Beyond the State? 348

Women 348
An informal society with informal politics 351
The Islamists 352
The rebellion in Casablanca 354
The need for a new consensus 355

10. ADJUSTMENTS 356

The economic crisis 356
Alienation from the political process 361
The Islamic movement 362
Women and power 364
Human rights 365
Arab allies and the Saharan war 366
The alliance with the West and with Israel 368
The Gulf War 370
Rebuilding 372
Liberalising the economy 373
Transition 374

The Return of the Travellers? 380

The shape of the land 380
A mosaic of cultural choices 382
Public mass culture 384
The mass culture of sport 386
A society with women 387
From Sultan to King 388

Appendix
Sultans and Kings of Morocco; French Residents-General; High Commissioners of the Spanish Protectorate 392

Bibliography 394

Index 413

ILLUSTRATIONS

View of Moulay-Idriss, 1920s, by Azouaou Mammeri 2

between pages 136 and 137

The murder of Dr Mauchamp, Marrakesh, 1907
Railway linking Melilla with iron ore mines at Seghanghan
Casablanca after French bombardment, 1907

between pages 176 and 177

Moroccan soldiers in the French army assembling in the early stage of the conquest
Moroccan soldiers embarking for France in the 1914-18 war
Tangier sea front, early 1920s
The Khalifa of the Spanish Zone

between pages 190 and 191

House of Walter Harris, Tangier
House of local army commander, Guercif
Two Rifi *qadis*, 1919
Shackle used to control Spanish prisoners of the Rifis, 1921
Rif bomb made from a tin can

between pages 226 and 227

Hotel patronised by French colons
Galeries Lafayette
General Mohamed ben Mizian

Hassan II mosque, Casablanca *facing page* 344

MAPS

Morocco in the nineteenth century 165
The division of Morocco into two Protectorates 189
The Rif war 220
Administrative divisions, 1940 221
The former Spanish Sahara 341
Greater Morocco 341

FIGURES

Exports and imports, 1885-1900 117
Moroccan trade during the Protectorate 189
Rainfall in Casablanca, 1950s 307
The relation between rainfall and G.D.P., 1970-82 324
Moroccan tourism in the economy 359

TABLES

Population of Moroccan cities, 1912 and 1921 179
National trade in Moroccan zones, 1929 197
Moroccans living abroad, 1986 370

PREFACE AND ACKNOWLEDGEMENTS

In 1970 Abdallah Laroui complained that the Maghrib suffered from

> [...] always having inept historians: geographers with brilliant ideas, functionaries with scientific pretensions, soldiers priding themselves on their culture, art historians who refuse to specialise, and, on a higher level, historians without linguistic training or linguists and archaeologists without historical training. All these historians refer the reader back to each other and invoke each other's authority. The consequence is a conspiracy which puts the most adventurous hypotheses into circulation and ultimately imposes them as established truths.[1]

The historians to whom Laroui referred in *The History of the Maghrib* were not Moroccans. Although there were Moroccan historians, and chroniclers, before colonial rule was imposed on his country, and some of them were certainly functionaries first and historians second, the jibe was about Frenchmen, whose writings were inseparable from the fact of colonial rule. His complaint about the self-referencing nature of their writing is a familiar one to anyone who has read Edward Said, though Laroui predates Said by some eight years. Clearer-sighted than Said, he went on to acknowledge that post-colonial Maghribi historians were no better: 'torn between political leaders, schoolteachers, and imitators of medieval historians, the reader can only console himself with the thought that, after all, the serene certainty of these men is no more unfounded than that of their adversaries, of whom as it happens they are more respectful than they should be'.[2]

Laroui went on, in 1970, to lay down the agenda for a new study of history of the Maghrib, a re-reading of the Maghribi past.[3] His 'attempt at a synthesis', as he called it, stretched back to the dawn of humanity, a timescale that included so many lacunae

1 Abdallah Laroui, *The History of the Maghrib: an Interpretive Essay*, trans. Ralph Mannheim (Princeton University Press, 1977), 3. The book was originally published in French in 1970.

2 *Ibid.*, 4.

3 *Ibid.*, 6.

that only an outline could be discerned. Laroui admitted to many problems, not least that of periodisation. Should the history of North-west Africa be seen in terms of dynasties, or of European divisions of time – 'Antiquity', the 'Middle Ages' and the 'Modern' periods – or in terms of waves of conquerors – Carthaginian, Byzantine, Arab, Turkish, European? The first option necessarily leaves much outside the city shrouded in darkness; the second is a time-frame that has little relevance to the flow of events in northern Africa, the third tends to exclude the conquered and so breaks the long-term continuities of the region (and, equally, largely excludes the Berber-speaking population).

And what should be the unit of analysis? Laroui's book was not about Morocco, but the three countries of the Maghrib: Tunisia, Algeria and Morocco: in appearance at least, a North African concept of space. This did take account of what the region shared: dynasties that crossed over what are now national boundaries; trade routes and agricultural patterns that knew no modern boundaries; a common religion, albeit one that stretched far beyond north-western Africa (and which Laroui does not mention in his introduction.) Yet such a North African concept of space happens to neatly coincide with the extent of French colonial rule, and excludes what is now western Libya, an Italian colony, but before that, as the Ottoman province of Tripoli, geographically and culturally part of the Maghrib.

Finally, Laroui's was a political history, limiting in itself, but one, he said, that was worth experimenting with 'while awaiting the development of an economic and social historiography'.[4] It was also a consciously *politicising* history, part of an effort to decolonise the past. But even as Laroui wrote, he complained that this effort was already degenerating into abstract criticism, because it was easier to criticise colonial historians than to provide the documentary material on which to base such reassessments.[5]

When Laroui wrote, the past and its interpretations were already the subject of political debate, not only between anti-colonialists and colonialists but also between left-wing and right-wing nationalists. In 1958, two years after independence, representatives of both wings of the nationalist movement published books about Moroccan history. One came from the right, ben Abdallah's *Les grands courants de la civilisation au Maroc,* equipped with an introduction by the historic leader of the bourgeois right-wing of the

4 *Ibid.*, 12.

5 *Ibid.*, 4.

nationalist movement, Allal El Fassi. The other was written by a young lawyer, Mohamed Lahbabi, and was provided with an introduction by the historic leader of the petty-bourgeois and working class left of the nationalist movement, Mehdi Ben Barka. El Fassi's laudatory preface delimits the discussion to a defence against colonialists who belittle Islamic civilisation – and the book continues in the same vein. It is a polemic, in which history becomes a nationalist vehicle for rescuing the past from the colonialist grip.[6] Lahbabi's book is quite different: its purpose is to rescue the Moroccan past from other Moroccans, to challenge the nature of the colonial state that has been inherited by the post-colonial regime.[7] It is an attempt to argue that the Protectorate that had claimed to preserve Moroccan sovereignty and political identity had in fact traduced it, that the democratic elements in the pre-colonial political system had been removed, that the creation of the sultan as a figure who embodied all power in Morocco was a typically French one. What was needed was a real reassertion of Moroccan identity against the winners in the war of independence. For Lahbabi, the attack on the French conception of Morocco was not an attempt to redress past colonial slights, but an attempt to fight a current political battle.

It is clear that the battle-lines being drawn here were more complicated than a mere European versus Moroccan conflict. It is undoubtedly true that French colonialist historiography, conceived as it was in a desire to demonstrate the instability and despotism of Morocco, also provided many of the materials for a later reappraisal of pre-colonial Moroccan history, particularly by publishing chronicles written by earlier, Moroccan, historians and the European sources of the Moroccan past. It also focused on areas that were particularly useful to its own endeavour, which were not covered in the chronicle histories: religious brotherhoods were a particular example, and the rural history of tribal structures was another.[8]

Moroccan historians were too few in number after independence, to do more than to dent the enormous weight of colonial historiography. In the 1960s some certainly tried to do so by con-

6 Ernest Gellner, 'The Struggle for Morocco's Past', *Middle East Journal*, 15 (1961): 79-90.

7 Mohamed Lahbabi, *Le Gouvernement marocain à l'aube du vingtième siècle*, 2nd edn. (Rabat: Les Éditions Maghrébines, 1975).

8 Mohamed El Mansour, 'Moroccan Historiography Since Independence', Michel Le Gall and Kenneth Perkins (eds) (Austin: University of Texas Press, 1997), 111-12.

centrating on Moroccan sources rather than on European ones and by taking a specifically nationalist perspective. Muhammad Manuni[9] relied upon Arabic sources to suggest that European intervention had strangled a nineteenth-century Moroccan renaissance at birth. Over a period of twenty years, beginning in the early 1960s, Germain Ayache, a Frenchman who took Moroccan nationality after independence, wrote a series of articles based almost entirely on Moroccan rather than European sources.[10] In them he drew a number of conclusions about the nature of the Moroccan nation – that there was a consciousness of a common identity well before colonialism that stretched far into the countryside and desert, and that even the remotest tribes owed allegiance, as well as taxes, to the sultan. This was a full-blooded rejection of the colonialists' history of disparate tribes controlled only with the greatest difficulty by a despotic sultan. Indeed, he blamed European intervention in the late nineteenth century for undermining the traditional system. Ayache was a Marxist, and his ideas parallelled many of those of Lahbabi: but they were also attractive to the Palace. Just as it had been under the colonial regime, history became a tool of the post-colonial state – the Royal Palace patronised historians, but in ways that legitimised itself. Equally, the ongoing French presence in Morocco meant that French historians continued to be active there, in the service of the new independent state.

In 1967 six historians, four of them French, came together to write a single-volume *Histoire du Maroc* that prefigured Laroui's by taking the history of the country from Roman times to independence.[11] It was essentially a high-school textbook, and an extremely good one. The authors spent no time philosophising about the nature of history or the relevance of periodisation (which would hardly have been suitable for the audience). Instead, they taught by example, by weaving questions of economic and intellectual history into the wider tapestry. Their framework was Moroccan-centred, although they recognised the wider Islamic and Maghribi context, and the legacy of European conquest. The book moved from pre-Islamic to Islamic Morocco, to the great dynasties of the al-Murabitun and al-Muwahhidun (Almoravids and Almohads)

9 Muhammad Manuni, *Mazahir yaqzat al-Maghrib al-hadith* (Rabat: Manshurat wizarat al-awqaf wa-l-shu'un al-islamiyya wa-l-thaqafa, 1973).

10 They are reprinted in Germain Ayache, *Études d'histoire marocaine* (Rabat: SMER, 1979).

11 Jean Brignon *et al.*, *Histoire du Maroc* (Casablanca: Librairie Nationale, 1967).

that coincided with the European Middle Ages, to the formation of a distinctly Moroccan identity after the beginning of the sixteenth century, under the pressure of European expansion, and finally to 'contemporary Morocco' – the nineteenth and twentieth century.

Yet there were problems with these approaches to history that blossomed in the years following independence. By rejecting the use of European archives, Ayache cut Morocco off from its international past, and by laying the blame for all Morocco's decadence on Europeans, he paradoxically (and certainly unintentionally) lessened the Moroccan role in making Moroccan history. One prominent, and more recent, Moroccan historian, Mohamed El Mansour, while he payed tribute to Ayache's influence and his effort to Moroccanise history, went on to describe the older scholar as an 'extremist' who failed to make clear how Moroccans themselves had participated in the country's collapse, and who put too much faith in official documentation.[12] This last charge was a strange, though not incorrect, one to make of a Marxist, for by doing so Ayache blunted the role of the common people in the making of Moroccan history.

By the 1970s the limitations of these approaches were already clear and a new generation of historians tried to reverse the focus on political questions, on the sultan and king, and the political parties of the independence period. To be sure, radical French historians – like Jacques Berque – had already set out down that road several decades before,[13] but Moroccan historians were also influenced by new trends in historiography that originated outside Morocco, particularly the *Annales* school. Even more important was the work of sociologists like Paul Pascon, another French radical who had taken Moroccan nationality. Pascon taught his students to link history and sociology in a way that shifted the emphasis away from the centre and on to local areas.[14]

This new social history, which called on the social sciences and literary and cultural theory, was also heavily influenced by American anthropologists and sociologists. In the late 1960s and early 1970s a number of American social scientists, and rather fewer historians,

12 El Mansour, 'Moroccan Historiography', 115-16.

13 Jacques Berque, *French North Africa: the Maghrib between Two World Wars*, trans. Jean Stewart, (London: Faber, 1967).

14 Paul Pascon, *Le Haouz de Marrakech*, 2 vols (Rabat: Centre Universitaire de la Recherche Scientifique, 1983). There is an abidged English edition: Paul Pascon, *Capitalism and Agriculture in the Haouz of Marrakesh*, trans. C. Edwin Vaughan and Veronique Ingman (London: Kegan Paul International [KPI], 1986).

wrote books and doctoral theses on Morocco, part of an expanding American interest in the Middle East and North Africa. Among the most influential was John Waterbury, whose book *The Commander of the Faithful*, published in 1971,[15] was an account of the Moroccan political and, to a lesser extent, financial elite in both sociological and historical terms. He explored the way they defined, and were defined by, the political culture of the country. Five years later David Hart, an American anthropologist who has spent much of his life working on tribal societies, and in particular those of northern Morocco, wrote a huge and scholarly study of a single tribe, the Aith Waryaghar,[16] and in the same year Kenneth Brown wrote an urban history and sociology of nineteenth-century Salé.[17] These books confirmed a shift in emphasis away from politics towards social history, but also towards very local histories. Nevertheless Hart's ideas on the political roles and organisation of tribes in particular were part of a generation of debate that was expressed in Gellner and Micaud's collection *Arabs and Berbers*, though the attention was sometimes given more by foreigners than by Moroccans.[18]

This new wave also challenged the French hegemony over Moroccan history, although many Moroccan scholars continued to be trained in France. Some Moroccans also studied in Britain in the 1970s, although, with a few exceptions, British interest in Morocco was relaxed. In any event this new wave of research, both by foreigners and by Moroccans (other Arabs paid little attention to Moroccan history) produced a great many tightly focused and localised studies, which left it open to the criticism that it became almost formulaic: a great deal was discovered of a descriptive nature, but it was not slotted into a more general framework, either theoretically or even as a narrative.[19] It did however open new areas of discussion: particularly about women and the poor.

Much of the discussion of women was also started by sociologists, but Fatima Mernissi, a Moroccan sociologist of world repute, helped bring the focus within a historical framework by publishing a book

15 John Waterbury, *Commander of the Faithful* (New York: Columbia University Press, 1970).

16 David M. Hart, *The Aith Waryaghar of the Moroccan Rif, an Ethnography and History* (Tucson: University of Arizona Press, 1976).

17 Kenneth L. Brown, *People of Salé: Tradition and Change in a Moroccan City 1830-1930* (Manchester University Press, 1976).

18 Ernest Gellner and Charles Micaud (eds), *Arabs and Berbers: From Tribe to Nation in North Africa* (London: Duckworth, 1972).

19 El Mansour, 'Moroccan Historiography', 118.

of biographies of poor and middle-class Moroccan women which was substantially based upon their own words.[20] Subsequently, Zakya Daoud wrote a full-length history of women in the Maghrib that referred feminist questions back to the overall economic and political narrative.[21] They were, however, twentieth-century accounts: only Mohammed Ennaji, one of Pascon's most prolific students, attempted to apply his teacher's sociological methods to the nineteenth century, in the context of his detailed study of slavery, another attempt to deal with a marginalised group.[22]

Similarly, work on urbanisation – particularly full length city studies of Rabat and Casablanca – was followed by Mohamed Salahdine's collection of biographical studies of people living on the edge of urban society: street traders, house-servants, and other players in the informal economy. The urban crisis that faced Moroccan society made these studies immediately relevant, and the search for the roots of the crisis pushed some researchers back into the past.

In the same vein, the political demands of the 1980s and 1990s led scholars, as well as activists, to write about the consequences of the political events for those who suffered from them, and particularly in terms of human rights. The reports of international organisations like Amnesty International and of Moroccan-based human rights organisations provided a detailed and frank account of mistreatment in prisons and restrictions of the freedom of expression. In a way, their concerns echoed those of European activists at the beginning of the century that linked human-rights abuses to the nature of the Moroccan state and so justified its overthrow and replacement by an allegedly more civilised regime. Not surprisingly, political analysis of the many misdeeds of the colonial regime had largely vanished during the Protectorate – except as a political campaign by nationalists. Only in the 1990s was there an attempt to look back over the colonial period to discover the roots of human rights abuses under the post-colonial regime, but nothing was written that resembled the long view of how the state controlled its subjects by force that Darius Rejali gave for Iran.[23] Abdellah Hammoudi, on the other hand, provided a crisp analysis of

20 Fatima Mernissi, *Doing Daily Battle: Interviews with Moroccan Women* (London: Women's Press, 1986).

21 Zakya Daoud, *Féminisme et politique au Maghreb* (Casablanca: Eddif, 1993).

22 Mohammed Ennaji, *Soldats, domestiques et concubines; L'esclavage au Maroc au XIXme siècle* (Casablanca: Eddif, 1994).

23 Darius Rejali, *Torture and Modernity: Self, Society and State in Modern Iran* (Boulder, CO: Westview Press, 1994).

authoritarianism in Morocco, connecting it to deeper structural relations in Moroccan society in which the 'state as arbitrator' manipulates divisions between social groups.[24]

Another area of Moroccan history only appeared in the late 1980s and 1990s as the full extent of the environmental crisis became apparent. This concentrated attention on the environmental history of Morocco once again was often localised – McNeill's study of the Rif,[25] or the articles in a collection edited by Swearingen and Bencherifa.[26] Only Swearingen's own history of irrigation in Morocco covered the country as a whole.[27] Equally importantly, from a methodological point of view, this last work illustrated the long-term continuities between the colonial and independent state. It may be that one reason why Morocco has been (and is) so very difficult to rule is that it is not an easy land to live in. The natural environment, and in particular the problems occasioned by unpredictable and irregular rainfall, as well as the ravages of human activity, have had a crucial effect on the political and economic policies of successive Moroccan rulers. They can be seen in the export policies of pre-colonial sultans (which helped to determine their relationship with European trading powers), in the irrigation policies of the colonial period that shaped the Protectorate administration's relationship with both the *colons* and the Moroccan population, and in the policies of the governments after independence that helped fix the pace of land reform (or lack of it), and once again determined the relationship with the developed economies. Some of this, of course, is the stuff of economic history, and well-enough explored; but some of it is environmental history in a broader sense and, in comparison, much less-known, with great lacunae in the historical narrative.

Against that environmental backdrop must be set not only the political narrative, but also an economic one. There have been several accounts of Moroccan economic history, particularly in the colonial period. Stewart's book, published in 1967, dealt with the colonial period and the morning of independence in macro-economic

24 Abdellah Hammoudi, *Master and Disciple: the Cultural Foundations of Moroccan Authoritarianism* (University of Chicago Press, 1997).

25 John Robert McNeill, *The Mountains of the Mediterranean World: an Environmental History, Studies in Environment and History* (Cambridge University Press, 1992).

26 W. Swearingen and Abdellatif Bencherifa (eds), *The North African Environment at Risk* (Boulder,CO: Westview Press, 1996).

27 Will D. Swearingen, *Moroccan Mirages: Agrarian Dreams and Deceptions, 1912-1986* (London: I.B. Tauris, 1988).

terms: it concentrated on the organisation of the economy, production and trade.[28] Miège's multi-volume work on the economic history of pre-colonial Morocco, published a few years earlier, did go into more detail about local economic activity, but it was still largely concerned with the trade with Europe.[29] This is an important consideration since for more than 200 years Europe has been Morocco's main trading partner, but it made it hard to understand the details of local trade and economic conditions. It was not until the 1980s that Moroccan and foreign researchers began publishing local studies of the economies of Morocco in the nineteenth century – Umar Afa's account of the Sous[30] and Daniel Schroeter's of Essaouira[31] stand out, but there was also a host of (particularly American) doctoral theses, some of which were never published.

Schroeter's book raised one of the other continuities of Moroccan history: the relationship between the Moroccan state and the Jews inside and outside Morocco. Since the late 1970s, a major historiographical effort has been put into understanding this relationship. How was a highly differentiated community, even after it had left the country, able to maintain such a close link to the trade relations and political developments inside Morocco? An examination of the role of the Jews in Morocco – only partly covered by Laskier's work (he largely ignored economics) – throws much light on the nature of the Moroccan state, economy and politics.[32]

What emerged from the enormous historiography of Morocco at the end of the twentieth century was a reflection of the society and the nation as a whole: a mosaic of material that illuminated the mosaic of cultural, economic and social interactions. But all the research that had been done on Moroccan history since the Brignon

28 Charles F. Stewart, *The Economy of Morocco, 1912-1962* (Cambridge, MA: Harvard Centre for Middle Eastern Studies, 1967).

29 Jean-Louis Miège, *Le Maroc et l'Europe* (1830-1894), 4 vols (Paris: Presses Universitaires de France, 1961-3).

30 Umar Afa, *Mas'alat al-nuqud fi tarikh al-Maghrib fi al-qarn al-tasi' 'ashar: (Sus, 1822-1906)* ([Agadir]: Jami'at al-Qadi 'Iyad, Kulliyat al-Adab w-al-'Ulum al-Insaniyah bi-Agadir, 1988).

31 Daniel Schroeter, *Merchants of Essaouira: Urban Society and Imperialism in Southwestern Morocco 1844-1886* (New York: Cambridge University Press, 1988).

32 Michael M. Laskier, *The Alliance Israélite Universelle and the Jewish Communities of Morocco, 1862-1962*, SUNY Series in Modern Jewish History (Albany, NY: State University of New York Press, 1983); and *North African Jewry in the Twentieth Century: The Jews of Morocco, Tunisia, and Algeria* (New York University Press, 1994).

collection of 1967 and Laroui's essay of 1970 had not produced a new synthesis or even a new narrative.

In consequence, some of the big themes of Moroccan history in the nineteenth and twentieth centuries had been not so much ignored as fragmented. When I began this book, I had no conception of the extent of these gaps in the story. Like most scholars who had worked on the history of Morocco, I had focused on the bit that I was dealing with and assumed that under the broad brush of generalisations there lay the more detailed elements from which a synthesis could be built. This was naive.

I discovered instead that there are enormous lacunae in the narrative; whole areas had not been touched upon. Some of these rather surprised me: the lack of a deep study of the Ba Ahmad period at the end of the nineteenth century, for instance, or of the Moroccan notability during the colonial period. Other gaps were less surprising. With the exception of women slaves – who, because they were treated as a commodity, were recorded in ways that free women were not – writing about the history of women is extremely difficult for the nineteenth century because of the limitations of sources. That is not quite so true of the history of the environment, for which there is scope for detailed studies of the nineteenth century and the early colonial period if the archives and other sources are re-examined; but the history of the environment is everywhere a new theme – and I am fortunate now to be working in Australia where many of the important questions about environmental history are being formulated. Some phenomena, such as organised team sports, barely existed before colonialism, so such a long-term view of them is clearly impossible. But, although football in particular captivates the emotions of huge numbers of Moroccans and excites both local and national feelings, no serious work has been done on it.

These considerations may help explain both why it took so long to write the book and some of its final shape. It seemed to me, as I read more and more widely, that the spine of most of the past narratives of Moroccan history – the concern with high-level political events, with who *ruled* Morocco – was not the only issue, that what was needed was to take account of these different approaches and knit them into a single narrative. At first sight that precludes any attempt on my part to impose an overall theory to explain or categorise Moroccan history. Attempts to do so are by their nature limiting, as they must focus on concepts that provide only a partial explanation.

There are nevertheless some themes. One is that the fragmented nature of the historical research is an unconscious (probably) reflection of the fragmented nature of Moroccan society as a whole. There is a history of Jews in Morocco, or of particular places or tribes or regions, or particular groups like women or the poor, or of particular religious brotherhoods, or of the governing elite precisely because those things *have* histories. They are identifiable units at the same time as they form part of the society as a whole. Part of the story is the way in which they interact with each other in the societal mosaic. Another part is the way they are *made* to interact.

One of the guiding forces in this enforced interaction is indeed the government structure, the Makhzan, and another important theme in the history of the nineteenth and twentieth century is the survival of the Alaoui dynasty itself. At the end of the twentieth century, Morocco is the only major country in the Arab-speaking world whose dynastic system of rule substantially predates colonialism, a fact that obviously calls for an explanation. The answer lies in the way in which the sultans, colonial rulers and kings have ably moved the tiles in the mosaic through the use of patronage, alliance, force and kinship in order to ensure, or at least allow their continued power.

Writing a book of this nature raises another question besides that of what it should cover. This is how it should be written. Following continuities through immediately suggests a chronological rather than a thematic framework, but what of the periodisation?

The starting point in 1830 was suggested by the importance for North Africa of the invasion of Algeria by French armies: that, for the first time, confronted Moroccans with the long-term problem of dealing with more powerful Europeans, disrupted the physical continuity of the Islamic *umma* and laid down a challenge that no Moroccan could avoid. It might be argued that in a book that seeks to go beyond the monarchy and the Morocco of the elites, it is rather surprising to fit the periodisation so much around the reigns of sultans and kings. Yet it is an essential feature of Moroccan history in the past two centuries that the death and accession of rulers have indeed marked important moments of change. The death of Moulay Abderrahmane in 1859 coincided with the defeat of his armies in the war with Spain and the introduction of an attempt at modernisation under his two successors. The death of Moulay Hassan in 1893 marked the collapse of the old system, to be replaced by a regent, an ill-prepared boy and his radical brother. The imposition of the French protectorate was accompanied by the imposition of a new Sultan, and his death coincided quite closely with the emergence of nationalist protest that led his son, Mohammed V, to take up a different mantle of leadership. Mohammed V's long reign is divided by two events: the beginning of the Second World War and the independence of Morocco, both of which marked turning points so crucial that they are obvious chronological milestones. It might be argued that his son continued many of the policies of the last years of Mohammed V's reign, yet the second half of the twentieth-century history of Morocco has been so marked by King Hassan's successful attempt to hold on to power that to focus attention elsewhere would be misleading. It was easier to choose a starting point than an ending point. For many Moroccans (not to speak of myriads of journalists and commentators) the death of King Hassan in July 1999 provided a moment for taking stock. Moroccan history thus melds indistinguishably into the present, but this is not a book of political science. We do not, of course, have the gift of hindsight to be able to deal with current events as historians. All that we can do is to see how these current events connect with what has gone before, to present them as the outcome of the main chronological themes.

The other principal consideration in writing this book has been to mitigate the effects of the periodisation by rulers by using, as far as possible, material that reflects the concerns of other groups in society. Mounia Bennani-Chraïbi, in her introduction to her account of young people in Morocco in the 1980s and 1990s,[33] wrote that an emphatic concern with the monarchy, the elites and the legitimacy of political movements and leaders has drowned out the voices of the middle class and the *déclassé* groups. She attempted to make those voices be heard by repeating them. This style of presentation is one that Fatima Mernissi has also used to great effect, and I do not think it a coincidence that both these authors are women: women are the archetypical excluded group from Moroccan history, and these two women sociologists are attempting quite literally to give them a voice. In any event, it is a stimulating approach, both for men and women. It is unfortunately also a difficult one to sustain: the voices of those outside the Moroccan elite are only occasionally heard directly before the current generation. I have, however, confined all my quotations to the words of contemporaries who participated in the events they are describing: Edward Drummond-Hay and Ahmad ibn Tuwayr, Salih el-Abdi and Ahmad al-Nasiri (though he was definitely part of the Moroccan elite), Ahmad el-Raisuni, Fatima Mernissi

[33] Mounia Bennani-Chraïbi, *Soumis et rebelles. Les jeunes au Maroc* (Casablanca: Editions le Fennec, 1994).

herself and Abdelmalek Lahlou, Mernissi's interviewees in the 1960s and 1970s and Rachida Yacoubi in the 1980s. If they occasionally repeat the assertions in the text, I make no apology for that: it is an attempt to anchor the assertions into some sort of personal experience.

When all is said and done, this is essentially a chronological history of Morocco in the past two centuries. It has no pretensions to an overall explanation; instead it tries to situate events in a context, to mark up the major themes, to outline the thrust of major events and perhaps, even in what it leaves out, to suggest areas where the study might be continued. In that sense, and also in the sense that the story is not over, it is strictly a provisional history.

Acknowledgments

First, I want to thank my family – Mun Wei, Sam and Sarah (in strict alphabetic order) – for their practical help and their tolerance over the long time in which this book was being written. I certainly would never have been able to do it without them.

Other people who have helped with suggestions, encouragement, information and ideas over the years are, in Morocco, Mohammed Chtatou, Mohammed el-Mansour, Abdelmajid Benjelloun, Rachida Yacoubi and Professor Chouki Binbin of the Royal Archives; in Britain, George Joffe, Michael Brett and Robert Drummond-Hay; in Spain, David Hart (a triple mention if that were possible), Rachid Raha and Vicente Moga; in the United States, Terry Burke, Ross Dunn and Daniel Schroeter; in the Netherlands, Paolo de Mas; in Singapore, Brian Farrell; and in Australia, Stephen Wheatcroft. If I were to expand on all the ways in which these people helped me, this acknowledgement section would be almost as long as the book, so I will leave it at that. I am really very grateful.

I made use of the services of the library of the University of Melbourne, the National Library of Australia, the Bibliothèque Générale in Rabat, the British Library in London, the Biblioteca Nacional in Madrid, and the library of the National University of Singapore. Some of the material here also reflects my visits to the archives of the Royal Palace in Rabat, the Gibraltar Government, the Public Record Office in London, the French Ministry of Foreign Affairs in Paris and (particularly) in Nantes, and the Spanish Foreign Ministry in Madrid. I thank the staff of all those institutions for their help over the years.

Since January 1996 I have been working in the History Department of the University of Melbourne and I would like to express my gratitude for the way in which my colleagues welcomed me and for the support of the successive heads of that department, and to Patricia Grimshaw and Peter McPhee, who have provided me with space and time, and, like Michael Dwyer of C. Hurst and Co., have not flustered me any more than I usually am by demands for immediate results.

Melbourne, July 1999 C.R.P.

GLOSSARY

abd (pl. *abid*) – slave: can be used in a religious sense in many names coupled with one of the names of God (e.g. Abd el-Rahman – 'servant of the Compassionate') or literally, in which case it often refers to black people. Many of the members of the army were originally black slaves and were referred to as the *Abid al-Bukhari*.

alim (pl. *ulama*) – literally, 'learned man'. Someone trained in the traditional Islamic sciences and qualified in Islamic law.

amir – title denoting something like 'prince, commander'. Sometimes given to governors of provinces or even of states (in Arabia).

Amir al-Muminin – 'Commander of the Faithful': the religious and political leader of the Islamic community, originally a title ascribed to the Caliph.

al-Azhar – Mosque-university in Cairo. The most important centre for the study of Islamic theology and law in the Sunni world. Founded in AD 972.

baraka – blessing, grace, charisma. Often attributed to certain individuals for their virtue or talent or birth.

bay'a – 'oath' of allegiance to the ruler. Implicitly, and sometimes explicitly, presented in contractual terms.

bilad al-makhzan – 'Land of Government': the area of Morocco that fell directly under the control of the Sultan and his Makhzan (*q.v.*), paid taxes and accepted his *qaids*. The distinction is from *bilad al-siba*.

bilad al-siba – 'Land of Dissidence'. Those areas which refused to pay direct taxes to the Makhzan or to accept direct control from the Sultan through his *qaids*. However, there were still relations between them and the Sultan.

Caliph – Anglicisation of the Arabic word *khalifa*. Literally means lieutenant, or successor, that is the successor to the Prophet Muhammad as the leader of the Muslim community (*umma*). The four 'orthodox' or 'rightly-guided' Caliphs, according to the Sunnis, were Abu Bakr (623-34), 'Umar (634-44), 'Uthman (644-56) and 'Ali (656-61). For the Shi'is, the first three were usurpers and 'Ali was Muhammad's directly designated successor. See also *khalifa*.

censaux (French) – commercial servants with semi-diplomatic immunity.

dahir – a decree issued by the Sultan.

faqih – jurist, expert in divine law.

fatwa – authoritative opinion by *mufti* on a point of Islamic law. Unlike the judgement of a *qadi* (*q.v.*) the *fatwa* has no legal weight in itself, but is taken into consideration when a legally binding ruling is given. It is simply a statement of what the *mufti* considers the law to be.

hadith – A report of traditions of the Prophet Muhammad or his companions. Collected *hadith* form one of the bases of Islamic law.

hubus – the Maghrebi term for *waqf:* A religious or charitable endowment set up, for example, to pay for the upkeep of a mosque or a hospital, usually taking the form of real property – land or housing – to provide revenue for the stated purpose. Once set up, it is theoretically inalienable.

imam – Literally the man who stands in front of the community in the mosque and leads its prayer. By extension, a leader of the Islamic community.

jaysh – 'army'. In Morocco applied to those tribes which provided troops to the Makhzan (*q.v.*) in return for tax and other concessions. These tribes also provided many members of the Makhzan personnel.

jihad – 'Struggle in the way of God'. In the Qur'an this probably refers to the first Muslim raids against pagan opponents. Later it came to be used for any war undertaken in the name of Islam against unbelievers or backsliders. Also used in a non-military sense.

jizya – head tax or poll tax paid by Christians and Jews.

khalifa – The Arabic word literally means 'deputy' and it is from this that the term 'Caliph' (*q.v.*) is derived. But the concept of deputyship could be used at less exalted levels for political or hierarchical deputies, such as the Sultan's immediate deputy, the *khalifa* of Marrakesh who was the effective governor of the Moroccan south, and was usually the Sultan's brother or son.

Maghreb/Maghrib – the direction in which the sun sets – used to designate the three north-west African countries of Morocco, Algeria and Tunisia, and often includes a fourth, Libya, as well. Adjectival use: Maghrebi. Distinguished from Mashriq (*q.v.*).

mahdi – the divinely guided leader, who according to early Muslim tradition, will one day come to restore true Islamic order.

majlis – assembly. In traditional Arab society, it refers to the regular audience held by a tribal chief. In modern Muslim societies the word is often used for parliaments and other similar bodies.

Makhzan – literally storehouse (of money) – the name for the pre-colonial Moroccan government.

Mashriq – the Arab East – Egypt and the Fertile Crescent in particular.

Moulay (Arabic: *Mawlay*) – literally 'my Lord', used to address and refer to a sharif or a sultan (unless he is named Muhammad, in which case the word Sidi is used)

marabout (*murabit*) – A man, not necessarily descended from the Prophet, popularly acclaimed as a 'saint', living or dead, recognised as having *baraka* (*q.v.*).

qadi – judge in a court administering the *shari'a.*

qaid – 1. governor of a tribe or city; 2. military rank.

sharif (pl. *shurafa*) – a man claiming patrilineal descent from the Prophet through his daughter Fatima and her husband Ali.

shaykh – 'old man', a title indicating respect. Most commonly used for learned teachers, but also for political rulers (esp. in Arabia) or for people of importance; an important leader in a tribe, village, guild etc. (cf. 'elder'), or a Sufi mystical master.

shari'a Islamic law.

simsars – see 'censaux'.

Sufism – a religious tradition (rather than a sect) found throughout much of the Muslim world. It emphasises the immanence of God, rather than his transcendental aspect. Originally a mystical form of Islam, it became a vehicle of popular piety and was organised into brotherhoods (*turuq*) which cut across social groups and geographic boundaries.

sunna – the 'beaten path' or customary practice of the Islamic community, drawn from the example of the Prophet and his Companions.

Sunni – those who believe themselves to be the followers of the true *sunna,* and thus form the mainstream or orthodox part of Islam, in contrast to the Shi'a. This is the dominant sect in Islam and universal among Moroccan Muslims.

Tanzimat – a general term referring to the reforms of administration and government undertaken in the Ottoman Empire in the period 1839-80.

tariqa (pl. *turuq*) – 'path' in other words a particular Sufi way to knowledge of God. Thus, by extension, an order or brotherhood following the teachings of a particular *shaykh.* The *turuq* were often associated with craft guilds.

ulama – see 'alim'.

umma – the Islamic community as a whole. Thus, by extension, used to mean the 'nation'.

Wahhabi – A sect of extreme puritans, followers of Muhammad ibn Abd al-Wahhab, an eighteenth-century reformer from the Arabian Peninsula, and now the dominant form of Islam in Saudi Arabia.

vizir – 'Minister', that is a minister of the Sultan and member of the Imperial Council. The chief minister ('Prime Minister') was the Grand Vizir.

zawiya – The local house of the *tariqa*, usually built around the tomb of a *murabit* (*q.v.*) with a mosque and teaching and accommodation facilities attached to it.

ABBREVIATIONS

AHN	Archivo Histórico Nacional, Madrid
AND	Archives de Nantes (Diplomatiques), Nantes, France
FBIS	Foreign Broadcasting Information Service
EIU	Economist Intelligence Unit
GGA	Gibraltar Government Archive
ICJ	International Court of Justice
PP	Parliamentary Papers
IMF	International Monetary Fund
PRO	Public Record Office
MAPR	Archives du Palais Royal, Rabat, Morocco.

TRANSCRIPTION OF ARABIC

In the eighteenth century, Joseph Morgan had this to say about his sources and their way of transcribing Arabic names: 'It gives me the Vapours to find people miscalled in such guise that they could not possibly know their own names if they were to hear them so mangled.' (Joseph Morgan, *A Complete History of Algiers* London: 1731) This seems a reasonable test: that people should be able to recognise their own names. Many modern Moroccans have quite a clear idea as to how their names should be transcribed into Latin characters, and they use it for the covers of their books and for official and semi-official purposes. The modern Moroccan monarchy has a series of official transcriptions not only of the present king's name, but also of those of his ancestors. It is a matter of politeness to preserve the form used by the individuals involved. In the rare cases where no common transcription of a name exists, I have used the transcription system used by the *International Journal of Middle East Studies* and its publisher, Cambridge University Press, and the same system for transcribing other Arabic words. In both cases I have suppressed the *hamza* wherever it would occur, and the *'ayn* except where doing so would cause confusion.

For place names, I have used the versions given in the *Times Atlas of the World,* and where the places concerned are too small to be shown there, the style used in the Michelin Map of Morocco. Readers have to be able to find places on a map. I have made an exception of Fez (not Fès), Tetuan and Marrakesh (not Marrakech), because these forms are more common in English.

Inevitably some inconsistencies will result from this, and I ask that these be excused. Any system of transcription is necessarily arbitrary, and I have tried to be as rational as possible.

1

1830

In the winter of 1829-30 Edward Drummond-Hay, the new British Consul in Tangier, went to Marrakesh to present his credentials. Escorted by the sultan's armed cavalry, he travelled down the Atlantic coast and then struck inland. After completing his official business, he made a short trip up into the snow-covered High Atlas and then returned across country to the coast at Rabat. From there, he followed the shoreline home. The whole trip lasted nearly three months.

Drummond-Hay's crescent-shaped route took him through forest, stony plain, cultivated fields and mountain villages. It missed the deserts, the Mediterranean coast and Fez, the other capital, but it was a most educational introduction to Morocco. Drummond-Hay, eager to learn, kept detailed records of his trip; a series of snapshots of his new home. A classically educated antiquarian, he searched assiduously for Roman and Phoenician remains and mused on the past. Comparing the poverty around him with an imagined glorious history, he saw a static society, slowly decaying.

The British consul was not the only traveller who left a record of his trip through Morocco that winter. From the far south, in what is now Mauritania, came Ahmad bin Tuwayr al-Janna.[1] This scholar from the remote oasis of Wadan was on his way to Mecca on pilgrimage, and he was embedded in a classical past quite different from that of Drummond-Hay. A devout Muslim, he sought the company of other Islamic scholars and traced his own family origins to Morocco seven generations before. Yet he too was a stranger, who saw Morocco with the eyes of an outsider. Neither man knew that change, sudden and biting deep, would very soon be thrust upon Morocco.

In June 1830, French armies captured Algiers, chief city of a province of the Ottoman Empire. All Muslim powers now faced the direct challenge of Europe, but the Moroccans had the Christian enemy on their borders, breaking the land link with the eastern

1 Ahmad bin Tuwayr al-Janna, *The Pilgrimage of Ahmad, Son of the Little Bird of Paradise: an Account of a 19th Century Pilgrimage from Mauritania to Mecca*, trans. H.T. Norris (Warminster: Aris & Phillips, 1977).

View of Moulay-Idriss, *c.* 1930, by Azouaou Mammeri.
(Private collection, courtesy Lynne Thornton, Paris)

cities of Islam. The universal Islamic community, the *umma*, which existed irrespective of political divisions, was physically parted. That winter of 1829-30 was the last before the deluge. The Morocco that the consul and the pilgrim saw, and tried to comprehend, would soon be lost.

The face of Morocco

The landscape was very striking. Although Ahmad bin Tuwayr paid little attention to it – he was more interested in the life of the intellect and the soul – Drummond-Hay, a minor Scottish aristocrat, was sometimes overwhelmed and at times appalled by the Moroccan countryside. His journal describes Nature run riot: 'Plain, fine rich soil covered with marigolds, thistles, artichokes, palmetto – and enamelled with white & small blue flowers, which a night's rain had brought forth in great beauty. Here & there patches of cultivation.'[2]

South of Larache, in the Rharb plain, the party made its way through fennel higher than a man, and the banks of the River Sebou were littered with so many round bitter gourds that these adult men stopped to play ball with them.[3]

The countryside was inhabited by a vast population of wild animals, and Drummond-Hay and his Moroccan hosts at once found a common passion, hunting.

> I took my gun & accompanied by Williams & a few Moors rode into the hills to left of track and saw much partridge but so wild could not get a shot.[4]

In the marshes the party hunted snipe, curlew, plover and larks[5] and at every opportunity, Moroccans and Britons alike chased wild boar.[6] The rivers and sea teemed with fish. At the mouth of the Sebou, north of Rabat, loads of shebel and mullet were landed from boats, and in a freshwater lake further up the coast fishermen speared large and very tasty eels.[7]

Yet the people were very poor. Although Drummond-Hay was horrified that the land was so poorly cultivated in 'this luxuriant

2 Bodleian MS Eng. hist. e. 349, 445.

3 *Ibid.*, e. 346, 95, 103.

4 *Ibid.*, e. 349, 388.

5 *Ibid.*, e. 346, 85.

6 *Ibid.*, e. 349, 418.

7 *Ibid.*, 476, 478.

but neglected country,' he soon realised that it was not in the least luxuriant. He passed through miles of stony waste, strewn with rocks or bits of slate, such as the Bahira plain north-west of Marrakesh (now a region of large-scale phosphate mining). The coastal soil was sandy, and of such poor quality that it had to be left fallow for one or two years between crops.[8] Nevertheless, even in the wasteland there were patches of cultivation. Near Azemmour, people had cleared the rocks from the land in order to plough it. Extensive palm-groves surrounded Marrakesh, and there were gardens around even the smaller settlements, like the insignificant village of Casablanca. A prominent shaykh had built acres of garden at Guérando in the rocky desert north-west of Marrakesh.[9] 'In short', Drummond-Hay remarked, 'it may be generally noted that wherever there be dooars [*duar* – the tented village of transhumant herders] in this region of the country (& in all indeed where the land admit it) there will be found patches of ploughed land.'[10]

The whole of the Atlantic plain, from the Rharb in the north to the Doukkala, Temesna and Sraghna regions between Casablanca and Marrakesh, was herding country. The Consul's party saw huge numbers of cattle and sheep all along the way. This transient way of life was forced on the inhabitants of the plains. Although the land was often perfectly arable, it was also very dry. In parts of Morocco the prevailing winds bring heavy rainfall from the Atlantic, as much as 2,000 mm. a year in the western Rif mountains, but less to the east and the south; the High Atlas around Marrakesh gets about 800 mm. The coastal plains are much drier and rain is unreliable. At times violent storms flood the dry riverbeds, but quickly drain away.[11]

Because of the uncertain rainfall, people sowed where they could in the rainy season and then moved on. Settled agriculture required irrigation which was only possible where groundwater could easily be tapped or in river valleys; and while Morocco has more rivers than anywhere else in north-west Africa, none is very big. Most are filled by Atlantic rain and melting snow and flow westwards out of the Rif and Atlas mountains towards the ocean. The Sebou and Oum er Rbia are relatively full for most of the year, but smaller rivers like the Tensift, Bou Regreg and Lekkous

8 *Ibid.*, e. 347, 230.

9 *Ibid.*, e. 346, 173, 179, 184; e. 347, 237; e. 348, *passim.*

10 *Ibid.*, e. 349, 422.

11 Swearingen, *Moroccan Mirages*, 8.

are little more than sluggish ditches in summer, though they can be raging torrents in winter.[12]

The Tensift nevertheless formed the spine of an intensive agricultural system in the Haouz plain near Marrakesh. Its web of tributaries supplied a complex system of irrigation, either by surface channels (*saquias*) or by underground canals (*khattara*) of the type famous in the Middle East as *qanat*.[13] Drummond-Hay heard the water rumbling away through the *khattara* many feet beneath him as he approached Marrakesh.[14] He saw how water from reservoirs supplied Rabat and Casablanca through underground aqueducts; at Tangier an aqueduct apparently of Roman origin was still in use in the 1830s.[15]

When Drummond-Hay's party visited the High Atlas in mid-winter it found valleys with fields of beans, barley and olive trees.[16] The villages overlooking them were surrounded by barren hills that abounded in game for the locals to hunt (and the Consul to dream about): lions, wolves, wild boar and Barbary sheep.[17] If the wolves did not eat them, sheep and goats grazed the hills.

He would have seen much the same on the Mediterranean coast, had he gone there. The isolated valleys of the Rif mountains were intensively irrigated, and in the plain facing the bay at Al Hoceima two small rivers supplied an extensive irrigation system that sometimes produced two crops a year of citrus fruits, figs, vegetables and cereals.[18] Since the seventeenth century the Rif had been losing tree-cover. This had caused erosion and gullying, and above these green oases loomed bare hills, suitable only for rough grazing.[19]

Many areas of Morocco were still forest in 1830. The Middle Atlas between Fez and Marrakesh was covered in trees and Drum-

12 Swearingen, *Mirages*, 17 gives an upper limit for the Sebou of 10,000 cubic metres a second in full flood and 3 cubic metres a second in high summer.

13 Paul Pascon, *Le Haouz de Marrakech*, 2 vols (Rabat: Centre Universitaire de la Recherche Scientifique, 1983), 1: 82-128; George Joffe, 'Khattara and Other Forms of Gravity-fed Irrigation in Morocco' in Peter Beaumont, Michael Bonine and Keith McLachlan (eds), *Qanat, Kariz and Khattara: Traditional Water Systems in the Middle East and North Africa* (Wisbech: Middle East and North African Studies Press – hereafter Menas Press – 1989), 195-210, reference here to 195-7.

14 Bodleian MS Eng. Hist. e. 348, 301-6.

15 *Ibid.*, e. 346, 145-9, 171; d.492, 165-8.

16 *Ibid.*, e. 349, 365, 407, 438.

17 *Ibid.*, 384.

18 Hart, *The Aith Waryaghar of the Moroccan Rif*, 31-3.

19 McNeill, *The Mountains of the Mediterranean World*, 99-101.

mond-Hay touched the edge of the great forest of Mamora that divided the Rharb from the Zemmour and Chaouïa plains around Rabat. It was much bigger than it is today: he was told that going inland it would take three days to cross.[20]

The consul's party failed to visit one region that had long been important in Moroccan history: where the southern and eastern sides of the Atlas mountains, denuded and barren, merge with the semi-desert and the Sahara beyond. Typical of this hot mountain landscape is the Jbel Sarhro, rising to more than 2,500 metres. Almost treeless, the terrain was so rocky as to make it impenetrable to anyone who did not live there. For those that did, such as the people of the Ait Atta, it provided summer pastures.[21] What rivers there are flow, if at all, into the Saharan sands. The valleys, though, have been irrigated for centuries and the Tafilalt oasis, more than 100 square miles of date palms, is an ancient settlement.[22] This is the site of Sijilmasa, a town at the northern end of the medieval gold-routes across the Sahara. To the west of the Jbel Sarhro, another long finger of oases follows the usually dry Drâa river from the High Atlas round the edge of the Anti-Atlas to the Atlantic. The only permanent river south of the High Atlas is the Sous. In the early nineteenth century Taroudannt, the 'capital' of the Sous region, and the Tafilalt were the limits of the sultan's effective political control. Yet these desert marches were the home country of both the Alaoui dynasty, whose sultan Drummond-Hay was visiting, and of the Saadi dynasty that preceded it in the sixteenth and seventeenth centuries.

Yet farther lay the semi-desert and the Sahara, where settled life was confined to oases, like those of the Tazeroualt in the Anti-Atlas. There, agriculture depended on a complicated system of underground *saquias* and land was so valuable that houses were only built where nothing could be grown, and the greatest care and skill were lavished on irrigation systems to produce dates of the highest quality. Yet the profits never repaid the investment in labour.[23] Further south, Guelmim in the early nineteenth century was little more than a fortified hamlet, perched on a hill and surrounded by dunes and ravines from which the underground

20 EADH Bodleian MS Eng. Hist. e. 349, 467; e.346, 115.

21 David M. Hart, *Dadda 'Atta and his Forty Grandsons: the Socio-political Organisation of the Ait 'Atta of Southern Morocco* (Wisbech: Menas Press, 1981), 4.

22 Ross E. Dunn, *Resistance in the Desert: Moroccan Responses to French Imperialism 1881-1912* (London: Croom Helm, 1977), 31-4.

23 Paul Pascon, *La Maison d'Iligh et l'histoire sociale de Tazerwalt* (Rabat: SMER, 1984), 9.

water-table could be tapped. It provided a base for the nomadic Tekna people.[24]

Ahmad bin Tuwayr, who came from even further south, reported that the Sultan asked him three questions about his homeland. One was about its agriculture: 'Are there date palms in your land?' The scholar replied that indeed there were and also wheat and barley, but in small quantities, not like Morocco.[25] Although Morocco must have looked lush to this Saharan, even in the best of times, Morocco was not an easy land to live off; and times were not always good. The most common problem was drought that sometimes affected much of the country, with horrendous results.[26] In 1826 Captain Beauclerk, a British officer attached to a medical mission to the sultan's court, saw skeletons lying beside the road, half-eaten by hyenas and vultures. They had died the previous year.[27] If drought did not bring starvation then locusts might: they did spectacular damage in 1799, 1813-15 and 1820.[28]

In this harsh environment, people organised to share scarce resources. Dams had to be built and maintained for irrigation, water had to be allocated, and the consequent arguments settled. Where transhumant herders roamed, pasture-land had to be shared and interlopers chased off.[29] On the edges of the Sahara, the population banded together and lived in walled villages (*qsars*); nomads fought side by side to defend their grazing grounds, or to raid the flocks of others; in mountain valleys communities protected water and arable land. Nobody could live alone.

Tribes

The second of the Sultan's questions to Ahmad bin Tuwayr was about his homeland's political structure. 'Are the Banu Maghfar in your land?' he asked, referring to one of the great Arabic-speaking

24 Mustapha Naimi, 'The Evolution of the Tekna Confederation: Caught between the Coastal Commerce and Trans-Saharan Trade' in E.G.H. Joffe and C.R. Pennell (eds), *Tribe and State: Essays in Honour of David Montgomery Hart* (Wisbech: Menas Press), 213.

25 Ahmad bin Tuwayr, *Pilgrimage*, 8.

26 Charles Bois, 'Années de disette, années d'abondance, sécheresse et pluies au Maroc', *Revue pour l'Étude de Calamités*, 26-7 (1949).

27 G[eorge] Beauclerk, Captain, *A Journey to Morocco, in 1826* (London: printed for Poole and Edwards ... and William Harrison Ainsworth ... 1828), 58.

28 Bois, 'Années de disette', *passim.*

29 John Brendan Godfrey, 'Overseas trade and rural change in nineteenth century Morocco: the social region and agrarian order of the Shawiya' (Ph.D. diss., Johns Hopkins University, 1985), 12-13.

warrior tribes of the Sahara.[30] Outside the cities, the tribe (*qabila*) and its various subdivisions was the basis of Moroccan life. Since it was, very broadly, territory that was at issue, both a tribe's members and outsiders defined it by the space that it controlled. Drummond-Hay, who must have been relying on Moroccan informants, identified the Chtouka and Chiadma tribes both by the land they occupied – '*Shtuka* and *Sheadma* are the names of the two tribes that yet inhabit and once with great numbers occupied an extensive district north and west of the river *Omm Errebeh*'[31] – and by how they worked together – 'The Shtuka & Shiedma were the two tribes that plundered the ship *Ann Lucy* on the coast near this place'.[32]

In reality, tribes seldom acted with one voice. Although in theory, a tribe's members were descended from a common ancestor, and the subdivisions – clans and lineages – formed a supposedly genealogical relationship, this was a fiction. Kinship relations were only real at the lower levels, but that was precisely where cooperation was really important. This genealogical structure provided the organising principle of a society in which individuals could only exist as members of a group, subsumed into a larger identity. Only a larger group could mobilise resources for production or defence. The lineage and the clan, working together, had to protect their members against outsiders, or there was no safety at all. Peace depended on keeping a rough balance between the competing groups, and councils of the most important men (shaykhs) of each lineage, clan or tribe agreed on how grazing rights or water or land were to be distributed. They mediated between groups when these arrangements broke down, and kept peace in the markets and on the roads leading to them. When war did break out, lineages and clans activated, or created, alliances with other lineages and clans, so that even then the balance might be preserved. Feuding often disrupted economic life, sometimes for long periods till political equilibrium was restored. Leaders provided protection and resources and were expected to share, generously, of their wealth. In this patriarchal society the followers, male and female, provided labour and children; what was required of them was submission to the authority of the shaykhs.[33]

30 Ahmad bin Tuwayr, *Pilgrimage*, 8.

31 Bodleian MS Eng. hist. e. 347, 198.

32 *Ibid.*, e. 346, 176.

33 The literature on the Moroccan tribe is vast. See in particular Jacques Berque, 'Qu'est-ce qu'une "tribu" nord-africaine?' in *Maghreb: histoire et sociétés* (Gembloux: Duculot, 1974); David Hart, 'Clan, Lineage, Local Community and the Feud in a Rifian Tribe' in Louise E. Sweet (ed.), *Peoples and Cultures of the Middle East: An*

Politics and religion

Sometimes an outsider was needed to mediate. Drummond-Hay's party passed numerous tombs, usually a small white-painted structure with a dome, sometimes decked out with flags. Generalising wildly, he described one such tomb as that of 'of one of their canonised fools or madmen',[34] ignorant or careless that Islam knows no canonisation. These were the tombs of holy men and women, known in Morocco as marabouts, who possessed the quality known as *baraka*. *Baraka*, often translated as 'charisma', is a mixture of personal holiness and inherited worth, and manifests itself in the purity of a marabout's life or good works. It could pass from father to son and also from uncle to nephew, or even father to daughter.

Once again the principle of genealogical descent appears as an organising principle of society. But descent was not the only way in which spiritual charisma could be transmitted. Alive, marabouts might work miracles, and transmit their *baraka* by touch; when they were dead, the same power was invested in their tombs. Alive, they were neutral figures who mediated in disputes; dead, their tombs became places of sanctuary from authority, or feuding neighbours.[35] Once inside a marabout's tomb, a fugitive was inviolable. In Salé, the consular party was attacked by a small mob throwing stones, some of whom were captured by the governor's soldiers, but two escaped: 'Soon after our return home I received a message from the Governor... that he had severally punished two of the rascals whom they had brought to him & then sent them to jail & that the 2 others who had taken refuge in the sanctuary were watched at the door by a guard of soldiers.'[36]

Some marabouts were adepts of forms of Islamic mysticism, Sufism. The great Sufi teachers of the past had laid down rituals and devotional practices for their disciples to follow, and so marked out a spiritual path towards knowledge of God. The Arabic word for 'path' (*tariqa*) is used for the Sufi brotherhoods that they

---

Anthropological Reader (New York: Natural History Press, 1970), 3-75; Ernest Gellner, *Saints of the Atlas* (University of Chicago Press, 1969); Henry Munson, 'On the Relevance of the Segmentary Lineage Model in the Moroccan Rif', *American Anthropologist*, 91 (1989): 386-400; Abdellah Hammoudi, *Master and Disciple: the Cultural Foundations of Moroccan Authoritarianism* (University of Chicago Press, 1997), 78-9.

34 Bodleian MS Eng. hist. e. 349 (unnumbered page facing 354).

35 Hammoudi, *Master and Disciple*, 138-9; Hart, *Aith Waryaghar*, 149, 190-1.

36 Bodleian MS Eng. hist. e. 346, 138.

established. This, too, was a form of spiritual genealogy – a master passing on his path to his chosen successors, and their closest disciples passing them on or branching off to form paths of their own. But it was also an exercise of power: the disciples of each *tariqa* shared forms of prayer and dress that distinguished them and gave them a common identity that crossed tribal and regional lines. They were also subservient to the leaders of the *tariqa* in a powerful relationship where once again descent and charisma were mingled. In the nineteenth century this meant that the houses of the brotherhoods, the *zawiyas*, not only provided services as hostels for travellers, sanctuaries for fugitives and refuges for the sick, but were also political nuclei, able, on occasion, to mobilise armed force to protect their interests. Scattered across the countryside were smaller *zawiyas* that had many of the same functions, and whose heads, like the marabouts mediated between feuding clans and lineages. This gave the marabouts and *zawiyas* local political influence, and endowed the heads of the *tariqas* with great political power which they used to build up extensive, and inalienable, land holdings and estates.[37]

Tariqas could be very powerful. The Nasiriyya *tariqa*, based at Tamgrout, dominated the Dràa valley. The Sharqawiyya, at Boujad near Tadla, held sway in the Middle Atlas. The Wazzaniyya, founded at Ouezzane on the southern edge of Jebala mountains in the mid-seventeenth century, had large estates in the Rharb, and Moulay al-Arbi, its head who died in 1850, lived in splendour and exerted influence far into the Sahara. The Darqawiyya, with its headquarters at Amjot on the southern edge of the Rif, had adherents in the countryside and among the poor; the rich joined the Tijaniyya, that emphasised wealth in this world as well as salvation in the next.[38]

The Tijaniyya was centred in a city, Fez, but most other *tariqas* were based in more inaccessible regions, in mountains and on the edges of the desert. A famous example was the *zawiya* of Sidi Ahmad ou Moussa at Iligh near Tazeroualt. Set in a stony semi-desert, it relied on a system of irrigation and landownership of such complexity that trees sometimes had different owners from the land on which they stood.[39] Conflict and strife always threatened

37 Hammoudi, *Master and Disciple*, 84; Abdallah Laroui, *Les origines sociales et culturelles du nationalisme marocain* (Paris: Maspéro, 1977), 150-4.

38 Mohamed El Mansour, *Morocco in the Reign of Mawlay Sulayman* (Wisbech: Menas Press, 1990), 160-3.

39 Pascon, *Maison d'Iligh*, 21-3.

in such a place and the role of the descendants of Sidi Ahmad as mediators gave them economic and political power in these desert marches.

Genealogical descent underpinned the authority of many of the leaders of the *zawiyas*. Most were descended from two great medieval Sufi teachers, Abu al-Hasan al-Shadhili (1175-1278) and Abd al-Salam bin Mashish (d. 1227/8) who was buried in northern Morocco on the side of a mountain, Jbel Alam. Both these masters were themselves descendants of the Prophet, and lineages originating with Muhammad controlled most of the *tariqas* by the early nineteenth century.[40]

The lineage of the Prophet was the most prestigious of all. His descendants, the sharifs, were given the honorific title of Moulay (roughly 'Lord') – unless their first name was Mohammed, when they were called simply 'Sidi Mohammed'. Idris I (788-793) and his son Idris II (793-828) set up the first sharifian dynasty in Morocco, established the city of Fez and founded there the greatest centre of Islamic learning outside Cairo, the Qarawiyyin mosque. Idris I's tomb, on Jbel Zerhoun north-east of Fez became the premier sanctuary of Morocco; that of his son, in the city itself, was only slightly less sacred. In the late fifteenth century, a family of sharifs from the Sous on the edge of the Sahara, the Saadis, joined the leaders of some of the stronger *tariqas* to attack the Spanish and Portuguese fortresses scattered along the Moroccan coast. They cleared away the Christian garrisons, apart from the scattering of Spanish military outposts on the north coast, and held back the Ottoman Empire, then at its zenith, to a line that is roughly the modern boundary between Morocco and Algeria. There were no boundary posts but Oujda was considered Saadi territory and Tlemcen was Ottoman, although these marches were not always peaceful.[41] The greatest of the Saadi sultans, Ahmad al-Mansur (1578-1603) also pushed far southwards into the Sahara desert and seized the gold-mines of Gao and the city of Timbuktu. It could be said that the boundaries of the 'Greater Morocco' that would be claimed in the twentieth century date from the events of the sixteenth.

40 El Mansour, *Mawlay Sulayman*, 160-73.

41 Hammoudi, *Master and Disciple*, 14, 54; Dahiru Yahya, *Morocco in the Sixteenth Century: Problems and Patterns in African Foreign Policy* (Atlantic Highlands, NJ: Humanities Press, 1981); Abdelatif Agnouche, *Histoire politique du Maroc. Pouvoir – légitimités – institutions* (Casablanca: Afrique Orient, 1987), 171-81, 202-6; David Seddon, *Moroccan Peasants, a Century of Change in the Eastern Rif, 1870-1970* (Folkestone: Dawson, 1981), 11-12.

The Saadis soon lost control of the Sahara. At the beginning of the seventeenth century, plague, drought and changes in patterns of trade destroyed the economy and the family fell apart. Civil war dragged on for over half a century until a new sharifian family, the Alaouis, took control. They too originated on the edge of the Sahara, in the Tafilalt oases. In the early seventeenth century, they gradually conquered the petty principalities, powerful *zawiyas*, local warlords, virtually autonomous city-states, and what remained of the Saadi dynasty in Marrakesh.[42] It was Moulay Rachid (1664-72) who completed the process, but his more powerful brother Moulay Ismaïl (1672-1727) consolidated it. He even organised attacks on the remaining Spanish garrisons on the north coast: the prison colonies of Ceuta and Melilla and the tiny islets at Peñon de Vélez and Al Hoceima; but he did not dislodge them. A contemporary of Louis XIV, whose daughter he unsuccessfully tried to marry, Ismaïl laid the basis of Alaoui power on sharifian prestige and armed force. He built up a huge army, financed by heavy taxation, which it helped to collect.[43] State power and taxation were so closely intertwined that the Arabic word for 'treasury', Makhzan, became synonymous with the government, its army and its officials.

The Sultan

Consul Drummond-Hay went to Marrakesh to meet the great-great-grandson of Moulay Ismaïl, Moulay Abderrahmane bin Moulay Hicham bin Sidi Mohammed bin Moulay Abdallah bin Moulay Ismaïl. In this lineage only Moulay Hicham had not been a sultan; Moulay Abderrahmane had succeeded his uncle Moulay Slimane in 1822. On the other hand, the sultan's great-grandfather, Moulay Abdallah, had been sultan five times, on-and-off. The dynasty may have been holy, but it was by no means stable.

Moulay Abderrahmane was more secure in his position than his great-grandfather, and he received the Consul in a dramatically simple ceremony:

> His Imperial Majesty came forth on horseback in a dress so plain that he might at little distance have been mistaken for any of his own more respectable Kaids; except that the number & silence of the attendants surrounding him & the great crimson umbrella (the only article of the kind which had yet [*sic*] seen

42 Agnouche, *Histoire politique*, 202-5.

43 *Ibid.*, 214-17.

> in the country) (which we had noticed to be held, but not expanded, in waiting for him near the gate & within the square at our past entrance) which was immediately raised above the Royal head, announced the first personage of the Empire. On entering the court the Sultan turned to his soldiers on either side saying *Allah elawenkoom*, literally, 'God help you'! to which they replied by a loud yet respectful exclamation *God bless the life of our Master* accompanied by a low bow from all and at the same touching their right knee.[...]
>
> The Sultan rode slowly forward, & then at a slight movement of his hand the men in our immediate front opened right & left. His Majesty then saying (something which I did not hear but intuited we should come forward) then we moved on a few paces, & halted, when I made at the same time as Seedy Muhammad a low bow, the monarch asked Seedy Muhammad 'Is that the Consul?' to which Seedy Muhammad having answered by pointing me out, His Majesty asked also for the interpreter who being indicated (standing on my left) the Sultan then said 'Tell him: "we are disposed to maintain the solemnly agreed & friendly alliance of our predecessors & yet further to add of our own efforts to the bonds of amity between us & them (the King & nation of Great Britain) with the help of God." '

Drummond-Hay struggled through a short formal speech and then 'the Monarch, making a very slight inclination of his head... turned round and rode quietly out of the square; & so soon as he passed the Gate of the enclosure we covered our head again'.

The sultan had said very little. Protocol, ceremonial, shouted prayers, and indirect conversation all kept him apart. His person was holy. This separateness and silence were noted by many, if not all, European visitors to the Moroccan court in the nineteenth century. The Sultan generally kept the same distance from Moroccans. His palaces were surrounded by high walls and even when he travelled on campaign his encampment was treated as a holy sanctuary to which few had access.[44] Yet some travellers did have direct access to the Sultan. Ahmad ibn Tuwayr was given a personal interview by Moulay Abderrahmane at which he discussed religious matters and Sufism in particular.[45] And in 1803, 'Ali Bey' (who was really a Spaniard named Domingo Badía y Leblich; he had disguised himself as a learned Muslim who had spent many years

44 Hammoudi, *Master and Disciple*, 73-5.

45 Ahmad bin Tuwayr, *Pilgrimage*, 8, 9.

in Europe) was ushered into the presence of Moulay Slimane and interrogated about European technology.[46]

Moulay Abderrahmane was more than a ruler, he was *amir al-muminin*, the Commander of the Faithful, the head of the Islamic community, the *umma*. That meant he had also to be a scholar and a religious expert. His task was to protect the 'Abode of Islam', *dar al-islam*, by ensuring that the *shari'a*, the holy law, was obeyed, that irreligious forces, inside and outside Morocco, were checked and that Muslims lived in peace and security.

Jihad and the right to rule

During the European Middle Ages, Christian states fought a crusade against Muslims. The response was *jihad*, holy war, a war for security not converts; Muslims did not fight a *jihad* against Jews, for no Jewish state threatened them until the twentieth century. During the seventeenth century the *jihad* was fought at sea, by corsairs, whom the Christian powers called pirates.

In the eighteenth century, corsairing was largely abandoned, partly for economic reasons. Most European powers signed treaties with the Moroccan sultans and in June 1786, the United States signed with Morocco its first foreign treaty. By the beginning of the nineteenth century, only Denmark and Sweden still bought immunity from attack for their ships with an annual tribute. Finally, in 1817, Moulay Slimane abolished the Moroccan corsairing fleet because it served no military purpose; his enemies complained that he had abandoned *jihad*.[47]

Inside Morocco, the Sultan's task was to uphold the law, and since this could not be done without order and security, it was but a short step to justify untrammelled power. Some legal scholars argued that order was so important that no challenge to the sultan's rule could be licit. No matter how unjust the ruler, rebellion was a far worse evil. The community had to have a head. At the end of his interview with the Moulay Abderrahmane, Ahmad bin Tuwayr said to him:

> 'My lord, my Shaykh – may God sanctify his spirit and illuminate his tomb – told me that there is a prophetic tradition which says, "He who dies, and who has not sworn homage to a *sultan*, dies the death of an ignorant pagan." Now, stretch forth your

46 Ibid., 7-9; [Domingo Badía y Leblich], *Travels of Ali Bey: in Morocco, Tripoli, Cyprus, Egypt, Arabia, Syria and Turkey: Between the Years 1803 and 1807 Written by Himself*, 2 vols (London: Longman, Hurst, Rees, Orme and Brown, 1816), 47.

47 El Mansour, *Mawlay Sulayman*, 17.

> hand to me, and I will swear my allegiance to you.' He stretched forth his hand, may God aid him.
> I said to him, 'I swear homage to you according to the *Sunna* of God and his Messenger, the blessing and peace of God be upon him. Oh, my lord, before I met you I used to pray pious prayers for you. Now I will do so even more.' He said to me, 'Your prayer for me is a prayer for all Muslims.' I said to him, 'My lord, that is so.'[48]

It is a revealing passage, for both sultan and scholar recognised that a truly Islamic society depended upon a hierarchy of power, but also on an exchange of religious fervour between master and servant.

The argument, which appealed to sultans, had a solid basis in the *shari'a*. The sultan claimed to be the *khalifa* (Caliph), a term that originated with the death of the Prophet Mohammed. Literally, it meant 'successor' or 'deputy' but there was some argument whether this signified merely the successor of the Prophet as leader of the community or whether it meant *khalifat Allah*, God's deputy on earth. The latter interpretation was a licence for virtually unrestrained power.[49] A rebel, in this view, was an enemy of God.

The claim to absolute power never went unchallenged, because the *shari'a* also held that the Islamic community should choose its leader on the basis of ability and suitability. In Morocco this was expressed in the oath of allegiance, the *bay'a*, that was given to a sultan at the beginning of his reign. When a city or a tribe swore allegiance it was usually simply recognising the status quo – the sultan had already taken power.

Even so, words were important. Moulay Abderrahmane had been given a *bay'a* in 1823 that referred to him by three titles: Sultan (that is a political leader), imam (effectively a religious leader) and caliph (the leader of the Islamic community). His authority as Sultan was limited by his territorial control (he did not rule the territory of the Ottoman Sultan next door), so caliphal responsibilities were thus distinguished from his political ones – in practice if not in theory.[50] But the word used for the oath, *bay'a*, is etymologically connected with commerce, and the contractual relationship sometimes became explicit. When the community had a real choice, the *bay'a* might contain conditions. The *bay'a* of Moulay Ismaïl's son, Abdallah, went: 'We have given you the *bay'a*,

48 Ahmad bin Tuwayr, *Pilgrimage*, 9.

49 *Ibid.*, 17.

50 Hammoudi, *Master and Disciple*, 66.

and we have given you power in order that you may direct us with justice and blessing, with fidelity and truth, that you should judge between us with justice'.[51] Abdallah did not fulfil those conditions. Hence: 'The notables met together and conferred about their position and that of the sultan. They brought a copy of the *bay'a* and scrutinised its conditions. They said "We did not give him the *bay'a* so that he could deal with us in this way." Then they announced that he was deposed.'[52]

This was easy to do when the sultan was weak and easier to justify, because weak sultans could not protect the *shari'a* or *dar al-Islam.*[53] It was much harder to justify, and much more dangerous, when the Sultan was strong. One very brave scholar, Hasan al-Yusi invoked the concept of justified rebellion against the immensely powerful Moulay Ismaïl, a man who brooked no dissent. In a famous letter, al-Yusi warned the Sultan,

> Let our Lord know that this world and everything in it are the property of God, may he be exalted, who has no associate. Men are but slaves of God, may he be praised, and women are his bondsmaidens. Our Lord [the sultan] is one of these mere slaves to whom God has given power over his servants in their trials and afflictions. And if he rules over them with justice and mercy and equity and reconciliation, then he is the lieutenant of God on earth and the shadow of God on his slaves, and he has high rank in the eyes of God, may he be exalted. And if he rules with oppression, and violence and haughtiness and tyranny and iniquity, then he is insolent to his master in his kingdom and reigns and has pride on earth without the right to do so.[54]

In short, while a sultan had to keep order, he had to rule justly. He was subject to the law, he did not make it: that was the prerogative of God alone; nor did he interpret it: that was the function of the *'ulama,* the scholars.

The 'ulama

The third of the Sultan's questions to Ahmad bin Tuwayr was 'Is there scholarship in your land?' To which the pilgrim replied:

51 Abu al-'Abbas Ahmad bin Khalid al-Nasiri, *Kitab al-istiqsa li-akhbar duwwal al-Maghrib al-Aqsa,* 9 vols (Rabat: Dar al-Kitab, 1956), 7: 128.

52 *Ibid.,* 7: 130.

53 C.R. Pennell, 'Tyranny, Just Rule and Moroccan Political Thought', *Morocco Occasional Papers,* 1 (1994): 13-42.

54 Al-Nasiri, *Kitab al-istiqsa,* 7: 82.

> 'My lord, all the sciences are to be found there, both exegesis and tradition, the recitation of them, skilled workmanship and artistry, jurisprudence and principles of law, logic and rhetoric and the study of Arabic, its grammar and its rules and its syntax.' He said to me, 'It is the very opposite in our land. Here scholarship is meagre.'[55]

Ahmad took this as a sign of the Sultan's modesty: for the deprecation was self deprecation. Ideally, the Sultan was a 'good' man, devout and a scholar (in Arabic, *'alim*, pl. *'ulama*). Many sultans were just that. Moulay Slimane had studied deeply, with some of the most respected scholars of the late eighteenth century.[56]

These men on whom the sultan so relied were the apex of a learned profession that began in the local mosque where children learned to read and to memorise the Quran by heart. Later on they might progress to higher levels of learning – studying jurisprudence, Quranic exegesis and Arabic grammar, and sometimes algebra and astronomy in the madrasas (religious colleges) of Marrakesh, or the great mosque-university of Qarawiyyin in Fez, the pinnacle of learning in north-west Africa. Learning meant years of rote memorisation of ancient texts and commentaries. Those who completed their studies became *'ulama*, scholars, who comprised the body of judges (*qadis*), notaries, teachers, and preachers and the clerical administrators of the state. Law and administration, religion and education were intertwined with social status: the learned pyramid stretched downwards from the *shaykh al-jama'a*, who advised the sultan to its base among the numerous, and much less skilled teachers in mosque schools and preachers in rural mosques. The higher levels, who were called upon to take part in the government and administration were usually drawn from scholarly families whose genealogies included famous scholars.[57]

This was a very conservative system. After years of studying religious texts, the higher *'ulama* had great prestige and political weight. If the Sultan asked them for a *fatwa*, a legal opinion about the validity of his actions, and they gave it in his favour, he benefited. If they opposed the Sultan, they could undermine him, although that was rare. Fear and the desire to avoid disorder ensured that they did not act until his power had collapsed, and even then they would not seek to overthrow the Alaoui family, but transferred

55 Ahmad bin Tuwayr, *Pilgrimage*, 8.

56 El Mansour, *Mawlay Sulayman*, 154.

57 *Ibid.*, 153.

their allegiance to another member of it. The *'ulama* could not exist outside the sultanian order.[58]

Even the most rebellious tribes held the person of the Sultan sacred. On one occasion Berber tribes defeated the army of Moulay Slimane; they put his military commanders to death, but escorted the Sultan to a nearby fortress.[59] On the other hand, family membership was not enough, for there were many Alaouis to choose among, all of whom could make a valid claim to the sultanate, since there was no rule of primogeniture. There was a real surfeit of legitimacy. When a sultan died, brothers and cousins scrabbled for power. At the end of the reign of Mohammed III (1757-90) things fell apart. For two disastrous years his son, Moulay Yazid, tried to appease a fractious and motley collection of allies; then a civil war began. It took six years for Moulay Slimane to overcome his various relatives in different parts of the country, and on his deathbed he obliged the *'ulama* of Fez, the most prominent merchants and part of the army to confirm his nephew Moulay Abderrahmane as his successor. In fact, violence marked the beginning of nearly every sultan's reign.[60] This helps to explain the makeup of the group that surrounded the Sultan.

The Makhzan

Around the sultan was a small group of members of his own family, rich merchants, *'ulama* and the leaders of the tribes who provided his military muscle. These formed the *dar al-makhzan* (or *dar al-mulk*), the household of the Sultan which accompanied him as he moved through the land. Power and influence in this coalition were carefully balanced between members of his family, tied by links of kin, and his political supporters, tied by links of service and dependence. Consul Hay carefully sorted out these groups before he arrived in Marrakesh and distributed his official presents accordingly.

He knew that certain members of the Sultan's family were crucial. The sultan's brother Moulay Mimun (who received four cuts of cloth, two pieces of finest muslin, four loaves of sugar, four pounds of tea, seven silk kerchiefs and a watch)[61] was the *khalifa* of Marrakesh, the sultan's deputy in the south. This was typical: governors

58 Hammoudi, *Master and Disciple*, 58.

59 Agnouche, *Histoire*, 211.

60 El Mansour, *Mawlay Sulayman*, 89-98, 219; Hammoudi, *Master and Disciple*, 62; al-Nasiri, *Kitab al-istiqsa*, 8:82-6.

61 Bodleian MS Eng. hist. e. 348, 318.

of major cities and important provinces were nearly always Alaouis. Moulay Slimane's son, Ibrahim, had several important military commands before he was killed putting down a rebellion in 1819. The sultan chose his nephew, Moulay Abderrahmane, the governor of Essaouira, to take his place as his intended successor, rather than another son who was governor of Tafilalt, or a brother who was governor of Tangier and then of Meknès.[62] But not all Alaouis were reliable, for their descent gave them a competing claim to the sultanate and some rebelled, like Abd al-Malik bin Idris, the governor of the Chaouïa, who rose against his cousin Moulay Slimane in 1797.[63] Thus important posts were also given to men who were not members of the family. Hay's information was accurate enough to know that he should give the two wazirs, or ministers, Hajj Talib bin Jallun and Sidi Muhammad bin Idris, larger presents even than Moulay Mimun; Ibn Idris, in addition to his tea and sugar and cloth received 'One gold watch with inner case enamel & outer tortoise shell set in gold with a double gold chain & by all in a red morocco case & tied up in a French silk kerchief'.[64] His colleague, ibn Jallun, was a merchant who had grown extremely wealthy first in the trans-Saharan trade and then in the maritime trade with Europe, and had bought huge estates around Fez.[65] The sultan courted him and other merchants for their money, because they were a political counterweight to the *'ulama* and because they were dependent on the sultan for their continued prosperity, which might make them his partisans.

In fact, non-Alaouis were at the centre of power for just this reason. Drummond-Hay presented two men with only a watch apiece less than the *khalifa*. One, whom the consul called the 'prime clerk' of the Sultan,[66] was Mukhtar bin Abdelmalik al-Jama'i, whose tribe, the Awlad Jama'i, was an important element in the Makhzan's army. Another, ibn Ghazi, came from the Zemmour tribe, that had rebelled against Moulay Slimane. Moulay Abderrahmane had bought off trouble by marrying ibn Ghazi to a former concubine of the dead Slimane, constructing a kinship relationship of sorts by doing so. He became the Sultan's closest confidant, rivalled only by the head of the palace administration, the chamberlain (*hajib*) Jilali bin Hammu whose father, Ahmad bin Mubarak

62 El Mansour, *Mawlay Sulayman*, 189, 219.

63 *Ibid.*, 95.

64 Bodleian MS Eng. hist. e. 348, 305, 317.

65 El Mansour, *Mawlay Sulayman*, 43, 60.

66 Drummond-Hay calls him Mocta el-Zamhi.

had been chamberlain to Moulay Slimane. Drummond-Hay gave him presents of roughly half the value of al-Jama'is, which probably annoyed him intensely. The rivalry of the Jama'is and the descendants of Ahmad bin Mubarak was an unhealed sore through the nineteenth century.

Drummond-Hay gave less valuable presents to the commanders of two important military groups (the *abid* and the Oudaia), to the commander of the palace guard (*qaid mashwar*) and to various clerks and court officials such as the commander of the Royal Hunt. But he did not reward the numerous lesser bureaucrats, nor the religious officials on whom the Sultan so much relied: the judges (*qadis*) and the teachers in the colleges and other educational institutions. There was a fairly small pool of 'Makhzan *'ulama*. In Tetuan various members of the Afailal family served as *qadis*, and under Moulay Slimane, an Afailal was imam of an important mosque, having studied under another *qadi*, Muhammad Carrazu, who had studied alongside Moulay Slimane when both were young.[67] In Fez, Moulay Slimane turned to members of the *'ulama* families with whom he had grown up. There were many *qadis* from the ibn Suda family, and one of its most senior members had led the Fasi *'ulama* in declaring for Moulay Slimane in 1792.[68] Ahmad ibn Tuwayr found that his own Sufi master had studied at the feet of another member of this family many years before.[69]

Some *'ulama* refused to serve, which was an act of disobedience that bordered on the rebellious: it denied links of patronage and dependency and made them independent of the Makhzan.[70] When Sidi Abd al-Karim bin Abd al-Salam bin Qarrish turned down the post of *qadi* of Tetuan, Moulay Slimane promptly exiled him to the edges of the Sahara, remarking that the scholar 'was a man of very cold character, and since it is very warm in Taroudannt, I have sent him there to see if he warms up a bit'.[71] Moulay Slimane also quarrelled with the leaders of the *tariqas*. His own rather austere faith was out of sympathy with pilgrimages to the tombs of marabouts, with *tariqas* that played music during their prayer-meetings and other extravagances of popular religiosity. Many *tariqas* objected when the sultan insisted on his right to appoint

67 Ahmed R'honi, *Historia de Tetuán* (Tetuán: Marroquí, 1953), 98, 165, 143-4.

68 El Mansour, *Mawlay Sulayman*, 90-1, 154, 193.

69 Ahmad bin Tuwayr, *Pilgrimage*, 14.

70 Hammoudi, *Master and Disciple*, 60.

71 R'honi, *Historia*, 144.

the heads of the *zawiyas*,[72] and they were unhappy when he sent his son, and presumed heir, Ibrahim to Mecca in 1812. Mecca was held by the greatest reformist movement of the time, the Wahhabis, austere doctrinaires who loathed marabouts and *zawiyas*. Although Moulay Slimane did not go nearly as far as they did, many *'ulama* worried all the same.[73]

Thus, while *'ulama* served as the Sultan's officials, and gave him ideological support, they were not necessarily his men. The army, too, was formed from elements that existed independently of the Makhzan, and had to be won over and incorporated.

The army

Moulay Abderrahmane's army was a ramshackle affair. In part it was tribal with *jaysh* (literally, 'army') tribes providing troops, largely cavalry, in exchange for the use of land and exemption from taxes. Two of the biggest *jaysh* tribes – the Oudaia, who garrisoned a fortress at the mouth of the Bou Regreg at Rabat, and the Cherarda, who lived in the Rharb plain, claimed descent from Arabs who had arrived in the Middle Ages. The Fahs tribe, who lived around Tangier, were originally Berbers from the Rif mountains, and the Cheraga, who included the Awlad Jama'i, had both Berber and Arab roots. They were all unreliable. Since they were only paid when they were actually fighting, they provided for themselves from booty. Sometimes they refused to serve, and sometimes they rebelled.[74]

There were also remnants of Moulay Ismaïl's black army, the *abid al-bukhari*. In the early eighteenth century he had formed these slaves (*abid*) into a standing army that would have no tribal loyalties. The *abid* turned out to be loyal only to themselves and when Ismaïl died in 1727, they helped ignite a civil war that lasted a generation. When Mohammed III (1757-90) restored order, he let the *abid* vegetate, although they continued to exist, supporting themselves as tradesmen or labourers. The senior officers became landowners and farmers.[75]

72 El Mansour, *Mawlay Sulayman*, 140-2.

73 *Ibid.*, 141-3.

74 Wilfrid J. Rollman, 'The "New Order" in a Pre-colonial Muslim Society: Military Reform in Morocco, 1844-1904' (Ph.D. diss., University of Michigan, 1983), 384-7; El Mansour, *Mawlay Sulayman*, 7, 218-19.

75 Rollman, 'New Order', 375; Allan Richard Meyers, 'The 'Abid 'l-Buhari: Slave Soldiers and Statecraft in Morocco, 1672-1790' (Ph.D. diss., Cornell University, 1974).

Sidi Mohammed and Moulay Abderrahmane relied on levies (*naiba*), which were furnished by non-*jaysh* tribes as a form of taxation. They went unpaid and even provided their own food and horses. When they were called into service, they were grouped into a *mahalla*, an expeditionary force that was sent to restore order or extract taxes.[76]

This was more a disorganised rabble than a reliable army. Moulay Slimane tried to reform it by giving new tribes *jaysh* status, by rebuilding the *abid al-bukhari* and by buying military equipment from abroad. Officers were educated in the palace, forming yet another quasi-familial link.[77] But powerful tribal confederations could field as many troops as he did and famine shattered his army. Drummond-Hay was told that the province of Doukkala that had supplied Moulay Slimane with 30-40,000 men a year, could now manage no more than 5 or 6,000.[78]

Even so, Drummond-Hay saw plenty of the *jaysh* and *abid*, for local governors provided an escort to the consular party while it travelled across their province. At Salé the governor met him with '500 cavalry and infantry who advanced to salute the Mission, bearing 3 standards, 1 yellow with a star and crescent with a border inscribed with sacred verses in green, another standard crimson, and another yellow'.[79] It was picturesque, but Sidi Muhammad bin Abd al-Malik bin Abu, the young commander of the escort provided by the Sultan, did not trust them. In one small village, he chased away the welcoming 'company of village infantry' before they could pose any threat.[80] This was a rather unreliable military machine; it was hard pressed even to collect taxes.

Finances

It was difficult to tax Moroccans. Rural people often refused to pay at all, and taxing townspeople created political, even ideological, problems. According to the *shari'a* only two taxes were legal: *zakat*, on livestock, and *ushur*, on the produce of the harvest. The proportions were precisely stated and were not high. One way of raising extra income was a system of sacking and reappointing men to government office. When a provincial governor was dismissed his

76 Rollman, 'New Order', 260-9.

77 Hammoudi, *Master and Disciple*, 56.

78 El Mansour, *Mawlay Sulayman* 24-5; Bodleian MS Eng. hist. e. 347, 202.

79 Bodleian MS Eng. hist. e. 346, 115.

80 *Ibid.*, 99.

property would be confiscated. When he was reappointed he would make up his loss by securing forced contributions from those he ruled, only to be relieved of his position and his fortune when he was again removed from office. This revolving system generated income for the sultan and forced the official to seek a return of the sultan's goodwill – it ensured obedience.[81] Even so, Sidi Mohammed found that he could not fill the Makhzan's coffers and persuaded the *'ulama* to let him levy additional, and temporary, taxes. He collected duties at the gates of cities and sold trading monopolies in hides, tobacco, sulphur or spices, at amounts that he arbitrarily determined. This form of taxation, which lacked any Quranic justification, was called *maks*, a word pregnant with pejorative connotations. Edward Lane's huge *Arabic-English Lexicon*, published in 1863, explained *maks* as 'generally, what the sultan's guards take wrongfully on an occasion of buying and selling' and quoted a tradition that the Prophet Muhammad had declared that: 'The taker of *maks* will not enter paradise.'[82]

The *'ulama* disapproved of non-Quranic taxes on principle, and Moulay Yazid abolished the *maks* to get their support; Moulay Slimane, himself an *'alim*, did not reinstate it. Instead, he turned to trade.

Trade and commerce

Bankrupt when his reign began, Moulay Slimane opened his ports to trade, although neither the sultan nor the *'ulama* much liked commerce with Europe. They believed that the *shari'a* forbade Muslims to trade with Christians, because horses, for example, or sulphur, might make the Christians stronger. The inhabitants of the cities loathed the grain trade, fearing that exports in years of plenty would mean that none was kept in reserve for years of want. Since hungry townspeople might riot, Moulay Slimane see-sawed between prohibiting the export of wheat and allowing it, in order to raise revenue.[83] In 1820 the urban mob in Fez, with the support of many *'ulama*, rioted against the grain trade and all but brought the Sultan down. They were joined by the informal urban militia, the *rumat*, and backed by opportunistic merchants who, once the rebellion was crushed, just as promptly switched sides. They were swiftly pardoned by the Sultan and some

81 Hammoudi, *Master and Disciple*, 52.

82 Edward William Lane, *An Arabic-English Lexicon, Derived from the Very Best Sources ...*, 2 vols (London: Williams and Norgate, 1877), 2: 2,729.

83 El Mansour, *Mawlay Sulayman*, 55-7, 69-70.

were given important positions: one became controller of the customs in Tangier, and another was made qaid (governor) of Fez, and Talib bin Jallun, richest of all, became the *wazir*. By the end of the century this merchant elite would dominate Moroccan political life. The descendants of ibn Jallun, the Benjelloun family, were particularly important.[84] The sultan needed rich merchants like them.

Moulay Abderrahmane was an enthusiastic advocate of foreign trade. As governor of Essaouira he had encouraged European merchants, and after he became sultan, consul after consul trekked down to Marrakesh; the Portuguese in 1823, the British in 1824, the French and the Sardinian in 1825.[85] Each signed a trade treaty, although Morocco had little to export because in 1825 the country began another cycle of poor rainfall and famine. However, there were plenty of opportunities for importers, and in 1826, 250,000 quintals of grain valued at 7 million francs was imported and largely paid for by the Makhzan.

To recoup his expenses Moulay Abderrahmane flirted with the idea of re-founding his corsairing fleet. In 1828 it captured some British ships – which were soon returned – and an Austrian one. The Austrian navy retaliated with force. In June 1829 they landed at Larache and burned Moroccan ships.[86] Trading was much safer than corsairing.

Moulay Abderrahmane did not trade himself, but relied on agents, the *tujjar al-sultan* ('merchants of the Sultan'), most of them concentrated in Essaouira, or Mogador, the southern port city that Mohammed III had built to funnel foreign trade into the Makhzan's hands. He encouraged merchants to settle there and act as his agents. Many were Jews, and by the time Drummond-Hay visited Morocco, there was a Jewish trading elite in Essaouira, and in other ports.[87]

Commerce and the British

Not all merchants were Jewish. Ibn Jallun and ibn Idris, Drum-

84 *Ibid.*, 192-208.

85 Jean-Louis Miège, *Le Maroc et L'Europe (1830-1894)*, 4 vols (Paris: Presses Universitaires de France, 1961-3), 2:31-2.

86 Al-Nasiri, *Kitab al-istiqsa*, 9:24-6; J.-L. Miège, 'La Marine marocaine au XIXme siècle', *Bulletin du comité marocain de documentation historique de la marine*, no. 2 (1956): 2-4.

87 Daniel Schroeter, *Merchants of Essaouira: Urban Society and Imperialism in Southwestern Morocco, 1844-1886* (New York: Cambridge University Press, 1988), 21-4.

mond-Hay's main contacts during his visit to the court, were important traders. At his first interview with ibn Idris, he gave the *wazir* a list of specific issues that the government in London wanted to settle: a long-running argument about the property of a deceased Moroccan consul in Gibraltar; the Royal Navy's request for permission to survey the Atlantic coast; and compensation for three ships wrecked and plundered by local inhabitants. Ibn Idris listened politely and promised to reply later. Over the next fortnight, the Consul visited the city, rode in the country, celebrated Christmas, bought goatskins as souvenirs, wrote despatches, visited a big market, did a bit of desultory hunting and mineral-collecting, and chafed at his inactivity. At the second interview, ibn Idris turned down all his main requests, with the greatest politeness and good humour. To make the best of a bad job, Drummond-Hay launched onto a discussion of general principles.

> Our grand object, I continued, was commerce; it furnished the sinews of our strength as it would theirs, if more liberally indulged; so that their wealth & prosperity was a matter of material interest to their friends, for we could never trade with them to such advantage to ourselves as when they prospered. I hinted moreover that they might discover, as we knew, and were examples of the truth of the proposition, – that a *commercial* navy was the only nursery whence could spring a national force upon the seas, that might bid defiance to insult.[88]

The consul and the *wazir* parted most amicably. Soon afterwards Drummond-Hay received a letter from ibn Idris, who told him that

> [...] having related all my conversation to the Sultan, H.I.M. had been vastly amused & satisfied saying that ye advice of the English consul was very good indeed for he had supported it by reasons undeniable. He had desired ... to express his satisfaction & to say that he much regretted the impolicy of his predecessors in destroying or allowing to go to ruin the naval force of Morocco, that he was only ... restrained at present by want of funds but so soon as they improved he would augment his naval force. That he would willingly extend his commerce & proposed to do so when he found his power sufficiently established to permit him with safety to admit more wealth to flow into channels which might at this moment be turned into danger to the state.

88 Bodleian MS Eng. hist. e. 349, 360.

Ibn Idris might want trade with Europe, but even though Drummond-Hay translated his title of *wazir* as 'prime minister', he had no executive power; he was no more than the ears and mouthpiece of the Sultan. Moulay Abderrahmane wanted trade too, but not at the expense of rebellion. His gnomic comment that wealth might 'flow into channels which might at this moment be turned into danger to the state' meant that trade might make rebels richer, not the Makhzan.

Rebellion

This was a reasonable fear. Foreign trade did indeed underpin powerful leaders in remote regions that the Makhzan could not control. One was Sidi Hashim, the Sharif of Iligh in the Tazeroualt oasis, on the fringes of the Sahara. Since agriculture was so precarious there, the Sharif engaged in commerce. He was a banker, lending and advancing capital, and a merchant, purchasing commodities in Essaouira and selling them at great profit in the markets of the Sous. His caravans brought slaves, gum Arabic, gold dust, and ostrich feathers from the southern side of the desert, and took back leatherwork and textiles from Marrakesh and European manufactures such as ironmongery, medicines and guns. He had great economic autonomy, although as head of the *zawiya* and a descendant of the prophet, the Sharif could hardly rebel against the *amir al-muminin*, the leader of the community.[89]

Another, Shaykh Bayruk of Guelmim, had no religious prestige. In the 1820s he turned his tiny settlement into an important trading centre by diverting some of the trans-Saharan trade. Relying on his own tribe, he established a web of trading posts across the Sahara and traded with Europeans on the coast. Indeed, he forced them to do business with him by holding for ransom European sailors shipwrecked on the coast. Control of commerce gave him political influence, which he increased by allying himself with local maraboutic families.[90]

Despite their autonomy, neither Bayruk nor Sidi Hashim was a threat to the Sultan. The danger was much more acute further north, in the Chaouïa. There, at the beginning of Moulay Slimane's reign, the leaders of the Abda and Doukkala tribes supported

89 Pascon, *Maison d'Iligh*, 43-8; Laroui, *Origines*, 137; Mohamed Ennaji and Paul Pascon, *Le Makhzen et le Sous al-Aqsa. La correspondance politique de la maison d'Iligh (1821-1894)* (Casablanca: Toubkal, 1988), 10.

90 Naimi, 'Tekna', 231, 234-6.

a series of pretenders who promised them a share of the export duties on grain.[91]

Ambitious local notables were only one source of trouble. The local governors and qaids whom the sultan had appointed were often avaricious, cruel or simply incompetent. To get rid of them, the tribes revolted. Since Moulay Abderrahmane refused to bow to outside pressure to remove his people, he faced several rebellions of this kind, some of which developed into something far worse. A rebellion by the Cherarda, that ended in 1828, began as a revolt against a governor; but its leader, al-Mahdi bin Muhammad al-Sharardi, capitalised on his name and announced that he was the 'expected Mahdi', who was destined to usher in a final thousand years of justice and peace before the world ended.[92] Millenarian revolts were dangerous because they usurped the very terms by which the sultan claimed legitimacy.[93]

Another danger came from inter-tribal rivalry. The endemic quarrel over resources led tribes that needed new territory to take over other peoples' grazing land. In the seventeenth century, the Ait Atta began moving relentlessly out of the Jbel Sarhro and posed such a threat to neighbouring tribes that a confederation, the Ait Yafalman ('People who seek the Peace'), was formed to oppose them.[94] It found not peace but years of fighting. The Rif coast was also beyond the sultan's control. In the mid-1840s, Drummond-Hay's chief bodyguard, bin Abu, wrote in a report to the Sultan that he could not restore order there because of 'the large number of the tribes and the enmity and rancour which exist between them and their lack of attention [to the Makhzan]...'[95]

Inter-tribal fighting and raiding was only a step away from banditry, and in the winter of 1829 Drummond-Hay travelled through several areas of bandit country. On the fringes of the great Mamora forest near Rabat, only luck prevented his baggage train being attacked and pillaged by people from the Zaër tribe, then in a

91 El Mansour, *Mawlay Sulayman*, 89-97.

92 Laroui, *Origines*, 158; al-Nasiri, *Kitab al-istiqsa* 9: 17-18

93 Laroui, *Origines*, 158.

94 Ross E. Dunn, 'Berber Imperialism: The Ait Atta Expansion in Southeast Morocco' in Ernest Gellner and Charles Micaud (eds) *Arabs and Berbers: From Tribe to Nation in North Africa* (London: Duckworth, 1972), 87-9; David Hart, *The Ait 'Atta of Southern Morocco: Daily Life and Recent History* (Wisbech: Menas Press, 1984), 6-7.

95 Moulay Abderrahmane to Busilham, 3 Dhi al-Hijja 1261/21 November 1845, MAPR Papers of Moulay Abderrahmane, series 2, 3-35.

state of rebellion.[96] Even close to Marrakesh, his party had to camp in a square, battlemented enclosure recently built by the sultan to provide protection for travellers.[97] Ahmad bin Tuwayr encountered the same problem: his journey was disrupted by intertribal fighting and the fear of robbers in the Wadi Dra'a, 'but God delivered us from them and from others besides'.[98]

Bilad al-siba and bilad al-makhzan

Not surprisingly, Europeans convinced themselves that Morocco was in a state of semi-permanent rebellion. In time, they elaborated a theory of a country divided into two political areas, *bilad al-makhzan*, the Arabic–speaking plains and cities, that obeyed the sultan and the *bilad al-siba*, the Berber-speaking mountains and deserts, that did not.[99]

This picture was too stark and sharply drawn, for most rebellions were temporary affairs and the term *siba* could be applied to urban rebellions too.[100] Although the Makhzan admitted that it could not control the Rif, it only mattered when that caused diplomatic problems. The 1799 treaty between Morocco and Spain excluded the Rif coast because it was impossible to prevent local people from attacking Spanish ships.[101] Otherwise, the Sultan was content to let the remoter regions well enough alone, since it was too expensive to maintain direct control over unproductive areas. He only required that the caravans get through, that bandits should not close the roads and, above all, that his leadership of the community be recognised in the Friday prayers, which was universally done. The 'dissident' areas still recognised the sultan, even if they took little notice of him in daily affairs. He was useful to them too. The Commander of the Faithful, the ultimate holder of *baraka*, could mediate their disputes, and the areas that he did control,

96 Bodleian MS Eng. hist. e. 349, 475ff; e. 346, 114.

97 *Ibid.*, e. 347, 257.

98 Ahmad bin Tuwayr, *Pilgrimage*, 2, 4.

99 Robin Bidwell, *Morocco under Colonial Rule: French Administration of Tribal Rule, 1915-1956* (London: Cass, 1973), 33; for a bald statement of the *siba-makhzan* distinction see Bernard Hoffman, *The Structure of Traditional Moroccan Rural Society* (The Hague: Mouton, 1967), 21.

100 K.L. Brown, 'Excursus sur l'insummission' in *Rivages et déserts. Hommage à Jacques Berque* (Paris: Sindbad, 1988), 99-109.

101 Clive Parry (ed.), *The Consolidated Treaty Series*, 231 vols (Dobbs Ferry, NJ: Oceana, 1969-81), 54:413-28.

the towns and plains, provided a refuge when feuding got out of hand, or the harvests failed.[102]

That is not to say that the sultan was happy that his direct authority was flouted. When he placed the Rif outside the treaty, and his authority, he also put it outside the *shari'a* in consequence. Educated men of the cities assumed that many inhabitants of the mountains and deserts were irreligious: their social behaviour, their morals, sexual and otherwise, their religious practices were all suspect. Most of the inhabitants of the mountains spoke one of three dialects of Berber, but it was not a written language and more than a millennium of Islam had made Arabic dominant in the towns and cities. Speaking Berber was, in the eyes of the elite, further evidence of lack of Islamic staunchness: they could not speak the language of the Quran.[103]

Yet Drummond-Hay found no evidence of disorderliness. When he visited the Berber-speaking Misfioua tribe in the High Atlas, he found the people most friendly: 'there was no tumult nor insulting manner, none of the jeers so usual with the *good* Musselmen of the towns. And this good behaviour was the more striking as we were doubtless the first body of Europeans that had for many ages, far indeed beyond their memory or knowledge entered their mountain recesses.'[104] Only when order broke down, did the sultan assert his authority.

Coercion and co-option

The sultan could contain rebels by breaking them, or by coopting them. The one did not exclude the other, and Consul Drummond-Hay witnessed both methods during his trip. Near Azemmour, amidst picturesque countryside, he saw the ruins of war and rebellion.

> The scenery was indeed such as the best taste would devise in an artificial wilderness of beauty but we were at the same time told that 2 years ago you could not pass thro' this district with less than 2,000 men. [...] Long walls on our right in several lines & about 3 feet high, said to have been built by the late rebels for their breastwork in front of their position. [...] It

102 Germain Ayache, 'La fonction d'arbitrage du Makhzan' in *Études d'histoire marocaine* (Rabat: SMER, 1979), 159-76.

103 C.R. Pennell, 'Makhzan and Siba in Morocco: an Examination of Early Modern Attitudes' in Joffe and Pennell (eds), *Tribe and State*.

104 Bodleian MS Eng. hist. e. 349, 411.

> is said that the rebels collected 9,000 men but the Emperor routed them on the first meet with about half that number of his troops. His Highness took 700 prisoners & cut off 170 heads which were as usual sent to the various provinces of the Empire.[105]

Closer to Marrakesh, his guides pointed out the distant ruins of the *zawiya* of Cherarda. The sultan had reduced it to ashes the previous year and allowed his troops to pillage what remained. The *wazir*, ibn Idris, was very satisfied and reported: 'More than 600 men have been taken prisoner, and everyone has enriched themselves from the goods, riches and treasure which were there.'[106] Pillage, like the exhibition of heads on the walls of the city, was a very public warning. Terror was an integral part of this system, humiliating a captured rebel as well as causing him pain. A common practice was to parade him round the town before killing him in a theatrical way.[107] But it was often cheaper and more useful to leave a rebel leader with his power and wealth virtually intact, if he agreed to come under the wing of the Makhzan. As the consular party travelled home, they passed through the Sraghna, whose pasha

> [...] is the descendant of several ancestors who have governed as almost independent chiefs & the present Basha is said not to have acknowledged any fealty to Mulai Abderachman until within these 2 years ... the Sultan is desirous of employing the strength of this basha to lower the pride & disposition to revolt which is suspected to exist in the Chief of the Rhamna.[108]

Even the leader of the Cherarda revolt was pardoned and, eventually, appointed as a governor.[109]

The towns

Drummond-Hay's 'good Musselmen' of the towns sometimes rebelled too. He only visited one really big town, Marrakesh, which had been devastated by plague thirty years before. Even before that it had been declining, shrinking inside its walls so that whole

105 *Ibid.*, e. 346, 177-83.

106 Al-Nasiri, *Kitab al-istiqsa*, 9:17-21; quotation from page 20.

107 Hammoudi, *Master and Disciple*, 63-4.

108 Bodleian MS Eng. hist. e. 349, 391-2.

109 Al-Nasiri, *Kitab al-istiqsa*, 9:21.

areas were left uninhabited.[110] The consul saw the rubble of a much larger city:

> We passed round the walls until we came to the market place of Thursdays called *Sok el Kemees* where we entered the city by the adjoining gate called thence the *Bab el Kemees* within which for several hundred yards we traversed heaps of undistinguishable ruins of tappia built dwellings which extended right & left to a nearly equal distance. [...] Piles of dirt, the refuse of life raised to the height [*sic*] of respectable hills much higher than the houses on the North & West of the city ... & upon our return home we mounted again near the noble *Jamaa l'-Kootoobea* one of these dunghills that we had ascended on a former day to feast our eyes with the melancholy but most impressive panorama of this ruined Capital.[111]

Even the vast royal gardens were dilapidated, although they were filled with fruit and decorative trees.

Despite the decay, Marrakesh was a great city, rivalled only by Fez. Their names were synonymous with Morocco. Edward Drummond-Hay, like many Europeans, referred to Marrakesh as 'Morocco city' and in other Arab lands Marrakesh was used as the name of the country. Only the Ottoman Turks (and modern ones, too) differed: they referred to Morocco as 'Fas'. In any event, the country was defined by its urban culture. Such cities had a life independent of the sultan, because they were only 'capitals' while he was in them. The capital could just as easily be a group of campaign tents. Marrakesh was a centre of administration, of learning and religion, and of commerce; its markets served the people of the surrounding countryside and its walls protected its citizens from them. Just outside its walls, Drummond-Hay visited the Thursday market where tribespeople came to buy and sell. On other days, pedlars from Marrakesh roamed the country markets.[112]

Power in the capital was held by the privileged class, the *khassa*. These were the *'ulama*, the important *sharifs*, the top Makhzan officials and rich merchants, men of wealth and authority, the people who 'bind and loose' (*ahl al-hall wa-laqd*), who signed the *bay'a* and made and broke sultans. From their families came governors and *qadis*. In large cities like Fez, Marrakesh or Tetuan they included descendants of people who had left Spain at the time

110 El Mansour, *Mawlay Sulayman*, 10-11.

111 Bodleian MS Eng. hist. e. 348, 324.

112 Schroeter, *Merchants of Essaouira*, 85-7.

of the Christian reconquest. Muhammad bin Abu, the commander of Drummond-Hay's escort, came from just such an Andalusian family.[113]

The commoners, the *amma*, provided much of the wealth. The towns were centres of industry: Fez was famous for its leatherwork, and its textiles, Salé for shoes. All towns had metalworkers. These artisans and craftsmen belonged to guilds that organised and helped administer their members.[114] Beneath them was a large unskilled, floating, population of casual workers and peddlers. But even they were not entirely disorganised, for just as the inhabitants of the countryside mountains and deserts had an identity only as members of tribes, so the inhabitants of the cities found protection and solidarity in urban groups based upon the patronage of a marabout, on the craft guilds, and in the irregular militias, the *rumat* that were organised on a neighbourhood basis.[115]

Moulay Slimane believed the *amma* had no political status at all, and sneered that they 'should rather count among the dead than the living'.[116] This was wishful thinking. For the most part the towns and cities were orderly, controlled by market officers (*muhtasibs*) and qaids by day; at night the gates were shut while an urban watch patrolled the streets.[117] But the *'amma* made dangerous rebels. Their faction leaders could mobilise them and, sometimes cooperate with factions among the *khassa*; in Fez, in 1820, an alliance of *sharifs* and the big Andalusian families found support among the militia,[118] and in 1831 the Oudaia troops revolted with the help of the urban mob. Throughout the nineteenth century the artisans, the militia and the flotsam of the streets were disorderly and rebellious, but they were not the lowest stratum in society. That, legally at least, was the lot of the slaves.

The slaves

Legal stipulation was one thing, reality quite another. Slavery was

113 El Mansour, *Mawlay Sulayman*, 12-13.

114 Roger Le Tourneau, *Fès avant le Protectorat: Etude économique d'une ville de l'occident musulman* (Casablanca: Éditions la Porte, 1949), 275-322; Kenneth L. Brown, *People of Salé: Tradition and Change in a Moroccan City 1830-1930* (Manchester University Press, 1976), 135-8.

115 El Mansour, *Mawlay Sulayman*, 202-8; Hammoudi, *Master and Disciple*, 78.

116 El Mansour *Mawlay Sulayman*, 11.

117 Brown, *Salé*, 45; Le Tourneau, *Fès*, 251-3; George Borrow, *The Bible in Spain* (London: Dent/Everyman, 1947), 510.

118 El Mansour, *Mawlay Sulayman*, 202-8.

a necessary part of a hierarchical society, particularly one organised along the lines of patronage: the master owned his servants in the most absolute sense, and it was part of the social order. Indeed the social order in part depended upon it. Slaves were a commodity that could be exchanged in a way that sealed links of obligation and patronage between the powerful and the less powerful. Husayn, the master of Iligh, on the edge of the Sahara, sealed his relationship with the sultan by sending him regular presents of slaves, as well as other products of the trade across the Sahara.[119] Slaves were employed as agricultural workers, pressing olives or building irrigation systems. But they were more commonly used as domestic servants.[120] Drummond-Hay noted that in the house of the Shaykh of Guérando, a rural notable who had managed to cultivate the stony ground on the way to Marrakesh, but was nevertheless hardly a rich man, the slaves mingled with the female members of his family:

> We passed through an inclosure of rude stone walls into a large tent where were several of his female slaves preparing the grain of cuscusoo. The chief ... pointed out to me his two wives, his two daughters & two sons. I did not understand there were more of his children in the party, altho' there were more young women, who might probably fill some other station not uncommon in this country into which I did not think it advisable to inquire.[121]

Many female slaves were indeed concubines, but the majority of women slaves worked as domestic servants. Male slaves were sometimes equally integrated into the family of their owner and acted as his agents. Many were given highly responsible tasks and were highly trained: some as secretaries and accountants, others as musicians, others as specialist gardners. Often the sultan's palace would send slaves to the houses of important provincial notables to be trained there, creating yet another line of patronage and clientage.[122]

The slaves themselves could develop strong personal relationships with their masters and Ahmad bin Tuwayr reported of a famous marabout with whom he stayed: 'When a lad of his died,

119 Ennaji and Pascon, *Le Makhzen et le Sous al-Aqsa*, 12.

120 Mohammed Ennaji, *Soldats, domestiques et concubines. L'esclavage au Maroc au XIXme siècle* (Casablanca: Eddif, 1994).

121 Bodleian MS Eng. hist. e. 347, 249.

122 Ennaji, *Soldats*, 30-4.

a valuable slave of his, on the day of the feast, he recited for him the Sūrā of Yāsīn. He prayed for him, and he told me to pray for him also.'[123]

This took on a particularly important political complexion in the Makhzan, where slaves were often high officials, particularly in the slave army, the *abid al-bukhari*.

Not all slaves reached such elevated status of course, and on occasion the agricultural slaves of powerful men were left to shift for themselves without food, and others were punished in the most savage manner.[124] Many of the men fled ill-treatment and became bandits, some sought refuge in *zawiyas*. This last was the choice of women too, some of whom were particularly badly treated by their owners, although not all women who fled were actual slaves: ill treatment at home on occasion led women to leave their tribe and take up residence in a neighbouring tribe or with a *zawiya*: this was frequent enough for one of the sultan's officials at the end of the century to write that 'every tribe at present has a certain number of women from another tribe'.[125]

We actually know very little indeed about the lives of Moroccan women in the early part of the nineteenth century, and what we do know is confined to those who were publicly visible – either to European travellers, or in the Moroccan archives dealing with slavery. In other words there are more glimpses of poor women than of rich ones. Outside the elite, certainly, Drummond-Hay's difficulty in distinguishing between slave women and free women may have been a reflection of the status of women generally.

The Jews

If slaves and women were set apart by their social status, Jews were set apart by their religion. In towns they lived in their own quarter, or *millah*. Drummond-Hay remarked how dirty were the streets of the *millah* in Rabat, and how sickly the inhabitants, although their houses were clean enough inside.[126] In Marrakesh it was the same: '[in] the dirty *Millah* or Jewery ... we noticed much activity in various tradesfolk, decent assortment of goods exhibited in the little shops & and air of business about this singular &

123 Ahmad bin Tuwayr, *Pilgrimage*, 5.

124 Ennaji, *Soldats*, 39, 58-9

125 *Ibid.*, 88 and 80 which is the source of the quotation.

126 Bodleian MS Eng. hist. e. 346, 138.

here unluckedly enslaved people.'[127] Even the small town of Settat had its Jewish quarter a 'miserable assemblage of dirty tattered tents', where between eighty and one hundred families lived precariously by cultivating 'a little land' and from commerce. They were too poor to move to a larger town.[128]

There were other Jewish communities in the mountains. When Drummond-Hay visited the High Atlas, he found a village where twenty-five out of the one hundred or so families were Jewish. The Shaykh of the Jews arranged picturesque dancing and a wild party, when the Consul got rather drunk. More usefully, the Shaykh gave him his first Berber word-list, for these rural Jews spoke Berber to their neighbours and Judeo-Arabic among themselves.[129]

Many of the poorer Jews who lived in the towns were migrants from the countryside, mostly small-scale artisans and shopkeepers, or hawkers and pedlars. There was also a Jewish upper class often descended from families expelled from Spain in 1492. They spoke a dialect of medieval Spanish and even had Spanish names: Parientes, Pinto and Toledano. They were bankers and merchants, the sort of people whom Mohammed III had encouraged to settle in his new royal port at Essaouira. There, they acted as his agents, because they were part of a trading community that stretched across the Mediterranean. Families like the Solals had members in Tunis, Genoa, Constantinople and Gibraltar; the Bensaudes had relatives in Gibraltar, Lisbon, Oran and London.[130]

Some of the sultans' Jewish agents graduated to semi-official positions. One Jew was chief of customs in Tangier in 1819 and another in 1826.[131] Drummond-Hay's suspected that his principal interpreter, Isaac Abensur, was working for the Makhzan:

> It appears to me that Isaac Abensur pumped me as much as he could ... about his desire the better to prepare a translation of my proposed address to ye Sultan, in order ... to prepare the Sultan & his advisers & thus pursue in order that course of espionage, for which doubtless he is well paid. This office of Interpreter must answer to him better than we would suppose

127 *Ibid.*, e. 348, 308.

128 *Ibid.*, e. 349, 428-30.

129 *Ibid.*, 369-74; Michael M. Laskier, *The Alliance Israëlite Universelle and the Jewish Communities of Morocco, 1862-1962* (Albany, NY: State University of New York Press, 1983), 12-13, 8-10.

130 Miège, *Le Maroc et l'Europe* 2:95-6.

131 M. Mitchell Serels, *A History of the Jews of Tangier in the Nineteenth and Twentieth Centuries* (New York: Sepher-Hermon Press, 1991), 7.

from the scant amount of his allowance as Interpreter to the Brit: Consulate...[132]

Yet, like the other European consuls, Drummond-Hay appointed Jews as agents and vice-consuls in the smaller ports. The British Vice-Consul in Rabat was a member of the Sumbel family that had connections with the Makhzan going back to Muhammad III's time.[133]

The Makhzan and the foreign consuls kept the Jews safe. In every town, the *millah* was close to the walls of the royal palace or the residence of the governor, even in a miserable place like Settat. Because the Jews had a revealed religion, the *shari'a* required the sultan to protect them, but it also made them subservient. They paid a special poll-tax (*jizya*), they were forbidden to mount horses or to carry arms, and in some towns had to take off their shoes when passing a mosque. In 1815 Moulay Slimane reiterated an old requirement that they wear special clothing; in a *qadi's* court, their word could not be accepted against that of a Muslim.[134] Instead, Jews had their own rabbinic courts to deal with inheritance, personal status, contracts and financial affairs. They could practise their religion and in each town, the rabbis and a council organised communal life, schools and welfare systems. A shaykh of the Jews collected taxes for the sultan.[135] This separateness did not prevent them from taking part in everyday economic life. In 1810 members of the guilds in Salé wrote to the sultan to defend the reputation of the market inspector (*muhtasib*). Of the 162 men who signed the letter, twenty were Jews.[136]

Yet many Muslims disliked the Jews and at times of tension urban mobs sacked the *millahs*; in the eighteenth century, this happened four times in Meknès alone. In the early nineteenth century so many Jews were working for foreign consuls that many Muslims suspected that Jews were agents of European powers. Reports spread that Jews had cooperated with the French during the occupation of Egypt between 1798 and 1805; they were even supposed to have helped to translate the Quran.[137]

132 Bodleian MS Eng. hist. e. 348, 293.

133 Schroeter, *Merchants*, 18.

134 El Mansour, *Mawlay Sulayman*, 15.

135 Laskier, *Alliance*, 12-13.

136 Brown, *Salé*, 138.

137 El Mansour, *Mawlay Sulayman*, 15.

Morocco as mosaic

Were the Jews part of Moroccan society or outside it? The question could be asked, in different ways certainly, about many of the elements of the political and social structure. In 1830 this was not a unitary system but, like most societies, a conglomeration of its parts. Yet those parts were, in a twentieth-century perspective, unusually autonomous. The ruling institution, the Makhzan, called in the support of several different hierarchies, and enforced obedience when it had to (and could). There was a tribal hierarchy in which some tribes obeyed the sultan and some did not, and this varied according to circumstance. There was a hierarchy of *tariqas*, some more prone than others to cooperate with the sultan. There was a religious and learned establishment and a military one, both to a large degree dependant on the Makhzan, but available for the use of whatever member of the Alaoui family controlled that Makhzan. These different groups were themselves fragmented, but also held together by the genealogical and patriarchal systems that defined them. Genealogy of kin underpinned both the tribal structure and the ruling family, and genealogical links helped to determine the divisions that factionalised them. A genealogy of knowledge, or the transmission of knowledge, differentiated the *tariqas*. These systems of coalescence and division were overlain by others based on mutuality, or at least patronage, and the exercise of force both by the sultan towards those he ruled and between segments of the tribes. The alternative to force was arbitration whose principles also ran through every level of society: from Makhzan to tribe, sultan to local marabout, there was an arbitrator available. This system was not chaotic, however it might have appeared to European observers like Drummond-Hay: it had rules of conduct that were defined externally and structurally by religion and by the logic of political relationships. Men, families and groups did not simply enter the political scene in an arbitrary fashion: indeed from the ruling family down to the qadis in charge of mosques, certain families had considerable longevity, and certain tribes and family factions were long-term participants. The Makhzan has been described as 'a stable system of organised violence',[138] and that could be applied more widely throughout society: to the tribal structure in the countryside, or to the factions in the cities. It was stable in that it could continue, provided that there was no outside force to throw out the balance between force and

138 Waterbury, *Commander*, 15.

patronage, between hierarchy and faction. The events of 1830 would show that there was such an outside force: Europe.

Most Moroccans mistrusted their neighbours to the north, although even the most educated Moroccans knew little about Europe. The Strait of Gibraltar divided two worlds, and eighteenth-century Moroccan ambassadors who wrote accounts of their trips made little attempt to distinguish between European cultures. Although they praised some social institutions like hospitals and military training, there was no equivalent of Drummond-Hay's hour-by hour, mile-by-mile account of his trip. Many aspects of European life horrified them, such as dances and public entertainments where men mingled with women and European religion was deeply, shockingly perverse: Catholicism's strange religious festivals, its monasticism, its papacy and priesthood, and above all its deification of Jesus Christ.[139]

A tiny elite of Moroccans knew Europeans quite well, for there had been peace treaties with European powers for centuries, and the Makhzan was accustomed to international law, despite its non-Islamic origins. For most of Moulay Slimane's reign, European consuls dealt with Muhammad bin Abd al-Salam al-Slawi, the governor of Larache, who signed himself *wazir al-bahar*, 'minister of the sea', which the Europeans translated as 'foreign minister'.[140] In 1801 he wrote to the French consul that the Berber guards at Agadir could not be expected to help a French ship because 'they are Berber people and do not know the way of the sea (*tariq al-bahar*)'.[141]

Foreigners were people beyond the ken of ordinary Moroccans, with some exceptions, The people of the Rif fought the Christians, but also traded with them because they needed to sell their produce; equally the Spanish, bottled up behind the walls of Melilla, needed food.[142] Christians were mostly feared. In 1827 when war started

139 Hassan Elboudrari, 'L'exotisme à l'envers. Les premiers voyageurs marocains en orient (Espagne, XVIIème-XVIIIème siècles) et leur expérience de l'altérité' in J.C. Vatin (ed.), *D'un orient l'autre: les métamorphoses successives des perceptions et connaissances*, (Paris: Editions du CNRS, 1991), 377-401.

140 El Mansour, *Mawlay Sulayman*, 19.

141 C.R. Pennell, 'The interpenetration of European and Islamic law in the western Mediterranean in the early nineteenth century', *British Journal of Middle Eastern Studies*, 21 (1994): 159-89, quoting AND Tanger AF 75, Hamid bin Abd al-Salam al-Slawi to [French vice-consul], 15 Jumada I 1216/19 Sept. 1801.

142 Henk Driessen, *On the Spanish-Moroccan Frontier: a Study in Ritual, Power and Ethnicity* (Oxford: Berg, 1992), 24-9, 33; C.R. Pennell, 'The Geography of Piracy: Northern Morocco in the Nineteenth Century', *Journal of Historical Geography*, 20, no. 3 (1994): 272-82.

between the French and the Ottoman province of Algiers, it was rumoured that this was a general attack on the Muslims of North Africa.[143] The Austrian landing at Larache in June 1829 frightened people even more, and the captain of a British naval survey ship who arrived the previous year found that his attempts to gain information 'were thwarted by their dread and suspicion of us'. A prophecy was circulating that 'in four years' time the Christians will conquer their country'.[144]

In fact, conquest was two, not four, years off, and it was Algeria, not Morocco that was invaded. But the waves would wash deeply across the land.

143 Phillipe de Cossé-Brissac, 'Les Rapports de la France et du Maroc pendant la guerre de l'Algérie (1930-1847)', *Hésperis*, 13 (1931): 35-203; reference here to 40.

144 Royal Naval Hydrographic Archive, Taunton, OD. AP.I/1, Extracts from Remark Books of Captn Boteler on Barbary Coast between August 18th and September 20th 1828, p. 1; S.L. 4 Boteler 1828-29 Captain's letters, H.M. Sloop *Hecla* at Santa Cruz de Tenerife, 30 Oct. 1828.

2

DEFEAT

The European Challenge

Despite all the predictions, the Christians landed in Algiers. Even so, Moroccans could not escape the consequences. After the Ottoman dey surrendered, on 5 July 1830, to a French army that had disembarked less than three weeks before, the sultan and his subjects had to choose between helping their co-religionists and living with their new and powerful neighbour.

Indeed, it was not long before foreign forces would invade Morocco itself. Twice, over the next generation, the Moroccan army would be defeated and Moroccan territory occupied, first by French and then by Spanish armies. Yet the occupation was never permanent at this stage. In an effort to cope with the danger, Moulay Abderrahmane did try to restructure his shaken Makhzan. He was not the only Muslim ruler who faced this problem, and to a limited extent he imitated the Ottoman Sultan or the Pasha of Egypt and tried to remake his financial and military systems. Only to an even more limited extent did he succeed: a really biting reform would have threatened the links of patronage and mutuality that underlay his own power.

There could, for example, be no real changes in the Makhzan that would call into question the legitimacy, or even the efficacy of the Alaoui system. There could be no changes that cost huge amounts, because there was no money in the treasury, and attempts to raise taxation threatened rebellion. Changes to the military structure undermined the system of tribal alliances on which the sultanate depended.

Yet the fact remains that Morocco was not occupied permanently by any European power. Part of the reason lay in the extreme difficulty of doing so: not the sultan's armies, but local, tribal, forces showed themselves well able to resist European invasion. That was a marker for the future: in the early twentieth century, the Rifis would show just what they were capable of against the Spanish and French. For the moment, the French army had come up against determined opposition in Algeria and French military leaders and politicians had no desire to engage in adventurism in Morocco. For its part, the British government had no intention of allowing such adventurism: the security of sea lanes into the Mediterranean required a weak state to hold the southern side of the Strait of Gibraltar rather than a powerful, European one. The balance of power in Europe kept Morocco free of European occupation: a western Mediterranean version of the Eastern Question that helped determine European chancelleries' attitudes towards the Ottoman Empire. That consideration brought British and French support for the Ottoman Sultan during the Crimean war in the 1850s, and incidentally forced both governments to cooperate in Morocco.

That did not mean that there was no European intervention in Morocco. Quite the contrary, it grew in commerce, in the economy and in politics. The government in London presided over the most powerful economy, and the most powerful navy, on earth and its agents in Morocco saw to it that British political and economic hegemony was extended there, through a series of treaties that lesser governments quickly imitated.

Yet the sultan and his agents did not passively suffer the consequences of this growing European intervention. Instead they tried to use it to their own advantage, if not always to the advantage of the people whom they ruled. The Makhzan's servants were able and experienced men, who would not willingly allow the system on which they depended to die. They traded, and they tried to manipulate the European powers, not always unsuccessfully, and often in a rather haphazard fashion: it was always difficult to fix on a single policy because all options offered advantages and problems. The French invasion of Algeria was just such a test.

The Algerian challenge

Before the landing, the French consul in Tangier had reassured the Makhzan that there was no threat to Morocco. Moulay Abderrahmane replied the war was nothing to do with him and even promised to provide supplies to the French forces. Afterwards he wrote to General Clauzel to congratulate him on his success.[1] The French army had not advanced beyond Algiers itself, so perhaps the city would remain just another European enclave on the north African coast, irritating and inconvenient like the Spanish garrisons, but not dangerous. It was not until June 1831 that the French prime minister announced that the whole of Algeria was to be

[1] De Cossé-Brissac, 'Rapports de la France', 10-11.

taken over, but even then French troops only occupied Algiers, Oran and Bône.[2]

Other forces did pull the sultan into the Algerian war. The collapse of the Turks left western Algeria with no effective ruler, so that Fez, Oujda, Taza, and Marrakesh were exposed if the French army did advance. Also, the pilgrimage routes passed through Tlemcen, the first Algerian town over the border, where the Fasi merchant class had important commercial interests. Shortly after Algiers fell, Muhammad Bennouna, a Tlemceni merchant from an old Fasi family, organised a deputation to ask Moulay Abderrahmane to accept a *bay'a* from Tlemcen.[3]

The sultan had no wish to tangle with the French army, so he referred the Tlemceni petition to the '*ulama* in Fez who provided him with the *fatwa* he wanted. They ruled that the inhabitants of Tlemcen had already sworn allegiance to the Ottoman Sultan and they could not change it now. The Tlemcenis were more than equal to the debate. In September 1830 they sent another letter arguing that the authority of the Sublime Porte no longer existed, and that its former representatives had been irreligious tyrants. They quoted an early fifteenth-century Moroccan commentator on the religious traditions (*hadith*): 'Thus al-Ubbi, in his commentary on Muslim, speaking of a case similar to ours, declared that if the imam is unable to ensure that his orders are carried out in some country, it is permissible to choose another in his place and proclaim him, and any delay in the proclamation will lead to damnation.'[4]

The French invasion of Algeria had made the old argument about the legitimacy of power and of rebellion newly relevant: a sultan's rule depended on him being just and protecting the *Dar al-Islam.* The arena had been marked out for the rest of the century. Many Moroccans agreed with the Tlemcenis and wanted to help struggling fellow-Muslims. Finally, in October 1830 the Sultan sent Moulay Ali bin Sulayman (at once his cousin and his brother-in-law) to take control of Tlemcen. He had 500 troops, hardly a great military enterprise.

The weakness of the Moroccan system now stood out starkly. Moulay Ali was appointed not because he was an experienced

2 Charles Robert Ageron, *Modern Algeria: a History from 1830 to the Present*, trans. Michael Brett (London: Hurst, 1991); Raphael Danziger, *Abd al-Qadir and the Algerians: Resistance to the French and Internal Consolidation* (New York: Holmes & Meier, 1977).

3 Miège, *Le Maroc et l'Europe*, 2:157-8; Danziger, *Abd al-Qadir*, 42-3.

4 Al-Nasiri, *Kitab al-istiqsa* 9:28-9. Al-Ubbi died in 1425.

military leader, but because he was an Alaoui. Although he was pious and loyal he was otherwise quite unsuitable. He was only fifteen years old, and an uncle of the sultan, Idris al-Jarari, the Governor of Oujda, was sent with him to help. Neither of these two men was politically adroit. Although his proclamations made great play with religious solidarity, Moulay Ali let local rivalries continue unchecked, while his troops pillaged the countryside instead of taking the citadel of Tlemcen, still manned by Ottoman troops. In March 1831 the sultan recalled both of them, but their replacement, ibn el-Hami, the governor of Tetuan, was no better.

The Moroccan intervention in Algeria made it clear that the Alaoui leadership could not orchestrate the popular feelings against the French to their own advantage. They were much too frightened to do so, and when a French warship appeared at Tangier in January 1832 the Makhzan hurried to negotiate. The Sultan agreed to withdraw his troops and Moroccan troops evacuated Tlemcen in May.[5] Before he left, ibn al-Hami appointed a new governor in the sultan's name. This was the local head of the Qadiriyya *tariqa*, Muhyi al-Din, who began to organise resistance to the French. In November he handed the leadership to his son, Abd al-Qadir, who was proclaimed *amir al-muminin*, Commander of the Faithful.[6] A *jihad* had begun in Algeria, beyond the Sultan's control, although it acted in his name.

The Makhzan's commerce

Meanwhile, the sultan tried to profit from the new order. In exchange for withdrawal from Tlemcen, the French had offered free trade across the frontier. Moulay Abderrahmane announced that he would sell grain to European buyers, opened ports that had previously been closed, such as Casablanca, lowered export taxes on wheat and allowed the export of wool.[7] There was plenty of demand in Europe. Grain, wool, skins, wax and gum all increased in price and Moroccan exports nearly doubled in value between 1833 and 1834. By 1836 they had risen by another 50%.[8] The Sultan took a personal interest. He himself tried to arrange for the importation of some Spanish sheep into Morocco in 1840, after a Fasi merchant reported on the quality and quantity of

5 Danziger, *Abd al-Qadir*, 44-5.

6 *Ibid.*, 51.

7 PRO FO 99/1 58-63, E.W. Drummond Hay to Palmerston, Tangier, 22 March 1838; Miège, *Le Maroc et l'Europe*, 2:44, 67, 84.

8 Miège, *Le Maroc et l'Europe*, 2:45, 67.

the wool on the sheep in Cataluña.[9] His son, Moulay Ahmad, the governor of the Chaouïa, encouraged Casablanca to begin growing from an almost derelict village into an active port: it handled 3% of Moroccan trade in 1836 and 10% in 1843.[10]

Since the sultan's purpose was to raise money without taxing the general population, he was anxious to keep control of trade for himself and his officials. So he barred European traders from the ports without his permission and forbade them completely from living in the interior. His preferred intermediaries were Jews, like the Corcos and Aflalo families of Essaouira to whom he advanced trading capital, or the Syrian Altaras family who linked Morocco with Marseille, Cyprus, Livorno, and India.[11]

Other Makhzan families had their own Jewish intermediaries. Fasi merchant houses joined with the Jewish merchant community in Gibraltar to supply Abd al-Qadir with powder and munitions. One participant in this profitable enterprise was Talib bin Jallun, the former chief *wazir*, whom Edward Drummond-Hay named as the richest merchant in the country in 1840. His real wealth came from commerce across the Sahara with Timbuktu; in the early 1840s it was estimated that Saharan products re-exported to Europe made up between 11 and 16% of total maritime exports from Morocco. Another prominent Saharan merchant was Muhammad Binnis who in 1840 controlled the mint in Fez, a useful synergy with the trans-Saharan gold trade. In 1838 Binnis purchased a licence to export oxen to Gibraltar in numbers far exceeding anyone else and, it was alleged, at a specially low price. Commerce was the principal support of the Makhzan.[12]

Despite the efforts of the sultan and the Makhzan trading families, Europeans did succeed in breaking into the Moroccan market with the help of Jewish merchants. Since so few of their own subjects lived in the ports, European consuls appointed ever more Jews as vice-consuls and consular agents. The resulting immunity gave them so much advantage that in the mid-1830s, the sultan tried to stop the practice, but the British, French and Spanish

9 AHN Estado, 5825 Expediente Tanger – 1840 "Sobre el envio de seis parejas de carneros para el Emperador de Marruecos", Beramendí to Evaristo Perez de Castro Tanger 4 Abril 1840.

10 Miège, *Le Maroc et l'Europe*, 2:182-3.

11 *Ibid.*, 88, 97.

12 *Ibid.*, 152, 155-8, 160-1; Mansour, *Mawlay Sulayman*, 219; Bodleian Library MS 494, 147; PRO FO99/1 58-63, E.W. Drummond Hay to Palmerston Tangier 28 March 1838.

governments simply ignored him.[13] The problem of foreign protection would overwhelm Morocco later in the century.

Local commerce

A much more immediate threat to the Makhzan's trade monopoly came from the fringes of Morocco. In the far south, Shaykh Bayruk at Guelmim and Husayn bin Hisham at Iligh started trading with Europeans through intermediaries, often Jewish. Bayruk contacted first the British traveller John Davidson and then the French Consul Jacques Delaporte, both of whom hoped to see their countries trading with Timbuctu. Davidson died trying to reach Timbuktu.[14] European merchants found that Bayruk was a kindred spirit whose thoughts on trade and government, as he expressed them to a French traveller, had a strongly utilitarian ring:

> A man should not simply wait for riches at home, he should go and seek them, carrying the produce of his country in order to exchange it with that of foreigners. In his wisdom God has given some people what is lacking elsewhere, obliging men to enter into relationships, uniting them by common interest and thus permanently banishing the spirit of war. If God has inspired us to nominate a chief from amongst us, he has done so in order to manage those relationships. Such a thing would not have been possible if every people did not have in its midst someone who could translate its desire to deal with others. Otherwise, how could two peoples communicate, if each member attempted to speak at the same time? Now the first duty of this chief is to guarantee peace and to encourage what is the root of all greatness. This is what I try to do by using the income which my position bestows upon me to dispatch trade caravans in all directions.[15]

On the Mediterranean coast, too, people seized new opportunities. The French invasion may have disrupted the coastal trade briefly, but not for long. Within a few years, small boats from the central and eastern Rif were plying between Tetuan and Algeria carrying wool, skins, wax and, of course, firearms. In the 1840s and 1850s, a marabout from the Banu Sa'id, Sidi Muhammad al-Hadary ran several boats and carefully built up relations with the French and the British consuls in Tangier, and the Spanish authorities

13 Miège, *Le Maroc et l'Europe*, 2:90-1.

14 Schroeter, *Merchants*, 161; Naimi, 'Tekna', 235.

15 Léopolde Panet, *Première exploration du Sahara Occidental. Relation d'un voyage du Sénégal au Maroc, 1850* (Paris: Le Livre Africian, 1968), 105.

in Melilla. These alliances were for his own commercial benefit, and he was extremely anxious that the sultan should not hear of them.[16]

The sultan disliked uncontrolled trading because it undercut the Makhzan's commercial operations and undermined his power. In 1845 Moulay Abderrahmane wrote to Husayn bin Hashim, Bayruk's rival at Iligh, asking him to try to stop Bayruk's contact with the Europeans. He said it was an 'innovation', and therefore a heresy,[17] but he was unable to rein in Bayruk himself.

Military weakness

The sultan turned to intermediaries like Husayn bin Hashim because he had little power of his own. His navy could not stop smuggling, much less face down any European threat. Indeed it could hardly put to sea at all. When, in 1837, he ordered the rotting hulks in Larache to be prepared to sail, the Spanish consul-general remarked perceptively that this was all a show; the sultan was trying to convince people, inside and outside the country, that he had more power that he really did.[18] In July 1841 three ships did set sail, armed with letters of marque to attack 'Christian' shipping,[19] which meant Spanish smugglers on the Mediterranean coast. One ship limped into Gibraltar and saluted the town, taking five minutes to load between shots,[20] but one of the others actually arrested an undoubted Spanish smuggler. This caused such a diplomatic storm that naval activity was afterwards abandoned. The Moroccan government could not control the waters off its coasts.

On land, the Sultan was more persistent. He re-equipped his army, largely from British sources. The Ordnance Department supplied 'one thousand stand of arms' and 4,000 bayonets in 1839; and, several times in the early 1840s, the Sultan instructed the Governors of Tetuan and Tangier to purchase gunpowder, guns and other matériel from Gibraltar.[21]

16 C.R. Pennell, 'The Maritime Trade on the Northern Morocco Coast in the Early Nineteenth Century', *Morocco* (n.s), 1 (1996): 85-96: Abdelmajid Benjelloun, *Fragments d'histoire du Rif oriental, et notamment des Beni Said, dans la deuxième moitié du XIXme siècle, d'après les documents de Mr Hassan Ouchen* ([Rabat]: Textes à l'Appui, 1995).

17 Ennaji and Pascon, *Le Makhzen et le Sous al-Aqsa*, 41.

18 Beramendí to Calatrava, Tanger, 2 January 1837, AHN Estado, 8364.

19 Dahir of Mawlay 'Abd al-Rahman dated 2 Jumada II 1257/ 22 July 1841, MAPR 6/5 – 2.

20 Beramendí to González, Tanger, 3 September 1841, AHN Estado 8365.

21 Woodford to E.W. Drummond-Hay, Gibraltar 28 June 1839 and Bridgeman to

These military preparations were intended to keep control inside Morocco and so to hold off European threats. In the 1830s and 1840s the Sultan sent several expeditions into the Rif, both to raise taxes and stop smuggling and to maintain the Makhzan guard at Badis that kept the peace with the Spanish in the fortress at Peñon de Vélez. After local people clashed with the Spanish in Ceuta in 1843 and 1844, he fortified that frontier too and forbade them any contact with the Spanish.[22]

Revolts

There were also rebellions to stop. In 1841 the Haha tribes rebelled and, no sooner had they been defeated than the Zaër and Banu Hassan tribes rose in the rich and fertile plains between Meknès and Rabat. In October, the Tafilalt rebelled and by February of the following year the Sous was in general revolt.[23]

The sultan's army could not stop these rebellions, and on occasion was responsible for them. The Oudaia army rebelled in Fez in 1832 and proclaimed Moulay Mohammed bin el-Tayyib, the sultan's cousin. The *abid* army supported the sultan, but it took two years before the revolt was crushed. The Oudaia was then demilitarised.[24] The Cherarda were equally lawless. Having

---

E.W. Drummond-Hay, Gibraltar 12 Oct. 1839, GGA CA 2/4, 104, 223; MAPR Series 5, file 4–38, Mawlay 'Abd al-Rahman to Muhammad 'Ash'ash, 19 Rabi' II 1256/ 20 June 1840; file 5–19, Mawlay 'Abd al-Rahman to Busilham bin 'Ali, 13 Muharram 1257/ 7 Mar. 1841; file 6–3, Mawlay 'Abd al-Rahman to Muhammad 'Ash'ash, 7 Rajab 1257/ 25 Aug. 1841 and 32, Mawlay 'Abd al-Rahman to Busilham, 29 Rabi' II 1258/ 9 June 1842; file 8–9, Mawlay 'Abd al-Rahman to Busilham, 16 Jumada I 1259/ 14 June 1843 and 15, Mawlay 'Abd al-Rahman to Busilham, 7 Jumada II 1259/ 5 July 1843; file 9–8 Mawlay 'Abd al-Rahman to Muhammad 'Ash'ash, 17 Jumada I 1260/ 4 June 1844.

22 Mawlay 'Abd al-Rahman to 'Abd al-Salam al-Salawi, MAPR Series 5 file 4–6, 8 Dhi al-Hijja 1254 / 30 July 1838); file 4–10 (13 Jumada II 1254/ 3 Sept. 1838); file 4–19, 12 Dhi al-Hijja 1254/ 26 Feb. 1839); Mawlay 'Abd al-Rahman letters to Busilham b. 'Ali, file 5–8 22 Shuwal 1256/ 17 Dec. 1840; file 6–16, 14 Dhi al-Qa'da 1257/ 28 Dec. 1841; file 6–19, 3 Safar 1258/ 16 Mar. 1842; file 6–23, 6 Safar 1258/ 19 Mar. 1842; file 6–30, 17 Rabi' II 1258/ 28 May 1842; file 7–13, 3 Ramadan 1258/ 8 Oct. 1842; file 7–23, 8 Muharram 1259/ 8 Feb. 1843; file 7–34, 19 Rabi' II 1259/ 19 May 1843; file 8–18, 7 Ramadan 1259/ 1 Oct. 1843; file 8–21, 12 Ramadan 1259/ 6 Oct. 184; file 8–38, 14 Rabi' I 1260 3 April 1844.

23 MAEF Nantes, Tanger, Anciens Fonds A1-3 bis 'Correspondance de la Direction Politique, 1839-1845', draft of a letter, de Nyon to [Guizot], Tanger, 3 July 1841; *ibid.*, draft of a letter, de Nyon to [Guizot] Tanger 17 Aug. 1841; *ibid.*, draft of a letter, de Nyon to [Guizot], Tanger 5 Oct. 1841; *ibid.*, draft of a letter, de Nyon to [Guizot], Tanger, 6 Feb. 1842.

24 Al-Nasiri, *Kitab al-istiqsa*, 9:32-41

put down the rebellion in the Tafilalt, they began murdering the women captives they had enslaved, leaving their bodies to be found in the environs of Fez.

The sultan dealt with some troublemakers severely and theatrically. One leader of the Oudaia revolt was thrown to the dogs, who ate up all of him 'apart from his feet with their chain'. Forty of the murderous Cherardis had a hand and foot cut off and were left to bleed to death. Rebels' heads were dispatched, packed in salt, to adorn the city gates of various towns.[25] However, when he had to, the Sultan bought off trouble. In 1840 he gave all the troops in Tangier an extra year's salary to quieten discontent.[26] This did not make for a reliable or competent army. Its nemesis came at Isly in 1844, when Abd al-Qadir's resistance dragged Moulay Abderrahmane back into western Algeria.

Defeat in Algeria

When Moroccan troops left Algeria in 1832, the Makhzan did not break links with Abd al-Qadir. The Algerian amir received arms, called himself the sultan's *khalifa*, and the '*ulama* in Fez provided him with *fatwas* that legitimised him and his statelet.[27] That state lasted nearly ten years, but when the French army mounted a full-scale attack in March 1840 it began to collapse. After fighting a guerrilla campaign from a movable 'capital' made of tents, he fled across the border in March 1842. But that was not the end of him: Moroccans flocked to join his army, and with these reinforcements he went home.[28]

Moulay Abderrahmane faced a dilemma. The French government threatened to invade if he did not cut the amir's supply routes,[29] but too many Moroccans supported Abd al-Qadir for their Sultan to abandon him. Abd al-Qadir used that popularity to crisscross the frontier and deliberately provoke the French forces. In June 1844 the French army occupied Oujda.[30]

25 *Ibid.*, 41; MAEF Nantes, Tanger, Anciens Fonds A1-3 bis, 'Correspondance de la Direction Politique, 1839-1845', Draft of a letter, de Nyon to [Guizot], Tanger, 6 February 1842; Bodleian MS Eng. hist. D 493, 67.

26 MAEF Nantes, Tanger, Anciens Fonds A1-3 bis 'Correspondance de la Direction Politique, 1839-1845', Draft of letter de Nyon to Thiers, Tanger 22 March 1840.

27 Laroui, *Origines*, 265-7.

28 Danziger, *Abd al-Qadir*, 223-8.

29 P.G. Rogers, *A History of Anglo-Moroccan Relations to 1900* (London: Foreign and Commonwealth Office, n.d.). 149.

30 De Cossé-Brissac, 'Les Rapports de la France', 99ff; Rogers, *History*, 151.

Finally, in August 1844, there was a short and decisive war. The French fleet bombarded Tangier and Essaouira, which was abandoned by the Makhzan officials and the army and then pillaged by the Haha and Chiadma tribes.[31] On the Algerian frontier, at Wadi Isly near Oujda, 30,000 men led by Sidi Mohammed, the Sultan's son, were routed by 11,000 French troops. The Cherarda *jaysh* contingents broke under the fire, pillaging the Moroccan camp as they fled. When Sidi Mohammed regrouped in Taza, he found that many of his men had been stripped and robbed as they fled through the countryside. The Moroccan army could not fight.[32] The Sultan sued for peace. He was fortunate that British mediation lightened the terms of the Treaty of Tangier.[33] The French handed back Oujda and did not demand an indemnity but they insisted on a definite border between Algeria and Morocco, and that Abd al-Qadir be declared an 'outlaw'. A dilemma would face every sultan for the rest of the century. Because any attempt to resist the Europeans would lead to defeat, all resistance was against the interest of the Makhzan, and had to come from dissident, 'corrupted', tribes. European forces would retaliate and further subvert Makhzan power. Since the sultan's authority depended on leading the defence of the *dar al-islam*, this quandary was bound to be destructive. As the chronicler al-Nasiri explained, the amir contributed to the destruction of Morocco.

At this time the intentions of Hajj Abd al-Qadir with regard both to *jihad* and 'to the sultan became clearly depraved. This was because his *jihad* produced no benefit, and because he craved complete independence and encouraged the tribes in the region to be corrupted.'[34] Six decades later the logic of this brutal spiral of illegitimacy would destroy Moroccan independence. Meanwhile, Moulay Abderrahmane tried to restore his authority and live with the new order.

The call for reform

To seal the peace, in 1845 the Sultan sent his ambassador, Abd al-Qadir Ash'ash, to Paris. Ash'ash's secretary was a young '*alim* from Tetuan, Muhammad al-Saffar, whose account is a revelation of

31 Schroeter, *Merchants*, 120.

32 Rollman, 'New Order', 546.

33 Rogers, *History*, 151-2.

34 Al-Nasiri, *Kitab al-istiqsa*, 9: 50.

the attitudes and preoccupations of the Moroccan elite after the defeat. In the heart of French power he was faced with the vigour of French civilisation and its works.[35] Al-Saffar was impressed. He disliked Christianity, but by no means everything that he saw conflicted with Islam. The ideas that wealth was a good in itself, that order made the government stronger and society more secure, that military strength underpinned order, that education was essential for social growth, were not alien to Islamic thought.[36] The French, al-Saffar observed, simply did these things better.

Particularly awesome was French military power. A march-past in Paris struck fear into the hearts of the Moroccan mission. Lines of infantry marching in time were followed by lines of artillery with their guns ready for action and then lines of cavalry with fluttering pennants. The Moroccans were duly intimidated:

> In comparison with the weakness of Islam, the dissipation of its strength, and the disrupted condition of its people, how confident they are, how impressive their state of readiness, how competent they are in matters of state, how firm their laws, how capable in war and successful in vanquishing their enemies – not because of their courage, bravery or religious zeal, but because of their marvellous organisation, their uncanny mastery over affairs, and their strict adherence to the law.[37]

All over the Islamic world, ruling elites had come to similar conclusions. First in Egypt, then in the Ottoman Empire, governments imported European military officers to train their new armies and European weapons to equip them. They called them the 'New Organisation' – *nizam al-jadid* in Egypt, *nizam-ı cedid* in Turkey. The *nizam* armies performed considerably better than the old ones, and pilgrims and travellers returning to Morocco from the east sang their praises. Muhammad Ali sent military textbooks to Moulay Abderrahmane.[38] In Algeria, Abd al-Qadir set up a regular European-style army in the 1830s and absorbed the lessons of French tactics. His counterpart in eastern Algeria, Hajj Ahmad Bey, did the same. Before the Battle of Isly, Abd al-Qadir warned Sidi

35 Muhammad al-Saffar, *Disorienting Encounters: Travels of a Moroccan Scholar in France in 1845-1846: the Voyage of Muhammad as-Saffar*, trans. Susan Gilson Miller (Berkeley: University of California Press, 1992), 9-17.

36 See Norman Itzkowitz, *The Ottoman Empire and Islamic Tradition* (University of Chicago Press, 1980), 88.

37 Al-Saffar, *Disorienting Encounters*, 193-4.

38 Laroui, *Origines*, 272.

Mohammed that he should not have brought large amounts of baggage and impedimenta and left them in pitched tents in front of the army. They would be the first target. He explained that French ways of fighting differed from those of the Moroccan army, but his words were ignored: the Moroccans were already too demoralised to heed them.[39]

Military reform

After the defeat at Isly, the Sultan and his son, Sidi Mohammed, set about building a *nizam* army of 50,000 men. The first battalion of infantry was duly set up in June 1845 with uniforms like those of *nizam* troops in the Ottoman Empire and armed with British flintlock muskets. By March 1846 there were nearly 3,000 of them, but they quickly deserted because they were not paid regularly and were badly clothed. By August 1846 they were down to about 400. Organisation needed more than training and uniforms.

In the summer of 1847, the *nizam* troops fought alongside the more numerous *jaysh* and *naiba* contingents against Abd al-Qadir, who had taken refuge in the eastern Rif, and was making diplomatic problems for the Sultan. They were defeated, and traditional and modern elements broke with equal ease.[40] This defeat destroyed the ideological basis for a *nizam* army. It had been justified as a more effective way of combatting the Christians, yet here it was fighting Abd al-Qadir, a Muslim who really was fighting the French. The *nizam* units now became part of the royal guard, but rudimentary training in the European style continued through to the 1860s.

It was easier to build fortifications and import weapons than train soldiers. Coastal fortresses were restored and rearmed, and new ones were built. But the 'new' arms were quite antiquated: surplus British flintlock muskets for the infantry and small calibre and smooth-bored field guns, too few in number to cause serious damage to any European troops.[41]

39 Al-Nasiri, *Kitab al-istiqsa*, 9: 51; On Hajj Ahmad see Abdeljelil Temimi, *Le Beylik de Constantine et Hajd Ahmed Bey (1830-1837)* (Tunis: Publications de la Revue d'Histoire Maghrébine, 1978), especially 56ff. and 63. On Abd al-Qadir see Danziger, and Bruno Etienne, *Abdelkader. Isthme des isthmes (Barzakh al-barazikh)* (Paris: Hachette, 1994), especially 134-41.

40 Rollman, 'New Order', 533-4; Hammoudi, *Master and Disciple*, 55; Al-Nasiri, *Kitab al-istiqsa*, 9:56-9.

41 Rollman, 'New Order', 566-7.

The modernisers

Reform only went so far: it did not touch the core of the Makhzan itself. Despite the defeat, the commander of the army was not punished in any way, certainly not removed. That would have taken the reform far too close to home: since the commander was Sidi Mohammed himself.[42] As in Algeria in 1830-1 an appointment had been made on dynastic lines.

Reform, proposed by Sidi Mohammed, was supported by a small group of Makhzan officials. Some had witnessed the French invasion of Algeria. Others were foreign Muslim military officers who came to Morocco to offer their services, former officers of Muhammad Ali's army for instance. Yet others were *'ulama* from the lower reaches of the Makhzan – the top *'ulama* were much more conservative.[43]

The modernisers spent much effort in writing books that all harped on the same theme. The Sultan should reorganise his army, with efficient training and administration and in sufficient numbers to hold back the threat of Christian invasion.[44] It was, they said, a religious duty to resist the infidel.

They also knew that reform of the army was not enough. In Turkey and Egypt the reformers had realised that modernisation depended on education in technical subjects. In Morocco the Sultan's son, Sidi Mohammed, studied mathematics and engineering as well as religious and literary subjects and arranged for technical books to be translated into Arabic. He was particularly interested in military text-books, and shortly after Isly he founded a military school, the *Madrasat al-Muhandisin* (School of Engineers). He even taught there himself at times. It had little effect on the old system for its very few graduates were given advisory, not command, positions.[45]

Sidi Mohammed's supporters were a group of Makhzan officials who knew Europe well, men like Abd al-Qadir Ash'ash and Busilham bin Ali Aztut. Abd al-Qadir Ash'ash, the ambassador to Paris in 1845-6, had commercial ties with the British and was extremely rich. Busilham, for many years the governor of Larache, had acted

42 Hammoudi, *Master and Disciple*, 51; Laroui, *Origines*, 247; Sir John Drummond-Hay, *A Memoir of Sir John Drummond Hay: Sometime Minister at the Court of Morocco, Based on his Journals and Correspondence* (London: John Murray, 1896), 79-80.

43 Archives du Gouvernement de l'Algérie, Aix-en-Provence, France, 30h26 Dossier 7, Roches to MAE Tanger 27 October 1848.

44 Laroui, *Origines*, 273-8.

45 Rollman, 'New Order', 57-76.

as Morocco's foreign minister in all but name and had made a fortune from the European trade.[46] In 1848 he became governor of Tangier, with a new title: Representative (*naib*) of the Sultan to the foreign powers. European consuls treated his office, the *Dar al-Niaba*, as the Moroccan foreign ministry, although his role was no more than to pass on messages to the Sultan. When Busilham died in 1851, he was replaced by Hajj Muhammad al-Khatib, who had lived for twenty-seven years in Gibraltar and then in Genoa. As a merchant, al-Khatib believed in freedom of trade and much preferred his diplomatic and commercial role to being the governor of the fractious city of Tangier. In 1854, at his request, the sultan confirmed him as *naib*, but handed the governorship to Muhammad bin Abd al-Malik bin Abu, Edward Drummond-Hay's old guard commander.[47] After escorting so many consuls, he was no stranger to Europeans either.

Not everyone trusted these cosmopolitan merchants. Many felt that they had too much to do with the unbelieving enemy. This was unjust. Al-Khatib's main purpose was to avoid trouble and to that end he was quite prepared to reject European demands. In 1854 the French navy wanted to conduct a hydrographic survey of the Straits of Gibraltar, but al-Khatib was reluctant to allow them to land men on isolated beaches in the Straits. It would infringe Moroccan law because no-one was allowed to land where there were no customs houses and it might lead to fighting with the tribes in the region.[48]

Disorder

To servants of the Makhzan, disorder was a paramount problem. Muhammad al-Saffar was deeply impressed by the public security of France: 'It happens that travel in this country is easy both day and night, with no strain or toil, because there is complete security. The traveller need not be afraid of thieves or brigands, and for that reason you will not see anyone carrying weapons other than a soldier.'[49]

Safety on the roads was one of the traditional touchstones of whether a Moroccan ruler was competent. The difficulty was to achieve it in a society in which tempers flared easily. In 1844,

46 *Ibid.*, 555-6.

47 Miège, *Le Maroc et l'Europe*, 2:279.

48 AND Tanger A 77, Al-Khatib to Jagerschmidt 24 Dhu al-Hijja 1270 [18 September 1854].

49 Al-Saffar, *Disorienting Encounters*, 95.

200 men of the Anjra and Banu Masawwar tribes near Tangier fought a battle over hunting rights, and a handful of people were killed.[50] In Tangier in 1840, there was nearly a free-for-all on the beach. Someone let off a gun carelessly during a powder play, and a bystander was slightly hurt and drew his knife. People in the crowd persuaded him not to kill the owner of the gun but had they failed, there could have been several deaths.[51] Tangier could be a violent town. In 1834 Moulay Abderrahmane instructed one of his officials:

> We order our respected servant Abd al-Rahman Ash'ash to arrest any unmarried layabouts whom he may find in the port of Tangier and put them in chains and inform us of it. They have become spies who do exactly what they want and then return to their country whenever they wish. Among the treacherous things they have done is [the case of] four of them who came to Mehedia at night and chose a boat from the port and got into it and fled. The people of the town saw them and pursued them and when they realised that they were being overtaken they threw themselves into the sea. They captured three of them and the fourth was eaten by the sea, and went to his [?] mother. Peace. 5 Sha'ban 1250.[52]

Virtually the same order was repeated for Tetuan in 1850.[53]

Makhzan officials did what they could. Tangier had a curfew after sunset, though it was not always rigorously enforced.[54] Disorder certainly increased after 1844, but it was hard to distinguish mass criminality from outright rebellion. What was the difference between the pillage of Essaouira by the Haha and Chiadma after the French bombardment, and the behaviour of the Amir and Zaër tribes around Rabat and Salé in 1849 when they 'assailed it with attacks and robbery, and committed the utmost depravity and rebellion on the roads and gardens?'[55] And how was rebellion to be distinguished from inter-tribal rivalry between the Ait Atta

50 Bodleian MS Eng. hist. D 493, 135.

51 *Ibid.*, D 493, 156ff.

52 MAPR series 4 – 3/17 Mawlay Abd al-Rahman to Abd al-Rahman Ash'Ash, 5 Sha'ban 1250/ 7 December 1834.

53 MAPR series 4-24/10 Mawlay Abd al-Rahman to Abd al-Qadir Ash'ash 1 Muharram 1267/ 6 November 1267.

54 Bodleian MS Eng. hist. D 493, 91.

55 Schroeter, *Merchants*, 120-1; Al-Nasiri, *Kitab al-istiqsa*, 9:60.

and their neighbours on the Saharan fringe?[56] Some tribes were almost permanently rebellious: for several years running after 1853 the sultan or Sidi Mohammed led an expedition against the Zemmour.[57]

In the Sous, Husayn bin Hashim of Iligh cooperated with the Makhzan the better to pursue his own local struggles, but in truth, Makhzan support was a broken reed. In 1855 Husayn attacked one group of rebels and the sultan congratulated him for 'acting for the good of the Muslims and the unification of religion'. Yet the following year, when he asked for help to collect the *zakkat* and *'ushur* taxes, the sultan complimented him on his zeal, but refused to send him troops.[58] There were simply none available.

British and French rivalry

The most dangerous disorder was that which drew the Makhzan into disputes with European governments. It had not much mattered in the 1830s that Rifis attacked Spanish ships because the Sultan could wash his hands of them, quoting the 1799 treaty that put the Rifis outside the law. But in the 1840s people on the Guelaya peninsula near Melilla started to attack British and French shipping, and that was much more dangerous. The British and French governments threatened to invade Morocco. On mature consideration, both governments dropped the idea; it would have been a thoroughly dangerous military adventure.

Instead both governments came to the same conclusion: that the best way to stop the attacks was to encourage greater Makhzan control of the Mediterranean coast. This would also open the region to commerce. Both the French and British Consuls-General considered the governor of Tangier, bin Abu, their friend and they encouraged him to punish the Rifis. In 1856 he took a large force into the region and stopped the piracy with brutally simple methods. He burned villages, destroyed crops, levied heavy fines and collected back-taxes. Then he appointed his own qaids in the region.[59]

Bin Abu played the French and British against each other quite successfully. Ever since 1830 British diplomats in Tangier had been trying to prevent a French invasion of Morocco by keeping the

56 Al-Nasiri, *Kitab al-istiqsa*, 9: 67-8.

57 *Ibid.*, 65.

58 Ennaji and Pascon, *Le Makhzen et le Sous al-Aqsa*, 51-2.

59 C.R. Pennell, 'Dealing with Pirates: British French and Moroccans, 1834-1856', *Journal of Imperial and Commonwealth History*, 21, no. 1 (1994): 54-83.

lid on any quarrel between the Makhzan and the French government. The Makhzan's officials therefore thought that they could count on British help. Palmerston played along and told Drummond-Hay to drop heavy hints about how British troops had helped the 'legitimate rulers' of Portugal, Afghanistan, and Turkey against rebellions.[60]

When it came to the point, British friendship was practically worthless. In 1841 the Governor of Tangier asked for help if the French attacked the town, saying that he supposed that the British government would protect the Moroccan Sultan as it had protected the Ottoman Sultan from Muhammad Ali, the Pasha of Egypt. He was turned down.[61] Yet the British government was willing to act as a mediator with the French.

British mediation was especially valuable after the defeat at Isly. In the summer of 1844, while British and Russian diplomats in Paris persuaded the French government to evacuate its troops, Edward Drummond-Hay went to Marrakesh and convinced the Sultan to make peace with the French. The extreme heat helped kill Drummond-Hay, but his son John took over. In quick order he brokered an agreement with Spain over the boundary at Ceuta that was unfavourable to Moroccan interests, and headed off a threat by the Swedish and Danish governments to send warships to attack Morocco by persuading the Sultan to stop demanding tribute. This second agreement was made with the assistance of the acting French Consul-General, Victor Mauboussin who, as it happened, was John Drummond-Hay's brother-in-law.[62] But in early 1845 Mauboussin was replaced by Edmonde de Chasteau, whose son-in-law Léon Roches acted as consular secretary, and who pursued an open rivalry with their British colleague.[63]

British mediation had consisted of persuading the Makhzan to give way on every issue, and the British government insisted that its friendship was dependent on trade. Palmerston told Drummond-Hay to explain this to the Makhzan:

> Nations cannot enter into real friendship with each other without that mutual intercourse which begets kindly feelings on both sides, and the most certain means which the Emperor could take to secure to himself the support of England on occasions

60 Francis Roseboro Flournoy, *British Policy Towards Morocco in the Age of Palmerston* (London: P.S. King, 1935), 65-6.

61 *Ibid.*, 64-6.

62 *Ibid.*, 100-7; Miège, *Le Maroc et l'Europe*, 204.

63 Miège, *Le Maroc et l'Europe*, 2:211-13; Flournoy, *British Policy*, 116-17.

> when he may require it, would be to encourage and facilitate to the utmost the commercial intercourse between his subjects and those of the Queen. For thus the whole British nation would grow to take an interest in the welfare of the Emperor, and the friendship between the two countries would rest on a broader and more solid foundation.[64]

But trade conditions were very difficult. Harvests were poor in 1845 and 1846, worse in 1847, only slightly better in 1848 and 1849. By 1850 people in Safi, Casablanca and Azemmour were starving. Stories came up from Marrakesh about people eating corpses, and the cities filled with hungry refugees from the countryside.[65] The currency collapsed; it fell 30% against the Spanish dollar in eight years (1845-53).

Senior members of the Makhzan relied on trade for much of their private income, public revenues relied on customs duties and grain was needed to supply the starving population. So tariffs were raised, export of grain was stopped, and monopolies were set up on new commodities and sold to important members of the Makhzan and their associates.[66] When British merchants in Gibraltar, Manchester, and London complained, John Drummond-Hay was told to press the Makhzan to change its policy.

By 1848, Drummond-Hay had managed to get both import and export duties reduced and British influence started to recover. In 1849 a fleet commanded by Admiral Napier arrived, threatening to retaliate in a minor commercial dispute and to deal with Rifi pirates. This assertion of naval power came just as French diplomacy fell into disarray after the revolution of 1848.[67]

In 1849 de Chasteau and Roches were replaced. The new team – Prosper Bourée as Consul-General and Charles Jagerschmidt as Secretary – were able men, but they never restored French preeminence. Then, in 1851, the Quai d'Orsay miscalculated badly. When a French ship was wrecked at Salé and pillaged by the hungry inhabitants, a war fleet was sent to bombard Rabat and Salé for eight hours. It actually caused very little damage, and the Moroccans used their own guns to some effect on the French ships, but Drummond-Hay persuaded the Makhzan to be concili-

64 Quoted in Flournoy, *British Policy*, 69-70.

65 Miège, *Le Maroc et l'Europe*, 2:220-4.

66 *Ibid.*, 239-241; Schroeter, *Merchants*, 123-5.

67 Flournoy, *British Policy*, 122-3.

atory because his government was also putting pressure on Paris.[68] John Drummond-Hay was laying the basis of a commanding British influence in Morocco that would last a generation. The thrust of his economic arguments began to sound more convincing. Battening down the economic hatches had not made the Makhzan any richer in 1851 than it had been in 1845. When he preached the benefits of free trade, he found an attentive audience among senior men in the Makhzan, and among influential merchants.

Opening Moroccan markets

The sale of monopolies had shut the merchants of Rabat, Essaouira, Tangier and Tetuan out of the markets. In Essaouira they protested so vociferously against the monopoly on skins – and engaged so effectively in contraband – that the Sultan's governor petitioned for it to be lifted.[69] When Drummond-Hay talked of free trade, merchants like Mustafa al-Dukkali became quite enthusiastically pro-British. This was pure self interest – al-Dukkali was a noted tax-farmer who had made a fortune by buying the right to collect taxes – but he had influence with the *wazir* al-Mukhtar al-Jama'i and was a close advisor of al-Khatib, the Sultan's minister for foreign affairs.[70] Drummond-Hay did not campaign alone. In 1848 a US naval frigate visited Tangier, and various important Moroccans went aboard. According to the American consul:

> On leaving the Frigate, an intelligent and prominent Moor, who is in the employ of the Emperor, and high in his confidence, was heard to exclaim to his companions 'America is the bravest, the greatest nation in the world – and what are we? We have a fine climate and a rich soil – we have lead and iron – gold and silver – and all the elements of national greatness – Yet see what we are compared with that great and powerful nation – Young America'.[71]

Consul Hyatt was flattered, which was doubtless the intention, and he too pushed for free trade. In 1849 he wrote to Busilham bin Ali, the sultan's *naib* in Tangier, telling him at length that free trade and lower duties were the basis of the prosperity of

68 *Ibid.*, 143-8 Al-Nasiri, *Kitab al-istiqsa*, 9: 62-3; USNA Microfilm T61/7, Brown to Webster, Tangier 4 December 1851; Brown, *Salé*, 176-9.

69 Schroeter, *Merchants*, 122-5.

70 Miège, *Le Maroc et l'Europe*, 2:277; Schroeter, *Merchants*, 124.

71 USNA – Microfilm T61/7, Despatches from US Consuls in Tangier, 1797-1906, Hyatt to Buchanan, Tangier, 8 December 1848, no. 8.

the United States. Busilham replied: 'I see the many riches your nation and commerce enjoys, with the produce of your country: all is so much to our pleasure, the more so knowing the friendship, tranquillity and peace that exist between the two potencies.'[72]

The riches of the trading powers gave other members of the Makhzan pause for thought. Muhammad al-Saffar had found French capitalism most attractive:

> The people of Paris, men and women alike, are tireless in their pursuit of wealth. They are never idle or lazy. [...] Even though they have all kinds of amusements and spectacles of the most marvelous kinds, they are not distracted from their work and give every moment its due. [...] Nor do they excuse someone for being poor, for indeed death is easier for them than poverty, and the poor man there is seen as vile and contemptible.[73]

Like Shaykh Bayruk, al-Saffar saw nothing immoral in being rich, but unlike the master of Guelmim, Muhammad al-Saffar was at the very centre of the Makhzan. In 1854 he became *wazir*,[74] just as the monopoly system was beginning to unravel. The Crimean War obliged the British and French consuls in Tangier to work together, which was not easy since Jagerschmidt and Drummond-Hay cordially hated each other,[75] but by the end of 1854 both of them were pressing the Sultan to allow the export of grain. The war had created a huge demand in Europe for wool and wheat and prices surged upwards, just when Moroccan harvests brought in bumper crops of grain. The merchants rejoiced in August 1855, when the Sultan agreed to the export of wheat.[76]

In March 1855 Drummond-Hay went to Marrakesh to present a draft commercial treaty that would abolish monopolies and lower duties. This, he told al-Saffar, would benefit both Morocco and Britain, since everyone gained from free trade; it was a world-wide phenomenon, the spirit of the times, and even the Ottoman Sultan had agreed to it.[77] Not all the Sultan's advisors were easily convinced.

72 USNA – Microfilm T61/7, Despatches from US Consuls in Tangier, 1797-1906, Hyatt to Clayton, Tangier, 12 October 1849, no. 14 enclosing Hyatt to [Busilham b 'Ali] Tangier 20 March 1849 and Translation, [Busilham b. 'Ali] to Hyatt. 9 Jumada I 1265/ 1 April 1849.

73 Al-Saffar, *Disorienting Encounters*, 153.

74 Khalid bin Saghir, *Al-Maghrib wa-Britaniyya al-'Uzma fi-l-qarn al-tasi' 'ashr* (Al-Dar al-Baida: al-Walada, 1990), 70.

75 Pennell, 'Dealing with pirates', *passim*.

76 Miège, *Le Maroc et l'Europe*, 2:280-307.

77 Bin Saghir, *Al-Maghrib wa-Britaniyya*, 83.

Hajj Muhammad al-Razini, the Moroccan consul in Gibraltar and a very rich beneficiary of the monopoly system, strongly counselled the sultan to resist Drummond-Hay's suggestions.[78]

Torn between conflicting advice, the Sultan temporised.[79] Drummond-Hay got an increased quota of bullocks to be exported to Gibraltar, but nothing much else. Instead, the Sultan agreed that Drummond-Hay and al-Khatib should continue the negotiations in Tangier. That took a long time, because al-Khatib had to refer everything back to the Sultan. Drummond-Hay laid siege to the *Dar al-Niaba* from mid 1855 to early 1856, badgering al-Khatib to a conclusion. Under instructions from Paris, the French consulate supported him and finally the whole consular corps went to al-Khatib to pressure him into accepting a new treaty.[80]

Al-Khatib may have agreed with many of Drummond-Hay's ideas about free trade, but when it came to the point, he proved a very effective negotiator. Over the months of discussion he changed several clauses of the proposed treaty. Drummond-Hay had to agree to limits on how many Moroccans could be employed in British consulates, and benefit from British protection. Al-Khatib refused to accept a clause allowing foreigners to own land in Morocco, citing similar prohibitions in Gibraltar, and Drummond-Hay gave way. Britons would only be allowed to rent property.[81] When a draft was referred to Moulay Abderrahmane, the Sultan insisted that he should be able to prohibit the export of grain if he thought it necessary.[82] Although the Moroccans were working from a weaker position, this treaty was not imposed on Morocco. It was negotiated. Nevertheless, the Treaty and Convention on Commerce and Navigation, signed on 9 December 1856, definitely favoured the British. Most monopolies were abolished, import duties were reduced to 10%, and maximum export duties were fixed. Most important of all, was an agreement that these benefits would later be extended to traders from other nations.

The rise of John Drummond-Hay

The Makhzan had virtually lost control of trade. In theory, this

78 *Ibid.*, 72; Rogers, *History* 164.

79 Schroeter, *Merchants*, 125.

80 Miège, *Le Maroc et l'Europe*, 2:307-10.

81 Bin Saghir, *Al-Maghrib wa-Britaniyya*, 85-106.

82 *Ibid.*, 106.

treaty was valid only for five years but in reality it was irreversible.[83] It also sealed British hegemony in Morocco for a generation. From now on, the British were at the forefront of a campaign to open Moroccan markets; that undermined the authority and the financial independence of the Sultan and made their influence over the Makhzan unstoppable. Britain was the biggest military and trading power in the world but its influence in Morocco was largely due to the Consul-General, John Drummond-Hay. For him the treaty was a personal triumph, and he was made a Companion of the Order of the Bath.[84] His knowledge of Morocco was unrivalled among European representatives. As a fifteen-year-old schoolboy he had visited his father in Tangier and learned both colloquial and classical Arabic. In 1840 he joined the Foreign Office and was posted to Alexandria and then to Constantinople, under Sir Stratford de Redcliffe, the architect of Britain's reform policy for the Ottoman Empire; there he learned Turkish. In 1844, aged twenty-eight, he returned to Tangier as a temporary assistant to his father, and when Edward suddenly died he took over as a stopgap and simply stayed on. He dominated Moroccan diplomacy for forty years.

By 1856, when the treaty was signed, Drummond-Hay had already outlasted four different French consuls (during his forty years in Morocco there would be ten heads of the French mission in Tangier). Other consuls were bound to him by personal links. The long-standing Swedish Consul was a friend and regular hunting partner of his father, and so were some of the US Consuls. He was married to the daughter of the Danish Consul. But his real success was with the Moroccans. Drummond-Hay's extraordinary linguistic ability brought him close to many officials, with whom he spent much time hunting wild boar. The Moroccan elite was quite prepared to hunt these dangerous pigs; they merely refused to eat them. One regular hunting partner was bin Abu, the Governor of Tangier. Another, Hadj Abdallah al-Amarti, the shaykh of a nearby village, was a go-between with Rifi pirates in 1856.[85] On several occasions Drummond-Hay arranged for important Moroccans to be treated by military doctors in Gibraltar and for British

83 Laroui, *Origines*, 250, Miège, *Le Maroc et l'Europe*, 2:307-23.

84 Rogers, *History*, 166.

85 C.R. Pennell, 'John Drummond-Hay: Tangier as the Centre of a Spider's web' in A. Bendaoud and M. Maniar (eds), *Tanger 1800-1956. Contribution à l'histoire récente du Maroc* (Rabat: Editions Arabo-Africaines, 1991), 107-34.

ships to carry their children on their way to Mecca.[86]

It was the rich who most benefited from these contacts, and from increased trade with Europe. The artisans and the poor had less cause to rejoice. Between August 1855 and August 1857 wheat prices in Rabat almost trebled and barley prices in Fez more than doubled. The fall in the value of the Moroccan currency and drought played their part, but the Europeans were an easily identifiable enemy, and there were anti-European protests in several towns in 1858. The value of the sultan's veto on exports was now seen. He banned the sale of wool and grain.[87] It took longer for the effects of growing European imports to be felt. Manchester cotton goods did flood in but the local industry was buoyed up by the world shortage of cotton during the American Civil War.[88] In 1858 the artisans of Salé and Rabat still produced shoes, leather, pottery and textiles in large quantities. The rich merchants built luxurious houses; life was good for builders and carpet makers.[89]

The physical environment

What riches there were, were not in the Moroccan countryside, so the rural population began to move. Some Rifis found employment on French farms in western Algeria, the beginning of the emigration that would become a principal support of the region in the twentieth century. Most people did not go so far, but sought jobs in port cities like Salé, Rabat, Tangier, Essaouira and Casablanca.[90] Once there, they had to be fed and warmed.

Firewood was a great problem. In the mid 1830s the shortage was already so acute in Tangier that the deputy governor asked the '*ulama* for a *fatwa* forbidding people from digging up the roots of bushes to burn. Edward Drummond-Hay, the biggest consumer of all (on his own avowal), pretended that this was an anti-Christian plot and threatened a diplomatic incident if he was not exempted from the prohibition.[91] The problem rang a clear bell with al-Saffar when he went to France in 1844:

86 E.g. GGA CA2/4, 124 Wilson to John Drummond-Hay, 6 June 1846; Rogers, *History*, 167.

87 Schroeter, *Merchants*, 144; Miège, *Le Maroc et l'Europe*, 2:341; Muhammad Daud, *Tarikh Titwan*, 5 vols (Titwan: Ma'had Mawlay al-Hasan, 1965), 3: 363.

88 Brown, *Salé*, 121; Miège, *Le Maroc et l'Europe*, 3: 535; Schroeter, *Merchants*, 128.

89 Brown, *Salé*, 128-31.

90 *Ibid.*, 122; Miège, *Le Maroc et l'Europe*, 3:23ff.

91 Pennell, 'Law'.

> Firewood is a matter of great concern with them.[...] They do not have open woodlands for gathering firewood, but each one cuts wood from his own property, planting trees in his fields and gardens for that purpose. A forest is the property of its owner and is not open to everyone.They have rules about the cutting of trees, one of them being that he who has a forest must divide it according to when the trees mature.[92]

The forests in the Rif were depleted by a burst of building in Fez,[93] and the forests of the Mamora by cork harvesters. When John Drummond-Hay went to Marrakesh in 1846 he noticed a great change since his trip with his father, nearly three years before.

> Alas, what a change since last I traversed this fine forest. Every cork tree, of which it is chiefly composed, had been barked, and nought remained but whitened and withered stems; a melancholy sight, and we English are the robbers: for this article of trade has been in great request of late years, and vessels are constantly loading bark at Laraiche, Tangier, and Tetuan, curious to say all bound to *Cork*, in Ireland; so from Cork it came, and to Cork it returns. I hear the sultan intends to put a stop to its further exportation, having lately witnessed the devastation of his forests.[94]

Moroccan views of Europe

Clearly, European trade was a mixed blessing, and Moroccan feelings about Europe were ambivalent at best. When al-Khatib, bin Abu, al-Saffar and others negotiated with Europeans, it was as equals, believing – as they did when they hunted together – that they shared a common ground. Centuries of diplomatic contact and international treaties ensured that they respected common rules. But even lower down the social scale, quite ordinary people believed they had equal rights to the Christians, although they did not share the same ideas.

In 1850 the US Consul-General released a former servant who had been falsely imprisoned by his predecessor. He did it in his consular court, according to the ideas of European jurisprudence. But the accused man's wife was a Rifi who acted according to the rules of *her* society. The Consul-General was startled when

92 Al-Saffar, *Disorienting Encounters*, 99.

93 McNeill, *Mountains*, 122, 307.

94 John Drummond-Hay, *Journal of an Expedition to the Court of Marocco in the year 1846* (Cambridge: printed by Metcalfe and Palmer, 1848), 9.

she sacrificed a lamb on the consular steps, splashing them with blood. In Rifi society that would have placed a strict obligation on him to come to her aid. European legalism and Rifi shame compulsions converged, and the man was released, and he and his wife remained, presumably, as secure in their attachment to Rifi ways as the US Consul-General was to his.[95]

It was a minor incident, but proof that illiterate Rifi servants, just as much as Makhzan officials, did not accept that European society was *better* than theirs. For most Moroccans, the Europeans were the unbelieving enemy, and Muslims should have nothing whatever to do with them. For men like al-Saffar, the European superiority was technical, not moral, and therefore perfectly compatible with Islam. Their religion was quite another matter. The French worshipped idols and believed that Christ was God, not a prophet:

> The figure of Jesus is portrayed in various ways: as a grown man, or a small boy in the lap or arms of Mary. In the church they pray to them both. If you ask one of them about his likeness, he will explain to you that it is God, or His son, or His mother if Mary is there. May [God] preserve them from that, and may He be raised high above what they say. The proof of our eyes only increased our insight into their unbelief, the falsity of their creed, and the stupidity of their reasoning. Thanks be to God who guided us to the true religion.[96]

While the Europeans were powerful, they were also underpinned by a political and religious system that was immoral.[97] That made the European powers even more dangerous, as the Spanish proved in 1860.

War with Spain

The War of Africa, as triumphalist Spanish historians later called it, was a border squabble blown up into a war. When General Leopoldo O'Donnell took over the government in 1858 the political system had all but collapsed and a victorious war seemed a good

95 Pennell, 'Interpenetration'.

96 Al-Saffar, *Disorienting Encounters*, 110.

97 Mohamed El Mansour, 'Moroccan Perceptions of European Civilisation in the Nineteenth Century' in George Joffe (ed.), *Morocco and Europe*, (London: Centre of Near and Middle Eastern Studies, School of Oriental and African Studies [SOAS], 1989), 43.

way of raising support.[98] The only enemy that the Spanish army could conceivably beat was Morocco. Traditional religious prejudices were used to whip up support and an incident easily manufactured. In any case, the bellicose commander in Melilla, Colonel Buceta, who hoped to expand the territory under his control, was already fighting a local war. When O'Donnell's new Consul-General, Juan Blanco del Valle, arrived in Tangier, he found that he was merely a mouthpiece whose job was to pass on increasingly radical demands for territory, and compensation for long-past pirate incidents. Under British pressure, each demand was conceded, only to be followed by another. The Spanish government was determined on war.[99]

The Makhzan had little choice. In August 1859 Moulay Abderrahmane died and was succeeded by Sidi Mohammed. This passed off with unaccustomed ease, but a new sultan could hardly begin by abandoning Moroccan territory. In Morocco as well as in Spain, popular opinion called for war.[100] Even the British government gave up expecting the Makhzan to make concessions, and the fleet was told to prevent any Spanish landing west of Ceuta that might threaten Tangier.

Accordingly, in November 1859, the Spanish navy landed to the east of Ceuta, and at Ouad Martin, the port of Tetuan. The campaign was a spectacular disaster. The army did not occupy Tetuan, and during the chaotic advance from Ceuta huge numbers of troops died of cholera. But the Makhzan's armies performed even worse. Inadequately armed, they could not fight the Spanish in open battle, and it was left to local contingents drawn from the tribes around Tetuan and Tangier to take the Spanish on, to deadly effect.

On 6 February 1860 Spanish troops at last occupied Tetuan. Racked by cholera, the army was in no condition to go much further, and O'Donnell hoped that the Sultan would agree to peace. When he refused to do so, Spanish troops marched wearily on towards Tangier.

This the British government would not allow. Despite official declarations of neutrality in London, Drummond-Hay and naval officers from Gibraltar had spent months providing technical aid

98 Manuel Espadas Burgos and José De Urquijo Goitia, *Guerra de independencia y época constitucional (1808-1898)*, vol. 11 of *Historia de España* (Madrid: Gredos, 1990), 83-4.

99 C.R. Pennell, 'The Moroccan Discovery of the Mediterranean Coast', *British Journal of Middle Eastern Studies*, 20, no. 2 (1993): 226-36.

100 Rollman, 'New Order', 598-9; Miège, *Le Maroc et l'Europe*, 2:359-602.

to the Moroccans. The US Consul commented that if the British Prime Minister's critics

> [...] had only known for a certainty who concocted the Moorish diplomatic notes, and had witnessed as I have done, the activity and anxiety of the British agent as he popped in and out of the Moorish batteries at Tangier, in company of an aide de camp of the Governor of Gibraltar and Capt. Riley of the British gunboat Lapwing who had superintended the placing of the Moorish guns in position to sink the Spanish squadron, together with other little incidents rather anti-Spanish in their nature, Lord John would have found some difficulty in sustaining my clever little colleague.[101]

When the Spanish army finally managed a Pyrrhic victory over the Moroccan army in the territory of the Ouad Ras tribe, British negotiators got both sides to agree to peace without much difficulty.

The Treaty of Ouad Ras, signed on 26 April was a disaster for the Makhzan. The British government had no wish to see Spanish control of the southern side of the Straits of Gibraltar, so it persuaded Madrid to leave, but at a terrible price to the Sultan. More territory was handed over around Ceuta and Melilla and yet more assigned for future Spanish occupation at Santa Cruz de Mar Pequeña, somewhere in the far south: no-one knew just where it lay. Several attempts were made to find Santa Cruz before it was eventually identified as the enclave of Ifni. Missionaries would be allowed to build a church in Tetuan and a commercial treaty that mirrored the 1856 treaty with Britain was promised. Finally, an indemnity of 100 million Spanish pesetas was to be paid by the end of the year.[102]

The moral of defeat

This defeat of 1860 was the real watershed in nineteenth-century Moroccan history, not the French invasion of Algeria in 1830, nor the defeat at Isly in 1844. Not a battle but a whole war had been lost. It showed that the rather limited efforts at reform had been quite insufficient: there was neither the money, nor the will to implement anything more far-reaching. Had that been attempted, it would have called into question a system based on a mixture

[101] USNA – Microfilm T61/7, Despatches from US Consuls in Tangier, 1797-1906, Brown to Cass, Gibraltar, 14 February 1860, no. 3.

[102] Germain Ayache, 'Aspects de la crise financière au Maroc après l'expedition espagnole de 1860' in *Études d'histoire marocaine* (Rabat: SMER, 1979), 97-138.

of authoritarianism and attraction, force and mediation, patriarchy and violence. Because that system could not distinguish between the Sultan as religious leader, as political leader and as an individual with personal interests, every setback, difficulty and injustice undermined his legitimacy. There were pressures too that no Sultan could control, because they stemmed from the relations between great, and not-so-great, European powers, and they concerned those powers' willingness to trade, which was essential if the Sultan was to have an income. This had drawn the Makhzan into a close relationship with the British government and its energetic Consul-General, who seemed to be the Makhzan's only friends, although they were not prepared to *do* very much.

In this difficult environment it would have been hard for any Moroccan ruler to have much success. Morocco was an agricultural country, dependant on factors beyond the sultan's control for its economic survival: on the weather and on external demand, for the Moroccan economy was becoming more and more subservient to the European world economy. The effects were sometimes even physical: environmental degradation as well as currency decline.

The war of 1859-60 left the Makhzan bankrupt. Spanish insistence on a commercial treaty confirmed that trade was part of European dominance, but the insistence on a religious presence convinced many Moroccans that this was a continuation of Christian attacks on the *Dar al-Islam*. The war showed that the Makhzan's armies were unable to fight the Europeans, and that the most effective protection of Islamic territory came from unorganised local tribal contingents. In short, it capped the decline of the previous thirty years of Moroccan history.

3

REFORM

The inheritance of the Spanish war

When the Spanish evacuated Tetuan in May 1862, they left three legacies. The first was hatred of the Spaniards. In Tetuan the Spanish had destroyed houses, desecrated graveyards, converted one mosque into a church and another into a hospital. According to John Drummond-Hay, a mosque was even used as a latrine.[1]

The second was a debt of 100 million pesetas. The indemnity to the Spanish government was to be repaid in two parts, half of it over a long term from the product of half the customs dues, and the other half at once. To do that, the Makhzan had to take out a foreign loan. In a series of complicated financial manoeuvres, bonds were floated in London, backed by the British government. They were to be repaid over the next twenty years, from money taken from the other half of the customs dues.[2] A debt to Spain was thus transferred to Britain, the greatest, but not the only, creditor of the Middle Eastern states. All through the middle years of the nineteenth century poorer Muslim countries on the eastern and southern shores of the Mediterranean were falling deeper and deeper into debt with richer Christian ones. The Ottoman state borrowed more than £200 million between 1854 and 1874, defaulted in 1876 and in 1881 had to suffer the tutelage of a Public Debt Commission with delegates from six European countries. In Egypt between 1862 and 1875 the government contracted debts of at least £47 million in Europe and perhaps another £28 million locally. It too defaulted and an international debt commission took over Egyptian finances in 1876. In 1882 British troops occupied Egypt and imposed an unofficial protectorate. Even closer to Morocco an international debt commission was imposed on Tunisia as early as 1868, and French occupation followed in 1881.[3]

[1] Rogers, *History*, 173; Al-Nasiri, *Kitab al-istiqsa*, 9:94; Daud, *Tarikh Titwan*, 3:216-18; *El Eco de Tetuan*, 1 March 1860.

[2] Flournoy, *British Policy*, 211-12; Rogers, *History*, 171.

[3] Roger Owen, *The Middle East in the World Economy, 1800-1914* (London: Methuen,

The third legacy was economic. The Treaty of Madrid in 1861 conceded to Spanish traders the same commercial privileges as the treaty with Britain had done in 1856.[4] The Spanish economy was feeble compared to the British, but this opened the door to other nations. The Belgian Consul negotiated a treaty in June 1862 and a year later the French consul did likewise.[5] This too was an experience shared with other Muslim states in the Mediterranean, as European traders led by the British forced their way into markets by insisting that tariffs be lowered and concessions to build the infrastructure be granted. All over the Middle East and North Africa local economies fell under the control of European bankers and traders, became suppliers of raw materials (cotton in Egypt, silk in Lebanon) and consumers of manufactured goods.

In Morocco the French consulate prepared a public proclamation – although it may never have been issued – to explain to Moroccans the benefits of belonging to a European-dominated international economy. It likened the Spanish evacuation of Tetuan to the European evacuation of Peking in November 1860 and so demonstrated the pacific intentions of all the European powers.

> You should reflect on the evacuation of Tetuan, an important town in Morocco, and of Peking, the capital of China, by victorious European armies, in order to understand the Europeans' conduct towards the Muslims and peoples of the East. Then you will understand that the Europeans had no intention of reducing those they had conquered to slavery and permanently seizing their countries.
>
> The purpose of the Europeans was to be able to help the progress of their commerce, to facilitate the export of their own manufactured goods and the importation of primary products which they needed, and finally to protect their merchants and the people of their country. Once they had gained these objectives, they took nothing else.[6]

Trade, it went on, benefited both sides. Europe provided manufactured goods for Morocco ('needles, scissors, razors, knives, blacksmith's

---

1981), 100-7, 126-8; Stanford Shaw and Ezel K. Shaw, *The History of the Ottoman Empire and Modern Turkey*, 2 vols (Cambridge University Press, 1977), 2: 223; Jean Ganiage, *Les origines du protectoral français en Tunisie (1861-1881)* (Tunis: Maison Tunisienne de l'Edition, 1969), 277-323

4 Miège, *Le Maroc et l'Europe*, 2: 382.

5 *Ibid.*, 2: 403-5.

6 Archives du Ministère des Affaires Etrangères, Quai d'Orsay, Paris, MD Maroc 10, 183-6.

tools ...') and in return Morocco sold its products to Europe ('animal skins, grain, oil, wool, silk, cotton, and beasts of burden...'). In times of famine, 'the Europeans come in their boats from every part of the Universe. When the price of grain goes up in one place, the Europeans are quick to bring it from far-away lands, in order to provide it for those who have none.'

This mutual dependency was divinely ordained: 'When matters are carefully considered, it will be recognised that the Christians and the Muslims need each other. [...] Every religion and every person of good sense is agreed that God did not create anything which was useless.'[7]

All this, except perhaps the divine aspects, was accurate enough. European boats did indeed bring food to Morocco in times of famine, European traders did open Moroccan markets, and European troops did withdraw. More than twenty years would pass before European armies again threatened Moroccan territory; meanwhile, European economic penetration first ate away the edges of Moroccan society, and then its political heart.

The aims of European diplomacy

This took time, for it was not until the 1880s that the colonial division of Africa began. Until then both the British and French, and later the Germans, sought to preserve the independence of non-European states, even if only as a fiction: the Ottoman Empire was too strong to take over, and its collapse might throw the European concert into disarray. Even when it came to Tunis, in the 1870s, the French ruled through financial domination not direct administration until they finally occupied the country in 1881. And when the British did finally occupy Egypt the following year they maintained the illusion of government through a consular 'adviser', Lord Cromer, and repeated declarations of respect for the 'rights' of other European powers and their subjects. In any event, the great powers tended to prefer indirect to direct rule as a matter of general policy.[8]

The French government could not have taken over Morocco even had it so wanted. In 1871 German armies paraded through Paris and half of Algeria revolted. Although some French officers in Algeria called for an attack on Morocco, to salvage national pride, or to avenge support for the rebels, the government would

7 *Ibid.*

8 R.E. Robinson and J. Gallagher, 'The Imperialism of Free Trade', *Economic History Review*, 5 (2nd series) 6 (1957): 1-15.

have none of it. Governor-General Chauzy was ordered not to meddle in Morocco. There were no resources to spare.[9]

The German Chancellor, Otto von Bismarck, was equally uninterested in Moroccan adventures. He was happy to build up political influence, and to increase German trade, principally in armaments, but no more than that. In 1877 he told the German Consul-General in Tangier: 'Morocco is the last country in the world where Germany would seek to establish a colony, for various reasons, the chief being that it would give rise to antagonism on the part of France, Spain and Great Britain.'[10]

The Spanish government, which might have wanted to take advantage of the victory of 1860, could not do so. In quick succession, the nearly bankrupt government was tied up in a war in Mexico, overthrown (1868), replaced by a temporary Italian king (1871-3), then by an equally temporary republic (1873-4) and then undermined by civil war. Even attempts to occupy Santa Cruz de Mar Pequeña were aborted since nobody knew where it was. In 1879 the single expedition that was sent to find out was beaten back by fierce waves and equally fierce resistance.[11]

Above all, the British government that ruled the most powerful imperial state and the richest trading nation, maintained its policy throughout the 1860s and 1870s of preserving Morocco from foreign occupation. Three principles governed British policy towards Morocco during these twenty years: that Moroccan markets should be open to commerce; that no other European state should control the southern shore of the Strait of Gibraltar; and, above all, that no money should be spent from the British Treasury to secure these aims. Self-interest determined that the British government champion the continued independence of Morocco, its stability and its financial viability.[12] Its local servant John Drummond-Hay worked tirelessly to help 'reform' the Makhzan and preserve Moroccan independence.

Despite the European stand-off, Sidi Mohammed IV and his successor Moulay Hassan knew that they would remain independent only if they were strong. They wanted to modernise the army, for which they needed money, so they were prepared to listen to Drummond-Hay's advice when they thought it was helpful – or when they had no choice. Equally they rejected his advice,

9 Parsons, *Morocco Question*, 38-41.

10 Quoted in *ibid.*, 55-6.

11 *Ibid.*, 27-8, 94-5.

12 Parsons, *Morocco Question*, 44-7.

when they could, if they felt that it went against their interests or might cause trouble. Yet they did not have a free hand. Powerful men, in the Makhzan and outside it, would resist changes that went against *their* interest, so the sultans were torn two ways.

Military reform

The shock of military defeat meant that the Makhzan turned first to military reform, and this remained the core of modernisation plans for the rest of the nineteenth century.

One man who lived through this was Salem el-Abdi. Born about 1863, the son of a soldier in the *abid al-bukhari*, he served first in the Makhzan's army and then in the colonial army of France, in which he reached the rank of *khalifa* (roughly, major) before he died in 1938.[13] One of his earliest memories was of accompanying the Qaid of the Abda, whose slave he was, to the court of Sidi Mohammed. The Sultan was 'a huge strong man with a powerful chest, but thin legs. He wore his hair long and curly, in the Berber style and did not shave his head. [...] He had a tanned complexion and big black eyes. He was both a scholar and a warrior.'[14]

Before he set about rebuilding his army this warrior-scholar turned to scholars for help. Ten important *'ulama* were asked to give *fatwas* declaring whether it was licit to adopt European weapons, tactics and methods of training the troops. This was a political ploy – Sidi Mohammed had already decided what he was going to do, but he needed the *'ulama* to convince other members of the Makhzan.[15]

Five replies have never been found, and may have been dissenting voices, but the remainder duly obliged. One of them, Muhammad al-Mahdi bin Suda, wrote that gunpowder, which was unknown to the Prophet, had been a praiseworthy innovation because it had allowed Muslims to extend their rule. Logically, when the *Dar al-Islam* was in danger, other innovations were permitted. Since other Muslim rulers had organised *nizam* armies, the Sultan of Morocco should do so.[16] This certainly struck a chord. In the

13 Louis Arnaud, *Au temps des mehallas au Maroc, ou le Maroc de 1860 à 1912* (Casablanca: Atlantides, 1952, i-iii and 1).

14 *Ibid.*, 2.

15 Al-Nasiri, *Kitab al-istiqsa*, 9:102.

16 Muhammad Manuni, *Mazahir yaqzat al-Maghrib al-hadith*, 2 vols (Rabat: Manshurat wizarat al-awqaf wa-l-shu'un al-Islamiyya wa-l-thaqafa, 1973), 1:269-71.

sixteenth century Moroccans had shown themselves very willing to use gunpowder.[17]

By 1869 the *nizam* army numbered 3,000 infantry and the artillery was growing too. The recruits came from both *jaysh* and non-*jaysh* tribes, and though men from the same region were often grouped in the same battalion it was not universal. The army was beginning to become Moroccan rather than factional.[18] The Sultan bought British shoulder arms and artillery, but also set up a gunpowder factory in Marrakesh, a first step in creating an industrial base for the army.[19] He turned to the British to train it. In 1870 the first group of students was sent to Gibraltar.[20]

The Sultan set great store by his army and it provided a path for the ambitious – Salem el-Abdi described how 'the army and the Makhzan soon swelled with importance. By 1285 (1868) these two supports of the throne were prospering.'[21]

When Sidi Mohammed died in 1873, his son Moulay Hassan continued to build up the army. By the end of his reign it had around 16,000 infantry, 12-15,000 cavalry and around 1,200-1,500 artillery. This was far short of the Sultan's intentions and only rarely were all the members of each battalion on full-time active service. They were paid very little, and even that did not always arrive.[22]

Moulay Hassan bought most of his weapons from Britain and France, but agents from many countries flocked to proffer their wares and the Sultan also bought shoulder arms from Austria, the United States, Germany and Belgium, to avoid offending any particular government. He also converted his father's powder factory into a cartridge factory, supervised by a Belgian, and built a rifle factory – the *Makina* in Fez – to make copies of Martini-Henry rifles under Italian supervision. It began production in 1893, turning out rifles very slowly and at an exorbitant price. Each rifle cost over 3,000 French francs to manufacture; imported Martini-Henrys cost around 50 Francs.[23]

Training was equally fragmented. Moulay Hassan sent students

17 Weston F. Cook, *The Hundred Years War for Morocco: Gunpowder and the Military Revolution in the Early Modern Muslim World* (Boulder, CO: Westview Press, 1994).

18 Rollman, 'New Order', 626.

19 *Ibid.*, 625.

20 Laroui, *Origines*, 282.

21 Arnaud, *Au temps des mehallas*, 3.

22 Rollman, 'New Order', 688, 693.

23 *Ibid.*, 707.

to the Royal Military Academy at Woolwich, and regular groups were sent to Gibraltar.[24] Since it was cheaper to bring the trainers to Morocco, in 1876 the Sultan hired a Briton, Sir Harry Maclean, who had resigned his lieutenant's commission in Gibraltar because of financial problems. Moroccan pay did not solve those problems, but he also sold arms on the side. Kaid Maclean, who dressed in an elaborate Arab-style uniform and spoke good Arabic, was an excellent soldier, and the Moroccans whom he trained, like Salem el-Abdi, admired him.[25] He was chief instructor of the infantry for thirty-two years.

Using the argument that Maclean was an agent of the British government, which he effectively was, the French government insisted that the Sultan accept a French military mission to train the artillery. Jules Erckman, its chief instructor, became a keen rival of Maclean's. Both men represented the interests of their governments. Maclean, with his theatrical emphasis on Moroccanisation, symbolised the British government's wish to strengthen Moroccan independence. Erckman and his successors epitomised an effort to bend Morocco to the will of the French government.

The German government insisted that it too should have a role, and in 1877 it was given responsibility for the coastal artillery. Krupp supplied vast 60-ton guns for Rabat at a cost of 1.9 million French francs. Starting in 1888, these took nearly ten years to install, partly because they were so big and partly because the technicians spun the operation out. The guns were fired twice, before their cement emplacements cracked.[26]

The guns were not only a military expense, but a diplomatic one. European governments struggled for influence in Morocco, but the Makhzan footed the bill. The Sultan even accepted Spanish and Italian military advisors. The Italians were asked to make the *Makina* work, but the Spaniards, aside from maintaining a single bridge, received no duties at all, and passed their time in drawing maps.[27]

Thus military reform that was intended to strengthen the Moroccan state against external aggression led to increased European involvement and heavier debt. Similarly, the Sultan might have hoped that the expansion of trade would make the Makhzan richer; instead it became poorer.

24 Rogers, *History*, 185-6; Miège, *Le Maroc et l'Europe*, 3: 225.

25 Arnaud, *Au temps des mehallas*, 123.

26 Rollman, 'New Order', 730-1.

27 *Ibid.*, 731.

Economic reform

Moroccan Sultans had for long financed themselves through foreign trade. Now it undermined them. John Drummond-Hay insisted on liberalising trade before he helped with any other reform. He demanded that clauses in the 1856 treaty that put severe limits on the Sultan's authority should be strictly honoured. Markets should be opened, and Europeans allowed to buy land in the interior. The Sultan had to wait six months before banning the export of produce, although he could not predict the size of the harvest. In 1860 Drummond-Hay complained that the Sultan had breached the anti-monopoly clause by selling a monopoly on fuller's earth (*ghasul*) to a prominent member of the Makhzan, Muhammad al-Madani Binnis. In 1864, he protested against interest-free loans to the Sultan's Jewish agents.[28] The preaching continued when Moulay Hassan succeeded his father. Free trade was for the good of Morocco; it would encourage agriculture and commerce, and only that could save Morocco from disaster.[29]

Agriculture was a most uncertain foundation. Droughts or floods, locusts or pestilence brought ruin and famine. Cholera followed drought that followed locusts in 1867-8, and some cities lost more than a tenth of their population. In 1878 drought on the Atlantic plains inaugurated five years of disaster: a general harvest failure, then cholera, then typhoid. Perhaps a quarter of the population of Tangier, and a third that of Larache, died, their numbers swelled by countless immigrants from the desolated countryside. Around three-quarters of the cattle round Casablanca died and nearly all around El Jadida. Famine returned to the far south in 1884 and locusts spread over the land in the following year.[30]

Certainly there were good years. After the Tetuan war, the economy boomed, helped by good harvests and the removal of trade restrictions. The American Civil War cut Europe off from supplies of American cotton and exports of raw cotton and woollen cloth soared, as long as the war lasted.[31] But demand fluctuated: exports of olive oil and almonds peaked in 1865 and then fell off.[32]

28 Bin Saghir, *Al-Maghrib wa-Britaniya*, 357-64.

29 *Ibid.*, 359, 364; Miège, *Le Maroc et l'Europe*, 3, 216; Drummond-Hay, *Memoir*, 314.

30 Bois, 'Années de disette'; Schroeter, *Merchants*, 197-8, 208; Mohammed M'rabet, 'Un millénaire de lutte contre le mort au Maroc, appreciation d'une thèse', *Revue Dar al-Niaba*, no. 36-27 (1990): 11-12.

31 Miège, *Le Maroc et l'Europe*, 2:502, 536, 323.

32 *Ibid.*, 531.

In the early 1870s, harvests improved, and the Moroccan economy entered one of its most prosperous periods in the nineteenth century. The balance of exports over imports was positive in every year between 1870 and 1877.[33] Increased exports meant there was more money to buy foreign cotton goods instead of local wool which the drought of the late 1860s had made so expensive. Imports of cotton cloth increased by a quarter between 1870 and 1877.[34] But when the droughts and disease returned in the late 1870s, foreign trade declined quickly (down from 58 million francs in 1874 to 40 million in 1878) and cotton imports did not pick up again until after 1883. Only grain imports grew in this period, because people were hungry; in 1878 grain made up 27% of total imports.[35] Harvests and disease dictated the pace of imports as well as exports.

While drought influenced what people wore, it had no effect on what they drank. Two commodities, tea and sugar, were immune from the influence of harvests. Tea had been a luxury item in the 1840s and 1850s, but by the 1870s it was a staple of Moroccans' diet and a vital part of their social life. In 1870 around 95,000 kg. of tea were imported, 275,000 kg. in 1884. Moroccans drink their tea heavily sweetened and flavoured with mint. The mint grew locally, but the sugar was imported, in equally huge quantities. By 1883 sugar made up just under 19% of all imports.[36]

The promise of the French consulate in 1860 was fulfilled: Morocco exported raw materials and imported manufactured goods, and grain in times of famine. British and French traders benefited the most. By the end of the 1870s British and French vessels made up 90% of all shipping in Moroccan ports, in roughly equal proportions. Portugal and Spain were far behind.[37]

Technological innovation

The Sultan, like his predecessors, tried to profit from the growth in trade by encouraging an increase in production. After he became Sultan, Sidi Mohammed began to experiment in growing cotton on his own estates around El Jadida and Drummond-Hay suggested he might import some Egyptian fellahs to help. The Sultan did

33 *Ibid.*, 3:237 – though the table seems to have been incorrectly formulated.

34 *Ibid.*, 2:535.

35 *Ibid.*, 3:424; M'rabet, 'Un millénaire', 13.

36 Miège, *Le Maroc et l'Europe*, 2:543-4; 3:247, 249, 417.

37 *Ibid.*, 2:506-8; 3:252.

not go as far as that, but he did distribute seeds to farmers and set up cotton ginning machinery in Marrakesh to process the fibres. In 1862 he imported British machines to process sugar.[38] A steam mill was set up in Tangier and a paper factory in Essaouira which would use the local esparto grass as the basic material. A printing press was imported which Sidi Mohammed eventually set up in Fez.[39] Moulay Hassan made plans to dig a coal mine at Tangier, using men brought up from the Marrakesh region where they were accustomed to dig irrigation tunnels.[40]

These efforts did not come to much. The refinery produced very little sugar but the steam mill at Tangier produced a lot of flour until its boiler blew up in 1872, and could not be repaired. Fatally, there was no overall plan, and projects were organised piecemeal, a factory here and a mill there without any real technological base. No Moroccan students were sent abroad to study technological subjects, as they had been in Egypt.[41]

The Sultan's aim was to increase revenue and so to strengthen his control. Drummond-Hay knew this and although his intentions were different – to build up the Moroccan infrastructure in order to make trade easier – what he told Sidi Mohammed was that better roads would allow his armies to move at greater speed. The sultan hired engineers to build roads and imported a prefabricated metal bridge for the Oum er Rbia, though it turned out to be too short. A new mole was planned for Safi, and the Sultan promised to repair the walls and harbour at El Jadida. In 1869 the Makhzan completed new quarters for merchants in Essaouira.[42] In 1877 Moulay Hassan agreed to Drummond-Hay's demands for port works at Essaouira, Tangier and Casablanca. Although these projects were later abandoned, a small quay was built at Tangier.[43] The Sultan refused to allow railway lines or land telegraph lines because tribesmen might attack them.[44]

38 Al-Nasiri, *Kitab al-istiqsa*, 9:122, 127; Pascon, *Haouz*, 44; Manuni, *Mazahir*, 1:78; Miège, *Le Maroc et l'Europe*, 3:117.

39 Germain Ayache, 'L'apparition de l'imprimerie au Maroc', in *Études d'histoire marocaine* (Rabat: SMER, 1979), 139-58; Manuni, *Mazahir*, 1:206-10; Miège, *Le Maroc et l'Europe*, 3:114, 117.

40 Bin Saghir, *Al-Maghrib wa-Britaniya*, 381.

41 Pascon, *Haouz*, 46; Ayache, 'Imprimerie'.

42 Schroeter, *Merchants*, 63-5, 128, 141-2; Miège, *Le Maroc et l'Europe*, 3:114-15; Al-Nasiri, *Kitab al-istiqsa*, 9:127.

43 Miège, *Le Maroc et l'Europe*, 3:218.

44 Bin Saghir, *Al-Maghrib wa-Britaniya*, 372ff.

Other services were provided directly by the consuls, often in competition with each other. In 1857 Drummond-Hay set up a post office in the British consulate in Tangier. The French did the same in 1860 and the Spanish in 1862. The French, British and Spanish all built hospitals in Tangier to treat both Moroccans and Europeans. By 1869 there were European doctors in virtually every Moroccan coastal town.[45] Sometimes the consuls imposed a development and made the Makhzan pay for it. Backed by treaty, a lighthouse was built at Cape Spartel, at the entrance to the Mediterranean. It was maintained and controlled by the consular corps, but at the Makhzan's expense although not one merchant ship flew the Moroccan flag.[46] By international consent, the Sultan lost control of his country, and paid for it while European traders benefited.

Administration

The clearest infringement of the Sultan's sovereignty came when Spanish officials were sent to the customs houses to help collect duties from which the indemnity would be paid. They stayed there for the next twenty-four years with Moroccan officials to shadow them. The need to reform the Makhzan's administration became clear. Sidi Mohammed began with Rabat. A *dahir* (decree) of 1861 set up a new corps of officials with new methods of operation and of record-keeping.[47] The following year the system was applied to the whole country: two *amins* (literally, 'secretaries') were appointed in each port, paid a monthly salary and made independent of the authority of the governor.[48]

This coincided with Drummond-Hay's own suggestions for reform, although it did not go nearly as far as he would have liked. Regular and sufficient pay for officials was something that the Makhzan simply could not afford. It was not a religious question, but a practical one; there was nothing un-Moroccan or un-Islamic

45 Miège, *Le Maroc et l'Europe*, 2:450, 468-70.

46 Treaty between Morocco and Spain November 1861, article XLIII; Convention as to Cape Spartel Light-house Between the United States, Austria, Belgium, France, Great Britain, Italy, the Netherlands, Portugal, Spain and Sweden and Norway, and Morocco. Signed at Tangier, May 31, 1865; ratifications exchanged February 14, 1867.

47 Manuni, *Mazahir*, 1:306-15.

48 Thomas Kerlin Park, 'Administration and the Economy: Morocco 1880 to 1980: the Case of Essaouira' (Ph.D. diss., University of Madison-Wisconsin, 1983), 201-2; Bin Saghir, *Al-Maghrib wa-Britaniya*, 399.

about administrative reform. Indeed, the need for honest officials was a constant theme of *fatwas* in nineteenth-century Morocco, largely because the new officials were not honest.[49]

Moulay Hassan reorganised the whole administration. In 1879 he increased the power of his top official, the *wazir*, who was now designated chief minister (*wazir al-a'zam*), and given charge of the bureaucracy: raising troops, levying taxes, appointing officials, taking charge of public order. Beneath him was a minister of finance, so that for the first time one man had responsibility for revenues as well as expenditures.[50] The sultan formalised an office of *wazir al-shikayat* ('minister for complaints'), to set right administrative and judicial abuses and oversee how *waqf* properties were administered. He appointed a minister for war (*wazir al-harb*) to take charge of the *mahallas*, the columns that were sent out across Morocco. But he demoted his representative in Tangier, the *naib*, whose daily contact with the consuls had allowed him to take on more and more power. The *naib* was now a mere functionary, under the Foreign Minister, the *wazir al-bahar*.[51] Yet the fundamental character of Moroccan government did not change. The power to make decisions rested with the Sultan, even in the most insignificant matters. Reform, for the Sultan, meant taking a firmer grip on power.

It was not enough to restructure the administration. The Makhzan had to become richer, a hard task when the very coins in which taxes were collected were tumbling in value.

Currency reform

After the war of 1860 all the reserves in the treasury were used to pay off the first half of the indemnity to Spain, and Moroccan gold coinage virtually disappeared. From then on, the currency system was based on silver and copper. In 1862 Sidi Mohammed decreed new exchange rates in terms of silver, but allowed the copper coinage to float. By doing so, he protected the Makhzan's income, because receipts in silver became relatively stable, but

49 Bin Saghir, *Al-Maghrib wa-Britaniya*, 403; Laroui, Origines, 285; Mohamed Kenbib, 'Changing aspects of State and Society in 19th-century Morocco' in Abdelali Doumou (ed.), *The Moroccan State in Historical Perspective 1850-1985* (Dakar: CODESRIA, 1990), 11-27.

50 Al-Nasiri, *Kitab al-istiqsa*, 9:122.

51 Mohamed Lahbabi, *Le Gouvernement marocain à l'aube du vingtième siècle*, 2nd ed (Rabat: Les Éditions Maghrébines, 1975), 140-80; Nicholas Michel, 'L'approvisionnement de la mhalla au Maroc au XIXe siècle', *Hespéris-Tamuda* 29, no. 2 (1991): 324.

the depreciation in the bronze coinage was passed on to the taxpayers. This was a recipe for speculation, both by Moroccans and Europeans.

The result was a system of parallel currencies. The poor used copper for buying, selling and paying their taxes, while the rich, the traders and the Europeans in the ports, used silver. Rapid inflation followed because the silver content of the Moroccan silver coinage declined (the silver *dinar* shrank from the 29 grammes laid down by the *shari'a* to between 26.8 and 28.25 grammes) and because of massive counterfeiting of copper coinage. Exchange rates between European and Moroccan coinage widened, and the Moroccan coinage decreased further in value. By the end of the 1860s, European coins had driven out the local currency, and the Spanish silver five peseta and the French silver five-franc piece became the main currency of Morocco.

Since customs duties were paid in European silver, revenue should have gone up; but the merchants demanded that the tariffs be reduced in order to compensate them. In 1869 Sidi Mohammed announced that he was returning to the system of coinage outlined in Islamic law. For a short while this made the Moroccan currency more valuable, but then it began to slide again. In 1877 Moulay Hassan again tried to bring the exchange rates down, and to remove the differences between the rates in Fez and Marrakesh that proved a gift to speculators.[52]

Although Sidi Mohammed had good religious justification for his reforms, he also had the support of John Drummond-Hay. In consequence, the French and Spanish consuls discerned a British plot to undermine their merchants (or speculators) and protested. They did the same when the Sultan tried to reform the status of protégés.

Protégés

Morocco had a magnetic attraction for speculators. It was not the respectable businessman from London or Paris who went to Morocco, for on the economic frontiers of Europe, and way beyond its political borders, there was unusual risk. Not all Europeans in Morocco were dishonest or criminal, but there were plenty of unscrupulous opportunists. From 1860 onwards the number

52 'Umar Afa, *Mas'alat al-nuqud fi tarikh al-Maghrib fi al-qarn al-tasi' 'ashar: (Sus, 1822-1906)* ([Agadir]: Jami'at al-Qadi 'Iyad, Kulliyat al-Adab wa-al-'Ulum al-Insaniyah bi-Agadir, 1988), 221-9; Ayache, 'Aspects de la crise', 129-37.

of foreigners grew steadily. In 1858 there were about 700 Europeans living in Morocco; by 1867 there were nearly 1,500.[53]

Since Europeans generally did not speak Arabic and had few local contacts, this provided new opportunities for Moroccans. The ideal job was in a consulate, as a translator, interpreter or household servant. Particularly valuable were the consular agencies in the smaller ports, often filled by Jewish merchants.[54] These were frequently sinecures: in Essaouira, Joseph ben Aaron, the consul for the Austro-Hungarian Empire in the 1860s, was succeeded by his son when he died.[55] There was virtually no trade between Austria-Hungary and Morocco, and no resident consul-general in Tangier: Sir John Drummond-Hay acted for the government in Vienna.[56] The US Consul in Essaouira was another rich Jewish merchant, and an Italian merchant acted for Portugal and for Norway and Sweden.[57] None of these countries conducted much trade.

Diplomatic status brought immunity from prosecution, taxation and military service. In theory, only two employees of each consulate were entitled to extraterritorial rights, but as soon as Abraham Corcos became US Consul in Essaouira he extended protection to his brother and to his nephew, an exporter of ostrich feathers.[58] This was usual practice. All foreign nationals had extraterritorial rights too, so Moroccans began to be naturalised as foreign subjects. Because nationality was hereditary, it was much prized. Felix Mathews, the American Consul, naturalised many people who had little or no direct connection with the United States, as did the Portuguese and Italian Consuls. Many of them were Jews.[59].

Logic determined that the local agents of foreign merchants' would claim protection. It was therefore extended to two *simsars* (*censaux* in French) or commercial servants of each merchant. Within a year of the Treaty of Madrid in 1861, the number of

53 Miège, *Le Maroc et l'Europe*, 2:481; bin Saghir, *Al-Maghrib wa-Britaniya*, 315.

54 Pascon, *Haouz*, 65-7.

55 Schroeter, *Merchants*, 44-5.

56 *U. S. Compilation of Treaties in Force*, 1904, p. 558, 'Convention as to Cape Spartel Light-house between the United States, Austria, Belgium, France, Great Britain, Italy, the Netherlands, Portugal, Spain and Sweden and Norway, and Morocco; Signed at Tangier, May 31, 1865; ratifications exchanged February 14, 1867'.

57 Schroeter, *Merchants*, 166.

58 *Ibid.*,

59 Parsons, *Morocco Question*, 79,67.

Spanish protégés had increased from ninety to 763.[60] The whole question of protégés was surrounded by so many uncertainties and abuses that all numbers are misleading. In 1877 the Consuls-General estimated that they had around 800 protégés between them, with the Spanish leading the pack, followed by France, Italy and Britain. But the real figure may have been three times as big. The US Consul acknowledged only thirty-seven, but unofficially Felix Mathews had more than 100 rich Moroccans under his protection in 1877.[61] Having spread through every port, protection followed European commerce into the countryside. The merchants were not allowed to settle in the inland cities, like Marrakesh, so they appointed agents; they were not allowed to buy real property, so they set up agricultural partnerships with Moroccans, some of which were faked and corruptly sold. The partners also claimed *de facto* immunity.[62]

By no means were all the protégés scoundrels. Some were respectable men, trying to protect their wealth against an often arbitrary government.[63] But the unscrupulous and ambitious latched onto the opportunities that protection gave them and did very well as a result. Among the most infamous was Abu Bakr bin al-Hajj al-Bashir al-Ghanjawi. A former camel driver on the route between Marrakesh and the coast, he became a *simsar* for a British firm in Safi, where he got a reputation as a fixer. By the early 1870s he was helping the British Vice-Consul to sort out commercial problems with Makhzan officials. This excited so much local envy that he took formal protection from the British Consulate-General in Tangier. In 1898 R.B. Cunninghame-Graham, a Scottish traveller and radical member of parliament, described him as 'known from the Atlas to Riff, and from the Sahara to Mogador, feared and disliked, and yet respected'.[64] He was certainly immensely rich: Cunninghame-Graham described how 'he showed me all his treasures in his palace in Morocco City, tapped on his iron chest, and said, "This one is full of gold, that is all jewels; this, again, is full of bonds;" and is assumed to have a hundred thousand

60 Miège, *Le Maroc et l'Europe*, 2:402.

61 *Ibid.*, 2: 263-4, 403.

62 Kenbib, 'Changing aspects', 17-19.

63 *Ibid.*, 22.

64 R.B. Cunninghame-Graham, *Moghreb-el-Acksa* (London: Century, 1988; first publi. London: Heinemann, 1898), 288.

pounds all safely tied up in Consols.'[65] Ghanjawi was not alone,[66] and greed knew no religious boundaries, for there were Muslim protégés and there were Jewish ones. Indeed, some Jews profited mightily from protection.

Jews

Jews, who once had acted as the Sultan's merchants, now found greater benefits by working for Europeans. Protection soothed the anxiety that their property might be expropriated, exempted them from the poll-tax to which only Jews were subject, and removed them from Moroccan jurisdiction in criminal cases, where they were not treated equally. They could settle down to business and steadily accumulate capital.[67] Rich Jews flocked to the protection of the Europeans and most of those who naturalised as Europeans were Jews, since few Muslims would take a step that meant formally abandoning Islam.[68]

Poorer Jews could not become protégés, but they found a protector in the Alliance Israélite Universelle (AIU). The Alliance was set up in Paris in 1860 by some of the most influential Jews in France, who included Alphonse Crémieux, a republican lawyer who had lobbied to extend French citizenship to the Jews of Algeria, and French protection to Maronite Christians in Lebanon. Consequently, the AIU was often identified as an agent of French influence, although it was designed to be a charitable organisation helping the Jews outside France.[69] In Morocco the Alliance concentrated on bringing 'moral progress', by which it meant education. Within a year the first AIU school, set up in Tetuan in 1862, had 162 pupils and a waiting list almost as long.[70] By 1897 there were Alliance schools in five cities, Tangier, Tetuan, Essaouira, Fez and Casablanca, educating over 1,700 pupils.[71]

The schools were in the port cities because foreign consuls supported them, and because the Jewish communities there were more liberal. Conservative Jews considered the education provided

65 *Ibid.*, 52.

66 For another example, see Misa'ud bin 'Abd al-Qadir al-Talawi as cited in bin Saghir, *Al-Maghrib wa-Britaniya*, 294-305.

67 Laskier, *Alliance*, 46; Kenbib, 'Changing aspects', 15-16.

68 Parsons, *Morocco Question*, 67.

69 Laskier, *Alliance*, 33-4.

70 *Ibid.*, 62.

71 *Ibid.*, 92-3.

by the Alliance to be far too secular. Although the schools taught Hebrew and biblical history, they concentrated on 'modern' subjects – European languages, geography and mathematics.[72] The Tetuan and Tangier schools even taught girls. Conservative rabbis accused the Alliance of de-Judaising its pupils, and forced the schools in Tetuan and Tangier to close for short periods.[73] In this clash of cultures the AIU's representatives were equally intolerant. The school director in Tangier accused the chief rabbi of superstition and ignorance,[74] and in 1892, the head of the Essaouira school complained: 'Living in a milieu of a profoundly backward and fanatical Arab population, speaking their language and practising their customs, the Jews of Mogador have acquired the predominant vices of their Muslim compatriots: ruse and hypocrisy.'[75]

The flavour of the AIU was predominantly French, because of the help given by French consuls in Tangier and Casablanca, although the Spanish consul in Tetuan helped with the school there and it worked in Spanish. Although English was taught in the other schools, this sometimes brought conflicts with the British consulates and British-inclined Jewish leaders. The school in Essaouira fell victim to this pressure in the 1870s, and the Board of Deputies of British Jews founded its own school there.[76]

In general, though, the rich British Jewish community focused its efforts in Morocco on welfare and political rights. After the Tetuan war, a leading London Jew, Moses Picciato, took to Essaouira funds that had been raised in Britain and the United States.[77] He was followed by the celebrated Sir Moses Montefiore, who was sent by the Board of Deputies to visit the Sultan. Sidi Mohammed agreed to enlarge the *millah* in Essaouira (which was not done) and in 1864 issued a *dahir* that ended corporal punishment for Jews and promised equality and justice, just as the Turkish Sultan had done six years before, in 1856. The Makhzan's officials were often less tolerant. Ahmad al-Nasiri, author of the *Kitab al-Istiqsa* chronicle complained that when the Sultan's *dahir* was issued, 'copies of it were taken and distributed among all the Jews of

72 *Ibid.*, 100-1.

73 *Ibid.*, 86-7.

74 *Ibid.*, 81-1.

75 Schroeter, *Merchants*, 59-60.

76 Laskier, *Alliance*, 62-3.

77 Schroeter, *Merchants*, 200.

Morocco, and they became insolent and reckless'.[78]

There was an element of truth in this: Drummond-Hay and other European consuls repeatedly complained of the abuses that a small minority of very wealthy Jews made of protection.[79]

The Madrid conference

Despite the abuses, the consuls continued to support both Jewish and non-Jewish protégés. They helped even the most shady traders when things went wrong. In 1864 a British company in Safi sold arms on credit to rebels of the Awlad Amran tribe, who promptly reneged on their debt. Drummond-Hay forced the Makhzan to pay it.

Simple carelessness, or ill-luck, led to endless complications. Since the Moroccan countryside was chronically insecure, it was clearly unwise for Europeans to visit it alone and unprotected. Yet they did so, and from time to time they were murdered. In 1864, after a British merchant was killed on an unauthorised visit to a religious ceremony, the Sultan punished the murderers, but Drummond-Hay demanded that local officials be sacked and publicly disgraced. On other occasions the Sultan had to pay an indemnity to the victim's family.[80] The pressure was endless. After a dispute between a Spanish protégé and Makhzan officials in 1866, Spanish warships were sent to Essaouira. Italian gunboats made a protest visit in 1869. Europeans in Morocco came to the conclusion that they could do as they pleased, since their consuls would always protect them.

The Sultan complained about loss of taxation and of authority. In 1863 Sidi Mohammed wrote a circular letter to the consuls asking them to help sort out the protection problem. The French consul obliged and negotiated the *Béclard Convention* that limited protection to specific individuals, excluding their families, and made it non-hereditary. Merchants were to be allowed only two *simsars* each. Agricultural protégés were not to be exempted from Moroccan law, although the consuls were to be informed if they were arrested.[81] Apart from the last provision, this was all supposed to be happening anyway, and it was ignored.

78 Al-Nasiri, *Kitab al-istiqsa*, 9:114.

79 Parsons, *Morocco Question*, 67; Rogers, *History*, 181; Kenbib, 'Changing aspects', 18.

80 Bin Saghir, *Al-Maghrib wa-Britaniya*, 264-6.

81 Parsons, *Morocco Question*, 64; 'Regulations Relative to Protection Adopted by Common Consent by the Legation of France and the Government of Morocco,

When he became sultan, Moulay Hassan asked the British government for support. In 1876 Lord Derby, the Foreign Secretary, assured a Moroccan ambassador to London that he wanted a solution to the protection problem, so in March the following year the *naib* in Tangier convened a conference of the consuls. Drummond-Hay may have helped to frame the Moroccan demands, but the Spanish, Italian and US Consuls refused them, and the French consul equivocated.[82]

Despite the support of the British Consul-General, the other European consuls ensured that the Tangier conference failed, and the initiative then passed from Moroccan hands. In May and July 1880 the British government organised an international conference in Madrid to settle the protégé problem.[83]

After protracted negotiations, this conference agreed to limit protected status. Neither criminals nor government officials could be named as protégés; their numbers would be curbed; and they could only live in the port cities; their status would not be hereditary; foreigners and protégés would pay agricultural and gate taxes. In return, foreigners would be allowed to own land, and if a native employee were arrested nothing would be done until the consul was informed. In reality, consuls and merchants only insisted on those articles that were advantageous to them and ignored the limitations. Instead of limiting foreign privileges, the Madrid conference extended them.[84]

Sir John Drummond-Hay alleged that some of his colleagues sought only to protect their privileges and their ability to grant protected status and naturalisation corruptly, in exchange for money. Other delegates responded that the British government merely wished to preserve its own influence in Morocco, and accused the British consul-general of conducting a personal vendetta against them.[85] In truth, they were not entirely self-serving. The AIU appealed to delegates and their governments not to expose Jewish protégés to risk, and this concern played its part in the reluctance to clamp down on protection. The Italian consul in Tangier,

---

August 19, 1863'

82 Parsons, *Morocco Question*, 70-9; Bin Saghir, *Al-Maghrib wa-Britaniya*, 309-12; Rogers, *History*, 188.

83 Parsons, *Morocco Question*, 79.

84 *Ibid.*, 79-86; Leland Bowie, *The Impact of the Protégé System in Morocco, 1880-1912*, (Athens, OH: Ohio University, Center for International Studies, 1970), 3.

85 Parsons, *Morocco Question*, 79, 67.

who may have been corrupt, did also champion Jewish causes.[86] Even Drummond-Hay declared that protection was a way of seeking security in a country where law did not exist.[87] In 1864 he had told Bargach, the *naib* in Tangier, that he was intervening in the case of the qaid of Demnate who was mistreating the Jews there because, 'I am the representative of a great nation, which has law, and we will not be silent about that'.[88] In his eyes the rule of law set the Europeans off from the Moroccans. However badly individual Europeans might behave, they could not be subjected to Moroccan law. The occasional common ground of the early part of the century had been abandoned completely.

The Morocco question

After the Conference of Madrid all common ground was irretrievably lost. From now on, Europeans decided the fate of Morocco and Moulay Hassan could no longer take any serious diplomatic initiative.

Morocco remained independent because no important European government wanted to force the pace and allow one of their number to take over the country completely. The French government wanted no foreign army on the Algerian border. Bismarck wanted to keep the mouth of the Strait out of French hands. Lord Salisbury, the British Prime Minister, told the French ambassador in 1891: 'It is in no-one's interest to raise such a serious question as the dismemberment of Morocco. There are enough combustible materials in Europe without manufacturing new ones.'[89]

Minor governments like those of Italy and Spain had fewer compunctions about disturbing 'sleeping dogs' in Morocco,[90] fearing that they would be excluded completely from the division of northern Africa. When French forces occupied Tunisia in 1881, the Italian government was horrified because there were more Italian than French settlers there. The Spanish government made empty threats to occupy Larache and Tangier and in 1884 Spanish troops did establish a tiny post at Villa Cisneros, on the tip of

86 Laskier, *Alliance*, 51, 54, 65.

87 Bin Saghir, *Al-Maghrib wa-Britaniya*, 402.

88 *Ibid.*, 289 quoting PRO FO 174/137, Drummond Hay to Bargash, Tangier, 7 November 1864).

89 Quoted in Parsons, *Morocco Question*, 397; see also 135 and 143.

90 *Ibid.*, 241.

the Dakhla peninsula in the far south of what would become the Western Sahara. The following year the Madrid government declared a protectorate over the whole coast from Cape Juby to Cape Bojador, a particularly vapid pronouncement since there was no money in the Spanish treasury.[91]

Neither the Italian nor the Spanish governments amounted to much on their own, and their search for allies met with only modest success. In 1885 the government in Berlin turned Madrid down, but in 1887 the British government did support a joint Italian and Spanish note to the Makhzan demanding that the Sultan make no territorial concessions without consulting them. Although the Sultan would use this demand for his own purposes a few years later, it was a sign that the minor powers were pulling the governments of major states like Britain into intervening in Morocco. The British government was determined to protect trade and markets.

Trade, protection, diplomacy and self-promotion

European imports into Morocco grew rapidly in the 1880s and early 1890s, but Moroccan exports faltered. In the 1870s Moroccan trade had mostly been in credit, but late in the decade it moved into deficit and never really recovered.[92]

The first sign was the decline of the trans-Saharan trade. Ostrich feathers now came from South Africa, salt was brought out through Dakar, gold and ivory from many places.[93] Only the slave trade escaped the trend; after the suppression of the Atlantic slave trade and the European occupation of most of the rest of North Africa, Morocco was one of the few remaining markets.[94]

Moroccan exports of agricultural goods were reduced in the late 1870s because the French and German governments adopted protectionist policies.[95] British purchasers found cheaper suppliers elsewhere. Indian skins and hides beat Moroccan produce in price and quality (many Moroccan skins came from animals that had died in the drought), wool was cheaper from South America and Australia, North America could supply grain in larger quantities

91 *Ibid.*, 95-6; Jacques Cagne, *Nation et nationalisme au Maroc: aux racines de la nation marocaine* (Rabat: Dar Nashr al-Ma'rifa, 1988), 204-5.

92 Miège, *Le Maroc et l'Europe*, 3: 237, 419.

93 *Ibid.*, 3:362-3.

94 Daniel Schroeter, 'Slave Markets and Slavery in Moroccan Urban Society', *Slavery and Abolition* 13, no. 1 (1992): 190-3.

95 Miège, *Le Maroc et l'Europe*, 3:381.

and Sardinian and Balearic almonds were better. Moroccan olive oil harvests were poor in the late 1880s and although agricultural exports picked up briefly in that decade, Morocco remained on the economic periphery of Europe as far as exports were concerned.[96]

That was not true of imports. In the 1880s, imported glassware, knives and candles became much cheaper. Sewing machines spread widely.[97] Petroleum imports through Essaouira doubled every year from 1888 to 1892. Matches spread throughout the country, pottery was imported from Britain, cotton from Britain and France.[98] Above all, tea and sugar continued their inexorable rise. By 1890, tea was the third biggest item of import and accounted for 5% of the total value. By 1895, sugar made up a quarter of all the imports of the country.[99]

As the competition between French, British and, increasingly, German traders increased, so did the rivalries of assertive European diplomats. Ladislas Ordega, appointed as French consul in 1882, was noted for his impulsiveness, vanity, and chauvinism. He was followed in 1885 by Charles Féraud, a much more upright man but virulently anti-British, and in the same year a new German Consul-General was appointed, the arrogant Charles Testa. By then, John Drummond-Hay was a declining force. His autocratic style sat badly with the many disreputable Britons ('foreign vultures', he called them) who arrived in Tangier in droves. Among them was Edward Meakin, on the run from a court judgement, who set up *The Times of Morocco* in which he attacked the British Consul-General. In 1885, Drummond-Hay retired, though he stayed on in Tangier until he died in 1893. Apparently his family in Britain wanted to keep him at arms' length. His successors were the apoplectic Sir William Kirby Green, who despised Moroccans, and Sir Charles Euan Smith (1891-4) who had helped establish a British protectorate over Zanzibar and was certain that he knew how to set Orientals to rights.[100]

With more trade and aggressive diplomatic support, the number of Europeans in Morocco grew from some 3,500 in 1886 to around 9,000 in 1894, most of them Spanish. By the 1890s there were

96 *Ibid.*, 3:398, 401; 4:420-3.

97 Edmund Burke, III, *Prelude to Protectorate in Morocco* (University of Chicago Press, 1976), 23; Miège, *Le Maroc et l'Europe*, 4:367.

98 Miège, *Le Maroc et l'Europe*, 3: 424-5; 4:391-5.

99 *Ibid.*, 2: 543-4; 3: 247, 249, 417; 4:388-9.

100 Parsons, *Morocco Question*, 111-29, 264-5, 398-401, 604.

about six times as many Spaniards as Britons, and twice as many Britons as Frenchmen.[101] Sir John Drummond-Hay claimed that the Britons were 'sometimes persons not of a very high standing'. That was true of other nationalities, too. A counterfeit Russian count claimed to set up diplomatic relations for the Tsar. A criminal Frenchman posed as a Muslim and claimed the Sultan's throne, and another Frenchman convinced the Makhzan that he was the legitimate consul for 'Araucania-Patagonia', under which disguise he was also presented to the President of France. He lived for some time in Essaouira by selling protection.[102]

Genuine consuls also awarded protection for diplomatic advantage. One recipient was the Sharif of Ouezzane, Si al-Hajj Abd al-Salam bin al-Arbi, whose father had invested in landed property near Tangier. The young *sharif* became close to European residents, and in 1873 he married an English governess in Tangier, Emily Keene. He was also a drunk, and by the early 1880s his extravagance had run him short of money. Although al-Hajj Abd al-Salam was hardly the epitome of a reputable *sharif*, many people venerated him because of his ancestry, and he had great political influence. In January 1884, on his own initiative, Ordega gave him French protection. Nearly five years later the *sharif* sold to Jules Jazulot, the head of the Parisian Printemps group, a large estate outside Tangier that was not his to sell: it belonged to the *tariqa*. Politics and diplomacy underlay this unrestrained financial knavery. John Drummond-Hay was not alone in believing that the *sharif* had made a secret deal with the French consul to take the Sultan's place if Moulay Hassan were overthrown.[103]

When trade and protection allowed people to escape the Makhzan's net, feelings among officials ran high, particularly when those concerned were Jews. Muhammad bin Husayn, the ruler of Iligh and an ally of the Sultan, complained in 1889 about a Jew whom he said had falsely accused him of kidnapping his wife and children. The following year he tipped the Sultan off about a Jewish merchant who had been caught smuggling ostrich feathers and guns. Yet he had also arrested a tribesman for murdering a Jew and beaten him until he confessed to the crime. Muhammad

101 Miège, *Le Maroc et l'Europe*, 3: 469; 4: 285-6; Bin Saghir, *Al-Maghrib wa-Britaniya*, 315.

102 Parsons, *Morocco Question*, 93.

103 Miège, *Le Maroc et l'Europe*, 4:239-43; Parsons, *Morocco Question*, 15-116; George Joffe, 'The Zawiya of Wazzan: Relations between Shurafa and Tribe up to 1860' in Joffe and Pennell (eds), *Tribe and State*, *passim*; Rogers, *History*, 203; Laroui, *Origines*, 251, 254; Emily Keene, Shareefa of Wazan, *My Life Story*, ed. S.L. Bensusan (London: Edward Arnold, 1912).

bin Husayn was not being inconsistent, he was simply trying to control 'his' Jews. The Jews, he complained, wanted to break free, and live in the new Makhzan town at Tiznit.[104]

Freedom eluded most Jews, who were neither protégés nor rich. While the richer Jews benefited from protégé status, the poor had to pay higher and higher proportions of the *jizya* poll-tax. Sometimes this was so heavy that the Makhzan could not collect it.[105] As ever more Jews moved out of the Sous, conditions in port cities like Essaouira and Salé got worse and relations between richer Jews and their poorer brethren became more strained. The Jewish community was still vertically divided by lines of patronage, so that it would be wrong to talk of class divisions growing up, but in the 1890s there were a few short-lived, and violent, outbursts in Essaouira and Salé.[106] The rich Jews had more in common with affluent Muslim Moroccans, and they formed many partnerships with Muslim merchants, jointly owning property, and running business ventures together.[107]

The rich and powerful

One place where Jewish and Muslim Moroccans cooperated was in the north of England. In the late nineteenth century, the Moroccan merchant community in Manchester included Jews and members of very prominent Fasi Muslim families: Guessus, Benjelloun and Binani among others.[108] Some merchants became so rich from the trade with Europe that they could join the elite of the Makhzan. Even so, the '*ulama*, the learned families, still looked down on them and intermarried with them only rarely.[109]

The upper reaches of the Makhzan were still filled by members of the Sultan's enormous family, since Moulay Hassan had numerous brothers. Moulay al-Amin led a *mahalla* to the Guelaya in 1880.[110] Moulay Umar was Governor of Fez for a time,[111] and Moulay

104 Ennaji and Pascon, *Le Makhzen et le Sous al-Aqsa*, 125, 169-70, 193, 162.

105 Schroeter, *Merchants*, 201.

106 *Ibid.*, 202-4.

107 Brown, *Salé*, 55, 157-9.

108 Fred Halliday, 'The *millet* of Manchester: Arab Merchants and Cotton Trade', *British Journal of Middle Eastern Studies*, 19, no. 2 (1992): 159-76.

109 Norman Cigar, 'Socio-economic Structures and the Development of an Urban Bourgeoisie in Pre-Colonial Morocco', *Maghreb Review*, 6, no. 3-4 (1981): 67-8.

110 Arnaud, *Au Temps des Mehallas*, 60.

111 Laroui, *Origines*, 355.

Uthman was Khalifa in Marrakesh in the early years of his reign.[112] Moulay Ali took a *mahalla* to the Banu Snassen in 1875 to put down a rebellion, and was defeated.[113] Moulay Arafa was wounded in a scuffle with the same tribe in 1876.[114] These were royal cannon-fodder, no more than attendant lords, although one of Moulay Hassan's brothers was always vital to him: al-Rashid, who was appointed khalifa of Tafilalt in 1862, and remained there for the next half century.[115] Eventually, Moulay Hassan came to rely on his sons. His favourite son, Abdelaziz, who was born in 1881 was pressed into service at a very early age. In 1893 he and his elder brother, Bilghith, were sent with a large gift of money to the sharifs of the Ait Atta and Tafilalt to reward them for their loyalty.[116]

Beneath the Sultan's immediate relations came families who had served the Makhzan in the past. One important faction consisted of the descendants of Ahmad bin Mubarak, whose family had provided a chamberlain for Moulay Abderrahmane and even Moulay Slimane. Abdallah bin Ahmad was chamberlain, then governor of Fez and finally Moulay Hassan's minister of war. His brother Musa was Mohammed IV's chamberlain and was succeeded, when he died in 1879, by his son Ahmad bin Musa who as 'Ba Ahmad' became the virtually all-powerful chamberlain of Moulay Hassan. A rival was the family of the Jama'is. Muhammad bin al-Arbi al-Jama'i, grandson of the secretary of Moulay Abderrahmane and son of a man who had briefly been *wazir*, became *wazir* in his turn in 1878. When he died in 1886 he was replaced by his brother al-Ma'ti, and another brother, Muhammad al-Saghir, became minister for war.[117] Mohammed IV sealed the relationship by marrying a daughter of al-Arbi al-Jama'i.[118] Such families also helped to fill the new posts that were created by the administrative reforms. Benjellouns served as *amins* of the tax houses in Fez[119] and the custom house in Tangier,[120] but there were more posts available

112 Al-Nasiri, *Kitab al-istiqsa*, 9:161.

113 *Ibid.*, 9:145.

114 Arnaud, *Au temps des mehallas*, 45, 69; al-Nasiri, *Kitab al-istiqsa*, 9:158.

115 Dunn, *Resistance*, 239.

116 al-Nasiri, *Kitab al-istiqsa*, 9:204-5.

117 Laroui, *Origines*, 84-6; Mustafa al-Shabi, *al-Nukhbat al-makhzaniyya fi Maghrib al-qarn al-tasi' 'ashar* (Rabat: Jami'at Muhammad al-Khamis, Manshurat Kulliyyat al-Adab wa-'Ulum al-Insaniyya, 1995), 31.

118 Arnaud, *Au temps des mehallas*, 5.

119 Cigar, 'Socio-economic structures', 66.

120 Bin Saghir, *Al-Maghrib wa-Britaniya*, 397.

than suitable candidates from the old elites. The newly- rich merchants made ideal substitutes because they knew something of European ways and because as traders they were anxious to profit from Makhzan service, so they would be less likely to stir up trouble. Equally importantly, they were not Jews: so many Jews had taken out protection with foreign consuls that they could not be relied upon.[121] Not all the new men were Fasis: the Razinis of Tetuan, and the Brishas of Essaouira provided recruits. Muhammad al-Tazi of Rabat, who returned to Morocco after twenty years abroad, was made head of the treasury in 1879. When he died in 1890 he was replaced by his brother, Abd al-Salam. Muhammad Bargach, a merchant from an Andalusian family, whose father had been one of the last corsair captains, headed the customs house in Casablanca, a minor post, under Moulay Abderrahmane but was *naib* in Tangier in 1860-86.[122]

Other posts were filled from the intellectual class. Ali bin Muhammad al-Simlali who had a traditional education first in the Sous, then in Essaouira and then in Marrakesh, and was a learned grammarian, became one of the Makhzan's most important polemicists. He defended *maks* taxes and trade with Europe, and was sent to the Algerian frontier to investigate French violations of the border.[123] Ahmad al-Nasiri, author of the great chronicle, the *Kitab al-istiqsa*, was born in Salé and studied in Fez, before returning to his home town first as a notary then as deputy to its *qadi*. In 1875 he entered the Makhzan's service and worked in the customs offices in Casablanca, Marrakesh, Azemmour, Tangier, and Fez.[124]

The Sultan also relied upon old Makhzan families to administer the cities. In 1883 Moulay Hassan wrote to his military governor in Marrakesh, Ahmad bin Dawud remarking, 'You are a servant, the son of a servant and from one of the houses of service from olden times.'[125] The Ash'ash family did finally lose control of the governorship of Tetuan in 1862/3, but other old Tetuani families remained. A member of the Afailal family, which included a past

121 Laroui, *Origines*, 105-6; Cigar, 'Socio-economic structures', 61.

122 Laroui, *Origines*, 105-7; Al-Nasiri, *Kitab al-istiqsa*, 9:166; al-Shabi, *al-Nukhbat*, 32, 35, 89.

123 Susan Miller and Amal Rassam, 'The View from the Court: Moroccan Reactions to European Penetration in the Late Nineteenth Century', *International Journal of African Historical Studies*, 16, no. 1 (1983): 25-38.

124 Brown, *Salé*, 76-7, 175ff.

125 Bin Saghir, *Al-Maghrib wa-Britaniya*, 301.

qadi of the city and several noted scholars, served in the customs service in Tangier, Tetuan, Melilla and Fez.[126] Yet the intake of recruits from a merchant and intellectual background led in the long run to a further shift in power away from the old military elite, a process that had begun under Moulay Abderrahmane.[127]

Rebels against the Sultan

Not every member of the elite was so loyal. Even the Alaoui family itself provided a ready-made line of pretenders among the descendants of Moulay Slimane who had been set aside when the sultanate passed to his nephew, Moulay Abderrahmane. In 1859 just as the Tetuan war was beginning and Sidi Mohammed settling on the throne, Moulay Slimane's son, also called Abderrahmane, tried to seize control. He was defeated with ease, as was his son, Abd al-Kabir, who tried his hand at the beginning of Moulay Hassan's reign.

The most dangerous threat from within the Alaoui family lay in the future, in the person of Moulay Hassan's son, Moulay Mahammad. At first he was his father's closest aide, khalifa of Marrakesh in 1888, and commander of a *mahalla* to Taroudannt in 1893.[128] Then, shortly after his return, he was dismissed, allegedly for mistakes he had made in military operations and a supposed lack of sympathy towards Islam. He was shut up in a palace, given a tutor to complete his education, and did not appear again.[129] After Moulay Hassan died, in the last years of the sultanate, Moulay Mahammad would become the rallying point of several rebellions. Until then revolts in the countryside and in the towns were a more immediate danger.

Economic deprivation inspired revolt. In the towns, artisans were impoverished by European imports that undermined traditional industries. In Salé in 1858 there had been fifty-three workshops weaving cloth or wool, but by 1885 cloth weaving had all but vanished. Dyeing, brocade making, and embroidery declined, and the export of shoes slumped, when markets in Egypt closed off. The soap industry of Rabat virtually disappeared in the 1880s, and pottery declined too. Some trades did weather the European storm and even profited from it. Salé's famous rush-

126 R'honi, *Historia*, 89, 151.

127 Bin Saghir, *Al-Maghrib wa-Britaniya*, 404-11; Laroui, *Origines*, 285.

128 Arnaud, *Au Temps des Mehallas*, 69; Ennaji and Pascon, *Le Makhzen et le Sous al-Aqsa*, 225.

129 Arnaud, *Au Temps des Mehallas*, 74.

mat trade was hardly affected at all. The demand for carpets increased, both from European and local buyers, and that brought more women into the commercial workforce; they did all the weaving and most of the processing of the wool. These women were not artisans, though, simply the cheapest labour that could be found, a sign of the general demotion of artisan industry. Many former artisans became unskilled marginal labourers, desperately seeking other employment.[130]

Some found it in the ports. Casablanca's population of around 4,000 in 1860 increased to around 9,000 by the late 1880s. There, and in Essaouira, the building trades prospered mightily as they did, to a lesser extent, in Salé and Fez. Merchants, grown rich through trade, built palatial residences.[131] Even with the decline of artisans' wages, in normal times people could struggle through.[132]

Times were not always normal. Famine brought floods of country people into the coastal cities in the hope of finding food. Usually, they were not disappointed: the sultan distributed grain, as he was expected to do, for the Makhzan was a storehouse not just of money but of food.[133] If he did not also protect the population by forbidding the export of grain, then there might be riots.

Full-scale urban revolts were rare but dangerous, especially if they were supported by the *'ulama*, who generally disapproved of the tax policies of the Makhzan. Since Spanish control of the customs houses syphoned off the Sultan's revenues, Sidi Mohammed resorted to extraordinary *maks* taxes to fill his treasury. The easiest tax to collect, a gate tax on goods entering the towns and ports, fell much more heavily on the towns than the countryside, and more on the poor than on the rich. In the eyes of the *'ulama*, these inequalities meant that the tax was illegal.[134]

When Sidi Mohammed asked the *'ulama* to issue *fatwas* to regularise his new taxes, many were reluctant to oblige. They believed that the truce with the Spanish government was itself illegal, and when Christians were attacking the *dar al-islam* taxes should only be raised to fight them, not buy them off.[135] Eventually Sidi Mohammed did find *'ulama* to produce the *fatwas* that he needed,

130 Brown, *Salé*, 130-2; Janet L. Abu Lughod, *Rabat: Urban Apartheid in Morocco* (Princeton University Press, 1980), 107.

131 Schroeter, *Merchants*, 207; Brown, *Salé*, 130-3.

132 Schroeter, *Merchants*, 208.

133 *Ibid.*, 197-8; Bois, 'Années de disette'.

134 Laroui, *Origines*, 292.

135 *Ibid.*, 292-4.

but they were from families long dependent on the Makhzan, and even then they hedged approval with hesitations and conditions.[136] The issue exploded in 1873, when Moulay Hassan became Sultan.

He was proclaimed quickly in Marrakesh, but the Fasi *'ulama* refused to give their *bay'a.*[137] Behind their refusal lay a revolt of small artisans and merchants, led by the tanners, against Muhammad bin al-Madani Bennis who collected the gate tax. They demanded that he and other Makhzan officials be punished before they submitted. The new Sultan would have none of it: he bombarded Fez and allowed his troops to pillage the city.[138] Then he asked for new *fatwas* in favour of *maks,* but most *'ulama* simply refused to reply. Even loyal Makhzan officials like the chronicler Ahmad al-Nasiri, who considered the rebels to be moral reprobates, described the *maks* as detestable.[139] As soon as he could, in 1885, when the Spanish overseers left the customs houses, the Sultan abolished the *maks.*[140] That was the sort of reform that urban Moroccans liked.

Tensions in Fez flared up several times during Moulay Hassan's reign. Many artisans belonged to the more popular and unorthodox *tariqas,* such as the Aisawiyya and Hamadsha and were supported by the same irregular urban militias, the *rumat,* who had revolted against Moulay Slimane. Militias also caused problems in Essaouira and perhaps elsewhere,[141] but the protests in the cities were nothing compared to the opposition in the countryside, the mountains and the deserts.

Siba

The countryside was the scene of some of the most dangerous challenges to Sidi Mohammed and Moulay Hassan. Some revolts were overtly religious, and even though they were fairly paltry affairs, they raised uncomfortable spectres because they took place in areas close to the Europeans. In 1862, before the Spanish evacuated Tetuan, a pretender (*rughi*) named al-Jilani found support

136 *Ibid.*, 291.

137 Al-Nasiri, *Kitab al-istiqsa*, 9:128.

138 Arnaud, *Au temps des mehallas*, 32-8; al-Nasiri, *Kitab al-istiqsa*, 9:136-41; Laroui, *Origines*. 130-1

139 al-Nasiri, *Kitab al-istiqsa*, 9: 294.

140 Laroui, *Origines*, 297; al-Nasiri, *Kitab al-istiqsa*, 9:179.

141 Laroui, *Origines*, 131; Schroeter, *Merchants*, 160, 207; Le Tourneau, *Fès*, 366.

among the Safyan tribe of the Rharb. In 1874 another pretender named Bu Azza al-Habri appeared near Oujda on the Algerian border. Both claimed to be miracle workers and al-Habri drew mysterious lines on the sand. Both were defeated, not by the Sultan's troops but by treachery. The guardians of the tomb of Moulay Idris at-Zerhoun cut off al-Jilani's head, and Moulay Hassan executed Bu Azza despite a safe conduct negotiated by the Sharif of Ouezzane.[142] Nevertheless, these religious revolts were short-lived, and did not cause nearly so much trouble as the endemic rebellion in the countryside.

In the late nineteenth century rural insecurity, which had always been a problem in Morocco, became the defining cliché of Morocco for European observers. The division between *bilad al-siba* and *bilad al-makhzan*, between the zones of rebellion and government, and the idea of institutionalised disorder in the mountains and deserts, seeped into European consciousness as more travellers made their way into the interior. In the early 1880s Charles de Foucauld travelled through Morocco disguised as a Jew and distinguished between submitted and unsubmitted tribes simply by whether he could travel freely through their territory or not.[143] Although the boundaries were much more fluid than that, the Makhzan's officials sometimes talked in similarly stark terms. Al-Nasiri said that the Awlad Abu al-Saba' near Marrakesh made a custom of rebelling; and Salem el-Abdi described the Banu Mtir as 'having the habit of submitting when the Makhzan was there and of revolting when its back was turned'.[144] Moulay Hassan himself connected rebelliousness and wickedness to linguistic difference when he described the 'devils and riff-raff, the Berbers of the Banu Mgild'.[145] Thus was political and social rivalry reduced to 'ethnic' terms.

In reality, rural insecurity grew from similar roots to rebellion in the cities. Famine was one: three years of bad harvests in the Atlantic plains preceded the general failure of 1867. By then, tribes had already attacked Salé, pillaged its gardens and effectively cut it off, except by access from the sea. In 1868 rebellion shook

142 Al-Nasiri, *Kitab al-istiqsa*, 9:108-9; Arnaud, *Au temps des mehallas*, 39-43; Laroui, *Origines*, 158.

143 Charles de Foucauld, *Reconnaissance au Maroc. Journal de route conforme à l'édition de 1888 et augmenté de fragments inédits rédigés par l'auteur etc.* (Paris: Société d'Éditions Géographiques, Maritimes et Coloniales, 1939).

144 Arnaud, *Au temps des mehallas*, 60; al-Nasiri, *Kitab al-istiqsa*, 9:138

145 Al-Nasiri, *Kitab al-istiqsa*, 9:134.

the countryside around Essaouira.[146] Banditry surged again in the terrible famine of 1878-84, but prosperity brought security. During the good harvests of the mid-1870s the Sultan himself wrote: 'The rains keep the people at work in the fields and distract them from banditry.'[147]

Taxation also caused revolts in the countryside. In 1873, the year that Fez revolted, gate taxes were imposed in Essaouira. A tribal revolt south of the city soon followed.[148] Once again, it is hard to distinguish revolts against unpopular taxes from revolts against the unpopular governors who collected them. The Banu Musa, on the plateau northeast of Marrakesh, rebelled against their governor in 1872. The following year the Banu Hasan near Rabat did the same.[149] A letter in the archives of Moulay Hassan explained: 'If the people of Morocco are in the habit of rising up against the governors for the slightest abuse, massacring them, looting their property and burning their casbahs, and do not hesitate to do it all over again whenever they feel themselves unjustly dealt with, that is precisely because they are a high-spirited and extremely proud people.'[150]

Both Sidi Mohammed and Moulay Hassan usually treated these high-spirited rebels with disdain.[151] They were more circumspect when a powerful local leader threatened them.

The rise of the big qaids

It had often happened that a single leader was able to seize local power by using the support of one tribal alliance to subdue others, but his power usually collapsed when rival lineages and alliances fought back. In the mid-nineteenth century this changed, and local warlords extended their grip over wider and wider territories and passed power to their successors. Unless their impact could be blunted, the sultan's power was at stake.

Three of the most important of these qaids emerged in the High Atlas mountains, south of Marrakesh. The first, Muhammad bin al-Hajj Ahmad built a fortified house in the Nfiss valley in

146 Brown, *Salé*, 122; Schroeter, *Merchants*, 164.

147 Mohammed Kenbib, 'Protégés et brigands dans le Maroc du XIXe siècle et début du XXme', *Hésperis-Tamuda* 29 (1991): 229, 236.

148 Schroeter, *Merchants*, 156.

149 Al-Nasiri, *Kitab al-istiqsa*, 9: 123, 135.

150 Quoted in Kenbib, 'Changing aspects', 25.

151 Laroui, *Origines*, 158.

the 1850s and spread his influence over the Goundafa tribe. During Sidi Mohammed's reign he defeated a small column sent by a local ally of the pasha of Marrakesh. Then he occupied Tinmel, the village from which the great medieval Almohad empire had originated. With the help of local allies, El Goundafi turned southwards, and by the time Moulay Hassan became sultan he controlled a large area. When the Sultan's new pasha in Marrakesh tried to bring him to heel, he fought off his *mahallas*, but made sure that the Makhzan's regular troops were returned unharmed, and sent his son, Taïeb, to Fez to explain that his quarrels were with the pasha, not with the sultan. It was a private affair. Moulay Hassan responded by making El Goundafi qaid of his tribe and in 1883 confirmed Taïeb as his successor.[152]

A little to the east lay the Glaoua tribe. Mohammed El Glaoui, the son of an exiled marabout, seized control in 1858, and the sultan confirmed him as qaid of his little domain. In 1886 he too was succeeded by his son, Madani El Glaoui, who expanded southwards, like the Goundafis, in order not to upset the Sultan. In 1893 Moulay Hassan stopped at the Glaoui home base at Telouèt. He was returning from Tafilalt with his *harka* and Madani gave him such a hospitable reception that the Sultan rewarded him with a Krupp cannon and modern rifles. These El Glaoui used to effect against local rivals.[153]

In the western foothills of the High Atlas, was the domain of the Mtouggis. Although an ancestor had been qaid of the Haha plains behind Essaouira in the late eighteenth century, by the mid-nineteenth century a rival, Hajj Abdallah U-Bihi, had displaced them. Only when the sultan removed Hajj Abdallah in 1868 was Hajj Umar al-Mtuggi able to reassert control southwards and eastwards. Even so, he was never popular with Sidi Mohammed and Moulay Hassan because there were so many complaints about his brutality. When in 1886 Moulay Hassan decided to break Al-Hajj Misaud El Mtouggi (M'Touggi), his *mahalla* was greeted not with guns but the most lavish feasting that its commanders had ever seen. Misaud won over Moulay Hassan with the richest presents and even had his wives give separate tributes to the wives of the

152 Robert Montagne, *Les Berbères et le Makhzen au sud du Maroc* (Paris: Félix Alcan, 1930), 277-8, 303-5, 328; al-Nasiri, *Kitab al-istiqsa*, 9:137; Arnaud, *Au temps des mehallas*, 44.

153 Montagne, *Berbères*, 330-1.

Sultan. The Sultan confirmed him as qaid and in 1890 he was succeeded by his nephew Abd al-Malik.[154]

These three powerful qaids would help to destroy the Makhzan after Moulay Hassan's death, but for the moment they posed no threat. To secure their own local power, they preferred to ally themselves with the Makhzan, not oppose it.[155] The Sultan, for his part, was happy to incorporate powerful lords on the marches of the Sahara where European interference posed very great dangers.

Disorder and resistance

Because of the European advance, remote and unproductive areas, that the sultan had long left alone, became very dangerous. In the oases of the Saharan south-east, in the regions beyond the Sous and in the Rif mountains along the Mediterranean coast, attacks on European troops or ships were likely to bring retaliation in their wake.

In the far south east, the authority of the *khalifa* of Tafilalt, Moulay Rashid, did not reach far into the desert. The people of the Touat oases, deep in the Sahara, paid no taxes, although they did send presents and occasional affirmations of loyalty to the Sultan, which was all that was needed until the late 1870s. Then, Algerians fighting the French started using the oases as a base and in the 1880s the Algerian leader Bu Amama settled in the Touat, supported by local tribal factions. The Sultan repeatedly reminded Bu Amama that he was on Moroccan territory and told him not to attack the French. In 1882-4 Moulay Hassan appointed a local *khalifa* over the Figuig oases, and in 1892 a local administrator over the Touat, but the raids on French positions and convoys continued.[156] The population refused either to pay taxes or to recognise the authority of the Sultan's qaids.[157]

On the other Saharan fringe, in the Sous, local leaders undermined the Makhzan's authority not by fighting but by trading with the Europeans. Mubarak Bayruk had died in 1859,[158] and in 1880, one of his quarrelsome sons, Mahammad opened a trading

154 *Ibid.*, 333-41; Arnaud, *Au temps des mehallas*, 66-8; al-Shabi, *al-Nukhbat*, 71.

155 Laroui, *Origines*, 159.

156 Bradford G. Martin, *Muslim Brotherhoods in Nineteenth Century Africa* (Cambridge University Press, 1976), 176-267.

157 Dunn, *Resistance*, 151-7.

158 Ennaji and Pascon, *Le Makhzen et le Sous al-Aqsa*, 9, 41-2.

station at Tarfaya. His partner was an eccentric British adventurer named Donald Mackenzie, who believed that 'Christianity and commerce going hand in hand into Africa would raise the unhappy natives from the depths of degradation, to freedom and happiness'.[159] Mackenzie was no realist. In 1877 he proposed a bizarre scheme to flood the Sahara and allow maritime access to the interior of Africa. Predictably, this led nowhere, so he decided to tap into the trans-Saharan trade by caravan. In 1879 he set up the North West Africa Company, and persuaded Mahammad Bayruk to 'cede' him a strip of land, two miles wide and eight miles long at Tarfaya. There he built his factory.[160]

Moulay Hassan did not believe that Bayruk had any right to cede Moroccan land, but the British government did not recognise his own claim to sovereignty.[161] The Sultan tried to interest the master of Iligh, Husayn bin Hisham, in reining in Bayruk and Mackenzie, but Husayn was a very autonomous subject and was negotiating on his own account with French and German representatives. These were possibly no more than feelers and Husayn probably hoped to do no more than bypass Essaouira and avoid paying customs dues to the Sultan. Certainly he protested his loyalty to the sultan and denounced his competitors, but he did little to help Moulay Hassan.[162]

Sidi Mohammed and Moulay Hassan could not bring south-western Morocco into their economic and political embrace. They simply had no money. For more than twenty years, between 1864, when Moulay Hassan led part of his father's army into the Sous, and the late 1880s the Makhzan's formal representatives were little more than intelligence agents. The only influence that the sultans could exert was by manipulating tribal rivalries, a dangerous tactic since groups could simply change sides. This precipitated a great deal of political disorder, disrupted trade, meant that taxes could not be raised and made it impossible to deal with foreign merchants and their machinations.[163]

159 Parsons, *Morocco Question*, 162.

160 *Ibid.*; Donald Mackenzie, *The Khalifate of the West, being a General Description of Morocco* (London: Simpkin Marshall, 1911), 163-72; Donald Mackenzie, *The Flooding of the Sahara: An Account of the Proposed Plan for Opening Central Africa to Commerce and Civilization From the North-west Coast, with A Description of Soudan and Western Sahara, and Notes of Ancient Manuscripts, &c.* (London: Sampson Low, 1877).

161 Parsons, *Morocco Question*, 163.

162 Ennaji & Pascon, *Le Makhzen et le Sous al-Aqsa*, 122-3.

163 *Ibid.*, 18-25.

In 1887, after the Spanish army set up their new post at Villa Cisneros, Moulay Hassan appointed his first *khalifa* over the Sahara, Shaykh Muhammad Mustafa uld Mamun, commonly called Ma al-Aynayn. Born in the 1820s or 1830s, Ma al-Aynayn came from a sharifian family in Walata, in what is now Mauritania. He was a Sufi scholar of great note and prestige. Even more importantly, he was well disposed towards the Makhzan, as his father had been before him. In 1873 the Sultan gave him property in Marrakesh to use as a *zawiya,*[164] and Ma al-Aynayn became a bulwark against French and Spanish expansion, an influence for unity among the Saharan tribes, and an agent of the Makhzan who upheld the sultan's authority in the Sahara. This helped lay the basis of Moroccan claims to Mauritania and the Western Sahara in the late twentieth century.

In northern Morocco, where local people intermittently traded and fought with both the Spanish in the garrisons and the French in Algeria, the Sultan's authority was also in danger. The treaties with Spain in 1861 had increased the territory of the larger garrisons, and two years later the Spanish government declared Ceuta, Melilla and the Chafarinas Islands to be free ports.

It was one thing to proclaim, quite another to make the proclamation real. The people of the Guelaya peninsula refused either to hand over their land to the enemy or to pay taxes on trade with that enemy to the Makhzan. So a small Makhzan army was sent to persuade them, by occupying the *qasba* (fort) at Selouane a few kilometres south of Melilla. Since it could do so only by landing in Melilla and advancing from the Spanish side of the frontier, this did not increase respect for the Makhzan among the Guelayis. Once it arrived, it could neither police trade nor prevent Guelayi attacks on Spanish positions. On the border intermittent raiding mixed strangely with commerce as big caravans linked Melilla with Taza and beyond. They traded in cattle tea, sugar, cottons, guns and ammunition.[165]

The flood of guns was truly tremendous. A French report of 1887 described Spanish merchants selling guns 'with no more concern than a grocer sells sugar'.[166] They became so cheap that by 1889, the French claimed, 50,000 guns a year were being sold

164 B.G. Martin, 'Ma' al-'Aynayn al-Qalqami, Mauritanian Mystic and Politician' in *Muslim Brotherhoods in Nineteenth-century Africa* (Cambridge University Press, 1976), 125-51; Odette de Puigaudeu 'Une nouvelle généalogie du cheik Ma' el-'Ainain u-mamr', *Héspéris-Tamuda* 12 (1971): 157-63.

165 Driessen, *On the Spanish-Moroccan Frontier*, 48-9.

166 Miège, *Le Maroc et l'Europe*, 4:106, n. 5.

on the Rif coast.[167] That made the entire coast even more difficult to control. In the mid-1870s Selouane was reinforced and qaids sent with troops to *qasbas* near Peñon de Vélez. But none were sent to watch over the garrison of Al Hoceima, in the territory of the powerful Banu Waryaghal tribe. Whatever tenuous authority the sultan had there was secured by holding local qaids to ransom when they came to Fez or Meknès, and by appointing qadis. One Waryaghli qadi was Abd al-Karim al-Khattabi whose son would lead the opposition to the Spanish in the 1920s.[168]

The Algerian frontier offered other opportunities. French farmers in the province of Oran needed seasonal labourers, and Rifis were happy to help. From the 1870s onwards many thousands of migrant labourers, from the Banu Snassen on the border, from the Guelaya and later from the central Rif, passed through Melilla. While they were away, between May and October, the burden of work shifted onto those who stayed behind, particularly women.[169] Smuggling was also lucrative because goods imported through the free port of Melilla had a ready market in eastern Algeria. Raiding was helped by the cascade of weapons and by the frontier itself, because the Banu Snassen, the most enthusiastic raiders, could retreat behind it after making their sallies into Algerian territory. French officers began to talk of advancing into Morocco up to the Moulouya river, for 'defensive' reasons. That was firmly stamped on by Paris, but hot pursuit was allowed.[170] In the Rif, as in the south-west, or the Sous, Moulay Hassan's authority was undercut because he could not prevent the European advance, or check the disorder that eased its way.

The Mahalla

Siba, then, had many faces: mere banditry, political protest, illicit war on Europeans and outright attempts to overthrow the sultan. It was hard to quell these rebellious subjects. Moulay Hassan, the

167 *Ibid.*, 4:106.

168 Hart, *Aith Waryaghar*, 354; Paul Pascon and Herman van der Wusten, *Les Beni Boufrah. Essai d'écologie sociale d'une vallée rifaine (Maroc)* (Rabat: Institut Agronomique et Vétérinaire Hassan II, 1983), 82; these authors respectively give 1875 and 1873 the date for the reorganisation of the Rifi governorate; see also C.R. Pennell, *A Country with a Government and a Flag: The Rif War in Morocco, 1921-1926* (Wisbech: Menas Press, 1986), 49.

169 McNeill, *Mountains*, 213, 274; Driessen, *On the Spanish-Moroccan Frontier*, 49; Hart, *Aith Waryaghar*, 89.

170 Parsons, *Morocco Question*, 198-9.

quintessential soldier-sultan, seemed always to be on the move at the head of his *mahalla.* The author of an anonymous hagiography of the sultan wrote: 'This prince had a passion for travel. In this he conformed to the old saying: "To live in a fixed habitation is the worst of misfortunes. The back of his horse is the right place for a Sultan." His greatest happiness was to do the night vigil. Through his resolution, men of good faith were seized with the desire to extirpate the wicked.'[171]

Europeans had a different perspective on this behaviour. For Pierre Loti it proved the antique quality of the Moroccan sultanate: 'The Sultan generally lives in his tent for six months of the year, a nomad by nature like his Arabian ancestors.'[172]

This was more image than reality. Moulay Hassan spent over three-quarters of his reign in one of the four main cities: Fez, Marrakesh, Meknès and, less frequently, Rabat.[173] Much of the remaining time he was travelling between them, often by the inland route between Marrakesh and Fez through Tadla. This did keep turbulent tribes in order. The ritual progress was dreaded by the tribes through which the *mahalla* passed because they had to feed it. Moulay Hassan's *mahalla* was huge: in 1883 it included 5,000 regular infantry, 8,000 cavalry and 3 or 4,000 irregular (*naiba*) troops. Tribes that did not provide food were ransacked. The *mahalla* that visited the Zaër in 1890 spent two days emptying the grain silos.[174]

These regular excursions were complemented by special ones, like those to the Sous in 1882 and 1886, to Oujda in 1876, to Tangier and Tetuan in 1889 and to the Tafilalt in 1893, areas where Europeans were active and Makhzan authority was weak. In 1882 the sultan sent a circular letter to provincial governors all over Morocco explaining that his expedition to the Sous was to a region that had not been in 'intimate relations' with the Makhzan for many years. He went on: 'The most important intention of this blessed trip was to protect the most sacred possessions of the Muslims of that region, to defend their country, their persons

171 [Anonymous], 'Chronique de la vie de Moulay el-Hassan', ed. L. Coufourier, *Archives Marocaines* 7 (1906): 348.

172 Pierre Loti, *Au Maroc*, (Paris, 1890) quoted in Daniel Nordman, 'Les expéditions de Moulay Hassan: Essai Statistique', *Héspéris-Tamuda* 19 (1990-1): 123.

173 Nordman, 'Les expéditions', 134.

174 Michel, 'L'approvisionnement', 329.

and their wealth from the desires of those who had designs upon it.'[175]

Because this was a political campaign, the impoverished Susis were not asked to feed the *mahalla*. A recently acquired steamer supplied the army by sea, not always very successfully. On the way back, much of the army starved. The army set out with 25-40,000 men and between fifteen and thirty artillery pieces, but it did little fighting. Moulay Hassan named qaids, collected taxes and received declarations of loyalty from various tribes. He reoccupied the old Makhzan base at Tiznit and built a new port at Assaka to divert trade away from the local partners of the Europeans. Once the army left Tiznit, the fortifications came under attack. In 1886 a smaller *mahalla* returned and forced Mackenzie and his people to leave Tarfaya, which caused endless arguments with Sir William Kirby Green about indemnifying the North West African company for its loss, but it did reestablish the Makhzan in the region.[176]

The great expedition to the Tafilalt in 1893 was sent because the sultan feared that disorder there would provide an excuse for French intervention. Between 15-30,000 men marched in a huge loop from Fez to Marrakesh via the Tafilalt oases. Again, it did little fighting, but it was greeted with loyal submissions and the payment of taxes, and so buttressed the sultan's claims to sovereignty.[177]

While Moulay Hassan was on his way to Tafilalt, fighting flared up near Melilla. Spanish troops trying to occupy yet more of the territory granted to them under the 1860 treaty had built a fort close to the tomb of an important local *marabout*, and the Guelayis attacked. Moulay Hassan sent his brother, Moulay Arafa to Selouane, not to help the Rifis but to stop them. The matter was settled diplomatically, but expensively: the Makhzan was obliged to pay an indemnity of 20 million pesetas.[178] If this raised doubts as to whether Moulay Hassan was able or willing to protect Islamic territory, his trade policy caused similar apprehensions.

Trade, treason and faith

In 1884 a Fasi *'alim* described merchants who went abroad for

175 Al-Nasiri, *Kitab al-istiqsa*, 9:176; Coufourier, 'Chronique', 338-9.

176 Ennaji & Pascon, *Le Makhzen et le Sous al-Aqsa*, 81-6; Coufourier 'Chronique', 339-42; al-Nasiri, *Kitab al-istiqsa*, 9:175-7, 180-2.

177 Al-Nasiri, *Kitab al-istiqsa*, 9: 202-5; Hart, *Ait Atta*, 159-61; Dunn, *Resistance*, 157-71.

178 Al-Nasiri, *Kitab al-istiqsa*, 9:205-6; Burke, *Prelude*, 30; Driessen, *On the Spanish-Moroccan Frontier*, 37; Coufourier, 'Chronique', 389.

trade as 'traitors'. Rumours circulated that European sugar was refined with the aid of pig's blood, an allegation that harmed the interests of rich merchants who imported it.[179] Muhammad al-Kattani even forbade members of his brotherhood to drink tea, saying (quite correctly) that it provided a basis for European control of the economy.[180] Behind this clash between the old religious elite and the new commercial one lay deep distrust of Europeans. In 1886 the European consuls again demanded that tariffs be reduced, and bans lifted on the export of livestock and grain. Although the governor of Fez had told the Sultan that merchants were buying so much grain to sell to Europeans that it would soon run short, Moulay Hassan asked the *'ulama* for a *fatwa* allowing him to lift the ban. They turned him down:[181] Eventually the Sultan and the *'ulama* compromised; the ban was lifted on grain for a trial period of three years, but not on exports of livestock. The *'ulama* covered their retreat from principle by declaring that the Sultan had greater knowledge than they, so that he should act as he thought fit.[182]

Not all the *'ulama* were so difficult and the Sultan could call upon able and vocal men to support him. Ali bin Muhammad al-Simlali and Ahmad al-Nasiri, who were part of an elite that depended for its wealth on trade with Europe and government service, were very willing to support peace with France and Spain. Al-Nasiri defended the Sultan's policies by arguing that it was absurd to forbid trade with the Christians on the grounds that this would help them become more powerful than the Muslims. They already were.[183]

Yet even al-Nasiri had an ambivalent attitude to the Europeans. He recognised the need for trade and the Europeans' technical superiority. He related with pride how Moulay Hassan's new palace was built with no expense spared. The carpets came from India and much of the furniture from Europe.[184] Everyone acknowledged the superiority of European weapons. Moulay Hassan's anonymous biographer, who clearly loathed Europeans, wrote: 'In matters concerning preparations for war and equipping the army, no previous

179 Cigar, 'Socio-economic structures', 67-8.

180 Burke, *Prelude*, 38.

181 Miller and Rassam, 'The View from the Court', 29; al-Nasiri, *Kitab al-istiqsa*, 9:142; Henry Munson Jnr, *Religion and Power in Morocco* (New Haven, CT: Yale University Press, 1993), 52.

182 Munson, *Religion and Power*, 52-3; Manuni, *Mazahir*, 473.

183 Miller and Rassam, 'The View from the Court', 29; al-Nasiri, *Kitab al-istiqsa*, 9:184.

184 Al-Nasiri, *Kitab al-istiqsa*, 9:144-5.

monarch of Morocco could rival him. Not content with having built up the stocks of cannons and material by buying it from Europe, in which he followed the policy of his ancestors, he planned to set up an arsenal in order to ensure a continuous supply.'[185] But few Makhzan officials actually liked the Europeans. Ahmad al-Nasiri talked of the 'unbelieving enemy'. Simlali described European protégés as 'blasphemous' and 'infidels'. Some *'ulama* went further: booklets and sermons circulated with titles like 'Letter about the scum who hold passports' and 'The disasters and ruin of those who hold passports' – the latter preached as a sermon in Moulay Hassan's presence.[186] For people like this, the solution was *jihad*. From the 1860s onwards calls for *jihad* were repeatedly made, especially by rural *sharifs* and *marabouts*. In 1863, a Darqawi *sharif* in the Tafilalt, Muhammad al-Arabi al-Madaghri, complained about Europeans flocking to the coast, buying property and spreading through the countryside. 'The Muslims have no alternative to fighting,' he wrote. 'Either they oppose unbelief so that the religion of God prevails, or they will be overwhelmed... The road to hell begins with putting trust in the enemies of religion.' No *jihad* followed, but in 1888 al-Madaghri returned to the fray, and directed another call to *jihad* at the Sultan, who ignored it.[187]

The Makhzan loosed its propagandists against the proponents of *jihad*. Al-Nasiri wrote that the Europeans were so strong that no battle against them could be won. Therefore any attempt to fight them was illicit because more Muslim territory would be lost.[188] Al-Simlali agreed: 'Past experience indicates that we cannot defeat the Europeans...whoever orders a *jihad* will bring ruin on himself.'[189] He blamed the protégés and the disorderly Moroccan population, who paid no taxes and were criminals: 'As for the mountains we do not even see the [tax] which God has made our due because they are beyond our reach. [...] All the tribes of Morocco are usurpers and thieves.'[190]

Al-Simlali had simplified the question to the old discontinuities: *siba* versus Makhzan, Berber versus Arab, mountain versus city. Like other important members of the Makhzan he was terrified

185 Coufourier 'Chronique', 355.

186 Manuni, *Mazahir*, 256-8; al-Nasiri, *Kitab al-istiqsa*, 9:189; Miller and Rassam, 'The View from the Court', 31.

187 Manuni, *Mazahir*, 276-8.

188 Al-Nasiri, *Kitab al-istiqsa*, 9:191ff.

189 Miller and Rassam, 'The View from the Court', 37.

190 *Ibid.*, 38.

of the tribes. With Moulay Hassan's death those terrors were unleashed.

The end of the old order

Moulay Hassan died on campaign in the summer of 1894. After returning from Tafilalt he had wintered in Marrakesh. There he fell sick, but the Ait Sakhman rebelled again and he organised two columns to deal with them. When Moulay Hassan set out a few days later, he was still sick, and by the time he reached the banks of the Oum er Rbia he was so ill that the army stopped for nine days. Close to death, the Sultan had his chamberlain Si Ahmad bin Musa, Ba Ahmad, call the other ministers together, and obliged the *wazir,* al-Ma'ti al-Jama'i, his brother Muhammad al-Saghir, the minister of war, and the minister of complaints (*wazir al-shikayat*), Si Allal Misfiwi, to sign a paper recognising Moulay Abdelaziz as the next sultan. This was largely Ba Ahmad's doing: he had bound the Jama'is, who headed the other main faction in the Makhzan, to recognise the new order in waiting. Later that evening, 7 June 1894, Moulay Hassan died. Ba Ahmad swore the inner circle to secrecy, fearing that if the news spread, hostile tribes would attack the column and destroy it. Camp was struck, and the column continued towards Rabat at its usual pace, as though the sultan were still alive.[191] The sacred separateness of the Sultan's person served one last time: few people were accustomed to see him, so that few expected to do so now.

When they finally reached friendly territory, Ba Ahmad proclaimed Moulay Abdelaziz, although Muhammad al-Saghir al-Jama'i hesitated before agreeing 'saying that Moulay Abdelaziz is much too young and that the real sultan would be Ba Ahmad."[192] In this, he was quite correct. The *mahalla* rushed to Rabat, the decaying body of the Sultan was buried, and messengers were sent out to proclaim his successor across Morocco. The inner circle soon fell out. On 10 July then Ba Ahmad turned on the Jama'is and arrested al-Ma'ti, Muhammad al-Saghir and their allies.[193] Then the chamberlain became *wazir* himself.

By imprisoning the chief minister and minister of war, Ba Ahmad secured his own position and that of the new Sultan, but he weakened the Makhzan. A very young Sultan would have to face

191 Arnaud, *Au temps des mehallas*, 75-9; Burke, *Prelude*, 41; Laroui, *Origines*, 78.

192 Arnaud, *Au temps des mehallas*, 87.

193 *Ibid.*, 87-90; Burke, *Prelude*, 41; Laroui, *Origines*, 78. PRO,PRO 30/33/4/19 Madean to Satow, Meknes 10 July 1894.

the same problems as his father without the assistance of two very experienced men. Moulay Hassan's Morocco was in great danger.

Of course, that danger was not simply the result of Ba Ahmad's deceptions, treachery and ambition. Three years later, in 1897, Ahmad al-Nasiri put the finishing touches to his chronicle, the *Kitab al-istiqsa.* He died soon after. His last lines summed up a generation and a half of reforms that had brought the country to the brink of disaster.

> Know also that power of these Europeans during recent years has increased to a shocking degree, making itself apparent to an unprecedented extent. The progress and improvement in their circumstances has rapidly increased, doubling and redoubling like grains of wheat in squares of a chess board, so that the state has fallen into a time of complete calamity. Knowledge of the results and limits of all this belongs to God, may He be exalted, who alone knows what is hidden. I know well what happens today and yesterday before it. But to things which tomorrow brings, I am blind.[194]

Not everyone blamed the Europeans alone. Many shared the feelings of the author of a letter denouncing the new elite that dominated the Makhzan:

> The reign of Moulay Hassan was a time of prosperity, happiness and good fortune. There was one black spot, however. This was the coming to the royal court of businessmen who have taken over the highest posts in the administration, grown mighty in the land, are influential and can make and unmake whom they choose. [...] Their mismanagement has given the Moroccan State a fatal blow. [...] The situation in the country has been worsened by the injustices and abuses perpetrated by other officials of the Makhzen.[195]

The failure of reforms?

This complaint reaches the heart of any understanding of whether the reforms did in fact fail. What were they intended to change?

The ruling institution, the Sultan and his Makhzan were not in question. Neither Sidi Mohammed nor Moulay Hassan wanted to change himself and they still relied on the same system of

194 Al-Nasiri, *Kitab al-istiqsa*, 9: 208.

195 Quoted in Kenbib, 'Changing aspects', 24.

kinship relations and patronage to secure the support of the centre, and diplomacy and arbitration or force to secure compliance elsewhere. What they sought, was to make themselves more powerful, and to a degree they succeeded. Moulay Hassan had tighter control over Morocco at the end of his reign than he did at the beginning of it. To an extent that was achieved by modernisation of his army and the purchase of better guns. But it was a tactic that was also open to other people within the Moroccan political system: they too could 'modernise' their local armies, and strengthen their local position as the big qaids did, and they too could trade with and profit from the Europeans. All this carried the price of increased European intervention, which for a considerable part of his reign actually underpinned both Hassan and his more powerful subjects.

The Europeans also pushed for 'reforms' and modernisation by which they meant improvement of the infrastructure and the removal of tariff barriers on trade. That did, coincidentally, help many individual members of the Makhzan, and it certainly advanced the position of European traders in Morocco.

Yet to argue that the 'reforms' and the modernisations succeeded would be to claim that there was no difference between the personal interests of individuals – including the sultan – and that of the Moroccan community as a whole. That was not how even Makhzan servants like al-Nasiri saw it. In their eyes Moulay Hassan was a great Sultan, but he could not stem the European advance by his military efforts. That was because the European advance in the late nineteenth century was achieved not through military but financial and commercial means. Every reform of the money or the army, every modernisation of the infrastructure drained the Moroccan treasury in the direction of Europe. It also left the Sultan ideologically vulnerable to those who equated modernisation with letting the Europeans in and the betrayal of the interests of the *umma*. This might have been a simplistic idea, but it was a perfectly coherent one. During the reign of Moulay Abdelaziz the Europeans and the Makhzan elites would fight over a weakened Morocco, and destroy it.

4

COLLAPSE

When Sidi Mohammed and Moulay Hassan became Sultans, there had been short periods of disorder, but the tanners' revolt in Fez and the efforts of dissident members of the Alaoui family were nothing to the mayhem that followed the proclamation of the new Sultan. Moulay Abdelaziz was thirteen years old, and depended on the *wazir*, Ba Ahmad. Many people wanted to proclaim his elder brother Moulay Mahammad instead, if only because that provided an excuse to rebel against a weak boy.

The core of the Makhzan had been removed. Moulay Hassan had been exceptionally able, but he left behind him endemic rebellion, economic crisis and the torments of steadily growing European pressure. Ba Ahmad was also a vigorous man and he did his best to hold things together by relying on the British for diplomatic support, on the big qaids to shore up the south and the judicious use of force and bribery. Yet the fatal flaw was the way in which his own position had changed. His authority under Moulay Hassan had derived ultimately from the patronage of the Sultan; but the Sultan had also been the patron of his rivals. In this rickety system the actors were interdependent. Now that Ba Ahmad no longer depended on the Sultan, he removed his rivals. Indeed the boy-Sultan was dependent upon him, and the *wazir* ruled unchallenged and unchecked.

If the legitimacy of the regime was fatally compromised, economic conditions were worse than before. For the first six years of Moulay Abdelaziz's reign, when Ba Ahmad was effectively regent, the *wazir* preserved the form of Moulay Hassan's policies without the content. He could only do so because the foreign threat, for a while, was reduced; but the balance of power in Europe was shifting.

BA AHMAD'S MOROCCO

The new Makhzan

As Moulay Hassan's chamberlain, Ba Ahmad had been a powerful man, and by his coup on the road from Marrakesh he had destroyed his main rivals, the Jama'is. Yet by a curious reversal he was weaker now that he that no longer derived his power from the Sultan, for the new Sultan was dependent on him. Not all the old talent was lost: Si Abdessalam el-Tazi remained the minister of finance, because he was a close associate of the *wazir*'s, but otherwise the Makhzan had become a virtual fief of the family of Ba Ahmad. One brother, Saïd, was the Minister of War, another, Idris, was chamberlain and a third, Mahammad, went as ambassador to France.[1] Such men were trustworthy but often inexperienced. In 1895 a Frenchman who knew the old Makhzan well, Dr Weisgerber, judged that Si Saïd was better at supervising the security of the *wazir*'s kitchen than at overseeing the army.[2] Si Mehdi el-Mennebhi, a relative of El Glaoui, who was the principal military commander, was competent but very young.[3]

The other props of the new regime came from the Alaoui family. Important military and political commands were assigned to close relatives of the Sultan including his brother Moulay Abdelhafid who was made Governor of Tiznit in 1897 and then *khalifa* in Marrakesh.[4] But another brother, Bilghith, succeeded in having the Chaouïa tribes proclaim him as sultan.[5]

Rebellion and repression

There was a much more dangerous claimant than Bilghith: his long-imprisoned brother Moulay Mahammad, who had the additional appeal of occasional fits of madness, which many people interpreted as signs of divine blessing. He was a fine rallying-point for rebels in the Rehamna, in the Haouz of Marrakesh. Since the qaids of the Rehamna had gone north with Moulay Hassan, their rivals seized the moment. In August, when the harvest was in, the Rehamna rebelled and were joined by other big tribes, such as the Doukkala, Chiadma and Abda. Then smaller tribes along the northern fringes of the High Atlas revolted. All declared for Moulay Mahammad

Ba Ahmad handled the rebellion poorly: when he arrested some rebels who had taken refuge in a *zawiya*, a real mass uprising

1 Arnaud, *Mehallas* 90; Laroui, *Origines*, 343.

2 F. Weisgerber, *Au seuil du Maroc moderne* (Rabat: Éditions la Porte, 1947), 70.

3 Burke, *Prelude*, 48; Weisgerber, *Au seuil*, 72.

4 Arnaud, *Mehallas*, 92, 94, 127; Burke, *Prelude*, 99, 115.

5 Arnaud, *Mehallas*, 92; Burke, *Prelude*, 42.

began. The rebels laid siege to Marrakesh but the governor distributed rapid-firing rifles to the urban population which were far superior to the locally-made muskets of the Rehmanis, and the city held out. In the spring of 1896 Ba Ahmad attacked and his cannon and machine-guns mowed the rebels down. On 7 March the triumphant Makhzan column entered Marrakesh. They carried with them an iron cage containing one of the rebel leaders, whom they had dragged from sanctuary in a *zawiya* and, according to a letter written by Ba Ahmad himself, brought before the Sultan

> Our Lord – victorious by the grace of God – contemplated him and assembled around himself the blissful armies and troops as well as the notables of the city and the caids of the tribes. They examined him in this predicament. Then he was forced to mount a lame camel, paraded bare-headed in the blissfull mahalla, and slapped, as God's anger struck him from all directions. Then he was put in chains; after his feet, hands and neck were fettered, he was thrown into an iron cage like a wild beast or a ferocious dog.[6]

Some said that the bars of this cage were made from the gun-barrels of his followers: the intention, as ever, was to humiliate as well as to destroy the defeated rebel, to show that the *Makhzan* was indeed still powerful.[7] When the Misfioua rebelled in late 1899, Ba Ahmad filled the roads with prisoners 'who marched in a line of 15 or 20 on each chain, with their wives and children dragging on after them. They were a pitiful sight on the roads along which they slowly staggered'.[8]

Fifty Misfioui heads decorated the walls of Fez.[9] Other rebels were severely flogged, then the terrible punishment of the salt was imposed upon them: their palms were cut open, and the cuts filled with salt; the fingers were then bunched backwards and the fist bound with wet sheepskin. When this dried the hand was forever a useless ball of flesh.[10]

In the central Rif, equally harsh treatment was meted out to the Buqquya tribe, who had rediscovered the delights of opportunistic piracy. The ferocious commander of the *mahalla* that was sent to deal with them, Bouchta el-Baghdadi, burned crops and

6 Hammoudi, *Master and Disciple*, 63-4.

7 Arnaud, *Mehallas*, 120.

8 *Ibid.*, 128.

9 *Ibid.*, 130.

10 Parsons, *Morocco Question*, 495.

houses, sent 400 prisoners to Fez, executed some prominent notables and imposed a huge fine.[11] The Buqquya took a generation to recover.

The theatrical violence was, as always, designed to show that the Makhzan was still powerful, and at first sight this violence did have a salutary effect, for the country became quiet. Throughout the latter 1890s, the road between Fez and the coast was usually open;[12] Fez was peaceful, and Meknès so secure that Moulay Mahammad was imprisoned there.

This was an illusion. Violence had to be used again and again because the Makhzan was weak, not strong. The *jaysh* tribes provided neither troops nor taxes and Ba Ahmad simply relied on local leaders to keep the peace.[13] In the south itself, the big qaids kept control.

The big qaids

Using his Krupp cannon, Madani El Glaoui spread his power southwards from Telouèt into the desert. Taïeb El Goundafi and Abd al-Malik El Mtouggi extended their reach as well.[14] The big qaids were better armed than their tribal opponents with guns they had bought or been given by Ba Ahmad. Yet although they acted in the name of the Makhzan their allegiance was very shallow. El Goundafi summed up his idea of loyalty by saying, 'Let us go and cut off the rebels' heads for the benefit of our families.'[15]

In the very far south, Ba Ahmad followed the old sultan's lead by allying himself with Shaykh Ma al-Aynayn. In 1896/7, the shaykh visited Marrakesh and Moulay Abdelaziz, it was said, gave him a million silver dirhams, joined his *tariqa* and gave him land for a new zawiya in Marrakesh. Ba Ahmad also subsidised Ma al-Aynayn's vast new religious centre at Es-Semara in the upper reaches of the bone-dry Saquïa el-Hamra (Rio de Oro). He gave money to

11 Hart, *Aith Waryaghar*, 355-6.

12 PP 1897, 92:26ff; PP 1898, 97:17ff and 265ff; PP 1899, 101:101ff; PP 1901, 83:15ff.

13 Burke, *Prelude*, 42; Edmund Burke, III, 'Tribalism and Moroccan Resistance, 1890-1914: the Role of the Aith Ndhir' in Joffe and Pennell (eds), *Tribe and State*, 133.

14 Montagne, *Berbères*, 334-6.

15 Gavin Maxwell, *Lords of the Atlas: the Rise and Fall of the House of Glaoua 1893-1956* (London: Longman, 1966), 59.

dig wells and plant palm groves and soon the place had around 10,000 inhabitants.[16]

Ma al-Aynayn had no equivalent in the far south east. Ba Ahmad sent troops to help Moulay al-Rashid, the *khalifa* of the Tafilalt, but the road to Fez was closed in 1896 and 1897 and even when it was open, protection-money (*zattata*) pushed the prices of transport to ridiculous heights.[17] Down in the far Saharan oases the tribes fought each other. Since Algerian rebels still sought refuge amidst the disorder, the French army pushed forward. In 1898 they set up the post of Fort-Mirabel near In Salah, one of the major oases.[18]

Ba Ahmad had no money to deal with these problems. The financial difficulties of Moulay Hassan's reign, collapsing currency, poor harvests and the European takeover of the economy just got worse.

Economic problems

In 1896 Ba Ahmad issued new silver dirham coins weighing 4.1 grams more than the commonly circulating Spanish twenty-five-peseta piece, but good money did not drive out bad. Merchants alleged that their size made them 'un-Islamic', and only agreed to overcome their scruples and use them if they were given a discount of 12%. New brass coins caused speculation because of local differences in exchange rates.[19] Foreign currency was no more reliable. In the mid-1890s a flood of very debased Philippine silver was smuggled in, and in 1898 the Spanish currency collapsed following the Spanish-American war.[20]

There was also debt. In 1894 the Makhzan owed Spain 14 million of the 20 million peseta indemnity for the Melilla skirmishes in 1893, and numerous smaller indemnities to European consuls for real or imagined wrongs. Arms had to be bought. Between 1893 and 1900, the Makhzan's expenditure doubled to 40 million francs.[21] Since it was hard to collect any more in taxes, Ba Ahmad relied on customs receipts to make up the difference.

16 Martin, *Brotherhoods*, 134-7.

17 PP 1897, 92:261ff; PP 1898, 97:217ff; Dunn *Resistance*, 166.

18 A.-G.-P Martin, *Quatre siècles d'histoire marocaine: au Sahara de 1504 à 1902, au Maroc de 1894 à 1912*, 2nd edn. (Rabat: Éditions La Porte, 1994), 29-31.

19 Burke, *Prelude*, 56-7; Afa, *Mas'alat*, 248-52.

20 PP 1897, 92:261ff ; PP 1899, 101:101ff.

21 Laroui, *Origines*, 339-40.

This was a forlorn hope. Moulay Hassan had died in the second year of a run of bad harvests that lasted for the rest of the decade. The British Vice-Consul in Larache reported that 1896 had been the worst year since the famine of 1877-9. The harvest had failed, locusts had destroyed the crops and the orange trees, cattle had died, there was no local trade because the Makhzan was in Marrakesh, and people were impoverished by heavy taxation.[22] There was famine in the Chaouïa in 1897 and in Oujda and the Sous in 1899. Trade slumped. The figures were as inaccurate as usual, but the educated guesses of British consuls pointed to declining imports and exports between 1894 and 1896, followed by a patchy recovery to the end of the century. Imports picked up so slowly that in 1900 Morocco again had a trade surplus; only tea and sugar outperformed the trend, hovering between 20-30% during the second half of the 1890s (see figure).

The pattern of trade was changing too. Economic activity shifted southwards towards Rabat, Casablanca, Essaouira, Azemmour and Safi, partly because the court was in Marrakesh and partly because of increased German activity in the south. By 1898 Germany was the third most important export partner. Although Britain was still the largest market, German commercial houses cut British cloth firms out of local markets.[23] At the same time European manufactures poured into the Moroccan market. The British Consul in Casablanca described a cornucopia of products:

> The rest of the import trade must be described under the heading of sundries, as no single item is of important value. They consist of deals from Sweden; coffee from London and Hamburg; cheap cutlery, carpenters' tools, nails and screws from Germany; brass candlesticks, sheet brass, and metal teapots, from Birmingham; iron girders from Belgium; tin-plates from England; cement from Germany and France; cheap glossy cloth from Germany; silk goods from France; enamelled table and toiletware, tea-glasses, bits and stirrup-irons of Moorish pattern, cheap locks, door latches and hinges and cheap petroleum lamps from Germany; matches from Italy and Belgium; confectionery and biscuits from the United Kingdom; woollen manufactures, drugs, oil, paint and dyes, from the United Kingdom and Germany; petroleum from America, via Hamburg and London; low grades of stationery from Germany and Belgium; cheap mirrors, per-

22 PP 1898, 97:217ff.

23 PP 1897, 92: 261ff; PP 1898, 97:217ff ; PP 1898, 97:265ff; PP 1899, 101:101ff ; PP 1901, 83:615ff ; PP 1897, 92:261ff.

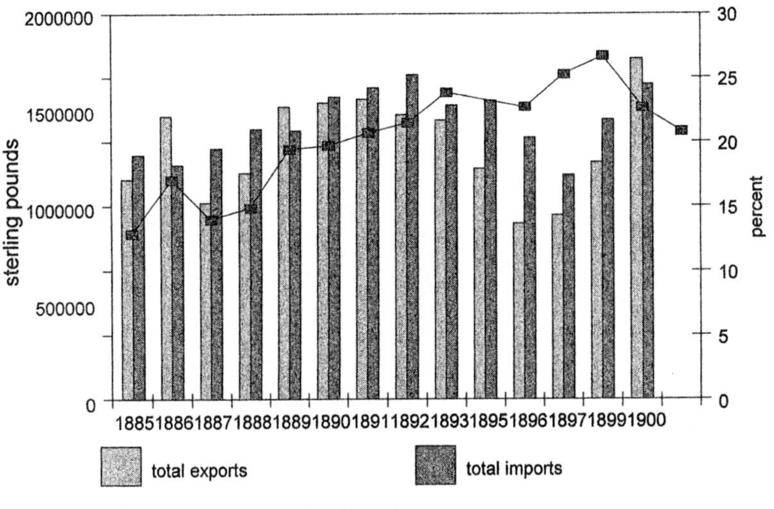

EXPORTS AND IMPORTS, 1885-1900

Note Figures for 1895 and 1898 incomplete so not included.
Source British Parliamentary Papers.

fumes and toilet soaps, from Germany; sacks and sacking used to come from Dundee, but now arrive direct from India, via London or Hamburg.

Those thin paper matches that cost the equivalent of one British penny for half a dozen boxes, brought instant fire to the hovels and tents of the poor. In their houses, wealthier Moroccans began sleeping on British bedsteads.[24] As the products of European factories dominated the lifestyle of Moroccans, so did European diplomats dominate the country's politics.

European diplomacy

At first Ba Ahmad had no great difficulties with foreign powers. No expert diplomat himself, he relied on the Foreign Minister Si Abd al-Karim bin Sulayman who, in his turn, looked to the British Consulate-General for support. Although the dashing Sir Harry Maclean had endeared himself to Ba Ahmad by getting word of Moulay Hassan's death to London by cable before the Sultan's death was known even in Rabat, the prime reason for

24 PP 1898, 97:265ff.

trusting Britain was that it seemed the least likely European power to disturb the *status quo*. Indeed, the British Minister in Tangier, Sir Ernest Satow, was almost helpful. In 1895 he agreed that if the Makhzan bought out the British North African Company, Mackenzie's factory on Cape Juby would be removed and his government would recognise Moroccan sovereignty over the coast and hinterland as far as Cape Bojador, something no other European government would do.[25]

No other European power was able or willing to supplant the British. The German government preferred British influence to a French takeover and its influence was anyway handicapped by two extraordinarily quarrelsome Consuls-General who made themselves deeply unpopular by turning each insult, each aggression and murder of German subjects into a full-blown diplomatic incident.[26] The French government, whose Consul-General in Tangier fell out with Ba Ahmad in 1895, wanted to avoid problems despite the odd incident on the Algerian frontier.[27] The minor powers did not matter. After the United States demolished what was left of the Spanish empire in 1898, the government in Madrid would have been thoroughly unpopular if it had tried any adventures in Morocco; in 1896, Italian imperial ambitions collapsed in front of Ethiopian guns at Adowa.[28]

Although the diplomatic pressure from European capitals was reduced, there was plenty of social and economic pressure from Europeans in Morocco. At the turn of the century, there were estimated to be some 9,000 foreign residents in Morocco. In 1901, the German consulate in Tangier reported only 147 subjects, and the Italian listed 53 families. Some of these foreign nationals had little connection with their supposed countries: the Brazilian consulate, headed after 1897 by a locally-born Jew, happily continued to sell nationality.[29]

25 Rogers, *History*, 231; Mackenzie, *Khalifate*, 203-4; Parsons, *Morocco Question*, 499-500; M. Brett, 'Don Roberto and the Tourmaline affair: British filibusters in the Canaries and Southern Morocco, 1875-1900 and the creation of the Moroccan Protectorate, 1912' in *II Aula Canarias y el Noroeste de Africa (1986)* 413-21; Weisgerber, *Au seuil*, 66, 80-1; Burke, *Prelude*, 49.

26 Parsons, *Morocco Question*, 407-8; Jean-Claude Allain, *Agadir, 1911* (Paris: Publications de la Sorbonne, 1976), 22-3; Germain Ayache, 'La Crise des relations germano-marocaines (1894-1897),' in *Études d'histoire marocaine* (Rabat: SMER, 1979), 249-92.

27 Parsons, *Morocco Question*, 500-1.

28 Allain, *Agadir*, 25; Parsons, *Morocco Question*, 497; Tomás García Figueras, *La acción africana de España en torno al 98 (1860-1912)* (Madrid: CSIC, 1966), 9-10.

29 Parsons, *Morocco Question*, 539-41.

Yet this small number of foreigners had disproportionate economic influence. Moroccans became indebted to them, either directly or at one remove, and were imprisoned at the request of Europeans and their protégés. Indebtedness reached deep into Moroccan society. In 1895 the British Consul in Casablanca described how a 'village blacksmith' who needed money to pay taxes, took a loan from a merchant, a protégé, in the form of sugar on credit, which he was to repay at harvest time. The merchant signed a chit for 2 hundredweight of sugar which the blacksmith sold to another merchant for about three-quarters the price of the sugar. Much of the harvest was tied up in advance in this sort of speculation.[30]

There was a new burst of protection. Between 1892 and 1902 the number of German *simsars* (native agents) in the Chaouïa rose from thirty-two to 217. In 1892 the American Consul in Casablanca had sixty-two *simsars* and in 1902, one big British trading house had more than sixty.[31] The effects were plain to the eye. More *gota'as*, adobe-walled farms, dotted the countryside, and fields were delimited with cactus hedges, to keep wandering cattle and sheep away from crops. Slowly, the physical signs of land ownership spread inland. Powerful members of tribes took over usufruct to land that had been collectively owned, and then assumed possession of it. Land that once had been left fallow between crops was cultivated for successive seasons by men who then asserted legal ownership. Even in the remotest parts, in the far north-east near Melilla, pressure from hill farmers led to the development of private property in the plain. Once land became private property, large estates began to grow, because the rules of inheritance fragmented land holdings so much that heirs began selling their plots to bigger investors.[32] In the Haouz of Marrakesh the Glaouis built up big estates and in the Rharb the Sharif of Ouezzane continued to buy land for his family in the name of his zawiya.[33]

As European economic power grew, so did interference in the way Morocco was governed. Ba Ahmad's all-too-public brutalities horrified humanitarians. Newspapers and books described the violence in graphic detail and European governments instructed their consuls to protest. British humanitarians concentrated on

30 PP 1897, 92:261ff.

31 Godfrey, 'Overseas trade', 214.

32 *Ibid.*, 281-93.

33 Pascon, *Haouz*, 51; Joffe, 'Zawiya of Wazzan', 3-7; Seddon, *Moroccan Peasants*, 64.

the slave trade, and the Howard League, a penal reform group, campaigned about conditions in Moroccan prisons.[34] In Morocco itself, European merchants in Safi organised the collection of locust eggs in 1896, by the simple expedient of buying them by weight. This brought the locust problem under control so successfully, that the following year they persuaded the government to follow suit. In 1898 the British Vice-Consul in Fez reported that a vaccination campaign had begun and by 1900, he was recommending a campaign of compulsory vaccination.[35]

Admittedly, there was a self-serving element in such proposals. Doctors were no longer the privileged confidants of Sultans and *wazirs*; now they were missionaries who hoped (with little success) to spread Christianity. Moreover, they made Morocco physically safer for Europeans and eased their political penetration.[36]

More and more Europeans were visiting Morocco. Tangier was now a health resort with sea bathing on a superb beach, an artistic colony and a high society revolving around the consulates. There was a flourishing European-language press notable for its sensationalism and inaccuracy, a telephone and electricity system. The many European hotels were filled by cruise liners that brought European and American visitors to view the sights of the mysterious and exotic Orient: the old walled city, the harem, the palaces and the picturesque cafés.

Europeans demanded better public services and insisted on running them. The Health Committee of the Diplomatic Corps supervised shipping and a Sanitary Association took charge of cleaning, and lighting and repaving the main streets. Europeans managed not only Tangier but the surrounding countryside. The boar-hunters of the Tangier Tent Club took control of hunting. Established in 1892, the club issued hunting permits, decided the off-season and oversaw the local Moroccan authorities in policing Moroccan hunters. Moroccans were excluded from traditional hunting activities and relegated to roles as bearers, beaters and supporters. A social distance evolved between Europeans and Moroccan hunters that had not existed in the days of Sir John Drummond-Hay.[37]

34 Khalid Ben Srhir and Mohamed Ennaji, 'La Grande Bretagne et l'esclavage au Maroc au XIXè siècle', *Hespéris-Tamuda* 29 (1991): 261-2; cf. Mackenzie, *Khalifate*, 110ff; Laroui, *Origines*, 340.

35 PP 1898, 97:241ff; PP 1898, 92:265ff; PP 1902, 108:665ff.

36 Jim Paul, 'Medicine and Imperialism in Morocco', *MERIP Reports* 60 (1977): 3-12; for Iranian examples see Rejali, *Torture and Modernity*, 49-50.

37 Budgett Meakin, *The Land of the Moors, a Comprehensive Description* (London: Swann Sonnenschein, 1901), 101-6; Priscilla Roberts, 'Nineteenth century Tangier:

European tourists even ventured into the interior. In 1897 Thomas Cook and Company added Fez to its list of destinations, although the numbers proved disappointing because it was so expensive.[38] In a British tradition of using eccentric, even stupidly dangerous, methods of travel, Budgett Meakin and a doctor friend travelled to Marrakesh by bicycle. No harm came to them, but they scared at least one Moroccan, who had never seen a bicycle before, and who cried out: 'Alas! Alas! Woe is me! The Christians have taken our country at last; why, here's a railway train! Woe to me! Woe to me!'[39] Or so Meakin said. He evidently thought such a tale of naivety amusing, but it was fairly typical of the growing European arrogance. Ba Ahmad sent an urgent message to the travellers in Marrakesh 'requesting us not to ride within the walls, and giving notice that such things did not belong in Morocco. But we had had our ride.'[40] The *wazir* and the countryman were both right. The bicycle became another tiny symbol of European domination.

ABDELAZIZ'S MOROCCO

The new regime

Ba Ahmad died on 13 May 1900. His brothers, Saïd, the Minister for War and Idris, the chamberlain, had died a few months before. The qaid of the palace, who was no relation, died shortly afterwards. Looking back, the Frenchman Dr Weisgerber concluded Ba Ahmad's death marked the end of the old Morocco.[41] In this he was correct. Although the new *wazir* was Ba Ahmad's cousin, and his brother became chamberlain, and the new qaid of the palace was the son of the old, and the finance and foreign ministers remained in office, the main props of the old regime had nevertheless disappeared; there was also a new Minister of War, the young Mehdi el-Mennebhi.[42] More than this, Ba Ahmad, for all his failings, represented the last attempt to apply Moulay Hassan's

---

its American visitors – who they were, why they came, what they wrote' in *Tanger 1800-1956, Contribution à l'histoire récente du Maroc* (Rabat: Editions Arabo-Africaines, 1991); Susan Miller, 'The Colonial Hunt in Nineteenth Century Tangier," in *ibid.*, 191-203.

38 PP 1898, 97:265ff ; PP 1901, 83:615ff.

39 Meakin, *Land of the Moors*, 438.

40 *Ibid.*, 441.

41 Weisgerber, *Au seuil*, 118-19.

42 Laroui, *Origines*, 343; Arnaud, *Mehallas*, 140.

policies of force mixed with patronage in the old context. Moulay Abdelaziz had neither the strength nor the money, nor the skill, to put them into effect, and probably did not want to anyway.

The new sultan sought to break with the past, both personally and politically. He celebrated his escape from the confines of the palace with a vast fireworks display in Marrakesh that culminated in a spectacular fiery elephant and a pink waterfall in the night sky.[43] Such frivolities fuelled sensationalist European reports of an improvident Sultan who was squandering the reserves of the state. That symbol of European civilisation that had so appalled Ba Ahmad, the bicycle, was wheeled into the palace for his harem and his ministers to ride. There was tomfoolery of the Marie-Antoinette kind: the Sultan and el-Mennebhi, the Minister of War, played at water-boatmen, ferrying the correspondent of *The Times*, Walter Harris, across the palace reservoir.[44] Masses of European fripperies were brought in, among them grand pianos, carriages and barrel-organs. Most of them were to moulder away unopened in their packing cases.[45]

Such stories amused some Europeans and appalled many Moroccans,[46] but they were exaggerated and masked the young Sultan's serious intent. He was young, certainly, but he was no fool: he had been educated by reform-minded religious scholars and sincerely wanted to restructure the country.[47]

So he appointed a new Makhzan, one which no single man dominated, but in which several strong personalities vied for power. The *wazir*, Si Feddoul Gharnit, was an elderly and extremely experienced in-fighter,[48] the Minister of Finance and Foreign Minister were unchanged, and el-Mennebhi remained as Minster of War. El-Mennebhi was very influential, for not only was he an agreeable companion but he also shared the Sultan's political ideas.

Abdelaziz's reforms

The Sultan and his reformists looked to the British to help modernise Morocco. In 1901, encouraged by el-Mennebhi and ibn Sulayman, the foreign minister, Moulay Abdelaziz announced a

43 Walter Harris, *Morocco that* Was (Edinburgh: Blackwood, 1921), 50.

44 *Ibid.*, 52.

45 *Ibid.*, 80.

46 Arnaud, *Mehallas*, 133.

47 Burke, *Prelude*, 47-8.

48 Arnaud, *Mehallas*, 140.

programme of reforms that closely resembled that proposed by John Drummond-Hay a generation before.

There was to be a cabinet government. A salaried civil service would oversee the collection of taxes and eliminate corruption. Everyone would pay a new tax, the *tartib*, on their agricultural produce and livestock. An embryonic consultative assembly would be formed of officials and merchants. There would be a huge program of public works: port facilities, roads, bridges, telegraphs, all paid for from the increase in tax receipts.[49]

This was really an attempt to create a new political and economic system in which responsibility and economic productivity would replace one based on patronage and social status. It was nothing short of a fundamental change in the way Morocco was governed, and it failed. The old system was one in which compliance was secured not simply through patronage, but through reciprocity: if powerful men were removed from access to the sultan, they had no reason to continue to support him, and Moulay Abdelaziz had no means to coerce them.[50]

The neat financial equation did not work out. Port works and continued arms purchases required huge amounts of money and brought big European commercial and financial firms enormous profits. By the beginning of 1903 the Gautsch company, a subsidiary of the French Schneider empire, had sold 20 million francs' worth of goods at an average profit of 25%. Such advantages could only be secured by corruption and rival corrupt groups emerged within the Makhzan, one pro-British (led by Kaid Maclean and el-Mennebhi) and one pro-French (led by ibn Sulayman).[51] Meanwhile, the Moroccan currency continued to collapse, so Moulay Abdelaziz tried to reform it yet again. He replaced the 29-gramme silver coinage with a 25-gramme dirham identical to the French and Spanish coins that circulated in Morocco. This time the merchants refused the new coins because they were worth less than the old. The dirham continued to slide, and inflation to rise. Rainfall was low in 1902-3 and the harvests of 1905 and 1906 were eaten by locusts.[52] It was an unfortunate time to change the tax system.

The new tax system was a disaster. It relied on salaried officials to collect taxes and since this deprived the rural qaids of their income, they did all they could to hinder it. The *tartib* may have

49 Burke, *Prelude*, 51.

50 Hammoudi, *Master and Disciple*, 53; Burke, *Prelude*, 52.

51 Burke, *Prelude*, 54-5.

52 Godfrey, 'Overseas trade', 271-2, 277-8; Bois, 'Sécheresses'; Burke, Prelude, 90-1.

fallen less heavily on those who already paid taxes but it required people who had never paid before to do so, and they objected. The '*ulama* protested that it was irreligious, and only in 1903 did the European consulates agree that their *protégés* should pay it. For two years, much of the *bilad al-makhzan* paid no taxes at all.[53] In need of funds, the Makhzan turned to European banks and so sealed French dominance of Morocco.

Morocco and the European Entente

In 1900 French forces occupied the Touat oases that lay right in the path of the railway the army was building into the Sahara. The only reason that French troops did not occupy more territory, was that the government in Paris feared European protests.

In reality, there was nothing to fear. The British government was preoccupied with the South African War and announced that it had no interest in what happened in Touat.[54] The German government only protested in the most measured terms because it wanted to avoid trouble. The Italian and Spanish governments concluded that France was about to emerge as the main power in North Africa, so the only way to salvage their position was to fall in line. One step at a time, a share-out of North-African spoils began, part of a wider division of influence and power in Africa, Asia and, crucially, in Europe.

The Italian government secured Libya. An agreement in December 1900 set aside this unprepossessing prize as a future Italian prerogative in return for recognition of future French preponderance in Morocco.[55] That June a convention had given Spain the even less attractive coast of the western Sahara, and tiny bits of land and islands in the Gulf of Guinea. In 1902 a draft Franco-Spanish treaty recognised future Spanish 'rights' over much of northern Morocco including Fez, and a further expanse of sand in the far south. It would come into effect if the Moroccan regime collapsed and the interests of order and security 'obliged' the European powers to step in, but the Spanish Prime Minister refused to sign it in the belief that the French and British governments would soon fall out and he might get even more by waiting.[56]

He was wrong. In the autumn of 1902 the British government

53 Burke, *Prelude*, 50-3; Laroui, *Origines*, 344-7.

54 Frank E. Trout, *Morocco's Southern Frontiers* (Geneva: Droz, 1969), 31; Nordmann, 'L'Armée de l'Algérie', 34-5.

55 Allain, *Agadir*, 25.

56 *Ibid.*, 25. García Figueras, *La acción*, 2:29, 65; Burke, *Prelude*, 70.

cleared the way for a French loan that secured French financial preponderance in Morocco.[57] Diplomatic hegemony followed, for European, not local, considerations were driving policy in Morocco. In April 1904, at the time of the Entente Cordiale, London and Paris settled outstanding overseas problems in Newfoundland, Siam, Gambia, Madagascar and, above all, Egypt and Morocco. Although the two governments still declared that they did not want to change the political situation in either Egypt or Morocco, or to obstruct free trade, they recognised that Egypt was primarily a British preserve and Morocco a French one. If it became necessary to step in to maintain financial stability and 'order', they would not get in each other's way. Realising it had been left behind, the Spanish government signed an agreement on much worse terms than it would have got in 1902. Now, when Morocco was divided, it would only receive the sands of Tarfaya in the far south and a tiny, rocky northern zone between Melilla and the mouth of the Ouerrha river. Although these arrangements were contingent on order breaking down, that was no real obstacle for order had already begun to collapse.

A generalised siba

It is hard to say whether the rebellions that spread at the time of Ba Ahmad's death were the causes or consequences of the failure of the Sultan's policy. Some disorder was mere banditry. In May 1901, when the Frenchman Dr Weisgerber travelled through the Chaouïa he found that the safe conduct issued by the Sultan was no use.[58] Moreover, the Makhzan was caught in a vicious circle: it could not collect taxes, so local people were able to build up financial reserves to resist Makhzan pressure in the future.

The reforms made things worse. Around Fez, the countryside collapsed in disorder. First the Ait Ndhir said that the new telegraph lines were a threat to the movement of their flocks and pulled them down. Then the *jaysh* tribes rebelled against the *tartib* tax. Finally the Aith Ndhir, helped by the Ait Yusi and Banu Mgild, besieged Meknès and cut the road to the coast.[59] At last, the Sultan moved from Marrakesh to Fez. Going by the coastal route, he sent out *mahallas* from the main column to repress rebels, but

57 Allain, *Agadir*, 26-7.

58 Weisgerber, *Au seuil*, 124-5.

59 Burke, 'Ait Ndhir', 134; Arnaud, *Mehallas*, 133.

when it moved on, the rebellions flared again. The troops, unpaid and unfed, simply deserted.[60]

The Makhzan had lost control of much of Morocco. In the central Rif this period would afterwards be known as the *ripublik* or *réfoublique*. The etymology and significance of the word are obvious: this was a time of struggles between local alliances, restrained only by local *marabouts* and a precarious balance of power. Factions that opposed the Spanish maintained the guard posts near Badis, Al Hoceima, and Melilla, while their rivals traded with the Spanish.[61] In the far south-east, some people traded with the French while others prepared to fight them. When French troops occupied the Touat, volunteers arrived in Tafilalt from as far away as Fez and Marrakesh, but when French units attacked Figuig in August 1903, the defenders were easily beaten off. The Sultan, far from fighting to protect the *Dar al-Islam*, actively worked to break up the column to prevent problems with the French.[62] Here as elsewhere, the only resistance to the French came from local groups that were acting autonomously; resistance to the Europeans was now synonymous with rebellion, although it was so factionalised as to be quite useless.

The big qaids

The only stability was in the south, where Si Madani El Glaoui, Abd al-Malik El Mtouggi and Si Taïeb El Goundafi made themselves the uncontested masters of the Saharan passes. The Glaouis raised taxes and lived in splendour in their stronghold of Telouèt. They were visited by adventurous European travellers with whom they went hunting: there was no question here of European control over hunting grounds. Thami El Glaoui, Si Madani's younger brother, entertained a Lady Grove with an extravagantly theatrical hunt and accommodated her in rooms decorated in opulent if garish taste, that were set aside for the Sultan should he happen to pass by.[63]

Farther south still, Ma al-Aynayn held the Mauritanian tribes as far south as Chinquit in a rough allegiance to the sultan. No European government recognised that allegiance, but many

60 Weisgerber, *Au seuil*, 129-30; Rollman, 'New Order', 815-16.

61 Pascon & van der Wusten, *Beni Boufrah*, 82-4; Hart, *Aith Waryaghar*, 359-61.

62 Dunn, *Resistance*, 176-200; Burke, *Prelude*, 46; Hart, *Ait Atta*, 161.

63 Maxwell, *Lords of the Atlas*, 76.

Mauritanian notables wanted it because the French army was pushing northwards from the Senegal river.[64]

In the north, a 'big qaid' of sorts emerged in the Jebala. Moulay Ahmad El Raisuni was a *sharif* of the lineage of Sidi Abd al-Salam bin Mashish, the famous Sufi buried on Jbel Alam south-east of Tangier. His family had a residence at Tazrut nearby. Although he was highly educated in traditional Islamic sciences, he turned to banditry, according to him, out of a sense of adventure and the desire to right wrongs. He adopted the bearing of the noble philosopher-bandit, who claimed that only a gold or silver bullet could kill him. As noble bandits should be, he was captured by treachery and imprisoned by Moulay Hassan in the most appalling conditions in Essaouira. Once Ba Ahmad died, powerful friends, including el Mennebhi, interceded for his release.[65]

After El Raisuni recovered his health he determined to take revenge on those who had betrayed him and became, in his eyes at least, an avenging protector of 'his' people, popular and free of control 'Against Europe on the one side and the Sultan on the other I protected the rights of the people, for they were my people'.[66] His method was to kidnap prominent Europeans and use them as bargaining chips. He captured the *Times* correspondent, Walter Harris, and went hunting with him in the hills, and Ion Perdicaris, an extremely rich Greek, who claimed American citizenship. This claim was untrue, but President Theodore Roosevelt threatened to declare war if Perdicaris was not released. Moulay Abdelaziz gave in and made El Raisuni Pasha of Tangier, because he could not afford a crisis with foreigners while he faced a serious rebellion in the mountains near Fez.[67]

The revolt of Abu Himara

The rebellion was led by a former Makhzan functionary who pretended to be Moulay Mahammad, the sultan's imprisoned brother. Jilani bin Idris had been educated at the Qarawiyyin, and was briefly a Makhzan secretary during the reign of Moulay Hassan. Ba Ahmad imprisoned him for forgery, but not before he had learned enough to carry off a credible imitation of Moulay Mahammad. Jilani was an accomplished mimic and magician.

64 Martin, *Muslim Brotherhoods*, 138-9; Trout, *Frontiers*, 156ff.

65 Rosita Forbes, *El Raisuni, the Sultan of the Mountains* (London: Thornton Butterworth, 1924), 40-65.

66 *Ibid.*, 66.

67 Burke, *Prelude*, 66; Forbes, *Raisuni*, 68-75.

When he was released from prison, he first went to Algeria and then returned to Fez in 1902, to a seething city. A British missionary, David Cooper, had been murdered when he appeared to violate the holy tomb of Moulay Idris II. The killer took refuge in the shrine, but Moulay Abdelaziz tricked him into leaving and had him executed.[68] Jilani noted the public fury that this treachery inspired and made for the mountains to launch his revolt.

He began by posing as a man of religion. Like many supposed *mahdis* in the past, he travelled the countryside on a she-ass, and so was nicknamed Abu Himara ('the man on the donkey'). He won support among credulous tribesmen with a series of ledgermains that he claimed were miracles, and then revealed the 'secret' that he was Moulay Mahammad, swearing those he told to silence, so that the news spread even more rapidly.[69]

The Sultan did not take Abu Himara seriously. In the spirit of the old Makhzan he gave the job of suppressing him to his young brother, Moulay al-Kbir. When Walter Harris protested that he was still a child, the Sultan replied that it was his turn to make a little money (by stealing the soldiers' pay and extorting fines from the tribes).[70] Not surprisingly, Moulay el-Kbir failed. When Abu Himara took Taza, its governor finally managed to convince the sultan that the pretender was dangerous:

> He has 15,000 horsemen who make up his regular forces, of whom many come from the Ghiata, and in addition all the contingents from the tribes in the east who have proclaimed him: the Hayaïna, the Beni Ouaraïn, the Tsoul, the Branes, the Metalsa ... and you say this man has no importance. He is an excellent warrior, loved and feared by his followers, educated and dangerous. I tell you the truth: if the Sultan carries on towards Marrakesh, Bou Hamara will take Fez without any difficulty, perhaps without firing a shot.[...]Prayers are being said in his name in the mosque in Taza.[71]

The Sultan put the real Moulay Mahammad on public show, but that did not sap the pretender's power. The Makhzan was so corrupt and divided that it could not even decide who would lead its army. In the end the Sultan sent three separate columns,

68 Burke, *Prelude*, 61. Al Khalloufi, *Bouhmara*, 45-47.

69 Arnaud, *Mehallas*, 159-63. AL Khalloufi, *Bouhmara*, 47-55.

70 Eduardo Maldonado, *El Rogui* (Tetuan: Instituto General Franco par la Investigación Hispano-Árabe, [1949]), 100.

71 Arnaud, *Mehallas*, 169.

20,000 men in all, and Abu Himara brushed aside the fears of his followers, telling them: 'These people would be dangerous if they had a single commander to lead them. But each column has its own leader, it is a flock of hens with no cock.'[72]

So it proved. The columns were all resoundingly defeated and el-Mennebhi finally insisted on complete control of the army. In January 1903 the Minister of War smashed the pretender's forces for the first time, and in May chased him out of Taza, albeit with some difficulty. Abu Himara escaped to the far north-east and set up in the old qasba at Selouane, close to the Spanish frontier at Melilla. From there he ruled for another five years, still pretending to be Moulay Mahammad, though no-one really believed him. He financed himself by commerce with Europeans.[73]

Abu Himara's short-lived threat pointed to future dangers. Claiming to be a member of the Alaoui family, his attacks on the corruption, disorganisation and irreligiousness of Moulay Abdelaziz's Makhzan had a powerful impact. But once the pretender had fled, el-Mennebhi received no reward. Instead, his rivals forced him out of his military command, and to avoid disgrace, he went on pilgrimage. When he returned, he settled quietly in Tangier. The Makhzan had lost its most successful and able military commander and even worse, it had cost so much to deal with the rebellion, that new loans were needed. This was a situation that benefited French interests.[74]

The rise of the French

The fall of el-Mennebhi, usually thought to have been pro-British, marked the rise of a faction that was generally considered to be pro-French. It included the Tazi family, one of whom was already finance minister, and a new minister of war, Mohammed Guebbas. After the Entente Cordiale was announced, the rumour spread among the tribes that 'England has sold Morocco to France.'[75]

72 Arnaud, *mehalla*, 174. Al-Khallouji, *Bouhmara* 60-3.

73 *Ibid.*, 183-95; Burke, *Prelude*, 164; Ross Dunn has written three important articles on Abu Himara: 'Bu Himara's European Connection: the Commercial Relations of a Moroccan Warlord', *Journal of African History*, 21 (1980): 235-53; 'France, Spain and the Bu Himara Rebellion, in Joffe and Pennell(eds), *Tribe and State*, 145-58; 'The Bu Himara Rebellion in Northeast Morocco: Phase 1', *Middle Eastern Studies*, 17 (1981): 31-48. Al-Khallouji, *Bouhmara*, 64.

74 Burke, *Prelude*, 65; Seddon, *Moroccan Peasants*, 107-9; Hart, *Aith Waryaghar*, 261-2.

75 Burke, *Prelude*, 72; Daniel Rivet, *Lyautey et l'institution du protectorat français au*

The effects were soon seen. In September 1903 Colonel Louis-Hubert-Gonçalves Lyautey took over as French army commander in Ain Sefra just over the Algerian frontier. Lyautey was a distinguished colonial officer and a theoretician of colonial penetration. His big idea, based on experience in Vietnam and Madagascar, was the 'oil slick'. The army would build posts on the edge of as-yet-uncolonised regions. These would show off French military power, and provide security, safe markets, and medical facilities that would win hearts and minds. Then French control would spread forward and the process would begin again. This apparently peaceful policy was backed by superior weapons and excellent intelligence.[76]

In October Lyautey decided to occupy the Moroccan settlement of Béchar, a base for attacks on French forces. After a storm of protest in the French press, and Moroccan complaints to the Quai d'Orsay, Lyautey withdrew his troops but it was clear that they would be back.[77]

Then came another blow. The French government forced the Banque de Paris et des Pays Bas consortium and Schneider and Company to organise a joint loan for Morocco. The *wazir* Gharnit, unable to play one company off against the other, had to accept most unfavourable terms. In June 1904 a new loan of 62.5 million francs was agreed, guaranteed by holding back 65% of Moroccan customs receipts for the next thirty-five years; agents of the French bank gained financial oversight of the customs houses. French officials now had the same sort of relationship with the Moroccan administration as the British had in Egypt, a veiled protectorate, and the Quai d'Orsay quickly prepared a programme of reforms of the economy, administration and army. In January 1905 a French mission led by Saint-Réné-Taillandier arrived in Fez to present this plan to a horrified sultan. Moulay Abdelaziz and Gharnit turned to the '*ulama* for support.[78]

Resistance to French influence

At the beginning of December, Moulay Abdelaziz had asked the Fasi '*ulama* for a *fatwa* concerning the employment of foreigners.

Maroc, 1912-1926, 3 vols (Paris: L'Harmattan, 1988), 1:177.

76 Bidwell, *Morocco*, 15-16.

77 Burke, *Prelude*, 75-6; Douglas Porch, *The Conquest of Morocco* (New York: Alfred A. Knopf, 1983), 74-6, 133-6; Dunn, *Resistance*, 204-9; Charles-André Julien, *Le Maroc face aux impérialismes, 1415-1956* (Paris: Éditions Jeune-Afrique, 1978), 50.

78 Burke, *Prelude*, 73-84; Allain, *Agadir*, 27-9; Parsons, *Morocco Question*, 518-19.

As he hoped, they replied that foreigners were the root of all the country's troubles and that the European advisors in the army should be dismissed. The sultan was less content when a delegation of '*ulama* went on to insist that he sever relations with France completely and dismiss Mohammed Guebbas and ibn Sulayman. This was much more than the Sultan wanted, and represented the views of more radical elements among the '*ulama*, led by Muhammad bin Abdalkabir al-Kittani, the founder of the last big *tariqa* to appear in Morocco. The members of the Kittaniyya were tribesmen, artisans and the urban poor attracted by el-Kittani's austere version of Islam.[79]

Al-Kittani was an old friend of the Sultan, who had paid for his pilgrimage to Mecca in 1903-4, but when he returned to Morocco he campaigned against the French reform proposals and by February 1905 was calling for *jihad*. In short, while he agreed with the Sultan's efforts to resist the French, he was not a tame '*alim*. The Sultan needed more malleable supporters.

He found them by convoking a Council of Notables (*majlis al-'ayan*) in late 1904, for which he cast his net much wider than the usual '*ulama* who provided *fatwas*. The invitation was sent to urban notables and merchants and to leaders of rural tribes, although it was very vague about the council's purpose:

> In the face of a matter of extreme importance we have been moved to write to all the tribes of our country so that each should name someone in whom they have confidence, from among the chiefs and notables, and that they should freely accept the best among them as their delegates, and send them to our royal residence to meet with the other notables of the country in order to deal with negotiations designed to find a remedy to this painful and important affair.[80]

Nothing was said about what the council was to discuss, largely because it was not meant to discuss anything. It was expected to echo the Sultan's objections to the French plans and thus lend them extra weight. Saint-Réné-Taillandier knew this and refused to allow the *majlis* to examine his proposals, though he did permit fifteen of its members to listen to his exposition, provided that they asked no questions.

The council's opposition to the French proposals allowed Moulay Abdelaziz to formally reject them, on 28 May, claiming that 'It

79 Burke, *Prelude*, 38, 78-80; Cagne, *Nation et nationalisme*, 394.

80 Quoted in Cagne, *Nation et nationalisme*, 407.

has not been possible for His Majesty to oppose the people.' He then suggested an international conference to discuss the Morocco question, a proposal that the *majlis* had made, although the idea came from Berlin.[81]

The conference at Algeciras

In Germany, the government was so perturbed by the Entente Cordiale that it decided to undermine it. The agreement on Morocco was a good place to begin, and a striking symbolic gesture became necessary. Kaiser Wilhelm II, who was cruising in the Mediterranean, stopped off at Tangier on 31 March 1905 and, after meeting representatives of the Makhzan and parading among the cheering populace, made speeches that reaffirmed the German commitment to the sovereignty of Morocco. His government followed with a demand for an international conference.[82]

If the German government hoped that the conference would internationalise the Morocco question, the Quai d'Orsay outflanked it by accepting the proposal and ensuring that the conference, far from limiting their room for manoeuvre, would widen it. The British government, a faithful ally, brought Madrid and Rome into line by pointing out that otherwise they risked losing their allotments in Libya and northern Morocco. Since the German government would not risk war, German and French diplomats eventually agreed on terms of reference that ensured that the French had won before the conference even started.

The conference began in the small southern Spanish port of Algeciras on 14 January 1906. On 7 April the final Act of Algeciras was agreed by the eleven European delegations, the US delegation and the Moroccans. The 123 articles were supposed to ensure 'order, peace and prosperity' in Morocco, and to preserve the sovereignty and territorial integrity of the sultan's dominions; no European country would predominate.[83] The reality was quite different.

To bring about 'order, peace, and prosperity' the European powers laid down a programme of reforms. The priority, as ever, was given to opening Moroccan markets. Foreigners received yet more rights to own property; export taxes on agricultural goods

81 Allain, *Agadir*, 32-3; Burke, *Prelude*, 84-5; Parsons, *Morocco Question*, 523-4.

82 Allain, *Agadir*, 32-3; Burke, *Prelude*, 84-5; Parsons, *Morocco Question*, 523-4.

83 *General Act of the Algeciras Conference relating to the Affairs of Morocco (Great Britain, Austria-Hungary, Belgium, France, Germany, Italy, Morocco, Netherlands, Portugal, Russia, Spain, Sweden, United States). Signed at Algeciras, April 7, 1906.*

were reduced; and import duties would be set by an international commission with a majority of European members. A three-man commission, two of them Europeans, would oversee the customs service. In the ports, a police force, manned by Moroccans, 'under the sovereign authority of his majesty the Sultan', would be commanded by a Swiss inspector-general with French and Spanish officers. The same illusion of sovereignty was maintained in the new state bank that would issue currency, act as the state treasury, and negotiate loans. A Moroccan High Commissioner would attend meetings of the board, but he would not be allowed to interfere. All employees would be citizens of the states that contributed the capital, which meant French control, since three quarters of the capital was French. Presented with a *fait accompli*, on 18 June 1906 the Sultan ratified an Act that removed his ability to make policy.

The consequences of Algeciras

One objective of the Act of Algeciras was to open the Moroccan economy to European participation. The giants of European industry quickly prepared their ground. The Compagnie Marocaine (a subsidiary of the French Schneider company) won contracts to build the port works at Casablanca and Safi in 1907,[84] but otherwise it was mining companies that were quickest off the mark. In 1907-8 two mining companies were founded in Spain (Compañía Norte Africano and Sociedad Española de Minas del Rif) and one in France (Union des Mines Marocaines). The French company was a cartel of some major names of European capitalism: Schneider, Krupp, and Guest, Keen, Nettlefolds; the Compañía Norte Africano was legally Spanish, but most of its capital was French; only the Minas del Rif company was purely Spanish – closely linked to Catalan capitalists and the Spanish Liberal Party, it could rely on government support in a crisis.[85]

Nevertheless, trade actually shrank in 1906/7 because of a brief recession in Europe and very poor harvests in Morocco. When in 1908 it started to grow again, the balance stayed firmly in the red. It was now that the French share of external trade overtook the British, making up more than 50% of the total, with about 30% of it coming across the Algerian frontier.[86]

84 Allain, *Agadir*, 140-1.

85 *Ibid.*, 79-84.

86 *Ibid.*, 166-73.

Thus the Act of Algeciras, which was supposed to open Moroccan trade to all European countries, principally benefited French commerce. Despite its Swiss inspector-general and some Spanish participation, the police force was controlled by French officers, regulated according to a French model and armed with French weapons. There were French agents in the customs houses, and the French military mission was re-established.[87] The other objectives of the Act, to ensure 'order, peace and prosperity', went by the board too. The Moroccan population stayed poor and the countryside and cities collapsed into disorder as the country lurched towards revolution.

The origins of revolution

The Act of Algeciras appalled many Moroccans who concluded that the only solution was to overthrow the Sultan. The obvious replacement was Moulay Abdelhafid, the Sultan's brother, who was *khalifa* of Marrakesh. He not only ruled the southern capital, but his mother came from an important family in the Chaouïa and he had good relations with Si Madani El Glaoui with whom he had spent the winter of 1904-5 huddled together discussing ways of preserving the 'security of Islam'. Above all he had good credentials both as a scholar and an opponent of the Europeans, for he had studied under Ma al-Aynayn.[88] He would make an excellent Sultan. Moulay Abdelhafid was too prudent to act quickly. He preferred to prepare the ground, and he spent 1906 building up alliances with local leaders. He even joined a *tariqa*, the Rimayya, noted for its dislike of Christians. But events carried him towards revolution, whether he was ready or not.

By 1907 a large part of the Moroccan population faced starvation. Locusts ate the crops in 1905 and 1906 and then the rains failed. Country people poured down into the ports where only the charity of European humanitarians, who rushed in grain, ensured that they did not die. But European charity did not lessen the general resentment of people who saw more and more of their land taken from them. Already by 1906 European protégés owned about 30% of all land within 50 km. of Tangier, and French companies bought up huge areas around Casablanca.[89]

Some of the poor expressed their frustration in individual acts

87 *Ibid.*, 207-9; Burke, *Prelude*, 89.

88 Burke, *Prelude*, 99-101; Martin, *Quatre siècles*, 397, 416.

89 Godfrey, 'Overseas trade', 293-6.

of violence: murders of and attacks on Europeans increased. In March 1907 a French doctor named Emile Mauchamp was murdered by a mob in Marrakesh.[90] In other cities, the poor rioted. The atmosphere in Casablanca was very tense: its population had grown rapidly in only a few years, and it was now the main port of Morocco, but there were no jobs for the people of the Chaouïa who had lost their land, for most of the port workers were Susis. Then, in July 1907, engineers of the Compagnie Marocaine that was building the port, started to construct a light railway through a cemetery. A train was derailed and rioting spilled through the town. The incidents in Marrakesh and Casablanca were eclipsed by the French response. On 26 March 1907 Lyautey retaliated against the murder of Dr Mauchamp by marching his troops into Oujda. On 30 July a French cruiser, the *Galilée,* stationed itself off Casablanca and shelled the town. The rioters sacked the European quarter, and the *Galilée* landed 2,000 colonial troops supposedly to restore order; instead, they joined in the pillage.[91]

Ellis Ashmead-Bartlett, a British war correspondent, described what he saw when it was all over:

> In the villa of Mr Murdoch, which I visited some days afterwards, the destruction was so complete that even the ivory had been stripped off the notes of the piano and the wires carried away. Not a chair or a table or a piece of pottery that had not been smashed to atoms, and anything that could not be removed had been wantonly destroyed.[...]The villa was first looted by the Moors, then by the townspeople, and afterwards the Foreign Legion and the Tirailleurs took anything that was left. I was gazing with wonder and disgust on the savage scene, when on the mantelpiece an object caught my eye, which alone had escaped the general destruction. It was a red book of great size and thickness, highly emblazoned, and the edges of the leaves covered with gold. I wondered what it could be, and why it had survived when all else had been destroyed. I picked it up, and found that it was an obsolete copy of 'Debrett's Peerage'; and it was not until I saw this record of the House of Peers had been respected and had remained inviolate amidst these hordes of barbarians, that I fully realised the innate

90 Burke, *Prelude*, 92; Julien, *Imperialismes*, 71.

91 Burke, *Prelude*, 96-98; Porch, *Morocco*, 147-59; André Adam, *Casablanca. Essai sur la transformation de la société marocaine au contact de l'Occident*, 2 vols (Paris: Centre national de la recherche scientifique, 1968), 27-8.

strength of the British Constitution, and how difficult it is to bring about a change.[92]

The irony of this moving scene was that Britain and its constitution were irrelevant. The French were in charge now and the response of their troops to Moroccan rioters who ripped apart pianos in the hopes of extirpating foreign influence was to join in the plunder and the pillage.

The revolution of Moulay Abdelhafid

As Moulay Abdelaziz's Makhzan collapsed, Ahmad El Raisuni, the bandit *sharif* of the Jebala, kidnapped Kaid Maclean. As usual, el Raisuni offered his captive unlimited hunting, good food, and even had a set of bagpipes brought up from Tangier to amuse the depressed Scot. But the *sharif* was adamant about the ransom: he insisted on being given British protected status, and this he was granted.[93]

The Sultan had lost control. When he sent a new pasha to Marrakesh, the Rehamna, the main tribe of the Haouz, rose in revolt and demanded that Moulay Abdelhafid claim the sultanate. In August the Chaouïa tribes around Casablanca sent him a letter to the same effect. Finally, Moulay Abdelhafid hesitated no longer. Encouraged by his mother, he announced on 16 August 1907 that he would accept the Sultanate if offered it and Si Madani El Glaoui at once proclaimed him.[94]

ABDELHAFID'S MOROCCO

The euphoria surrounding the proclamation hid the many different objectives of those who supported Moulay Abdelhafid. Sharifs and *'ulama*, who were taxed for the first time, fulminated against the *tartib; jaysh* tribes objected to paying taxes too, and rebelled. People in and around Casablanca saw Europeans and their *protégés* buying up land; they responded by rioting. Townspeople in Marrakesh watched in disgust as Europeans sauntered where they had never dared to walk before and how, when they were murdered, their assassins were dragged from sanctuary and executed. What united these people was disdain for an illegitimate sultan who was dependent upon the Christian Europeans.

92 Ellis Ashmead-Bartlett, *The Passing of the Shereefian Empire* (Edinburgh: Blackwood, 1910),48-9.

93 Arnaud, Mehallas, 226-8; Forbes, *Raisuni*, 83-95.

94 Burke, *Prelude*, 106.

The murder of Dr Mauchamp, Marrakesh, 1907.
Sensationalised in the French press, it provided the pretext for the occupation of Oujda by troops commanded by Lyautey.
Source: News magazine (author's collection).

The Events of 1907-9
Above Train on the railway linking Melilla with the iron ore mines at Seghanghan. (Postcard, c. 1908, author's collection.)
It was attacks on these workings and on the railway line that led to the Spanish invasion of north-western Morocco in 1909.
Below Casablanca after the French bombardment, 1907. (Postcard, author's collection)

Salem el-Abdi later declared that Moulay Abdelhafid was an opportunist.[95] El-Abdi was a French apologist, of course, but it was certainly true that no one could control such disparate groups, and he did not even have the support of all the *'ulama* in Marrakesh. The chief qadi only signed the first *bay'a* at the point of Madani El Glaoui's pistol, or at the points of his henchmen's daggers according to another version.[96]

Not surprisingly, Moulay Abdelhafid preferred to rely on personal loyalties and ties of kin rather than on such an unstable coalition. Soon after he was proclaimed, he married a daughter of Si Madani El Glaoui and a daughter of Muha u Hammu al-Zayyani, whose powerful Zaïane confederation controlled the road to Fez.[97] He then built up a Makhzan of big qaids. El Glaoui was Minister for War, Aissa ibn Umar al-Abdi, Pasha of Safi and head of the Abda confederation, was Minister of Foreign Affairs, and El Mtouggi was *wazir al-shikayat.*[98]

Moulay Abdelhafid was a politician, not a military commander. He stayed in Marrakesh, organising fund-raising missions to Germany and trying to convince visiting French journalists that he was not really anti-French: a forlorn hope, but hardly the action of a rampant jihadist.[99] It was his energetic cousin, Moulay Muhammad bin al-Rashid, who led 3,000 men to the Chaouïa in mid-September. Moulay Abdelaziz's army, led by Bouchta el-Baghdadi, melted away when those men who were not caught in the mud deserted and sold their guns to the rebels. Moulay Abdelaziz decided that his life was in danger and on 12 September he moved to Rabat and the protection of the French fleet.[100]

By November many northern tribes had declared for Moulay Abdelhafid and on 15 December, rebels forced their way into Fez, converged with the mob and sacked the tax houses, the markets, the French Post office and the Jewish *millah.* The ringleaders were the artisans, the tanners, shoemakers and weavers whose spiritual leader was Muhammad bin Abdalkabir al-Kittani. When the mob reached the Qarawiyyin, other *'ulama* were forced to support them. After two weeks of calm, there was more rioting on 30 December and the *'ulama* signed a *fatwa* deposing Moulay Abdelaziz. On

95 Arnaud, *Mehallas*, 233.

96 Munson, *Religion and Power*, 67-8.

97 Arnaud, *Mehallas*, 245.

98 Burke, *Prelude*, 107.

99 *Ibid.*, 112.

100 Burke, *Prelude*, 108-11.

3 or 4 January 1908, they approved a *bay'a* proclaiming Moulay Abdelhafid. Not all of them did so willingly, as even al-Kattani's supporters admitted.[101]

The *ba'ya* bluntly stated what was usually only implied, that the sultan's rule was conditional. It began conventionally enough by declaring that Moulay Abdelhafid was fit to occupy the caliphate and the imamate. Significantly, the title of Sultan was not mentioned, for this *bay'a* sought a new model of government, one that recast the leadership of the state in terms of the early Islamic caliphate.[102] Like Moulay Abdelaziz, the signatories sought to replace the old model with a new one, although theirs was intended not as modernisation of the system, but its recasting in an ancient mould. It was no longer a recognition of the Sultan's power – rather, it conferred power upon him – more a vague demand that he should work for the good of the community, the requirement that was emphasized. This was a programme of action with specific policies: to take care of the organisation of armies and the defence of the strongholds on the coast. 'He must do his best to repair the damage done to his subjects by the Act of Algeciras, even more so since the community has not approved its conditions and has not recognised the legality of those who represented it.'[103]

It continued in the same bald prescriptive way: the border regions, Oujda and Casablanca must be recovered; protection must be ended; the Sultan should only seek advice from the Ottomans or other independent Muslim states; concessions, monopolies and *maks* taxes must be suppressed; honest men should be appointed to religious offices; unjust governors should be dismissed; saints, *sharifs* and the *'ulama* should be honoured. In short 'He must be merciful, wise and seek only to do good. His subjects know that they will only survive the crisis that faces them through the solicitude of the Sultan.'[104] Muhammad bin Abdalkabir el-Kittani and his supporters had not consulted Moulay Abdelhafid before they framed these demands. Like all utopias, this one was impossible to fulfill.

The bay'a compromised

Moulay Abdelhafid could not break relations with the Europeans,

101 Munson, *Religion and Power*, 70-1; Cagne, *Nation et nationalisme*, 422; Burke, *Prelude*, 93-117.

102 Hammoudi, *Master and Disciple*, 66-7.

103 The text of the *bay'a* is in Cagne, *Nation et nationalisme*, 437-44.

104 Quoted in *ibid.*, 455-6.

since he did not have any. As far as European capitals were concerned, Moulay Abdelaziz was still the legitimate Sultan and all the income from the customs went to his hands. In order to secure the recognition of the European powers, and so defeat his brother, Abdelhafid had to make compromises that amounted to a rejection of the *bay'a.*

The first compromise was with his father-in-law, Muha u-Hammu al-Zayyani, who eased his passage along the difficult route through the Middle Atlas to Meknès and Fez, where he arrived on 2 June. This was a strategic necessity, since it outflanked the increasingly beleaguered Abdelaziz, but in return, he had to make al-Zayyani's son pasha of Fez al-Bali, which was unpopular. The tottering sultan managed a last great effort. He sent a sizeable *mahalla* southwards and it almost reached Marrakesh before it was stopped in a battle at Bu Ajiba on 19 August. Two days later Moulay Abdelaziz fled to Casablanca and abdicated. In October he took out a lease on Walter Harris's old house in Tangier and retired.[105]

More compromises followed, as the rest of Morocco joined the new sultan. By 6 September *bay'as* had been sworn in Safi, Oujda, and El-Jadida. In Tangier, the task was overseen by el-Mennebhi and El Raisuni.[106] El Raisuni explained himself in typically self-righteous terms: 'At that time we all thought Mulai Hafid... was a good Moslem and sincere, so I wrote to him saying that I would proclaim him as Sultan among the tribes, and he agreed, sending me the act of proclamation and ordering me to pitch my camp at Akbar el Hamara in the centre of the country.'[107]

What was really at stake was money. El Raisuni wanted a governorship under the new dispensation and he was not disappointed. He was given Asilah and most of the western Jebala, on condition that he renounce his British protégé status and supply Moulay Abdelhafid with 1.5 million pesetas in taxes. The *sharif* soon recouped his expenses and set about building a beautiful palace by the sea shore in Asilah.[108] One and a half million pesetas were certainly useful, but nowhere near enough. So Abdelhafid ignored the *bay'a*'s principles again. When he reached Fez, he imposed *maks* taxes.[109]

Finally, he sought European diplomatic recognition, in order to receive the customs receipts that were piling up in the Banque

105 Martin, *Quatre Siècles*, 485; Burke, *Prelude*, 118, 122.

106 Martin, *Quatre Siècles*, 490-1, 493.

107 Forbes, *Raisuni*, 97.

108 *Ibid.*, 103-4.

109 Martin, *Quatre Siècles*, 485, 487-99.

d'État. The French government demanded that first he should promise to honour all Moroccan debts, accept the Act of Algeciras and all existing treaties, and write a letter to be read in every mosque in Morocco calling an end to *jihad*. The British and the German governments got the last demand toned down, and on 7 December Moulay Abdelhafid agreed. On 5 January 1909 he was recognised by the diplomatic corps as sultan. Almost a year after the *bay'a* had been sworn in Marrakesh, he had the 12 million francs in the Banque d'État and the enmity of al-Kittani.[110]

Moulay Abdelhafid knew well how dangerous al-Kittani might be and in March 1909 closed down his *zawiya* in Fez. Al-Kittani fled to the Middle Atlas and what he imagined was the security of the Ait Ndhir, where he had many followers. But he also had enemies there, who caught him and sent him back to the capital in chains, where shortly afterwards he was flogged to death.[111]

He was buried at night to avoid trouble, but other enemies of the regime were dealt with very publicly. The Sultan's brother Moulay Mahammad, that perennial alternative Sultan, escaped and took refuge with the Zaër tribe, near Rabat. They proclaimed him Sultan in October 1908, but he was quickly recaptured, brought to Fez in chains and paraded in rags through the city and the palace before disappearing again into oblivion. Rumours spread that he had been killed, although he survived until 1946.[112] His secretary during his brief rebellion was publicly tortured in the palace courtyard: in front of a large crowd, his beard was plucked out, his head shaved and his hands were disabled by the salt torture. He was then led away to die.[113]

Two months earlier, in August 1909, Abu Himara had been destroyed with equally spectacular violence. He had over-reached himself, for after settling in Selouane in 1902 he had slowly run out of money (a problem that afflicted real sultans too). In 1907 he sold two concessions in the Banu Bu Ifrur near Melilla to Spanish companies: the Norte de Africa company was allowed to mine lead, and the Minas del Rif company to mine iron. He also permitted both companies to construct railways to take the ore to Melilla. In August 1908 Abu Himara tried to occupy the central Rif, where there were supposed to be more minerals, but

110 *Ibid.*, 498-500; Burke, *Prelude*, 138.

111 Burke, *Prelude*, 133-4; Burke, 'Ait Ndhir', 136-7; Munson, *Religion and Power*, 74.

112 Burke, *Prelude*, 130; Martin, *Quatre Siècles*, 499; Arnaud, *Mehallas*, 260.

113 Lawrence Harris, *With Mulai Hafid at Fez* (London: Smith, Elder, 1909), 145.

the Banu Waryaghal, the most powerful tribe in the region, threw him out. In a final effort he moved on Fez 'to begin again his old comedy' as Salem el-Abdi scathingly put it.[114] Moulay Abdelhafid captured him, and after many of his troops had been publicly tortured to death in a variety of horrible ways, Abu Himara himself was brought into the capital in a cage. After being kept on public view for a fortnight he was thrown to the lions in the royal menagerie. They were too well fed to do more than maul him, so eventually a servant put him out of his misery and his body was burned.[115]

Humanitarians in Europe were appalled. Newspapers in France and Britain heaped opprobrium on the Sultan and organisations like the Howard League for Penal Reform in London campaigned vigorously for greater European control over Morocco.[116] Moulay Abdelhafid refused to give way. For him the appalling punishments were not only a way of punishing his enemies, but spectacular proof of his sovereign power.[117]

Salafiyya

The limitations it placed on his sovereign power were good reason for the new Sultan to dislike the *bay'a.* In fact, its provisions went further than most *'ulama* desired, for religious reformers in Morocco tended to focus their attention on matters of personal behaviour rather than become involved in political activism.

The roots of religious reformism in Morocco stretched back to the later decades of the previous century. Scholars and travellers who returned from pilgrimage brought back the teachings of the Egyptian scholar Muhammad Abduh and his disciple Rashid Rida, and copies of their famous journals, *al-Urwa al-Wuthqa* and *al-Manar.* Abduh and Rida taught that the only way to overcome European domination was to return to a genuine Islam, the Islam of the 'virtuous forefathers', *al-salaf al-salih,* hence the name Salafiyya.[118]

114 Arnaud, *Mehallas*, 272.

115 *Ibid.*, 272; Burke, *Prelude*, 136-7; Hart, *Aith Waryaghar*, 363-7; Ross E. Dunn, 'France, Spain' 156-7; *idem.*, 'The Bu Himara Rebellion'; Maldonado, *Rogui*, 346ff; Seddon, *Moroccan Peasants*, 109; Garcia-Figueras, *Acción*, 2:268; Carlos Martinez de Campos, *España Bélica el Siglo XX Marruecos* (Madrid: Aguilar, 1969), 63. There are numerous accounts of the capture and death of Abu Himara. An overview is in Porch, *Morocco*, 207-11.

116 Mackenzie, *Khalifate*,113-35.

117 Cf. Rejali, *Torture*, 26-7, 177.

118 John P. Halstead, *Rebirth of a Nation: the Origins and Rise of Moroccan Nationalism*

Some of the Salafis' teachings were quite controversial in Morocco, for they condemned the Sufi brotherhoods and maraboutism. When one of the first men to be inspired by the Salafiyya, Abdallah bin Idris al-Sanusi, returned from pilgrimage in the 1870s and began to preach strict conformity to the *shari'a*, some '*ulama* were horrified and accused him of denying sainthood and miracles. Although he had the patronage of Moulay Hassan, they forced him into exile. Moulay Abdelaziz recalled him, and even after the abdication of this sultan, who was notorious for his inclination towards the Europeans, he and el-Sanusi remained on good terms. El-Sanusi believed that personal faith and conduct were more important than political action.[119]

Even firebrand Salafis like Muhammad bin Jafar al-Kittani posed no great danger to the Sultan. In 1908 this son of the man who presented the anti-European demands to Moulay Abdelaziz and cousin of the founder of the Kittaniyya, published *Nasihatahl al-Islam* (Frank Guidance to the People of Islam), a virulent attack on the 'enemies of Islam', the Europeans, who should be opposed by *jihad*, and on unjust rulers, who had reneged on their duty to lead and were unfit to remain in power. According to him, all rulers were liable to be corrupt and all *marabouts* were suspect. *Al-Nasiha* was one of the most widely-read books in early twentieth-century Morocco, not least because at least 600 copies were printed rather than distributed in manuscript. Among those who read it and became close to its author was the future Rifi leader, Muhammad bin Abd al-Karim al-Khattabi, who studied at the Qarawiyyin. Yet while al-Kittani criticised marabouts and sultans, he also wrote a book praising saints and worked on a guide to *hadith* literature that Abdelhafid proposed. This last effort may have been self-preservation. At first he refused to have anything to do with Abdelhafid, but when the new sultan flogged his cousin to death, he changed his mind. Even so, he did not stay long at court; in 1910, believing that the French were about to occupy Morocco, he moved to Madina. For all his fiery writing, Muhammad bin Jafar al-Kittani chose migration in order to avoid living under non-Muslim rule over the duty to fight *jihad*, and did nothing to persuade the Sultan otherwise.[120]

1912-1944, (Cambridge, MA: Harvard University Centre for Middle Eastern Studies, 1969), 119-22; Munson, *Religion and Power*, 101-2; Cagne, *Nation et nationalisme*, 170-5; on Abduh and Rida, see Albert Hourani, *Arabic Thought in the Liberal Age* (Oxford University Press, 1970), 130-160 and 222-4.

119 Munson Religion and Power, 86-7.

120 *Ibid.*, 87-95, 98.

Moulay Abdelhafid also won the support of another quietist Salafi, Abu Shuayb al-Dukkali. He had returned to Morocco around the time of Moulay Abdelhafid's revolt, after having studied at al-Azhar mosque in Cairo and then serving the Sharif of Mecca. He too preached in the Qarawiyyin on the need for a literal interpretation of the Quran and *hadith*, but he insisted Muslims must not fight the French. Since they could not win, it would only lead to more Islamic territory being occupied; a realistic approach, but hardly a radical one. In response, Moulay Abdelhafid showered him with money, a house and the job of *qadi*.[121]

In general, these activist Salafis emphasised correct personal conduct over *jihad*, a school of thought with which Moulay Abdelhafid had a good deal of sympathy. He too was a scholar, concerned to implement the *shari'a*, but as Sultan he knew that *jihad* would make matters worse. Moulay Abdelhafid's attitude to Sufism was similarly ambivalent. After being deposed, he swore to be the Sufi disciple of Muhammad bin Jafar al-Kittani, although he had crushed his cousin's *tariqa*.[122]

Constitutional nationalism

The alternative to religious reform was political nationalism. In 1905 the Japanese destroyed the Russian fleet and showed that an 'eastern' nation could defeat a 'modern western' one. To many Asian and African nationalists it was the Japanese constitution that was the key to success, and a constitution became their goal too. Iranian nationalists drew up a constitution in 1906 and two years later the army of the Ottoman Empire forced Sultan Abdülhamit II to reinstate the constitution that he had suspended in 1878.

Detailed knowledge of constitutional ideas was very rare in Morocco. Only a few Egyptian nationalist and constitutionalist newspapers circulated although among their readers were members of the El Mokri family who were about to rise to great prominence.[123] In 1908 Moulay Abdelhafid encouraged a short-lived newspaper, *al-Fajr*, edited by a Syrian Christian, and two other Syrian Christians, the brothers Arthur and Faraj-Allah Nemour, produced another Arabic-language paper in Tangier, *Lisan al-Maghrib*.[124]

121 *Ibid.*, 87, 98.

122 *Ibid.*, 95; Burke, *Prelude*, 135.

123 Cagne, *Nation et Nationalisme*, 374-5.

124 Berque, *Prelude*; Laroui, *Origines*, 380, n.29; Cagne, *Nation et nationalisme*, 380.

Thus the Ottoman Empire became a land of promise for both a small group of Moroccan reformers and for their Sultan. It was an Islamic great power that was both a counterweight to the European powers and an answer to the demand in the Fez *bay'a* that Moulay Abdelhafid rely on Muslim experts. This was one of the few conditions that he had any real desire to fulfill and he turned for help to the revolutionary Committee of Union and Progress (CUP) government in Istanbul. The CUP was anxious to oblige as part of its attempt to extend its propaganda outside the Ottoman Empire. In southeast Asia this was done through Ottoman consuls, but European pressure ensured that there were none in Morocco, so a military mission was sent instead, in November 1909. It was only in Morocco for a brief period, again because of French pressure, but that was long enough to set in motion a very small constitutionalist movement.[125]

Two constitutions were written, both very shadowy documents indeed. One was never circulated, and its text was only published in 1970. It was clearly modelled on the 1906 constitution of Iran. A consultative council (*majlis al-umma*) made up of elected representatives of tribes and regions would have law-making powers but the sultan would retain final authority. There would be a strong army to protect the country, sound finances administered on European lines, and a legal system in conformity with the *shari'a*. The unknown author was almost certainly an Arab from the east.[126]

The other proposed constitution, published in Tangier in 1910, was more extensive. It established personal liberty, security of property and free primary education. It called for a consultative assembly with an elected chamber, the Council of the Nation (*majlis al-umma*), and an appointed Council of Notables (*majlis al-shurafa*). Together they would oversee the administration and finances, albeit without any legislative power. The Sultan was to wield absolute sovereignty and appoint the ministers. This constitution was clearly based on the restored Ottoman Constitution. It appeared in the *Lisan al-Maghrib*, and its Syrian-Christian editors may even have helped to write it.[127] Half a century later this document would be claimed by the nationalist leadership as part of the constitutional

125 Burke, *Prelude*, 141-2; Jean Deny, 'Instructeurs militaires turcs au Maroc sous Moulay Hafidh' in *Mémorial Henri Basset. Nouvelles études nord-africaines et orientales* (Paris: Geuthner, 1928), 219-27 reproduces the reminiscences of one of the Turkish officers.

126 Cagne, *Nation et Nationalisme*, 479-84; Laroui, *Origines*, 378-80.

127 Burke, *Prelude*, 132; Cagne, *Nation et Nationalisme*, 484-95.

tradition in Morocco, but at the time it had very little resonance. Constitutional theorising, or indeed Salafi activism, was less urgent than the immediate danger of invasion by Spanish and French armies. Moulay Abdelhafid may have been recognised as the Sultan by the European powers, but that did not prevent them from taking over yet more of his territory.

The Spanish and French advance in the east

After Abu Himara's miniature state near Melilla collapsed, local tribes attacked the mine workings and the railway that he had signed away. In July 1909 the Spanish government called up its reserves and moved inland to protect its holdings. Like the war for Tetuan in 1860, this was a very slow affair and it took eighteen months for the Spanish troops to occupy the Guelaya Peninsula and the Banu Bu Ifrur. Their advance was not resisted by regular troops, since Moulay Abdelhafid had refused to send any, but a *sharif* of the Banu Bu Ifrur, Muhammad Amziyyan led a spirited local *jihad.* The Spanish army was inadequately equipped, poorly trained and abysmally led, and it behaved execrably. The British war correspondent Ellis Ashmead-Bartlett described its operations:

> We passed over a splendid, rolling, cultivated plain, dotted with villages and farms, amidst pleasant groves of fig-trees and prickly pears. Each one was visited in turn by detachments of infantry or cavalry and set on fire, whilst the engineers placed dynamite cartridges under the houses, leaving fuses to explode them after the troops had left. In a few hours this beautiful smiling country was nothing but a mass of smoking hamlets, and looked as if some great veldt fire had broken out. This work of destruction was very uncongenial to the Spaniards, and on all sides I heard expressions of regret that the exigencies of war should render it essential: it is, however, part of the price which barbarism pays for the blessing of civilisation.[128]

Such action was unlikely to win the hearts and minds of local people, although the Spanish army needed to do just that. By calling up the reservists, the government sparked an anarchist rising in Barcelona, the *Semana Trágica,* that brought it down. After that, the government refused to commit troops to fight in Morocco,[129] so the army was forced to adopt political tactics that

128 Ashmead-Bartlett, *Passing*, 428.

129 Pennell, *Government and Flag*, 41-2; Martínez de Campos, *España Bélica*, 62-116; García Figueras, Acción, 2:313-61; Germain Ayache, *Les origines de la guerre du Rif*

were vaguely similar to Lyautey's oil-slick, though not as well organised. In this endeavour, smoking hamlets did not help.

To be sure, Spanish military intelligence did win over some local leaders, including the *qadi* of the biggest tribe of the central Rif, the Banu Waryaghal. Abd al-Karim al-Khattabi had supported Moulay Abdelhafid in 1908 and obtained a *bay'a* for the new Sultan from his tribe, but Muhammad his eldest son, after studying at the Qarawiyyin, had entered Spanish service in 1907 as a *qadi* of the Muslim community in Melilla. Muhammad would later inflict on the Spanish army the most serious defeat of a colonial army in twentieth century Africa, but other recruits to the Spanish proved more constant. In the Banu Bu Yahyi tribe, the Spanish army educated the son of an important shaykh, Mohamed ben Mizian, gave him military training and a commission. Eventually, he rose to the rank of general and after independence became the first chief of staff of the Moroccan army.[130]

Similar things were happening around Tafilalt. In July 1907 a local *jihad* had begun, quite disastrously, as it proved, for it encouraged the French to advance. When Moulay Abdelhafid was proclaimed, he won many supporters, although they were disappointed by his letter telling them to stop the *jihad*. Scattered fighting and raiding continued, but there was no leader.

Lyautey spread his oil-slick of French influence. Among the people he attracted to the French cause was a previously insignificant man, Mohammed Oufkir, who eventually won himself a prime position in the protectorate administration. His son served in the French army and became Minister of Defence in the Moroccan government after independence.[131] Even before the French and Spanish had taken over Morocco, the foundations of the post-colonial state were being laid.

The economic crisis

While French and Spanish troops nibbled at Moroccan territory, European creditors drained the treasury. Moulay Abdelhafid could not fulfil his *bay'a* by recovering the lost lands, nor by ending the debt.

The new sultan needed money. He had recognised the Act of Algeciras, which had undermined his authority, but customs

(Rabat: SMER, 1981), 137-9.

130 Pennell, *Government and Flag*, 49-50.

131 Dunn, *Resistance*, 230-42.

dues alone were not enough. Abdelhafid needed foreign loans. Between January and April 1909 negotiations in Fez and in Paris produced a proposal to reorganise the Moroccan debt, at the price of increased French control over the Chaouïa and Oujda where only the fiction of Makhzan authority would be maintained. The sultan refused to accept these conditions, under the illusion that international recognition and the defeat of Abu Himara had made him more secure, but in February 1910 the French government put an end to his tergiversations. It demanded that he accept the accord within forty-eight hours, or French troops would seize the customs houses in Casablanca, Rabat and Azemmour, and yet more territory on the eastern frontier. Moulay Abdelhafid agreed at once. On 3 March 1910 the accords were signed in Paris.[132]

The new accords required the Makhzan to pay the costs of the French occupation of Casablanca and Oujda, and allowed French officers to organise local government there. They had already begun to recruit Moroccans for new regiments of the French colonial army (*goums*), where they mixed men from different tribes. More land would be made available to foreigners. The loan drained the Sultan's treasury still further. For 90 million francs, the Makhzan renounced to the French the remaining forty per cent of customs revenues that it still controlled, all indirect taxes, all receipts on state monopolies (tobacco and cannabis) and all receipts on Makhzan lands within 10 km. of the coast. Only Makhzan receipts from the *tartib* and traditional gifts to the Sultan by the tribes remained.[133] Since neither of these amounted to much, the Sultan's financial autonomy had now ended.

The French take-over

As if to celebrate the end of the Makhzan's control of finances, foreign trade roared ahead, almost doubling (to 227 million francs) between 1910 and 1912, but the trade deficit grew from 15 million to 130 million francs between 1911 and 1912, with French commerce accounting for more than half of the total.[134]

Yet more foreigners flocked to Morocco. Even Australians con-

132 Burke, *Prelude*, 138-43; Allain, *Agadir*, 49-57.

133 Burke, *Prelude*, 144; Driss Maghraoui, 'Moroccan Colonial Soldiers: between Selective Memory and Collective memory', *Arab Studies Quarterly*, 20, no. 2 (1998): 21-42.

134 Allain, *Agadir*, 170-2.

sidered buying land to farm sheep, timber and wheat; an Australian report of 1911 praised almost everything except the 'natives',

> [an] indolent, lazy lot, much given to talk and little work, and they must have degenerated from former times ... the native people form the greatest obstacle in the way of the rapid development of the country: they are in possession of the land in large numbers and how to get them off and turn it to the best account is, I consider, the greatest problem that will have to be solved.[135]

The problem, so redolent of home, was being solved at that very moment. By 1911 Europeans, mainly French and Germans, owned 9,140 hectares in the area around Casablanca.[136]

At the same time French interests seized control of the Moroccan government. In the summer of 1910 there was a new Makhzan, dominated by the El Mokri family. Mohammed ben Abdesselam El Mokri, who as Minister of Finance had negotiated the Paris accords, became minister for foreign affairs; one son, El-Taïeb became minister of finance, another, Mukhtar, became Pasha of Tangier and a third, Ahmad, became pasha of Fez. Only the *wazir*, Madani El Glaoui, was not pro-French.[137] The French delegate on the customs board, Gaston Guiot, took control of administration and recruitment.[138] In the countryside French occupation forces in the Chaouïa extended their political control.[139] In November 1910 a new French military mission led by Colonel Emile Mangin, began restructuring and retraining the Moroccan army. He appointed French officers in the cavalry and artillery, but the infantry was less malleable, so Mangin stood it down and re-employed only those he thought reliable. The troops chafed at his strict discipline and found that even though Mangin tried to ensure that they were paid regularly, they were financially worse off.[140]

By 1911 French banks controlled the Makhzan's finances, French armies occupied large parts of the countryside, and French officials much of the administration. But the Sultan's subjects were beyond control.

135 HAC Webb to R Tilden Smith, 1911, National Library of Australia Ms1576.

136 Mohamed Salahdine, *Maroc: tribus, makhzen et colons, essai d'histoire économique et sociale* (Paris: L'Harmattan, 1986), 59.

137 Allain, *Agadir*, 196; Laroui, *Origines*, 406; Burke, *Prelude*, 153-4.

138 Allain, *Agadir*, 200-1.

139 Burke, *Prelude*, 156.

140 Porch, *Morocco*, 213-17; Burke, *Prelude*, 148-9.

The revolt in the north and the French occupation of Fez

Since nearly all regular taxes went to the French, Moulay Abdelhafid tried to raise extraordinary levies. His position was now worse than that of his brother in 1908, for he had reneged on the ideological expectations that had brought him to power. He soon faced a rebellion much like that he himself had led. The political situation was turning full circle.

In the Middle Atlas, south of Fez, the Ait Ndhir still resented the murder of al-Kittani. When, in January 1911, French officers executed two soldiers for desertion, that caused more disgust: many of the infantry came from the region. In February the Ait Ndhir organised a meeting attended by representatives of many Middle Atlas tribes who agreed they would kill El Glaoui at the celebrations to mark the birth of the Prophet in March.

The Cherarda revolted prematurely, but when El Glaoui and Mangin set out to crush them a full scale rising ensued. On 11 March the Ait Ndhir besieged Fez, and many northern tribes joined them. They demanded the dismissal of El Glaoui, the abolition of the French military mission, regular and low taxation, the end of new military regulations and qaids that were chosen by their tribes. On 15 April the *'ulama* of Meknès proclaimed a brother of Moulay Abdelhafid, Moulay Zein; the *'ulama* of Sefrou followed their lead in May. His Makhzan was drawn from local notables so it had a predominantly Berber character, although one minister was a British protégé, and another was an old acquaintance of Walter Harris. Fez was now besieged by over 6,000 rebels.[141]

The French government had already decided to intervene. At the end of April a large expeditionary force, much of it made up of Moroccan *goum* troops, had grouped at Kénitra, avowedly to protect the European community trapped in Fez. On 4 May, under pressure from the French Consul in Fez, Henri Gaillard, Moulay Abdelhafid asked for military assistance to relieve the Europeans.[142] The same message was given by General Moinier, the commander of the French column, in a letter to the tribes through whose territory he would have to pass:

> Calm your spirits, O Moslems, and listen to the truth. Yes, we have landed a great number of soldiers and guns, but not to conquer lands, for we have enough. What we wish, for upon

141 Burke, *Prelude*, 157-160, 162; Burke, 'Aith Ndhir', *passim*; Porch, Morocco, 213-15; Laroui, *Origines*, 407-9.

142 Burke, *Prelude*, 163-71; Allain, *Agadir*, 253-77; Porch, *Morocco*, 213-22; Julien, *Imperialismes*, 84-5.

> this we shall never give way, is that our European brothers who live among you no longer have their lives and property threatened. To end these outrages and this violence, His Sharifian Majesty has called upon the harkas of his tribes who have rallied in great numbers. And we are here only to offer our guns to support the defenders of order and of the traditional authority of the country.[143]

This was humbug, for burdened down with a huge supply train, Moinier's column advanced too slowly to end any atrocities. He reached Fez on 21 May.[144] This was not really a humanitarian rescue mission, for French forces went on to occupy Meknès on 8 June, and Rabat on 9 July. Four days after occupying Meknès, General Moinier was ordered *not* to do so, but military commanders were now making policy. The occupation of Fez was no less than a French *coup d'état*, disguised by the support of the Sultan.[145]

The de-internationalisation of the Morocco question

The occupation of Fez was accompanied by a concerted French attempt to de-internationalise the Moroccan question. As the Fez rebellion gathered strength, El Mokri completed negotiations for a new loan. On 13 March a new agreement made more promises to undertake financial reform, to impose the *tartib* in progressive stages, and to institute a programme of public works. The most important promise of all was that, if it proved necessary, the Sultan would call on French troops to restore order: a clause that provided the legal basis for intervention two months later.[146]

While the British government publicly supported its ally, Madrid complained that it had not been consulted over the new loan, and that the French occupation of Fez broke the accords of 1904. It talked of a separate Spanish area in northern Morocco, and after a Spanish protégé was murdered in Larache, Spanish troops were landed there on 8 June. On 12 June they occupied Ksar-el-Kebir as well.[147] This did not greatly worry the French government, but the reaction from Berlin was more disquieting. On 1 July the German government sent a naval cruiser, *Panther*, to Agadir,

143 Quoted in Porch, *Morocco*, 224.

144 *Ibid.*, 225-8.

145 Julien, *Imperialismes*, 85; Porch, *Morocco*, 233.

146 Allain, *Agadir*, 297; Burke, *Prelude*, 165-166.

147 Allain, *Agadir*, 301-10; García Figueras, *Acción* 2:364; Julien, *Imperialismes*, 85; Burke, *Prelude*, 171-2.

supposedly to protect German interests and mineral prospectors in the Sous. This appeared as a threat to occupy the Sous, and the Agadir Incident briefly brought Europe to the brink of war; but with British support, the affair ended peacefully enough. In November 1911 the French government ceded French territory near the Congo River in exchange for a German agreement to a French protectorate in Morocco.[148]

The imposition of the French Protectorate

While the diplomatic road was being paved, construction of the edifice of French power in Morocco had already begun. Having occupied Fez, General Moinier and Consul Gaillard set about rebuilding the Makhzan. Their ideas differed: Gaillard and the Quai d'Orsay believed that the old Morocco should be governed through its own elite and that French troops had officially acted to restore the authority of the Sultan; Moinier, an officer of the Armée d'Afrique, thought that indirect rule was inefficient, and preserved local tyrants in power.[149] Such distinctions were matters of form not substance, masking personal and ministerial rivalries. In the end, Gaillard ensured that the Makhzan did just what he wanted and Moinier imposed obedience in the name of the Sultan.

Gaillard's local elite was of his own making. Si Madani El Glaoui was replaced as *wazir* by Mohammed El Mokri. When told that the Sultan had dismissed him, El Glaoui replied: 'He has dropped me. May God drop him,' and with that curt comment retired to Telouèt. His brother Thami was removed as Pasha of Marrakesh, but became a French *protégé* and was allowed to keep all his property in the city.[150] That generosity laid the basis of future cooperation.

Moinier's troops, acting in the Sultan's name, had defeated Moulay Zein by the middle of June,[151] but the countryside remained disordered. Dr Weisgerber travelled from Marrakesh to Fez in June 1911 and his party was attacked even in the area that was occupied by French troops. He spent

> [...] five hellish days crossing the burned-out plain of the Beni Ahsen and the bare hills of the Cherarda, surrounded for most of the way by a cloud of thick dust, harassed by flies, fleas and mosquitos and above all by the Zemmour who sniped at

148 Burke, *Prelude*, 172; Allain, *Agadir*, 320-420;

149 Porch, *Morocco*, 238; Burke, *Prelude*, 172-3.

150 Burke, *Prelude*, 176-7; Porch 239; Arnaud, *Mehallas*, 300-1.

151 Arnaud, *Mehallas*, 300.

> our Spahis from a few hundred yards off, along a road marked by the bodies of animals so advanced in putrefaction that a blind man could have followed it with ease.[152]

In Fez, he heard talk of local *jihads* in the Middle Atlas and found Mangin hard at work training the Moroccan army.[153] In January 1912 the French government approved the creation of a new Moroccan army of 15,000 men.[154]

On 16 March the French minister in Tangier, Henri Regnault, set out for Fez, carrying the text of a treaty of protectorate. His purpose was not to negotiate and his enormous supply train included 300 bottles of champagne, 1,000 bottles of wine, fifty-four packets of toothpicks and material for a gigantic fireworks display. Obediently, the sultan succumbed, but the protectorate was not the one that he had hoped for. It resembled not the British veiled protectorate in Egypt that would have granted the Makhzan autonomy in areas like justice and administration, but the French protectorate in Tunisia, where the Bey was reduced to a cypher. The Treaty of Fez, which Moulay Abdelhafid signed on 13 March 1912, guaranteed the religious authority of the sultan but did not set out how this was to be secured. It guaranteed the secular sovereignty of the sultan, but delegated all his powers to the protectorate government. It allowed French troops to operate anywhere and gave French administrators control of foreign affairs.[155] It emptied the sultanate of practical content, or so it seemed.

The haemorrhaging Makhzan

In reality, practical content had been seeping out of the Makhzan ever since the death of Moulay Hassan. The old sultan's death had destroyed the basis on which the political system had rested. Ba Ahmad had become powerful because of the patronage of the sultan, and though he was pre-eminent, it was as part of a group that included his rivals the al-Jama'is. In the first weeks of the new and very young Sultan's reign he destroyed those rivals and replaced them with nothing outside himself: he changed from being part of a system of patronage to being its centre. The source of legitimate patronage had gone and what was left was the form of the old system, a simulacrum of Moulay Hassan's policies, and

152 Weisgerber, *Au seuil*, 253.

153 *Ibid.*, 259.

154 Porch, *Morocco*, 240.

155 Burke, *Prelude*, 180-1; Porch, *Morocco*, 240.

the use of force, which became a weapon of weakness, not of strength.

When the *wazir* died, Moulay Abdelaziz attempted to rule according to a new system. That was his inclination, but he had little choice anyway, for his father's system could no longer work. But neither could his new system, for without the networks of patronage, there was no reason for the old clients to cooperate.

The *bay'a* given to Moulay Abdelhafid represented a third model of government, one that was also designed to replace what had been lost. It too was structured in new terms: Moulay Abdelhafid was a caliph but not a sultan. Legitimacy would come not from the possession of power, but from adopting the right policies. But without the power to impose them, this was a hopeless prospect. Abdelhafid himself did not accept the premises of the *bay'a* anyway, and seems to have tried to return to the system that had collapsed, based upon patronage, kin, alliances and force. By doing so, he destroyed his own ideological legitimacy and replaced it with nothing.

All three heads of the Makhzan, the *wazir* and the two sultans, were essentially powerless, because they did not have enough money. Financial power was leeched away by European demands and loans; and the economy on which any Moroccan system would have to be based was progressively taken out of Moroccan hands.

While this was happening, the French and to lesser effect Spanish armies were nibbling away at Moroccan territory in the Sahara. The loss of Touat was the first stage in a process that would define Moroccan frontiers along more restricted lines, leaving the memories of a greater Morocco to be resurrected in the late twentieth century. Apart from this, the European takeover (in a general sense at first then to all practical purposes French) was achieved by indirect means. The exigencies of European diplomacy meant that the French state could only take over Morocco if it pretended otherwise, so treaties were drawn up that preserved Spanish 'rights' and balanced the interests of other European governments. The theoretical obstacle to French rule – the sultanate – became the pre-requisite for their takeover.

The Treaty of Fez gave the French government authority but very little power. The cup it had seized was very nearly empty. To take possession of Morocco, it would have to conquer it.

5

CONQUEST

The conquest of Morocco was not simply a matter of enforcing a military presence: the past few years had shown all too clearly that an army could traverse a region and restore 'order', only for rebellion to flare up as it moved on. What was needed was a transformation of the state itself, its extension not just through military control, but through detailed administrative, social and legal means into every corner of the country. The first paragraph of the Treaty of Fez pronounced: 'The government of the French Republic and His Majesty the Sultan agree to institute in Morocco a new regime that will allow those administrative, judicial, educational, economic, financial and military reforms that the French government will judge useful to be introduced into Moroccan territory.' It went on 'This regime will safeguard the religious conditions, the respect and traditional prestige of the Sultan, the practice of the Muslim religion and the religious institution, particularly the religious endowments.'[1]

That first article not only set out the nature of the changes that would be put into place, but also separated them into two parts: modernisation and preservation of the past, with the first decided upon solely by the French authorities, and the second made contingent upon their presence. That duality would mark every political relationship under the protectorate until the modern and the pre-colonial state became fused in the independence struggle.

Over the previous half-century Moroccan Sultans had tried to reformulate the political and economic system. They had failed because no Makhzan that operated on lines of clientage and kinship as well as force and patronage could simultaneously alter relationships and survive. The amounts of force and money that it could mobilise were never sufficient. But now that had changed: the French protectorate could call upon, and even form from Moroccan men, a modern well-equipped army that depended not on the

[1] See text of the Treaty of Fez in Moulay Abdelhadi Alaoui, *Le Maroc du traité de Fès à la libération, 1912-1956* (Rabat: La Porte, 1994), 247-8.

acquiescence of tribal leaders bought by patronage, but on wages paid to soldiers. It could also change the nature of patronage to a much simpler formula: it would now consist of allowing local notables to continue in their local power. Qaids would no longer have to balance competing interests among those they ruled, and so they became agents of a colonial state disguised in the garb of the pre-colonial one. These considerations even included the sultan, whose position would be guaranteed by the protectorate even as its old powers were taken away.

Thus Moulay Abdelhafid was dependent on the French; yet he resented them. He was powerless, but still leader of the *umma.* Senior members of the Makhzan were just as unhappy, and men like Taïeb El Mokri deluged the British Mission with complaints.[2] At the bottom of the social scale, the French-trained army resented its trainers, and the urban and rural population wanted nothing whatever to do with the French. The French authorities set about resolving these contradictions with a determined single-mindedness, backed by the resolute use of force against those who would not conform to their wishes.

The Fez mutiny

The infantrymen rebelled first. French discipline, training and pay policy had set off the first siege of Fez in 1911 and now they led to a second. A Moroccan soldier killed a French officer who had publicly rebuked him and was court-martialled and shot. Moulay Abdelhafid sent a letter to be read out in the mosques in the hope of calming the protests that this provoked; it merely made clear that he was a prisoner of the French. On 17 April the French commanders announced new regulations that required recruits to carry knapsacks, which they felt as a humiliation, to obey commands in French, and to accept a cut in pay. An eclipse of the sun on the same day was taken as a signal to mutiny and the mob joined in. European businesses and the *millah* were looted, and many Europeans were killed. After French artillery bombarded the city, and French troops, along with some loyal Moroccan soldiers from the *goum* regiments, had restored order, General Moinier declared martial law.[3]

With Fez cowed into servility, deserters fled into the countryside. North of the city, a Darqawi *sharif,* Sidi Muhammad al-Hajjami, organised a *jihad* and another *sharif,* Sidi Rahu, led a rising to

2 Burke, *Prelude,* 182.

3 Porch, *Morocco,* 248-49; Burke, *Prelude,* 183.

the south, in the foothills of the Middle Atlas. Together, they prepared to besiege Fez.[4] In these dangerous moments the first Resident-General, Hubert Lyautey, arrived in the capital.

Lyautey in Morocco

The title 'Resident-General' was an indication of the ambiguous nature of the protectorate institution: the new controller of Morocco's destiny supposedly did not govern, he merely resided.[5] But however much this symbolised the indirect nature of rule in the Protectorate, it was contrasted with the reality that the new Resident was a soldier, however much the Quai d'Orsay might have preferred a civilian: the country had to be conquered by its new Resident. A diplomat, the Comte de Saint-Aulaire, was indeed appointed as Délégué des Affaires Etrangères, effectively Lyautey's secretary, but he was an enthusiast for Lyautey's strategy of political penetration backed by force, an enthusiasm born of long diplomatic experience in Morocco. A third member of Lyautey's team was recruited in Casablanca: Colonel Henri Gouraud, who had gained a reputation as a daring colonial soldier in the Soudan. The day after they reached Fez, on 24 May, the tribal alliance attacked.[6]

Al-Hajjami besieged Fez while Sidi Rahu took on Sefrou and El-Hajeb. This was quite different from the agglomeration of factions that attacked Fez in 1911. Lyautey telegraphed to Paris: 'It can be affirmed that the column which operated June 1st and 2nd around Fez had to deal with an almost homogeneous army, having only one flag and one soul, whose various elements obeyed voluntarily to one discipline and affronted death for the same idea.'[7]

He responded with a mixture of force and politics. In Fez itself he bought support by giving salaries to important '*ulama*, and by freeing Fasis who had taken part in the riots; outside the walls he attacked. On 1 June Gouraud tore al-Hajjami's *mahalla* to pieces with shrapnel shell, and mopped up the rest of his supporters on 6 July.[8] But Sidi Rahu still controlled the Middle Atlas, and

4 Burke, *Prelude*, 183-7; Porch, *Morocco*, 236-247.

5 Hammoudi, *Master and Disciple*, 110.

6 Porch, *Morocco*, 251-2; Alan Scham, *Lyautey in Morocco: Protectorate Administration, 1912-1925* (Berkeley: University of California Press, 1970), 14; C. V. Usborne, *The Conquest of Morocco* (London: Stanley Paul, 1936), 174-7; Burke, *Prelude*, 187-90.

7 Quoted in Burke, *Prelude*, 192.

8 Usborne, *Conquest*, 181-2; Burke, *Prelude*, 193-4; Porch, *Morocco*, 255-7

Lyautey, worried that the Sultan might slip out of Fez and join him, decided that Moulay Abdelhafid had to be removed.

The abdication of Moulay Abdelhafid.

Lyautey had already shifted the court to Rabat, leaving the sultan's brother, Moulay Youssef, as *Khalifa* in Fez. But when Moulay Abdelhafid tried to use his vestigial powers and refused to sign decrees (dahirs), Lyautey decided to remove this resentful and unreliable man. The Sultan drove a hard bargain, and on 12 August only agreed to abdicate in exchange for an annual pension equivalent to £15,000 and the right to live in Tangier. Before embarking on the French cruiser *Du Chayla,* Moulay Abdelhafid made a last gesture: he smashed the imperial seal and the royal parasol. The French would have to provide new symbols of the Sultan's authority, along with a new Sultan.[9]

That new Sultan, Moulay Youssef, was proclaimed without difficulty in the towns which the French controlled: Fez, Rabat and Casablanca. In the far south, Marrakesh and the surrounding plains and mountains relapsed into the *siba* typical of a change of regime.

El Hiba

In the Sous, *siba* became revolution. On 3 May, Ahmad Haybat Allah, popularly known as El Hiba, proclaimed himself *imam al-mujahidin.* This son of Ma al-Aynayn called for a *jihad* against both the French and the Alaouis, the restoration of the *shari'a,* the abolition of *maks* taxes and the creation of an Islamic society. He gathered so much support in the Sous and the High Atlas that even big qaids like El Mtouggi joined him, to avoid being swamped. Swathed in blue, Saharan tribesmen swept into Marrakesh on 14 August. On 18 August El Hiba himself arrived, and was proclaimed Sultan.[10]

He got little further, although Sidi Rahu in the Middle Atlas promised support, and Spanish Consulates in Morocco offered encouragement because of their government's resentment of the unilateral French take-over.[11] The alliance of tribal factions, big qaids and urban merchants that gave him Marrakesh was unstable. The qaids objected when he prohibited all but Quranic taxes, because it cut their income, and the merchants were overwhelmed

9 Burke, *Prelude,* 197-8; Usborne, *Conquest,* 186-9.

10 Burke, *Prelude,* 199-204; Porch, *Morocco,* 202-64; Usborne, *Conquest,* 189-90.

11 Burke, *Prelude,* 205.

by the flood of virtually worthless Saharan coins and by the wild behaviour of the desert warriors. Claiming the interests of morality, El Hiba demanded that all unmarried girls should be married off to his men, which did not endear him to the population of Marrakesh.

On 29 August a military expedition that El Hiba's brother, Mrebbi Rebbo, had led north was turned back by the French army. Now, French emissaries found it quite easy to persuade the big qaids to change sides. On 6 September, French forces defeated El Hiba's main army at Sidi Bou Othman, some 35 km. north of Marrakesh. The next morning, the city was relieved and El Hiba fled back to the Sous.[12]

Despite the military success, El Hiba had deeply worried Lyautey because his movement was driven by an ideological commitment to Islam and rejected the Alaoui family on which the protectorate was to be based. The Resident-General needed to fix the French in power and Moulay Youssef in position.

The theory of Protectorate

The Treaty of Fez was a rather ill-defined outline of indirect rule, promising to respect religion and the sultan but putting only very vague limits on French policy. It was for French officials to decide the nature and pace of reforms. Lyautey's ideas of spreading French influence through cooperative local officials, which he had elaborated on the Algerian frontier a decade before,[13] fitted nicely with these ideas about colonial rule.

French colonial policy had evolved since the invasion of Algeria in 1830. The idea of assimilation, of turning the colonised people into Frenchmen by educating them in the political, judicial and economic values of France, had crumbled in the face of its cost and the realisation that the 'natives' would swamp the 'real' French population.[14] The policy had shifted towards association: the French army would impose control, but the institutions of the conquered would be preserved and local leaders accommodated and made dependant upon the French. A few natives would be allowed to

12 *Ibid.*, 204-9; Porch, *Morocco*, 264-8; Usborne, *Conquest*, 190-4.

13 Edmund Burke, 'The Image of the Moroccan State in French Ethnological Literature: a New Look at the Origins of Lyautey's Berber Policy' in Gellner and Micaud (eds), *Arabs and Berbers*, 182-3.

14 Martin Lewis, 'One Hundred Million Frenchmen: the "Assimilation" Theory in French Colonial Policy', *Comparative Studies in Society and History* 4 (1961-2): 129-53.

evolve into French nationals provided they showed their loyalty for France.[15] Lyautey was particularly influenced by the examples of indirect rule by the British in India and Nigeria, and the Dutch in Indonesia, while Tunisia and Egypt provided examples near at hand of working through a local dynasty.[16]

The Algerian experience provided a received wisdom for use in Morocco. It divided Arabs from Berbers and assigned to each a series of characteristics that were apparently based on scientific principles but which were really little more than prejudices that justified colonial methods and created a hierarchy of local populations. The Arabs were not esteemed; as nomads, they could not be incorporated into the European economic structures, and as religious fanatics they could not be incorporated into the secular French Republic. Their patriarchal society was alien to republican and democratic values, and they were racial newcomers, who had swamped the original Berber inhabitants. Those Berbers were much more attractive. Natural democrats, they lived in settled agricultural societies, just like French peasants. They were unenthusiastic Muslims, preferring customary law to the *shari'a*. Although they fought hard against French occupation, once conquered they made much better collaborators than the Arabs.[17] This was largely self-serving: even if the Berbers were Frenchmen-in-waiting, little effort was made to open the door to them; but such mythology could be useful in Morocco.

The first French administrators relied on this 'Algerian Vulgate' because they knew very little about Morocco, despite the Mission Scientifique du Maroc having collected information since 1903. From 1908 it had been headed by Édouard Michaux-Bellaire, a former French consul in Morocco. He was a prolific writer, who by 1911 had published more than twenty articles in *Archives Marocaines*, the Mission's scholarly journal, and others in the *Revue du Monde Musulman.* They covered subjects from taxation and alchemy to *fatwas* and genealogy. The Mission's aim was supposedly academic, but the Mission sought to 'know' Morocco in order to control it. Michaux-Bellaire's most influential contribution was

15 Patricia M.E. Lorcin, *Imperial Identities: Stereotyping, Prejudice and Race in Colonial Algeria* (London: I.B. Tauris, 1995), 6-8.

16 Faouzi M. Houroro, *Sociologie politique coloniale au Maroc: cas de Michaux Bellaire* (Casablanca: Afrique Orient, 1988), 120; Bidwell, *Morocco*, 68, 166; see also Edmund Burke, 'La Mission Scientifique au Maroc', *Bulletin economique et sociale du Maroc* 138-9 (1979): 37-56.

17 Charles-Robert Ageron, *Politiques coloniales au Maghreb* (Paris: Presses Universitaires de France, 1972), 110ff; Lorcin, *Imperial Identities*, 130 ff.

to build into an incontrovertible truth the idea of a sharp divide between *bilad al-siba* and *bilad al-makhzan*, and between Arab and Berber, and to suggest how a French administration might bring them into a single political structure that it could dominate.[18]

Lyautey believed that the Berbers would rather submit to a 'state' controlled by the French, than to the traditional Makhzan that had never dominated them before. The way to win them over was to promise to respect customary law.[19] Thus, preservation of the Makhzan and of local identities were complementary, not contradictory, policies, that were underpinned by practical considerations as well as theoretical and ideological precepts. With all this mind, Lyautey set about designing the structure of the Protectorate.

Government in the French Protectorate

Moulay Youssef made an ideal sultan. Virtually unknown outside Fez, he was beholden to no-one except Lyautey, and had no political ambitions of his own. When he heard that he was to be Sultan, he protested in tears. This was a decent man, well-educated, intelligent, courteous and with a reputation for piety, but outside Fez he was widely despised as a creature of the French. Disapproving *'ulama* and notables delayed his proclamation for a day in Tetuan and Larache, and in Essaouira he was only proclaimed when the French threatened to bombard the city. To avoid compromising him, Lyautey kept Moulay Youssef at arms' length and had him live for the first three years in Fez and Marrakesh, in a Moroccan and Muslim environment, rather than the Europeanised cities of the coast. When he did move him to Rabat, it was to a palace within the Almohad ramparts, and in sight of Lyautey's Residency: the two wings of the protectorate resided side-by-side. In outward form it was unclear who was paramount, an ambiguity that Lyautey both fostered and respected.

As colonial rulers did so often, Lyautey invented or revived Moroccan traditions that associated the Sultan with his country's past. The annual 'Id al-Kabir was celebrated in a style not seen since the time of Moulay Hassan: Moulay Youssef sacrificed the sheep in the name of the *umma* as a whole, symbolising his leadership of the country. Bands played the Moroccan, not the French anthem and the Moroccan flag flew over public buildings. Lyautey always treated the *amir al-muminin* with the greatest respect and

18 Houroro, *Sociologie*, 141-2. Burke, 'Image', 184-5

19 Burke, 'Image', 194-5

courtesy, paying him elaborate public compliments; he was equally polite in private: letters to friends described Moulay Youssef in effusive terms.

Moulay Youssef learned quickly, although he knew nothing of political affairs at first. After an early discussion of state matters, when his only request was for a garage for his car, a French officer commented: 'This Sultan is a passive man, always happy to agree.' Yet by 1914 St-Aulaire was expressing surprise at his political abilities. Moulay Youssef was never entirely supine: he always refused to sign any *dahir* that introduced the guillotine into Morocco, for instance.[20]

The French even controlled the Sultan's personal household. Si Kaddour Ben Ghabrit, an Algerian, was Head of Protocol, and another Algerian, Si Mohammed Mammeri, was his deputy and tutor to the young prince, and future King, Mohammed. Moulay Youssef did manage to have an old friend, Thami Ababou, appointed as chamberlain (*hajib*) and he would come to be the great rival of Hadj Mohammed El Mokri, who was almost permanently the *Grand Vizir* (*wazir al-azam*).[21]

At first Lyautey wanted to sack El Mokri, whom he thought blatantly corrupt and unreliable and, worse, too 'European' to be *wazir*. His sons, Si Taïeb and Si el-Mukhtar, were quickly removed as minister of finance and pasha of Tangier, in October 1913, Hadj Mohammed himself was replaced by Mohammed Guebbas, who had succeeded el-Mennebhi as minister of war in 1904. But by 1917 El Mokri was back, to remain *Grand Vizir* for the rest of the Protectorate. This was a role of primary importance because he oversaw the qaids, appointed Makhzan officials, and issued decrees.[22] Much of the rest of Makhzan was discarded: between

20 The description of Moulay Youssef in this and the preceding paragraph draws on: Bidwell, *Morocco*, 65-9; Alaoui, *Maroc*, 50-1; Julien, *Impérialismes*, 103-4; Scham, *Lyautey*, 57-60; William A. Hoisington, *Lyautey and the French Conquest of Morocco* (Basingstoke: Macmillan, 1995), 45; Rivet, *Lyautey*, 166-75; Mohamed El Alami, *Mohammed V: histoire de l'indépendance du Maroc* (Rabat: Les Éditions A P I, 1980), 39-40; Hammoudi, *Master and Disciple*, 110.

21 El Alami, *Mohammed V*, 46-7; Joseph Luccioni, 'L'avènement de Sidi Mohammed ben Youssef au trône du Maroc, 1927', *Revue de l'Occident Musulman* (1972): 124; Jean Wolf, *Les secrets du Maroc espagnol. L'epopée d'Abd-el-Khaleq Torrès* (Casablanca: Eddif, 1994), 159; Marthe and Edmond Gouvion Saint-Cyr, *Kitab aayane al-Marhrib 'l-akca. Esquisse générale des moghrebs de la genèse à nos jours et livre des grands du Maroc* (Paris: Paul Geuthner, 1939), 260-2.

22 Abdeslam Baita, '"Reversion to Tradition" in State Structures in 19th Century Morocco' in Abdelali Doumou (ed.) *The Moroccan State in Historical Perspective*, (Dakar: CODESRIA, 1990), 36-7; Hoisington, *Lyautey*, 142; Rivet, *Lyautey*, 3:175-7;

October 1912 and August 1915, Lyautey abolished the ministries of foreign affairs, finance, and war. Yet some ministries were strengthened. A ministry of *habus* was created to manage religious endowments, and the *wazir al-shikayat* (minister of 'complaints') became Minister of Justice, no longer a righter of wrongs, but responsible for the *shari'a* courts. The first such minister was Mohamed Hajoui, a specialist in Islamic law, and the head of the Moroccan delegation to the Algerian frontier delimitation in 1904.[23] Yet even in these Islamic ministries, Moroccans had little control, for a parallel administration, the Secrétariat-Général du Gouvernment Chérifien, shadowed them and ran the technical services. Every department of modern government – finance, public works, health, communications, education, justice, agriculture, land use (*Eaux-et-Forêts*), commerce, industry and mines, labour, social affairs, public security and ancient monuments – was run by French administrators.[24] The two systems ran in parallel and the boundaries between them were the boundaries of modernity. A system that was supposedly designed to help the Moroccans develop denied them any understanding of how that was to be done.

At local level, the Protectorate changed some personnel but did not recast the old order itself. The Pasha of Salé, Hajj el-Taïeb el-Sobeïhi, who had been appointed in 1905 and died in 1914, was replaced by his son Hajj Muhammad, who remained in this post until 1958. The pasha of Fez was Buchta el-Baghdadi who, in 1898, had violently suppressed Rifi piracy.[25] In Casablanca, the pasha was replaced by Hadj Omar Tazi, Moulay Abdelaziz's finance minister, who had been excluded from politics during the reign of Moulay Abdelhafid and had made a fortune in trade in retirement. The merchants, so important in Casablanca, liked him, although the rest of the population was quite indifferent; the French accompanied his appointment with a twenty-one-gun salute.[26] All these men were shadowed by the civilian *contrôleurs civiles* who

---

El Alami, *Mohammed V*, 46-7; *Times*, 10 September 1957; *Bulletin Officiel du Maroc*, 15 Novembre 1912; Gouvion, *Kitab aayane*, 258-5; PRO FO371/2970/180371, White to Balfour, Tangier, 1 September 1917.

23 Abdallah Laroui, *Esquisses historiques* (Casablanca: Centre Culturel Arabe, 1992), 115; Baita, 'Reversion to Tradition'; Gouvion, *Kitab aayane*, 266-7.

24 Rivet, *Lyautey*, 1:175-81; Halstead, *Rebirth*, 36-40; Baita, 'Reversion to Tradition', 36.

25 Brown, *Salé*, 164-5; Jacques Berque, *French North Africa: The Maghrib between Two World Wars*, trans. Jean Stewart (London: Faber and Faber, 1967), 166-7; Gouvion, *Kitab aayane*, 754-5.

26 Hoisington, *Lyautey*, 140-3.

ensured qaids collected taxes properly, qadis ran their courts efficiently, public works were carried out and agriculture was administered without disputes between Moroccans and Europeans.[27] Their military equivalents in the Service des Renseignements, carried out the same functions in the forward areas.[28]

The big qaids

Under French supervision, the Makhzan exercised a control that it had never enjoyed before the Protectorate. Yet Lyautey also preserved the big qaids and incorporated them into the system, just as preserving local 'aristocracies' was an essential feature of that most perfect example of indirect rule, British India. It was also a practical policy, for the big qaids had been most useful in ending El Hiba's occupation of Marrakesh. Expediency and ideology were once again combined.[29] Lyautey knew that the big qaids were not very savoury characters and he told Paris that they 'must be controlled in a discrete fashion, but strictly and all the time. Our presence cannot be a cloak, under any circumstances for a return to old abuses, that would run the risk of infuriating the population and inciting it to rebel.'[30]

Lyautey did not right wrongs. After El Hiba left, Thami El Glaoui was reappointed Pasha of Marrakesh, a post he would hold for forty years. Objections from tribesmen and urban notables were simply ignored, because he was far too useful and El Hiba was still dangerous.[31] In the early summer of 1913 the Glaouis and El Goundafi contributed troops to a *mahalla* led by Moulay Zein, the Sultan's brother, that chased El Hiba from Taroudannt. They received the Legion of Honour as their reward.[32]

Lyautey briefly considered trying to turn El Hiba himself into a big qaid ruling the Saharan tribes between the Atlas and Mauritania,[33] but there was no need. French troops moving northward from Senegal entered Ma al-Aynayn's old capital at Es-Semara in February 1913, blew up the council hall and destroyed the library. Although they then pulled back, El Hiba was confined

27 Scham, *Lyautey*, 71-4, Bidwell, *Morocco*, 166-8.

28 Bidwell, *Morocco*, 161-2.

29 Rivet, *Lyautey*, 1:184-7, 199.

30 Quoted in Bidwell, *Morocco*, 104.

31 Rivet, *Lyautey*, 1:189-90.

32 Bidwell, *Morocco*, 107-9; Rivet, *Lyautey*, 1:191.

33 Rivet, *Lyautey*, 1:95.

to a guerrilla struggle in the Anti-Atlas.[34] For the big qaids, French support brought greater rewards than the Legion of Honour. French troops helped them to regain control over tribes that had slipped away during the El Hiba interlude, despite local opposition. That brought the opportunity to invest in land on a big scale.[35]

There were no big qaids in the Middle Atlas, so the French turned to the leaders of the big *tariqas* such as Abdelhay El Kittani, who was happy that the French had overthrown Moulay Abdelhafid, the murderer of his brother. El Kittani preached against the Salafiya in the Qarawiyyin,[36] but he had little political influence among the Middle Atlas tribes. Only one man had real local power there, Muha U Hammu, and he refused to co-operate. Moreover the local French commander, General Henrys, had less sympathy for notables than did Mangin in the far south. He thought they were oppressors.[37]

Thus it was that two elements of the pre-colonial order, the big qaids and the *tariqas* were maintained and incorporated into the system. But a process was beginning by which they would be fundamentally changed. By being incorporated into the colonial structure, they no longer had to apply rules of patronage and mediation that had applied before the protectorate. There were no local limits to their power, only the demands of the French. This allowed them to grow virtually unimpeded in wealth and power unless the colonial authorities decided otherwise.

The origin of the Berber policy

General Henrys, who had served in Algeria, applied the Kabyle myth to Morocco. He promised the Beni Mtir, who were reluctant to submit, that instead of being ruled by representatives of the Makhzan, they could run their affairs according to their own customs, be ruled by their own councils (*jama'as*), and regulated by customary law.[38] This mixture of pragmatism and the ideology of colonial rule in Algeria underpinned the third strand in French administration in Morocco: the Berber policy. It was soon embodied in a *dahir* (11 September 1914) whose first article stated: 'The

34 Tony Hodges, *Western Sahara: The Roots of a Desert War* (Westport, CT: Lawrence Hill, 1983), 61.

35 Rivet, *Lyautey*, 1:189-94; Bidwell, *Morocco*, 77.

36 Bidwell, *Morocco*, 149.

37 Rivet, *Lyautey*, 1:194-9.

38 Burke, 'Image', 188-91; Rivet, *Lyautey*, 1:198-9; Bidwell, *Morocco*, 50-1; Baita, 'Reversion to Tradition', 44.

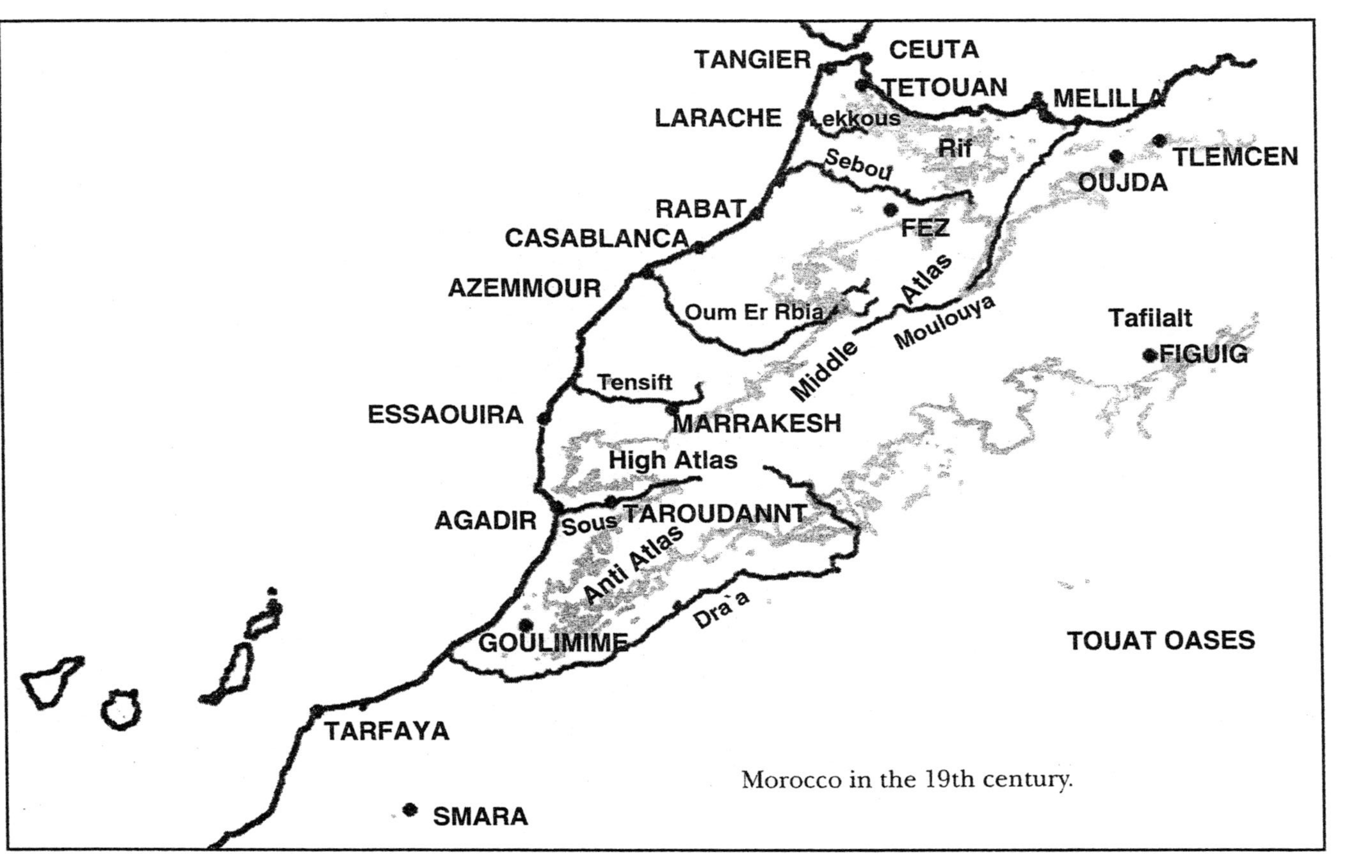

Morocco in the 19th century.

tribes referred to as being of Berber custom, are and will remain governed and administered in accordance with their own laws and customs, under the supervision of the authorities.'[39] The second article left the authorities to decide which were the Berber tribes and what rules and laws would be applied to them. It was only clear that the authority of the Sultan was to be set at naught.[40]

Circumstance, pragmatism and ideology combined to produce a dual system of rule. Some territories would come under the Makhzan, others under local rulers, either the big qaids, or Berber customary systems, but the French controlled them all, with two exceptions.

The Spanish Protectorate

The Spanish government insisted that its 'rights' be recognised. On 27 November 1912, after eight months of negotiations, the Treaty of Madrid set up a Spanish sub-protectorate, with its capital in Tetuan. It had two parts: some 20,000 sq. km. in northern Morocco, stretching from just south of Larache to the Moulouya river, and another 23,000 sq. km. around Tarfaya, in the far south. Ifni, still unoccupied, and the enclaves were excluded.[41] These were merely shapes on the map. One large tribe, the Beni Zeroual, was cut in two, but since no European had ever been there, no one knew.[42] For the moment it was more urgent to devise constitutional arrangements that preserved the fictional sovereignty of a Sultan whose empire was divided between two European powers.[43]

The solution was the 'Zone of Spanish Influence' that mirrored the French zone. The Sultan delegated authority to a *khalifa*,[44] the 'permanent emanation' of the 'legal personality' of the sultan, as the treaty had it. He issued *dahirs*, had his own Grand Vizir, ministers of finance, justice and *habus*, and his court had its own *hajib* and other officials. The government of Spain 'protected' him, through a high commissioner who headed a Spanish civil and military ad-

39 Ageron, *Politiques coloniales*, 122.

40 Halstead, *Rebirth*, 69; Ageron, *Politiques colomiales*, 121-2.

41 José María Cordero Torres, *Organización del Protectorado Español en Marruecos*, 2 vols. (Madrid: Editora Nacional, 1942), 1:17; Ricardo Donoso-Cortés, *Estudio geográfico político-militar sobre las zonas españolas del norte y sur de Marruecos* (Madrid: Libería Gutenberg, 1913), 58-64.

42 Donoso Cortés, *Estudio*, 86-93; Pennell, *Government and Flag*, 22.

43 Cordero Torres, *Organización*, 1:72-73.

44 Quoted in Alaoui, *Maroc*, 249.

ministration that was responsible for order, security and the panoply of technical 'services' – health, communications, commerce, industry and so on.[45]

This Spanish protectorate was even more a fiction than the French. An official description of the public administration of the Spanish zone, published in 1942, stated baldly: 'There is no practical interest in discussing whether the Khalifa is coordinate with or subordinate to the High Commissioner, since his every act presupposes the consent of the High Commissioner.'[46]

Consequently the Spanish authorities chose as *khalifa,* a thoroughly obscure first cousin of Moulay Youssef named el-Mehedi ben Ismail. Otherwise the Spanish, like the French, kept the old elite in place. The pasha of Tetuan was Hajj Ahmad Torres, son of a former *naib* of Tangier. When he died in 1920 his successors included two men, Abdel Carim Lebbadi (Abd al-Karim al-Abbadi) and Abdussalam ben al-Husain al-Bujari (al-Bukhari), who had been pashas before the Protectorate. Hajj Abdussalam Bennuna, minister of finance from 1922 onwards, was the grandson of an important diplomat, Hajj Abd al-Salam Brisha.[47]

The international zone in Tangier

The Spanish government was not the only foreign power that had to be satisfied. The consular corps had run Tangier for much of the nineteenth century, and now the governments of Europe, supported by that of the United States, demanded a system of international control; the principle had already been recognised in the Treaty of Fez. Of course, the fictional authority of the Sultan had to be maintained.

Eventually negotiators from France, Spain and Britain, worked out yet another variation on the protectorate theme. The Sultan's representative, the *Khalifa,* would uphold Islamic law and preside over a Committee of Control consisting of the consuls. A municipal assembly, partly appointed and partly elected with a handful of Muslim and Jewish members, would run daily affairs. The officials would be Europeans, appointed in proportion to their country's trade, number of nationals and investment in Tangier. There would be three separate legal systems: European, Muslim and Jewish, and two police forces: a Spanish-commanded military police and

45 Cordero Torres, *Organización,* 1:119-50.

46 *Ibid.*, 1: 120.

47 R'honi, *Historia,* 91-8; Wolf, *Secrets,* 149-50.

a civilian police commanded by a Frenchman. To satisfy the British, Tangier was never to be fortified.[48]

The beginnings of conquest

It was one thing to write treaties, quite another to make European rule a reality. In the cities, once the rising in Fez had been put down, active opposition fell silent. Passive resistance continued. In Salé some people shut themselves in their houses in order never to see Christians. One man spent every evening counting his beads and repeating, 'The infidels have come, Islam has perished.' Such extremely personal ways of coping with conquest posed no threat to the French.[49]

The mountains, valleys and deserts had to be conquered, and there was far more fighting than politicians in Paris and Madrid had been led to expect. Lyautey's political penetration relied on the resolute use of force when it was needed, and it often was. Ideology (the desire to work through local agents) and practicality (the desire to limit French casualties and save money) meant that Lyautey relied on Moroccan troops to conquer their own country. New Moroccan units of Tirailleurs (riflemen) and Spahis (infantry) were set up in June 1912. Above all, the goums were expanded and the process of changing from local security units into a major fighting force was begun.[50]

Some notables and their clans were 'attracted', as French terminology had it, by self-interest, considerations of financial gain or political advantage; others chose to fight. Some fought on principle, often long after personal advantage would have determined that they submit. There were local *jihads* in the Rharb in 1912 and the Ouerrha valley in 1913. Among the Fishtala in 1912 there was even someone who pretended to be Abu Himara, and who was joined by former *nizam* infantrymen who had mutinied in 1912. Men who had served in *nizam* units since the end of the nineteenth century had often been thoroughly detribalised, and when they were sacked by the French instructors in 1911 and 1912, the mini *jihads* in the mountains gave them the chance to do what they knew best: to fight and to make a small living through raiding.[51]

48 Graham H. Stuart, *The International City of Tangier*, 2nd edn. (Stanford University Press, 1955), 61-5.

49 Brown, *Salé*, 188-91; Rivet, *Lyautey*, 2:94-5.

50 Maghraoui, 'Moroccan colonial soldiers'.

51 Rivet, *Lyautey*, 2:96-7.

Some members of the *tariqas* resisted too. Although most of the leaders of the Darqawiyya cooperated with the French, many ordinary Darqawis supported the *jihad* led by the mysterious Al-Shinqiti who proclaimed himself sultan in Taza in 1913. The Hadawiyya, a thoroughly heterodox *tariqa* whose long-haired, kif-smoking adepts were often very dirty, violently disliked the French. But most Moroccans loathed their millennarian ideas.[52]

Some of this resistance was dangerous, and Lyautey moved cautiously, sometimes too cautiously for his more hotheaded officers. He was soon proved right: Colonel Charles Mangin lost men when he was forced to withdraw from Tadla, which he had occupied in March 1913, against Lyautey's orders.[53] For Lyautey, Taza was a more important prize because it opened the corridor between Fez and the Algerian frontier. After it was occupied, on 16 May 1914, Lyautey was able to turn on the powerful Zaïane confederation led by Muha u Hammu.[54] Even then the Zaïane carried on fighting, as did al-Shinqiti who fought on in the mountains until the end of the First World War. Throughout the campaigns in Morocco, a lesson was driven home to French and Spanish commanders: possession of a fixed position did not guarantee its security.[55]

Yet by mid-1914 Lyautey had lifted the siege of Fez, taken Marrakesh from El Hiba, broken through the Taza corridor and pushed opposition into the mountains. The French Makhzan held what Lyautey described as 'le Maroc Utile'.[56] The resistance was disunited. In the winter of 1912-13, the Zaïane asked for help from the Ait Ndhir, but not all the clans agreed. Eventually the Ait Ndhir clans were peeled away from the alliance and by the end of 1914 the whole tribe had surrendered.[57]

The Spanish zone

Disunity also undermined resistance to the Spanish. Tetuan was occupied in February 1913, and on 27 April the new *khalifa* entered his new capital, alongside the new High Commissioner, General Alfau. Moulay el-Mehedi, the British Consul reported, received 'the same honours as are usually accorded to the Sultan, the Royal

52 *Ibid.*, 2:106-7.

53 Porch, *Morocco*, 283-4; Usborne, *Conquest*, 202-5.

54 Porch, *Morocco*, 285-6; Usborne, *Conquest*, 209.

55 Usborne, *Conquest*, 209-10; Rivet, *Lyautey*, 2:106-7.

56 Porch, *Morocco*, 285-8; Usborne, *Conquest*, 211.

57 Burke, 'Ait Ndhir', 140-1.

umbrella, lance bearers and all the paraphernalia of State being employed. This produced a bad effect on the tribesmen, who interpreted it as indicating a complete separation of their district from the rest of Morocco and its subsequent incorporation in Spain.'[58] The tribesmen were right, and several groups of Rifis arrived to help the fight, but their leaders quarrelled or were bought off with money.

The Spanish army spent lavishly to buy support. In the central Rif they gave a large monthly pension to Abd al-Karim al-Khattabi, the qadi of the Banu Waryaghal and in 1913 they awarded a medal to his son Muhammad, the future Rifi leader, who was qadi in Melilla.[59] The Khattabis were locally important but only Ahmad El Raisuni had any wide influence, and attempts to deal with him were an absolute failure.

El Raisuni was resentful that the Spanish authorities had not appointed him *khalifa*. They did appoint him as pasha of Asilah, but they undermined his authority. In January 1913 General Miguel Fernández Silvestre, the commander in Larache, was so appalled by the conditions in El Raisuni's jail that he stormed into the *sharif*'s presence and ordered him to release the prisoners. El Raisuni refused, and explained:

> Spain has other and greater purposes than to interfere with our justice. The Sheria law permits my actions, no, insists on them. You should uphold my authority, not weaken it, as has been your purpose for a long time. Spain swore to support our religion and our law. You misunderstand your mission. You have no more right to meddle with our traditions and our customs than I have to tell you that the food you eat is unclean. To each country its laws![60]

This was a notion of indirect rule that Silvestre could not understand. Here was the logical contradiction of protectorate ideology revealed most clearly. A commanding general was asked to agree to actions in his subordinates of which he disapproved. Silvestre, an unsubtle man ordered his men to see that the prisoners were released, and that summer, El Raisuni stockpiled supplies at his family home at Tazrut in the Jebala. As his support grew,

58 PRO FO881/10423 'Morocco Annual Report for 1913', 17.

59 Pennell, *Government and Flag*, 46-9; Germain Ayache, *La Guerre du Rif* (Paris: L'Harmattan, 1996), 31-9

60 Forbes, *Raisuni*, 153.

he was proclaimed 'Sultan of the jihad'.[61] El Raisuni was no El Hiba, but rather a well-educated bandit who might have made an excellent big qaid had the Spanish known how to manipulate him. Instead, he fomented endless trouble.

Although warfare took up most of the energies of the Spanish and the French, Lyautey was intent on more than conquest. He wanted to change Morocco and for that he needed money, investment and a new legal infrastructure.

Land as a commodity

Lyautey despised the French peasants who settled in Algeria ('The mentality of Huns. [...] They have neither humanity nor intelligence).'[62] If allowed into Morocco, they would undermine his idea of protectorate. Large companies were much more likely to cooperate with the Protectorate government and invest on a large scale. Besides they already owned many thousands of hectares on the Atlantic plains and in the Haouz of Marrakesh.[63]

Big companies would invest nothing unless their property was secure, so the Protectorate government set about registering land and turning it into a saleable commodity. As a first step, roads, rivers, beaches, collective tribal land and forests were turned into Makhzan property. Then, in August 1913, a dahir established procedures for registering private land. The Spanish authorities did the same the following year. Then, as much property as possible was taken into Makhzan ownership, so that it could be made available for sale. Former Makhzan domains were clawed back from powerful men like El Mokri, who had no choice but to agree. In July 1914, *jaysh* land was made inalienable, and all Moroccan surface water was placed in the public domain on the pretext that collective ownership was closer to the spirit of Islam.[64]

Lyautey intended these policies to encourage large-scale farming but even he could not keep all French colons out of Morocco. In the first year of the protectorate, 29,000 Europeans arrived to settle, many of them in coastal cities like Casablanca.[65]

61 *Ibid.*, 155.

62 Bidwell, *Morocco*, 202.

63 Charles F. Stewart, *The Economy of Morocco, 1912-1962* (Cambridge, MA: Harvard Centre for Middle Eastern Studies, 1967), 75; Pascon, *Haouz*, 2:415; Bidwell, *Morocco*, 201-2; Salahdine, *Maroc*, 161.

64 Bidwell, *Morocco*, 205-7; Stewart, *Economy*, 72; Salahdine, *Maroc*, 139-42; Pascon, *Haouz*, 2:449; Seddon, *Moroccan Peasants*, 123; Swearingen, *Mirages*, 45.

65 Scham, *Lyautey*, 134.

New cities

Once a scruffy village, Casablanca in 1913 was an ugly urban sprawl of 59,000 people and the busiest port in Morocco, and had the country's first big factories (tobacco and cement). Wooden and tin shacks mingled with stone and brick buildings, but Lyautey wanted this to be his economic capital, so it would have to be properly planned. Casablanca would not do as a political capital: it was too uncouth and had no imperial history. Fez was unhealthy, difficult to reach and isolated from the economic boom of the coast. Rabat was the best choice.[66]

In building his New York City and his Washington DC, as he called them,[67] Lyautey was determined that traditional Moroccan madinas should be preserved and European architecture should be made 'tolerable' to the Moroccans by using local architectural idioms. To execute his plans, Lyautey recruited a young French architect, Henri Prost. Prost eventually designed nine European quarters in Morocco (Casablanca, Rabat, Fez, Marrakesh, Meknès, Sefrou, Ouezzane, Taza and Agadir), but his first task, in April 1914, was to draft a dahir laying down the building regulations of the Protectorate. These insisted that the style, scale and materials of new buildings should harmonise with traditional Moroccan architecture. The aesthetic was literally only a façade, for the buildings themselves conformed to the latest European thinking. The height of the walls was fixed to a European norm, the positioning of windows and types of roofs to European standards. For all their Moroccan decorative flourishes, these were buildings for Europeans to live in. Moroccans lived in the *madinas*, from which Europeans were excluded by quite different building regulations that made the houses unsuitable for them. Since the regulations also determined who was allowed to build in each area, and how construction syndicates were to be organised, the two communities were kept apart. The French *ville nouvelle* with an Arab face surrounding the Moroccan *madina* stood for the protectorate as a whole.[68]

The legal façade

The treaty of Fez promised to respect Moroccan religious institu-

66 Gwendolyn Wright, *The Politics of Design in French Colonial Urbanism* (Chicago: University of Chicago Press, 1991), 101; Abu Lughod, *Rabat*, 138-9; Halstead, *Rebirth*, 78, 80; Adam, *Casablanca*, 1:31, 57.

67 Wright, *Politics*, 94.

68 *Ibid.*, 100-5; Abu Lughod, *Rabat*, 145-7; Adam, *Casablanca*, 61.

tions. Outwardly this was done: mosques were forbidden to non-Muslims, and Lyautey made a point of respecting the sanctity of the holy town of Moulay Idris, north of Fez which had always been closed to Christians. Although it was now open to European visitors, he refused to enter. But he could still see it through the eyes of one of the first Muslim Algerians to be trained in European schools of painting. Azouaou Mammeri was the brother of Si Mohammed Mammeri, the tutor of young prince Mohammed. After studying under a French painter, Léon Carré, he became professor of drawing in Fez in 1916, and eventually an important colonial official responsible for traditional arts. Thus a Muslim used European artistic forms to transmit pictures of Muslim holy places which the European ruler would not visit.[69]

Equally the Protectorate preserved the *shari'a* , the essence of Muslim identity, while being determined to control it. An early decree, in October 1912, gave the new minister for justice control of the Islamic courts, and the task of choosing, supervising and, if necessary, removing qadis, but French advisors would ensure that this was done properly. In July 1913 another dahir took all but civil cases right out of the qadis' hands and reorganised their administration along French lines.[70] The *shari'a* courts had a Muslim form, but a French bureaucracy.

In August 1913 a French court system was set up to deal with commercial law and all cases involving Europeans, even those that also involved Moroccans; under no circumstances should a European be exposed to Islamic law.[71] Although the theory of protectorate implied the primacy of Moroccan institutions, European courts took precedence over Muslim ones in practice. This enabled the French authorities to claim that consular courts were no longer necessary and most foreign governments soon abandoned consular jurisdictions; only the British and the American governments refused to agree.[72] It was hard to reconstruct a whole legal system. Before Berber customary law could be defined, Jewish rabbinical courts reformed or criminal courts established for the

69 Roger Benjamin (ed.), *Orientalism – Delacroix to Klee* (Sydney: Art Gallery of New South Wales, 1997), 246; Berque, *Mahgrib*, 73. See this book's jacket cover.

70 Scham, *Lyautey*, 177-9.

71 *Ibid.*, 169 ff.

72 Mohammed Kenbib, 'European Protections in Morocco, 1904-1939' in George Joffe (ed.), *Morocco and Europe* (London: Centre of Near and Middle Eastern Studies, School of Oriental and African Studies, 1989), 48-9; Scham, *Lyautey*, 169.

Muslim population, the outbreak of war in Europe brought everything to a virtual halt.[73]

In August 1914 the French army had occupied most of 'useful' Morocco but had barely begun the conquest of the Berber and mountain areas. The Spanish army controlled only Tetuan and some patches around Melilla and Larache. There was the skeleton of an administrative and political system in both zones, but no more than plans for Tangier. There had been some economic and social modernisation in the French zone, but little in the Spanish. The question, in August 1914, was how much even of this would survive.

THE FIRST WORLD WAR

When war broke out, the international regime for Tangier was abandoned. Eventually, the German and Austrian Consuls were expelled, German property was expropriated and German citizens were told to leave. There was no international administration, indeed there was no real administration at all. Public health and security disintegrated, the port was closed, food ran short. Tangier virtually fell apart.[74]

The French Protectorate rested on firmer foundations. Moulay Youssef publicly supported France,[75] but the Paris government told Lyautey that his first priority was to help save the motherland: 'The fate of Morocco will be decided in Lorraine.' This pretentious message was followed by orders to send half the French army home and withdraw all garrisons from the interior except those that were keeping open the Taza corridor. Lyautey knew that a withdrawal would become a rout, so he refused to do it. He still sent home 50,000 troops, but replaced them with settlers, Senegalese troops and Moroccans. He used *jaysh* troops from the Cherarda and Cheraga in the Rharb in 1915 and in 1916, but otherwise Moroccans were recruited into the regular forces. By November 1918 they formed about a quarter of the whole army in Morocco.

That was not the only use that the French army made of its colonial troops, for they were sent to defend France itself. In 1910 Charles Mangin, Lyautey's aide, had proposed that a *Force noire* of African colonial troops should be set up to defend the

73 Laskier, *Alliance*, 155-6; Scham, *Lyautey*, 181, 186.

74 Stuart, *Tangier*, 66-9.

75 Bidwell, *Morocco*, 67.

metropolis. Although it was not fully mobilised until 1917 when Clemenceau came to power, the first regiments of Moroccan Tirrailleurs were sent in 1914. The number of *goum* regiments increased from fourteen to twenty-five by the end of the war; 34,000 Moroccans fought in France where they suffered casualties far out of proportion to their numbers, a fate shared by other colonial forces who, physically unprepared and poorly led, were used in the most terrible battles on the Somme.[76]

Lyautey held French positions but he made no major advances for the first two years of the war. The commander at Khénifra demonstrated why in November 1914. When he disobeyed orders and tried to capture Muha U Hammu, the operation went badly wrong and big columns had to be sent to relieve him.[77] Instead, Lyautey concentrated on political and economic action. He had roads built to the areas that his army controlled and in September 1915 organised a big trade fair, the Casablanca Exhibition, to impress Moroccans with French self-confidence and convince the French government that Morocco was useful to the war effort.[78]

This worked. In 1916 some French troops were sent back to Morocco and Lyautey returned to the offensive. The most important operation, completed in June 1917, was to send three columns to smash through the narrow neck of the Middle Atlas near Midelt and split the resistance.[79] This was done against the orders of the government in Paris since Clemenceau wanted to draw men from Morocco to fight in Europe. It was also done without Lyautey to oversee it: between December 1916 and May 1917 he was recalled to Paris for a short and unsuccessful spell as minister for war. General Gouraud, who did the detailed planning,[80] used Moroccan troops to conquer their own country for the French.

The big qaids

During the First World War the greatest allies of the Protectorate were the big qaids. On 2 August 1914, at a meeting in Marrakesh, Si Madani El Glaoui led the others in promising to help the war effort, saying that the defeat of France would destroy the big qaids

76 Rivet, *Lyautey*, 2:20-1; Porch, *Morocco*, 263; V.G. Kiernan, *European Empires from Conquest to Collapse, 1815-1960* (Leicester University Press, 1982); Maghraoui, 'Moroccan colonial soldiers'.

77 Usborne, *Conquest*, 218-9.

78 *Ibid.*, 218, 222; Scham, *Lyautey*, 28.

79 Rivet, *Lyautey*, 3:59-60; Usborne, *Conquest*, 231-2.

80 Scham, *Lyautey*, 30-4.

too. El Glaoui made it a matter of honour, brushing aside the suggestion of his brother Si Thami that they should bargain for a better deal: 'We are the friends of France, and to the very end we shall share her fortunes be it good or bad. That is my sworn word.' El Mtouggi, more succinctly, told Mangin: 'You hold the sea, we will hold the land.' In return, El Mtouggi had a free hand over the territory south west of Marrakesh, while El Glaoui controlled the mountain passes to the east. In January 1917 El Goundafi, at the head of 5,500 irregulars, backed by four French battalions, chased El Hiba deeper into the desert. El Goundafi became governor of the Sous and spent the war, with a single French advisor, Colonel Justinard, building roads and raising troops. Meanwhile the Glaoui brothers received huge amounts of money and arms from the French, and their prestige grew rapidly.[81]

In the areas without big qaids, policies were more confused. In November 1916 a dahir set up councils (jemaas) to represent tribes in the Berber areas. While this fulfilled the promise of preserving Berber identity, the Residency-General was at the same time busy appointing local qaids in the same tribes. So the councils had no power, for fear they would undercut the qaids' authority.[82] There was similar confusion in the French administration. In 1917 The Direction des Affaires Indigènes was set up to oversee all political work in the Protectorate, while the Direction des Affaires Civiles took charge of administrative matters. It was soon found that the two could not be separated.[83]

Social policy of the French Protectorate

Having secured the French position politically and militarily, Lyautey put off most urgent changes until the war was over, unless they could not be avoided. In 1914 the Protectorate government had announced that Berber areas would be administered according to customary law, and to quieten opposition in the Berber mountains this was done. A system of local judicial councils (*jemaas judiciares*) was set up to administer civil cases. Criminal law came under the qaid.[84]

81 Morsy, 'El Hajj Thami el Glaouï, un grand caïd contre le sultan et l'indépendance marocaine' in Charles-André Julien (ed.) *Les Africans* (Paris: Éditions J. A, 1976), 72; Bidwell, *Morocco*, 110; Maxwell, *Lords of the Atlas*, 145-7; Rivet, *Lyautey*, 2:69, 177; Usborne, *Conquest*, 231.

82 Baita, 'Reversion to Tradition', 44-5; Scham, *Lyautey*, 123, Bidwell, *Morocco*, 284.

83 Bidwell, *Morocco*, 162-3.

84 *Ibid.*, 273.

Above The French army in Morocco was largely made up of Moroccans. Here are seen 'partisans' from the Beni Ourain assembling in the early stages of the conquest. *Below* Moroccan troops embark for France to fight in the1914-18 War.

Colonial Morocco
Above Tangier (postcard, early 1920s). Note the late 19th-century buildings facing the sea and the newer square building on top of the hill. Tangier had attracted European expatriates since the end of the 19th century. *Below* The Khalifa of the Spanish zone, shaded by the umbrella that was the prerogative of Alaou sultans, enters the Plaza de España, Tetuan. (Author's collection)

Little money was spent on education although there was some administrative tinkering. Islamic education was put under the Minister of Justice in 1915. The following year, a Conseil Supérieure de l'Enseignement des Indigènes was set up with the *grand vizir*, minister of justice and various Muslim notables, and their French shadows as members, but it did very little. Islamic learning was not stagnant, but there was not very much of it – perhaps 700 students in the Qarawiyyin in Fez and 400 in the Yusufiyya in Marrakesh by the late 1920s. This was only partly because of lack of funds, because the informal structure of the Qarawiyyin and Yusufiyya mosque in Marrakesh made it difficult for the French to find a structure that they could take in hand. They did try to discourage the annual festivals in Fez and Marrakesh of the 'Sultan of the Students', when students had an opportunity to make satirical speeches and do other politically unsettling things, but they could not ban the festivities outright. Modern education was hard to find, both because Lyautey had no wish to educate large numbers of Moroccans into political opposition, and because many Moroccans simply did not want their children to be educated by Christians. Only a few modern primary schools were set up, mainly in Casablanca; there were fifty-eight of them in 1917 and they had very few pupils – by 1930-1 there were still only 1,618 Moroccan students in French secondary schools.[85]

Education was really provided for political reasons, to educate the sons of the Muslim, Arab-speaking elite. The first two 'Schools for the Sons of Notables' (Écoles des Fils de Notables) were set up in 1916 and fed into the even more restricted secondary schools, the Collèges Musulmans at Fez (founded in 1914) and Rabat (1916). Their purpose was to bind the fathers more closely to the French system, and to produce in the sons a loyal class of young men to help run the bureaucracy. They would be fluent in French, since only language and religion were taught in Arabic.[86] Even so, the notable fathers had to pay fees, which the fathers of pupils in the first Écoles Franco-Israélites did not, because the Protectorate administration was competing with the Alliance Israélite Universelle for the loyalty of the Jewish community.[87]

85 Rivet, *Lyautey*, 2:241-2; Bidwell, *Morocco*, 242-3; Dale Eickelman, *Knowledge and Power in Morocco* (Princeton University Press, 1985), 85-91.

86 Halstead, *Rebirth*, 100-6; Rivet, *Lyautey*, 2:242-6; Scham, *Lyautey*, 151-56; Bidwell, *Morocco*, 230-42.

87 Laskier, *Alliance*, 156; Halstead, *Rebirth*, 100.

Nothing much was done about Moroccans' health apart from coping with emergencies. There were typhus outbreaks in the coastal cities in 1914 and 1916, so the rubbish was cleaned off the streets, garbage burned and war waged on rats by offering a bounty as had once been done for locusts. European inhabitants sheltered behind *cordons sanitaires* around the European areas of the cities, and house servants and state employees were compulsorily vaccinated. Many Moroccans considered this to be sanitary despotism, not benevolence. Apart from the medical regulation of prostitutes very little personal medicine was received by the Moroccan population. Indeed, Moroccan cities were becoming more unhealthy than ever, as cars belched exhaust and churned up dust on unmade streets.[88]

Even land surveying, vital for the colonial economy, slowed down, although the legislative and administrative bustle did not. In 1915 a Conseil Supérieur de Habous was established to register land controlled by religious endowments. In 1916 and 1917 the first steps were taken to whittle away collective land and to clear the way for economic exploitation of forest clearings but there was little distribution of land during the war since the demand was not great and immigration was restricted.[89]

The wartime economy

Although little land was distributed, France needed food and the resurrection of the 'granary of Rome' was never more urgent. One of the Protectorate's irrigation experts, Paul Penet, coined what became the catch phrase of Moroccan agriculturalists, 'not a drop of water to the sea', as the objective of the water management system. Such a huge undertaking needed careful preparation and surveys of resources, and during the war not a single drop of water was *prevented* from reaching the sea.[90]

Even so agricultural exports to France boomed (from 31 million francs in 1914 to 114 million in 1918).[91] The tax system provided the encouragement. During the war the *tartib* was extended through most of 'Maroc Utile', but rebates were given to anyone who cleared land for European-style colonisation. That did not, of course, include many Moroccans, so they still paid the *tartib* and had to

88 Rivet, *Lyautey*, 2:224-38. Bidwell, *Morocco*, 259-60

89 Bidwell, *Morocco*, 205-17; Pascon, *Haouz*, 2:457. Scham, *Lyautey*, 77; Stewart, *Economy*, 134-5.

90 Swearingen, *Mirages*, 38-9.

91 Stewart, *Economy*, 38-9; Salahdine, *Maroc*, 72, 175, 237.

increase production to do so.[92] The wartime shortage of shipping encouraged the local industrial processing of agricultural products, such as flour milling.[93]

The infrastructure grew during the war. The narrow-gauge military system between Casablanca and Rabat was opened to civilian traffic in 1916, which made it easier to move agricultural products along the coast, where the cities were growing fast.[94]

POPULATION OF MOROCCAN CITIES

	1912	*1921*
Casablanca	12,000	110,000
Azemmour	6,000	22,000
Safi	8,000	26,000
Rabat-Salé	44,000	58,000

Source: Figures drawn from Abu-Lughod, *Rabat*, 153.

The new port at Kénitra, the Resident-General's personal project, was renamed Port Lyautey in his honour; by 1921 it had 10,000 inhabitants. Inland cities grew more slowly, because fewer Europeans wanted to live there. Henri Prost ensured that government structures preserved the required Moroccan architectural idiom. Some impressive architecture was the result: the Grand Place (later renamed the Place Lyautey) in Casablanca and the Collège Musulman that was built in Rabat in 1916 with copious use of horseshoe arches. Lyautey also made sure that the ruined Merinid city at Chellah, outside Rabat, was preserved.

While a Moroccan past and a Moroccan façade were preserved, there were few houses for real Moroccans to live in. The first *bidonville* (shanty-town) appeared in Port Lyautey as early as 1912. Prost tried to persuade industrialists to build garden suburbs for their workers in Casablanca, but most inhabitants of the *bidonvilles* had no regular employer. When he tried to make *habus* property available, much of it was appropriated to build a new palace for the Sultan or seized by *Makhzan* officials and merchants.[95]

Fortunately for Prost, Moroccans who sought work had alternatives to the cities. Recruits were sent to France to fight, and to work as civilians, mainly in war-related industries. Many Rifis

92 Abu Lughod, *Rabat*, 193; Salahdine, *Maroc*, 149-50; Stewart, *Economy*, 82-3, 101.

93 Stewart, *Economy*, 123, 128.

94 J-C Allain, 'Les chemins de fer marocains du protectorat français pendant l'entre-deux-guerres', *Revue d'Histoire Moderne et Contemporaine*, July-Sept (1987): 427.

95 Wright, *Politics*, 154-6.

left the Spanish zone for Algeria, to work on the big estates around Oran.

The Spanish zone

In the Spanish zone, economic activity came to a standstill, like virtually everything else. In May 1915 the High Commissioner, General Marina, was replaced by General Francisco Gómez Jordana, who halted practically all military advances and almost all civilian activity. By 1919 only 200 boys were being educated in the Melilla area, hardly a record of great success since it was intended that by educating their sons local notables might be won over. Hospitals were not built, few roads constructed.[96] In January 1919 a Spanish deputy told the Cortes: 'The reports of our maladministration of our zone fade before the reality. At the outbreak of war, Spain took over from the German company which was operating the port of Larache all their material, but nothing whatever has been done. [...] In all our zone the insecurity is absolute.'[97] Jordana agreed but blamed government policy that 'has paralysed our action during this period, which may be considered wasted, making pointless, for the most part, much of the political work carried out.'[98] This was disingenuous. More than 82% of the budget was dedicated to military expenses, and the army sat still.[99]

Instead of advancing, the army tried to buy support. The pensions of Rifi notables increased quickly, in the hope that they would supply intelligence and stir up enough trouble to push the tribes into a debilitating civil war.[100] This policy was basically flawed, as one pensioner explained to Spanish military intelligence in 1916:

> Know also that those who eat your money and declare that they are friends of Spain are liars; they are evil and treacherous, for they know ... that if the Spanish nation does come down upon the Rif and settle its troops there, the monthly salary which they now take will no longer remain. And for this reason they never advise you truly; on the contrary, they always deceive you.[101]

96 Pennell, *Government and Flag*, 62-3.

97 Quoted in *ibid.*, 63.

98 Gomez-Jordana y Souza, 132.

99 PRO FO 371/2970/107057, Hubert White to Balfour, Tangier 21 May 1917.

100 Pennell, 'Anual' 76; Pennell, *Government and Flag*, 56.

101 Quoted in Pennell, 'Anual', 78.

The war gave Moroccans a choice of European paymasters. German military intelligence hoped that the Spanish zones would serve as a base from which to attack the French and maintained a network of spies and saboteurs in Larache. It also had agents in Melilla, who may have included Muhammad bin Abd al-Karim al-Khattabi, the future Rifi leader who was then the city's qadi. He was so openly anti-French that even the Spanish felt obliged to imprison him in 1915. In the far south, the lonely beaches provided landing sites for German agents and arms going to the Sous.[102]

El Raisuni tried to play off the Spanish against the Germans, and had been in contact with the German consul in Tangier whom he hoped would be a conduit to Istanbul. This was opportunism, not Muslim fellow-feeling, as he told his biographer: 'Germany wished to unite all of North Africa under the Commander of the Faithful [the Turkish Sultan]. Turkey is not popular in Morocco, though all men prayed publicly in the mosques that she might win the war, but her rule is better than that of Europe and Stamboul is far away. Each country would have its Khalifa, and all the tribes would have been united under one ruler.'[103]

El Raisuni doubtless hoped that he would be that *khalifa*, but he was careful to do nothing irrevocable and after warning his followers against an alliance with the Germans, he made a quiet compact with Jordana. He would help Spanish troops open the road between Tangier and Tetuan and rule the plains, in exchange for a free hand in the mountains.[104] El Raisuni was never a big qaid in the French sense, because he did not depend on European support. He was a self-made man, and if his popularity slipped, no Spanish forces would help him. So he cooperated enough to remain unmolested, but not enough to ruin his reputation as sultan of the *jihad*.

German military intelligence did not trust El Raisuni either, but pinned its hopes on Abd al-Malik Muhyi al-Din, the grandson of the Algerian leader of the 1840s, Abd al-Qadir. A former Ottoman army officer, Abd al-Malik had helped Abu Himara, and served as an inspector of native police in Tangier. After the Ottoman victory at Gallipoli he slipped into the Rif with 1,000 men, mainly

102 PRO FO371/2970/154893, White to Balfour 27 July 1 917; Pennell, *Government and Flag*, 53-4.

103 Forbes, *Raisuni*, 182.

104 *Ibid.*, 193, 209; see also Edmund Burke, 'Moroccan Resistance, Pan-Islam and German War Strategies, 1914-1918', *Francia* 3 (1975): 434-64.

deserters from the 1911 mutiny in Fez, and a German advisor named Albert Bartels. Two Turks arrived later. Yet Abd al-Malik was never happy with the Germans.[105] Bartels complained: 'On one occasion he expressed his apprehension that in the event of a German victory in Europe, Morocco would become a German possession. His dream, however, was to establish an independent Morocco under his leadership.'[106]

Abd al-Malik caused the French much anxiety in 1917 and 1918, but the end of the war put paid to such dreams, although it was some time before everyone believed that the French really had won.[107]

MOROCCO AFTER THE FIRST WORLD WAR

Restructuring the administration

The end of the war allowed Lyautey to consolidate the Protectorate. The years after 1918 saw the flowering of his system, even before the military conquest was completed. Two quite separate societies had to be accommodated within the administration. As more colons migrated to Morocco after the war, they demanded that their voice be heard. Lyautey was willing to allow them that much. In March 1919 he set up a Council of Government with representatives from chambers of commerce and agriculture in the settled areas; later delegates from the municipalities were added and in May 1923 a second chamber of pro-French Moroccans was added. But all it could do was discuss: it could make no decisions on laws or budgets.[108]

Another urgent task was to simplify the administration of the tribes. The Direction de Affaires Indigènes was given charge of virtually everything that concerned the Moroccan population: disposal of 'jemaa lands, agricultural loans, order and security. It had a strict military chain of command from the generals who commanded huge regions to junior officers in charge of *circumscriptions* who controlled the qaids who collected the taxes, administered justice and managed collective land. Even the best qaids were usually illiterate, and many were corrupt. Yet when, in 1920, the

105 Pennell, *Government and Flag*, 51-3; Rivet, *Lyautey*, 2:108-9; Albert Bartels, *Fighting the French in Morocco*, trans. H. J. Stenning (London: A. Rivers, 1932), *passim*.

106 Bartels, *Fighting*, 108.

107 Pennell, *Government and Flag*, 64.

108 Scham, *Lyautey*, 75.

Grand Vizir El Mokri suggested that they should be trained in the Collège Musulman, Lyautey turned him down. It would be more difficult to remove a qaid who had a diploma. Unreliable and corrupt qaids were certainly removed from time to time but they were always hard to control because they knew their areas far better than officers of the Affaires Indigènes did, and easily dominated the jemaas.[109]

Those jemaas were never really important, because French administrators found the qaids easier to manage, for all their faults. Among the 'tribes of Berber custom', the full force of the separatist policy now came into play. French native affairs' officers were disciplined for using Arabic not French and there was much exaggerated talk of a 'Franco-Berber race', even of converting the Berbers to Christianity. Lyautey had no use for this last idea, but he opposed anything that strengthened Islam among the Berbers. The new Berber schools that were set up after 1923, and the Berber teachers' college in Azrou, rigidly excluded Islamic materials from their curricula.[110]

The Spanish authorities may have distrusted the French but they admired their organisation, so they imitated it. In each tribe there was a military officer, an *interventor* of the Oficina de Asuntos Indígenas who oversaw the qaids. The only real difference was that the system applied to the whole Spanish zone, not just the Berber areas.

In the south of Morocco, French control was tightened as the big qaids were gradually abandoned and replaced by a single 'super' qaid, Si Thami el Glaoui.

The end of the big qaids and the rise of Si Thami El Glaoui

El Mtouggi and Taïeb El Goundafi were growing old. Both died in 1928, but their power had already been cut away; by 1925, Affaires Indigènes offices had been opened in their fiefs. Only one great family survived.[111]

The head of the Glaoui family was still young. Si Madani, the patriarch, had died in August 1918, supposedly of heartbreak when his favourite son Abd al-Malik, one of very many children, was

109 Bidwell, *Morocco*, 81, 95-6, Baita, 'Reversion to Tradition', 41-2.

110 Scham, *Lyautey*, 66-70, 84; Halstead, *Rebirth*, 72-3.

111 Bidwell, *Morocco*, 114-16; Rivet, *Lyautey*, 2:184.

killed in fighting near Demnate. Lyautey at once confirmed Si Thami as pasha of Marrakesh and head of the family.[112]

Si Thami sent his troops into battle beside the French army. In January and February 1919 and in July 1920, they were in action against the Ait Atta, but that bellicose tribe defeated him in 1922. That ended his career as a field commander, but his political career was only just beginning.[113] In 1921 Si Thami had visited Paris and caused a sensation. His stylish behaviour won him a reputation for splendour and romance in the French Empire rather like that of some of the grander princes of British India, but this could not entirely head off the criticism in the press concerning his activities in Marrakesh. As pasha, he was building up enormous wealth through corrupt land deals. From the early 1920s Si Thami acquired huge estates around Marrakesh and in the coastal cities. In 1926 and 1927 he paid 7 million francs for a block of flats in Casablanca and another 2 million for the old estate of Ion Perdicaris in Tangier. He took a cut from most commercial undertakings in Marrakesh – even the city's 22,000 prostitutes paid him part of their earnings – and engaged in large scale fraud. In 1927 he cheated a Marseilles company of 500,000 francs in an olive oil deal.[114]

Because he was corrupt, the French found him useful, for there was little possibility of Si Thami abandoning them. In times of danger, he was a bulwark of French power. Moreover, he was the only person who could hold in check the qaid of Telouët, the old Glaoui heartland. This was his nephew, Si Hammu, who was appallingly cruel and strongly anti-French. The French army could not control him because he had prevented the road up to Telouët from being laid, stopped telegraph lines from being installed and ensured that no French officer was sent there.[115]

Si Thami's only guiding principle was self-interest, but other Moroccan servants of the French were not always so self-serving. Many were indeed corrupt, but others were genuinely concerned to modernise and reform the state under colonial auspices, recognising that it brought real advantages.

112 Rivet, *Lyautey*, 2:177; Bidwell, *Morocco*, 111; Maxwell, *Lords of the Atlas*, 148-9; Morsy, 'Glaoui', 72; Pascon, *Haouz*, 2:324.

113 Hart, *Ait Atta*, 165-6; Usborne, *Conquest*, 238; Morsy, 'Glaoui', 73-5.

114 Bidwell, *Morocco*, 112, 114-15, 120; Rivet, *Lyautey*, 2:181; Maxwell, *Lords of the Atlas*, 153-9; PRO FO 371/ 12694, W7802/600/28, Ryan (C-G Rabat) to Sec of State., Rabat 10 August 1927and W10065/600/28, Gurney (C-G Tangier) to Chamberlain, Tangier 18 Oct 1927; Pascon, *Haouz*, 2:325.

115 Pascon, *Haouz*, 2:325; Maxwell, *Lords of the Atlas*, 153-9.

Reform under colonialism

For some, particularly Salafis, cooperation with the Protectorate was perfectly compatible with reforming society and modernising the economy.

In 1923 Ahmed R'honi, the Minister of Justice in the Spanish zone, who had studied in the Qarawiyyin under Muhammad bin Jafar al-Kittani, and Abdussalam Bennuna, the Minister of Finance, put forward a proposal to open more schools for Moroccans. Bennuna also proposed commercial cooperation with European partners in order to build up the finances of a Moroccan bourgeoisie. He founded a pottery factory with Spanish partners, an import agency with German partners, and in 1928, the 'National Electric Cooperative' to supply the *madina* of Tetuan with electricity. Bennuna was in contact with Tal'at Harb, the virtual founder of economic nationalism in Egypt and the creator of Bank Misr, although Bennuna was more willing to link up with European capital, and disliked Bank Misr's reliance on interest. Bennuna was motivated by a mixture of religious piety, commercial entrepreneurship, and Salafi-inspired belief in education and reform. Such motivations were mutually reinforcing, not mutually exclusive.[116]

Mohamed Hajoui, as minister for education in the French zone, tried without much success to modernise the Qarawiyyin. Hajoui, a philosopher, wanted to respond intellectually to the colonialist challenge. Education in the *sunna* and *hadith*, he claimed, could provide the basis of a society radically different from the old: progressive, commercially oriented, open to free trade. Only an erroneous interpretation of the *shari'a* stood in the way of Islamic capitalism. Hajoui's ideas were both a criticism of his own society and a spirited answer to European supremacists who said that Islamic societies lacked bourgeois values.[117]

Thus in the early years of the protectorate, Salafi leaders saw their responsibility to reform Islam and Moroccan society rather than to battle against the colonialists. Yet any emphasis on an Islamic and a Moroccan identity would eventually cause conflict with the colonial authorities. It surfaced, inevitably, in education.

116 R'honi, *Historia*, 11-13; Wolf, *Secrets*, 152-3; Jamal Eddine Benomar, 'Working Class, Trade Unionism and Nationalism in Colonial Morocco' (Ph. D. diss. University of London, Birkbeck College, 1992), 261.

117 Laroui, *Esquisses*, 115-21.

The Free School movement

In 1921 Salafi activists founded several schools in Fez, the ancient headquarters of Islamic learning. Others were soon set up in Rabat, the new capital, Salé and Casablanca. In 1924 the first school was founded in Tetuan. Others followed in Marrakesh and Kénitra. Among the early teachers in Fez were several products of the Qarawiyyin such as Allal El-Fassi, Mohamed Ghazi and Mohammed bel-Arabi el-Alaoui, a qadi who also taught in the Qarawiyyin and in an Ecole des Fils de Notables. All would later become important nationalist leaders, but for the moment they concentrated on education.

They called these establishments 'Free Schools' not because the pupils paid no fees, but because they were free of French control. They provided a modern Islamic education in Arabic. The Quran, ethics, *hadith* and Islamic history were taught alongside geography and mathematics and, in some schools, science.[118]

While the schools were not overtly nationalist, their effect most certainly was. Autonomous of French control, they emphasised pride in an Islamic civilisation that had been denigrated by its conquerors. They taught a return to true Islamic values with a pronounced modernist tinge. This was a profoundly urban movement, because the countryside was untouched by Salafi ideas, and indeed by education of any sort. Some of the countryside was still untouched by French and Spanish occupation, and armed struggle continued there.

'Useful' and 'Necessary' Morocco

In 1920, with the world war over, Lyautey gave himself three years to accomplish the 'total submission of Morocco, leaving no areas of dissidence.'[119] This was much too optimistic: the French government was short of money and needed troops to help occupy the Rhineland, not Morocco. So the Resident-General concentrated on the subjugation of 'Useful Morocco' (*Le Maroc Utile*), areas with some economic worth for agriculture, mining or providing water, and of 'Necessary Morocco', the areas needed to protect it. The rest could wait.[120]

118 Halstead, *Rebirth*, 161-2, 278-80; Brown, *Salé*, 82; Munson, *Religion and Power*, 102-3.

119 Rivet, *Lyautey*, 2:63, quoting Lyautey.

120 *Ibid.*, 2:63-4; Usborne, *Conquest*, 239.

The priorities were the Middle Atlas and the *Tache de Taza* (home to the Zaïane and Beni Ouarain confederations). In 1922 a pincer movement encircled the Zaïane, and resistance began to crumble; by the end of 1922 most of the Zaïane had submitted. Lyautey was promoted to Marshal of France. In 1923 French columns cut the *Tache de Taza* in two and broke the power of the Beni Ouarain.[121]

These advances were hard fought. A picture is sometimes painted of a conquest in which massive force overawed the Moroccans into passivity, or at best into formalised battle that salvaged their honour but led to few deaths.[122] This was not true of the operations in the *Tache de Taza* and the Middle Atlas: in 1923 there were 21,000 French troops in the field against 7,000 Moroccans, and on one bad day the French lost sixty-five dead. In fact, most of these dead were Moroccans, for Lyautey's use of French troops was strictly limited.[123] They were limited also as to the area in which they operated, and Lyautey's concentration on 'Usfeul Morocco' left the control and even the status of peripheral areas open.

The boundaries of Morocco

Morocco was not the only battleground for the French colonial army, which was also trying to take control of the Saharan portions of its colonies of French West Africa (Afrique Occidentale Française, AOF) and Algeria. Imposing order on nomads meant pursuing them across the desert, an occupation in which boundaries meant little, even in so far as anyone knew what the boundaries were.

Some borders had been fixed by the French and Spanish governments in 1912. These defined the Tarfaya district as part of the Spanish Zone of Protectorate, and the territory to the south – the Saquïa el-Hamra – as being Spanish territory, though that last provision was a change of policy of sorts: until then the French government seem to have regarded Moroccan territory as stretching down at least to the Saquïa el-Hamra valley itself (in other words the northern part of what would become the Spanish Sahara.)[124]

The boundaries between different French colonies were less clear. The differences between Algerian, AOF and Moroccan ter-

121 Usborne, *Conquest*, 242-3; Halstead, *Rebirth*, 115.

122 Bidwell, *Morocco*, 34-5.

123 Usborne, *Conquest*, 243; Bidwell, *Morocco*, 35; Rivet, *Lyautey*, 67; Maghraoui, 'Moroccan colonial soldiers'.

124 Trout, *Frontiers*, 200-15.

ritory were defined by military operations, and in the 1920s forces based in Algeria advanced further into the desert. There they came up against nomadic and semi-nomadic tribes that roamed through huge areas. The movements of the Ait Atta confederation extended from the Jbel Sarhro to the south east as far as Touat, which French troops had occupied in 1900, and the nomadism of the great Reguibat confederation spread from Tindouf across to the Atlantic coasts.[125]

While there was never any formal definition of political boundaries, Algerian military maps appeared in 1923 showing all of the north-western Sahara as far as the Dràa valley as part of Algerian territory. This was very vague, and apparently designed to be temporary, since it was assumed that eventually Moroccan jurisdiction would be extended over much of this territory, but the process of dividing the Sahara between Algeria, Spain and the AOF had begun.[126]

Yet such border issues and desert skirmishes were extremely unimportant at this stage, for a more immediate threat had arisen in the Rif mountains north of Fez. It would provide the greatest challenge of all to the Franco-Spanish Protectorate.

THE RIF WAR

The attack on El Raisuni

Moments before he died, in November 1918, General Jordana completed a memorandum in which he demanded more troops, more supplies and proper air support before real 'pacification' could take place. His successor as High Commissioner, General Dámaso Berenguer, got them.

In February 1919 Berenguer attacked El Raisuni and sent troops deep into the Jebala. Although El Raisuni's men beat the Spanish at Ouad Ras in July 1919, it was an isolated triumph. Spanish troops pushed forwards and on 15 October 1920 occupied the holy city of Chaouèn, where no European had openly set foot before. By the beginning of July 1921 Berenguer had cooped up El Raisuni in Tazrut. Then, much to his own surprise, El Raisuni was saved by the Rifis.[127]

In the summer of 1921 a coalition of Rifi tribes broke the

125 *Ibid.*, 218-29; Hart *Ait 'Atta*, 14.

126 Trout, *Frontiers*, 229-46.

127 Pennell, *Government and Flag*, 87-8; Ayache, *Guerre du Rif*, 51.

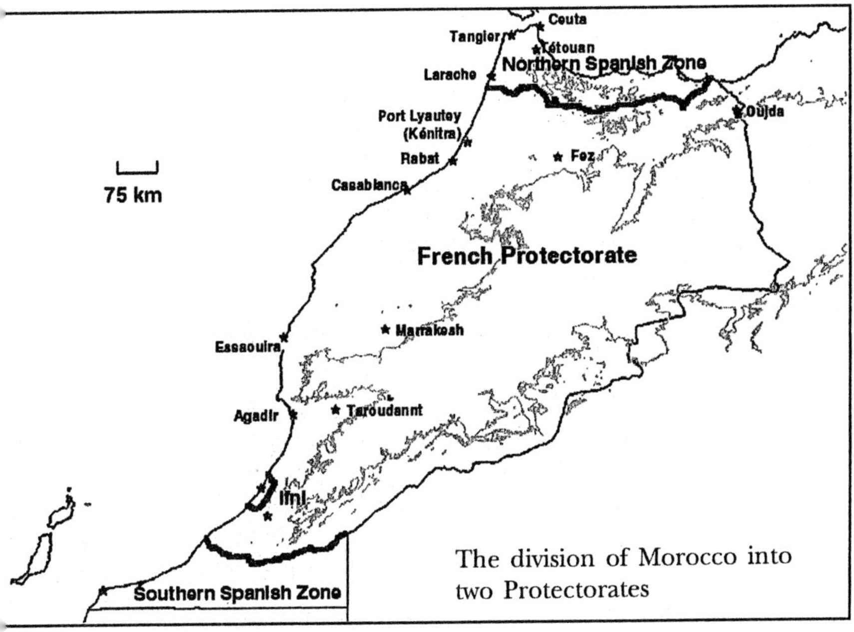

Ceuta
Tangier
Tétouan
Northern Spanish Zone
Larache
Port Lyautey
(Kénitra)
Rabat
Fez
Oujda
Casablanca
75 km
French Protectorate
Marrakesh
Essaouira
Agadir
Taroudannt
Ifni
Southern Spanish Zone

The division of Morocco into two Protectorates

Thousand Francs
5000000
4000000
3000000
2000000
1000000
0
1926
1927
1928
1929
1930
1931
1932
1933
1933
1935
1936
1937
1938
TOTAL
Britain
France
Spain
Japan

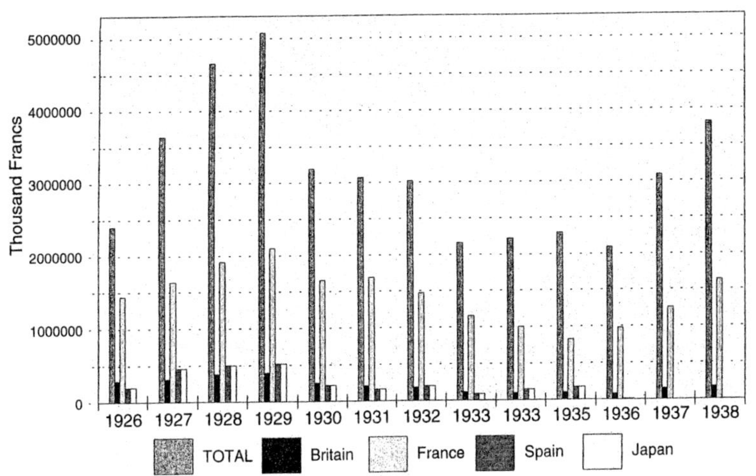

Moroccan trade during the Protectorate (all zones)

Source: Great Britain, Dept. of Overseas Trade

Spanish army. For two years Spanish forces had been advancing westwards from Melilla across the desolate Garet plain.[128] Temporary alliances that were stitched together to oppose them were ineffective, but the enemies of Spain in the Banu Waryaghal, the biggest tribe in the Rif massif, turned on the Spanish pensioners in their midst, and demanded that they break off relations or see their houses burned. Among the first to obey was the richest, Abd al-Karim al-Khattabi; in early 1919 he called home his younger son Mahammad from Madrid where he had been studying mining engineering. His elder son, Muhammad bin Abd al-Karim, returned from Melilla where he had been a qadi, disillusioned from his imprisonment during the war and inspired by Salafi ideas of social and religious reform. He was determined to stop the Spanish advance.[129]

Ibn Abd al-Karim's organising genius transformed the opposition. By January 1921 he had formed the nucleus of a modern army. In May, he used it to capture a Spanish blockhouse on an isolated hillock named Dahar Abarran. On 25 July he attacked the main Spanish forward base at Annoual. Annoual was badly situated in a valley surrounded by high hills and the 4,000 Spanish troops were ordered to withdraw. They panicked; as they fled eastwards towards Melilla, the tribes around them rose. By 9 August, at least 10,000 Spanish troops were dead, including their commander, General Manuel Fernández Silvestre (some said by suicide); another general, Felipe Navarro, was one of hundreds of prisoners in Rifi hands. It was the worst defeat of a colonial army in Africa in the twentieth century.[130]

Over the next year the Spanish army slowly recaptured lost ground, and by the end of 1922, they were back at their old forward positions.[131] They got no further, because ibn Abd al-Karim had taken firm control of the Rif mountains. His supporters had captured a huge stock of weapons (20,000 rifles, 400 mountain guns and 129 cannons) as well as 400 Spanish prisoners. In January 1923 ibn Abd al-Karim ransomed the prisoners for 4 million pesetas and used the money to train a regular army and set up a regular administration. He armed it with the captured weapons, appointed qaids in every tribe and clan that he controlled, and in February 1924 had himself declared Amir of the Rif.[132]

128 Martínez de Campos, *España Bélica*, 207-23.

129 Pennell, *Government and Flag*, 67.

130 *Ibid.*, 83-4; Usborne, *Conquest*, 251-3; Ayache, *Guerre du Rif*, 84-92, 131-59.

131 Pennell, *Government and Flag*, 98, 110; Ayache, *Guerre du Rif*, 189-205.

132 Pennell, *Government and Flag*, 110-16.

European pseudo-Moroccan architecture in Morocco
Above The ornate residence of Walter Harris in Tangier, where Moulay Abdelaziz resided after falling from power. *Below* The more austere residence of the colonel in charge of the district (*cercle*) at Guercif, western Morocco.

The Rif War.
Above Two *qadis* (1919) — the future Rifi leader Muhammad bin ‘Abd al-Karim al Khattabi (*standing*) and his father, considered to be one of the Spanish army's principal agents in the Rif.
Right shackles used to control Spanish prisoners of the Rifis after the Annoual disaster in 1921. *Below* Rif bomb made from a tin can. (Museo de la Legion, Ceuta)

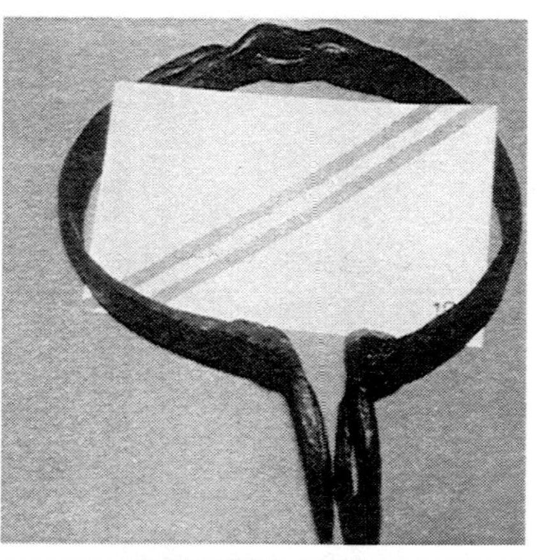

Instead of tackling ibn Abd al-Karim the Spanish commanders decided to finish off El Raisuni. In August 1922, the *sharif* finally agreed to disband his forces and retire to Tazrut. There, immensely fat and very sick, he was visited by Rosita Forbes, the Englishwoman who wrote his biography.[133]

Having won the Jebala, the Spanish army promptly lost it. Recriminations over the defeat at Annoual brought down the Spanish government in 1924 and General Primo de Rivera, the dictator who took over, wanted to abandon Morocco completely. A vigorous campaign by African Army officers like Francisco Franco persuaded him merely to withdraw to secure positions, but that meant abandoning the interior. The retreat from Chaouèn between October and December 1924 cost the Spanish army another 10,000 men. Rifi forces occupied the city when the Spanish left it, so this became yet another victory for ibn Abd el-Karim. The Rifis also took El-Raisuni. Bloated with dropsy, he was placed on a litter, carried to the coast, loaded on to a boat and transported to the Rif. There he died on 3 April 1925.

Fired by success, and impelled by the need to secure food supplies, Rifi forces turned south and, on 12 April 1925, attacked Lyautey's front line. By 5 June Rifi forces were 40 km. from Fez, yet the city did not rise and the front was held.[134] After Marshal Pétain, the hero of Verdun, took overall command, Lyautey resigned; on 5 October he left Morocco for ever.[135]

The attack on the French zone forced the French and Spanish governments to bury their differences. On 8 September 1925 a huge amphibious operation landed 16,000 Spanish troops on the coast of the Banu Waryaghal, near the site of the future town of Al Hoceima. It took them nearly a month to advance 8 km. inland to Ajdir, the Rifi capital, even though the Rifis had no more than 5,000 men. Other Spanish troops closed in from the east and French troops advanced from the south. During that winter's blockade the Rifis starved.[136]

In the spring of 1926 ibn Abd al-Karim tried to negotiate a peace, but the French and Spanish governments were less than half-hearted. The combined attack began again on 8 May with

133 Forbes, *Raisuni, passim.*

134 Pennell, *Government and Flag,* 183-9.

135 Usborne, *Conquest,* 296-7.

136 Martínez de Campos, *España Bélica,* 306-9; Pennell, *Government and Flag,* 199. José E. Alvarez, 'Between Gallipoli and D-Day: Alhvcemas, 1925', *Journal of Military History,* vol. 63, 1(1999): 75-98.

123,000 men and Rifi resistance finally crumbled. On 26 May ibn Abd al-Karim surrendered to the French, who hustled him off to an eventual exile in the Indian Ocean island of Réunion. He was afraid that if he had surrendered to the Spanish they would have executed him.[137]

The expectations of the Rifis and their leader

Muhammad bin Abd al-Karim is such a towering figure that it is easy to forget that the resistance started before he assumed command and continued briefly after his defeat. Although he led it, the first impulse came from below, and although it was his disciplined men who attacked at Abarran and Annoual, it was the mass rising that overwhelmed the Spanish troops as they fled back across the baking Garet plain in midsummer. Popular enthusiasm and sheer euphoria carried the Rifis forward at every stage, and ibn Abd al-Karim's support came from his success and his personal magnetism. An American journalist who visited the Rif in early 1925 was harangued by a Rifi qaid:

> And the Rifi killed and killed and killed, until there were one hundred and sixty-four thousand million Spaniards dead upon the field ... and Generan Barro [*sic* – General Navarro] and all the *coroneles* and *tenientes* and many thousands and thousands of men worked for the sultan on the roads and as slaves. The sultan is very great: the sultan is Lord of Islam. The sultan can defeat all enemies in battle. The sultan has many millions of fighting men who will sweep that French and the English and all the Christians out of the Arab's country.[138]

Ibn Abd al-Karim did not have millions of men, nor was he Sultan, but such expectations dragged him into the fatal attack on the French zone. The ballads people sang to celebrate the victories were a stronger motivation than any ideology,[139] for they extolled an immediate purpose, to remove the Christians. As ibn Abd al-Karim knew well, this was really a popular *jihad*, and he

137 Pennell, *Government and Flag*, 215-16.

138 Vincent Sheean, *Adventures among the Rifi* (London: Geo. Allen & Unwin, 1926), 47.

139 Pennell, *Government and Flag*, 81-2; Mohamed Chtatou, 'Bin 'Abd al-Karim in the Rifi Oral Tradition of Gzenneya' in Joffe and Pennell (eds), *Tribe and State*, 193-5; Hart, *Aith Waryaghar*, 375; C.R. Pennell, 'The Responsibility for Anual: the Failure of Spanish Policy in the Moroccan Protectorate 1912-21', *European Studies Review*, 12 (1982): 67-86.

played on those feelings, although he personally believed that *jihad* was a medieval anachronism. After the war, ibn Abd al-Karim complained that most Rifis had seen his leadership as a temporary expedient before restoring the traditional tribal structure of society.

His own objectives were quite different. At the beginning of the war he told his closest supporters that he wanted to set up 'a country with a government and a flag', and his government documents referred to a 'République Rifaine' or in Arabic, *al-jumhuriyya al-rifiyya.* Yet the *bay'a* that named him Amir of the Rif, in February 1924, closely resembled those given to sultans of Morocco, not because he wanted to supplant Moulay Youssef – there is no evidence for of that – but because he modelled his state on the traditional Makhzan.[140]

Most of his ministers were members of his family: his uncle Abd al-Salam was minister of finance, his brother Si Mahammad was his *khalifa,* and his minister of foreign affairs, two ministers of the interior, minister of marine and his personal secretary were relations by marriage.[141] Significantly, outsiders provided the ideological spine of the state. Men like the chief legal officers, the minister of justice and the chief *qadi,* were responsible for the strict imposition of the *shari'a,* which they did with a will. Men were obliged to pray five times a day, murderers were executed, people who got into fights were imprisoned, men and women were prosecuted for slander, and men for sodomy and for reneging on a promise to marry. One man was even imprisoned for wife-beating.[142]

Imposition of the *shari'a* served a practical purpose too, because only a single system of law could supplant fragile tribal alliances and guarantee unity.[143] That was also why ibn Abd al-Karim's army, with its hierarchy of ranks and defined command structure, was more reliable than the groups of irregular fighters raised on the old rotating basis among the tribes, even though these did much of the fighting. To make central control even more effective, ibn Abd al-Karim constructed an extensive telephone network and road system, both of which were built from scratch, in part by Spanish prisoners.[144] Neither his authoritarian control, nor his

140 Pennell, *Government and Flag,* 110-16.

141 *Ibid.,* 126.

142 C.R. Pennell, 'Law, Order and the Formation of an Islamic Resistance to Colonialism: the Rif, 1921-1926', *Revue d'Histoire Maghrébine,* 21-2 (1981): 23-39.

143 Pennell, 'Law, Order', 23-39; Pennell, *Government and Flag,* 144-7.

144 Pennell, *Government and Flag,* 130-3.

imposition of the *shari'a* were popular with ordinary Rifis, but ibn Abd al-Karim was a Salafi, and, like Hajoui, the reforming Minister of Justice in the French Protectorate, believed that *nizam* was more than military modernisation.

As might have been expected of a Salafi, he gave education a high priority. Years later the nationalist leader Allal El-Fassi would jibe that ibn Abd al-Karim founded no schools, but his mosque schools taught mathematics and advanced pupils studied Muhammad bin Jafar al-Kittani's book *Nasihat ahl al-Islam.* There was even an attempt to teach girls, one of many changes in the life of Rifi women. Women did most of the agricultural work, and played an important role in spying on the Spanish (and in spying for the Spanish). On occasion they fought too.[145]

A mixture of practical and ideological reasons determined ibn Abd al-Karim's distaste for the *tariqas.* After the war he complained in *al-Manar,* a journal edited by the Egyptian Salafi Rashid Rida, that the shaykhs of the *tariqas* had undermined him. The leaders of the Darqawiyya certainly fled to French protection when Rifi forces took their headquarters at Amjot, although individual *marabouts* and shaykhs did support him. Personal power was the most important consideration, even if it was dressed up in religious language. El Raisuni , surrounded in Tazrut, eloquently brushed aside ibn Abd al-Karim's invitation to join him:

> Close your eyes and take stock, and you will see that this is an ocean that you cannot cross, for this is no way to make war. To make war in accordance with the law, you must first respect your brothers, then you must respect the law, respect the habus, in that way you can make war on the Christian and God will help you. Moreover, the image fades and only reality remains. Our only desire is peace and to avoid the shedding of blood which is today quite useless.[146]

Ibn Abd al-Karim's response was equally uncompromising:

> You should know, oh Sharif, that we are quite aware of what you are. You aspire only to personal greatness, scattering over your brothers the filthy mud of the Christians. Your love for them is public knowledge. Your rejection of your faith is public and notorious... As a result of this, soon, very soon, we will

145 Munson, *Religion and Power*, 93; Pennell, *Government and Flag*, 150; C. R. Pennell, 'Women and Resistance to Colonialism in Morocco: the Rif, 1916-1926', *Journal of African History*, 28 (1987): 107-18.

146 Pennell, *Government and Flag*, 178-9.

come upon you and those who would defend you. This is our last letter to you.[147]

Here were two different concepts of Islam: custom and respect for *sharifs* on the one hand, and the demand that all resources be put at the disposal of an Islamic government on the other. Yet ibn Abd al-Karim received no support from the Salafi '*ulama* in Fez, even when his men were only 40 km. away.[148] They saw the Rifi episode as the last flutter of rural resistance, and did nothing to help while the French and the Spanish combined to crush it. In the end, ibn Abd al-Karim failed for much the same reasons as Moulay Abdelhafid and Moulay Abdelaziz had failed. The old systems which they tried to replace were crumbling in the face of the European onslaught, but the new systems with which they tried to replace them could not mobilise the support, though patronage or kinship or force, that was needed to hold off a modern European army and economic system.

Yet their military success did not mean that the two colonial powers were now able to work together. The Franco-Spanish alliance was born of necessity and not friendship, for nothing could alleviate the bitterness of Spanish resentments dating back to 1912 or even to 1904. The rivalry was played out openly in Tangier.

The international zone reborn

Since the First World War had ended any German interest in the future of Tangier, the French government claimed that the city should remain under the sultan's sovereignty, in other words French control, while the Spanish government demanded that past injustices be rectified by incorporating Tangier into the Spanish zone. The British government, the third major player, wanted Tangier to be internationalised in order to protect the Strait of Gibraltar, and the American administration was determined to maintain an open door trade policy. Both London and Washington wanted to hang on to their old capitulatory rights, and keep their *protégés*.

These contradictory claims were complicated but unimportant compared with the settlements in Europe and the Middle East, so they were put on one side. Only when Benito Mussolini revived Italian resentments at the carve-up of 1904 was a conference convened in London in June 1923. On 14 May 1924 the French, Spanish and British governments ratified a new Statute of Tangier

147 *Ibid.*, 179.

148 *Ibid.*, 179-81.

and invited other states to adhere to it. Most did so, but Mussolini refused until it was modified, a success he achieved in 1928, in true nineteenth–century style, by sending an Italian fleet to parade off Tangier.[149]

The Statute was an unwieldy compromise, neither administratively effective nor in the interests of the Moroccan inhabitants of Tangier. It resembled the aborted arrangements of 1914, except that it gave even less power to the Sultan's representative. A Mandoub (*mandub*), a mere commissioner, now had authority over Muslim affairs and presided over the International Legislative Assembly that replaced the Municipal Council. That body's decisions were subject to veto by a council of European consuls. Day-to-day management was given to the Administrator, who controlled the budget, the police, the bureaucracy and public works. Since the first administrator was a Frenchman, and the Mandoub was given the assistance of a French 'Sharifian Advisor', the French government prevailed. Spanish demands were accommodated, but never satisfied, with second-in-command posts in many parts of the administration.[150] The other posts were also distributed not on the basis of competence, or even of numbers, but of political convenience. Although only a handful of Belgians lived in Tangier, their government demanded its own judge in the already overstaffed Mixed Courts. Walter Harris, the *Times* correspondent, caustically suggested that the Belgians be given half a judge, either physically or mentally handicapped and paid half a salary, but a Belgian was appointed to command the police instead. It was an absurd system. The Legislative Assembly used three languages – Arabic, French and Spanish, but only the Jewish members could understand all three, and the Mandoub could understand only one. British, French, and Moroccan post offices sold sixty-one denominations of stamps to a population of about 60,000.[151] The administration was usually short of money, and the port company, an independent undertaking, could not raise capital, so that in 1930 a jetty projected to be 960 metres long was abandoned when only 500 metres had been built.[152]

149 Kenbib, 'European protections', 49-53; Claire Catherine Spencer, 'The Zone of International Administration of Tangier (1923-35)' (Ph.D diss., SOAS, University of London, 1993), 135-67; Stuart, *Tangier*, 75-83, 98-9.

150 Spencer, 'Tangier', 167-216.

151 *Ibid.*, 269; *Times*, 22 June 1925; Great Britain, Department of Overseas Trade, *Survey of Economic Conditions in Morocco 1928-1929* (London: HMSO, 1930).

152 Spencer, 'Tangier', 335-9; Stuart, *Tangier*, 171.

The 40,000 Muslims, about two-thirds of the population, paid a disproportionate share of the taxes and received little benefit. Urban construction was concentrated in the European parts of the city, and Muslim medical services were so minimal that in 1927 charitable Europeans had to organise a relief committee. In the Mixed Courts, Moroccans received harsher sentences than Europeans for the same crimes, and were mistreated by the police. Some were tortured, electric shocks from telephone batteries being a favoured method since they left no trace. The European occupation of Morocco, for all its humanitarian pronouncements, had not ended torture; it had only ensured that it was done more scientifically and in secret.[153]

Divided economies

In the rest of Morocco, the Spanish and French zones became separate economic fiefs. By 1929 France and Spain took more than 50% of the trade of their respective zones (see table).

NATIONAL TRADE IN MOROCCAN ZONES, 1929(%)

	France	*Spain*	*Britain*	*USA*	*Germany*
French Zone	52	6	9	6	5.5
Spanish Zone	16.5	55	7	4.5	5.5
Tangier	39.5	8.5	7.5	9	

Source Great Britain, Department of Overseas Trade, *Survey of Economic Conditions in Morocco.*

The trade of Tangier was more balanced but was of minimal economic importance, except to its inhabitants. The port that, in 1906, had taken 19% of all Moroccan imports now took 4%. Even the Spanish Zone had little economic consequence. Its share of the total trade of Morocco was 11% of imports and 7% of exports. France accounted for nearly 48% of the trade of the whole country, for Morocco was a French economic enterprise.[154]

Lyautey and his economic advisors gave the Makhzan command of the heights of the Moroccan economy, and then tied it to that of France. In 1920 the Moroccan ('Hassani') currency was taken out of circulation and replaced by notes denominated in francs issued by the Banque d'État. On 1 January 1922 the Moroccan

153 Spencer, 'Tangier', 283-4; Stuart, *Tangier*, 139; FO 371/12694/1224/28, Gurney to Chamberlain, Tangier, 17 February 1927.

154 Rivet, *Lyautey*, 3:113; Víctor Morales Lezcano, *El colonialismo hispano-francés en Marruecos* (Madrid: Siglo XXI, 1976), 102, 191.

franc, legally a separate currency, was tied to the French franc at parity. The Banque d'État itself was taken over by French interests. Frenchmen occupied the former seats of German and Austrian directors and bought out Russian interests. By 1920 the Banque de Paris et des Pays Bays controlled most of the share capital.[155]

Non-French capital was largely excluded from the rest of the economy by a variety of ruses. Only French-owned companies were allowed to invest in minerals (such as lead, manganese, cobalt and zinc) and, especially, in railways, even though that delayed the line between Morocco and Algeria until 1929. On other occasions the state favoured private French companies, as in the coal and iron industries, by directly investing in them. Sometimes production was simply nationalised in the name of the Moroccan government, as happened in 1920 when Lyautey set up the Office Chérifien des Phosphates. Phosphate production rose from just over 8,000 tonnes in 1921 to more than 1.7 million tonnes in 1930, when it directly provided 17% of state revenue, and yet more in indirect taxes. Because of phosphates, the current accounts were in credit for most of the 1920s, which reduced Lyautey's dependence on Paris for cash, and gave him still greater political leeway.[156]

Despite the profits from the phosphate industry, most of the Protectorate's revenue came from taxes and customs dues, and notwithstanding the grumbling of the European settlers, the real weight of those taxes fell upon Moroccans.[157]

Taxation and land sales

In 1925 the *tartib* produced just over 21% of government revenue. Moroccans paid most of it because in 1923 farmers using modern methods (mainly Europeans) were rebated half the tax. It was collected by the qaids with relatively little supervision, and great enthusiasm because they were paid 6% of the proceeds. As a result many Moroccans were forced into debt, at usurious rates of interest, often more than 50% per annum. Harvests were mortgaged in advance, and Moroccans lost land when they failed.[158]

155 Mohammed Bouarfa, *Le Rial et le Franc* (Rabat: INMA, 1988), 147-64, 169-70.

156 Allain, 'Chemins de fer'; René Hoffherr, *L'Économie marocaine* (Paris: Sirey, 1932), 177; Stewart, *Economy*, 118-23; Salahdine, *Maroc*, 258-9; Rivet, *Lyautey*, 3:141.

157 Rivet, *Lyautey*, 3:188.

158 Salahdine, *Maroc*, 152-4; Rivet, *Lyautey*, 3:215.

It has often been said that Lyautey opposed large-scale colonisation on the Algerian pattern, and despised colons.[159] But he did not stop the colons' advance. By the end of 1925 they had acquired just under half a million hectares, half the total area they would occupy when the Protectorate ended in 1956. When Lyautey left Morocco, half the job had been done.[160] The process quickened under Lyautey's successor, Théodore Steeg. Steeg was a Parisian politician, a senator, and had been Governor General of Algeria since 1921; he had greater sympathy for colons.[161] He even set up a third chamber in the Council of Government for those settlers who had no voice in the Chambers of Commerce and Agriculture.[162]

Until just after the First World War, most of the land that was made over to Frenchmen went to 'official settlers,' mainly companies. After the war, individual colons arrived in ever larger numbers, and put great pressure on the Protectorate to release land. It became necessary to mobilise collective land. A dahir in April 1919, whose avowed purpose was to regulate the administration, development and alienation of jamaa land, passed ownership of much collective land to the state, which then sold it to settlers.[163] Lyautey and his economic advisors were happy to do this, provided that individual colons had access to capital and could bring the land up to European levels of cultivation.[164] Individual colonisation became quite common around Marrakesh, but in the Rharb and Chaouïa large colonisation companies like the Compagnie Marocaine bought big holdings. New companies were set up by old Morocco hands capitalising on their contacts with powerful Moroccans. In 1920 Eugène Regnault went into partnership with Moulay Abderahman al-Kbir, yet another brother of the Sultan and a former rebel against Moulay Abdelhafid, now tamed by the economic opportunities provided by the Protectorate. In 1925, Regnault set up the Compagnie Marocaine d'Exploitation Fermière Agricole, which was partially financed by large French and Algerian

159 E. g. by Scham, *Lyautey*, 130 and Bidwell, *Morocco*, 202.

160 Rivet, *Lyautey*, 3:216.

161 *Ibid.*, 3:221-3; Abdelkrim Belguendouz, 'La colonisation agraire au Maroc et ses méthodes de pénétration', *Revue juridique politique économique du Maroc* 4 (1978): 115-151, reference to 149.

162 Scham, *Lyautey*, 75.

163 Rivet, *Lyautey*, 3:221-3; Bidwell, *Morocco*, 210; Belguendoz, 'Colonisation', 145; Wright, *Politics*, 64.

164 Pascon, *Haouz*, 2: 453.

banks and included St-René Taillandier among its directors.[165]

In the Spanish zone, there was less land suitable for colonisation. Individual farmers settled in the Al Hoceima plain on land confiscated from ibn Abd al-Karim and his followers, and in the plains around Melilla. The only big agricultural enterprise was the Compañía Agrícola del Lucus founded in 1927 to farm in the area around Larache.[166]

The development of capitalist agriculture

To clear the land and irrigate it, the new owners needed a large workforce, a lot of money and new supplies of water. The Protectorate's administration extended the power of the state to ensure that these necessities became available.

Surface water had been taken into public domain in 1914, and in 1919 underground water and marshes were added. This was justified by a specious argument based on respect for Islamic law. Since, in theory, the Sultan owned all the water and only ceded usufruct rights, the customary law that determined actual usage was un-Islamic. In practical terms that shifted access to the water supply away from Moroccans to the Makhzan or, in reality, the French colons.[167]

Slowly, water that had been used by tribal groups was diverted towards settler land, albeit as surreptitiously as possible, to avoid political problems. *Khattaras* were particularly encouraged because less water was lost through evaporation, and it was easier to prevent water being siphoned off. But they were also expensive, and therefore the state provided most of the funds, which increased its leverage still further.[168]

Yet even this did not provide enough for the colons. Individual colons began sinking so many private wells that the water-table fell and the streams dried up. In August 1925 the Protectorate administration banned private prospecting for water, and in the following month announced an alternative strategy. Rather than divert water to colons, more water would be supplied from dams.[169]

Théodore Steeg, Lyautey's successor, raised a loan of 400 million francs in Paris and in 1927 started building dams on the Oued

165 *Ibid.*, 2:475-7.

166 Seddon, *Moroccan Peasants*, 123.

167 Swearingen, *Mirages*, 45.

168 Pascon, *Haouz*, 2:500, 503; Swearingen, *Mirages*, 46.

169 Swearingen, *Mirages*, 46-8, 51-4; Pascon, *Haouz*, 2:526.

Beth in the Rharb and the Nfis in the Haouz. Others followed near Casablanca and Kasba Tadla. This '*politique des barrages*' was not designed to benefit Moroccans, apart from a few big landowners like El Glaoui. Irrigation allowed European farmers to concentrate on high value crops like oranges, apricots and grape vines. By 1929 there were 9,500 hectares of vines.[170]

Ordinary Moroccans benefited from modern irrigation only in the sense that their traditional water-rights upstream from the dams were left alone. Traditional water systems supplied land cultivated by traditional tools, such as light ploughs that did not remove deep-rooted weeds. Moroccan farmers herded sheep and goats in traditional ways and grew traditional crops: almonds, olives, date palms, and above all, wheat, barley and maize. They could not do otherwise because Moroccans had very little access to capital to invest in new crops or new tools. Lyautey did set up some Sociétés Indigènes de Prévoyance to provide credit at low interest but the amounts they gave were too small to make much difference. Agriculture as practised by Moroccans was almost a museum-piece except that the area devoted to cereals increased by nearly 50% (from 2 to almost 3 million ha.) between 1919 and 1920.[171]

Moroccan farmers had to increase cereal production because they were caught in a vicious circle. They grew crops that were not so dependent on irrigation, and relied on uncertain rainfall. With lower returns, they had little or no capital to invest in modernisation and therefore paid a heavier *tartib* than European farmers. Not all of them were able to grow more grain; more and more Moroccans were forced onto marginal land, either in the mountains or the less fertile parts of the plains, and transhumant tribes saw their grazing lands cut away. In the nineteenth century the Marmoucha had, in some years, driven 120,000 sheep into the plains round Fez; by 1931 they were only allowed to take 37,000.[172] Those who could not cope at all had to work for others.

Employment

There was plenty of work on the new estates, clearing the land, irrigating, tilling and sowing it and harvesting the crops. In 1935 it was estimated that a medium sized *colon* farm employed about fourteen Moroccan families, and the figures would have been broad-

170 Stewart, *Economy*, 98.

171 *Ibid.*, 92-5, 98. Swearingen, *Mirages*, 46-8, 51-4; Pascon, *Haouz*, 2:526, 528; Bidwell, *Morocco*, 224-8.

172 Belguendouz, 'Colonisation', 151; Stewart, *Economy*, 151; Berque, *Maghrib*, 119.

ly similar in the 1920s. Men were also needed to build roads and railways, to work in the mines and build the cities. To their astonishment, the Protectorate authorities, the colons and French businessmen found that they were short of manpower.

The first migrants to the cities behaved like temporary exiles from their rural homes: they returned home at harvest-time and in the sowing season. Since colonial planning did not allow the *madinas* to expand, many migrants settled in *bidonvilles* on the edges of cities and acted as casual labour rather than a salaried permanent workforce.[173] Some new migrants engaged in commerce on their own account. In Salé the market grew so quickly that it was moved outside the walls. Itinerant traders no longer took so many goods to the rural markets, since rural people came to shop in town instead. In many cities Susis began to dominate the grocery trade,[174] and became the butt of numerous jokes about their allegedly hard-headed attitudes.

In 1929 an enquiry discovered that there were 30% fewer workers than the big agricultural estates and the construction industry needed. As a result, male wages increased by 15-20% between January 1927 and January 1929. This was not a situation that the authorities welcomed. They encouraged the qaids to recruit labourers forcibly and to oblige those who left their work to return; Si Thami El Glaoui was an enthusiastic user of forced labour. In 1927 the Office Chérifien des Phosphates started to use convict labour. Other employers hired women instead; they worked in the Casablanca docks, in the construction industry, and above all, on the agricultural estates, where they did much of the sowing and harvesting. This did not help the shortage of labour either, because women were paid less than men, so they kept wages low. Their menfolk often migrated, either to France or to Algeria, despite two decrees, in 1924 and 1928, that forbade them to do so.

Male migration put an even greater part of the burden of productive labour on to women and the social effects of bringing women into the workforce were striking. Moroccan women who worked outside the home were not respected, so that only those who had no alternative, like divorced women and the very young, would do it. Some found employment as maids in European houses, and the name 'Fatma' soon came to be a generic word for all

173 Abu Lughod, *Rabat*, 160, 200.

174 Brown, *Salé*, 127, 153.

Moroccan maids.[175] Others, who worked for European companies were particularly exploited. In 1926 and 1928, government decrees limited the work of women and children to ten hours a day, but those rules were generally ignored, just like others about safety at work. There were no inspectors, and it was hard to supervise a temporary workforce recruited through intermediaries in the countryside and organised on a tribal basis.[176]

Moroccan workers had no one to represent them. Although they outnumbered European workers in the same big industrial companies that would later prove such a fertile recruiting ground for trade unions, virtually no attempt was made to organise Moroccan workers in the 1920s. Indeed, after Moroccans joined strikes in Casablanca, Kénitra and Rabat in 1918-19, they were banned from taking part in 'European' industrial disputes. The trade unions that grew up in the 1920s were for European employees of the civil service, banks, hotels, education sector, and the post office. In 1926 the railway workers struck in Casablanca and Kénitra, and there were demonstrations in Khouribga. Moroccans did not take part, but they watched with great interest. The only Moroccans who did join trade unions, at the very end of the 1920s, were Jews.[177]

The Jews and Zionism

After decades of education by the Alliance Israélite, many Jews thought they should be treated like Europeans. In Tangier they almost were, since the international regime in the city gave Jews a formal position in the administration.[178] In Spanish Morocco, Jewish traders virtually monopolised the textile industry and traded all over Morocco and beyond, in Gibraltar and Britain.[179] In the French zone, younger Jews left the millahs of the old towns like Fez and Essaouira for the new towns of the coast: Casablanca, Rabat and Kénitra. They started dressing in European clothes, moving up the social scale and asking for French citizenship.[180]

The AIU had campaigned for citizenship since 1912, saying

175 Wright, *Politics*, 74; Salahdine, *Maroc*, 202-10; Benomar, 'Working Class', 113-17; Hoffherr, *L'Économie*, 45-6; Pascon, *Haouz*, 2:466-8, 538; Abu Lughod, *Rabat*, 203.

176 Albert Ayache, *Le mouvement syndical au Maroc*, 3 vols (Paris: L'Harmattan, 1982-), 2: 41-2, 45.

177 Benomar, 'Working Class', 193-8; Ayache, *Mouvement syndical*, 2:53-7.

178 Serels, *Jews*, 123-5.

179 Driessen, *On the Spanish-Moroccan Frontier*, 93-4.

180 Abu Lughod, *Rabat*, 153, 198-9;

that Islamic law discriminated against Jews and that naturalisation was permitted in Algeria. General Lyautey, who abominated the Algerian experience, had no time for this argument and accused the leaders of the very gallicised Alliance of trying to undermine French authority.[181] This was an absurd allegation, and by the 1920s it was counterproductive. It was cheaper for the French administration to subsidise AIU schools than to run another system to compete with them, so in 1924 the two sides agreed to merge. This was also politically expedient for both sides since they now faced a competitor for the loyalty of Moroccan Jews: Zionism.[182]

Outside Morocco, the AIU and the Zionists had always disliked each other intensely. The founding father of Zionism, Theodor Herzl, thought that the Alliance's assimilationism and internationalism were foolish, while the leaders of the Alliance reckoned Zionists were separatist extremists. In Morocco, Alliance leaders treated Zionist propagandists – few in number until the War was over – with contempt and disdain. The creation of the Mandate for Palestine and its proclamation as a homeland for the Jews, changed things. In April 1919 Rabbi Pinhas Cohen set up a Zionist Office in Marrakesh to distribute propaganda and collect money; it even sold land in Palestine to hopeful emigrants. Small contingents left from Fez and Meknès between 1919 and 1921, mocked by Alliance leaders who said that they were going not to a promised land but one of grinding poverty. Lyautey clamped down on Zionism, and visits by Zionist agents were closely watched and sometimes obstructed, but he could not ban them completely since the French government had been favourable towards Zionism. Although Zionists found life easier under Lyautey's successor, Steeg, who was a civilian, many French officials mistrusted the Zionists. Some asked whether the freedom Zionists enjoyed in the Spanish Zone, where they were even allowed their own newspapers, was another Spanish effort to undermine the French Protectorate. Some simply disliked Jews. Others feared the effect on Muslim Moroccans; Zionism might excite feelings against Jews and so cause trouble or, even worse, it might encourage Moroccan nationalists to emulate it.[183]

181 Laskier, *Alliance*, 163-5.

182 *Ibid.*, 152-62, 171-5.

183 Zvi Yehuda, 'Zionist Activity in Southern Morocco, 1919-1923', *Revue des Etudes Juives*, 144, no. 4 (1985): 363-8; Laskier, *Alliance*, 197-200; David Cohen, 'Lyautey et le sionisme', *Revue française d'histoire d'outre-mer*, 67 (1980): 269-99; Serels, *Jews*, 120-3.

The bases of nationalism

It was true that the campaigns against the British Mandate in Palestine itself had distant echoes in Morocco; collections were made for Palestinian Arabs during the revolt of 1929. The Middle East was certainly a source of nationalist ideas, especially once the resistance in the Rif had ended, but so was France. In any case, the small nationalist group started to grow. By 1926 some of the Free Schools, set up by Salafi-inspired nationalists, had been in existence for five years and their graduates, like those of the *Écoles des Fils de Notables* and the *Collèges Musulmans*, had gone on to study elsewhere. Some went to France, and their names were a roll-call of the future leaders of the independence movement: Abdelkader Benjelloun, Mohammed El-Fassi, Mohamed Hassan Ouazzani, Ahmed Réda Guédira. In the cafés on the Left Bank, they met radical and socialist French intellectuals and students from Tunisia with whom they set up the *Association des Étudiants Musulmans du Nord de l'Afrique* in 1927. At first this was purely a welfare organisation but it soon moved on to educational affairs and then, inevitably, politics.[184] Appalled, the Protectorate authorities tried to limit the numbers studying languages or law, subjects that they believed to be thoroughly subversive. Louis Brunot, the French director of education, told one young man, Omar Abdeljalil, that he could only go to France if he studied agriculture in a provincial university. Abdeljalil duly studied in Montpellier, became an agronomist and later a prominent nationalist leader.[185] Other Moroccan students went to Cairo, mainly to the secular Fuad I University rather than the religious al-Azhar, and in 1928 Abdussalam Bennuna, the reform-minded Minister of Justice in Tetuan, organised a group to study at al-Najah secondary school in Nablus in Palestine. Some people, like Ahmed Belafrej and Mekki Naciri, studied both in Paris and in Cairo.[186]

When these graduates came home, they set up groups of like minded young men to develop their new ideas further. In late 1925, helped by teachers in the Free School Movement, notably Allal El-Fassi, Mohamed Ghazi and, above all, by the qadi Mohammed bel-Arabi el-Alaoui, they established their first group in Fez, and

184 Halstead, *Rebirth*, 171; Julien, *Impérialismes*, 157; Leon Borden Blair, *Western Window in the Arab World* (Austin: University of Texas Press, 1970), 22-3.

185 Halstead, *Rebirth*, 107, 112, 170-1, 278-88.

186 *Ibid.*, 125, 278-88; Abdelmajid Benjelloun, *Approches du colonialisme espagnol et du mouvement nationaliste marocain dans l'ex-Maroc khalifien* (Rabat: Okad, 1988), 106; Wolf, *Secrets*, 135.

then in Rabat. In Tetuan, Bennuna and Mohammed Daoud, a prominent local historian, set up another group in August 1926. All the members swore oaths of secrecy on the Quran, but although they adopted names like *al-Muslihun* (Reformers), La Ligue Marocaine and *Ansar al-Haqiqa* (Defenders of the Truth), they were hardly subversive groups of plotters. They were really discussion groups debating ideas they culled from newspapers and books.[187] It was not Moroccan publications that they discussed, because there were virtually none. The authorities limited Arabic newspapers to a few information sheets, although they themselves produced several mimeographed papers; one called *Umm al-Banin* was set up by Allal El-Fassi in 1926 and another called *al-Widad* ('Friendship') was put out in Salé. These were so clandestine that hardly anyone got to read them. But newspapers and books were smuggled in from Egypt and Tunisia, often through the British Post Offices,[188] which had survived along with British protection and consular courts, and which the Protectorate authorities could not censor. They learned of the ideas of Sa'ad Zaghlul in Egypt and Shaykh Abdelaziz Thaâlibi in Tunisia. Thaâlibi's book, *La Tunisie Martyre*, published in 1920 had a wide following among these Moroccan intellectuals. They agreed with his gradualism and the call of the Liberal Constitutional Party (Destour) not for independence but for self-government with full civil rights, a constitution, equal pay for men and women, freedom of the press and compulsory education. Mohamed Hassan Ouazzani particularly admired the polemics of the Egyptian al-Kawakibi against tyrannical rule and many nationalists later acknowledged the impact of Qasim Amin's call for a degree of female emancipation and education. New layers were being added to the underlying Salafi ideas.[189]

Politics was only part of the story. The Arabic literary revival of the previous half-century deeply interested young Moroccans, for many plays and novels treated historical themes that were close to their hearts. Muhammad Ashama'u opened a bookshop in Salé in 1927 that sold classical Islamic texts, modern histories of the Crusades and the great Islamic empires, and Arabic translations of European classics, particularly French novels. He and his friends

[187] Allal Al-Fasi, *Al-harakat al-istiqlaliyya fi-l-Maghrib al-'Arabi* (Tangier: 'Abd al-Salam Gassus, [n. d.]), 139; Benjelloun, *Approches*, 102-3; Julien, *Impérialismes*, 158; Halstead, *Rebirth*, 166-7; Blair, *Western Window*, 21-2.

[188] Halstead, *Rebirth*, 55-7; Brown, *Salé*, 196; al-Fasi, *Al-Harakat*, 129.

[189] Lisa Anderson, *The State and Social Transformation in Tunisia and Libya, 1830-1980* (Princeton University Press, 1986), 99; Benjelloun, *Approches*, 105; Halstead, *Rebirth*, 127-9.

also set up a drama club; another theatrical group in Fez produced Molière's *Tartuffe* in which the sanctimonious villain was made up to look like Abd al-Hay El-Kittani, who was widely disliked for his lectures in the Qarawiyyin in which he attacked the Salafiyya. They also put on dramas about Saladin, the conquest of Andalusia, a translation of Shakespeare's *Romeo and Juliet* and a play they wrote themselves called *Science and its Fruits.*[190] French officials and colons sneered at the literary scene in Salé and at half-educated natives who aped the manners of their betters: the 'tainted little terrors of Slawi society' was one phrase, but these cultural nationalists were much less chauvinist than their French masters. They picked and chose from European and Arab culture what they liked or needed. In the process they sometimes scandalised their elders, who were suspicious of their command of French. Even simple things could cause scandal. One of the Tetuani youths who went to Nablus shaved off his beard before he left, and hid at home while waiting to depart the next day. Others changed into European clothes only when the party landed in Spain. Young men like these challenged both the ideas of the older generation of Moroccans and the colonialism of the Spanish and French. Some of those who had grown up in the first half-generation of European colonial rule were equiping themselves with ideas of changing Moroccan society and opposing their colonial masters, mixing a longing for the past glory of their own culture with the political ideas of Europe. In 1930 the first political crisis in colonial Morocco struck the first spark of a nationalist movement.

The Protectorate in question

One challenge came from a man whom the French had almost created as their tool, the Sultan himself. In 1926 and 1927, British diplomats warned London that Moulay Youssef was showing signs of independence, resisting French demands 'which he conceived to be unjust'.[191] Behind this lay a clash of personalities. Moulay Youssef disliked Steeg, who followed Lyautey in the Residency, for allowing in more and more French settlers, and because he was not as sympathetic as Lyautey had been. When the Sultan asked the French government to remove Steeg, and the request was turned down, he barred the Resident-General from the Palace.

190 Brown, *Salé*, 196-7; Wolf, *Secrets*, 155; Halstead, *Rebirth*, 127; Bidwell, *Morocco*, 149.

191 PRO FO 371/ 12696, W10886/10711/28, Rapp to Chamberlain, Rabat 26 Nov 1927.

Consequently, Steeg had no knowledge of how serious matters were when Moulay Youssef fell ill, and he was quite unprepared for the Sultan's death.[192]

The brief succession struggle that followed the Sultan's death on 11 November 1927 was fully in accordance with Moroccan tradition in that officials divided behind rival candidates, except that some of the participants were French. The Director of the Resident's Military Cabinet, General Mougin, and the palace chamberlain (*hajib*), Si Ababou, backed Moulay Youssef's eldest son, Idris; M. Marc, the *conseiller* of the Sharifian government, and the Grand Vizir, Mohammed El Mokri, supported his youngest son Sidi Mohammed. El Mokri had no great affection for Sidi Mohammed whom he had belittled and humiliated at every turn, but he loathed Ababou, and Sidi Mohammed was so young that both the Vizir and the French administrators assumed that he could be easily manipulated. The day after his father's death, Sidi Mohammed was given his first *bay'a* in the palace in Fez. Dutifully, the rest of Morocco followed, though without noticeable enthusiasm.[193]

Although political cognoscenti in Rabat at first dismissed the new Moroccan Sultan as an insignificant boy, Mohammed V soon showed that he had a mind of his own. In July 1928 he snubbed the Mandoub of Tangier, alleging gross errors of politeness and protocol and, more seriously, overruled the choice of a judge to the court in Casablanca. Pointedly, he demanded a man who had a reputation for honesty rather than the administration's candidate.[194]

Trouble was brewing outside the palace too, with murmurings that Islam was in danger. This was exacerbated by a senior French official who distributed Arabic biographies of Jesus, and by the Bishop of Rabat who made foolish assertions about the need to convert Moroccan Muslims. The brother of Omar Abdeljalil, the agronomist who would soon emerge as an important nationalist leader, did convert to Christianity and there were many protests; one group even retaliated by getting the Bishop's secretary drunk and announcing he had converted to Islam. These might all have been no more than isolated incidents, had they not seemed to

192 Al-Fasi, *Al-harakat*, 132; Julien, *Impérialismes*, 159; PRO FO371/ 11918/ W1116/ 827/ 28, Ryan to Chamberlain, 16 November 1926.

193 Luccioni, 'L'avènement', *passim*; El Alami, *Mohammed V*, 51-2; Wolf, *Secrets*, 159-60.

194 PRO FO 371/ 13403, W5843/11/28, Ryan to Sec. of State, Rabat, 12 June 1928 and W11/11/28, Gurney to Sec. of State, Tangier, 22 Dec 1927.

fit in with a more general French attack on Islam, in which the encouragement of Berber separatism seemed to accompany the de-Islamisation of the Berbers.[195]

A society of dualities

On the surface this was a strange development: the ideology of the Protectorate had loudly proclaimed French respect for Moroccan society, sovereignty and culture. That did not fit with the de-Islamisation of the Berbers, but it did square with French colonial theories about North Africa that divided Muslim society into two – Arab and Muslim (and Makhzan) versus Berber and partially Muslim (and *siba*). They were still part of the same reality – a constructed reality, certainly, but one that the French Protectorate's ideology recognised as being the essence of Morocco.

Yet that division of Muslim society into two was only one of the many dualities that the Protectorate produced. One of the most striking was economic: the agriculture of the bulk of the Moroccan population was confined to unirrigated land, producing food for the Moroccan market and received very little investment; very heavy investment, on the other hand, was directed into the modern agricultural economy, that was dependant on irrigation and produced crops for export, but this was largely the province of European colons and agricultural companies. Yet the division was not absolute: prominent and rich Moroccans, qaids and heads of *tariqas* also participated in the modern sector. Similarly, the French-Moroccan duality split the 'modern', European, elements of administration and law, from their 'traditional' Moroccan elements. Yet the contradictions were part of a single Protectorate entity: the Resident-General was the protector of the Sultan, who remained sovereign. Both Sultan and Resident-General were interdependent within the Protectorate system, but that led to the ideologically confusing situation of a liberal European state proclaiming its respect for Moroccan sovereignly by supporting political and social codes that were thoroughly illiberal: the rule of the big qaids for example, or the refusal to let Moroccans join trade unions.

Those trade unions were symptoms of a much more subtle duality within the French system, for the French side was deeply fissured. French colonialism in Morocco was founded on the interests of big French companies (mining, electricity) and those of the organs of the state (posts, education). Yet the activities of unions, that only existed because Morocco *was* under French

195 Halstead, *Rebirth*, 72-3; Julien, *Impérialismes*, 159.

control, clearly competed with those of the state and the companies. Indeed, the unions had potentially a greater common interest with Moroccan employees than with French employers – except that without the French Protectorate and the French companies there would be no French workers in Morocco in the first place. Similarly, on the Moroccan side, the exploited peasants began to flee the qaid–ruled countryside for the French-built and administered towns.

The dual pattern was repeated in the military struggle. In the French Protectorate the inhabitants of the Berber mountains fought French armies consisting mainly of Moroccans that sought to incorporate them into a Makhzan that in its turn sought to divide them off. In the towns the early nationalist movement sought not to get rid of the French but to recreate Moroccan society, an idea that in the 1930s would become a call for a 'real' Protectorate. The early nationalists needed European knowledge, and they refused support for the one successful Salafi-inspired attempt to oppose the colonial regimes: that of ibn Abd al-Karim in the Rif mountains. There, once again, was the attempt at a 'modernised' state, organised to protect Muslims from Christian domination, opposed by many of just those it sought to protect.

The very existence of the Spanish Protectorate was another duality: until the events of 1925 united them, the Spanish and the French were more at loggerheads than allies: a Protectorate system that was set up to preserve Spanish interests was resented by both sides. It was in these contradictory circumstances, in 1930, that the French administration promulgated a decree that formally divorced Arab from Berber-speakers, and the nationalist movement took off.

6

NATIONALISM

Although many Moroccans had misgivings about French and Spanish rule, this hardly amounted to a nationalist movement. During the 1920s Moroccan opposition to the Protectorate had been fragmented: armed opposition had faded out in the cities in the very early days of the occupation, although it continued in the mountains. In the Rif, opposition was organised, at least by its leaders, along the lines of religious reformism; elsewhere it followed the segmentary patterns of pre-colonial rural Morocco. Political opposition in the cities was very small until the end of the 1920s, because the number of Moroccans with a modern education was very small. This group rejected the sharp division between 'modern' and 'traditional' knowledge, and in its free schools religious subjects and technical subjects were taught side by side: the division between reformers inside the Protectorate system and outside of it was not so great.

The decade that followed would see the emergence of an organised political nationalist movement that brought together elements of pre-colonial Moroccan society, particularly the Alaoui sultanate, and the modernisations of the protectorate. In addition, it created links with the nationalist movements in the Arab east, and was influenced by Egyptian political thought, as well as by radical nationalist movements in Algeria, contacts with them having developed as a result of common French rule. These international contacts did not stop at nationalism. As a result of colonial rule, Moroccans were not only more deeply embedded in the European economic system than ever, but at the end of the decade they would be dragged as soldiers into European conflicts, first into the civil war in Spain and then into the Second World War.

The decade began badly. In early 1929, locusts ate the leaves of two-thirds of the fruit trees in the Sous, and by the end of the autumn drought had killed a third of the cattle and a fifth of the sheep. In the spring of 1930, the locusts returned for a second season.[1] French policy piled affliction upon distress. On

1 PRO FO371/15001/W1297/679/28, Vaughan-Russell to Stonehewer-Bird, Mar-

19 April 1930 a plan was announced to divide the waters of the River Fez at its entrance to the city, which appeared to divert water from Moroccan inhabitants to the French settlers. On 9 May there were protest meetings in six of the biggest mosques; 10,000 people demonstrated and the Resident-General, Lucien Saint (appointed in 1929), ordered the plan dropped. Although he berated the demonstrators for not using 'proper channels' to voice their dissent, the cancellation of the plan was convincing proof that demonstrations were more effective than those proper channels.[2] Although these were the only street protests in the spring of 1930, discontent was growing over taxation, colonisation and land. In Salé, notables were disillusioned with French rule because there were no jobs for their sons in the administration.[3]

In this touchy climate, on 16 May 1930, the French authorities promulgated a dahir to regulate the application of Berber customary law. Its supposed purpose was to tidy up the confusion that surrounded the eighty-one *jemaas judiciares*. These were functioning smoothly enough, but had no proper legal standing. The Residency wanted to regularise things and at the beginning of December 1929 had set up a commission to study the workings of Berber justice. Some members of the commission had wanted to replace the *jemaas judiciares* altogether, and bring Berber 'customary law' into line with French law. This, they believed, would help to assimilate the Berbers and divorce them from Islam. The Affaires Indigènes department vigorously opposed the idea, and its head, General Noguès, stoutly declared that 'the Berbers love their judicial system'; it would be better to 'consecrate what already exists'. The Director of Sharifian Affairs agreed, saying that it would be easier to persuade the Sultan to sign a dahir that recognised what was already in place.[4]

This last argument carried the day, and the decree was presented to the young sultan as an attempt at legal tidying-up. It removed some judicial power from the *jemaas judiciares* and set up new customary tribunals to deal with civil, inheritance, commercial and property cases according to 'local custom'. 'Tribal chiefs' would deal with minor criminal matters according to French law, and

rakesh, 31 Jan 1930; W1164/679/28 Makereth to Ryan, Fez, 6 January 1930; W527/527/28, Watkinson to Gurney, Tetuan, 2 January 1930; W4189/4189/28 Report on Sous for 1930.

2 PRO FO371/15002/W5591/679/28, Makereth to Rapp, Fez, 21 May 1930.

3 PRO FO371/15002/W8827/679/28, Rapp to Henderson, Rabat, 22 August 1930.

4 J. Luccioni, 'L'élaboration du dahir berbère du 16 Mai 1930', *Revue du Monde Musulman et de la Méditerranée* 38 (1984): 75-81.

civil matters according to customary law. Appeals tribunals, run by French officials, would review their decisions. Yet this was not merely tidying up. It was really a radical change of practice, since in the mountains and deserts, 'criminal' cases – violence and theft – never had come before courts at all, let alone been subject to outside review, Islamic or otherwise. It was a radical change in theory too, for the customary ways of solving disputes had never before been transformed into a system: in precolonial Morocco the only legal system was the *shari'a.* Here it seemed was another nail in the coffin of the Islamic identity of the Berbers.[5]

Sidi Mohammed had no choice but to sign. He was still very inexperienced, and it would have been hard for him to stand up to the Resident-General, who insisted on the decree, against the advice of senior officials including, it was said, the *grand-vizir* Mohammed El Mokri.[6] Outside the palace, though, the protests soon began. In Salé, Abd al-Latif al-Subihi, a former official interpreter, organised demonstrations; and a special prayer, traditionally used in times of drought and famine, was recited in the main mosques. Its words were changed for the new circumstances; 'Oh God the Benevolent (*ya latif*), we ask of you mercy in what fate has brought and that you do not separate us from our Berber brothers.'[7]

The *Latif* prayer was repeated in Meknès, Tangier and Casablanca and, above all, Fez.[8] Demonstrations began there in early June and continued through July. Because they were peaceful, the French authorities found them hard to stop. In mid-July Mohamed Hassan Ouazzani, who had led a demonstration, was invited to make his case to the pasha, el-Baghdadi. When he did, he and two others were promptly arrested and flogged. Allal El-Fassi was arrested on the same day. They were soon released and El-Fassi and Ouazzani drafted a memorandum to the Sultan that demanded the abrogation of the Berber dahir, the establishment of a unified judiciary, the use of Arabic as the national language and the end of Christian missionary activity. Sidi Mohammed listened to the delegation that presented the memorandum on 27 August, with tears in his eyes, and promised to consider their demands, but El Mokri brushed

5 Julien, *Impérialismes*, 160; Halstead, *Rebirth*, 71; Berque, *Maghrib*, 218-19.

6 Robert Montagne, *Révolution au Maroc* (Paris: France-Empire, 1951), 183, 187; Ageron, *Politiques coloniales*, 136.

7 Brown, *Salé*, 198-201.

8 Halstead, *Rebirth*, 181. Ageron, *Politiques coloniales*, 137-8.

it aside. Allal El-Fassi, and Ouazzani were arrested again and not released until October, when the demonstrations died down.[9]

Leaflets were circulated in the streets, or were pasted to the walls of mosques. One poster concentrated on the threat to Islam:

> Six months ago you came to know all too well, and discerned all too clearly, the determination of the government of the French Protectorate to remove our Berber brothers from the realm of Islam, to separate them from the bosom of the religion of the Prophet and to prevent them from appealing to the very laws that God sent down to put an end to primitive customs. This they did as a step on the road towards converting them to Christianity and making them embrace the cross.[10]

When the Islamic Society of Fez sent an appeal to various foreign consuls, it repeated these assertions, but it added new themes suited to a foreign diplomatic audience: that the dahir contravened the Treaty of the Protectorate because it divided the Sultan's sovereignty; that floggings were 'against all the laws of humanity and Muslim law;' finally, the letter insisted, the Berbers were Moroccans despite the linguistic differences.

Tactically, the disorganised nationalist groups had a unifying issue for the first time, one that brought together anger over water rights, the threat to Islam and the tyrannical behaviour of the French authorities. It was this mixture of ideas that gave the agitation against the dahir its significance. In the past, such complaints had justified revolt, but the nature of the French Protectorate had changed the meaning of revolt: it now required not the Sultan's deposition, but his return to the political arena. The duality underlying the Protectorate was challenged by the assertion that Morocco was made up of the various groups that lived in it and had always done so: to divide them was a French and Spanish colonialist project. The nationalist delegates who presented their letter to Sidi Mohammed asserted that the Almohad and Almoravid dynasties which had spread Islam in Morocco had been Berber, and that Jews were Moroccans too, although there was 'no third religion for Moroccan subjects'.[11] The rejection of dualism went as far as to challenge the fundamental colonialist division between the 'traditional' and Moroccan, and the 'modern' and French.

9 Halstead, *Rebirth*, 185-6; William A. Hoisington, *The Casablanca Connection: French Colonial Policy 1936-1943* (Chapel Hill: University of North Carolina Press, 1984), 33-4; al-Fasi, *al-Harakat*, 146-8; Ageron, *Politiques coloniales*, 139.

10 PRO FO371/15740/420/28, Edmonds to Henderson, Rabat, 28 April 1931.

11 PRO FO 371/15002/ W9726/679/28, Rapp to Henderson, Rabat, 16 Sept 1930.

The legal argument talked of the laws of Islam and humanity, appealed to European concepts of international law and asked for a 'real' Protectorate, not its overthrow. Even that most fiery Salafi, Mohammed bel-Arabi el-Alaoui, never attacked the Protectorate in his impassioned lectures at the Qarawiyyin, only the policies that put Islam in danger, although some of his students demonstrated so enthusiastically that they were jailed.[12]

Nor could the Protectorate be neatly classified as 'modern'. It merged such 'traditional' political characters as the rural qaids (redefined along new lines) with the technocratic and bureaucratic French colonial state of trained soldiery, police, railway workers and postmen. And the qaids were certainly not removed from the economic benefits of French rule: with government support they could clear peasants off the land and amass large fortunes and land-holdings.[13] So did the leaders of the *tariqas* who supported French rule: in the Abda region in 1931 all the five qaids were members of the Tijaniyya, Nasiriyya or Wazzaniyya. The *tariqas* profited from the relationship: a cooperative shaykh like Sharif al-Nasiri was allowed to collect contributions and so became wealthy.[14] One of the most powerful *tariqa* leaders of all, Abdelhay El-Kittani, who was also lecturing at the Qarawiyyin, attacked Salafi ideas vehemently. Still nourishing his unbending dislike of the Alaouis because Moulay Abdelhafid had flogged his brother to death, he associated himself so thoroughly with the French as to become their most important agent after Si Thami El Glaoui.[15]

Yet the huge membership of the *tariqas* was not necessarily as pro-French as the leaders. At Souk El Arbaâ in the Rharb in the 1930s the local Tijani shaykh was considered a subversive,[16] and during the demonstrations against the Berber dahir the British Consul-General in Rabat warned there might be trouble in mid August at the time of the main pilgrimages of the Aisawiya and Hamadsha. Although it failed to materialise, the French authorities were not sanguine about *tariqa* opposition.[17] There were very good reasons why the Salafis, who disapproved of Sufism, should refrain from attacking the *tariqas*, for it would have been impolitic.

The reaction of the Berbers themselves in the great swathe

12 Munson, *Religion and Power*, 103-4.

13 Hammoudi, *Master and Disciple*, 105-7.

14 Bidwell, *Morocco*, 146-7.

15 *Ibid.*, 149.

16 Berque, *Maghrib*, 145-6.

17 PRO FO371/7862/679/28, Rapp to Henderson, Rabat, 25 July 1930.

of territory that the French army now occupied was more muted, although many of them certainly did not like the dahir. When the French authorities backed down slightly and announced that any tribe that *wanted* to place itself under the *shari'a* would be allowed to do so, delegations came from the Zemmour and Ait Yusi to demand just that. Their members were promptly arrested.[18] The only effective Berber opposition to the French came from the regions that had not yet been occupied. There, the fight went on.

The final stages of conquest

There was some irony, but no contradiction, in that, while Arabic-speakers rioted in the cities against a dahir that split the Berbers away, some Berbers continued to resist being united to the rest of Morocco by the French army. It was another example of the dualism that the Protectorate regime had fixed into Moroccan life.

In any event there was now a real division between *makhzan* and *siba.* The mountains south of Marrakesh, in the Middle and High Atlas were still unconquered, as were the deserts beyond. This was hard land to fight in, but the French High Command was anxious to finish the job. For the moment they had a lot of troops at their disposal. In 1929, the Algerian lobby in Paris, anxious to secure the right of hot pursuit of 'bandits' into Moroccan territory, had agreed to set up a joint military area, the *Confins Algéro-Marocains.* Here, Moroccan and Algerian commanders would cooperate and turn overwhelming force against some of their oldest and most tenacious opponents, men who would not easily submit. It was a highly personalised conflict in these last stages, fragmented and very bitter.

The new campaign that began in 1930 lasted five years. First, the Middle Atlas south and south-east of Kasba Tadla, was encircled. In the summer of 1930 French forces took the heights on the north side of the Oued el-Abid, the northernmost of several river valleys running east–west through the Middle Atlas. The following year they took the valley itself, and in the summer of 1932 pushed over the next ridge into the valley of the Asif Melloul. That third autumn there was heavy fighting on the high and remote plateau overlooking Lac Tislit (Isly), till Sidi el-Makki, a famous and determined opponent, surrendered in September 1932. Meanwhile other forces moved in to the south and east, occupied Zagora,

18 Al-Fasi, *al-harakat*, 145.

and then pushed north. In January 1933 French forces moved into the Tafilalt and occupied the castle at Rissani of another old enemy, Bel-Qasim n-Gadi, who escaped. This left the resistance encircled in a large *tache* around Jbel Sarhro and a smaller one on Jbel Bou Gafẹr, where Aissa u-Ba Slam fought on hard until he surrendered in March 1933; Bel-Qasim n-Gadi surrendered the same month.

French progress was so slow because the terrain was extremely difficult, and the resistance was tenacious indeed. Each group was a distillation of the most irreconcilable opponents who had withdrawn further into the mountains, rather than surrender, men who were battle-hardened and extremely determined. This was not 'oil-slick penetration', in the supposed style of Lyautey, but a series of hard-fought battles. Of those who made their last stand with Sidi el-Makki in the high plateau in August 1932, General Guillaume wrote: 'All the professional bandits and deserters from our native troops had come together in an extraordinary grouping that had over 1,000 warriors armed with rapid-fire rifles, well supplied with ammunition, whose atavistic spirit of independence and xenophobia had brought them close to madness.'[19] Leaving aside the exaggerated chauvinism, Guillaume had reason to be impressed. The thousand-odd Ait Atta fighters who stood with Aissa u-Ba Slam in Jbel Bou Gafer came from every clan of that enormous tribe, even those that had already submitted.[20]

These intractable fighters took very heavy casualties – several hundred of Sidi el-Makki's supporters died near Lac Tislit, 3,000 were made prisoner and 5,000 head of cattle were confiscated by the French army.[21] But the French army had to mobilise huge forces for these final campaigns. Against Sidi el-Makki they deployed fifteen infantry battalions, twelve artillery batteries, and four squadrons of aeroplanes. For the final push in 1934, they used 40,000 men: twenty-six infantry battalions, seven motorised cavalry units, eight plane squadrons and a battalion of tanks. The brunt of the fighting was done by Moroccan troops, who took most of the casualties. Although the number of casualties was never given one estimate is that around 23,000 goumiers were killed in the 'pacification' of Morocco.[22]

19 Guillaume, *Berbères*, 372.

20 Hart, *Ait Atta*, 179-83.

21 Guillaume, *Berbères*, 382-3.

22 *Ibid.*, 323-5; Usborne, *Conquest*, 322-8; Maghraoui, 'Moroccan colonial soldiers', 24.

The parts of Morocco that remained unsubmitted now lay in the far west, between the coast and the foothills of the Anti-Atlas, and in the desert further south. This was not all French territory. In March 1934 the Spanish general Osvaldo Capaz finally occupied the enclave of Ifni that the treaty of Ouad Ras had assigned to Spain in 1860, seventy-four years before. In May he pushed southwards, occupied Ma al-Aynayn's old base at Es-Semara, and met with French forces moving north from Mauritania. The conquest of Morocco was over.[23]

The roots of future problems

The aftermath was very long. In January 1995 an old French artillery shell killed two shepherd boys, one aged nine and the other thirteen, when they threw it into a fire.[24] The geopolitical consequences also resonated into the 1990s. 'Dissidence' had ended, but 'banditry' continued in both Morocco and Algeria so, in May 1934, the government in Paris reorganised the military region known as the *Confins Algéro-Marocains* that covered territory in the north-western Sahara administered by Algeria, Morocco and *Afrique Occidental Française*. It stayed in existence until Moroccan independence in 1956. In this land of military and nomad raids, frontiers had no effective meaning, so the Moroccan frontier south of Tafilalt was left undefined. Certainly from 1934 onwards, a line labelled 'Presumed southern frontier of Morocco' appeared on official Moroccan maps, which ran straight from the south-eastern corner of Spanish-ruled Tarfaya north-east to Ighli on the Oued Souara. This was clearly no more than an administrative convenience, for the best the French army could do in nomad country was to hold the watering holes along the northern edge of the desert. From there, helped by the Algerian army, they might check raiding and perhaps tax passing nomads. The border did make it clear that the Sahara south and west of Béchar was definitely in Algerian territory, even though no formal disposition was ever made. But that was not the end of the story, since there were several subsequent disputes in the later 1930s over the extent of Moroccan control, with the Residents-General pushing to extend Moroccan claims, even, in one case, as far as Tindouf itself.[25]

Thus, the completion of the conquest consummated the identity

23 Guillaume, *Berbères*; Usborne, *Conquest*, 314-22; Hart, *Ait Atta*, 169-83; Hodges, *Western Sahara*, 64-5; Trout, *Frontiers*, 286-9.

24 Reuter report dated Rabat, 7 January 1995.

25 Trout, *Frontiers*, 327-52.

of pre-colonial Morocco. French forces took on the role of the Makhzan in establishing control over the desert fringe, albeit rather more successfully. It also limited Morocco territorially, but not definitively, laying the ground for argument a generation later. The Moroccan population certainly knew little of all this, and they had a more immediate problem: conquest had unified Morocco during a deep world economic depression.

The economic crisis

The world slump that began in 1929 took some time to affect Morocco. Its agriculturally based economy made it less vulnerable than the industrialised countries that took the first shock.[26] Yet France, Morocco's largest trading partner and ruler, was one of those industrialised countries, so when the crisis did bite in 1931, it bit deep.

The figures are stark. Between 1929 and 1935 the exports of the whole of Morocco dropped by 49% and imports by 57%. The mineral industry collapsed: phosphate exports went down from 1.7 million tonnes in 1930 to 900,000 tonnes in 1931, when nearly every mine in French Morocco cut production and lead and zinc mines shut down completely. The construction industry dropped by 53% between 1929 and 1934 and wheat prices fell by 55% between 1930 and 1933.[27]

In the international zone of Tangier trade declined by half and in the Spanish zone by 53% between 1929 and 1935. The Compañía Española de Minas del Rif, the biggest company in the northern zone, stopped production for a while.[28] Only companies of the get-rich-quick variety stayed in business: the Compañía Colonizadora haphazardly stripped cork trees in the Jebala because it had no land title and wanted to maximise its returns. Around Al Hoceima the tizra tree, that provided a valuable dye, almost disappeared because of unregulated felling.[29]

26 René Gallissot, *Le patronat européen au Maroc. Action sociale, action politique, 1931-1942* (Casablanca: Eddif, 1990), 55.

27 The figures are derived from successive numbers of Great Britain, Department of Overseas Trade, *Survey of Economic Conditions in Morocco* (London: HMSO, 1930-9). Gallissot, *Patronat*, 55-62, gives different figures for total trade but the percentage fall, 49%, is much the same.

28 Figures calculated from successive numbers of Great Britain, *Survey of Economic Conditions in Morocco* Victor Morales Lezcano, *España yel norte de África: el protectorado en Marruecos (1912-1956)* (Madrid: U.N.E.D, 1984), 161.

29 PRO FO371/19706/W2779/1839/28, Report on a tour from Tetuan to Melilla by Mr Monck in November 1934.

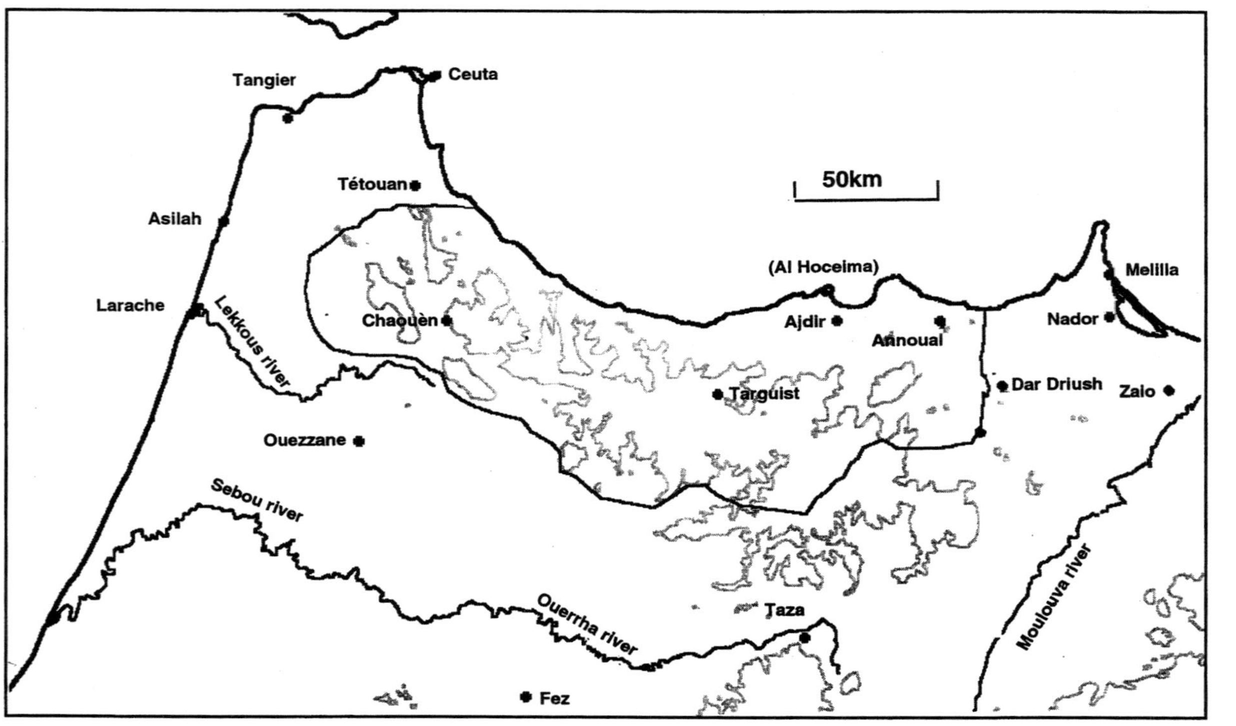

Above The Rif War (showing approximate boundary of Rifi state, September 1925).
Below Administrative divisions, 1940.

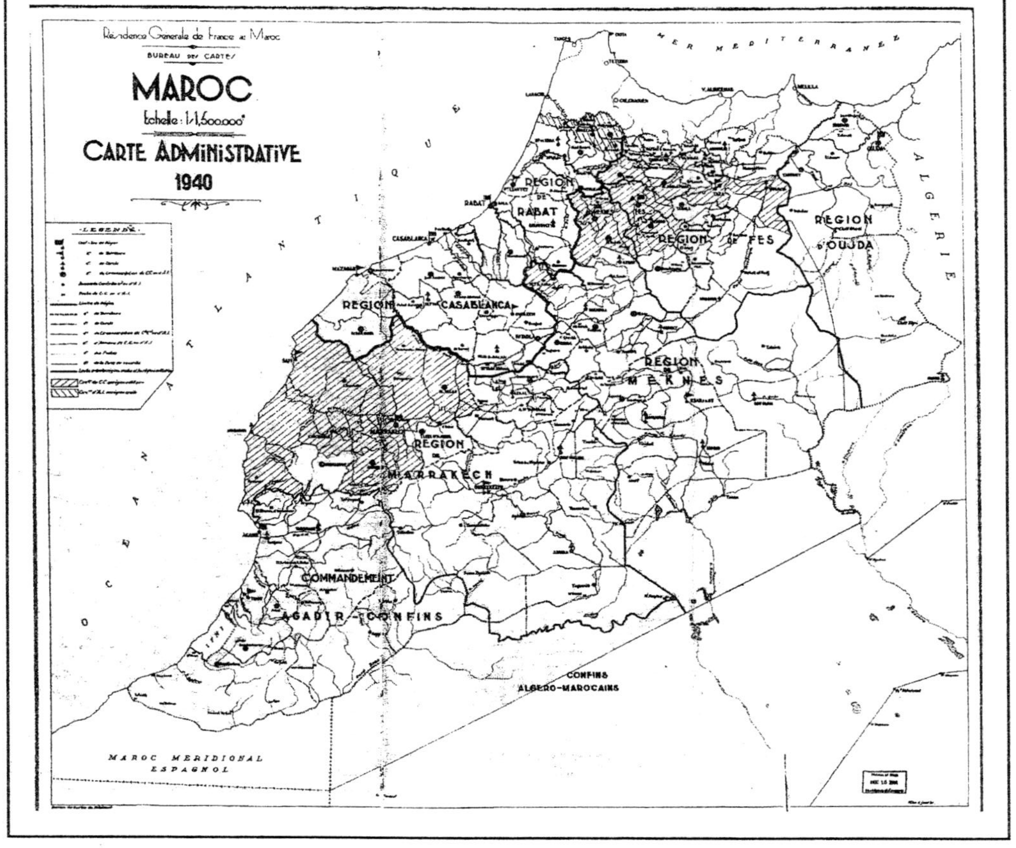
Résidence Générale de France au Maroc
BUREAU DES CARTES
MAROC
Echelle: 1/1,500.000
CARTE ADMINISTRATIVE
1940
LEGENDE
MER MEDITERRANEE
ALGERIE
OCEAN ATLANTIQUE
REGION DE RABAT
REGION DE FES
REGION D'OUJDA
REGION DE CASABLANCA
REGION DE MEKNES
REGION DE MARRAKECH
COMMANDEMENT AGADIR-CONFINS
IFNI
CONFINS ALGERO-MAROCAINS
MAROC MERIDIONAL ESPAGNOL

To the world crisis was added a typically Moroccan phenomenon: the weather. Rainfall was generally well below average in 1931, when people in the Spanish zone could not plant their seed, and again in 1935, although December 1933 brought very heavy flooding.[30]

Into these depressed markets thrust a newcomer. Japanese imports were one of the few growth areas, up from 2.2% of imports to the French zone in 1932 to 10% in 1935. In the process, Japan overtook Britain, the United States, Spain and Germany to become Morocco's second-largest trading partner after France.[31] By the early 1930s imports of Japanese plastic shoes were cutting a swathe through Moroccan artisanal shoemakers, whose traditional markets at home and in the eastern Mediterranean were declining. In 1872 shoe shops in Salé had employed 3,000 workers, in 1929 only 116 people were still producing the traditional slippers. As for the potters, by 1930 there were none at all left in Salé.[32]

New industries did not replace the old. Few Moroccans had access to capital, so they depended on European firms for employment, but during the slump these firms cut wages, increased working hours and sacked employees to reduce costs. The Office Chérifien des Phosphates and *La Manutention Marocaine*, which ran the port in Casablanca, both cut their workforce heavily. In 1934 there were an estimated 10,000 unemployed Moroccans in Casablanca; the unemployed population of the *bidonvilles* could not be counted.[33] Between 1928 and 1931 the labour market shifted from one where it was hard to find workers to one where it was hard to find jobs.

Women workers were still in demand, no longer because of a shortage of labour but because they could be paid less. Conditions were often appalling: women in the sardine factories in Safi and Agadir stood for eight to ten hours a day with their feet in water. Despite these sacrifices, family income declined from a rough estimate of 10-25 francs a day in the late 1920s to as low as 3 francs in 1935. The cost of living did drop too, but not as fast as wages.[34]

30 Jean Le Coz, *Le Rharb, fellahs et colons: étude de géographie régionale*, 2 vols (Rabat: Ministère de l'Education Nationale, 1964), 1:150, 199, 200; National Climatic Data Center, Global Historical Climatology Network Data: Precipitation Data for Casablanca; Mimoun Aziza, 'La década trágica del Rif. El hambre y sus consecuencias sociales en los años Cuarenta', *El Vigia de Tierra* 2/3 (1996/7): 237-44.

31 Great Britain, *Survey of Economic Conditions in Morocco*.

32 Brown, *Salé*, 129-30; Stewart, *Economy*, 136.

33 Gallisot, *Patronat*, 70-4.

34 *Ibid.*, 68-71; Zakya Daoud, *Féminisme et politique au Maghreb* (Casablanca: Eddif,

In the countryside, the general rate of wage decline was about the same as the cities – about 60% between 1930 and 1935 – but rural wages were a little over half of those of the *bidonvilles.* Rates in the Spanish zone were slightly lower still.[35]

The rural population was rising beyond the level that the rural economy could sustain. The 1936 census, the first to cover the whole of the French zone, put the population at 6.2 million. An estimate in 1921 had put it at 4.3 million, which was probably too low, but it does seem likely that the population increased by 1.5 – 3% a year in the 1920s and 1930s. By 1935 yet more people were coming on to the labour market, producing the chronic unemployment problem that has bedevilled Morocco ever since.[36]

Many Moroccans simply moved to the cities. The *bidonvilles* were poor, but opportunity was still greater than in the countryside. In 1931 Henri Prost, the *éminence grise* of urban planning, declared the *bidonvilles* to be the greatest problem besetting planners. Rabat-Salé increased in size from about 80,000 to about 115,000 people between 1931 and 1936. Some did move into the *medinas,* where big houses were subdivided among the poor, but most settled in huge *bidonvilles* like Douar Jdid, where life was very precarious. They had no legal title and rents were often very high. People survived by keeping chickens, cattle and goats, or by cultivating the ground. Some even lived in tents. Yet, while people in the *bidonvilles* clung to their rural origins, they also mixed their identities: even in the early 1930s Douar Jdid was housing people from the Rharb, the Sahara and Chaouïa.[37]

In the Spanish zone, population pressure led to more intensive cultivation, and in the countryside in the far north-east people began to exchange tents for mud and stone houses. In the Jebala, where population densities were forty to fifty per square kilometre and in Melilla where they reached more than eighty, many people emigrated. By 1931, around ten per cent of the adult male population of the eastern Rif was migrating seasonally to Algeria: 'swallow-type migration' as the Spanish administration rather expressively called it. Wages in Oranie were twice what they were in the Rif, even up to seven or eight times as much for really unpleasant

1993), 249.

35 Pascon, *Haouz,* 2:511; Gallisot, *Patronat,* 67-8; Louis Milliot, 'L'exode saisonnier des riffains vers l'Algérie', *Bulletin Economique du Maroc* 1, no. 5 (1934): 313-21.

36 Gallisot, *Patronat,* 74; Abu Lughod, *Rabat,* 204.

37 Abu Lughod, *Rabat,* 208-9, 211; Wright, *Politics,* 154; Gallisot, *Patronat,* 73; M. Naciri, 'Quelques exemples d'évolution des douars à la périphérie urbaine de Salé', *Revue de Géographie du Maroc* 8 (1965): 133-47.

jobs. This migration did not mix people of different origins. Jobs were arranged by brokers from each tribe, or informally by other members of the tribe in tea shops dotted along the Algerian roads.[38]

How the colons coped

Poor weather and the world crisis did not spare the colons. A typical farm in the Rharb lost half its harvest in 1935.[39] Yet, in the dual economy, the settlers could still protect themselves by exerting political pressure on the Protectorate authorities to shift more of the burden onto the Moroccan population.

The support of the Protectorate authorities was vital. The Act of Algeciras made tariff protection difficult, but the government restricted foreign wheat imports in 1928 and 1933 by claiming the needs of 'public order'. The Protectorate also took over the debts of farmers who had defaulted, but obliged them to sell their crops to the state in return; it also set quotas for vegetables, guaranteeing their sale in French markets. Moroccan farmers had no such privileges and in the 1930s provided less than 10 per cent of the soft wheat exported to France.[40]

Yet the quotas were too small to sustain colon agriculture. In the late 1920s, colon farmers and agricultural promoters had decided that citrus fruits would be the best export earner. California was the model, similar in climate, soil and rainfall, so various propagandists, notably the president of the Casablanca Chamber of Agriculture, went to America and came back with glowing reports and a new dream. Morocco would no longer be reborn as the granary of Rome, but as a Mediterranean California. The Protectorate administration helped. In 1932 it set up the *Office Chérifien de Contrôle et d'Exportation* whose job – apart from research and education – was marketing: it would inspect fruit and vegetables for export and only pass produce of the highest quality, which it would advertise abroad. The 'Maroc' label on fruit began at this time, as a seal of quality, and so began a policy that would turn Morocco into the world's second largest exporter of oranges by the mid-1980s. This benefited colons almost entirely, for it was they who planted the citrus trees – over 2,000 ha. between 1929 and 1932. Only a very few, very wealthy Moroccan landowners took part.

38 Seddon, *Moroccan Peasants*, 127; David Seddon, 'Labour Migration and Agricultural Development in Northeast Morocco: 1870-1970', *Maghreb Review*, 4, no. 3 (1979): 69-77; Milliot, 'L'exode saisonnier', 315.

39 Le Coz, *Rharb*, 2:547.

40 Stewart, *Economy*, 89-92, 96-7.

Even the European agricultural pressure groups could not persuade the Protectorate to spend any money on big capital projects. Although irrigation was a necessary part of the Californian dream, big irrigation projects were mostly put on the back burner in the early 1930s.[41]

The Protectorate supported employment for French settlers by making sure that only French (not Italian or Spanish) enterprises won what construction contracts there were. It also started a renewed program of public works, and that too benefited the French population. In 1934, 256 workers were employed on municipal public works projects in Meknès. Not one was Moroccan.[42]

Working-class French trade-unionists were not entirely grateful. The employers vigorously opposed their demands for labour-protection laws, a minimum salary and eight-hour day, partly for fear that their Moroccan employees would demand the same. European employers were particularly successful at holding down Moroccan wages, hiring ever more Moroccans on a daily basis, and so excluding them from the protection of the very basic labour laws. They strenuously resisted reductions in Moroccans' working hours and even imposed compulsory overtime without pay. The organisation representing building contractors explained, in a memorandum to the labour department, that a ten-hour day was necessary because Moroccan workers were not productive: 'All our workers are natives, apart from the foremen, and no native does enough work to obtain normal output in eight hours.' A ten-hour day was even in the interest of Moroccan workers, the memorandum continued. It kept the employers in business, and it allowed Moroccan workers to work for themselves during slack periods. With such cheap labour the European community weathered the crisis, more easily than the French in France and much more easily than the Moroccans. In 1934 the average European income in Morocco was around 17,400 francs a year. It was 5,500 in France. A Moroccan, if he was lucky enough to *be* employed full time, had a salary of about 1,500 francs a year.[43]

Yet the colons were not satisfied. Henri Ponsot, who became Resident-General in 1933, clashed with business leaders because he refused to revise the Act of Algeciras and allow full tariff protection for their produce and manufactures. He told them that the world economic crisis was too serious to make changes just then,

41 Swearingen, *Mirages*, 59-86.

42 Gallisot, *Patronat*, 77-9.

43 *Ibid.*, 91.

but his real fear was probably that tariff barriers would integrate the Moroccan economy even further with that of France, which would undermine the administrative independence of the Protectorate.[44]

Despite these setbacks, the colons were more and more creating their own image of Morocco. Although immigration tapered off after 1931, those who had arrived in the 1920s were now well settled. They lived without much contact with the Moroccans, apart from their servants, who ideally did their jobs as silently as possible. They lived in European-planned cities, worked in European companies or the administration, and travelled in cars or first-class railway carriages. Even colonial architecture was changing. By the end of the 1920s, a new generation of French architects, influenced by Le Corbusier, were designing severely modernist buildings, like the courthouse and the railway station in Rabat, that took little account of local styles and disdained Lyautey's 'pseudo-Moorish' style.[45]

In Spanish-controlled Morocco, the municipal architect of Melilla, Enrique Nieto, also opted firmly for modernism, on the grounds that Melilla had never been an 'Arab city'. In the Protectorate itself the new town of Villa Sanjurjo was being built on Al Hoceima Bay, under the guidance of a military native affairs officer, Emilio Blanco Izaga. His public buildings certainly used North African motifs, but very eclectically. Blanco used what he considered to be 'Berber' designs in order to build up a Berber rather than Arab or Spanish identity, sometimes with peculiar results. Since Rifi homesteads were more atomised than he cared for, the Native Affairs Office at Arba Taourirt in the mountains of the central Rif was modelled on Berber collective storehouses in the far south of Morocco. When completed in 1940, it did not find favour with his superiors. In Villa Sanjurjo itself, the plan for a parallel Rifi 'garden city' was quickly abandoned because there was not enough water. Moroccans were actively discouraged from settling there and almost the only buildings that were completed for Moroccan use were a qaid's office and a prison.[46]

44 Hoisington, *Casablanca Connection*, 110-11.

45 Abu Lughod, *Rabat*, 205-6; Wright, *Politics*, 138-9.

46 Juan Román, *Fragmentos de una conversación sobre Alhucemas* (Melilla: Ayuntamiento de Melilla, 1994), 24; Antonio Bravo Nieto, 'L'architecture coloniale espagnole du xxème siècle au Maroc', *Revue Maroc-Europe* 5 (1993): 159-76; Antonio Bravo Nieto, *La construcción de una ciudad europea en el contexto norteafricano. Arquitectos e inginieros en la Melilla contemporánea* (Melilla: Ciudad Autónoma de Melilla, 1996), 463.

Colon life in Morocco
Colons brought French customs with them, and lived apart from the Moroccans. Men and women relaxed in the open at hotel tables (*above*), while Galcries Lafayette (*below*) provided them with department stores. (Author's collection)

General Mohamed ben Mizian
The highest-ranking Moroccan soldier in the Spanish colonial army. He fought with great bravery on the Ebro front during the Spanish Civil War, and rose to the rank of general. He was chief of staff of the Moroccan army after independence.

Protest and nationalism

Segregation led to violence. Moroccan workers expelled from public works' sites in Casablanca in 1933 threw stones at the Europeans who remained. When salaries were eaten away by 'fines' imposed by employers for supposedly bad behaviour, or when middlemen took too large a cut, there were more riots: in Port Lyautey (Kénitra), on the Fez to Tangier railway, and at Kasba Tadla in 1933 and again in 1935.[47]

Rage did not threaten the Protectorate because too few Moroccans worked in the modern sector. The protests over the Berber *dahir* in 1930 had undermined French prestige as no reasoned criticism could ever do, but the nationalists were not able to keep up the momentum of popular fury. They were still too few, and they were a very mixed group, who had been subjected to a medley of intellectual and political influences. Some had been educated abroad, some in France and some in the Arab east; others in Morocco, in the traditional *madrasas* and the Qarawiyyin and a few in the French schools of the Protectorate.

Young men who had studied in Paris had been exposed to the traditions of the French Enlightenment and Republic and to the more recent ideologies of the Parisian left. Some had joined Mesali Hadj's trade union organisation *Etoile Nord-Africaine* that was heavily influenced by the Communist Party. Few of them were really communists, but they learned how to build a party organised in cells and, back in Morocco, they used the model to organise what would become the *Kutlat al-Amal al-Wattani* (National Action Bloc).

In the summer of 1930 a secret society called the Zawiya was set up, first in Fez and then in Tetuan and Rabat. At its core were nine men, a bare majority of them with a modern education, either from France (Mohamed Hassan Ouazzani, Omar Abdeljalil, Ahmed Belafrej and Mohammed Lyazidi) or from French schools in Morocco (Mohamed Diouri); three were products of traditional Islamic universities – the Qarawiyyin or al-Azhar (Mohamed Ghazi, Allal El Fassi, Hassan Bouayad); and one came from a Quranic school (Ahmed Mekouar). Between 1930 and 1933, they attracted followers in Rabat, Salé, Port Lyautey, Casablanca, Safi, Marrakesh and Tangier, and to preserve security they organised them into cells; collectively this outer circle of activists was known as the *Taifa*. Their numbers were very small, between thirty and forty

47 Gallisot, *Patronat*, 80, 82; Fouad Benseddik, *Syndicalisme et politique au Maroc* (Paris: L'Harmattan, 1990), 117-18.

in the first two years. The French-educated made up most of the top leadership while the propagandists and organisers in the cities were largely Muslim educated.[48]

The most successful propagandist, Allal El-Fassi, organised a boycott of a French-owned tobacco company that had sacked its Moroccan workers and made fiery speeches to the students of the Qarawiyyin. The French authorities were nervous about intervening in a sensitive religious environment, but in August 1933 they silenced him, by refusing to let him return after a trip abroad.[49] Allal El-Fassi apart, the activities of the Zawiya in the early 1930s centred on the Free Schools that the Salafis had set up in the previous decade. This was both for ideological reasons and because it was almost the only way in which Moroccan children *could* be educated. The French record was paltry. Few Moroccans could attend European French schools. One who did was Mehdi ben Ahmed Ben Barka, the son of a small shopkeeper in Rabat, who sat at the front door of a French school for three months until the headmaster's wife intervened and got him admitted. He was extremely bright; he won a place first at the Collège Moulay Youssef in 1934, when he was fourteen, and then at a French Lycée in Rabat and gained his baccalaureate in mathematics in 1939, at the age of nineteen. By 1940, 1,400 Moroccans had passed the baccalaureate exam, but places were always hard to find. The Protectorate stopped opening *Ecoles des fils de notables* in 1929 and only one *Collège Musulman* was added in Marrakesh in 1936. The Berber policy produced a teacher's training college, the *Collège Berbère* at Azrou in 1931 but its academic level was minimal. For the less affluent, there were thirty-seven *écoles urbaines* and forty-four *écoles rurales* in the whole country in 1937. There were also seventeen girls' schools that concentrated on inculcating 'clean, orderly economical household habits'.[50]

Only one major activity built up a mass following in the early 1930s: a scouting movement. The first troop was formed in 1931, and became popular at the end of 1933 when the Rabat troop recruited the Sultan's son Hassan, then five years old. They made him honorary president and renamed themselves 'Hassani scouts'. The aim was overtly political: they concentrated on drilling boys

48 Halstead, *Rebirth*, 192-3; Agnouche, *Histoire*, 159.

49 Al-Fasi, *al-Harakat*, 154-5.

50 Halstead, *Rebirth*, 105-9; Daoud, *Féminisme*, 243; Zakya Daoud and Maâti Monjib, *Ben Barka* (Paris: Editions Michalon, 1996), 64, 69-70, 74.

in paramilitary style rather than taking them on camps and nature rambles in the countryside.[51]

Otherwise the early nationalists were elitists, pinning their hopes for change on winning support in France, particularly on the parliamentary left, in the hope of influencing the government. This was a perfectly practical objective, but it was hardly a challenge to French domination. The nationalists recruited the help of Robert Longuet, his father Jean (a socialist deputy and a grandson of Karl Marx), Georges Monnet and the left-wing Minister of Education of the Spanish Republic, Fernando de los Rios. These four men financed a journal, *Maghreb*, that began publication in Paris in July 1932.[52] The main contributors were Moroccans – Ouazzani, Abdeljalil and Lyazidi, and Belafrej, the editor[53] – and its back cover displayed an elaborate Moroccan-style design and an appeal in Arabic that announced:

> Moroccans, this journal has been set up to defend your rights and to make your voice be heard, to express your demands and your experiences, in the knowledge that your country needs such a project to be brought to fruition.
>
> In truth, a right that is lost because no effort is made to seek it or an injustice that is suffered in silence are a form of death. To seek a right is to live. It is your duty to take note of the content of this journal, to immerse yourself in its breath, to broadcast its principles and to help in distributing it.[54]

Moroccans in Morocco could do nothing of the sort, since the Protectorate authorities promptly banned it, and aside from the cover, the whole magazine was in French.[55] So was a little book about the Berber dahir that Ouazzani published in Paris in 1931, under the ironic pseudonym of 'Mouslim Barbari',[56] a play on Berber and Barbarian.

Between 1930 and 1933, Ouazzani was the secretary of the pre-

51 Leon Borden Blair, *Western Window in the Arab World* (Austin: University of Texas Press, 1970), 23.

52 Mohamed Hassan Ouazzani, *Combats d'un nationaliste marocain*, 2 vols (Fès: Fondation Mohamed Hassan Ouazzani, 1989), 1:96-7; Halstead, *Rebirth*, 197; al-Fasi, *al-Harakat*, 152.

53 Halstead, *Rebirth*, 207.

54 Quoted in Ouazzani, *Combats*, 1:101.

55 Blair, *Western Window*, 26.

56 Mouslim Barbari, *Tempête sur le Maroc ou les erreurs d'une 'politique berbère'* (Paris: 1931); Halstead, *Rebirth*, 207; Ouazzani, *Combats*, 2:17-18.

eminent Arab nationalist thinker, Shakib Arslan. Arslan, a Lebanese, lived in Geneva and at the moment when Italian forces were crushing the Libyan resistance under Umar al-Mukhtar, recommended that Libyans work with the Italians not against them.[57] Similarly, Moroccan nationalists hoped to work with the French, protesting against the injustices of French rule, not French rule itself. 'Mouslim Barbari' asked rhetorically: 'Are we not under the aegis of France, the France that made the Revolution of '89, executed kings to achieve the liberation of peoples, went through the great war to save civilisation from the "German barbarians"?'[58]

When Ouazzani set up in 1932 the first nationalist newspaper to be published in Morocco itself, *L'Action du Peuple*, it too was written in French, and complained that the French authorities had betrayed the ideals of the Protectorate.[59] The Protectorate authorities disagreed that they had betrayed any ideals, and quickly banned the paper.[60] They did allow an Arabic-language journal *Majallat al-Maghrib*, founded by Muhammad Salah Meissa in 1932, that carried Salafi-inspired articles by members of the Makhzan elite – particularly Hajoui, the minister for education.[61] In 1935 *Majallat al-Maghrib* published articles on Moroccan nationality, on charitable societies and, above all, on education. A series of articles on the need for women's education was sparked by an anonymous article signed by 'A Girl'. This turned out to be a fifteen-year-old, Malika El-Fassi, who shortly afterwards married her cousin Mohammed El-Fassi, who was already a prominent nationalist. Echoing the Egyptian thinker Qasim Amin, she wrote of the importance of educating the mothers of future generations as the first priority, but she also hinted at larger ambitions, pointing out that when the Arabs had been great, there had also been famous women scholars.[62]

Majallat al-Maghrib also provided an idea that won mass support. In 1932 it proposed an annual festival to celebrate the ruling dynasty, a *Fête du Trône*. In September 1933 it repeated the idea,

57 Juliette Bessis, 'Chekib Arslan et les mouvements nationalistes au Maghreb', *Revue Historique* 259 (1976): 477-81.

58 Quoted in Ouazzani, *Combats*, 1:222

59 *Ibid.*, 2:21, 33.

60 Al-Fasi, *al-Harakat*, 154.

61 Alaoui, *Maroc*, 70.

62 *Majallat al-Maghrib*, issues for 1935. The initial article on education is in the number for Dhu al-Hijja 1353/March 1935; Latifa Akharbach and Narjis Rerhaye, *Femmes et Politique* (Casablanca: Le Fennec, 1992), 20; Daoud, *Féminisme*, 244.

which was picked up by *L'Action du Peuple* and won the support of the Pasha of Salé. That gave it respectability, and on the anniversary of Sidi Mohammed's succession, 18 November, students at the Qarawiyyin sent telegrams of support to the Sultan and food was distributed to the poor of Marrakesh in his name. Since the Protectorate authorities could hardly suppress expressions of loyalty to the sultan whom they protected, they made the day a public holiday in 1934.[63]

The nationalists were grouping around Sidi Mohammed as a symbol of the nation, a role that he was keen to take on. He gave Allal El-Fassi an audience in February 1934 and told him: 'The rights we have lost were the result of those who held responsible positions in the past having no knowledge of the methods they should follow. From now on the country will lose no more rights. Moreover, I will work to retrieve what has been lost.'[64]

Sidi Mohammed did not say what were the rights that had to be regained, but the nationalists were less concerned to discuss detail than to capitalise on Sidi Mohammed's popularity, which was real enough. When he visited Fez on 10 May 1934, a huge crowd greeted him, shouting 'Long live the King' and 'Long Live Freedom'. Sidi Mohammed was no longer a sultan, but a king, a modern sovereign, who would be able to repudiate the past, and in particular the Treaty of Fez, that assigned to him the title of Sultan and so confined everything Moroccan to the traditional, the oriental and the antique.[65] While the title did not become official until independence more than two decades later, this was the first stage in resolving the duality between the Moroccan and the modern roles of the state.

In April, during celebrations to mark the Prophet's birthday in Tangier, young men in the processions sang verses praising Islamic culture and calling on people to awake and 'forget the past'. The Mandoub jailed some of the poorer participants and banished some of the richer. He even physically assaulted one of the accused.[66]

63 Halstead, *Rebirth*, 199; Alaoui, *Maroc*, 71-2; al-Fasi, *al-Harakat*, 163 claims that the idea was purely that of the nationalists and dates it to 1933. Alaoui 's date of 1932 as the first time the suggestion was raised is confirmed by PRO FO371/18556/W10683/196/28, Vaughan-Russell to Bullard, Marrakesh, 28 Nov 1934.

64 Al-Fasi, *al-Harakat*, 158-9.

65 Alaoui, *Maroc*, 73; Halstead, *Rebirth*, 199; al-Fasi, *al-Harakat*, 161-2; Hammoudi, *Master and Disciple*, 113.

66 PRO FO371/18554/W7218/33/28, Gardner to FO, Tangier, 30 July 1934.

British consuls reported that public sympathy was swinging behind the nationalists and the Sultan, but the French authorities treated the nationalists with contempt, as mere agitators with no political programme. In fact, leading members of the Zawiya were already working on just that. In the summer of 1933 Lyazidi, Ouazzani, Abdeljalil and others formed a committee to draft a Plan of Reforms.[67] It was published in Arabic in Cairo in September 1934 and in French in Paris in November. On 1 December Abdeljalil and Ouazzani, flanked by Longuet and other French politicians, presented it to Pierre Laval, the Foreign Minister. In Rabat, Mohamed Ghazi presented a copy to the Sultan, and Lyazidi, Diouri and Allal El Fassi took one to the Resident-General.[68]

The Plan de Réformes

The *Plan de Réformes* called not for independence but for a true application of the Treaty of Fez, a real Protectorate. Its long preamble explained that Moroccan sovereignty had not been extinguished in 1912, and that under the treaty, the Sultan continued to embody the Moroccan identity. The purpose of the Protectorate was reform, which was also the wish of the Moroccan population, so that a 'real' Protectorate was therefore a democratic demand. Nowhere was there any recognition of a possible conflict between these democratic ideals and the authority of the Sultan.

The main body of the plan dealt with different areas of reform: economic (finance, tax and the reform of agriculture), social (health and education) and political (administrative and public liberties and democratic electoral rights). Teasing out the various influences on these proposals is next to impossible. They were the common currency both of nationalists throughout the Arab Middle East and of reformers on the European left: redistribution of land and the establishment of experimental farms, the abolition of corporal punishment, free compulsory primary and secondary education for both boys and girls, equal treatment of Moroccan and French state functionaries.

French practice would provide the administrative and legal structure for the courts; French electoral systems would be used for municipal government and a national assembly; the French min-

67 Al-Fasi, *al-Harakat*, 165; Halstead, *Rebirth*, 191-2; Alaoui, *Maroc*, 74; Agnouche, *Histoire*, 260; PRO FO371/18554/W4900/33/28, Ellison to Edmonds, Fez, 14 May 1934.

68 Al-Fasi, *al-Harakat*, 165; Halstead, *Rebirth*, 212-13; Alaoui, *Maroc*, 75; Agnouche, *Histoire*, 260.

isterial system would provide the model for the Moroccan cabinet. Yet the reasoning drew on Islamic theory and Moroccan political traditions. The separation of the executive and judicial powers of the pashas and qaids was justified in terms of the *shar'ia.* Despite the call for elections and a cabinet, the absolute power of the Sultan was maintained.[69]

This was a project of intellectuals, the products of the Salafiyya and the Free Schools they had founded in the 1920s: the allies of Arab nationalists in Geneva and Cairo, Nablus and Jerusalem sympathisers with the French left or the Italian right. It caught the imagination of the educated young, but more traditional members of the Moroccan elite, Moroccan officials of the Protectorate and many *'ulama,* felt threatened. People like the Fasi *'ulama* who demanded in 1937 that women be prohibited from walking in the streets dressed only in a djillaba rather than a full veil, or the Pasha of Rabat who forbade women to walk the street unaccompanied by a man, would have no sympathy for women's education or equal rights before the law.[70] Neither did Henri Ponsot, the new Resident-General, who superciliously remarked that the plan 'would make a good doctoral thesis in law'.[71] Unwittingly he had put his finger on a truth: the *Plan de Réformes* marked yet another step by the nationalists down the path of resolving the duality of the protectorate: Islam and democracy converged: in that both demanded the application of modernisation, but in the interests of the community.

Politics in the Spanish zone

The authorities in Tetuan were less snobbish. They wanted to encourage the nationalists, for entirely self-interested reasons. Despite the Rif war, many Spanish officials still felt that the French Protectorate was a competitor, not an ally, and hoped to use the nationalists against their rivals. In August 1930, hoping to exploit the protests over the Berber dahir, Shakib Arslan, the intellectual doyen of the Arab nationalist movement, planned to visit Morocco. The French authorities would not admit him, but he went to Tangier and then Tetuan, where he met members of the elite, including Abdussalam Bennuna, Muhammad Daoud and a young student named Abdelkhalek Torrès, the son of a former Pasha of Tetuan.

69 Halstead, *Rebirth,* 214-30; Alaoui, *Maroc,* 75-7; Al-Fasi, *al-Harakat,* 165-70; Agnouche, *Histoire,* 260-2; Daoud, *Féminisme,* 243.

70 Daoud and Monjib, *Ben Barka,* 69; Daoud, *Féminisme,* 242.

71 Alaoui, *Maroc,* 77.

Ahmed Belafrej, Mohammed El-Fassi, Omar Abdeljalil and others came up from the French zone. In September 1930, after Arslan returned home, Bennuna set up a nationalist group that functioned for a while as the Tetuan branch of the Zawiya.[72]

Stirring up trouble for the French satisfied wounded Spanish pride, but it also had practical benefits. In the turbulent domestic politics of Spain, Morocco was a central issue. In 1931 the monarchy fell, partly because of the continuing after-shock of the Annoual disaster a decade before. A republic was declared on 14 April 1931, and within weeks several prominent *Africanista* officers were arrested, including General Dámaso Berenguer, the High Commissioner at the time of Annoual. A young general, Francisco Franco, became his rather unwilling defence counsel.[73] Morocco loomed large in right-wing politics as a result. Between 1931 and 1936, swings between governments of left and right on the Peninsula and frequent changes of High Commissioner in Tetuan meant that Spanish administrators sought Moroccan support, and being friendly to the nationalists was part of this, although there was no intention of giving concessions of any value. Many promises were made, but few were kept.

Immediately after the republic was declared, left-wing and anarchist trade unions in Tetuan organised a mass demonstration. Moroccans joined in, waving not socialist or anarchist flags, but the Moroccan green star on a red field. Crowds mobbed the first civilian High Commissioner, Luciano López Ferrer, when he arrived in October 1931.[74]

Members of the elite did not run through the streets, but Bennuna and others organised a delegation to Madrid on 3 June and presented a petition to the new president, Nicolás Alcalá Zamora. The 800 signatories wanted reforms: municipal councils with elected members, an elected council for the whole zone to control the budget, a free press, freedom of association, more primary schools in the villages and secondary schools in the towns.

72 Wolf, *Secrets*, 168-71; Halstead, *Rebirth*, 192; Abdelmajid Benjelloun, 'Les developpements du mouvement nationaliste marocain dans la zone nord sur le plan international', *Revue d'Histoire Maghrébine*, 14, nos 45-46 (1987): 31-74.

73 Paul Preston, *Franco: a Biography* (London: HarperCollins, 1993), 76-7.

74 Wolf, *Secrets*, 175; María Rosa de Madariaga, 'The Intervention of Moroccan Troops in the Spanish Civil War: a Reconsideration', *European History Quarterly*, 22, no. 1 (1992): 67-97; Abdelmajid Benjelloun, 'La part prise par le mouvement nationaliste marocain de la zone d'influence espagnole dans le processus de libération du Maroc', *Revue d'Histoire Maghrébine*, 13, nos. 43-44 (1986): 5-42.; PRO FO371/15745/W8271/4220/28, Chafy to Gardner, Tetuan, 7 July 1931.

This was the first time in either zone that nationalists had presented a coherent series of demands to their European rulers.[75]

Alcalá Zamora accepted all the demands, but before the delegation set out, the British Vice-Consul in Tetuan had commented in his report: 'I gather that it is the intention of the Spanish Authorities to let this Moorish Commission talk and do nothing.'[76] So it turned out. A dahir did grant freedom of association and of the press, and the municipal councils were elected, but within a year they had been abolished on the pretext that they misused funds.[77] Freedom of the press and political activity turned out to mean only freedom to criticise the French, but northern nationalists made the best of the opportunity. Mass demonstrations in Tetuan marked the second and third anniversaries of the Berber dahir.[78] Even this freedom did not last long. López Ferrer's successors knew little about Morocco, and Spanish army commanders and the French in Rabat persuaded them to rein in the nationalists.[79] Yet no move was made against the rising star of the nationalists, Abdelkhalek Torrès.

Torrès was young and energetic. At the age of twenty-three in March 1932, he founded the Association of Muslim Students in Tetuan. In quick succession he helped set up a girls' primary school, a nationalist newspaper, *al-Hayat,* a worker's welfare organisation, *Dar al-Amal,* that was a trade union in disguise, and organised a scout troop.[80] Although he kept on good terms with senior Spanish officials (and even joined the Freemasons, who had great influence in the Republic), he made virulent attacks on the French in his newspaper and in public speeches. He was an excellent speaker. He organised a boycott of French products and in December 1934 sent telegrams to Sidi Mohammed supporting the *Plan de Réformes* and reaffirming the loyalty of the north.[81] When Abdussalam Bennuna died in January 1935, Torrès became the most important nationalist leader in Tetuan.[82]

75 Benjelloun, 'Developpements'; Halstead, *Rebirth,* 201; Wolf, *Secrets,* 176-7;

76 PRO FO371/15745/W7093/4220/28, Chafy to Gurney, 3 June 1931.

77 Wolf, *Secrets,* 181-2.

78 Benjelloun, 'Developpements'; Wolf, *Secrets,* 182-3

79 Al-Fasi, *al-Harakat,* 157-8

80 Wolf, *Secrets,* 182, 190-1; Halstead, *Rebirth,* 236. Carmen Ruiz Bravo-Villasante and Amin al-Rihani, *Un testigo árabe del siglo XX. Amin al-Rihani en Marruecos y en España (1939), 2 vols* (Madrid: Cantarabia, 1993), 2:191.

81 Wolf, *Secrets,* 191.

82 Ibid., 190-1; Halstead, *Rebirth,* 236.

Torrès caused little trouble to the Spanish administrators. The cities were quiet and after the Rif War the army had successfully turned many of its rural enemies into allies. Many of the Spanish qaids had been prominent members of ibn Abd al-Karim's administration.[83] They were closely supervised by officers of the military Native Affairs Office, some of whom grew very expert. Colonel Emilio Blanco Izaga, who came to the Rif in 1930, and later became head of Native Affairs in the Rif, was an anthropologist of great expertise. The army also recruited many Rifi men into the Regulares regiments, whose Spanish officers were nearly all right-wing.[84]

In late 1934 General Francisco Franco, now a personal aide to the conservative Minister of War, transported huge numbers of Regulares to the Peninsula to smash a socialist and anarchist uprising in Asturias. This had a special symbolism for Spaniards, because Asturias was the only region of Spain that the Muslims had never conquered. It was a savage business and afterwards the Spanish left's attitude to Moroccan affairs varied between the dismissive and the openly racist. When the Popular Front took power in June 1936, speakers at victory rallies in Ceuta and Melilla called Moroccans 'the armed force of the reactionaries'.[85]

Sport and popular culture

Even nationalists acknowledged the many beguiling aspects of French culture, some of which also captured the imagination of people of the *bidonvilles* and the *medinas.* Organised sport was one. There was nothing new about displays of physical prowess: hunting was an old Moroccan delight and the rich quickly took to golf after the first course opened in Tangier in 1914. Si Thami El Glaoui, ignoring water restrictions, built a golf-course in Marrakesh in the 1920s on which he achieved a handicap of four. He pursued his passion with distinguished partners, Winston Churchill among them.[86] Some Salafi-inspired nationalists already understood that sport was an important part of a modern education for boys, and even in some cases, for girls. One rich man set

83 Hart, *Aith Waryaghar*, 402. *Historial de la harka Melilla* (Melilla: Tipografía la Hispana, [n.d.]).

84 David Hart, *Emilio Blanco Izaga, Colonel in the Rif*, 2 vols (New Haven, CT: Human Relations Area Files, 1975), 7-10; Madariaga, 'Intervention', 73.

85 Preston, *Franco*, 103-5; Benomar, 'Working Class', 249-54.

86 Maxwell, *Lords of the Atlas*, 193; Hassan Rahmouni, (ed.), *La grande encyclopédie du Maroc* (Rabat: GEI, 1987) 1:113.

up a special school for his daughter and her friends, where her uncle gave physical education classes.

A girl from the respectable middle class would not compete in public for several decades. But barefoot boys, who had kicked about old tennis balls or bags filled with sand in the 1920s, joined the football teams organised by the colons' clubs in the 1930s, or founded their own. Football allowed talented boys to escape from the squalor of the *bidonvilles*. Larbi Benbarek was the most famous. Born in the medina of Casablanca, he began playing football for a small-time local team at the age of sixteen. Only when he joined the Casablanca second division club *L'Idéal* did he first put on boots, to his great discomfort. He was so talented that in 1937 he played for Morocco against France. The French won, but Olympic Marseille promptly recruited him.[87] Other clubs in France and Spain acquired Moroccan players.

Boxing was an alternative means of escape. Benbarek's great friend was Marcel Cerdan, the son of a colon butcher from Casablanca. In 1939 Cerdan became middleweight champion of the world and, colon or not, the hero of Moroccan boys. The lightweight Lahcen, from Marrakesh, also used boxing as a way out of poverty, although in his case the result was fatal: he died in the ring in 1943.

While Moroccans made great players, sport was administered by Frenchmen and most football clubs kept Moroccans off their committees. The *Club Nautique* in Casablanca even refused to let Moroccans swim in their pool. Not all clubs were so restrictive, and from 1930 onwards a few Moroccans did become expert swimmers and even took part in French national championships. Finally, in 1937 a group that had been excluded from the *Club Nautique* organised their own swimming club, Widad Athletic Club. Two years later they set up a football team that quickly became the club's most important activity.[88]

Widad Athletic Club's name came from the title of an Egyptian film starring Umm Kalthoum. The cinema and popular music, two other products of European and American technology, had a mass following in Morocco. The huge new cinemas – the Vox in Casablanca was the biggest in North Africa when it opened in 1932 – were extremely cheap and attracted big audiences to American blockbusters like *Tarzan* and Egyptian musicals starring

87 Abdelmalek Lahlou, *Casablanca à l'heure de l'opération Torch et de la Conférence d'Anfa*, (Casablanca: [n.p.], 1993), 85-6; Rahmouni, *Encyclopédie*, 1:42.

88 Lahlou, *Casablanca*, 80-95; Rahmouni, *Encyclopédie*, 1:43, 65, 77.

Umm Kalthoum or Abd al-Wahhab. Egypt was the birthplace of Arab mass culture, and when Moroccan singers imitated Egyptian popular songs, they forged a stronger link with the Arab east than the Salafiyya ever could. Sometimes the cinemas put on live comedy programmes that were more specifically Moroccan: comedians satirised the favourite targets of the townspeople: rich Fasis, money-grubbing Susi shopkeepers, stupid peasants and vicious, exploitative Europeans.

In the 1930s a mass-culture was born in the cities that fused American technology and spectacle, European diversions like football, Egyptian tastes and Moroccan symbols. Football developed a team identity, disciplined and cooperative, in which players stood out purely because of their skill. It became a vehicle of popular nationalism: in matches against French teams the fans identified themselves as Moroccans, forgetting or ignoring tribal, linguistic or even religious distinctions, for Jews were as keen on football as Muslims. Football also created heroes who were not intellectuals, not politicians and not from the elite: they represented the aspirations of the young men of the *medinas*.

Educated Moroccans benefited even more from modern opportunities. Classical Andalusian orchestras were set up, and one Moroccan traditional musician, Mohammed ben Khadir, gave a concert of Andalusian music in the United States in 1932. This was not mass culture, of course, but it was often nationalist, like the theatre groups in Salé and Fez. The teenaged Mehdi Ben Barka joined a drama group in Rabat and a singing group that recorded nationalist songs for the radio.[89]

The small Moroccan middle-class also had money to spend on new consumer products. *Majallat al-Maghrib*, the mildly reformist Arabic-language magazine, carried advertisements for Philips radios and Radiola radiograms, for Oldsmobile cars and OTOX fly-killer (complete with a graphic illustration of a fly), for Richefleur eau-de-Cologne and for a whole series of products to cure modern ills: Enos Fruit Salt ('If you eat too quickly...'), Aspirin, Vittel and Vichy mineral waters, their Moroccan competitor, Oulmès, and a brand of pure grape juice ('It cures the liver and brings back strength'). The Compagnie Paquet's advertisement showed the Sultan boarding one of its ships on his way to France.[90] These advertisements signalled the beginnings of a cultural change, though almost no Moroccans went so far as to wear European

[89] Lahlou, *Casablanca*, 67-73; Daoud and Monjib, *Ben Barka*, 66.

[90] *Majallat al-Maghrib*, 1935, *passim*.

clothes. Modernisation of clothing and specifically the introduction of hats, was a leitmotif of the modernisation of Iran and Turkey in the late 1920s and early 1930s, but those were countries ruled by nationalists who wanted to meet the European challenge aggressively. The French had no interest in encouraging this, or any, sort of nationalism, so the forces of the state were mobilised to preserve what it called Moroccan traditions.[91] Yet the advertisements also signalled the slow emergence of a Moroccan middle class. In 1935, the year of their appearance, more Moroccans could afford such things, and the middle class was beginning to grow, although most people were still very poor.

The limits of economic growth

When the world economy picked up in the mid 1930s, so did that of Morocco, although Europeans benefited more than Moroccans and the French zone more than the Spanish.

The weather held things back, as usual. Over much of the country harvests were dreadful in 1936 and 1937. In 1937 famine was so widespread that Théodore Steeg, the former Resident-General, was recalled to write a report on the crisis; he estimated that 1.4 million people, one quarter of the Muslim population, needed urgent state assistance and that half a million were actually destitute. In the Spanish zone, the harvest in 1937 was 35% of the average for 1936-46. By 1938 the cattle were dying and typhus ravaged the undernourished population. Bands of displaced peasants wandered the countryside, spreading the disease and dying by the roadsides. Inflation made people even poorer.[92]

Inflation, ironically, was the product of economic recovery. Exports from the French zone started to increase in 1936 and imports rose too. Japanese products, in particular, continued to find larger and larger markets and by 1938 they made up nearly a tenth of all imports.[93] The export recovery was based on minerals like phosphates, coal and zinc, and on cash-crops such as citrus fruits, since irrigated land was less affected by drought. This fed through into inflation. Demand pushed up the price of wheat, and between 1936 and 1938 the general price index in Casablanca rose by

91 Hammoudi, *Master and Disciple*, 108.

92 Le Coz, *Rharb*, 2:547; Patrick Berges, 'D'une guerre à l'autre: Le Maroc espagnole dans la tourmente (17 juillet 1936-septembre 1940)', *Revue Maroc-Europe* 1 (1991): 107-33; Hoisington, *Casablanca Connection*, 83-4; Seddon, *Moroccan Peasants*, 132; Ayache, *Mouvement syndicale*, 1:154; Swearingen, *Mirages*, 97-8.

93 Great Britain, *Survey of Economic Conditions in Morocco.*

just over half. The Moroccan franc, tied to the French currency, declined in value. In the northern zone, the Spanish Civil War drove prices up by over 400% between 1935 and 1943, and shrank the peseta from forty to the British pound in 1935 to seventy in February 1939.[94]

Moroccan workers' salaries did not keep pace and by the late 1930s five out of six family budgets in Fez were running at a deficit.[95] Most industrial jobs were part-time. In 1937 the statistical office estimated that the 'principle industries' employed 68,000 Moroccans, but only 'several thousand' had full-time jobs.[96] They lived in the *bidonvilles* that were now spreading to the new towns in the European agricultural and mining regions and in local administrative centres, places like Sidi Kacem, and Souk el-Arbaâ in the Rharb, Khouribga, and Louis-Gentil (now Youssoufia) on the road to Marrakesh. In the Spanish zone, Nador tripled in size between 1935 and 1940.[97] Life in the *bidonvilles* was harsh and all members of the family had to work, even married women, although female wages were very low. A male weaver in Fez, who might earn 5 francs a day, needed the extra 1½ francs made by his wife to scrape by.[98] Europeans were not hit as hard. Irrigated farms, that did not depend on the vagaries of rainfall, did exceptionally well in the droughts.[99] Indeed, vineyards were so successful that they produced too much wine. In 1936 the Protectorate government put limits on the number of vines that could be planted, but in exchange it bought up the surplus, which it turned into alcohol products or destroyed. Thus, colons were subsidised for producing waste. The state also financed the mining industries. The Bureau de Recherche et de Participation Minières, set up in 1927 to back the coal and iron industries, was extended to cover all minerals except phosphates. As the world economy picked up so did production and by 1939 the colons were mostly back in credit.[100]

Not all finance came from public sources. Increased production

94 Gallisot, *Patronat*, 155-6, 159; Salahdine, *Maroc*, 259; Le Coz, *Rharb*, 1:437; Seddon, *Moroccan Peasants*, 131.

95 Gallisot, *Patronat*, 156.

96 Hoisington, *Casablanca Connection*, 99; Gallisot, *Patronat*, 158-9; Pascon, *Haouz*, 2:536.

97 Gallisot, *Patronat*, 158; Le Coz, *Rharb*, 2:853-5; Seddon, *Moroccan Peasants*, 133.

98 Gallisot, *Patronat*, 157.

99 *Ibid.*, 158; Le Coz, *Rharb*, 2:582.

100 Stewart, *Economy*, 99, 119; Berque, *Maghrib*, 98.

had to be processed, so processing companies began investing in land and large estates started setting up their own plants. Agricultural capitalism was taking root. Most of these agro-businesses were European-owned, but some were controlled by a few very rich Moroccans. The Glaouis, a fixture in the Haouz, brought others up on their coat-tails. By 1935, Demnati Husayn, a former factory worker in France, was one of the principal capitalists of the Moroccan south. In Fez the Mernissi family made money through links with high French finance, and at a less exalted level, many bourgeois Fasis moved to Casablanca in the late 1930s to build up their fortunes.[101] Such people had political influence, could rely on the Protectorate authorities to help them, and borrow money from banks. Most Moroccans had none of these advantages, nor did French skilled workers and state officials, but they could exert pressure through political parties and trade unions.

The strikes of 1936

Théodor Steeg had allowed ordinary colons a voice in the Council of Government, and in June 1934, the socialist members walked out, protesting that the government had broken its promises to apply French labour legislation about a minimum wage and maximum hours. The Resident-General, Henri Ponsot, who had been appointed the previous year, was no friend of Moroccan nationalists, but now he succeeded in turning the French community against him as well. He placated the socialists with vague promises that were nevertheless specific enough to infuriate the industrial and commercial bosses who were already complaining about his refusal to change the tariff system. Ponsot kept none of his promises to the left and so alienated them. On 21 March 1936, having infuriated nearly the entire French population, he was replaced by Bernard-Marcel Peyrouton.[102]

Peyrouton was the employers' great hope. When he arrived, he was cheered through the streets by expectant crowds of middle-class Frenchmen. He declared that he would not legalise trade unions, claiming that otherwise he would have to legalise unions for Moroccan workers too; that was inconceivable, because they would soon swamp French members. He was quite right about this, but union power was growing. In June 1936 strikes in

101 Pascon, *Haouz*, 2:521-2; Berque, *Maghrib*, 173, 240.

102 Ayache, *Mouvement syndicale*, 132-3; Albert Ayache, 'Les grèves de juin 1936 au Maroc', *Annales Economies Sociétés Civilisations* 12, no. 3 (1957): 423.

metropolitan France helped bring to power Léon Blum and the Popular Front.[103]

Within days strikes began in Morocco. On June 11 the European trade union leadership called out all the workers in Cosuma, the sugar works in Casablanca, because the management refused to negotiate with a workers' association that had Moroccan Muslim members. Blum refused to let Peyrouton expel the leaders from Morocco. In the negotiations that followed, the workers won higher salaries, the right to strike and annual leave, although Europeans were still paid much more than Moroccans. Cosuma employed many Europeans, but when workers in the phosphate mines at Khouribga, most of them Moroccans, came out, the Foreign Legion broke the strike. In Casablanca the street-cleaners, all Moroccans, walked out and 240 were sacked and seventeen of the leaders were sent to prison by a summary pasha's court. This pattern of sacking and imprisoning Moroccan strikers but negotiating with Frenchmen continued under Peyrouton's successor, Noguès, who was appointed in October 1936.

GENERAL NOGUÈS AS RESIDENT-GENERAL

Noguès was appointed to restore order, a role he was well equipped to play. An old *protégé* of Lyautey on the Algerian frontier in 1909, he had served with distinction during the First World War and afterwards joined the military staff of President Alexandre Millerand. From then on he alternated between France and north Africa as governor of Fez during the Rif War, *Directeur Générale des Affaires Indigènes* during the Berber Dahir riots and army commander in Algiers in 1933. Here was a prominent colonial soldier who would have no truck with Moroccan rebels. But he was one of Lyautey's men too, and unsympathetic to the colons, who were particularly wary of the new Resident-General, when they saw how the left wing parties heaped praise upon him.[104] Their fears were soon borne out.

Trade unions for the French

First, Noguès legalised the Communist Party and then the trade unions. At the beginning of 1937, the first legal trade union federa-

[103] Ayache, *Mouvement syndicale*, 1: 140.

[104] Halstead, *Rebirth*, 232; Hoisington, *Casablanca Connection*, 13-27; Georges Oved, *La Gauche française et le nationalisme marocain 1905-1955*, 2 vols. (Paris: L 'Harmattan, 1984), 2:101-2.

tion was formed. A year later, the *Union des Syndicats Confédérés du Maroc* had 15-20,000 members, mainly employed by the state or the concessionary companies like the railways or the mines. As a result, it was easier to negotiate better hours, salaries, and working conditions in the state than the private sector and in 1937 and 1938 there were many strikes, especially in the building trade, where many of the workers were Moroccans.

The dahir that legalised the unions implied that only French workers were supposed to join them, but did not say so specifically. This made Moroccan membership illegal without specifically banning it, apparently a deliberate ambiguity on Noguès's part.[105] For practical and ideological reasons, the trade union leadership had no interest in excluding Moroccans. In January 1937 building employers refused to recognise a trade union, most of whose members were Moroccan, and French union leaders organised a strike. *Maroc Socialiste*, the left wing paper, talked of a Moroccan proletariat 'becoming conscious of their dignity. They no longer want to be beasts of burden.' The first Moroccan socialists began to appear, one of them a postman.[106]

When Moroccan workers struck in the phosphate mines at Louis Gentil (Youssoufia) and then in Khouribga, Noguès sent in the police, the Foreign Legion and finally the Tirailleurs Sénégalais. The government talked of the 'deplorable example' that European strikers gave to the 'natives.'[107] Finally, on 28 June, a dahir explicitly forbade Moroccans to join trade unions. In words written by the French, the Sultan decreed that: 'It will have the most serious consequences if we allow our subjects to be exposed to the temptation of removing themselves from the authority of our Makhzan by infringing the strict laws that regulate associations and trade unions.'[108]

The unions lost a third of their membership. In their place Noguès tried to provide an alternative, under Makhzan control. On 28 July a corporation for Moroccan bus and transport workers was established, presided over by Si Thami El Glaoui, a thoroughly

105 Ayache, *Mouvement syndicale*, 167; Benseddik, *Syndicalisme*, 160. The text of the dahir is in *Bulletin Officiel*, 1 Janvier 1937, 'Dahir du 24 Décembre 1936 (9 Chaoual 1355) sur les syndicats professionnels'.

106 Ayache, *Mouvement syndicale*, 1:184-5

107 *Ibid.*, 1:194, 247-51.

108 *Bulletin Officiel*, 15 Juillet 1938, 'Dahir du 24 Juin 1938 (25 Rebia II 1357) complétant la législation sur les associations et sur les syndicats professionnels'.

unconvincing trade unionist.[109] It was too late anyway. Moroccan unionists may have been few, but they had tasted membership of a mass movement, organised on national lines. The resident-general's economic policies had similarly unintended results.

Economic reform

Noguès wanted Moroccans to become richer. He was committed to Lyautey's vision of developing Moroccan society, and also feared they might riot or turn to nationalism. So he diverted resources towards Moroccans by leaving more money in their pockets. Noguès abolished housing taxes in the cities and market taxes in the countryside. He also put more funds into the Sociétés Indigènes de Prévoyance that Lyautey had set up to provide credit at low interest to Moroccan farmers. Although this added to rural debt, interest rates were very low, and by 1938 peasants were able to repay them. Most importantly Noguès extended irrigation to Moroccan farmers and made laws that prevented too much Moroccan land being alienated to Europeans. Irrigation projects that benefited Moroccans were started around Tadla, and schemes in the Tafilalt increased the land under cultivation fivefold in one year.[110]

In the more explosive cities Noguès adopted similar tactics. He tried to revitalise the old guilds in order to undercut the trade unions and to direct grants to artisans. Artisanal manufacture revived as a result. New techniques of weaving were adopted, new mixes of cloth and new colours which, although duller than traditional designs, were more in tune with changing tastes. Potters began producing more 'European' designs and tanners began experimenting with eucalyptus bark, despite the strictures of some conservative '*ulama* in the Qarawiyyin that such innovations were irreligious.[111]

To pay for all this, Noguès increased taxes in consumption, which shifted some of the costs from the Moroccan to the European population, and obtained a huge subsidy of 120 million francs from Paris. The Spanish zone was equally dependent on funds from the metropolis, since two-thirds of its revenues came from Madrid.[112] Finally Noguès tried to increase customs receipts. After

109 Ayache, *Mouvement syndicale*, 1:250-1.

110 Hoisington, *Casablanca Connection*, 79-87; Swearingen, *Mirages*, 98-107.

111 Hoisington, *Casablanca Connection*, 94; Berque, *Maghrib*, 283-4

112 Hoisington, *Casablanca Connection*, 79, 84; Morales Lezcano, *Norte de Africa*, 167.

Japan, Britain and the United States were the major trading partners of French Morocco. Japan had no treaty relations, but trade relations with Britain were still regulated by John Drummond-Hay's treaty of 1856. In 1937 Noguès persuaded the British government to abandon the capitulations, consular courts and protected status, and in 1938 he negotiated a new trade treaty that returned tariff authority to Morocco. By 1939 only the US government still held out, saying that a new trade treaty would close the 'open door' that had been guaranteed under the Act of Algeciras.[113] But trade with the United States represented only 4% of the total for the French zone, so that by 1939 Noguès had fulfilled two of the main diplomatic objectives of the pre-colonial Makhzan – tariff autonomy and the abolition of protected status. This made it easier for nationalists to believe that Noguès was committeGd to a 'real' Protectorate, and they returned to the reform projects that his predecessors had rejected.

Noguès and the nationalists

Soon after Noguès was appointed, Omar Abdeljalil and Ouazzani went to Paris to present their reforms to the Quai d'Orsay. In October 1936, while they were away, Allal El-Fassi and Mohammed Lyazidi called the first conference of the *Kutla* in Rabat. As a result, El-Fassi became president, and although Ouazzani was elected secretary, the two men fell out. Otherwise, the conference was a success.

Early hopes were soon dashed. The Quai d'Orsay temporised, and the Residency banned a second meeting of the Kutla in Casablanca in November. That led to rioting, the Pasha of Casablanca arrested El-Fassi, Lyazidi and Ouazzani and demonstrations spread to Rabat, Salé, Fez, Taza and Oujda. By the end of the month over 200 people had been arrested,[114] and this silenced the protests. The Quai d'Orsay, anxious that things should stay calm, lest German propagandists profit from disorder, told Noguès to 'cut the ground from under the feet of nationalism ... For the moment the Frenchmen in Morocco do not count ... Morocco must be governed for the Moroccans ... and some decisive measure must prove it.'[115]

The decisive measure was an amnesty and the liberalisation

113 Kenbib, 'European Protections', 51-3; Hoisington, *Casablanca Connection*, 127-8.

114 Hoisington, *Casablanca Connection*, 41-2; Oved, *Gauche*, 2:101-4; Halstead, *Rebirth*, 235; al-Fasi, *al-Harakat*, 187-8.

115 Quoted in Hoisington, *Casablanca Connection*, 56.

of the press, which the nationalists interpreted as a sign of weakness. In January 1937 they reorganised the *Kutla* as a formal political party, with Allal El-Fassi as the president of its executive committee. It promptly split. Most longstanding nationalist leaders, like Ahmad Belafrej, Omar Abdeljalil, Allal El-Fassi, Mohammed El-Fassi and his new wife Malika, who was not a formal member, stuck together. But Mohamed Hassan Ouazzani, angry that he had only been appointed secretary, and not president, resigned in February.[116] Allal El-Fassi, who was president, and Ahmed Belafrej, the new secretary, carried the day. Within two months they recruited over 6,000 new members and set up an Arabic language weekly.[117]

This was not what Noguès had intended. On 18 March 1937 he banned the *Kutla*, after less than three months, as an open party. Yet he did not ban its newspapers and it reformed under a new name, the National Party for the Realisation of Demands (*al-Hizb al-Watani li-Tahqiq al-Matalib*), with virtually the same executive. Ouazzani formed a party of his own, the National Action Party (*Hizb al-Amal al-Watani*), which he claimed had a more radical program, although he was driven more by personal rivalry with El-Fassi than by ideology.[118]

The policies of the Hizb al-Watani

The program of the *Hizb al-Watani* was founded on two big ideas. The first was that modernisation of the economy and the political system, elections and the separation of powers accorded with the *shari'a*. The second was that monarchy was the natural form of government in Morocco and the throne was the symbol of the nation.[119] Yet its specific policies were reformist. The education of women, the encouragement of Moroccan industry, the development of property rights, the replacement of the *bidonvilles* with proper living quarters, freedom under the law, and an end to the rule of El Glaoui, were, none of them, incompatible with a reformed Protectorate. Yet the French had no stomach for the party's campaigns in support of the Palestinian Arabs nor for their demand that the Berber policy should be abolished, that Arabic

116 Ibid., 56-7; Halstead, *Rebirth*, 239-40; al-Fasi, *al-Harakat*, 191-2; Alaoui, *Maroc*, 77-8; Akharbach and Rerhaye, *Femmes*, 20.

117 Hoisington, *Casablanca Connection*, 56.

118 Halstead, *Rebirth*, 244-5.

119 Halstead, *Rebirth*, 242-7; Hoisington, *Casablanca Connection*, 57; al-Fasi, *al-Harakat*, 198-9.

be taught in Berber areas, and the *tariqas* reined in.[120]

Campaigns and suppression

Many of the stated policies of the party – industrialisation, property rights, political and legal freedoms – were more immediately in the interests of the emerging middle class, and its leadership was drawn from that class. There was certainly no interest in the fate of Moroccan trade unionists. Yet the party needed popular support, and there was considerable anger on the streets. After protests about water supplies in Marrakesh and Sefrou, there was rioting in Meknès in September 1937 over a plan to divert water supplies in a way that seemed likely to deprive Muslims of water. The party made much of this, but the Legion and the Tirailleurs Sénégalais repressed the demonstrations, and thirteen Moroccans were killed. Other cities provided different flashpoints: the visit of a senior French official in Marrakesh; a proposed Catholic pilgrimage in Khémisset; and celebrations to mark the birthday of Mouley Idris, the founder of Fez, in October.[121] All these popular focuses of discontent were seized upon by *Hizb al-Watani*.

After the Fez demonstrations, Noguès sent troops into the *medina*, shut down nationalist newspapers and again banned the *Hizb al-Watani*. On 29 October, following an incendiary speech by Mohamed Hassan Ouazzani in Fez, almost the entire nationalist leadership was arrested. Over 400 people were jailed and the most important leaders exiled: El-Fassi to Gabon, and Ouazzani, Lyazidi and Mekouar to the Sahara. Belafrej, who was abroad, stayed there.[122] The *Hizb al-Watani* was destroyed, but the events of 1937 had shown that it could take real advantage of popular issues to win wide support, both in the countryside and in the cities. Moreover, the nationalist movement was not entirely silenced, but shifted to a new arena: the Spanish zone.

The Spanish Civil War and the Spanish zone

After the Popular Front was elected in Spain in June 1936, Abdelkhalek Torrès re-formed the Tetuan branch of the *Kutla* as a political party, the Party of National Reform (*Hizb al-Islah al-Wat-*

120 Al-Fasi, *al-Harakat*, 199-208.

121 Ibid., 209-14; Hoisington, *Casablanca Connection*, 65-7; Halstead, *Rebirth*, 247-9; Alaoui, *Maroc*, 79.

122 Hoisington, *Casablanca Connection*, 73; Halstead, *Rebirth*, 250-1; al-Fasi, *al-Harakat*, 221-2. Alaoui, *Maroc*, 79; Blair, *Western Window*, 29.

tani). One prominent member was Mekki Naciri who had been expelled from the French zone earlier that year.[123]

Tumultuous events were beginning in Spain, or rather in Spanish Morocco. The army rose against the Popular Front government on 17 July. By 19 July, the rebels held the whole of the Spanish zone. Left-wingers were busily repressed, in the style typical of southern European fascism: olive-oil purges for the less important and executions for those considered more dangerous. Many were shot in Melilla and Nador and their bodies left by the roadsides. Tetuan was held for the rebels by Lieutenant-Colonel Juan Beigbeder, Director of the Native Affairs office, while General Francisco Franco and other *Africanista* officers fought in Spain.[124]

Torrès saw the civil war as an opportunity. First he tried negotiating with the legitimate, republican government in Madrid, but to no effect. The Spanish left detested Moroccans for their role in Asturias two years before, and the government was unwilling to upset their Popular Front allies in Paris by backing Moroccan independence.[125]

The Spanish nationalist 'capital' in Burgos had more to offer. Morocco was the home base of the rebel leaders, where their companionship had been formed, a source of men for their armies and foreign exchange from mineral exports. They were happy to court Torrès. Beigbeder appointed him to the new post of Minister of Habous, legalised his Islah party, and allowed him to recruit members. By the end of 1936, nearly 9,000 had joined up. On Radio Tanger, Quiepo de Llano, a prominent insurgent general, promised independence for the Spanish zone.[126] Torrès created a youth wing to his party and gave it green shirts, following current European and Middle Eastern fashion.[127]

The honeymoon was short. Torrès's autocratic style and his extreme Francophobia alienated Mekki Naciri, who formed his own party, supported by Beigbeder, who was now High Commissioner, on the principle of divide and rule. When Naciri's party, the *Hizb al-Wahda* (Party of Unity) grew too strong, Beigbeder underwrote the Liberal party, led by El Raisuni's son Khaled, the pasha of Larache. The policy differences between Naciri and Torrès

123 Wolf, *Secrets*, 198; Berges, 'D'une guerre', 116; Halstead, *Rebirth*, 258.

124 Berges, 'D'une guerre', 108-9; Román, *Fragmentos*, 27, 64.

125 Al-Fasi, *al-Harakat*, 180-1; Wolf, *Secrets*, 203; Halstead, *Rebirth*, 238; Madariaga, 'Intervention', 89-90; Bessis 'Chekib Arslan', 484.

126 Wolf, *Secrets*, 205; Halstead, *Rebirth*, 238-9.

127 Bessis, 'Chekib Arslan', 484; Wolf, *Secrets*, 206-7; al-Fasi, *al-Harakat*, 183.

were minimal. Both wanted civil liberties and efficient administration functioning in Arabic and both talked of the Alaoui family as the embodiment of national unity. Neither was particularly democratic; Torrès wrote in his newspaper in 1937 that 'Moroccan people are not suited for democracy'.[128] The differences were largely personal.

Now that he was weakened, the Spanish allowed Torrès a certain leeway. He organised demonstrations marking the Berber dahir in 1938, conducted a literacy campaign in 1939 and attended an Arab Interparliamentary Conference in Cairo. To win support in the Middle East, the Tetuan authorities welcomed a small stream of visitors from the Arab east and set up a residence for students in Cairo.[129] Beigbeder had incorporated Torrès and the nationalists into the Spanish system.[130] But the importance for the war effort of winning over a few urban nationalists was paltry in comparison to the troops provided to Franco by the rural tribes.

Somewhere between 60-70,000 Moroccan troops fought for Franco during the Civil War and the Regulares regiments won a prominent place in the victory parade through Madrid in 1939. Franco even had his own personal 'Moorish guard'. One man stood out: Mohamed ben Mizian, whose service history was a roll-call of the battle-honours of Franco's army: the University City in Madrid during the winter of 1936-7, the relief of the siege of the citadel at Toledo, Oviedo, Teruel, Castellón, the Ebro and Catalonia. He finished the war as a full colonel.[131]

Ben Mizian's career was pushed by Beigbeder, who also put great efforts into recruiting ordinary troops. His task was made easier by the poverty of the Rif and the great depth of control achieved by the Native Affairs officers, and backed by a clever propaganda campaign that honoured the Rifis' role in fighting the atheistic 'Reds'. Service in Spain had a psychological attraction too. This was the first generation of Rifi young men who had been disarmed and lacked the opportunity to demonstrate their manhood. Now they could do so, and on the home ground of

128 Benomar, 'Working Class', 259, quoting *Al Hayat* 23 Aug 1937; Berges, 'D'une guerre', 116-17; Halstead, *Rebirth*, 256-9; Ruiz Bravo-Villasante and al-Rihani, *Testigo*, 276.

129 E.g. the Lebanese Christian, Amin al-Rihani. Wolf, *Secrets*, 207; Benjelloun, 'Developpements', 186, 205; Ruiz Bravo-Villasante and al-Rihani, *Testigo*, 213.

130 Hoisington, *Casablanca Connection*, 147.

131 Hugh Thomas, *The Spanish Civil War*, 3rd edn. (Harmondsworth: Penguin, 1977), 415-17, 486-9; Preston, *Franco*, 186, 189, 225, 230, 237; Muhammad Hajji (ed.), *Mu'allamat al-Maghrib* (Salé: Matabi'Sala, 1989-), 3:760-1.

those who had so recently defeated their fathers in battle. It was an enticing prospect.[132]

The Rif was the main recruiting ground, which helped keep the region quiet by extracting much of the male population, but there was a state of almost permanent surliness in the Jebala and Ghumara. There was even a full-blown rising in the Beni Ahmad in November 1936, and women of the Khlut tribe burned down a recruiting office after rumours that all their men had been kidnapped for the army.[133] Even volunteers from the Rif had mixed feelings. Rifi soldiers departing for the peninsula sang a ballad:

> *Guard your belt and put another one over it*
> *For we are going to Spain to die.*
> *Spain has a bloodfeud and its 'villages' are divided*
> *Franco and the 'Reds' are both fighting for them!*
> *Spain is crawling [with people], and Madrid is full*
> *I am sorry for you, in my spirit and in my soul!*[134]

The words were truer than the balladeers knew. Spain seethed with foreigners, Moroccan volunteers for Franco were taking part in the first stages of an international conflict that culminated in the Second World War. The deepening international crisis already had other more numerous victims, notably the Jews whose persecution in Germany had already begun.

Privileged or underprivileged Jews?

Jews in Morocco were relatively safe. Despite Franco's pro-Nazi sympathies, his government left the Jews alone. The Alliance Israélite Universelle operated freely and in the French Zone, helped financially by the Protectorate, it extended Jewish education into the 'near south' – places like Beni Mellal and Taroudannt.[135] This close relationship made the Alliance appear to be the Protectorate's agent. Education in AIU schools was in French, and by 1936 around a quarter of the 16,000 Jews in the French Zone were literate in French or could speak it reasonably well.[136] Rural Jewish children began to adopt French hairstyles and girls began to be given French

132 Hart, *Aith Waryaghar*, 416; Madariaga, 'Intervention', 77-80, 88ff; Berges, 'D'une guerre', *passim*; Abdelmajid Benjelloun, 'L'enrôlement des marocains dans le rangs franquistes', *Revue Maroc-Europe* 7 (1994): 219-34.

133 Berges, 'D'une guerre', 121; Madariaga, 'Intervention', 81-3.

134 Hart, *Aith Waryaghar*, 417.

135 Laskier, *Alliance*, 161-9.

136 *Ibid.*, 269, 281.

first names – the fashion took longer to spread to boys. Young educated Jews found jobs in big European companies and banks and a few trained in professions such as pharmacy, law and medicine. The first Moroccan inhabitant of Casablanca to qualify as a doctor was a Jew, Léon Benzaquen.[137]

Despite this cosy relationship, the Protectorate government refused to allow Jews to become French citizens. It knew that the Sultan would not accept any further loss of sovereignty. Some officials were as frankly racist in their attitudes towards Jews as they were towards Muslims, the colons often more so. George Orwell, who visited Marrakesh in 1938, encountered some extraordinary 'dark rumours' about the Jews. One Frenchman told him:

> 'Yes, *mon vieux*, they took my job away from me and gave it to a Jew. The Jews! They're the real rulers of this country, you know. They've got all the money. They control the banks, finance – everything.'
> 'But', I said, 'isn't it a fact that the average Jew is a labourer working for about a penny an hour?'
> 'Ah, that's only for show! They're all moneylenders really. They're cunning, the Jews.'[138]

This was absurd, because most Jews were grindingly poor. Orwell used his eyes and saw real destitution in the *millah* in Marrakesh:

> I was just passing the coppersmiths' booths when somebody noticed I was lighting a cigarette. Instantly, from the dark holes all around, there was a frenzied rush of Jews, many of them old grandfathers with flowing grey beards, all clamouring for a cigarette. Even a blind man somewhere at the back of one of the booths heard a rumour of cigarettes and came crawling out, groping in the air with his hand. In about a minute I had used up a whole packet. None of these people, I suppose, works less than twelve hours a day, and every one of them looks on a cigarette as a more or less impossible luxury.[139]

In the *millah* in Rabat, 28% of the labouring Jewish population were out of work in the mid-1930s.[140] These poor Jews, the 75% whom the Alliance did not reach, were fruitful ground for Zionist

137 *Ibid.*, 289; Lahlou, *Casablanca*, 64.

138 George Orwell, *The Collected Essays, Journalism and Letters of George Orwell*, 4 vols (Harmondsworth: Penguin, 1970), 3:429.

139 *Ibid.*, 3:428.

140 Gallisot, *Patronat*, 157.

propagandists. From 1930 onwards, Zionist activity spread to the smaller towns. Great play was made of the success of the agricultural schemes and the Zionist settlements in Palestine, but few Moroccan Jews migrated to Palestine before the Second World War.[141]

There was an unexpected result of the European conquest of Morocco: Moroccan Muslims were participating directly in the European crises and Moroccan Jews were subjected to colon racism. The boundaries between the colonised and the colonising communities were becoming less stark. Muslims from the countryside moved into the towns – mixing Arab and Berber – where they worked for French companies, played and watched European sports like football, and fell victim to the disasters that afflicted the French economy; Rifis joined the Spanish army and fought for Franco in Spain. More and more women moved out of the home into the formal, or even the informal economy.

As those boundaries became more fluid so the political boundaries hardened. At the most simple level, involvement in football and other sports encouraged an expression of nationalism. A nationalist movement, founded in the small but growing Moroccan middle class, had begun. Paradoxically, it was in part the creation of the colonial authorities, at least in the Spanish zone. At the same time, institutions of colonial rule took on a national character because they embraced the whole country. At a deeper level, the nationalists' central premise was founded in the very treaty that had set up the Protectorate. A promise that, after a period of reform, real sovereignty would be returned to the Sultan, led them to demand just that. Sidi Mohammed, whom the French authorities had appointed as their sultan, became a symbol of national unity. So, when the decade began with violent opposition to the Berber dahir, the nationalists called not for the overthrow of the Protectorate but for it to be properly organised. By the end of the 1930s, some of them had elaborated a political program that called for the extension to Moroccans of political freedoms and constitutional systems that were rooted both in French ideas and those of reformist Islam. These ideas were the territory of the leadership, but they could draw upon a widespread discontent with economic circumstances. But the good practical reasons behind their acceptance of some European values and ideas, modernisation above all, were accompanied by a perception of interest: these nationalists came from the small middle-class, the one sector that was beginning to reap some advantages from modernisation, particularly in the

141 Laskier, *Alliance*, 210-11.

form of education. The struggle for control of the leadership of the nationalist movement was also a struggle over the interests of the leaders concerned.

In this way, by September 1939, the colonial state in Morocco had laid the foundation of the national state that would succeed it. The one was still immensely more powerful than the other, but the Civil War in Spain had already shown that European power was fragile; and within months of the beginning of the wider European conflict, the collapse of the French army and Pétain's surrender left the colonial state splintered and prone.

7

WARS

For half a generation, between 1939 and 1956, war was the constant in Moroccan life. The actual fighting mainly took place elsewhere: in Europe, Palestine and, potentially, on the great fault line between the communist and liberal blocs running through eastern Europe. Only the briefest of battles were fought in Morocco during the Second World War, and Algeria was the epicentre of nationalist struggle in the 1950s. But the struggle in Morocco in the late 1940s and the early 1950s did produce its own spiral of violence, as the colons who briefly captured the colonial state attempted to deny both the rationale of the Protectorate and the authority of the French Republic. Sixteen and a half years of global conflict had left their mark on Morocco when it became independent in 1956. They moulded a nationalist movement in which a conservative monarchy was allied to radical supporters of democracy and revolutionary nationalism.

THE SECOND WORLD WAR IN MOROCCO

On 3 September 1939 an end to European rule seemed far away. Franco ruled Spain, and Noguès had broken the nationalist movement. On 4 September Sidi Mohammed declared unconditional support for France in a letter read in all the mosques:

> From this day forward until the banner of France and its allies is covered in glory, we owe them our unreserved support. We will drive no bargains about supplying them with our resources, we will stint them no sacrifice. We were joined to them in times of peace and plenty and it is only right that we should remain at their side during the trials that they are undergoing, from which they will emerge, we are convinced, both victorious and great.[1]

Such a declaration of loyalty was also a declaration of solidarity and, in the end, of equality. The French were now allies, not

[1] Quoted in Alaoui, *Maroc*, 80.

rulers, and Moroccan soldiers would 'remain at their side'. For the future, the King's approval of Moroccan participation in the war in Europe, and beyond, would provide another national symbol. For the present, Moroccans hurried to enlist, as did Tunisians and Algerians, for economic opportunity was as great an incentive as the urgings of the Sultan. In the Spanish Zone, where hunger had already brought great misery even before 1939, the Spanish authorities recruited soldiers as a form of famine relief. In September 1939 North Africans made up fifty-three per cent of the French colonial army: Moroccans formed three of the fourteen divisions, and one of five cavalry brigades. By the time the French government surrendered in 1940, 47,000 Moroccans had been recruited, of whom more than 2,000 were killed and 18,000 made prisoner. There were also 23,000 irregular troops – *goumiers* – some of them very irregular indeed. People joined up to escape criminal prosecution and one group consisted of former bandits and sheep-stealers from the Tafilalt and Jbel Sarhro. They mainly served in Morocco, though one unit was sent to the Libyan frontier with Tunisia.[2]

The war undermined French authority in Morocco. During the phoney war, when French troops did not fight, they looked weak; when they did fight, they lost. Noguès wanted to fight on after the fall of France but he would not brand himself a rebel, so he sided with Vichy.[3] He arrested sympathisers of the Free French under General de Gaulle, refused to talk with British envoys, and promised the German government to defend the Atlantic coast. In exchange, no German troops were stationed on Moroccan soil. Even so, General Weygand, Pétain's commander-in-chief in Algiers accused him of lukewarm loyalty – though Weygand himself was talking to US representatives.[4]

Some of Noguès's officers chafed at the armistice, and did not demobilise the Moroccan troops whom they brought home. Instead they disguised them as 'sharifian guards' and kept them in service while caches of weapons were squirrelled away in the mountains. But the furtiveness and deception did not raise the general reputa-

2 Christine Levisse-Touze, 'La contribution du Maroc pendant la seconde guerre mondiale (1940-1945)', *Maroc-Europe*, 7 (1994): 212-13; Jacques Augarde, 'Les forces supplétives pendant les campagnes du Maroc et la libération de la France', *Maroc-Europe* 7 (1994): 199; Maghraoui, 'Moroccan colonial soldiers'; Aziza, 'Década trágica', 239.

3 Hoisington, *Casablanca Connection*, 163, 165-75; Luella Hall, *The United States and Morocco* (Metuchen, NJ: Scarecrow Press, 1971), 881.

4 Hoisington, *Casablanca Connection*, 180-91; Hall, *United States*, 891, 894, 897.

tion of France.[5] Noguès behaved as though nothing had happened and carefully maintained the fiction of Moroccan sovereignty. The Sultan reciprocated by assuring Noguès that he would not seek to profit from the disaster: 'We Moroccans do not stab those who are wounded. We do not betray our friends.'[6]

The war in the Spanish zone

General Franco openly supported the Nazis but kept Spain legally neutral. Although the German government had hoped for more than benevolent neutrality – the capture of Gibraltar would have been welcome – the Spanish treasury was empty and the army was ruined.[7] Franco refused to fight unless the German government provided arms and money and agreed to expand the Spanish empire in Africa. When France collapsed in 1940 he demanded that Vichy hand over areas north of Fez and Oujda at once, and told the Italian government that eventually he wanted all of Morocco, part of Algeria, an expanded Spanish Sahara and more territory in the Gulf of Guinea. In September 1940 Franco's brother-in-law, Ramón Serrano Suñer, visited Berlin and spoke of Spain's need for '*Lebensraum*'.[8] This was grand imperial folly: a bankrupt state and a shambolic army could not administer such huge territories. In any case, the German government did not need Franco that much: in the spring of 1941, after great Axis victories in North Africa, Goebbels dismissed Franco's offers of help as the posturings of 'a totally conceited loudmouth'.[9]

Although Franco built huge fortifications facing the French Zone and the Mediterranean, to guard against any allied attack,[10] the Spanish empire made only one tiny gain. On 14 June 1940, as the German army occupied Paris, Spanish troops marched into Tangier. Franco's excuse was that Tangier's neutrality was threatened by a supposed Italian invasion, but his real purpose was to incorporate Tangier into the Spanish zone, and to show off

5 Levisse-Touze, 'La contribution', 214; E.G.H. Joffe, 'The Moroccan Nationalist Movement: Istiqlal, the Sultan and the Country', *Journal of African History*, 26 (1985): 301; Leon Borden Blair, *Western Window in the Arab World* (Austin: University of Texas Press, 1970), 45.

6 Quoted in Alaoui, *Maroc*, 80.

7 Preston, *Franco*, 347-50.

8 *Ibid.*, 363, 377, 402.

9 *Ibid.*, 414, 424, 429.

10 Antonio Marquina Barrio, 'El Plan Backbone España, bajo dos amenazas de invasión', *Historia* 16, no. 79 (1992): 11-22.

to Hitler. But, since Spain was still neutral, the German and Italian, and the British, US and French consulates carried on – although what government the French Consul represented was a moot point.[11] Tangier quickly filled up with spies, providing a living for a small swarm of émigrés and for Moroccan nationalists who carefully played off both sides. Although they knew he had little liking for Franco, the authorities in Tetuan gave Abdelkhalek Torrès leeway to attack the French, and he used it. When France fell his supporters paraded a coffin through the streets, covered with a French flag that they then ceremonially burned.[12] But Torrès's newspaper deprecated the occupation of Tangier and he sought help from the German Consul in Tetuan. In January 1941 Torrès went to Berlin to meet Goering and Himmler and plans were hatched to incite a revolt in the French zone. The Spanish government even helped a nationalist emissary go through Ifni to raise the Sahraouis. Long afterwards, in the late 1970s, this man claimed that he had been playing a double game, hoping to raise opposition to the Spanish as well as the French.[13]

While Torrès flirted with the Germans, his rival Mekki Naciri became an agent of the British Special Operations Executive (SOE). Because Sir Samuel Hoare, the British Ambassador in Madrid, wanted to prevent the Spanish government from becoming more hostile to the Allies than it already was, he prohibited the SOE from sabotage and confined it to political work in Morocco. This consisted of devising anti-German rumours of the most bizarre kinds, and funding apparently friendly nationalists like Naciri.[14]

In the south, the SOE netted a bigger, and more slippery fish. By May 1941 it had established Si Thami El Glaoui as an SOE agent, equipped with the absurd code-name of 'Algy', although his controller complained that it was hard to get him to do very

11 PRO, HS3/205, M. B. Miluc [??] to Semtob I. Cohen, British Merchants Morocco Association; Iain Finlayson, *Tangier. City of the Dream* (London: Flamingo, 1993), 63ff.; Preston, *Franco*, 403, 406; Morales Lezcano, *Norte de África*, 133-4; Hall, *United States*, 889-892.

12 Halstead, *Rebirth*, 259-60; Wolf, *Secrets*, 223, 227.

13 Abdelmajid Benjelloun, 'La deuxième guerre mondiale, les nationalistes marocains de la zone espagnole du Protectorat et les possibilités de libération du Maroc' in *Approches du colonialisme espagnol et du mouvement nationaliste marocain dans l'ex-Maroc khalifien* (Rabat: Okad, 1988), 221-3; Wolf, *Secrets*, 227-8.

14 PRO HS3/205, Note to C.D. from A.D.4, 11 May 1942; Gort to Nelson (WO), Gibraltar, 28 Mar. 1942; HS3/203, W Strang to Taylor, FO, 9 June 1942; HS3/215, For rumour mongering eg Cypher – 'Special (Venom)' no 371, 23 Sept. 1942; HS3/204, Secret 424, 28.10.41.

much.[15] German sympathisers were more common in the *bidonvilles*. In early 1942 the SOE made these less-educated people the target of a bizarre plan to distribute obscene gramophone records libelling Hitler's sexual prowess. It was stopped before it could backfire.[16] British intelligence also proposed expensive plans to supply Tanger with pharmaceutical supplies ('*good practical* propaganda') and other goods like teapots, tea glasses and broadcloth. The government in London ignored them, and the Moroccan population, that depended on the Spanish zone for supplies, suffered terribly after the harvest collapsed in 1940. In the Spanish zone, rural markets had no sugar or tea, no eggs, chickens, oil or vegetables, although Spanish residents were better provided for than their compatriots in the Peninsula. By August 1941 drought and epidemics had brought Moroccans in the northern zone to their knees: some people were reported to be eating grass, others gathered in the cities and died of hunger.[17]

In the French zone, the war had at first stimulated the economy. More than 100,000 Moroccans found jobs in France and French industrialists opened factories in Morocco, hoping that they would be far away from the fighting. Since shipping space was limited, light industries substituted for imports: the local textile industry grew quickly, even though its products were more expensive than foreign ones. Moroccan entrepreneurs, if they had money to invest, grew rich too. The Sebti family cannily bought large stocks of foodstuffs and textiles before the war and made a huge profit by selling them when prices went up.[18]

After the fall of France the boom collapsed. Harvests were poor until 1944, the phosphate market disappeared, and most of the migrants were sent home.[19] In 1942 the French authorities req-

15 Maxwell, *Lords of the Atlas*, 198; PRO HS3/204, Copy of Report from A/DB to H dated 30 May 1941; HS3/205 Q2 to CD, 7 July 1941 and HS3/204 'Resumé of an interview between Si Mohamed the 2nd son of the Glaoui and W.Kirby Green an SOE agent on 25:6:42'.

16 Hoisington, *Casablanca Connection*, 202; al-Fasi, *al-Harakat*, 229-230; PRO HS3/205, Lt. Col. Sutton to Bruce Lockhart, 28 April 1942, 'Most Secret'.

17 PRO HS3/205, Report from A/Db to H No 1009, 29 June 1941 (presumably from Gibraltar); Finlayson, *Tangier*, 62-6; Román, *Fragmentos*, 30; Berges, 'D'une guerre', 127-9; Morales Lezcano, *Norte de África*, 195, 197; Aziza, 'Decada Trágica', 238-9.

18 Le Tourneau, *Fès*, 439; John Waterbury, *Commander of the Faithful* (New York: Columbia University Press, 1970), 100; G. Pallez, 'Les Marchands Fassis', *Bulletin Economique et Sociale du Maroc*, no. 51 (1951): 571.

19 Stewart, *Economy*, 159, 131, 130, 123; Swearingen, *Mirages*, 75, 113-24; Abdallah Baroudi, *Maroc, impérialisme et émigration* (Rotterdam: Editions Hiwar, 1989), 40-2,

uisitioned stocks of grain and flour, and rationed them. Afterwards, Moroccans called this '*L'année du bon*', the year of the ration ticket, when many nearly starved. Because the infrastructure was not properly maintained, malaria returned to the French zone and there were epidemics of bubonic plague in the Sous in 1940, in the countryside around Marrakesh in 1941, and worryingly close to Casablanca in 1942. Stringent quarantine kept plague out of the cities, but the typhus bacillus found the *bidonvilles*, factories and mines all too favourable, and struck in Casablanca and Rabat in 1943. The prophylactic campaigns seemed to the Moroccans like tyranny; in Rabat, streets were sometimes blocked off so that people could be forcibly vaccinated. The *cordons sanitaires* imposed on houses and villages stricken with plague forced people into virtual lazarettos, where they feared they would die.[20]

In the summer of 1942 Si Thami El Glaoui's son told a British agent that the forced sale of oil, cereals and wool to the French authorities, forced labour, and shortages of tea, sugar and other necessities had caused widespread discontent. His father suggested that after the war the Protectorates should be replaced by an advisory body organised by the British and American governments.[21]

The third player: the United States

Since the fall of France, American agents had been working to prevent Morocco from falling into German hands. At the end of December 1940, Robert Murphy, who had spent ten years at the American embassy in Paris, was sent to seduce Noguès with promises of supplies. Noguès turned him down, but Murphy stayed on to lead an intelligence organisation. He and his men, posing as vice-consuls, prepared the way for Operation Torch, the invasion of North Africa.[22]

On 8 November 1942 American troops landed on the coast of Morocco. In the first wave, 65,000 men landed, and there were as many again behind them. They were supported by more than 300 warships, and planes operating from carriers. Noguès, loyal

73; Hall, *United States*, 896.

20 Daniel Rivet, 'La recrudescence des epidémies au Maroc durant la deuxième guerre mondiale: essai de mésure et d'interprétation', *Héspéris-Tamuda*, 30, no. 1 (1992): 93-109; Daoud, *Féminisme*, 244; Hall, *United States*, 901; Blair, *Western Window*, 49.

21 PRO HS3/204, 'Resumé of an interview between Si Mohamed the 2nd son of the Glaoui and W. Kirby Green an SOE agent on 25:6:42'.

22 Hoisington, *Casablanca Connection*, 195-200; Hall, *United States*, 891, 903-13.

to Vichy, and anxious not to provoke the Germans, told his troops to resist but they had poor equipment and not all of them would fight: the commander of the Casablanca division went over to the Americans and Sidi Mohammed told the Moroccan units that they had no duty to fight the Americans. The only real battle was at Kénitra and on 10 November, after a confused hodgepodge of orders and counter orders from Vichy and Algiers, Noguès surrendered.[23]

The American troops made a striking contrast with the dour and defeated French. The victorious army brought a cornucopia of material delights: essentials that had been short for two years, like flour, food, matches, and pharmaceuticals, and consumer goods like perfumes, chewing-gum, cigarettes and cigars, that were sold on the black market. Most excitingly, they brought Coca-Cola, bottles of which became prized possessions for Moroccan boys. Many ordinary Moroccans thought the American troops were simply nicer people than the French they knew. A Moroccan, twenty years old at the time, later described how: 'The Americans meant nothing to me ... but I could see a difference. They played around with the Moroccan kids – gave them gum and candy.'[24]

The older generation was less impressed. In the *medina* of Fez, grave middle class patriarchs worried about the threat to Moroccan society. Fatima Mernissi, who grew up in such a household, recalled:

> Father, who was a pragmatic man, was convinced that our deadliest threat came not from the Western soldiers, but from their suave salesmen peddling innocent-looking products. He therefore organised a crusade against chewing-gum and Kool cigarettes. As far as he was concerned, smoking a tall, thin, white Kool cigarette was equivalent to erasing centuries of Arab culture. 'The Christians want to transform our decent Muslim households into a market place,' he would say. 'They want us to buy these poisonous products they make that have no real purpose, so that we turn into a whole nation of ruminating cattle. Instead of praying to Allah, people stick dirt in their mouths all day long.'[25]

23 Hoisington, *Casablanca Connection*, 225-30; Levisse-Touze, 'La contribution', 215; Blair, *Western Window*, 55-62.

24 Annie Lacroix-Riz, *Les protectorats de l'Afrique du Nord entre la France et Washington* (Paris: L'Harmattan, 1988), 11; Lahlou, *Casablanca*, 143-9; Blair, *Western Window*, 70, 76.

25 Fatima Mernissi, *The Harem Within: Tales of a Moroccan Girlhood* (London: Bantam, 1995), 191.

Affluent urban families like the Mernissis kept their womenfolk at home, yet inside the house, women shared the odd surreptitious cigarette and put on lipstick when they could. Some, like Fatima Mernissi's mother, dreamed of greater freedoms still, and believed that

> [...] the whole crusade against chewing-gum and American cigarettes was in fact a crusade against women's rights as well. When I asked her to elaborate, she said that both smoking cigarettes and chewing gum were silly activities, but men opposed them because they gave women opportunities to make decisions on their own, decisions which were unregulated by either tradition or authority. 'So you see,' said Mother, 'a woman who chews gum is in fact making a revolutionary gesture. Not because she chews gum per se, but because gum chewing is not prescribed by the code.'[26]

The landings were a turning point in many Moroccans' lives. Years later, a poor Middle Atlas woman who was working in Casablanca changed her date of birth to 1942 to make herself appear younger – 'She liked that date because she remembered the American landings at Casablanca and the rumpus that it caused.'[27]

The Jews during the Second World War

Many American soldiers were Jews, powerful, glamourous men who bore arms in a victorious army. This was a heady time for Moroccan Jews. Boys hung around American bases, girls in Casablanca learned American dances, socialised with the troops, and sometimes married them.[28]

The landings liberated Moroccan Jews. Although after the war some Jews testified in Noguès's favour, he had applied Vichy laws. Jewish refugees were interned in the Sahara in camps guarded by the Foreign Legion, and decrees forbade Jews from living in the European quarters (though this was not rigidly enforced) and banned Jews from journalism, banking and teaching in government schools. Ration quotas for Jews were set at less than those given to Muslims. Anti-Jewish racism was deeply embedded in the French army and among the *colons*. Yet the decrees did not wind up Jewish

26 *Ibid.*, 197.

27 Christine Daure-Serfaty, *Rencontres avec le Maroc* (Paris: La Découverte, 1993), 82.

28 Lahlou, *Casablanca*, 150.

religious organisations and the schools of the Alliance Israélite Universelle carried on by raising money locally, possibly with secret help from some French officials.[29] Sidi Mohammed helped, too. Steeled by a vision of the Prophet in a dream, he told the German armistice commission that he would not allow them to round up his Jewish subjects. This put him in very good standing with the American Jewish community after the war and laid the basis of good relations with the international Jewish community.[30] While an Alaoui Sultan protected the Jews and the US army released them from internment, the French were left on the sidelines. In late 1944 the Residency complained that Jewish leaders hoped that 'under American protection, they will be able to escape the authority of the Makhzan authorities which they tolerate more and more unwillingly.'[31]

The meeting at Casablanca

It was not just among the Jews that the French looked paltry. Noguès kept his word to General Patton, the US commander, and maintained order and organised labour for the ports and the transport of supplies. Patton did not deliberately try to humiliate him, but even when the two generals waited on the Sultan for the *Fête du Trône*, the American eclipsed the Frenchman.[32] In any event, the Sultan favoured the Americans. Shortly after United States troops landed in November, President Roosevelt had the good manners to write and thank the Sultan for his help.[33] In January Roosevelt and Winston Churchill arrived in Casablanca for a conference at a beach hotel. The private discussions about the conduct of the war did not concern Morocco, but the Americans staged a meeting and a public banquet with Sidi Mohammed that most certainly did. Roosevelt's exact words are unknown, because no one took notes, but the recollections of King Hassan, then

29 Laskier, *Alliance*, 181-2.

30 Hoisington, *Casablanca Connection*; 192, Ayache, *Mouvement syndicale*, 1:285; Laskier, *Alliance*, 178-81; Serels, *Jews*, 159; Hassan II, *The Challenge*, trans. Anthony Rhodes (London: Macmillan, 1978), 88; Lahlou, *Casablanca*, 101; H.Z. Hirschberg, *A History of the Jews in North Africa*, 2 vols (Leiden: E. J. Brill, 1981), 2: 322-3; Blair, *Western Window*, 65-6.

31 Laskier, *Alliance*, 178; quotation of Note of 6 December 1944 in Archives du Ministère des Affaires Etrangères, vol. 122B (Amérique) is from Lacroix-Riz, *Les protectorats*, 17.

32 Lahlou, *Casablanca* 157-61; Lacroix-Riz, *Les protectorats*, 11; Hoisington, *Casablanca Connection*, 239.

33 Blair, *Western Window*, 67, 68.

fourteen years old and overwhelmed by the distinguished company, reflect what his father understood Roosevelt to have said:

> The President said he thought the colonial system was out of date and doomed. Winston Churchill considered this too outright a statement. He also pointed out that after the French conquest of Algeria, Great Britain had been 'the guardian of the integrity of the Cherifian Empire' for half a century. In short, he tried to gloss it over.
>
> Roosevelt replied that this was not 1820, or even 1912. He foresaw the time after the war – which he hoped was not far off – when Morocco would freely gain her independence, according to the principles of the Atlantic Charter. After the war, he said, the politico-economic situation of human society must be reorganised. The United States would not put any obstacle in the way of Moroccan independence; on the contrary, they would help us with economic aid.[34]

This quickened the hopes of Moroccan nationalists. Two weeks after the Casablanca meeting, Torrès, who had abandoned the German cause, and Mekki Naciri, who never had joined it, drew up the first manifesto for Moroccan independence. They sent a letter to Roosevelt demanding an end to both protectorates, lower taxes and the return of political liberties.[35] They were echoed in the newspaper *La Voix Nationale* by Ahmed Réda Guédira, a future foreign minister, who praised the United States and described the glowing future of a 'liberal democratic economy'.[36] That summer its editor, Abdelatif Sbihi, formed the Roosevelt Club so that members of the Moroccan political elite could meet senior members of the American military. The members included Guédira, three other future ministers and the Sultan's brother, Moulay Hassan.[37]

Other important Moroccans streamed through the American and British Consulates. Si Thami El Glaoui brought messages from Sidi Mohammed, asking for diplomatic recognition and suggesting joint American and British 'protection' of Morocco along with the French. (Spanish involvement was added as an afterthought.) There was talk of the Atlantic Charter and self-determination; Sidi Mohammed proposed through an intermediary that he should

34 Hassan II, *The Challenge*, 31.

35 Wolf, *Secrets*, 233-4.

36 Blair, *Western Window*, 79.

37 *Ibid.*, 99.

declare war on Germany and Italy, and personally told Robert Murphy that he wanted friendly relations with the United States.[38]

All this left the British and American governments unmoved. Churchill may have disliked General de Gaulle, but he had no wish to break up the French empire. For Cordell Hull, the US secretary of state, de Gaulle was a much more important ally than Sidi Mohammed, more certain to preserve the three huge American bases at Casablanca, Port Lyautey and Marrakesh on which the War Department had lavished millions of dollars.[39] So Hull turned down the offer to declare war and announced that European colonies could only be independent when their leaders could govern themselves properly.[40]

The Istiqlal manifesto

In November 1943 Lebanese nationalists showed that they could do just that, by declaring Lebanon independent. Earlier that year Algerian nationalists had issued their own manifesto and Reform Plan and this encouraged Ahmed Belafrej, Omar Abdeljalil, Mohammed El-Fassi and others to begin drafting a manifesto calling for independence. They carefully cultivated the American consul in Rabat. When he asked 'if their movement enjoyed the sultan's approval ... they replied that they had reason to believe that he was informed about their plans and that they hoped to obtain his support'.[41]

Sidi Mohammed did share many of their ideas, particularly about education. In 1942 he appointed Mehdi Ben Barka, who had returned from Algiers with a degree in mathematics, as one of Prince Hassan's tutors and in 1943, at the Sultan's request, he wrote a report saying that girls should be given a modern education. Sidi Mohammed gave short shrift to the member of a delegation of *'ulama* who impertinently declared that 'educating girls was like giving more poison to a viper that was already full of venom'. The Sultan retorted that his mother was no viper, and that reason was the best antidote to poison. In 1944 he entrusted the education of his fourteen-year-old daughter, Lalla Aïcha, to the doyen of

38 Daoud and Monjib, *Ben Barka*, 86; US Department of State, *Foreign Relations of the United States* Washington: US Government Printing Office, 1943, 4:738-45.

39 Lacroix-Riz, *Les protectorats*, 13-15; Blair, *Western Window*, 107-8.

40 Halstead, *Rebirth*, 261; US Department of State, *Foreign Relations* 1943, 4:741.

41 US Department of State, *Foreign Relations*, 1944 5:527-8; Halstead, *Rebirth*, 261-2; al-Fasi, *al-Harakat*, 246-7.

the Salafis, Si Mohammed bel-Arabi el-Alaoui.[42] The Sultan was clearly in the nationalist camp.

Belafrej and his comrades worked fast. On 11 January 1944 they published the manifesto of a new party, to which they gave the blunt name *Istiqlal* (Independence). They no longer demanded reform of a Protectorate that had deprived Moroccans of economic and political power. Now that Moroccans had fought in the war for democracy, the Atlantic Charter guaranteed them self-determination. The manifesto made four demands: an independent Morocco under Sidi Mohammed; that Sidi Mohammed himself should negotiate independence; that Morocco should sign the Atlantic Charter and take part in the peace conference; and that the Sultan should establish a democratic government.[43]

This was a recipe for constitutional monarchy but it was otherwise quite vague in its details because the fifty-six signatories were in agreement on independence but not much else. Some were products of the Qarawiyyin, like Mohamed Ghazi, but most had received a modern education. There were old nationalist leaders like Belafrej and Abdeljalil, although Allal El-Fassi who was still exiled in Gabon did not sign. There were conservatives from old Makhzan families – a Jama'i, and a Benjelloun among them – and men from the new middle class, journalists, state functionaries, lawyers, teachers and doctors. Some were markedly left-wing, like Mehdi Ben Barka, Abderrahman Youssoufi and Abdallah Ibrahim.[44]

Morocco under the Free French

General de Gaulle had no sympathy for constitutional monarchy, democracy or independence and carried on as though nothing had changed. The Resident-General whom he appointed in June 1943 was an old colonial official, Gabriel Puaux, once High Commissioner in Lebanon and Syria.[45] The colons supported him and so, apparently, did the Catholic Church, which talked of setting up a bishopric in Fez. This plan fell through when the man picked for the see turned out to be a drunken French sergeant in the

42 Daoud and Monjib, *Ben Barka*, 79; Daoud, *Féminisme*, 244-5.

43 Alaoui, *Maroc*, 86.

44 For texts of the manifesto, see Halstead, *Rebirth*, 281-5 (English), Alaoui, *Maroc*, 263-6 (French), and al-Fasi, *al-Harakat*, 249-50 (Arabic); Daoud and Monjib, *Ben Barka*, 84; Ayache, *Mouvement syndicale*, 2:87.

45 Hoisington, *Casablanca Connection*, 243; Julien, *Impérialismes*, 190; al-Fasi, *al-Harakat*, 245; Hall, *United States*, 956.

2nd Moroccan Tabor, the victim and then participant in a farcical chain of mistaken identities.[46]

Sidi Mohammed was wary in the face of this determination. On 13 January he summoned his ministers and they advised caution. Only Mohammed bel-Arabi el-Alaoui, the minister for justice, openly favoured Istiqlal and declared independence to be a religious necessity. Puaux was unyielding. He insisted that the Sultan tell his ministers that 'the word independence must disappear from their hearts and their mouths'. But el-Alaoui refused to back down and said that he was tired of acting like a 'carnival monkey that stands when told to stand and sleeps when told to sleep'. So Puaux dismissed him and exiled him to Tafilalt, where he had been born. On 28 January eighteen leaders of the new party were arrested for 'consorting with the enemy', that is, with the Germans, a strange charge in a Protectorate that had surrendered to Vichy.[47]

It was also a mistake, for the manifesto had popular support. There was rioting in Salé, and in Rabat demonstrators even stormed the palace. In Casablanca troops fired on crowds, and in Fez women went onto the roofs of their houses and threw boiling water and flowerpots onto the police and Tirailleurs below. Some women demonstrated in the street too, and a few were shot. Malika El-Fassi, the wife of Mohammed El-Fassi the tutor to Crown Prince Hassan, helped to organise the opposition, and another tutor, Mehdi Ben Barka, was sentenced to two years' imprisonment. Prisoners were tortured, and some were summarily executed.[48]

The repression stopped the rioting but Puaux's own reform plan, issued in October, failed to gain any support. He promised to recruit more Moroccans (but only when they were trained), to produce a new penal code (he never promulgated it), and to extend property rights to farmers (nothing was done). He merely strengthened the pashas and the qaids, the main agents of repression. Istiqlal's leaders liked only one aspect of the plan: a dahir that set up schools for Muslim girls.[49]

46 K. Sinclair-Loutit, 'The Bishopric of Fes', *Morocco* (n.s.) 1 (1996): 116-28.

47 Alaoui, *Maroc*, 86-92; Munson, *Religion and Power*, 104-5; Julien, *Impérialismes*, 190-1; Muhammad al-Wadi 'al-Asfi, *Al-salafi al-munadil: al-shaykh Muhammad bin al-'Arabi al-'Alawi* (al-Dar al-Baida: Dar al-Nashr al-'Arabi, 1986), 72-3; al-Fasi, *al-Harakat*, 257-8.

48 Al-Fasi, *al-Harakat*, 258-66; Julien, *Impérialismes*, 191; Alaoui, *Maroc*, 92-3; Akharbach and Rerhaye, *Femmes*, 22-3; Daoud and Monjib, *Ben Barka*, 86-7.

49 Stéphane Bernard, *The Franco-Moroccan Conflict 1943-1956*, trans. Marianna Oliver *et al.* (New Haven: Yale University Press, 1968), 26; al-Fasi, *al-Harakat*, 269-74; Alaoui, *Maroc*, 93; Julien, *Impérialismes*, 191; *Foreign Relations* 1944 5:527-31, Mayer to Secretary

Sidi Mohammed helped devise the education decree. The sultan was becoming more popular by the month and his connections with rural notables simply bypassed French control. When he visited Marrakesh in February 1945 big crowds chanted 'Long live the King, long live the nation![50]

French colonial power was starting to crack. Rural notables observed that the French officers sent to administer them were simply less and less suitable. The captain in charge at Azilal for most of the war, who spoke excellent Arabic and had a superb network of informers, dabbled in the black market with Moroccans' ration coupons; the local qadi referred to him as a 'human devil' because of his 'loose morals'. Inflation was terrible. In early 1944, the qadi of Bzu, a small town on the lower slopes of the High Atlas, reckoned that barley cost 10,000% more than it had in 1942, chickens 1,500% more, and sugar a startling 28,000%. Tea drinking was no longer cheap.The Protectorate authorities demanded forced labour and early in 1944, requisitioned the entire olive-oil crop and much of the wheat crop.[51]

De Gaulle did try to regain Sidi Mohammed's trust. He invited him to Paris and together they watched the victory parade on 18 June. It included many Moroccan troops. Three-fifths of the French forces that landed in Italy were Moroccan. Moroccan troops also fought in Corsica, southern France, Germany and Austria. Hammou ou Amehzane, a grandson of their old enemy Muhar u Hammu, had carried the tricolour at the head of French troops that marched into Rome. His friend, Sub-Lieutenant Mohammed Oufkir, son of the man the French had attracted in the Tafilalt on the eve of the Protectorate, was awarded the Croix de Guerre and the American Silver Star. Si Thami El Glaoui's son died of wounds received at the Battle of Monte Cassino. The 2nd Tabor was the most decorated unit in the whole French army.[52]

De Gaulle decorated the Sultan with the cross of the Companions of the Liberation, a medal that Churchill only received in 1958 and Roosevelt never did. Yet Sidi Mohammed was unmoved. He agreed that French rule had done much for Morocco but the

---

of State, Rabat, 5 January, 1944.

50 Alaoui, Maroc, 94; Bernard, *Franco-Moroccan Conflict*, 30; Eickelman, *Knowledge and Power*, 143.

51 Eickelman, *Knowledge and Power*, 140-5.

52 Morsy, 'Glaoui', 84 90, Pascon, *Le Haouz*, 2: 316d; Augarde, 'Les forces supplétives', 201-3; Levisse-Touze, 'La contribution', 216; Bernard Pujo, *Juin, Maréchal de France* (Paris: Albin Michel, 1988), 162; Sinclair-Loutit, 'Bishopric', 117; Claude Clément, *Oufkir* (Paris: Jean Dullis, 1974), 50, 64-5.

time had come to make the 'transition between the Morocco of former times and a free, modern state... '[53]

A very unmodern problem had just reappeared: famine. As usual, the immediate cause was the weather. In Port Lyautey (Kénitra) rainfall in 1945 was half what it would be in a good year. Crop yields dropped to nearly one-fifth of normal and epidemics and starvation followed. Families trekked out of the mountains towards the ports where the French authorities were distributing food. The American government helped too, and the qadi of Bzu wrote in his diary, 'Because of the great dollar, people were freed from famine. People thanked God for what the Americans did and recognised the greatness of the American empire.' American aid stopped the epidemics with huge quantities of DDT, and in Tanger, a private American citizen, the millionairess Barbara Hutton who was a longtime resident, set up soup kitchens to feed the thousands who flooded in from the Spanish zone. There, things were so bad that in one small tribe, Tafersit, the death rate went up from 22% to 61% between 1944 and 1946. For years afterwards, Rifis called 1945 the 'year of hunger'.[54]

De Gaulle had promised Sidi Mohammed to replace Puaux, but his government fell in January 1946. It was a socialist administration that, on 2 March 1946, appointed the new *Resident-General* Eirik Labonne, an undoubted liberal.[55]

MOROCCO AFTER THE SECOND WORLD WAR

The liberal experiment

On 22 July Labonne presented his manifesto to the French sections of the Conseil de Gouvernement, the advisory assembly that Lyautey had originally set up to give a hearing to the concerns of the colons. The Moroccan section added later was not present to hear him. To this unsympathetic audience he talked in gushing terms of helping the Moroccan population:

> *Feed* them! At last the fairy of the rains has poured her torrents over the bone-dry land, filling the hearts of men with the marvel

[53] Bernard, *Franco-Moroccan Conflict*, 31-2; Alaoui, *Maroc*, 94-6; Jean Lacouture, *De Gaulle: the Ruler 1945-1970* (New York: W.W. Norton, 1992), 94.

[54] Hart, *Aith Waryaghar*, 417; Swearingen, *Mirages*, 121-2; Le Coz, *Rharb*, 2:150, 200, 3: 514; Rivet, 'Epidémies'; Román, *Fragmentos*, 65; Eickelman, *Knowledge and Power*, 146; Aziza, 'Década Trágica', 241.

[55] Alaoui, *Maroc*, 95-6.

> of hope. [...] The crops will be good. *Clothe them*, and at once: ordinary families, workers have not enough cloth to cover themselves. Then *house them*. We must increase the rate of building.[56]

His audience was unfavourably impressed, for the war had disrupted the colon economy too. Although the textile industry had grown, mining was paralysed by a shortage of capital and lack of markets. Exports of citrus fruits had held up but the wine industry nearly collapsed after a phylloxera plague in 1943. Labonne's solution, state intervention and industrialisation though joint Moroccan and French companies, smacked of socialism and weak-kneed appeasement of the nationalists. The representatives of the leading colons and the commercial bosses walked out.[57]

Now the logic of the simple Moroccan–French duality could clearly be seen to have broken down: the highest representatative the French Republic had publicly put the Moroccan population's interests before those of the local French population, and the representatives of that population turned their backs on him. This was an empty gesture, since without the support of the Resident-General the colons had no other recourse: unlike the French nationals in Algeria they had no seats in the National Assembly. For the rest of the Protectorate the colons' attempt to control the Residency despite the policies of whatever weak government was ruling in Paris would be the most important theme of settler politics.

Yet Labonne was right. At first, the ruined French infrastructure and industry soaked up Moroccan unemployment, but not for long. The remnants of traditional industry had disappeared – in 1938, 200,000 pairs of slippers had been exported; in 1948 that figure was 13,000. In the drought of 1943 Moroccan farmers in some parts of the country had lost 60-70% of their livestock. Worse still, it was clear that this was no mere cyclical failure, for Moroccan peasant agriculture had reached its limits and production was falling as the soil became exhausted. Technology had not trickled down to the peasants. Shock treatment was needed to kick Moroccan agriculture into life.[58]

The *Secteurs de Modernisation du Paysannat* project that began in 1945 was supposed to modernise rural life at one go: model

56 Guy Delanoë, *Lyautey, Juin, Mohammed V. Fin d'un protectorat* (Casblanca: Eddif, 1993), 40.

57 Julien, *Impérialismes*, 197; Alaoui, *Maroc*, 96; Daoud and Monjib, *Ben Barka*, 102-3.

58 Le Coz, *Rharb*, 2:553; Stewart, *Economy*, 95, 100, 123, 131; Salahdine, *Maroc*, 256-9, Baroudi, *Maroc*, 42; Joffe, 'Moroccan Nationalist Movement', 304.

farms would be built, surrounded by schools, clinics and irrigation system; tractors would cultivate the land and harvest the crops. But there was not enough money and the scheme was opposed both by the colons who feared that the cost of labour would rise, and by the Moroccan rural elite who worried that their authority would be diminished. By 1956 only 75,000 of the 440,000 ha. that were earmarked for this treatment had been developed.[59]

Labonne's political liberalism failed too. Istiqlal dismissed his promise to create a national assembly with French and Moroccan representatives, since they did not want to share power.[60] Both colons and nationalists interpreted it as political weakness when he released political prisoners and legalised parties. Istiqlal grew stronger when Allal El-Fassi returned from Gabon, took over the leadership, and founded a daily newspaper, *al-Alam.* Belafrej returned from Corsica. Mehdi Ben Barka, now the administrative secretary of the Istiqlal, began a frenetic round of teaching, organising boy scouts' troops and propagandising among college students. Mohamed Hassan Ouazzani re-founded his own party, now called the *Parti Démocratique de l'Indépendance* and a Moroccan, Ali Yata, became secretary-general of the Communist Party, and started recruiting Moroccan workers. The Istiqlal set up its own union in competition, the Union des Syndicats du Maroc.[61]

Labonne's officials undermined him. Philippe Boniface, the regional commissioner for Casablanca, and Colonel Jean Lecomte, head of the Interior Department, were extreme supporters of the colons.[62] Against their advice, Labonne allowed Sidi Mohammed to travel to Tanger in a symbolic journey of national unity.[63] By doing so, he sought to win Sidi Mohammed's friendship, but the day before he left, Senegalese Tirailleurs rampaged through Casablanca after a quarrel, perhaps over women, perhaps over insults hurled at them by street-urchins. While the police stood aside, several hundred Moroccans were killed and rumours spread that Boniface had planned it to prevent the trip.[64]

59 Swearingen, *Mirages*, 125-42.

60 Alaoui, *Maroc*, 97; Oved, *Gauche*, 238-9.

61 Ayache, *Mouvement Syndicale*, 2:23-4; Alaoui, *Maroc*, 99-104; Daoud and Monjib, *Ben Barka*, 95-7; Muhammad Darif, *al-Ahzab al-siyasiyya al-maghribiyya* (al-Dar al-Baida: Ifriqiya al-Sharq, 1988), 58.

62 Bernard, *Franco-Moroccan Conflict*, 43.

63 Julien, *Impérialismes*, 199; Alaoui, *Maroc*, 105-6.

64 Julien, *Impérialismes*, 199; Alaoui, *Maroc*, 105-6; Daoud and Monjib, *Ben Barka*, 103; Bernard, *Franco-Moroccan Conflict*, 55-56; Blair, *Western Window*, 134.

The Spanish zone

The Sultan's journey caught the Spanish authorities on the horns of a dilemma of their own devising. During the war they had encouraged Moroccan nationalists, and Franco still sought Arab friends to compensate for his diplomatic isolation. In December 1945 he received Torrès in Madrid and allowed the Khalifa to see off a delegation to the Arab League. The results were most gratifying: Azzam Pasha, the Secretary-General of the League, talked of the Arab world's friendship for Spain.[65]

Things moved to a different tune in Tetuan. In March 1945 Franco had appointed a new High Commissioner, General José Enrique Varela Iglesias, an old *Africanista* with a reputation for brutality. While the dictator courted the Arab League, Varela tried to check the nationalists. He prohibited public gatherings and banned suspected nationalists from travelling to the Rif.[66] Any who went there were summarily punished:

> The punishments were in public ... they whipped them with a rope that the owner of the Hotel Faro kept always ready, soaked in salt water. They didn't punish peasants from the local tribes in this way, for fear of reprisals. It was outsiders that they made an example of, people who came from Melilla or Tetuan, whom they identified because they wore jackets or cut their hair in the European style. That is to say those who didn't shave their heads or didn't wear a fez, or who wore the 'nationalist fez', who were assumed to belong to the Nationalist Party.[67]

To Varela's disgust, Franco allowed Sidi Mohammed's trip. The train was cheered all along the route and even worse, the Khalifa declared in a speech of welcome at Asilah: 'Morocco is one nation and has only one sovereign. [...] The Moroccans living in the Spanish zone express their allegiance to His Majesty Mohamed V, Commander of the Faithful and only leader of Morocco.'[68]

65 Preston, *Franco*, 535-6, 543, 554, 560; Wolf, *Secrets*, 235-6; Morales Lezcano, *España y el Norte de Africa*, 250.

66 Preston, *Franco*, 467, 527; Morales Lezcano, *Norte de África*, 139, 141; Wolf, *Secrets*, 235-38.

67 Román, *Fragmentos*, 29.

68 Wolf, *Secrets*, 238-40.

The visit to Tangier, 1947

In Tangier, Sidi Mohammed began a political campaign. He had promised to be emollient but the massacres in Casablanca changed that. His first speech was on 10 April, in the garden of the Mandoub's residence, when he talked of Morocco's role in the Arab world, and lauded the Arab League. He said that the French 'weigh us down with the yoke of iniquity and oppression' and thanked the American government for 'their part in delivering us from oppression'. The next day, at Friday prayers, his sermon described how Islam guaranteed justice and individual freedom. Later, Prince Hassan gave a speech directed at Moroccan youth, focusing on national unity, and Princess Lalla Aïcha, her hair uncovered, spoke about social unity, of the need for everyone to work together.[69] She at once became a heroine to Moroccan women. Fatima Mernissi's mother extolled a princess who made speeches in Arabic and French and wore 'both long caftans and short French dresses'.[70] The four speeches made up one message: Morocco was an Arab country whose Sultan was dedicated to political and personal freedom and friendly towards the Western alliance.

Some members of the royal party organised a meeting of the Roosevelt Club at the El Minza Hotel, the best in town. The speeches were explicitly pro-American and implicitly anti-French. Before he left, the Jewish community in Tangier presented Sidi Muhammad with a tea-set of sterling silver, and the inhabitants of Tetuan gave a silver map of Morocco and a gold case containing earth from the Spanish zone.[71] The symbolism was clear.

Labonne's tactics of appeasement had failed. In May 1947 the French government sacked him and appointed General Alphonse-Pierre Juin instead.[72]

The Indian summer of settler colonialism

Juin gave the settlers just what they wanted: investment in the modern economy and a tough line with nationalists. Land in the Rharb and the Haouz of Marrakesh was made available to new immigrants, many of them demobilised soldiers who had served under the Resident-General in Italy. Money flooded in; almost

69 Alaoui, *Maroc*, 105-8; Hassan II, *The Challenge*, 37-8; Julien, *Impérialismes*, 200; Wolf, *Secrets*, 240-1.

70 Mernissi, *Harem Within*, 190.

71 Al-Fasi, *al-Harakat*, 307; Blair, *Western Window*, 135.

72 Julien, *Impérialismes*, 201.

one third of the money invested in Morocco in the whole period of the Protectorate was invested between 1949 and 1953. About half was raised locally from taxes, the rest from long-term loans, from American spending on the three big airbases and from private investors who found Morocco particularly attractive. It was spent on the infrastructure: port, railway construction and irrigation, and on agricultural and urban real estate. New dams provided hydro-electric power and irrigation for vineyards and orchards.[73]

This did benefit the Moroccan rich, who invested in landed property, but also in commerce: in 1946 and 1947 sixteen new companies, entirely Moroccan owned, were started in Fez alone. But the colons were the great beneficiaries, while the Moroccan poor suffered. Between 1950 and 1956, exports of wine, citrus fruits and phosphates all soared, but exports of olive oil, a peasant product, slumped. Inflation was already running at an annual rate of 32% in 1949 when controlled prices of milk, oil and soap were raised. At average wage rates it took a woman a day's work to earn enough to buy a kilo of carrots.[74] With even more to lose than before, the colons expected the Protectorate to crush Moroccan nationalism. Juin set to with a will, supported by the French Foreign Minister, Georges Bidault, a socialist who believed that Moroccan nationalists were obscurantist opponents of the benefits of French civilisation.[75]

Juin's Moroccan allies were virtually colons themselves, men like Si Thami El Glaoui who had abandoned his brief flirtation with nationalism. In 1953 he took dividends of around 53 million francs from the cobalt mines at Bouazer, and 38 million from the manganese mines at Imini. He owned three olive-oil factories and four fibre factories. In 1958 his family interests were reckoned at over 27,000 ha. of irrigated land in the Haouz. All this was topped up with involuntary presents from those he ruled. In 1949 one community, with a population of only 1,450, made several gifts totalling 20,000 francs.[76] He had much to lose if the French left. Juin was quite comfortable with this, because it conformed with a romantic view of an autocratic Moroccan society. In 1951 Juin wrote the approving preface to a biography of Qaid El Goundafi

73 Pujo, *Juin*, 255; Le Coz, *Rharb*, 2:458, 461, 508, 525; Pascon, *Haouz*, 2:486; Pallez, 'Les marchands', 570; Ayache, *Mouvement Syndicale*, 2:11-14.

74 Salahdine, *Maroc*, 254; Stewart, *Economy*, 123; Swearingen, *Mirages*, 132-9; Ayache, *Mouvement syndicale*, 2:40, 51.

75 Alaoui, *Maroc*, 111; for Bidault's views on Morocco see Julien, *Impérialismes*, 206.

76 Pascon, *Haouz*, 1: 326-30; Julien, *Impérialismes*, 225-6; Bidwell, *Morocco*, 123-4.

that, denying twenty years of nationalist protest and modernist Islam, presented the real Morocco in terms of Berber warriors drawn from the Middle Ages, a folkloric Morocco that had nothing to do with modernism, nationalism and democracy.[77] He did pay lip-service to the idea of Protectorate and progress towards independence and even announced that the government would be given 'representative institutions'. This turned out to be a proposal to water down the powers of Makhzan ministers by setting up a new council, with French as well as Moroccan members to shadow them, and establishing a third Moroccan college in the Council of Government with appointed members who would not be allowed to legislate. He even proposed that the Sultan delegate legislative power to the *grand vizir.* Sidi Mohammed refused to sign the decrees on the grounds that legislative power 'is given to us personally by the people and it is illegal for us to set aside the responsibility that that entails'. In any event, he went on, the proposal 'had nothing democratic about it, because a real democratic reform would be to give legislative power to an elected assembly'.[78]

This sophisticated blend of Islamic concepts of power flowing from the community and European ideas of legislative democracy, was countered in the crassest fashion by Protectorate officials who distributed a series of anonymous Arabic tracts that made scurrilous accusations about the Royal Family.[79] Eventually Jean Lecomte, the Director of the Interior, was sacked for this. In December 1947 Sidi Mohammed complained to President Auriol about Juin's behaviour and insisted that he wanted real democracy for the Moroccan people, not the counterfeit variety that the Resident-General proposed.[80]

The broad nationalist coalition

These were not mere words. The monarch shared many ideals with the leadership of the Istiqlal, such as determined advocacy of modern education for girls. In 1945 he had founded a school for the daughters of 'notables' in Rabat and his own younger daughters had a French governess. Girls' education was spreading: in 1945 twelve Muslim girls entered secondary school in Rabat, there were 193 the next year and 7,000 in 1947. In 1949 the

77 Hammoudi, *Master and Disciple*, 113-19.

78 *Ibid.*, 113.

79 Julien, *Impérialismes*, 220; Alaoui, *Maroc*, 115; Pujo, *Juin*, 257.

80 Alaoui, *Maroc*, 114.

first Moroccan girl received her baccalaureate. In a more ordinary middle-class household, Fatima Mernissi's mother insisted that she leave her little Quranic school and attend one run by Ibrahim al-Kittani, a veteran of the struggle against the Berber dahir. There, Fatima learned geography and mathematics, French and Arabic and nationalist songs that she sang to her family while dressed up as Princess Aïcha.[81]

So many women were taking part in the nationalist movement that Istiqlal created a new women's association, the *Akhwat al-Safa* (Sisters of Purity). Its congress in Fez in 1948 discussed unequal treatment in marriage, polygamy and divorce, passed resolutions against child-marriage, infanticide, abortion and prostitution, and demanded equal treatment in the *shari'a* courts. Some Istiqlali leaders went further. When Mehdi Ben Barka married that year, he held separate receptions for men and women guests but he took his wife on honeymoon to Ifrane, a resort high in the Middle Atlas, and encouraged her to get rid of her veil, cut her hair and wear European clothes. This was revolutionary behaviour in mid-century Morocco.[82]

When Ben Barka was not revolutionising his family life, he was radicalising Moroccan youth. He set up scout groups, theatre clubs and above all, football teams. Football was now extremely popular and Widad Athletic Club won the North African Championship in 1948, 1949 and 1950.[83]

The trade unions were also growing quickly, which troubled conservative nationalists from old Fasi elite families. In September 1948 *al-Alam* declared that the notables should lead the unions, for mass action would be 'a danger for the mentality of the country, its traditions and its wholesome customs'.[84] But during the *Fête du Trône* in November 1949, Sidi Mohammed stressed the importance of workers' interests and *al-Alam* became suitably complimentary about 'the importance of the role of the workers in the life of the Moroccan nation'. This was papering over the cracks: Abdullah Ibrahim was sacked as editor of *al-Alam* because of an article in which he praised Ho Chi Minh.[85]

81 Daoud, *Féminisme*, 246; Mernissi, *Harem Within*, 207-8; for al-Kittani see Julien, *Impérialismes*, 171 and Halstead, *Rebirth*, 179.

82 Daoud, *Féminisme*, 247-8; Daoud and Monjib, *Ben Barka*, 108-9.

83 Daoud and Monjib, *Ben Barka*, 96, 101-2; Rahmouni, *Encyclopédie*, 1:211.

84 Ayache, *Mouvement syndicale*, 2:27-8 quoting, *al-'Alam* 11 September 1948.

85 *Ibid.*, 2:28-9, 57, 89, 91, 96.

The foreign policy of the nationalists

The Ho Chi Minh affair posed a serious question: should Istiqlal identify itself with the capitalist or the communist side in the Cold War? The US government now had no interest in ending French rule in Morocco. That would put at risk supplies of vital minerals: lead, cobalt and manganese; and the important military bases and French rule were bulwarks against 'Stalinist Communism' which sought to place formerly dependent territories into the orbit of Moscow'.[86] In December 1950 the American and French governments agreed that the air base at Port Lyautey (Kénitra) could be substantially rebuilt and new bases constructed at Ben Guerir, Sidi Slimane and Nouasseur (near Casablanca). This was so expensive that Congress later carried out an investigation into the corruption, incompetence and bad management.[87] Despite the agreement being made without Sidi Mohammed even being informed, the sultan did not complain. Even Allal El-Fassi grudgingly acknowledged that an independent Morocco would allow the bases to continue, and he stressed that Istiqlal was anti-communist.[88]

In any case, the alternative to the United States was not necessarily the Soviet Union. Both left-wingers like Mehdi Ben Barka and right-wingers like Allal El-Fassi placed their hopes in the Arab League. In February 1947 Maghribi nationalists in Cairo, where the League had its headquarters, set up the Office of the Arab Maghrib with the purpose of coordinating propaganda and agitation against French rule.[89] Despite this rather vague job description, within three months it managed a spectacular propaganda coup. In May Muhammad bin Abd al-Karim al-Khattabi, who was on his way from Réunion to France, was spirited off his ship at Suez, borne to Cairo in triumph, received by King Farouk and lodged at the Egyptian government's expense. He and his brother became chairman and deputy chairman of the Committee for the Liberation of North Africa, an umbrella body that was set up largely to give them a role.[90]

None of this actually threatened colonial rule, but it embarrassed the French and Spanish governments and heartened the nationalists.

86 US Department of State, *Foreign Relations* 1949, 6:1,785.

87 Blair, *Western Window*, 146-51.

88 US Department of State, *Foreign Relations* 1947:681, Pasquet to Sec. of State, Rabat 7 May 1947, Secret; *ibid*, 684, Caffery to Sec. of State, Paris, 17 May 1947; Lacroix-Riz, *Les protectorats*, 49-64, 55, 70-2, 82.

89 Daoud and Monjib, *Ben Barka*, 105; al-Fasi, *al-Harakat*, 322-5, 336.

90 Al-Fasi, *al-Harakat*, 339-52; Hart, *Aith Waryaghar*, 400-1.

It also tied Moroccan nationalism more closely to broader Arab nationalism. That worried the Residency, because of the conflict between the Arabs and Israel.

Morocco and Israel

After the war, Zionist activity in Morocco increased. Clandestine branches of the Haganah were set up and the Zionist intelligence service Mossad le-'Aliya smuggled migrants out of Morocco, for the French Residency firmly opposed migration to Israel.[91] Some French officials were instinctively anti-Jewish, but Juin had more practical concerns. He wanted to preserve a Jewish community that was still mainly pro-French and he had no wish to hand a propaganda card to the Moroccan nationalists.[92] During the Israeli war of independence in 1948, nationalists organised a boycott of Jewish shops, and Allal El-Fassi's wife and other prominent women, collected jewellery to sell for the war effort. Sidi Mohammed, who had protected Moroccan Jews during the Second World War made speeches calling for Arab unity against Israel.[93] On 7 June 1948 rioters in Oujda looted Jewish property and killed eight Jews. This was not a pogrom and the leaders of Istiqlal condemned the attacks.[94] Yet they could not abjure the rioters and raised money for the defence of those whom the French eventually arrested.[95]

Eventually, diplomatic pressure forced Juin to change his policy of preventing Jewish emigration and in 1949 an Israeli organisation, Cadima, set up its headquarters in Casablanca to organise orderly, but discrete, emigration to Israel. As a result, Cadima's task was certainly less nerve-wracking than Israeli efforts to evacuate Jews from other, independent, Arab states. In the Arab east, Operation Magic Carpet was carried out in far more clandestine fashion. By the time it was wound up after Moroccan independence, Cadima had arranged the emigration of tens of thousands – one estimate is 92,000 – of Jews.[96]

91 Laskier, *North African Jewry*, 87-91.

92 *Ibid.*, 107-8.

93 Ibid., 94, 91; Laskier, *Alliance*, 313-14.

94 Laskier, *Twentieth Century*, 92, 96-7.

95 *Ibid.*, 99.

96 *Ibid.*, 111; Agnès Bensimon, *Hassan II et les juifs. Histoire d'une émigration secrète* (Paris: Seuil, 1991), 52.

The campaign against Sidi Mohammed

Juin saw French power slipping away in Morocco as it had done in Vietnam. His most serious challenge came not from radical Arab nationalists but from a quiet and reasonable sultan, who impressed President Auriol with his moderation when he spent a month in Paris in the autumn of 1950. To fight him, Juin plotted with the most reactionary figures in Morocco. One was Abdelhay El Kittani, leader of the Kitaniyya *tariqa* whose ill-will towards the Alaoui family dated back to 1909 when Moulay Abdelhafid had flogged his brother to death. Even so, he joined up with Juin's other ally, Si Thami El Glaoui, whose brother had helped Moulay Abdelhafid to power.[97]

Si Thami brought things to a head in an audience with Sidi Muhammad. He may not actually have said 'You are not the sultan of Morocco – you are the Sultan of the Istiqlal', but that is what rumour reported. Sidi Mohammed at once banned him from his presence. El Glaoui complained to Juin, and returned to Marrakesh to organise a rebellion. On 26 January 1951 Juin demanded that the Sultan dissociate himself from the Istiqlal on the grounds that order was breaking down. The Sultan replied that he was above party matters, and refused. If he did not, Juin replied 'I will depose you myself.' Horrified, the government in Paris told him to calm things down, but Juin replied that El Glaoui's supporters were acting perfectly reasonably when they trekked north and camped under the walls of Fez. 'Since they have neither newspapers, nor a political party to represent their views, their wishes were ignored... The Protectorate Authorities therefore asked the native chiefs to express their sentiments by the most suitable means.' French rule was in peril, he explained.[98] Auriol felt obliged to back his Resident-General.

On 25 February, to avoid being deposed, Sidi Mohammed signed the decrees that put Juin's proposed reforms into effect. Several Makhzan ministers were sacked and Ben Barka was exiled.[99] Only then did Juin send El Glaoui's Berbers home. But his success rebounded against him, for Sidi Mohammed appeared as a martyr and the protests in the cities got worse. Any occasion now provided an opportunity for agitation. On May Day there were demonstra-

97 Munson, *Religion and Power*, 105; Julien, *Impérialismes*, 229-32; Pujo, *Juin*, 265-9.

98 Bernard, *Franco-Moroccan Conflict*, 83-4; Alaoui, *Maroc*, 119-23; Julien, *Impérialismes*, 234-6; the quotation is from Pujo, *Juin*, 271.

99 Julien, *Impérialismes*, 238-9; Alaoui, *Maroc*, 125-6; Maxwell, *Lords of the Atlas*, 210; Ayache, *Mouvement syndicale*, 2:108; Pujo, *Juin*, 273.

tions in Meknès, Fez, Kénitra and Oujda. When Widad Athletic Club's football team beat a French football team the crowds exploded with joy; and during a match against an Algerian team, the army and police surrounded the ground and trained a machine gun on the crowd. Juin's position quickly became untenable and a successor, General Augustin-Léon Guillaume, was appointed in August 1951. Juin went on, in October, to become NATO commander in central Europe, a suitable job for a Marshal of France. Guillaume had only four stars, and Juin hoped that he might continue to exercise influence through this surrogate.[100]

Guillaume as Resident-General

Guillaume was conscious of the difference in rank and embarrassed by his peasant origins, and his insecurity made him bluster. 'Fighting is my business,' he announced, 'I know how to avenge an insult.'[101] Of the nationalists he said, 'I will make them eat straw.'[102] He relied heavily on Boniface, still head of the Casablanca region, and on Si Thami El Glaoui and Abdelhay El Kittani. This reactionary cabal knew well enough that if the nationalists won, their careers would be finished. They were supported by the colon newspapers that conducted a noisy campaign for democratisation, by which they meant the promulgation of decrees setting up municipalities that colons would control. Juin kept a watchful eye from a distance, and when he was installed as a member of the French Academy in June 1953 he brazenly took Si Thami El Glaoui as his personal guest to dinner with the Immortals.[103]

Even within the Academy, Juin had his critics, François Mauriac among them, and newspapers of all political complexions joined the fray. *Le Monde, Le Figaro* and *L'Humanité* campaigned against Boniface. The French Catholic press joined in, and the Apostolic Delegate in Morocco wrote a pastoral letter in February 1952 supporting the nationalists.[104] President Auriol and the Foreign Minister, Robert Schumann, talked of upholding the Treaty of Fez,

100 Alaoui, *Maroc*, 125-7; Julien, *Impérialismes*, 239-40; Bidwell, *Morocco*, 124; Ayache, *Mouvement syndicale*, 2: 110-11; Lahlou, *Casablanca* 94-5; Pujo, *Juin*, 274-6; Bernard, *Franco-Moroccan Conflict*, 94.

101 Bernard, *Franco-Moroccan Conflict*, 95.

102 Daoud and Monjib, *Ben Barka*, 116.

103 Bernard, *Franco-Moroccan Conflict*, 95, 101-3, 166; Julien, *Impérialismes*, 246-7; Daoud and Monjib, *Ben Barka*, 116; Maxwell, *Lords of the Atlas*, 222.

104 Alaoui, *Maroc*, 134-5; Oved, *Gauche*, 263-4, 269-70.

so that 'we can bring about reforms'.[105]

Guillaume could not silence the President of the Republic and the Foreign Minister, so he ignored them. He turned on the trade union movement hoping to break the alliance between French communists and their Moroccan comrades. In October 1951 the Moroccan Secretary-General of the Conféderation Génerale du Travail, Mahjoub ben Seddik, was imprisoned for two years for 'encouragement to murder' – he was falsely alleged to have called for a holy war; in December the French Secretary-General, René Toussaint, was heavily fined. But that winter there were strikes all over Morocco: butchers in Oujda, fishermen in Safi, metal-workers in Rabat and innumerable disputes in Casablanca, the most politicised city in the country.[106]

Sidi Mohammed was even harder to silence because his responses were measured and moderate. In his speech from the throne on 18 November 1951 he called for a new agreement between a sovereign Morocco and France based on mutual friendship. In March 1952 he sent a memorandum to Guillaume demanding an end of the state of siege, full private and public liberties, and the establishment of a Moroccan government to negotiate with the French authorities. This temperate approach had little to recommend it to Guillaume, for it would have gutted the legal basis of French rule. Only in September did he reply, and then only to repeat the pseudo-democratic demands for joint municipalities that Sidi Mohammed had rejected before. The next month the Sultan quietly repeated his willingness to negotiate, once the Treaty of Fez had been cancelled.[107]

By the end of 1952 President Auriol had despaired of Guillaume's intransigence, but the Resident-General was the catspaw of the most hardline colons and administrators, and of Si Thami El Glaoui, who wanted him to remove the Sultan.[108] The opportunity was not long in coming.

The Protectorate's coup d'état

Events in another North African country now affected Morocco. On 5 December 1952 French terrorists assassinated a Tunisian

105 Julien, *Impérialismes*, 248-9, 252-3; Alaoui, *Maroc*, 135; Daoud and Monjib, *Ben Barka*, 116.

106 Ayache, *Mouvement syndicale*, 2:127-46.

107 Bernard, *Franco-Moroccan Conflict*, 103-5; Alaoui, *Maroc*, 129-30; Julien, *Impérialismes*, 256.

108 Julien, *Impérialismes*, 255-6.

trade union leader, Ferhat Hached, and Moroccan unions, backed by Istiqlal, called a general strike. On 8 December several Europeans and many Moroccans were killed in demonstrations and Boniface spread false rumours about European women being raped and killed. In an atmosphere of lynchings and shootings, several hundred more people died. The Istiqlal and Communist parties were banned, around 400 of their members were arrested and many French citizens were expelled. Only Ouazzani's PDI was left alone, protected by the Residency's chief Moroccan security man, Mohammed Oufkir.[109]

Paris did nothing. In January 1953 the government fell and Georges Bidault again became Foreign Minister. The right-wing colons, greatly heartened by the return of their apologist, set up their own terrorist group that came to be known as Présence Française.[110] Policy was now being made in Rabat and Guillaume even stopped sending regular reports about the meetings of the Council of Government back to the Quai d'Orsay. He and Boniface talked openly of dethroning the sultan.[111]

If that were to be done, the Protectorate administration needed Moroccans to engineer it. The Residency helped set up a Confederation of Brotherhoods in Eastern Morocco whose leadership talked of the need to protect Islam and the *tariqas* from the innovations of an irreligious Sultan. Their slogans were revealingly frank: 'Long live General Guillaume, long live Franco-Moroccan cooperation, long live the brotherhoods!' On 23 February, over the protests of the Quai d'Orsay, they demonstrated outside El Glaoui's palace.[112]

At the beginning of April the tireless El Kittani organised a Conference of Religious Orders of North Africa, attended by more than 1,000 delegates from fifteen *tariqas* and 200 *zawiyas*. Only by quick intervention from Paris, was it prevented from calling for the overthrow of Sidi Mohammed.[113] On 21 May El Glaoui presented a petition signed by 250 pashas and qaids, six heads of religious orders and thirty-one 'notables' which accused Sidi Mohammed of lack of religious devotion and demanded his deposi-

109 Clément, *Oufkir*, 90.

110 Julien, *Impérialismes*, 271.

111 *Ibid.*, 262-3; Alaoui, *Maroc*, 131-5; Bernard, *Franco-Moroccan Conflict*, 123-5; Ayache, *Mouvement syndicale*, 2:147-62; Daoud and Monjib, *Ben Barka*, 118-20.

112 Julien, *Impérialismes*, 269; Bernard, *Franco-Moroccan Conflict*, 147.

113 Bernard, *Franco-Moroccan Conflict*, 148; Alaoui, *Maroc*, 139.

tion. El Glaoui was an unlikely theologian, but since the French government fell that same day, the plotters had a free hand.[114]

El Glaoui now travelled to London to attend at Queen Elizabeth's coronation as a personal guest of his old golfing partner, Winston Churchill. But a personal guest was not an official one, and El Glaoui did not receive the knighthood he craved, nor were his lavish gifts accepted. On 31 May, before this humiliation took place, the pasha took the opportunity of a stop in Paris to announce that the sultan had been overthrown. This was a little premature because 300 *'ulama* in Fez signed a repetition of their *bay'a* to Sidi Mohammed. Even the *grand-vizir*, El Mokri, issued an acerbic circular, saying that the pashas and qaids 'were invested by the sultan to represent him in the towns and in the countryside' and had 'no right to rise up against the central power and thus go against all the most basic rules of hierarchy'. They also had 'no competence to comment on the general policy of the government of His Majesty, and even less on religious questions with which they had never had any concern'.[115]

El Mokri's letter may have been for show. In any event, neither he nor Guillaume, who was on a rest cure in Vichy, nor the government in Paris had any control over events in Morocco. Boniface and his supporters were running the Protectorate and they welcomed Si Thami with a Roman triumph when he returned from France. Guillaume rushed back, surrounded the palace with troops and demanded that the Sultan sign the decrees instituting his reform programme. On 13 August the Sultan did so and legislative authority passed into the hundred-year-old hands of El Mokri.[116] But El Glaoui still insisted that the supposedly irreligious Sultan must be replaced. He had a suitable substitute. On 14 August his tractable qaids proclaimed an obscure cousin of the Sultan, Moulay Mohammed ben Arafa.[117]

Ben Arafa, a grandson of Sidi Mohammed IV, was hardly well-known even within the Alaoui family. The urban population, who had never heard of him, rioted at once. In Oujda, men from the Beni Snassene killed several Europeans, shattering the fantasy of the 'good countryside' that opposed the nationalism of the towns.

[114] Julien, *Impérialismes*, 287.

[115] Alaoui, *Maroc*, 138-9; Bernard, *Franco-Moroccan Conflict*, 150-1; Julien, *Impérialismes*, 288; Maxwell, *Lords of the Atlas*, 220-1.

[116] Alaoui, *Maroc*, 143-7; Bernard, *Franco-Moroccan Conflict*, 156; Maxwell, *Lords of the Atlas*, 226-9.

[117] Julien, *Impérialismes*, 290-300; Alaoui, *Maroc*, 148; Bernard, *Franco-Moroccan Conflict*, 158.

So El Glaoui marched his men north again, saying that they were so infuriated with the Sultan that he could not stop them. Guillaume now had the excuse that he needed. Claiming that he could not maintain order he asked the French cabinet for permission to remove the Sultan, and the ministers agreed.[118]

Sidi Mohammed refused to abdicate, so he was deposed. On 20 August French policemen took him, and his two sons, from his palace at gun-point. They were first flown to Corsica, then to Madagascar, where they lodged in a semi-derelict hotel in the spa town of Antsirabé. Later that evening, El Mokri proclaimed Moulay Mohammed Ben Arafa as Sultan.[119]

The ben Arafa interlude

The new Sultan may have been proclaimed but only those who had to, signed a *bay'a.* The pashas of Agadir, Salé, El Jadida and Sefrou did so and one hundred notables in Meknès presented theirs, very suitably, to the local French commander. An *'alim* in Marrakesh was bastinadoed until he signed. Many *'ulama* refused. The Pasha of Fez refused to seek an audience with ben Arafa, and was sacked, and the doyen of the Salafis, Sidi Mohammed bel-Arabi el-Alaoui was imprisoned for recommending that the new sultan 'should be killed in accordance with our *shari'a,* which says that if *bay'as* are made to two khalifas, the second one should be killed because he is a devil.'[120]

Plenty of humbler *'ulama* agreed. In the little High Atlas town of Bzu, the qadi found his mosque under siege at the time of Friday prayer:

> When I got to the msalla, I saw members of the Foreign Legion on a ridge overlooking the assembly, with machine guns turned on us. By the time the sermon was over, everyone was in tears. [...] I got to 'in the name of the Sultan', then I coughed. I didn't pronounce the sermon in the name of any sultan... to have said it in the name of Muhammad bin Yusif would have been sedition to the French. To have said it in the name of Muhammad bin 'Arafa would have been a lie. It would have been against

118 Alaoui, *Maroc*, 151; Bernard, *Franco-Moroccan Conflict*, 160-6; Julien, *Impérialismes*, 304.

119 Bernard, *Franco-Moroccan Conflict*, 161; Julien, *Impérialismes*, 304-10; Hassan II, *The Challenge*, 49-50.

120 Julien, *Impérialismes*, 310; Abderrahim Ouardighi, *La grande crise franco-marocaine, 1952-1956* (Rabat: [n.p], 1976), 33-4, 38; the quotation is from Munson, *Religion and Power*, 106-7.

the shari'a. So I said nothing clearly. And everyone went away weeping. The French were very afraid that night. Before morning, sixteen people were arrested in Bzu.[121]

When a group of women saw Sidi Mohammed's face in the moon, the news spread from market to market and village to village, quite independently of any modern media, for no radio broadcast would carry it. Within a month an account of the miracle had reached Tiznit in the foothills of the Anti-Atlas.[122]

There was terrorism in the cities. Trains were derailed, telephone lines cut. On 11 September bel-Arabi's wish nearly came true: Mohammed Ben Arafa was stabbed on his way to lead Friday prayer in Rabat. His assailant, a house painter, probably acted alone. Groups like the Committee of the Black Hand, made up of artisans, workers and small shopkeepers, set off bombs. Between 20 August and 31 December 1953, fifty-three people died, many of them in a huge explosion in the Central Market of Casablanca on Christmas Eve; since Sidi Mohammed had been exiled on the 'Id al-Kabir, the bombers considered this fitting revenge.[123]

Allal El-Fassi broadcast encouragement to the terrorists from Cairo, but the internal leaders of Istiqlal condemned the bombings, if they were free to do so, for many were in jail. Alternative leaders were coming forward, often men who had been loyal servants of France. Abdelkarim el-Khatib, a Casablanca doctor, went to Europe to raise money to buy guns. Mahjoubi Aherdane, an officer in the French army and married to a French woman, refused to sign the petition calling for Sidi Mohammed's overthrow and was told by the French Contrôleur Civil, who sacked him as qaid of Oulmès, 'From now on, I shall regard you as an enemy of France.' M'Barek Bekkaï, the Pasha of Sefrou openly supported Sidi Mohammed but the French authorities did not risk removing him. Even the ultra-loyal Mohammed Oufkir began to think about building links with Madagascar.[124]

121 Eickelman, *Knowledge and Power*, 152.

122 Julien, *Impérialismes*, 335.

123 Alaoui, *Maroc*, 163-4; Ouardighi, *La grande crise*, 52-4; Julien, *Impérialismes*, 342-3; Daoud and Monjib, *Ben Barka*, 122-3; Blair, *Western Window*, 177; Clément, *Oufkir*, 96-9. Casualty figures should be treated with caution: Ouardighi gives 20 dead in the explosion in the market in Casablanca, Julien gives 18, Daoud and Monjib give 25.

124 The quotation is from Bernard, *Franco-Moroccan Conflict* 87-9; Waterbury, *Commander*, 238; Clément, *Oufkir*, 91-8; Blair, *Western Window*, 171.

The nationalists in the Spanish zone

In Tetuan the High Commissioner, Rafael García Valiño, refused to recognise Ben Arafa. He insisted, in the name of public opinion, that the name of Sidi Mohammed be mentioned in Friday prayers, not that of the 'false' Sultan.[125] Public opinion did not usually trouble the Spanish government, but both García Valiño and Franco knew that the army was too defective in arms and supplies to repress the nationalists. It was more advantageous to court them and perhaps garner Arab votes for the Spanish application to join the United Nations. Less realistically, García Valiño and Franco believed that maintaining the sovereignty of Sidi Mohammed might even win them supporters in the French zone, with the alluring possibility of extending Spanish control southwards. These were absurd calculations, but realism was never a hallmark of Spanish colonialism in Morocco.[126]

Torrès encouraged these illusions. He suggested that the Khalifa might be proclaimed regent of all Morocco, in the absence of Sidi Mohammed, and García Valiño seized on the idea and arranged an elaborate ceremony in January 1954. The Khalifa developed a convenient illness, and did not attend, but the many notables who did took the opportunity to declare their loyalty to Sidi Mohammed. Even after this neat doublecross, the Spanish authorities appointed Torrès Minister of Justice, and let him set up a nationalist radio transmitter that could be heard in Marrakesh. His supporters were permitted to celebrate the *Fête du Trône* and to declare a 'day of national mourning' on the anniversary of Sidi Mohammed's exile. García Valiño even let Torrès import guns and supplies, helped by the Egyptian military attaché in Madrid, and allowed armed groups fighting the French to use the Spanish zone as a base.[127]

War in the French zone

In the winter and spring of 1954, shadowy terrorist organisations with melodramatic names – Lions of the Liberation, Black Hand, Black Crescent and Secret Organisation – waged urban warfare. In February someone tried to blow up El Glaoui. Someone else threw a grenade at Ben Arafa in Marrakesh and in late May, Guil-

125 Julien, *Impérialismes*, 320-1; Wolf, *Secrets*, 277.

126 Preston, *Franco*, 642-3; Wolf, *Secrets*, 278-9; Román, *Fragmentos*, 36.

127 Julien, *Impérialismes*, 321; Zaki M'Barek, *Résistance et Armée de Libération. Portée, politique, liquidation* (Tangier: [n.p.], 1986), 33, 43; Wolf, *Secrets*, 281.

laume was nearly assassinated there. Women carried bombs, and befriended American soldiers on the bases and obtained arms. Présence Française responded with counter-terrorism and policemen took to torture. A special volunteer force, made up of El Glaoui's Berbers, patrolled the *medinas* like an occupying army.[128]

Fifty-five supposed members of Black Hand were charged with numerous crimes including murder. They replied through their lawyer, Jean-Charles Legrand, that they were fighting a patriotic war: 'For us, it was a holy war for King and Country: *Djihad lil malik ou lel bled.* [...] We want Independence, we want the freedom of our Country.' Legrand added as an aside: 'Gentlemen, this is a tragic argument: these are the very words that we taught to these people.'[129]

The French government, desperate for a political solution replaced Guillaume with Francis Lacoste. Then, almost immediately, it collapsed, after the defeat at Dien Bien Phu in Vietnam on 7 May 1954. Its successor, headed by Pierre Mendès-France, was just as unstable and Lacoste was no use as a negotiator. In his first speech Lacoste said he would end the cycle of violence and repression by establishing order, but did not explain how he would do so without repression.[130] He did replace some senior officials but Boniface, who had retired the previous year, remained in unofficial control of security and the violence and assassinations spiralled on. In August there were riots in Fez, in Sidi Kacem (Petit-Jean), Kénitra, Khémmisset and, of course, Casablanca. Most of the 161 dead were Moroccans.[131]

Lacoste quickly lost the initiative. By October the military courts had begun to release political prisoners for lack of evidence, among them Mehdi Ben Barka, Abderrahman Bouabid and several people accused, without any foundation, of mass rape and murder. The Istiqlali leaders promptly contacted Sidi Mohammed in Madagascar and worked out a plan to transfer power to a Council of the Throne in which all sides would have a voice. Lacoste would have

128 Julien, *Impérialismes*, 343; Ouardighi, *La grande crise*, 52, 56, 70-7; Daoud, 254; Blair, *Western Window*, 173-4.

129 Jean-Charles Legrand, *Justice, patrie de l'homme. Défenses devant les Tribunaux militaires du Protectorat, 1953-1955* (Casablanca: Editions Maroc, [n.d.]), 116.

130 Bernard, *Franco-Moroccan Conflict*, 213; Alexander Werth, *The Strange History of Pierre Mendès-France and the Great Conflict over French North Africa* (London: Barrie, 1957), 211.

131 Ouardighi, *La grande crise*, 84-9; Bernard, *Franco-Moroccan Conflict*, 215; Julien, *Impérialismes*, 369.

none of it, and proposed his own bizarre version of García Valiño's plan: to put the Khalifa of Tetuan on the throne and so unite Morocco under joint French and Spanish rule. Neither the nationalists nor the Sultan would accept that.[132]

The government in Paris now had an even more important battle to fight. On the night of 31 October-1 November 1954, Algerian nationalists began a revolutionary war, and this became the issue of over-riding importance. After the Mendès-France government fell on 5 February 1955, a new cabinet led by Edgar Faure agreed to prepare for independence in Tunisia, and to compromise in Morocco. Faure knew that his army could not fight more than one war.[133]

Faure certainly could not rely on Lacoste to win him any battles. The Resident-General's response to the formation of an entirely Moroccan trade union confederation, the Union Marocaine du Travail (UMT) in March, was to ban it.[134] The violence was getting worse, because, for all his denials, Lacoste was allowing counter-terrorists to operate freely. They plotted to murder Gaullist deputies in France, threatened newspaper owners in Morocco, and in January 1955 even assassinated an honest policeman named Forestier who threatened to expose them. By June 1955 a full-scale counter-terrorist war was underway, fought by police officers and encouraged by Boniface and El Glaoui. It culminated in the murder on 12 June of Jacques Lemaigre-Debreuil, a liberal businessman and newspaper owner who ran a brave press campaign against the counter-terrorists.[135]

At the same time, in the countryside, the qaids were returning to precolonial systems of punishment, that depended upon public humiliation of the accused. In the Sraghna, a qaid had two nationalists, who were suspected of planting a bomb, plucked in front of him; that is, his retinue pulled out the hair of their beards in bloody tufts, before they were taken to Marrakesh for the more formal investigation of the authorities.[136] Such behaviour certainly disgraced the two nationalists in front of the rural population, but it also caused resentment. It was clear that the despotism

132 Bernard, *Franco-Moroccan Conflict*, 222-32; Julien, *Impérialismes*, 377-80; Alaoui, *Maroc*, 174-5.

133 Bernard, *Franco-Moroccan Conflict*, 239; Julien, *Impérialismes*, 289, 393-4.

134 Julien, *Impérialismes*, 403.

135 *Ibid.*, 386-7, 396, 403-4; Werth, *Mendès-France*, 211-12; Bernard, *Franco-Moroccan Conflict*, 248-9; Alaoui, *Maroc*, 182

136 Hammoudi, *Master and Disciple*, 130.

of the Protectorate, and the contradictory ideology of reform that covered it had both run their course.

The murder of Lemaigre-Debreuil convinced Faure to remove Lacoste. On 20 July he appointed Gilbert Grandval, who had a reputation for being a hard-headed man of action. He began by sacking the most reactionary officials, and purged the security services. Mohammed Oufkir became his trusted confident. Sensing betrayal, the colons in Casablanca rioted, burned and looted Moroccan shops, lynched several Moroccans and tried to do the same to Maître Legrand, who had defended many Moroccan political prisoners; he shot back with a revolver. Grandval stood down the police and put Casablanca under martial law, administered by the Foreign Legion.[137]

Grandval then released forty-three prisoners and proposed a new peace plan to Ben Arafa. The latter, who was only too happy to oblige, would resign and hand over to a Council of Regency chaired by El Mokri. A Moroccan-led government would negotiate independence, and Sidi Mohammed would move to France. But it all took too long and the bombs continued, as the second anniversary of the Sultan's exile approached. On 20 August itself there was appalling violence. There were massacres, not in the big cities but in supposedly loyal Berber areas such as Oued Zem, a little town northeast of Marrakesh, where ninety-five *colons* were murdered. The French authorities claimed that tribesmen had 'lost their heads', but years later one of the participants told an audience of local notables (and an American anthropologist) that they had gone to the town armed. The massacre had been planned because Oued Zem was the local centre of Présence Française; this was part of a tit-for-tat series of massacres that the French Foreign Legion capped by killing 300 'rebels'.[138] On 22 August Grandval resigned.[139]

Aix-les-Bains

Back in Paris, Edgar Faure was putting the finishing touches to his own policy: the complete independence of Morocco. On the day of Grandval's resignation a conference opened at Aix-les-Bains,

137 Julien, *Impérialismes*, 423-5; Bernard, *Franco-Moroccan Conflict*, 252; Werth, *Mendès-France*, 214-18; Clément, *Oufkir*, 103.

138 Bernard, *Franco-Moroccan Conflict*, 283-4; Julien, *Impérialismes*, 435; Alaoui, *Maroc*, 189-90; Werth, *Mendès-France*, 218-19; Daoud and Monjib, *Ben Barka*, 126-7; Eickelman, *Knowledge and Power*, 31-2.

139 Julien, *Impérialismes*, 433.

attended by representatives of El Glaoui and El Kittani, and by delegations from Istiqlal and the PDI. On 27 August 1955 it produced a plan very similar to that of Grandval; Sidi Mohammed, still in Madagascar, accepted it on 5 September.[140]

Unfortunately, the new Resident-General was the least suitable man to put this plan into effect. The aristocratic General Pierre-Georges-Jacques-Marie Boyer de la Tour du Moulin had spent much of his life in Morocco, was a protégé of Marshal Juin and had allies among the hardline colons. He made Mohammed Oufkir, who had served under him in Vietnam, his aide-de-camp, although Oufkir was no longer reliable: he had switched sides to Sidi Mohammed.[141] Boyer de la Tour procrastinated over the resignation of Ben Arafa who only left for Tangier on 1 October.[142] The following day, the Liberation Army struck for the first time.[143]

The Liberation Army

In March 1955 a group of fifteen militants of the Maghrib Office in Cairo had landed near Nador in the Spanish zone. They included Moroccans, Egyptians and Algerians – notably Houari Boumeddienne, later President of Algeria – and they brought arms to start training the Liberation Army of the Arab Maghrib (Armée de la Libération du Maghreb Arabe). They declared that their immediate aim was the restoration of Sidi Mohammed, but with the ultimate intention of ending European rule in North Africa. Nevertheless, García Valiño financed their office in Tetuan.[144]

These fighters paid little attention to Istiqlal. Mehdi Ben Barka did win over one important guerrilla commander, Mohammed Basri, the head of a group known as *al-Munazzama al-Sirriyya* (the Secret Organisation), who was nicknamed *al-faqih*' (the learned one) because he was a respected Islamic scholar. But the Liberation Army leaders had no connection with the Istiqlal or broke their links with it. Mahjoubi Aherdane was one, and Dr el-Khatib another. A third was Batoul Sbihi who had organised the women's section

140 Alaoui, *Maroc*, 196-204; Julien, *Impérialismes*, 431, 437-8; Bernard, *Franco-Moroccan Conflict*, 300-1; Clément, *Oufkir*, 111.

141 Alaoui, *Maroc*, 205-7; Julien, *Impérialismes*, 439-40.

142 Werth, *Mendès-France*, 224.

143 Daoud and Monjib, *Ben Barka*, 140.

144 Alaoui, *Maroc*, 210-11; Ouardighi, *La grande crise*, 115-17; Zaki M'Barek, 'La désertion des soldats marocains de l'armée française à l'Armée de Libération du Maghreb (A.L.M.). Rôle militaire, inpact psycho-politique (1955-1956)', *Maroc-Europe* 7 (1994): 239ff.

of the Istiqlal in Salé before she fled to Tetuan.[145] The main operational commanders, Abbès Messaâdi, a Berber from the Middle Atlas, and Abdallah Sanhaji, declared that they recognised only Sidi Mohammed and most of their men agreed. Many were illiterate youths, shoe-shine boys, touts and street toughs, but some were former soldiers in the colonial army, motivated by religion. One tract distributed among Moroccan soldiers talked of *jihad* and apostasy: a believing Muslim should not kill another believer: Another, directed at Moroccan officers, said: 'You should do your duty towards your nation, towards your Islam and towards your Arab identity.' Such propaganda was quite successful, and there were many deserters from the French army. One was a corporal who had served in Madagascar as well as Morocco.[146]

The return of the King

On 17 October Boyer de la Tour finally set up the Council of the Throne. Its members included Si Bekkaï, the former Pasha of Sefrou and the centenarian El Mokri. Two days later a former Pasha of Fez, Si Fatmi bin Sliman, was asked to form a government. For the first time since 1 September 1917, a total of 15,388 days, El Mokri was not head of the government. His career as *grand vizir*, that had started before the French Protectorate began, finished less than five months before it ended.[147]

The Protectorate was now running down fast. Présence Française held its last rally on 10 October and on 25 October Si Thami El Glaoui told the Council that he would welcome the return of Sidi Mohammed. On 29 October the Sultan left Madagascar and two days later he settled into the Château de la Celle-Saint-Cloud near Nice. His interpreter there was Mohammed Oufkir, who became a close companion of Prince Hassan. On 4 November the French government agreed that he could return to Morocco as Sultan, and the next day he and President Pinay issued an agreement that Morocco would be a democratic, constitutional monarchy, an independent state 'joined to France by the permanent links of an interdependence freely agreed and defined'. Finally Si Thami El Glaoui came, prostrated himself at the Sultan's feet and protested his loyalty. Sidi Mohammed forgave him. This was the Pasha's last public act. With cancer of the stomach in

145 Daoud and Monjib, *Ben Barka*, 136-7.

146 M'Barek, *Résistance*, 87-9: M'Barek, 'La désertion', *passim*.

147 Alaoui, *Maroc*, 219-21; Bernard, *Franco-Moroccan Conflict*, 328-9.

its final stages, he returned to Marrakesh and died there on 31 January 1956.[148] On 8 November Boyer de Latour resigned and André-Louis Dubois became the last Resident-General.[149] His role, he said, was that of executor: 'we are trustees in bankruptcy'.[150] But there were several creditors.

The rivalries were apparent on the day that Sidi Mohammed returned to Morocco, 16 November 1955. Mehdi Ben Barka, the socialist nationalist, greeted him at the airport but Mohammed Oufkir, the colonial army officer who had appointed himself aide-de-camp, drove him into town. Hundreds of thousands of cheering people lined the route, marshalled by two militias: one was Istiqlali, organised by Ben Barka, the other formed by members of Ouazzani's Parti Démocratique de l'Indépendance.[151]

Sidi Mohammed's speech, two days later, to mark the *Fête du Trône* offended no-one. He promised an 'end of the trusteeship and of the Protectorate, and the beginning of an era of full independence' and that an independent government would set up 'democratic institutions that were the product of free elections, and founded on the principle of the separation of powers under a constitutional monarchy.'[152]

On 22 November the Council of the Throne resigned, and El Mokri lost his final public functions; on 7 December Si Bekkaï formed a coalition cabinet to lead Morocco to independence. It had twenty ministers, nine from Istiqlal, six from PDI and five independents. A Jew, Léon Benzaquen, was Minister for Posts and Telegraphs; Réda Guédira, a prominent member of the Roosevelt Club was a minister of state; and the aged Salafi, Mohammed bel-Arabi el-Alaoui, was made Minister for the Throne and a personal advisor to Sidi Mohammed. Si Bekkaï, who had no intention of breaking relations with Paris, announced: 'We will be the allies of the French people, because it is a democratic people, fundamentally anti-colonialist, and because we know that Franco-Moroccan cooperation will be loyal, fruitful and close'.[153]

On 11 February he and Dubois signed a protocol that left administrative power largely in the hands of French officials, although

148 Maxwell, *Lords of the Atlas*, 261-2; Morsy, 'Glaoui', 99; Clément, *Oufkir*, 117-19.

149 Alaoui, *Maroc*, 226-8.

150 Bernard, *Franco-Moroccan Conflict*, 339.

151 Daoud and Monjib, *Ben Barka*, 145-7; Hassan II, *La Mémoire d'un roi. Entretiens avec Eric Laurent* (Paris: Plon, 1993), 173.

152 Bernard, *Franco-Moroccan Conflict*, 340ff.

153 *Ibid.*, 343; al-Asfi, *Al-salafi*, 119; Laskier, *Twentieth Century*, 171.

legally they were no more than advisors. They were needed because when Morocco became independent from France on 2 March 1956, the country was far from settled. Great swathes of the countryside were effectively in open rebellion and terrorist bands roamed the cities.

The Liberation Army professed loyalty only to Sidi Mohammed, not to the coalition of bourgeois urban nationalists who occupied government ministries. Its fighters wanted the French to leave, completely, and they wanted revenge on their former collaborators. The second was easily done. On 19 November the deputy Pasha of Fez was lynched inside the royal palace and his body burned. Allies of El Glaoui were murdered while their old protector lay dying.[154] Supplied from Algeria, the Liberation Army rampaged through the northern part of the French zone. Istiqlal tried to rein them in. Allal El-Fassi spoke over the radio from Cairo, and the left-wingers Mehdi Ben Barka, Abdallah Ibrahim and Mohammed Basri '*al-Faqih*' tried to extend party control over the Liberation Army and the shadowy Black Crescent that was dominated by Communists and members of the PDI. They had little success.[155]

Independence from Spain

The Liberation Army finally broke with Spain. Franco's emotional involvement with Morocco would not let him contemplate independence. Two weeks after Sidi Mohammed returned to Rabat, the dictator who had once said 'Without Africa, I can hardly explain myself to myself' was still confidently predicting that Moroccans would not be ready for independence for twenty-five years.[156] But on 9 January 1956 Torrès resigned as a minister in the Khalifian government on Sidi Mohammed's instructions and on 10 January Dubois met García Valiño at Larache and left him in no doubt that Spanish rule would have to end.[157] Even then Garcia Valiño tried to persuade Torrès and the *Khalifa* to allow the northern zone to continue. Both refused.[158] An extraordinary story circulated that the High Commissioner had tried to drug Torrès and pack him off to a lunatic asylum. True or not, it suited the air of unreality in Tetuan. On 2 March when the French zone became independent,

154 Alaoui, *Maroc*, 233.

155 Ouardighi, *La grande crise*, 133-4; M'Barek, *Résistance*, 106-8.

156 Preston, *Franco*, 643, 652.

157 *Ibid.*, 643-4.

158 Wolf, *Secrets*, 296-301.

the Spanish authorities hung on in Tetuan.[159] Rumours spread that the Spanish Legion would hold the northern zone by force, and Tetuan erupted into rioting. Typically, Franco blamed communists,[160] but the nationalists were moving under their own steam. On 16 March Torrès and Allal El-Fassi met in Tanger and agreed to unite their parties.[161]

Franco had tried for so long to use Moroccan nationalists to undermine French rule that he could hardly believe that they would turn against him. But bereft of collaborators, he finally invited Sidi Mohammed to Madrid to transfer power. It was a glum occasion for the Caudillo, although the Moroccan side was gracious. On 7 April independence was formally agreed. The international zone of Tangier was abolished in July, although it would retain special administrative status until July 1960.[162]

In the northern zone itself both Moroccans and settlers experienced independence in starker ways. Some years later women in the central Rif told a visiting Englishwoman about the miraculous auguries of the great event:

> Long ago in the days when miracles and other equally amazing things happened, there were men who walked along this very path and some said they saw a horse and rider gallop *up* the cliff. Not everyone had the gift to see this vision for it foretold something extraordinary or dreadful would happen. [...] Once there was a great famine and the horse and rider were seen then; and then just before Independence they were seen again.[163]

The Spanish inhabitants of Villa Sanjurjo, a few miles down the road, had less warning. They first heard about Moroccan independence when the government loudspeaker in the town square announced it and told them that their town was now called Al Hoceima. The civilians quickly packed and returned to Spain.[164]

The Spanish authorities took longer to leave. They handed over civilian administration quickly enough, but the army still oc-

159 Julien, *Impérialismes*, 482-3; Wolf, *Secrets*, 298-9;

160 Preston, *Franco*, 644; Wolf, *Secrets*, 308-10.

161 Wolf, *Secrets*, 300; Daoud, *Féminisme*, 170.

162 Preston, *Franco*, 644; Wolf, *Secrets*, 313-15; Alaoui, *Maroc*, 240-1, and 272-3 reproducing the Hispano-Moroccan agreement of 7 April 1956; *Keesing's Contemporary Archives*, (1956): 15,110.

163 Ursula Hart, *Behind the Courtyard Door: The Daily Life of Tribeswomen in Northern Morocco* (Ipswich Press, 1994), 138.

164 Román, *Fragmentos*, 37.

cupied defensive positions in the mountains around Melilla as late as March 1960.[165] They did not leave the enclaves at all, or Ifni and the Spanish Sahara, none of which Madrid considered to be Moroccan: but the Army of Liberation did, so Spanish commanders also insisted on holding on the Tarfaya region as a buffer zone.[166]

Independence undefined

Independence came grudgingly from both colonial rulers, but in quite different ways. In the French Zone, the government in Paris had to overcome the opposition of the settlers; in the Spanish zone the settlers were not consulted but merely told. This was a consequence of the difference in character between the Spanish and the French states. For all its weakness and division, the French Republic was democratic and demanded an adherence to law and constitutional procedures. Franco's government was a dictatorship that acknowledged no such limits. Yet it was the need to adhere to law that undermined the French Protectorate. The Treaty of Fez, nearly half a century before, had as its premise that the government of a powerful European state would oversee the modernisation and reform of Morocco. But the events following 1939 demonstrated that the French Republic was not powerful and was unable to oversee reform.

The importance of the defeat of 1940 was critical, because it destroyed the duality on which the administration of the Protectorate was based. Not only had French armies been defeated but Moroccan armies were called upon to rescue France. Sidi Mohammed turned the logic of Protectorate on its head when he talked of standing at the side of France. This new logic was reinforced by the Casablanca conference in early 1943. The French armies had now been defeated in Morocco itself, or had collapsed from within. In their place stood a new paladin: the United States, proclaiming the utility and the desirability of freedom, and demonstrating its effectiveness in everything from the winning of victories and the provision of food, to the supply of lipstick, Coca-Cola and cigarettes.

With the war over, the Moroccan elite, King and nationalists, had agitated or negotiated their way out of colonial dependence

165 Juán Diez Sánchez, 'Fin del protectorado de España En Marruecos: repliegue a Melilla de las Fuerzas del Tercio Gran Capitán, Iº de la Legión', *Trapana*, número extraordinario (1995).

166 Hodges, *Western Sahara*, 80.

on their French and Spanish protectors, and into a political relationship, but still a dependent one, with the United States. That would carry with it its own contradictions, because of the American relationship with Israel and size of the Jewish community in Morocco.

It also opened up new stresses in Moroccan society. Sidi Mohammed's legitimacy came from the past, as a sharif, an Alaoui and as Commander of the Faithful. Yet his role had been recast by the Protectorate and confined to religion, while his customary lines of allegiance and patronage were taken over, subsumed or re-created by the French officials of the Protectorate; all possibility of force was entirely removed. Before he could reign in his own right, the Protectorate had to end and he would have to take control of the colonial state, its lines of patronage and its use of force. That meant that he would have to take on the mantle of a modern nationalist, a role that anyway agreed with his personal ambitions to continue to modernise Morocco.

But the nationalist arena was also occupied by other forces. The Istiqlal and the PDI, who had their origins in the Salafiyya had provided the intellectual and organising ability, and authored the political justifications, for the independence movement. It was they who forged the links with the Arab nationalist movements outside Morocco that mobilised diplomatic and, to an extent, military, support for the independence struggle. Yet these middle-class, urban nationalists had little in common with the inhabitants of the countryside. For the rural population, the main focus of loyalty was still Sidi Mohammed and deeper-seated ties of loyalty and patronage still centred around him. The rural resistance of the Liberation Army was largely beyond their control as a result, even though they had helped to arm and motivate it. Even in the cities, while the nationalist parties were able to mobilise the urban poor on occasion, as they had done in 1937, or even the trade union movement that had grown out of French syndicalisation, they never really controlled the demonstrations. The nationalist leaders were even split over who was to lead the movement, and thus have access to power when independence came.

That was a highly contested question, because there was no agreement on the specific shape that Moroccan society should take after independence. There was wide agreement that independence had to be achieved in the whole country, which meant uniting all the various pieces that the colonial regimes had divided up, but the issue of the Saharan boundaries remained unresolved. Apart from Tunisia, the other states of north-west Africa were not yet independent and the French government was still drawing their boundaries. Beyond that, agreement was less certain. The future economic system was unclear: the unions and the left-wing nationalists wanted much more radical policies than the mainstream of Istiqlal. That, and the Israeli-Palestinian conflict, raised questions about future choices between the United States and the Soviet Union. The modernisation of the economy, and the stresses of war had brought women into the political and social arena, although the more conservative parts of the nationalist movement, and certainly the religious establishment had no enthusiasm for this. There were also powerful men in the countryside, through whom the French had ruled, and who were still needed as administrators and agents: they were nervous of the new political forces that might deprive them of their authority and wealth.

It was these contests that made Sidi Mohammed so crucial. He could mediate between the nationalist groups, he had clearly supported the education of women, but equally clearly he was a devout Muslim. By assuming the leadership of the colonial state he might reassure the rural qaids by reasserting bonds of patronage. Yet while he was called upon to stand above the political fray, and arbitrate between these various groups, he also had to join the fight for power on his own account, which would mean manipulating and coercing them as well. He was a political actor, and of necessity, sought access to the levers of power and force. These conflicting ties would be the fulcrum of the political balance after independence.

For the moment, of course, these problems were hidden by the general euphoria. On 18 November 1956 Sidi Mohammed made his first speech at a *Fête du Trône* in an independent state. Morocco, he said, had been reborn: 'Today we celebrate the Feast of the Throne that links us to our glorious past and the most brilliant epochs of our civilisation. Thus these three national festivals recall for us memories of glory, victory, rebirth and liberty.'[167]

Even so, the wars had not ceased, hot ones in Algeria and in the Arab East and cold ones on the ideological divide between capitalism and socialism. Inside Morocco, the new political leadership would soon be challenged by violence.

167 Mohammed V, 'The First Anniversary of the King's Return to Morocco' (Speech of November 18, 1956) in I. William Zartman (ed.), *Man, State, and Society in the Contemporary Maghreb* (London: Pall Mall Press, 1973), 113.

8

INDEPENDENCE

Just over a year after independence, Mehdi Ben Barka echoed the king's celebration of a glorious past by writing the preface to an academic book about the pre-colonial political structures of Morocco.[1] Mohamed Lahbabi's *Moroccan Government at the Dawn of the Twentieth Century* was no mere theoretical discussion; it was part of the political argument over what Morocco should become.[2] Morocco, unlike other newly-independent African states, was not a creation of colonial map-making, but a political entity that had existed long before colonialism. In regaining its independence, Lahbabi asked, what exactly was it regaining? In his opening paragraphs Lahbabi made his opinions very clear:

> In 1956 Morocco regained its sovereignty and independence. Now, after a long interruption, it has a truly Moroccan government which exercises power. It is proper to ask by what means Morocco has regained its independence, since the Protectorate had as its official aim to introduce the Moroccan state to a modern government and modern institutions. This aim was to be attained by the reform of the old Moroccan government, a reform which would result in making it more effective. The history of these past fifty years, while rich in both plans for reform and their completion, has not ended in the modernisation of the old Moroccan government. Quite the reverse, these reforms have served to eradicate the national government and effectively replace it with the government of a foreign state.
>
> Thus the reforms of the Protectorate had a result quite the opposite of the official aims. They have served, in reality, as a screen for the liquidation of Moroccan institutions, a screen which has been convenient both because of its effectiveness and because of its hidden nature.[3]

1 Mohamed Lahbabi, *Le Gouvernement marocain à l'aube du vingtième siècle*, 2nd edn (Rabat: Les Éditions Maghrébines, 1975).

2 Ernest Gellner, 'The Struggle for Morocco's Past', *Middle East Journal* 15 (1961): 79-90.

3 Lahbabi, *Le Gouvernement marocain*, 7.

Lahbabi argued that the Protectorate had introduced absolute monarchy into Morocco, and so betrayed the Treaty of Fez. The nature of Moroccan sovereignty had been changed, not preserved and strengthened. If Morocco were to be truly independent, the organisation of the state would have to be returned to its original bases. Lahbabi was no political Luddite. He did not seek to recreate the pre-colonial system of government; that had been sadly inadequate.[4] Instead he wanted to recover the sovereignty of the people. His argument was based on two theses: that there had always been a specifically Moroccan form of politics in which 'the Moroccan monarch is a Sultan, but he is also a Caliph', an idea that he sustained by adapting elements of classical Islamic orthodoxy to the Moroccan situation, and that the Caliphate in Morocco was a mission that was carried out through the exercise of defined and limited powers.[5]

The mission of the pre-colonial Sultan was to defend the law and the community. To do this correctly he would have to consult the *ʿulama* over matters of importance, and to make their *fatwas* the basis of his dahirs. 'The Sultan-Caliph is a "governor", not a legislator, nor *a fortiori* a constituent. What powers of government he has, are held through a sort of popular delegation in the Moroccan tradition'.[6] If this sultan did not carry out this mission, he could be deposed. These were ideas that the *ʿulama* of Tlemcen had expressed to Moulay Abderrahmane over a century before, but the institution of the *bayʿa* was now being used to justify popular sovereignty. Because the *bayʿa* was given by different communities acting independently, it was in effect a referendum, a plebiscite on the new government. Orthodox Islamic practice, which had underpinned the *bayʿas*, was now shown to contain the essence of an electoral system in which the authority of the community put limits on a sultan's power:

> The political events in Morocco which marked the years 1951-6, make the question of the 'sovereignty of the Sultan' more and more arguable and fragile. It is impossible, without the consent of the community, to impose a Sultan and a political system of 'full sovereignty for the Sultan' which can only be realised through the alienation of Moroccan sovereignty. It is, therefore, very difficult to deny the reality of popular sovereignty. The 'Sultan of Morocco' belongs to a very short period, and one

4 *Ibid.*, 182.

5 *Ibid.*, 27.

6 *Ibid.*, 39.

which has been superceded. He has given way to the 'Sultan of the Moroccans'.[7]

The role of the King

In his speech from the throne two days after his return from exile Muhammad V declared, 'Our first objective is the constitution of a Moroccan government that is responsible and representative.' Its mission would be to create 'democratic institutions through free elections, founded on the principle of the separation of powers, in the framework of a constitutional monarchy that recognises for Moroccans of every religious faith the rights of citizenship and the exercise of public and trade union freedoms.'[8] But this required, as both he and Lahbabi well understood, that the King step back from the political struggle and adopt at best the role of an arbitrator or mediator, or even a symbol. Yet the years leading up to independence had made the Sultan more than that, and as King, Mohammed V was the direct heir of the colonial state: the Protectorate had left no other political structures outside the palace and the network of rural and urban administrators. This was in fact closer to the reality of the pre-colonial system than Lahbabi might have wanted to avow: the monarch was both arbitrator and participant in the political struggle. That he was now a king, rather than a sultan, was an assertion of the modernisation of the Moroccan administrative system that gave him more power, not less.

To this had to be added the King's extraordinary personal charisma. Sidi Mohammed was extremely popular in Morocco. It was not just that he was the hero of the independence struggle because of his defiance of the French and his exile in Madagascar, nor that he was *amir al-muminin*, but because the two roles were contingent on each other: he was a hero because he was commander of the faithful, and commander of the faithful because he was the hero of independence.[9] In the struggle that followed that prestige was crucial, although the most urgent question was to take control of the institutions of force.

The levers of coercive power

Allal El-Fassi was a popular man too, who was cheered wherever

7 *Ibid.*, 67.

8 Quoted in Agnouche, *Histoire*, 310.

9 Hammoudi, *Master and Disciple*, 16-17.

he went.[10] Shortly after independence, he wrote: 'There are only three powers in Morocco: the first is the Istiqlal, the second power is that of the Army of Liberation and the third is that of the palace. And if we consider that the Army of Liberation derives its strength from the Party and belongs to it, there are really only two powers: Istiqlal and the Palace or the throne.'[11]

He was not wrong that Istiqlal and the palace were the two main contenders for power, but his assessment of the balance of power was no more than bravado, or wishful thinking. Istiqlal did not control the Army of Liberation, the only organised military force in Moroccan hands, and certainly not the multitude of independent rural guerrilla units and urban terrorist groups that knew no logic beyond violence. In the spring and early summer of 1956 it was hard to distinguish between political violence and criminality. Some targets were clearly political: members of El Glaoui's family and entourage and local leaders of both the Istiqlal and Ouazzani's PDI were killed in Fez and Kénitra. Other arguments between terrorist groups melded into turf disputes between racketeering gunslingers. In Casablanca the Black Crescent fought with mobsters.[12]

There was no police force or army to stop them. Instead, party militias posed as police – Ben Barka set up the Istiqlali *Shabab Nizam* (Youth of Order), rightly believing that a police force was a central element of power.[13] Sidi Mohammed thought so too, and in May decreed a Moroccan police force and named as Director of the Sûreté Nationale Mohamed Laghzaoui, one of the most important financiers of the Istiqlal during the independence struggle. But Laghzaoui had never been a member of the executive committee and he was close to the palace. The policemen came mainly from the old colonial police force, together with some former guerrillas. With the help of French 'advisors', the new Moroccan security service began dismantling the urban terrorist network.[14]

The Royal Armed Forces were set up in the same way. Ahmed Réda Guédira, one of the founders of the Roosevelt Club, and

10 *Ibid.*, 16-17, 129.

11 Quoted in Darif, *al-Ahzab*, 85.

12 Douglas E. Ashford, *Political Change in Morocco* (Princeton University Press, 1961), 162-3; Daoud and Monjib, *Ben Barka*, 170-1.

13 Daoud and Monjib, *Ben Barka*, 171-2; Ashford, *Political Change*, 162.

14 Ashford, *Political Change*, 163-4; Majdi Majid, *Les luttes de classes au Maroc depuis l'Indépendance*, (Rotterdam: Editions Hiwar, *1987*), 14; Waterbury, *Commander*, 84.

another figure close to the palace, became the first Minister of Defence. The first Chief-of-Staff was Crown Prince Hassan. Moroccan officers in the colonial armies provided the core: Brigadier-General Ben Hamou Kettani, the highest-ranking Moroccan officer in the French army, General Mohamed Ben Mizian, his equal in the Spanish army, and Major Mohammed Oufkir were prominent among them.[15] Because of the way in which the colonial forces had been made up, these senior officers were drawn from a particular social group: most were from the families of notables, particularly rural qaids, and many were of Berber origin. They had little in common with the urban middle-class Arab nationalists. By relying on such men and placing them directly under the authority of the Crown Prince, the army was, at one and the same time, placed above the political struggle, and the palace was allied with alternative structures of power.[16] There was a strong Berber presence among the 14,000 troops who hurriedly assembled for the first parade on 14 May 1956 since most of them came from the colonial forces, along with some units of the Army of Liberation. The latter's military leaders (such as Abdallah Sanhaji) and its political spokesmen (Dr el-Khatib and Mahjoubi Aherdane) had declared that they were loyal only to Sidi Mohammed and would lay down arms only on his instructions. When he gave those instructions, most of the fighters obeyed. By the end of July, 10,000 former members of the Army of Liberation had trekked down to Rabat.[17]

It took rather longer for the Army of Liberation to be completely extinguished as a military force. Only two important military leaders of the Army of Liberation, '*al-Faqih*' Mohammed Basri and Hassan el-Araj, openly lined up with Istiqlal, but plenty of others wanted to carry on fighting, for the liberation of Morocco was not, they believed, complete. One group moved southwards, gathering support along the way, and became the Army for the Liberation of the Sahara. It intended to attack the Spanish army in Ifni, Tarfaya and the Western Sahara, but first it linked up with anti-French forces in Mauritania.[18]

15 I. William Zartman, *Morocco: Problems of New Power* (New York: Atherton Press, 1964), 65-8; Daoud and Monjib, *Ben Barka*, 170; Ashford, *Political Change*, 180; M'Barek, *Résistance*, 135.

16 Hammoudi, *Master and Disciple*, 25-6.

17 Daoud and Monjib, *Ben Barka*, 174; Ashford, *Political Change*, 175; M'Barek, *Résistance*, 116; Zartman, *Problems*, 72-4.

18 Ashford, *Political Change*, 176-7; M'Barek, *Résistance*, 122; Hodges, *Western Sahara*, 75-6; Trout, *Frontiers*, 419; Daoud and Monjib, *Ben Barka*, 177-8.

Allal El-Fassi and Ben Barka claimed to speak for the Army for the Liberation of the Sahara, and even though this was little more than opportunism, the Army and Istiqlal did have similar territorial ambitions. In April 1956 El-Fassi told *Le Monde* that Moroccan territory should include Mauritania, a good part of Algeria and even Mali. In June he proclaimed that while Morocco was independent it was not completely unified. There still remained 'Tangier, the Sahara from Tindouf to Colomb-Béchar, Touat, Kenadza, Mauritania. [...] The frontiers of Morocco end in the south at Saint Louis-du-Sénégal!' In July *Al-Alam*, the party newspaper, published a map showing just those frontiers. Mehdi Ben Barka was more circumspect, and preached support for the Algerian Front de Libération Nationale (FLN) with which he had good contacts; FLN units operated from Moroccan territory.[19]

The first targets of the Army for the Liberation of the Sahara were the French posts around Tindouf in Algeria and the iron workings at Zouerate (Fort Gourade) in Mauritania. Spanish territory provided a safe haven since the Spanish generals had so few troops that they were reluctant to fight.[20] In July 1957 the ill-equipped Spanish army was dragged in anyway when French troops began hot pursuit into Spanish territory. In November the Liberation Army responded by invading Ifni and the following month Spanish troops retreated to a defensive perimeter around Sidi Ifni town, a dusty, flyblown place with no port and a virtually unserviceable airfield. There they stayed for the next twelve years. Spanish troops did regain control over most of the Sahara, helped by the French army and the weather. A terrible drought broke the back of Sahraoui resistance when the Liberation Army failed to supply their local volunteers with water.[21]

It was only when the Liberation Army of the Sahara had crumbled that the Royal Moroccan army was able to step in. In April 1958 the Spanish government handed over the southern province of Tarfaya, although Oufkir turned up late to the actual ceremony because he thought it necessary to argue with Spanish commanders about his route into Tantan. General Ben Mizian received the hand-over alone.[22]

19 Trout, *Frontiers*, 416-19; Daoud and Monjib, *Ben Barka* 167, 172; Hodges, *Western Sahara*, 85-6, from which El-Fassi's remarks are quoted.

20 Hodges, *Western Sahara*, 75-6; Rafael Casas de la Vega, *La Ultima Guerra de Africa* (*Campaña de Ifni-Sáhara*) ([Madrid]: Servicio de Publicaciones del Estado mayor del Ejército, 1985), 78-9, 91.

21 Hodges, *Western Sahara*, 79-81.

22 Casas de la Vega, *Ultima Guerra*, 538; Zartman, *Problems*, 84-5.

The entrenchment of Istiqlal

Istiqlal's popularity was not swamped by its loss of the levers of force. It certainly managed to hold off the challenge of other political rivals. Ouazzani's Parti Démocratique de l'Indépendance might have been a serious problem: it grew fast in the first months of independence, setting up branches across the country, even in country districts, and by the end of 1956 had more than 150,000 members. It played on local resentment at the flood of Istiqlali officials descending on the countryside.[23]

In October 1956 Istiqlal successfully defended itself by persuading the King to give it more posts in the coalition government, including the Interior Ministry, and to promise to hold elections at an unspecified date. This was a useful vagueness, since it gave the party's leaders time to organise. On the left wing, Mehdi Ben Barka, whom Sidi Mohammed appointed president of an interim National Consultative Assembly, built support in the trade unions and student organisations and took the opportunity to make dramatic gestures, like his voluntary work project to build the Route de l'Unité, a road linking Taounate in the former French zone with Ketama in the old Spanish zone.[24] On the party's right wing, the more conservative ministers had time to entrench themselves in control of the state.

None of this pleased Istiqlal's opponents. 'People were becoming afraid of the Istiqlal party', the qadi of Bzu remembered, nearly twenty years later, 'because if the Istiqlal said someone was against them, the man might be dead soon after'.[25] Members of the PDI complained that they were harassed, arrested and even murdered by government agents. In January 1957 Mohamed Hassan Ouazzani wrote to the King, saying that things had been no worse under the French.[26]

Then, in October 1957, the historic leaders of the Liberation Army, Dr el-Khatib and Mahjoubi Aherdane, tried to set up a third party, the Mouvement Populaire. They drew on the Army's supporters in the countryside and the Berber areas, people who had little in common with the urban middle class Arab nationalists who dominated Istiqlal. Istiqlali officials used one legal fiddle after another to prevent them from registering their party until, in

23 Darif, *al-Ahzab*, 91-2; Waterbury, *Commander*, 234.

24 Daoud and Monjib, *Ben Barka*, 158-62.

25 Eickelman, *Knowledge and Power*, 160.

26 Darif, *al-Ahzab*, 93-4; Daoud and Monjib, *Ben Barka*, 157; Zartman *Problems*, 17.

April 1958, the non-Istiqlali members of the government and the Prime Minister, Bekkaï, resigned in protest.[27]

In the new government, Istiqlal took virtually all the ministries and Ahmed Belafrej, the General Secretary, became Prime Minister.[28] Even Ahmed Réda Guédira lost his job. The full power of the state was now turned on Istiqlal's opponents. The PDI's newspapers were banned, and leaders of the Mouvement Populaire were arrested after an emotional demonstration over the reburial of their hero Abbès Messaâdi, one of the military leaders of the Liberation Army. Rumour had it that Ben Barka had murdered him, which he did not deny, merely saying that the death was 'the result of the laws of the underground struggle'.[29]

Rural rebellions

Whether or not Ben Barka was involved it handed a political opportunity to the palace. The murder caused fury in the Rif, which was already caught in a deep economic crisis, caused partly by very low rainfall, but mainly by the aftermath of independence. The border with Algeria was closed, so emigration was no longer easy; there was no colonial army to enlist in and economic integration with the rest of Morocco pushed up prices. Above all, there was resentment at Istiqlal which monopolised the administrative posts and filled them with outsiders who spoke Arabic and French, not Berber or Spanish. At the time of the ceremonial reburial of Abbès Messaâdi, Istiqlal offices were attacked and rebels occupied the town of Al Hoceima. The rebels demanded the return of Muhammad bin Abd al-Karim and as a corollary that all foreign troops leave Morocco, American as well as Spanish.

Prince Hassan took time to prepare his men but when he did move, in late 1958, it was with great ferocity. Using 20,000 troops, some of whom made an amphibious landing at Al Hoceima, he crushed the rebellion. The only winner was Prince Hassan, since Istiqlal lost all influence in the Rif.[30] A similar set of resentments against Istiqlal in the Tafilalt, lacking only the murder of a popular hero, had led Addi ou Bihi, the governor of the province, to

27 Darif, *al-Ahzab*, 112; Waterbury, *Commander*, 238; Daoud and Monjib, *Ben Barka*, *193*.

28 Zartman, *Problems*, *20;* Daoud and Monjib, *Ben Barka, 193.*

29 Daoud and Monjib, *Ben Barka*, 173-5 according to which the original phrase was: '*Hadha Khad li les lois de la clandestinité.*'

30 Zartman, *Problems*, 87-01; Hart, *Aith Waryaghar*, 428-43; Daoud and Monjib, *Ben Barka*, 205-7; Seddon, *Moroccan Peasants*, 176-81.

rebel in 1957 with what some said was the secret encouragement of the palace. This rebellion was also crushed by Prince Hassan's army.[31] In both cases rebellion had the dual effect of strengthening the power of the palace and breaking that of the Istiqlal in rural Morocco.

The economics of independence

The third element in the undermining of Istiqlal was economic. French rule had left the legacy of a rich economic infrastructure. In 1953 exports and imports totalled over 9 million tonnes, more than ten times what they had been in 1923; there were 1,600 km. of railway track and 15,000 km. of all-weather roads; the huge port at Casablanca handled 84% of trade.[32] Some of the exports were agricultural, the product of 35,000 ha. of irrigated land, although another 246,000 acres could have been irrigated from all the dams the French had built.[33] The other major export was minerals: nearly 4 million tonnes of phosphates alone in 1952.[34] This was a valuable legacy, and in 1978 King Hassan would write in his autobiography, 'Those who assert that in the years between 1910 and 1935, "France turned Morocco into an underdeveloped country" know perfectly well that they are lying.'[35]

Yet the inheritance was very unequally distributed. French colonial rule had created great discrepancies. There was a tiny educated elite, for instance, and a vast illiterate mass. In 1959 89% of Moroccans were illiterate, and only two women in a hundred knew how to read and write. It was hard to change this: since only 0.6% of Moroccans had anything better than a primary education, who could teach? Every year another 50,000 were added to those who should have been in school, but, in 1959, less than 35% of them actually were.[36]

The same tiny elite scooped the economic spoils of independence. About half a million Moroccan families had no land at all, and many struggled to survive on tiny unirrigated plots of less than 4 ha. The rich owned the good land: nearly 6,000

31 Rémy Leveau, *Le fellah marocain – défenseur du trône*, 2nd edn (Paris: Presses de la Fondation Nationale des Sciences Politiques, 1985), 24; Waterbury, *Commander*, 236-7; Zartman *Problems* 79-82; Hammoudi, 19.

32 Stewart, *Economy*, 149, 152, 159.

33 Swearingen, *Mirages*, 140-1.

34 Stewart, *Economy*, 123.

35 Hassan II, *Challenge*, 90.

36 Daoud and Monjib, *Ben Barka*, 222.

Europeans and 1,700 Moroccans had 1.3 million acres between them.

The Europeans' land was not appropriated, for no government wanted to exacerbate both the flight of capital and French farmers; it was bad enough anyway – 200,000 of the 500,000 Europeans left between 1956 and 1960.[37] And no government wanted to redistribute the land of rich Moroccans unless they were political enemies, like the Glaouis. Omar Abdeljalil, the Istiqlali Minister for Agriculture for the first eighteen months of independence, was himself a large landowner. Even the left-wing Ibrahim government that came to power in 1958 limited land redistribution to state land. Even then, the civil service was able to ensure that only a small area was distributed and that those who did get land had the usufruct only, not the full title.[38]

For its part, the palace saw a stable rural landowning class as one of the essential foundations of its authority in the countryside, particularly if those landowners could be made dependant upon the patronage of the palace. So investment in the countryside, largely financed by foreign loans, was used as a way of distributing rural favours.[39] Istiqlal's effort at rural reform, *Opération Labour* (Operation Plough) in 1957, was supposedly designed to make Moroccan small-holdings more productive, but in reality was an attempt to extend government authority. Small-holdings were joined into bigger units that would be ploughed by government tractors and sowed with crops prescribed by the Ministry of Agriculture. The scheme was to be self-financing: loans would be free in the first year but then had to be paid back. This failed. As ever, part of the problem was the climate. The weather was abysmal in the first year, when floods and frost brought down yields, and rainfall slightly lower than average in the next two years.

But the worst problem was that the plan was ill-conceived, authoritarian and badly run. Fertilisers were not used, or were of the wrong type, and corruption led to seeds being sold rather than distributed.[40]

37 Johan Beyen *et al.*, *The Economic Development of Morocco: Report of a Mission Organized by the International Bank for Reconstruction and Development at the Request of the Government of Morocco* (Baltimore: Johns Hopkins University Press, 1966), 15; Jean-Paul Azam and Christian Morrisson, *The Political Feasibility of Adjustment in Côte d'Ivoire and Morocco* (Paris: OECD, 1994), 86.

38 Swearingen, *Mirages*, 142-6; Zartman *Problems*, 119-52.

39 Hammoudi, *Master and Disciple*, 25, 30.

40 Swearingen, *Mirages*, 149-51, 184.

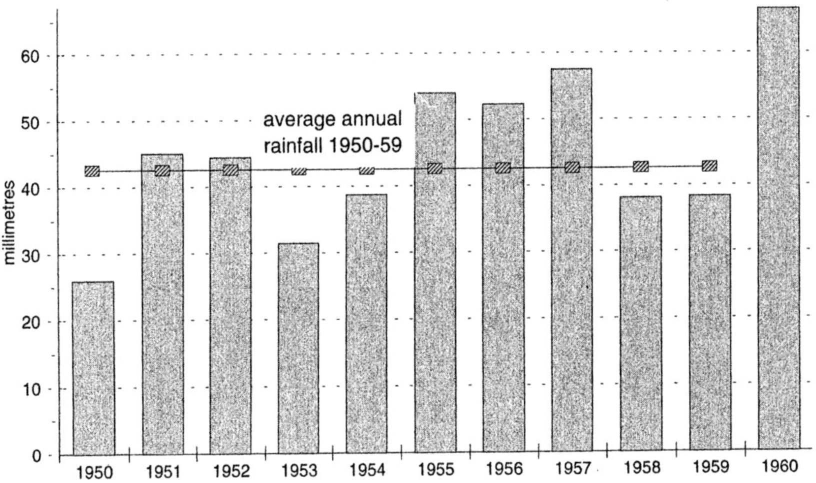

RAINFALL IN CASABLANCA, 1950-1960

Source: National Climatic Data Centre.

Istiqlal undermined

Despite such failures, Istiqlal was still a powerful force. Allal El-Fassi was immensely popular and Ben Barka moved across the world stage, making much of his contacts with the Algerian FLN and Néo-Destour, the Tunisian nationalist party. Inside Morocco, too, he set the pace. As President of the Assembly he organised a commission to investigate the origin of collaborators' fortunes. In August 1958, the commission named 170 qaids and other former officials, whose property was confiscated, either in whole or in part. They included Abdelhay El Kittani, Khaled El Raisuni, Hajj Mohammed El Mokri and several members of the Glaoui family.[41]

This had great popular appeal, but the radicals did not control the government. They demanded 'democratisation of the institutions', by which they meant elections, limits on royal power, and an end to the US bases, but they got none of it. The Belafrej government needed US economic aid ($50 million was granted in 1958), so it could not close the bases, which in any case provided

41 Daoud and Monjib, *Ben Barka*, 193-4; Ouardighi, *La Grande Crise*, 147-53 gives a full list of those whose property was confiscated.

other local benefits – education, help with municipal services and flood relief – and put money into the regional economy.[42] Even local elections were too much for the government, which feared that its candidates might lose. The Palace would not relinquish control of the army and police.

The Union Marocain du Travail (UMT) was dissatisfied too. Since it had always supported Istiqlal, it now expected benefits for its members, but it did not get them. Within weeks of the inauguration of the Belafrej government, the first that Istiqlal clearly controlled, the UMT had organised a general strike in Rabat, over the sacking of workers in a carpet factory. By the autumn of 1958 there were strikes across Morocco.[43]

The king encouraged the Istiqlal to split by supporting the left. On 24 December 1958 he appointed Abdallah Ibrahim, the union leader, as prime minister. Allal El-Fassi retired to Tanger in disgust, but the new government was not as radical as it appeared. Supporters of the palace were given the security ministries and Mehdi Ben Barka remained excluded. On 25 January 1959 Ben Barka resigned from the party executive and formed the National Confederation of the Istiqlal Party which he hoped would renew the Istiqlal. It drew most of its supporters from the big cities: Casablanca, Marrakesh and the capital. Ben Barka denied that this was a split: he called it a 'clarification and a reconversion', an attempt to transform the Istiqlal into a 'structured, homogeneous party, capable of playing a role in the execution of the work of reconstruction'. These were mere words. The old guard – Allal El-Fassi and others – refused to be homogenised and restructured. Instead, they set up their own autonomous trade unions to compete with the UMT. Almost simultaneously, in February 1959, the Mouvement Populaire was finally registered as a legal political party, and in September the split on the left was completed with the establishment of a new party, the Union Nationale des Forces Populaires (UNFP).[44]

Ben Barka still insisted that this was *not* a party but a 'Union' and its inaugural congress was held under the misleading slogan '*la hizbatiyya ba'da al-yawm*' ('from today on, no party spirit'). The first secretariat included men from the Mouvement Populaire, the PDI and even from the old *Munazzama al-Sirriyya* (Secret

42 Blair, *Western Window*, 252-64.

43 Daoud and Monjib, *Ben Barka*, 199-203; Waterbury, *Commander*, 186-7; Leveau, *Le fellah marocain*, 40-2.

44 Daoud and Monjib, *Ben Barka*, 215-20; Waterbury, *Commander*, 188, 243.

Organisation), the guerrilla group with which *al-Fqih* Basri had fought the French. Abdallah Ibrahim and several ministers joined too, so that the government was now led by the UNFP, not Istiqlal, though its authority was no greater than before. Indeed it was less, for now that the national movement had divided, the palace had even more influence.

MOROCCO'S PLACE IN THE WORLD

In the years immediately following independence the dualities of the colonial period were displayed in different ways. The internal political struggle saw the palace simultaneously continuing the active political role that it had taken up during the independence struggle, adopting the role of neutral arbitrator positioned above the political fray while exercising influence through patronage and coercion, and taking on the mantle of the successor to the colonial state. The nationalist movement, particularly Istiqlal, disintegrated, unable to coordinate its urban middle-class base with its supporters in the trade union movement or to extend its influence very far into rural Morocco.

Yet these conflicting pressures were not just internal. International circumstances imposed new demands that pulled the Moroccan political actors in different directions. Since independence did not break reliance on foreign landowners and foreign aid, there were great limitations on the government's diplomatic freedom of action.

The Israeli-Palestinian conflict and the Moroccan Jews

The extent of these limitations was shown in July 1956 when Nasser nationalised the Suez Canal, and made himself a popular hero across the Arab world. The Moroccan government broke off relations with France when British and French forces invaded Egypt. Accordingly, French aid came to a halt. When the US government condemned the invasion, that bolstered Sidi Mohammed's instinctive pro-American feelings, for the King had no sympathy for communism. But the United States was also the main ally of the state of Israel, and that caused problems.[45]

Neither the King nor the leadership of Istiqlal was anti-Jewish. The left wing had good contacts with the World Jewish Congress and many Moroccan Jews supported Istiqlal. David Azoulay and other Jews formed a special group, al-Wifaq, with allies of Mehdi

45 Blair, *Western Window*, 204-5.

Ben Barka.[46] There was a Jewish minister, Léon Benzaquen, in the first government and several young Jews with university degrees had important jobs in the administration. A Jew was a director of the National Irrigation Office, another was rector of the science faculty in Rabat. When Mohamed Laghzaoui was director of the Office Chérifien des Phosphates, one of his closest aides, Abraham Serfaty, was Jewish; Salomon Azoulay was a member of the Consultative Council of the Supreme Court and another Jew was a judge in the same court. Many Jews, such as David Amar the leader of the Conseil de Communautés Juives du Maroc, identified closely with the King.[47] One, Charles Bensimhon, wrote:

> The Jews, be they of Berber origin or those who came to [Morocco] in search of refuge all consider this country as theirs. There are several strong bonds which attach us to this land: the mother country, the fertile soil, or families and friends, the climate and the familiar horizons. [...] More than the native soil ... one single sentiment which we cherish in our hearts is the deep love for Muhammad V.[48]

Yet this was the voice of the elite, and many other Jews made quiet plans to leave.[49] The government tried to stop them. It had no desire to lose people who were economically necessary nor to provide troops for the Israeli army, and within four months of independence it closed down the offices of Cadima, the Israeli migration organisation. The political director of the Interior Ministry told the World Jewish Congress that the government preferred having 250,000 Jews inside Morocco to 70 million Muslims complaining about their emigration.[50] But the same government also wanted to join the United Nations and needed American aid, and when Benzaquen threatened to resign over the emigration issue, the cabinet split and the King decided to let the people already in the transit camps leave.[51]

After Morocco joined the Arab League in 1958, migration became difficult again, and Mossad began a secret campaign to smuggle Jews out through the Spanish enclaves and Gibraltar, some

46 Laskier, *Twentieth Century*, 168-77.

47 Armand Lévy, *Il'était une fois les juifs marocains* (Paris: L'Harmattan, 1995), 146-7; Laskier, *Twentieth Century*, 191; Waterbury, *Commander*, 127-8.

48 Quoted in Laskier, *Twentieth Century*, 188.

49 *Ibid.*, 170.

50 *Ibid.*, 195.

51 *Ibid.*, 181-5, 192.

by night on ships. It was dangerous: forty-two migrants died when the boat *Pisces* taking migrants from Al Hoceima bay to Gibraltar capsized in January 1961. Between 1957 and 1961 Mossad took nearly 18,000 Jews out of Morocco. By 1960 a Jewish community that had numbered over 211,000 in 1947 was reduced to around 162,000.[52] Not all of them went to Israel: at least 30,000 settled in France, the United States and Canada, and in the future they would come to have considerable influence in diplomatic dealings between Morocco and Israel.[53]

The war in Algeria

Suez was not the only problem that disturbed the relationship with Paris. The Algerian struggle was a popular cause in Morocco, supported by Ben Barka and the left wing of Istiqlal, but also by Ouazzani's PDI. In the summer of 1956 the UMT threatened to strike in support of their Algerian comrades.[54] The King sympathised too, and in October 1956 he sent a plane to carry Ahmed Ben Bella, leader of the Front de Liberation Nationale (FLN), from Tunis to Morocco but French security services forced the plane to land in Algeria and kidnapped him. That provided another reason to break off diplomatic relations.[55]

As early as July 1956 the French army had closed the frontier to try to prevent the FLN from using Morocco as a base. That turned the line of French posts between Figuig and Tarfaya into the *de facto* border and even though the new Moroccan government did not recognise it, there was not much it could do to change it. In May 1958 Rabat agreed to freeze the frontier as it stood, and there it remained.[56]

The Algerian FLN ignored the frontier. Moroccan territory provided a refuge for fighters from *Wilaya V*, the FLN's military district in western Algeria, that was run from 1957 onwards by Colonel Houari Boumedienne, with the same dour efficiency he would later show as President of Algeria. The FLN recruited in the refugee camps that were filled with those who had fled '*regroupement*', the French policy of filling huge concentration camps with

52 *Ibid.*, 204, 218-30; Bensimon, *Hassan II*, 86-106; Baroudi, *Maroc*, 45.

53 Bensimon, *Hassan II*, 214.

54 Ashford, *Political Change*, 318.

55 Alistair Horne, *A Savage War of Peace: Algeria 1954-1962* (London: Macmillan, 1977), 158-61; Hassan II, *La Mémoire*, 83.

56 Waterbury, *Commander*, 54, 175; Trout, *Frontiers*, 420-5; Hassan II, *La Mémoire*, 42.

Algerian peasants, who became very hungry, and thus willing recruits. Even though King Hassan later insisted that the Algerians always behaved correctly on Moroccan territory, the Moroccan government could not control them, since the Royal Armed Forces did not take up positions along the eastern frontier near Oujda until 1958. After the Algiers coup destroyed the Fourth French Republic and brought General de Gaulle to power, there were rumours that the French army would re-invade; the Moroccan army could not have stopped them if they had.[57] For all the declarations of friendship between Morocco and France that had marked independence, international relations between the two states had got off to a rocky start.

The Cold War

Pulled by conflicting alliances with America and France, all the governments in the first years of independence tried to steer a course between the Western and Eastern blocs. Yet non-alignment was impossible, not only because of international tensions but because of the rivalries of Moroccan politicians. Réda Guédira and other members of the old Roosevelt Club supported the United States, while their enemies on the left attacked the US military bases. Nationalist feelings ran high after rumours spread that US marines had used Nouasseur base as a staging post on the way to intervene in the brief civil war in Lebanon in July 1958. The UMT threatened a general strike and the PDI attacked the Istiqlal for doing nothing to stop such an infringement on sovereignty.[58]

The Belafrej government and its successors could not square the circle. They could not disavow nationalism, but they needed US economic aid.[59] The palace was just as torn. The King was fundamentally pro-American but his son Hassan, who was Chief of Staff of the Moroccan army, resented the refusal of the US Naval Attaché ever to meet him, ostensibly because he had 'kept the Sixth Fleet waiting for three hours'. There was certainly a strong anti-monarchist feeling in the American embassy.[60] Prince Hassan might have been happy to see the number of bases reduced, since that would boost his nationalist credentials, but he did not want it to happen at once, or to see many bases closed at the

57 Horne, *Savage War*, 221, 225, 228, 325-9; Hassan II, *La Mémoire*, 83; Zartman, *Problems*, 44, 93.

58 Quoted in Zartman, *Problems*, 44.

59 Blair, *Western Window*, 223; Ashford, *Political Change*, 316.

60 Blair, *Western Window.*, 243, which reproduces the quotation.

same time. He had his wish. In late 1959 the Pentagon lost patience with the interminable negotiations and announced that it would evacuate the air bases, but not the naval base at Kénitra, within five years.[61]

The triumph of the palace

Crown Prince Hassan was able to present himself, quite reasonably, as the man who had negotiated an end to the bases, and so stole the nationalist parties' clothes. It was the culmination of half a decade in which political power and popularity shifted decisively towards the Palace.

Independence had come without a constitution, an elected assembly, or any legal way to check the power of government. While Istiqlal dominated that government, it had made very little effort to change any of this. But with his unchallengeable personal prestige, Sidi Mohammed and his son had created state institutions that were independent of Istiqlal's control, the army and police force, and thus made sure that Istiqlal did not govern alone. Unlike many newly-independent countries in Africa, Morocco did not become a one-party state. The palace became powerful by arbitrating the disputes of lesser institutions and indeed by making many of them, such as the Mouvement Populaire or the Guédira group, into its political clients. Even the UNFP was dependent on the King. When Ibrahim became Prime Minister in December 1958, dedicated followers of self-interest shifted their allegiance to the new party, because Mohammed V seemed to favour it. Since this weakened the Istiqlal, it suited the needs of the palace.[62]

Putting the UNFP in power also helped to tame its radicals. They now exercised responsibilities that they could not handle, and had to take decisions that they did not like. These left-wingers presided over the repression of former comrades who had not been tamed. In September 1959 Ibrahim banned the Communist Party; in December *Fqih* Mohammed Basri and Abderrahmane Youssoufi, the editor of the UNFP newspaper, were arrested and the paper banned under the new press code. An editorial had said that the government should be responsible to public opinion, and for this they were charged with giving offence to the King, disturbing public order, incitement to crime and undermining the security of the state. Both were released within six months,

61 *Ibid.*, 252-64.

62 Waterbury, *Commander*, 217-18.

but the warning was clear enough. In January 1960 Mehdi Ben Barka was harassed into voluntary exile.[63]

Then, on 29 February 1960, an earthquake destroyed three-quarters of Agadir and killed between 10-12,000 people. Prince Hassan took charge – somewhat ruthlessly, since he ordered that looters be shot. But he was extremely efficient at having the dead buried and the city cordoned off, and with American help he set about relief work. American troops arrived within a day and aid poured in from private sources in the United States, flown in US navy planes.[64] But the goodwill was quickly wasted because of the way in which the US air force handled the evacuation of the bases. It did not notify the Moroccan government exactly when it was leaving the base at Boulhaut before it departed on 4 March, and on 22 June the garrison left the air defence headquarters at Rabat unannounced, so that Moroccan forces walked into empty buildings the next day.

The Ibrahim government could not profit by these gaffes, because it was out of office. In May 1960, when the Prime Minister tried to bring the Sûreté Nationale under his control, the King sacked him, made himself Prime Minister, and appointed Crown Prince Hassan as his deputy and Minister of Defence. The rest of the ministers were 'independents' – King's men – and tame members of the Istiqlal. The issue was not just security. Morocco's very first elections, for local councils, were days away and the palace was worried that the left might win too many votes.

Even so, the UNFP took 23% of the seats and did well in Casablanca and Rabat. Istiqlal won about 40% of the seats, mainly in the old cities like Fez and Meknès and in parts of the countryside. The Mouvement Populaire won 7%. It was an imperfect poll, and badly organised, but it was the first time that anyone had ever asked Moroccans who should govern them and around three quarters of them expressed an opinion. In some of the big cities more women turned out than men and fourteen women even stood as candidates, though not one was elected.[65]

In any event it was no triumph for the men of the Palace.

63 Abdelaziz Bennani and Abdellah Eloualladi, *Liberté de presse et de l'information au Maroc – limites et perspectives* (Rabat: Organisation Marocaine des Droits de l' Homme, 1995), 137-8; Daoud and Monjib, *Ben Barka*, 238-45.

64 Blair, *Western Window*, 271-7; K . Brown and A Lakhsassi, 'Every Man's Disaster – the Earthquake of Agadir: a Berber (Tashelhit) Poem', *Maghreb Review* 5, nos 5-6 (1980): 125-33.

65 Bernabé López-García, *Procesos electorales en Marruecos (1960-1977)* (Madrid: CSIC, 1979), 13-15; Waterbury, *Commander*, 219-20; Daoud, *Féminisme*, 262.

Indeed, the US State Department concluded that the regime would soon collapse. Desperate for support, the King gave an interview to an American magazine in September entitled 'Why I like Americans', and General Kettani offered all sorts of facilities to the United States navy in exchange for training. Crown Prince Hassan told an American diplomat that he wanted to 'hold the reins' in Africa to prevent 'communists' from taking over and asked for warplanes with which to do it.[66] He did not get them because he continued to talk of non-alignment, so in November Prince Hassan turned to the Soviet government which agreed to supply MiG-17 fighters, Ilyushin bombers and other equipment with which to start the Moroccan air force. The Cold War had provided a new friend, albeit a temporary one.[67]

These diplomatic wrangles were far removed from the concerns of most Moroccans – if indeed they heard of them. For them the Agadir earthquake had been a much more immediate disaster. The metaphorical aftershock inspired a Berber poet in a desert oasis 320 km. south of the ruined city to muse upon its deeper meaning. For him it was the end of the world, a tragedy that respected neither religion, wealth, gender nor age. It was a sign of God's omnipotence. The government was not even mentioned: it was not part of the picture.

REFRAIN
Praise be to God, the exalted
Whenever you come-O

Agadir has been destroyed.
Woe

All those who were there
They hadn't accomplished their ambitions,
Arab and Berber,
Whoever had entered it
Jews died
And Muslims, with a curse,
Children ***died***

Destruction is like a wadi.
Time, it gets up and leaves.

Buried in it someone's thousands.
They died, all the people, none escaped.

The tribe, totally obliterated.
Nothing was finished,

66 Blair, *Western Window*, 281-5.

67 *Ibid.*, 287-290.

No one escaped it.
Never again would get out.
And Christians too on that day,
And those who were righteous.
And women too on that day.

A few days short of a year later, a single death had an equally emotional impact, one that also transcended politics.[68] On 26 February 1961 Mohammed V died unexpectedly during very minor surgery on his nose. Over the previous twenty years this man had become a national hero, a symbol of Morocco even to his critics. Sidi Mohammed's face had been seen in the moon. His political legacy to his son Hassan was not easy, for his was a hard act to follow.

68 K. Brown and A. Lakhsassi, 'Every Man's Disaster the Earthquake of Agadir: a Berber (Tashelhit) Poem', *Maghreb Review*, 5, 5-6 (1980), 125-33.

9

KINGSHIP

Within hours of Sidi Mohammed's death, male members of the Alaoui family assembled to swear allegiance to his son. One was el-Amine, last surviving son of the first Hassan, who had died more than half a century earlier. Another aged uncle, Moulay Uthman, the Khalifa of Fez, collapsed and died almost immediately after performing his last act of loyalty.[1] The senior members of the Alaoui family were now very old, but the new King was only thirty-one. A younger generation was taking power, and without a rival brother, cousin or uncle to trouble the succession. Although Sidi Mohammed's death was unexpected, the transition had been well prepared.

The new king took care that there should be no striking break with the past. A month after he came to the throne, he appointed new qaids in the countryside, men who had already been approved by his father. He explained to the press that 'it would have been a great wrong to reexamine their candidatures and so, knowing the care that had been given to drawing up the list, He had affixed His seal to the dahir with His eyes closed, trusting in the choices of His August Father.'[2]

Tradition legitimised King Hassan and he consciously emphasised his religious authority and responsibility. For the first years of his reign, the King rode a white horse every Friday to the mosque to lead the community in prayer. Later he found other ways to exercise his religious role. During Ramadan, he instituted the Hassanian Lectures – a series given by religious scholars from across the Islamic world, as well as prominent Moroccan figures. The king presided over each lecture.[3]

The same tradition glorified the Alaoui family. Five months after he came to power, he held a triple marriage for his sisters

1 *Le Petit Marocain*, 28 Feb. 1961.

2 *Ibid.*, 23 March 1961.

3 *Hassanian Lectures, Lectures on Topics Related to the Exegesis of the Quran and the Tradition and Delivered before HM King Hassan II over the Holy Month of Ramadan of 1407 AH (1987)* ([Rabat]: Ministry of Waqfs and Islamic Affairs, 1408/1988).

Lalla Fatima Zohra, Lalla Aïcha and Lalla Malika. This was a splendid event with which to open his reign, and because it also included fifty ordinary Moroccan couples who were marrying at the same time,[4] the ceremony emphasised the links between the King and his subjects. The same notion was expressed every year at the 'Id al-Kabir, when King Hassan assembled the most important people of the capital city and, dressed in a white jellaba, prayed and then slaughtered a ram. The ritual was then repeated by the governor of each province, and then by the head of each family.[5] The King was thus brought symbolically into each household. On other occasions his subjects came to him. Every March, on the anniversary of his accession, delegates from all over the country formally renewed their *bay'as* of allegiance, and foreign ambassadors presented their compliments.[6]

Such ceremonies were religious and political, domestic and national: they bound courtiers, local and national politicians, and scholars into personal loyalty to the King who, as the constitutions declared, is Commander of the Faithful and whose male descendants are to rule Morocco after him. Yet the same constitutions declared that sovereignty resides in the people, that the judiciary is separate from the executive, that men and women are equal citizens before the law, and human rights are to be guaranteed. There was nothing un-Islamic about these provisions – those who proposed the sovereignty of the *umma* in early nineteenth-century Tlemcen would have had no difficulty identifying with their spirit.

Symbols were not enough. The formal legitimacy given by appealing to the past, to religious and traditional leadership, was only ever one aspect of the power of a sultan, and was even more the truth in the case of a king. The King was a modern ruler, his position was defined by a constitution, and like all constitutions Morocco's was concerned not only with who was to wield power but how this was to be done. That there were five constitutions during King Hassan's reign is evidence enough of how difficult it was to conserve and maintain power. Faced with internal challengers and external enemies, the King needed friends at home and allies abroad. Governing independent Morocco was as difficult as it had been for the Sultans and imperialists of the past, but it was deftly done.

4 PRO FO443/186, McAndrew to John, 24 Aug. 1961.

5 M. E. Coombs-Schilling, *Sacred Performances: Islam, Sexuality, and Sacrifice* (New York: Columbia University Press, 1989), 225.

6 Moumen Diouri, *A qui appartient le Maroc?* (Paris: L'Harmattan, 1992), 224.

King Hassan's government

When he came to the throne, King Hassan did so as his own prime minister, and remained as such until November 1963. Thus he oversaw the reshaping of Moroccan political structures, while exercising a virtual monopoly on power through the army, the police, a muzzled parliament and a compliant countryside under the control of his supporters. During this period, although the idea of the King as arbiter was advanced in the first Moroccan constitution (and was accepted in a referendum), in reality political life was closely controlled by the palace. The King took over not only the mantle of the colonial state but its methods of rule.[7]

The politics of elites

The French and Spanish Protectorates had ruled the countryside largely through local notables who were given official positions as qaids and allowed to develop their wealth through landholdings. For them and the French, the urban nationalists were natural enemies, and during the rural rebellions just after independence, people had complained that 'outsiders', allied with Istiqlal, had forced themselves on rural communities. While still Crown Prince, Hassan had used the excuse of these rebellions to exclude the Istiqlal and secure a rural base. When he became King, the palace relied on the same families that had worked with the French and Spanish to provide qaids for the new regime and members of the parliaments of the 1960s and 1970s.[8] The rural administration remained much as it had been in Protectorate times. Over it the King placed a small group of young Berber technocrats, many of whom had been educated in the Berber College at Azrou at the end of the colonial period. Their job was to oversee the rural qaids rather as French officers once had done, and they became governors or top bureaucrats in the countryside.[9]

Although there was a measure of local government, communal councils were barred from formulating political views, or indeed any views 'foreign to the objects of local interest'. They had no executive function; while they allocated the budget, most of the money came from Rabat. In short, they had few responsibilities. In 1963 the entire activity of the council of the poor north-eastern town of Zaio was to build a public lavatory, repair a school and

7 Hammoudi, *Master and Disciple*, 23.

8 Leveau, *Le fellah marocain*, 50-1.

9 *Ibid.*, 28.

community centre, and help put up three pre-fabricated schools.[10] Political activities in the communes were questions of personalities, not policies.[11]

In the urban areas, the elite was just as important. It was so small that it was almost an extended family. Its members married each other and were educated together. University in Paris often followed the École Moulay Hassan in Casablanca, a school so closely connected to the regime that one of its principals became an ambassador and another the director of the Royal Cabinet, the King's private office.[12] In a country where more than 80% of the population was illiterate, that was a powerful bond.

This social cohesion overlay any ideological differences or any boundaries between civilian and military, government service and commerce, management and unions. The intermarried families of Ben Sliman, Khatib, Boucetta, Boujibar and Hassar included the head of the Ministry of the Interior's troops, a member of the executive committee of the UMT, an ambassador to Saudi Arabia, a Director-General of the Royal Cabinet, a member of the executive committee of the Istiqlal, the president of the Mouvement Populaire, a leader of the Parti Socialiste Démocratique, the director of a parastatal board, and a member of a Rifi family related to Muhammad bin Abd al-Karim al-Khattabi's Minister for Foreign Relations.[13]

A Ben Sliman had been Foreign Minister before the Protectorate, and while there were no Mokris or Glaouis, many historic families were still prominent. During King Hassan's first decade, cabinets included members of the Guessous and Bargash families. The Benjellouns were prominent in banking and nationalised industries. Men from the newer elite that had helped to win independence were coopted by marriage.[14]

Yet although many of these men – there were no women – aligned themselves with the Palace, others, long-time nationalists, were less enthusiastic. If Hassan was to hold on to power, they had to be neutralised.

10 *Ibid.*, 59; Seddon, *Moroccan Peasants*, 279.

11 Leveau, *Le fellah marocain*, 41.

12 Marais, *Classe Dirigeante*, 718; Benhaddou, *Maroc*, 194.

13 Waterbury, *Commander*, 107-8; Octave Marais, 'La classe dirigeante au Maroc', *Revue Française de Science Politique* 14 (1964): 720.

14 Clement Henry Moore, *Politics in North Africa: Algeria, Morocco and Tunisia* (Boston: Little, Brown, 1970), 332-9; Waterbury, *Commander*, 95.

The regime and its enemies

The greatest force in neutralising opposition in the early years was Mohammed Oufkir, who was first chief of police and then Minister of Defence. He created a powerful and centralised police force that acted with scant regard for either outside control or human rights. The main torture centre was housed, with a deliberate irony, in the magnificent former palace of El Mokri.[15]

Oufkir's nominal boss was Ahmed Réda Guédira, Minister of the Interior in a government in which the King was his own prime minister. The first cabinet included Istiqlal, the PDI and the Mouvement Populaire as well as 'independents' like Réda Guédira who were really the King's men. Men got power as members of factions or independently, but none was ever allowed to build up a power base of his own.

Mehdi Ben Barka, who was excluded, did have a popular power base, as he showed in May 1962. When he returned from exile, throngs of supporters cheered him through the streets. At the UNFP Congress, he electrified his supporters by attacking the rich, 'feudalism' and international imperialism. He denounced corruption and injustice and demanded a constitution that would allow the masses to participate in power. He was not a republican, but the King well knew that his idea of monarchy was modelled on that of Britain, not on a French presidency with the trappings of kingship, so Ben Barka was too dangerous to bring into the fold.[16] King Hassan, helped by a small group of loyalists, drafted the first Moroccan constitution to ensure that power remained in his hands.

The first constitution

Playing on symbolism, the first Moroccan constitution was proclaimed on 18 November 1962, the anniversary of Sidi Mohamed's return. Morocco was to be a constitutional monarchy, but the King would be supreme, legitimised by his religious role. The constitution, by insisting on a multi-party system, fragmented the political opposition.[17]

The Mouvement Populaire and Istiqlal backed the constitution, but the UNFP called for abstention in the referendum to ratify

15 Clément, *Oufkir*, 181-3.

16 Daoud and Monjib, *Ben Barka*, 259-78.

17 Waterbury, *Commander*, 258-9; J-C. Santucci, *Chroniques politiques marocaines (1971-1982)* (Paris: Editions du CNRS, 1985), 17; López García, *Procesos*, 16.

it, saying that it gave too much power to the king. The ever-fiery Mohammed bel-Arabi al-Alaoui bluntly called for it to be rejected. It was un-Islamic, he said, to give right of primogeniture to the King's son; the constitution's proponents were swindlers and its supporters, cowards.[18] He told a crowd in Fez a short parable:

> It is said that a lion, a wolf and a fox were hunting, and caught a zebra, a gazelle and a hare. The lion said to the wolf: 'Divide the game among us!' 'It is very easy', said the wolf. 'The zebra will be for your lunch, the gazelle for me, and the hare for the fox.' The lion was furious and killed the wolf with one blow. He then asked the fox to proceed with the division of the spoils. 'My Lord,' answered the fox, 'the zebra will be for your lunch, the gazelle for your dinner, and the hare will be your snack in between.' [...] The lion asked: 'How did you come up with such a division?' 'It was the death of the wolf, my Lord, that inspired me.'[19]

The characters were easily identifiable: the lion, of course, was the King, whose offer to share power was a trick; the wolf was anyone who demanded his due, and would end up in Dar el-Mokri's dungeons; the cowardly fox was Istiqlal. This was unfair: the Istiqlalis were motivated just as much by the desire to pose as the party that had 'won' the referendum, and scoop the spoils.[20]

In any event, the King won the referendum. In December 1962 85% of electors ignored the UNFP's call for a boycott, and only 2.5% voted against.[21] Chastened, the UNFP set about campaigning for the elections in May 1963 with such gusto that Guédira was worried that they might win: 'We had built a house that would be inhabited by our adversaries; we had to make room for our friends', he said.[22] He quickly organised his Front pour la Défense des Institutions Constitutionelles (FDIC), really more of a list than a party, with its candidates selected in Rabat because they rarely had much of a local base. Its policies were vague and its propaganda centred on generalised protestations of loyalty to King Hassan. Istiqlal talked of loyalty too, but to the memory of Mohammed V; Abdelkhalek Torrès, standing in Fez, used photographs of himself with the late King, Nasser and ibn Abd al-Karim. The UNFP's

18 Al-Asfi, *al-Salafi*, 139; Munson, *Religion and Power*, 111.

19 Quoted in Munson, *Religion and Power*, 111.

20 Daoud and Monjib, *Ben Barka*, 281.

21 *Ibid.*, 281; López García, *Procesos*, 17; Waterbury, *Commander*, 259.

22 Waterbury, *Commander*, 258.

candidates talked of a revolutionary struggle and of corruption, schools, hospitals, economic development and employment; for them the King was absent.[23]

The elections showed that the King was present, for the FDIC won the most seats. This was done with the direct, or indirect assistance of local officials, and apparently the widescale harassment of opposition parties.[24] Yet even the whole-hearted support of local administrators could not win all the elections for the FDIC, because Istiqlal and the UNFP were very well implanted in some regions. At the end of the day, when their seats were combined, they were the equals of the FDIC. Although the elections provided a house for the King's friends, they could not occupy all of the rooms. So the government resorted to repression. Prominent members of the UNFP and the union movement were arrested, tortured, charged with plotting to kill the King, tried and, in March 1964, condemned. Abderrahmane Youssoufi was imprisoned, but *al-Fqih* Basri, Omar Benjelloun, a Marxist union organiser for the UMT, and Moumen Diouri, a star witness for the prosecution who dramatically recanted and recounted his many tortures, were all sentenced to death; so, in his absence, was Mehdi Ben Barka. Eventually, the King commuted the sentences, but promoted Oufkir to be Minister of the Interior.[25]

Repression did not silence the protests, and since parliament provided no forum, they shifted to the streets. When, in March 1965, the education ministry forbade older students to go to school, on the grounds that school was for children, rioting students joined the inhabitants of the *bidonvilles* to set Casablanca on fire. General Oufkir directed the suppression from a helicopter while, according to one story, he sprayed the rioters with a machine-gun. Speaking on the radio, the King blamed the teachers for encouraging students to rebel. 'There is no danger for the state', he told them, 'as grave as that of the so-called intellectual. It would be better if you were all illiterate.' On 7 June he suspended the constitution and prorogued the parliament. He would rule by decree.[26] This

23 Leveau, *Le fellah marocain*, 78-9.

24 See *Ibid.*, 138-9 for a description of how this was done in the area around Rabat and the Zaers region; Waterbury, *Commander*, 261.

25 López García, *Procesos*, 18-21; Waterbury, *Commander*, 261-2, 293-5; Daoud and Monjib, *Ben Barka*, 287-94; Gilles Perrault, *Notre ami le roi* (Paris: Gallimard, 1990), 74-84; Majid, *Les luttes*, 30; Munson, *Religion and Power*, 133; Daure-Serfaty, *Rencontres*, 70.

26 Waterbury, *Commander*, 263, 311-13 Clément, *Oufkir*, 217-22; Daoud and Monjib, *Ben Barka*, 321-2; Santucci, *Chroniques*, 18-19; Perrault, *Notre ami*, 88; Munson, *Religion*

was the culmination of the process that centred all direct power in the King's hands. His role as arbiter was almost completely compromised, because there were no political groups between whom he could mediate. Political control became a matter of repression and patronage, with the King once again his own prime minister.[27] As a result he had to face the economic crisis directly and that was serious indeed.

The economic crisis

'Faced with a choice between an intelligence report and the weather bulletin,' King Hassan told Eric Laurent, a French journalist who interviewed him in 1993, 'I will put the intelligence report on one side.'[28] He was right. Political peace was directly affected by the weather because irrigated land produced crops for export, not food for Moroccans. The staple foods, wheat and barley, were grown on unirrigated ground and when the rains failed, the

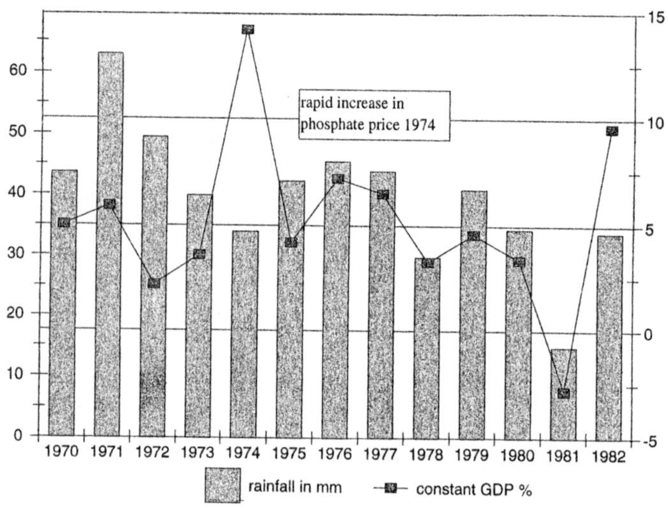

THE RELATION BETWEEN RAINFALL AND G.D.P., 1970-82

Source: National Climatic Centre; World Bank.

---

and Power, 134; I. William Zartman, 'King Hassan's New Morocco' in I.W. Zartman (ed.), *The Political Economy of Morocco* (New York: Praeger, 1987), 5.

27 Hammoudi, *Master and Disciple*, 23.

28 Hassan II, *La Mémoire*, 230.

economy shrank, and political problems grew. The GDP, and in consequence, political security have indeed generally tracked rainfall. Yet the independent government concentrated on irrigated agriculture for export, rather than developing the traditional agricultural sector.

King Hassan came to the throne on the ruins of Operation Plough and, spurred on by flooding in the Rharb plain in 1963, he opted firmly for large-scale irrigation, a *politique des barrages.* In 1968, backed by enthusiastic support and loans from the World Bank, the government announced that it would fulfill the colonialist dream of one million irrigated hectares by the end of the century. In fifteen years (1965-80) eighteen dams were completed and another eight were started, and between 1965 and 1986 irrigated land increased from 123,800 ha to 471,000 ha.[29] Some dams also produced electricity and helped flood control. This grand project of independent Morocco was commemorated with great names from the Moroccan past. Dams were named after Moulay Youssef, the King's grandfather; Mansour Eddahabi, the greatest of the Saadi Sultans; Idris I, the founder of Fez; and Sidi Mohammed ben Abdellah, the Alaoui Sultan who built Essaouira.

The King was proud of these dams. As he told Laurent; 'I know that Algerian officials made sarcastic remarks about me: "Look at him planting his tomatoes, while we plant our oil." I let them say it, and thought to myself: "I wish you luck when you have to eat hydrocarbon steaks."'[30]

The Moroccan agricultural economy certainly performed better than that of Algeria, but it did not feed the population. While the modern agricultural sector, 10-15% of the arable lands, gave 85% of produce, this was in export crops like citrus fruits, wine and fresh vegetables. Farming on unirrigated land stagnated. Cereal production, in decline since the 1930s, continued to fall after independence, and in 1960 Morocco became a net importer of cereals and has remained so ever since.[31]

Since foreign customers set the prices and imposed import controls, political independence did not bring economic independence. There was no free market. In 1958 France joined the

29 Swearingen, *Mirages*, 161-72.

30 Hassan II, *La Mémoire*, 139.

31 Swearingen, *Mirages*, 184; Habib El Malki, *Trente Ans d'Economie Marocaine, 1960-1990* (Paris: CNRS, 1990), 91-6; Rhys Payne, 'Food Deficits and Political Legitimacy: the Case of Morocco' in Stephen K. Commins, Michael F. Lofchie and Rhys Payne (eds), *Africa's Agrarian Crisis: the Roots of Famine* (Boulder, CO: Lynne Rienner, 1986), 153.

European Common Market and by 1970 the European Community as a whole was the biggest trading partner (61% of exports and 51% of imports).[32] Although the EEC gave preferential terms to poorer states on its periphery, it protected its markets by controlling imports of some of the very products that the Moroccan government encouraged farmers to grow. In 1969 the first association agreement with the EEC excluded fresh vegetables and wine. On the other hand, the agreement slashed tariffs on citrus fruits, about one-sixth of total exports, and gave concessions on olive oil. In return, the Moroccan government made only token reductions in customs duties; the benefit largely fell to the Moroccan side.[33]

The real problem was lack of capital. The King early identified himself as an economic liberal, but it took a generation to trek from state control towards a market economy. The argument that the state should provide investment capital because even the richest individuals could not finance industrial growth guided economic planning in the 1960s and '70s.[34]

Government economic plans, usually for five years, sometimes for three, were often abandoned: the Moroccan economy was too fragile to sustain them. The first Five Year Plan (1960-4) tried to shift away from the colonial economy through agricultural development, administrative reform, the expansion of education and the development of basic industry. It could not be done. Poor harvests kept growth in GDP below 4% a year, so money was borrowed, budget deficits grew, foreign exchange reserves were exhausted and a trade deficit developed.[35] In 1964 the IMF advanced $1.3 million, in exchange for a new Three-Year Plan to restore stability.[36]

Priority was now given to industrialised agricultural development and tourism rather than industry, but that still needed capital. In the 1968-72 Five Year Plan, agriculture consumed 22% of state investment. Parastatal companies grew and new state-controlled

[32] Economist Intelligence Unit (EIU), *Morocco to 1992: Growth against the Odds* (London: Economist, 1987), 15; Saleh M. Nsouli and Saleh M. Eken, *Resilience and Growth Through Sustained Adjustment: The Moroccan Experience*, 115-16 (Washington, DC: International Monetary Fund, 1995), 115-16; Ali Bahaijoub, 'Morocco's Argument to Join the EEC' in George Joffe (ed.), *North Africa: Nation, State, and Region* (London: Routledge, 1993), 235-46; Richard Pomfret, 'Morocco's International Economic Relations' in Zartman (ed.), *Political Economy*, 175.

[33] Pomfret, 'Economic Relations', 174-6;

[34] Hassan II, *La Mémoire*, 140.

[35] El Malki, *Trente Ans*, 18; Beyen *et al.*, *Economic Development*, 25-39.

[36] Beyen *et al.*, *Economic Development*, vii; El Malki, *Trente Ans*, 18.

monopolies were created.[37] The *Office Nationale de Transport* (ONT), established in 1963, was a huge bureaucratic empire. An application to run a trucking company had to be submitted to the provincial governor's office and then approved in detail – the number, type and capacity of each vehicle and where it would operate – by a commission, headed by the Prime Minister with members representing no fewer than nine ministries.[38] This cumbersome system also provided many opportunities for corruption.

Although economic growth during the 1960s averaged 4.4% a year, exports did not grow enough to pay for imports of food. By the early 1970s inflation was rising, and external debt was growing – in 1972 it equalled nearly 23% of the value of GDP. Disaster was staved off by fairly good harvests in 1973 and 1974 and a rise in phosphate prices. Morocco was the largest exporter of phosphates in the world, and the government resolved to imitate OPEC. It forced up the price, from $14 to $63 a tonne, and spent the increased income on subsidising food for the cities, on vast capital investment in irrigation and on military expenditure. But the gap between rich and poor was widening. In 1968 the richest tenth accounted for a quarter of consumption; in 1972 they consumed 37%. The share of the poorest tenth went down from 3.3% to 1.2%. Then the economy disintegrated. In 1974 inflation reached 17%; the following year the phosphate price collapsed and the harvest was poor. The country people were not producing enough food.[39]

The crisis in the rural world

Because the Palace relied on local notables, there could be no thought of land redistribution.[40] Some notables farmed with tractors and combine harvesters, for which they alone had sufficient collateral to raise capital, but their economic relations with the rural population still depended on sharecropping to provide labour. This made them rich up to a point, but prevented agricultural production from being intensified because they did not dare to

37 Azam and Morrisson, *Political Feasibility*, 86; El Malki, *Trente Ans*, 18-19.

38 Mohamed Salahdine, 'The Informal System in Morocco: The Failure of Legal Systems' in Lawrence Chickering and Mohamed Salahdine (eds), *The Silent Revolution: The Informal Sector in Five Asian and Near Eastern Countries* (San Francisco: ICS Press, 1991), 18-19.

39 El Malki, *Trente Ans*, 19; Azam and Morrisson, *Political Feasibility*, 86-7; Payne, 'Food Deficits', 158.

40 Leveau, *Le fellah marocain*, 65; Payne, 'Food Deficits', 157.

disturb, by enclosing the land, the rural universe on which their patronage depended.[41] The modernisation of the countryside came from outside. Rural *communes* were connected into the electricity grid and telephone system, schools were built, police stations opened. The staff were mainly outsiders, who began to form a lower middle class in the countryside. Some of the local population entered the modern economy too, setting up grocery shops in the villages and small repair shops for bicycles or radios. Others laboured for richer men or, short of work and land, entered the modern world economy in a more definitive manner, by emigrating.[42] Most migrants still went to France, where cheap labour was still needed and Algerian migrants were no longer popular. When the crisis of 1968 brought chaos to the streets of France and congealed the economy, migrants sought new destinations: Belgium, Germany, the Netherlands and Spain.[43]

The government encouraged them to go. Successive economic plans relied on emigration to bring in foreign exchange, reduce unemployment and train the workforce at no cost. That last hope was a delusion; more than half the migrants from the Rif and the Sous, the main sources, were illiterate and another 29% had only studied in Quranic schools. So European employers used them as manual labourers in agriculture and industry rather than train them. Migrants did send back a lot of foreign exchange, the equivalent of nearly 18% of the total import bill in 1974, and they relieved rural unemployment so effectively that in parts of the Rif and Sous there was a shortage of labour.[44]

The migrants, of course, left not to swell state coffers but to benefit themselves. They were poor, agricultural labourers and small artisans, people who, in 1971, spent less than 60% of the monthly average per household and they came from poor regions, the Sous and the Rif.[45] In the northern provinces, 31% of households relied on migrants as their principal source of income. 'France, gentlemen, is a sea of money', a Rifi told some Dutch geographers in the early 1970s.[46]

41 Hammoudi, *Master and Disciple*, 38-9.

42 Seddon, *Moroccan Peasants*, 253-4.

43 Baroudi, *Maroc*, 47-9.

44 Ibid., 53; W.F Heinemeijer, *et al.*, *Partir pour rester. Incidences de l'emigration ouvrière à la campagne marocaine* (Amsterdam: Université d'Amsterdam, Institut Socio-Géographique, 1977), 27-9.

45 Heinemeijer, *Partir*, 13; Baroudi, *Maroc*, 86, 149.

46 Heinemeijer, *Partir*, 61, 82, 92; Hart, *Aith Waryaghar*, 94-5.

The crisis in the cities

Not everyone went as far afield as Europe: the majority of rural migrants stayed inside Morocco, but moved to the cities, the population of which increased by 4.5% a year, almost double the general increase of the whole country (2.6%). By 1971 Casablanca was the third biggest city in Africa. In ten years, its population had grown from 965,000 to 1.5 million. Rabat-Salé, half the size, grew at much the same rate.[47] Even smaller towns expanded. In the depressed north-east, Nador grew from 4,806 in 1960 to 32,000 in 1971; Segangane, a minuscule settlement in the arid countryside nearby, went from 1,800 to 7,600.[48]

Within the towns, the rich also migrated. In order to get as far away from the poor as they could, rich families moved out of their houses in the *madinas* of the old cities into new, and safer, suburbs on the outskirts. In al-Anfa in Casablanca or Agdal in Rabat, they built villas behind high walls.[49] Yet the *bidonvilles* could not be ignored. The 1968-72 Five-Year Plan shifted capital expenditure away from housing towards agriculture, infrastructure and tourism, so the government began to allow 'auto-construction' in the shanty towns.[50] A whole uncontrolled economy developed: unofficial agents subdivided the land, unofficial builders worked openly but concealed their identities. Kiosks and semi-legal taxi drivers serviced a population of petty government officials, small artisans and those who worked in the informal economy: street peddlers selling single cigarettes, packs of tissues and cigarette lighters, parking wardens, barbers and circumcisers, unofficial tourist guides, repairers of clothes and soes. Many people lived by their wits and their numbers grew and grew; by 1971 around 69% of the urban working population was in the informal sector.[51]

If these people were hungry, they might flood out of their *bidonvilles* into the streets and squares of the more respectable parts of town. In 1967 King Hassan went to the United States to ask for food aid and was given $12 million.[52] Subsidies from abroad underpinned subsidies at home. The Prime Minister's office

47 Abu Lughod, *Rabat*, 248.

48 Seddon, *Moroccan Peasants*, 244.

49 Ali Benhaddou, *Maroc: les élites du royaume: essai sur l'organisation du pouvoir au Maroc* (Paris: L'Harmattan, 1997), 196-206.

50 Abu Lughod, *Rabat*, 254-7.

51 Salahdine, 'Informal sector', 34; Mohamed Salahdine, *Les petits métiers clandestins 'le business populaire'* (Casablanca: Eddif, 1988), 27-32, 34-7.

52 Payne, 'Food Deficits', 153.

fixed the prices of oil, dairy products, flour and sugar, which kept them low during the 1960s and 1970s. That helped reduce urban wages which benefited both the slowly-growing industrial sector and the government, the largest employer of all. But the real reason was political, to prevent the inhabitants of the *bidonvilles* from rioting. The ability to feed the population had become one of the tests of the legitimacy of the regime.[53]

The second constitution

King Hassan knew that he could not rule alone and, shaken by the riots of 1965, he tried to reconstruct a political consensus. Specifically, he attempted to bring Ben Barka back into the system. Using a suitably mathematical metaphor, he sent him a message: 'I want my old mathematics teacher to come back, because I have an equation to solve in Morocco'.[54] Ben Barka procrastinated, but in the autumn he decided to return. Oufkir was appalled and on 29 October 1965 Ben Barka was kidnapped on a Paris street and killed. President de Gaulle alleged that not only Oufkir but King Hassan was involved, and broke off diplomatic relations. Others claimed that the French security services had helped their Moroccan colleagues but both the President and the King denied any knowledge of the affair. In 1992, when interviewed by Laurent, the King said that the murder of Ben Barka was part of a plot against him: every time he tried to seek a rapprochement with the politicians, Oufkir foiled it.[55]

Oufkir certainly preferred the King to be isolated and dependent upon him, and now he had his wish. In July 1970 Istiqlal and the UNFP boycotted the referendum for a new constitution which created an acquiescent parliament; nearly two-thirds of the members were indirectly elected. When an electoral turnout of 93.15 per cent approved it by 98.7 per cent of the vote, allegations of vote-rigging were all too credible and UNFP and Istiqlal formed an alliance, the National Block (*al-Kutla al-Wataniyya*), to boycott the subsequent parliamentary elections. Those were won by independents.[56]

53 *Ibid.*, 162-3.

54 The wording here is from Hassan II, *La Mémoire*, 106; Daoud and Monjib, *Ben Barka*, 322 has a slightly different form of words, but to the same effect.

55 Hassan II, *La Mémoire*, 105-20; Daoud and Monjib, *Ben Barka*, 326-48; Clément, *Oufkir*, 221-49.

56 Zartman, 'New Morocco', 5; Santucci, *Chroniques*, 21, López García, *Procesos*, 22-4.

With no effective parliament, King Hassan was the centre of the political system. While a civilian bureaucracy and a military wing kept order, power was exercised though patronage on such a grand scale that corruption became the keystone of the regime. Corruption kept the rich loyal, allowed lesser officials to add to their meagre incomes and kept the poor obedient, for virtually every activity required contact with bureaucrats who had to be bribed.[57]

The Skhirat coup

Even General Oufkir, the Minister of the Interior with virtually unchecked powers, could not keep things quiet. As the economic crisis got worse and unemployment went up, the unions and students organised strikes and demonstrations.[58] Men on whom the King relied began looking to their own interests. Senior military officers were dismayed at civilian placemen who got more of the spoils than they did, at the slow rate of promotion, and at a system that was so unstable as to put their own security at risk. When the King ignored his Director of the Royal Military Household, General Medboh, who complained that corruption was undermining the system, the general began plotting to seize power. He intended, apparently, to control the government, while keeping the King on the throne, but there may have been another plot, a coup within the coup, for an unnamed conspirator to take power for himself.

In July 1971 a group of army cadets stormed the King's sea-side palace in Skhirat where he was celebrating his birthday with ambassadors, politicians, and the glitterati of French high society. Many people were killed, but the coup failed. The King and his brother faced down the cadets in the coolest fashion. Moulay Abdallah, his jellaba soaked in his blood, openly dared the rebels to shoot him, and King Hassan, after spending hours cooped up in a room in the palace, seized a moment's hesitation by some of the cadets as the chance to take the initiative. 'I shouted, "Why do you not kiss my hand? Have you become quite mad all of you, my children, the soldiers of my royal army?"' This so shook the cadets that they stopped to kiss his hands. Spotting Oufkir among the prisoners, the King shouted, 'General Oufkir, stand

57 John Waterbury, 'The Coup Manqué' (Hanover, NH: American Universities Field Staff, Africa, 1971, Report 1); John Waterbury, 'Endemic and Planned Corruption in a Monarchical Regime', *World Politics* 25 (1973): 533-55.

58 Santucci, *Chroniques*, 19-23.

up! I delegate to you all my civil and military powers! Take charge of all this!' The King's courage and Oufkir's cold-bloodedness ended the coup. Medboh and many others were killed or executed, and yet more were imprisoned in terrible conditions in remote desert castles, where they died after years of suffering. Then the blame was laid on Arab nationalists, inspired by Colonel Qathafi of Libya. In fact, most senior officers were Berbers, trying to protect their positions.[59]

Dissatisfied members of the elite were hard to root out or even identify. Oufkir himself, that most trusted officer, may have known about the coup and waited until he knew which side had won. King Hassan made him Minister of Defence, which the general considered a demotion. But Oufkir disliked even more the king's attempts to rebuild bridges to the opposition. In 1972 a third, more liberal constitution was proposed, with two thirds of the Chamber of Deputies elected, although the King could still rule by decree.[60] The constitution was approved by a 98% majority of a 92.9% turnout, but the bridge-building failed: the *Kutla* boycotted the referendum and refused to accept the result.[61]

The second coup

Now both the opposition and Oufkir were disgruntled, and the regime was less secure than ever. On 16 August 1972 air force jets attacked the King's plane, but once again, he survived in the most dramatic fashion. His pilot pretended that Hassan was mortally wounded, and when the seriously damaged plane landed at Rabat, the king coolly commandeered a private car and drove into town. While aircraft shelled his palace, he went to Skhirat, took a bath, and rallied his forces. By evening the coup was over. The next day Oufkir committed suicide, or so it was said; other rumours had it that the King shot the general himself. This coup was dismissed as no more than Oufkir's personal attempt to seize power, and his family disappeared into extremely harsh imprisonment for the next two decades.[62] In 1973 Hassan appointed a new security chief, Driss Basri.

King Hassan's escape, for a second time, increased his reputation

59 Waterbury, 'Coup Manqué'; Clément, *Oufkir*, 266-308; the quotation is from Perrault, *Notre ami*, 117-40.

60 Santucci, *Chroniques*, 40-1; Zartman, 'New Morocco', 5; Clément, *Oufkir*, 274-80.

61 López García, *Procesos*, 24.

62 Santucci, *Chroniques*, 45-7; Perrault, *Notre ami*, 157-63; Hassan II, *La Mémoire*, 166-72.

for luck, *baraka*, but luck would not keep him in power. In 1973 a left-wing plot was discovered and members of the UNFP were arrested.[63] Yet Hassan knew he had to rebuild the Moroccan political system and forge a common purpose with the nationalist opposition. After 1972 an attempt was made to do that by mobilising support around the issue of Moroccan identity, by restating the nationalist concept of the independence of *all* of Morocco as a single state. The big issue for the rest of the 1970s was the Sahara, which occupied Basri quite as much as security.

Morocco's expanding limits

When King Hassan came to the throne, Morocco was an island, surrounded by the French colonies of Mauritania and Algeria, and the Spanish Sahara. Algerian independence in March 1962 merely substituted a new rival for an old master. In the final bloody stages of the war, while European colons hunted down Muslim Algerians like animals, and the French army fought them both, a left-wing faction seized control of the FLN. In the first months of independence a civil war broke out.[64]

The left wing won and Ahmed Ben Bella became the first President. This heartened the Moroccan left and Ben Barka talked in incendiary terms of breaking the rich bourgeoisie, the feudalists, and the big landowners. He demanded land reform, a workers' revolution, and anti-imperialist solidarity.[65] The King and Oufkir were appalled and sent Moroccan 'auxiliaries' to invade Algeria and restore Morocco's lost territories. The disunited Algerian army threw them out. In September 1963 the Moroccan army occupied Tindouf while the Algerian army took Figuig. The Organisation of African Unity, saying that independent African states should accept colonial boundaries, got both sides to withdraw, but the colonial regime had never exactly defined where the boundaries were.[66]

This put paid to Maghribi unity. Ben Bella attacked the Moroccan dynasty in a speech so virulent that it still rankled with King Hassan thirty years later.[67] From exile Ben Barka furiously condemned the war as a betrayal 'not only of the dynamic of the Algerian

63 Santucci, *Chroniques*, 54-8; Zartman, 'New Morocco', 6.

64 Ageron, *Modern Algeria*, 124, 129-31; Horne, *Savage War*, 505-40; Trout, *Frontiers*, 425-6.

65 Daoud and Monjib, *Ben Barka*, 273; Clément, *Oufkir*, 186-8.

66 Hodges, *Western Sahara*, 93-4; Trout, *Frontiers*, 428-9.

67 Ageron, *Modern Algeria*, 137; Hassan II, *La Mémoire*, 86.

revolution, but, in a general sense, of the whole Arab Revolution for liberty, socialism and union, and of the entire world movement of national liberation'.[68] The King, of course, did not agree and neither did Istiqlal. It insisted that Morocco would only be truly independent when all its territories were re-united. That included parts of Algeria as well as Mauritania and the Spanish Sahara.

Mauritania was extremely poor. It had virtually no infrastructure beyond the iron mines and the railway leading to them, and for most of the colonial period had been ruled from Senegal; the capital, Nouakchott, was quite new. At the United Nations, M'hammed Boucetta, an Istiqlali who was Moroccan Ambassador, said that Mauritania was a fiction, a surrogate for French control, a West African Katanga.[69] But the UN and the OAU both admitted Mauritania and the dispute rumbled on until the end of the decade. In 1965 King Hassan even appointed a cousin, Moulay Idris bin Hassan, as Minister for Saharan and Mauritanian affairs,[70] but Mauritania was never a popular nationalist cause outside the Istiqlal. The UNFP was as scathing about the Mauritanian enterprise as it had been about the Algerian one.[71] The Spanish Sahara was quite another matter.

The Spanish Sahara

The Spanish Sahara was as unlikely an independent state as Mauritania. Its economy was minimal, and there was little sense of political identity. Since the late 1940s the Spanish government had known there were phosphates in the Sahara; there might be oil too, and there were certainly rich fishing grounds off-shore.[72] Twelve oil companies, Spanish and foreign, explored for oil but by 1968 all of them, even ENMISA, a state holding company, had given up.[73] Fishing was more successful (the value of the catch increased from less than 10 million pesetas in 1959 to nearly 60 million in 1965), but the fishing company was poorly managed and hardly ever made a profit.[74] Even the phosphate industry took

68 Quoted in Hodges, *Western Sahara*, 96.

69 Damis, *Conflict*, 17; Hodges, *Western Sahara*, 90.

70 Moore, *Politics*, 337; Hodges, *Western Sahara*, 111.

71 Hodges, *Western Sahara*, 90-1, 96.

72 Javier Morillas, *Sahara Occidental. Desarollo y subdesarollo* (Madrid: El Dorado, 1990), 228, 253.

73 *Ibid.*, 214-26.

74 *Ibid.*, 188-92.

a long time to get started. Exports only began in 1972, after the longest conveyor belt in the world, 100 km. long, was built to transport the rock from the mines at Bu Craa to the coast.[75] What little investment there was in the colony's infrastructure came from ENMISA, which changed its name to Fosfatos de Bu Craa in 1969, rather than the government.[76]

By 1974, when Spanish rule ended, there were only 480 km. of metalled road. The 28,010 inhabitants of Laâyoune, the capital, made up more than a third of the population (73,497 persons), and lived in what the authorities classified as 'fourth-class' houses, 'suited to their way of life' or in an extensive *bidonville*. Garbage piled up round the stagnant lagoon, and male youths smoked hashish in the abandoned Spanish forts that ringed the capital. Medical services were quite good, but only a few children went to school: 2,700 out of a school-age population of around 35,000. Half the population was under the age of fifteen, the literacy rate was 5%, unemployment was nearly 60%.[77]

Deprived of income, the Sahraouis were also deprived of power. In 1961 municipal councils were set up in Laâyoune and Villa Cisneros and Saharan representatives got seats in Franco's virtually powerless parliament. In 1967 a territorial assembly, the Yemaa (*jamaa*), was set up, manned by tribal leaders loyal to Spain. Even they had no power; the governor-general told them, 'Your job is to tell us about matters of general interest to the territory.' He made the laws and Spanish officers enforced them.[78]

But in 1960, in this age of decolonisation, the UN General Assembly resolved that all peoples had the right to self-determination. Within a few years virtually every British and French colony in Africa gained independence; only the moribund Portugese empire and the Spanish Sahara lingered on. King Hassan threatened Madrid with the 'virus of self-determination' and complained to the United Nations. In November 1965 the General Assembly resolved that both the Sahara and Ifni should be 'liberated from colonial domination'. It did not specify who should take over. In December 1966 that was cleared up: Ifni would be Moroccan, and 'in conformity with the aspirations of the indigenous people of the Spanish Sahara and in consultation with the Governments

75 *Ibid.*, 254; Damis, *Conflict*, 12, 25.

76 Morillas, *Sahara Occidental*, 175, 227.

77 *Ibid.*, 199, 242, 195; Damis, *Conflict*, 12; John Mercer, *Spanish Sahara* (London: George Allen & Unwin, 1976), 207-8, 210.

78 Hodges, *Western Sahara*, 139-41; Damis *Conflict*, 13.

of Mauritania and Morocco and any other interested parties' the Spanish authorities would hold a referendum to determine the local inhabitants' wishes.[79]

In 1969 Madrid handed back Ifni, a colony that the army could not defend, and was not worth keeping anyway. The Saharan question was ignored. True, it was raised several times during the 1960s and a paper independence movement, the *Frente de Liberación del Sahara Bajo Dominación Española* was founded in 1966, but there was little action beyond rodomontade. Neither the Spanish nor the Moroccan governments wanted to break relations; Madrid provided too much economic aid to Rabat, and King Hassan was anti-communist. In 1971 Franco sat stony-faced through an exposition on the Sahara that lasted two hours, and merely responded, 'What you ask of me, Your Majesty, is suicide, towards which neither I nor Spain are disposed.' Then he asked the King if he would like to wash his hands before lunch.[80]

Other governments also had an interest in the Saharan question. The Mauritanian President, Mokhtar Ould Dada, talked about a 'Greater Mauritania', a supposed common culture shared by Arabic-speaking tribes between the Senegal River and the Drâa valley. The idea helped to build unity at home, and to hold back Moroccan expansionism.[81] The Algerian government, which also feared Moroccan expansionism, protected Ould Dada for much of the 1960s. To the Moroccan government, that looked like dangerous encirclement.[82]

The Saharans themselves had no political voice. In 1967 Mohammed Bassiri founded the *Harakat Tahrir Saqia al-Hamra wa Wadi al-Dhahab* (Movement for the Liberation of Saguia el-Hamra and Oued ed-Dahab). Bassiri, the son of a nomad, had studied briefly in Casablanca, travelled in the Arab east and was inspired by Arab nationalism. But when his movement organised a demonstration in 1970, the Spanish authorities crushed it and Bassiri disappeared, never to be seen again.[83]

Elsewhere, Arab nationalism was reaching a high-water mark. In September 1969 Muammar Qathafi organised a coup in Libya. Little more than a year later his hero, Nasser, died and the colonel

79 Hassan II, *La Mémoire*, 185; Hodges, *Western Sahara*, 105-7

80 Hassan II, *La Mémoire*, 186-7.

81 Damis, *Conflict*, 30; Laila Khalil Badi', *Adawa wa-malamih min al-Saqiyya al-Hamra wa-Wadi al-Dahab (al-Sahara al-Gharbiyya)* (Beirut: Dar al-Masira, 1976) 79.

82 Hodges, *Western Sahara*, 113; Hassan II, *La Mémoire*, 185ff.

83 Hodges, *Western Sahara*, 154-5.

tried to assume his mantle. The Sahara confused Qathafi. He wanted to overthrow reactionary regimes like that of Morocco, and loudly praised the attempted coups in 1971 and 1972; but he dreamed of Arab unity, and could not support the creation of yet another Arab state. In February 1972 he resolved the contradiction by offering military aid to Mauritania.[84] This posturing only mattered because Morocco was so unstable. More than ever it was vital for the King to rebuild a political consensus.

From 1973 onwards the King again began to emphasise nationalist ideas. Moroccan troops joined the Syrian army on the Golan Heights during the October war; at home, government newspapers campaigned for the return of the Sahara to 'the motherland'. In July the king organised a conference in Agadir with the presidents of Algeria and Mauritania which declared 'unwavering attachment to the principle of self-determination' for the Sahara.[85] There was no contradiction, because Moroccan officials believed that the Saharans would vote to join Morocco, and the principles of the UN and of the Moroccan nationalist movement could both be satisfied.

The road to the International Court

Yet some Saharans were already drifting out of control. In 1971 a small group of students in Rabat began talking of liberating the Sahara by force. One of them was El-Ouali Mustapha Sayed, the son of an impoverished seamstress and her handicapped husband. He had grown up in a squatter camp near Tan-Tan, but had recived a primary education, and then scholarships for secondary education in Marrakesh, Taroudannt and Rabat. In 1970 he entered the law school of Mohammed V University, but had little in common with middle-class Moroccan students. When the police cracked down on his group, in May 1973, he and a few others fled to the desert and set up a new liberation movement, the Frente Popular para la Liberación de Saguia el Hamra y Rio de Oro (Polisario, for short). Within days they had attacked a remote Spanish military post, and in October 1974, having opted for bigger targets, they sabotaged the conveyor belt to the Bu Craa mines and stopped the export of phosphates.[86]

84 John Wright, *Libya: a Modern History* (London: Croom Helm, 1981), 208; Hodges, *Western Sahara*, 118; Badi', *Adawa*, 84-5.

85 Santucci, *Chroniques*, 54; Hodges, *Western Sahara*, 119; Badi', *Adawa*, 82.

86 Hodges, *Western Sahara*, 157-63; Damis, *Conflict* 40; Carlos Ruiz Miguel, *El Sahara Occidental y España. Historia, política y derecho – análisis crítico de la política exterior*

Elsewhere in Africa, the last remnants of imperial rule were falling away. After the coup in Portugal in 1974, the new government quickly dismantled the country's ramshackle empire. In Spain, General Franco was afflicted by numerous illnesses and incipient senility. His weak, squabbling and vacillating ministers were concerned only to salvage for themselves what they could from a dying regime. The struggle for the spoils now began in earnest.

In May 1974 the nationalist opposition in Morocco organised mass rallies demanding the return of the Sahara, and the King announced that 1975 would be devoted to the 'territorial liberation of Morocco'. But the Spanish government insisted on a referendum that would include the option of independence, which was not at all what King Hassan had in mind. Secretly, an agreement was made with Ould Dada to divide the Sahara between Morocco and Mauritania once the Spanish left. Publicly, in September, the Moroccan government persuaded the UN to refer the Moroccan and Mauritanian claims to the Sahara to the International Court of Justice even though the court could only give an advisory opinion, not a judgement, because the Spanish government refused to accept its jurisdiction. Instead, the Spanish government persuaded the UN to send a mission to the Sahara to canvass the opinions of its inhabitants.[87]

Madrid and Rabat had reckoned without the Polisario and the Algerian government. The UN mission was greeted by crowds of demonstrators waving Polisario flags and shouting '*Fuera España*!' (Spain out!), making it noisily clear that they wanted independence. On 23 May 1975 the government in Madrid announced that it would transfer sovereignty 'in the shortest time possible'. It did not say to whom. Inside the colony, Polisario refused to cooperate with a Spanish plan to patch together an alliance between the Yemaa, Polisario and a tame 'independence' party of their own. Outside, the Algerian government that in July had apparently agreed to partition between Morocco and Mauritania, in August started calling for self-determination and lobbying for Polisario at the OAU. Algiers was still worried about being encircled.[88] Then,

---

española (Madrid: Dykinson, 1995), 89.

87 Damis, *Conflict*, 50-4; Hodges, *Western Sahara*, 179; Santucci, *Chroniques*, 77-8; Preston, *Franco*, 774-7; Cour Internationale de Justice, 'Sahara Occidental: requête pour avis consultatif, ordonnance du 3 janvier 1975', *Receuil des arrêts, avis consultatifs et ordonnances* (1975), 21-4.

88 Ruiz Miguel, *Sahara Occidental*, 91 Damis, *Conflict*, 57-9; Hodges, *Western Sahara*, 204-7.

on 14 October, the UN mission reported in favour of Polisario's demand for independence.

The opinion of the International Court, delivered two days later, was just as unsatisfactory. It had been asked two questions: was the territory really subject to no state (*terra nullius*) when the Spanish colonised it, and, if not, what legal ties linked its inhabitants with those of Morocco and Mauritania? The Moroccan lawyers argued that there was a historic religious allegiance to the Sultan, and used the colonial theory of *bilad al-siba* to claim that the Sahara was *siba* territory, but Moroccan all the same. The Mauritanian government argued for a common historic identity between the tribes of the two territories. Had these arguments been carried there would have been no question of independence, and Moroccan sovereignty could be restored peacefully.

Instead, the Court found that, while there were indeed historic links between the Moroccan Sultan and the inhabitants of parts of the Western Sahara, and similar ties with Mauritania, they were not ties of sovereignty. The Sahraouis had the right to self-determination. King Hassan moved quickly. On 16 October he declared on national television that the court had acknowledged traditional links and, ignoring the caveats, that these validated the claim to sovereignty. He called on the Moroccan people to liberate the Sahara peacefully by marching across the border; the Spanish army would never fire on an unarmed procession.[89]

The Green March

The King asked for 350,000 volunteers for this Green March, a figure that equalled the number of people born in a single year. In three days 524,000 had come forward. The opposition parties rushed to support him, as did the PLO and many Arab governments. The US government, disliking the left-wing rhetoric of the Polisario, made no objection. When the marchers crossed the border on 6 November, the Spanish army simply withdrew. Its commanders refused to fire on civilians, but there was no one to tell them to do so anyway because on 18 October Franco had finally collapsed, although he lingered for another month, with only fleeting moments of consciousness. The general who had once said that he could not explain himself without Africa was dying, and his empire died with him. On 14 November the Spanish, Moroccan and Mauritanian governments agreed to administer the Sahara jointly

89 Damis, *Conflict*, 54-8; Cour Internationale de Justice, 'Sahara Occidental', 40-9; Badi', *Adawa*, 158-60; Ruiz Miguel, *Sahara Occidental*, 95-9.

until 28 February 1976. Then the territory would be split between Morocco and Mauritania. On 18 November, the Cortes ratified the agreement, and the following day Franco's life-support machines were turned off. He died on 20 November.[90]

By 12 January Moroccan troops and the tiny Mauritanian army had occupied their allotted areas. Polisario could not stop them, although with Algerian help it held off the Moroccan army in a pitched battle at Amgala, a way station on the route to the refugee camps it was setting up just across the Algerian border, from where it began a guerrilla campaign.[91] On 26 February, two days early, Spanish rule ended.

THE NEW MOROCCO

Morocco was now a united country; united as a territory, and moved by a common purpose that both the nationalist parties and the King could embrace. The coups had passed, and the principal torturer, Oufkir, was dead. A new age of democracy, common purpose and prosperity seemed to be dawning. But the war in the Sahara went badly, the economy improved not at all, and democracy proved to be a delicate plant. By the end of the decade the country was seething again.

The Saharan war

On 28 February 1976 Polisario proclaimed the Saharan Arab Democratic Republic. It talked of national liberation, of 'the will of our people', and of 'the rights of man, territorial integrity and established frontiers', and attacked Moroccan and Mauritanian colonialism. In November 1975, Polisario claimed, sixty-seven of the 102 members of the old Spanish Yemaa had met at Guelta Zemmour and declared Polisario to be the 'sole legitimate representative of the Saharaui people'.[92]

Despite the resonating echo of the Arab summit in Rabat, in October 1974, that had designated the Palestine Liberation Organisation the sole legitimate representative of the Palestinian people, Polisario did not enjoy the diplomatic support of the Arab states. But it found it easier than the PLO to liberate territory. Although it could not retake the towns, its guerrilla campaign

90 Preston, *Franco*, 76-8; Damis, *Conflict* 59-68.

91 Damis, *Conflict*, 71-3; Hodges, *Western Sahara*, 232.

92 Charles D. Smith, *Palestine and the Arab-Israeli Conflict*, 2nd edn (New York: St. Martin's Press, 1992), 235, 271; Santucci, *Chroniques*, 110; Damis, *Conflict*, 74.

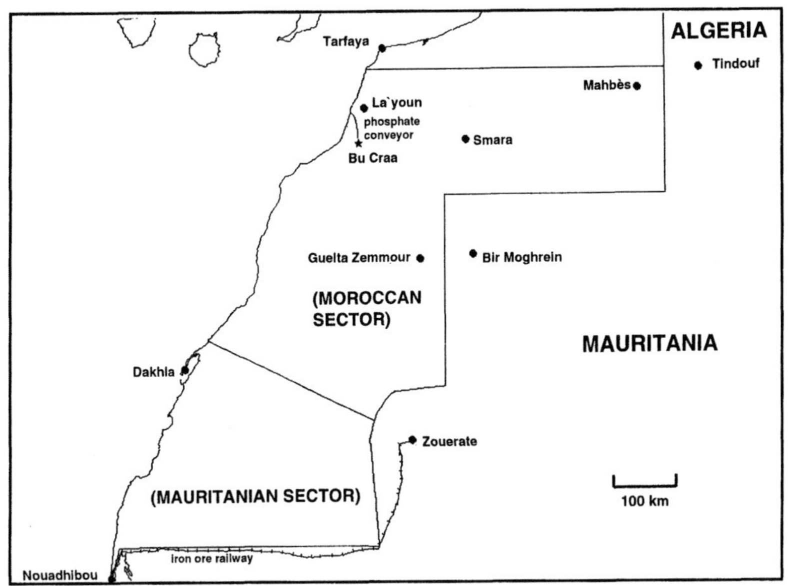

Above The former Spanish Sahara, divided between Morocco and Mauritania, 1975

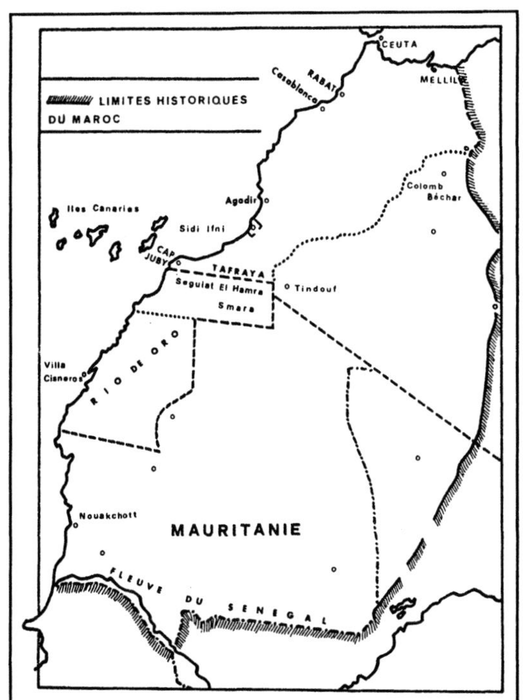

Greater Morocco, as described by Allal El Fassi and others

Source Rachid Lazrak, *Le contentieux territorial entre le Maroc et l'Espagne*, Casablanca: Dar El Kitab, 1974.

was remarkably successful. By the summer of 1976 Polisario units had broken the conveyor belt, and attacked Laâyoune. During the next two years, Polisario began operating big columns of a hundred or more armoured vehicles, heavily laden with Soviet-made weapons. They disrupted the conveyor belt again and again, expelled the Moroccan army from inland posts like Mahbès and Amgala, and even operated far into Morocco, 240 km. from the old border.

Guerrilla warfare could not expel the Moroccan forces, but it certainly put paid to Mauritanian control. Within months of occupying its sector, Mauritania's tiny army was in difficulties. In June 1976 Polisario units raided Nouakchott and went on to attack the iron mines at Zourate and the railway line linking them to the coast, not once but many times.[93] By 1978 defence spending was consuming 60% of the entire Mauritanian budget and although rich, right-wing, Arab states like Saudi Arabia and Kuwait underwrote the deficit, Mauritania hovered on the edge of bankruptcy. In July 1978 a group of junior officers overthrew Ould Dada and accepted Polisario's offer of a ceasefire. There was another coup in April 1979, and in August the Mauritanian government signed a peace treaty that recognised Polisario as the 'sole legitimate representative of the Saharan people', and occupied the Mauritanian zone. The Moroccan army moved southwards.[94]

Now the Moroccan army faced Polisario alone, and these were effective guerrillas indeed. In January 1979 they attacked the Moroccan town of Tan-Tan, so very successfully that Moroccan papers talked of a 'national catastrophe'. In August, Polisario attacked Moroccan troops in Dakhla (Villa Cisneros under the Spanish). The Moroccan army held them off, but later that month at Lebouiarat, it lost 1,500 men to Polisario and enough equipment to supply a whole regiment. In October Polisario attacked Es-Samara, Ma al-Aynan's old capital, and was beaten off by brand-new Moroccan Mirage F-1 jets, but over-ran Mahbès on the road between Algeria and Es-Samara.[95] After three years, the Moroccan army was on the defensive.

The diplomacy of the new Morocco

The Moroccan air force's Mirage jets came from France, but it

93 Santucci, *Chroniques*, 112; Damis, *Conflict*, 71-3, 83-4.

94 Damis, *Conflict*, 84-9; Santucci, *Chroniques*, 173; Ruiz Miguel, *Sahara Occidental*, 131-2.

95 Damis, *Conflict*, 95; Santucci, *Chroniques*, 174-5.

was the Algerian government that supplied Polisario, gave it bases in the refugee camps near Tindouf, and provided diplomatic support at the OAU and at the UN. By July 1980 twenty-three African states had recognised the Saharan Arab Democratic Republic, although it still controlled virtually no territory.[96]

Algerian support for Polisario ended any hope of inter-Maghrib cooperation, although the Moroccan government did not much care. There was nothing to cooperate over. Between 1976 and 1980, Moroccan exports to the other Maghrib countries were never more than 2% of the national total; imports did not exceed 0.2%. Instead, Rabat sought support from the Arab east and in particular from the King of Saudi Arabia, the major source both of oil and aid.[97] Since the great Arab cause was Palestine, the Moroccan government began to play an active role, which was no great hardship since that too was common ground with the nationalist parties. During the Six Day War in 1967 Istiqlal had insisted that troops be sent to help in the fighting, but the war was over before they arrived. Moroccan public opinion shared the Arab feeling that this was a collective tragedy, and during the 1973 war Moroccan troops fought in the Golan and Sinai.[98]

Moroccan help against Israel won Arab support but did not please the American government. From the mid-1970s, the United States was the main source of weapons for the Moroccan army. Washington stipulated that American arms should not be used outside the borders of the country, which included the Sahara but this caused little difficulty. Even during the short period in 1978 and 1979 when President Carter insisted that the restrictions be honoured, there were still none on purely defensive equipment, and French sources provided the rest: Mirage jets, Puma helicopters, Exocet missiles, AMX light tanks and military instructors.[99] The Ben Barka affair had been forgotten, and now King Hassan referred to President Giscard d'Estaing as his '*copain*'. Even ignoring military assistance, by 1975 Morocco received more French bilateral aid than any other country.[100]

All this tied King Hassan to the western bloc. Despite his good relations with the Soviet leadership in the 1960s, the Soviet govern-

96 Damis, *Conflict*, 82, 90, 92.

97 Miguel Hernando de Larremendi, *La política exterior de Marruecos* (Madrid: MAPFRE, 1997), 301.

98 *Ibid.*, 307.

99 *Ibid.*, 216; Damis, *Conflict*, 122-3.

100 Hernando de Larremendi, *La política*, 216, 250-8; Damis, *Conflict*, 122-3.

ment was always closer to Boumedienne's regime in Algeria. Yet the King was careful not to break relations, and in 1974 he sent Ali Yata, the leader of the proto-Communist Parti du Progres et du Socialisme, to plead the Saharan cause in Moscow, although to little effect.[101] In 1978 he signed with the Soviet Union what he later described as 'the contract of the century'. This was an agreement that bartered a fishery deal and the supply of phosphates against a hard currency loan of $2 billion and technical assistance for the phosphate industry. It was the largest commercial deal ever signed between the Soviet Union and a developing country.[102]

The Moroccan Jews

King Hassan tried to use Jewish intermediaries to win support for the Saharan cause in America; he despatched a delegation of influential Moroccan Jews in 1975.[103] Although most Moroccan Jews had emigrated, this was still the biggest community in the Arab world and its elite had close links to the palace. Until 1965 a Jew was cabinet secretary of the Minister of Defence, an unimaginable phenomenon elsewhere in the Arab world, and Sam Benazeraf, an immensely rich Casablanca financier, who had been cabinet secretary to the Minster of Finance in the first Bekkaï government, still played golf with King Hassan. David Amar, who had helped Jews emigrate to Israel, was so close to the King that at the time of the coup in 1971 he briefly fled abroad.[104]

It was the poor and middle-income Jews who had left, although even they did not cut their links. A few even disliked Israel and returned between 1975 and 1978 at the King's invitation.[105] Others reestablished their traditional life in an urban Israeli environment. Between 100,000 and 150,000 pilgrims, 2-3% of the entire Jewish population of Israel visited the grave of a particularly pious Rabbi of Moroccan origin, Israel Abu-Hatseira, on the anniversary of his death.[106] Yet others maintained a psychic link, for one popular pilgrimage site had no tomb at all. In 1973 a forestry worker

101 Hernando de Larremendi, *La política*, 231-9.

102 Damis, *Conflict*, 129.

103 *Ibid.*, 48.

104 Laskier, *Twentieth Century*, 203, 213, 242-3, 250; Bensimon, *Hassan II*, 162-3; Waterbury, *Commander*, 128.

105 Laskier, *Twentieth Century*, 124, 252.

106 Yoram Bilu and Eyal Ben-Ari, 'The Making of Modern Saints: Manufactured Charisma and the Abu Hatseiras of Israel', *American Ethnologist* 19, no. 4 (1992): 672-87.

The Hassan II mosque in Casablanca.

dreamed that a famous Moroccan Jewish saint had appeared to him, so he dedicated a room of his apartment in Safed to this man, with a marble tablet in place of the unavailable gravestone.[107]

Both sides valued these links. In 1970 the President of the AIU declared that to allow the Moroccan Jewish community to disappear would be against Israeli national interests,[108] and the king boasted to Laurent that he did not need a secret service to pass messages to the Israelis: 'The Moroccan Jews living in Israel come back here frequently, and the messages are passed in such a way that there is no need for codes. It is perhaps the most faithful and the most secret way to communicate.'[109]

Morocco became a meeting ground for Israeli and Arab leaders. The Israeli Prime Minister, Yitzhak Rabin, visited in 1976, and General Moshe Dayan started secret contacts in September 1977. He travelled to Marrakesh, toured the markets disguised in a wig, a moustache and dark glasses, and talked to King Hassan about arranging talks between Israel and the Arab states. Shortly afterwards he returned to meet the Egyptian Deputy Prime Minister, Hasan al-Tuhami, as part of the groundwork for President Anwar Sadat's visit to Jerusalem in November 1977.[110]

King Hassan played no part in the peace negotiations themselves but his role as an intermediary won not only American gratitude, but a recognition that Morocco was important. The diplomacy of the post-Saharan period was a great success.

The economics of the new nationalism

The economic results were far less satisfactory. There was no rapid economic growth and living conditions fared little better. The 1973-77 Five-Year Plan aimed for a growth rate of 7.5%, based on increasing exports by 10% a year. Because the local capital base was so small, the state would provide capital investment in irrigation and tourism.

This statist economic policy did not help the poor. In 1973 300,000 ha. of foreign-owned land were expropriated, in order

107 Eyal Ben-Ari and Yoram Bilu, 'Saints' sanctuaries in Israeli development towns: on a mechanism of urban transformation', *Urban Anthropology* 16, no. 2 (1987): 252-72.

108 Quoted in Laskier, *Twentieth Century*, 250.

109 Hassan II, *La Mémoire*, 264.

110 Hassan II, *La Mémoire*, 264-72; Moshe Dayan, *Breakthrough: a Personal Account of the Egypt-Israel Peace Negotiations* (London: Weidenfeld & Nicolson, 1981), 38-54, 91-7; FBIS, 3 April 1984, Israel I4 quoting *Ma'riv*, 2 April 1984.

to 'Moroccanise' the economy, but the Moroccan landlords were indistinguishable from the former French ones, except that senior army officers, politicians and urban merchants were even more likely to be absentees. Two big holding companies, jointly owned by the state and exceptionally wealthy individuals such as the royal family, controlled 40% of the orchards and 80% of the vineyards.[111] They received the benefits of investment in irrigation – between 1975 and 1980 eight major dams were opened providing 263,000 ha. of irrigable land, but 60% less was invested in dryland farming which provided most of the food and employed most of the agricultural labour force. The electrical supplies and the flood control that went with the dams certainly benefited people more generally,[112] but the rainfall was unobliging and harvests were poor in 1975 and 1977 and mediocre in 1979 (see Table on page 312).

The government had little room to manoeuvre. The Saharan war was very expensive. Between 1972 and 1980, defence expenditure rose from 2.8% of GNP to 6.1%, and *per capita* expenditure on defence increased by nearly 30%.[113] Imports cost more too. After the second oil shock in 1978-9, the external debt shot up, but the phosphate price collapsed. In 1977 the European Community, sunk in depression, put ceilings on imports of Moroccan textiles and reduced olive oil imports almost to nothing. In 1978 it cut tomato imports to about half what they had been in 1973.[114]

In 1978 economists in the Central Bank who had warned of inflation and of the danger of gambling on the phosphate price, were able to insist on a stabilisation plan that emphasised austerity. Public spending was cut and private sector investment was encouraged to replace it. The King praised the plan saying it was conceived by Moroccan officials, not foreigners, but it failed partly for that very reason. The high spending ministries raised loans easily enough from international banks flush with the huge deposits of the oil-producing countries, so that foreign debt carried on rising. Even though big tax increases tamed budget deficits, inflation remained above 10%, growth slumped and public enterprises continued to lose money.[115]

The poor suffered. By 1978 the ratio in income between the

111 Swearingen, *Mirages*, 180.

112 *Ibid.*, 166-7.

113 World Bank, *World Development Report 1983* (New York: Oxford University Press, 1983), 198, Table 26.

114 EIU, *Morocco to 1992*, 18-21.

115 Azam and Morrisson, *Political Feasibility*, 92-3.

top 5% of the population and the bottom 50% was 1:12. By the end of 1980 it was predicted that it would be 1:24.[116] Those who had jobs fought back. The miners, the vanguard of worker resistance in 1974 and 1975, were joined by civil servants, teachers and health workers who affiliated to the left-wing trade union federation, Conféderation Générale du Travail. In 1978 there were strikes by primary and secondary school teachers, railway workers, bank employees, postmen, hospital employees, civil aviation workers, dockers and textile workers.[117]

A political opening in the new Morocco?

It was these protests that brought down the government, not the political parties. In 1974 a political opening had indeed begun; the Communist party was re-launched as the Parti du Progrès et du Socialisme (PPS), Istiqlal held a national conference to choose a new leadership (Allal El-Fassi had died the previous year) and the Casablanca branch of the UNFP renamed itself the Union Socialiste des Forces Populaires (Socialist Union of Popular Forces – USFP). But the Saharan war had tamed the main opposition parties all of which supported it enthusiastically. Only some student activists and Marxist-Leninists refused to do so, and they were given brutal treatment. In November 1974 members of the *Ila-al-Amam* (Forwards) group were arrested, and tortured. They included Abraham Serfaty, a Jewish Marxist-Leninist and former technician in the Phosphates Office. In 1977 he was sentenced to life imprisonment at a mass trial in Casablanca of 178 Marxist-Leninists who were prevented by the president of the court from communicating with their defence lawyers. Since many of its own members were still in jail, the USFP leadership made only the most muted protests.[118]

With the opposition silenced or domesticated, parliamentary elections were held in June 1977. The election was carefully managed and all the main parties (including the neo-communist PPS) were given seats, but the 'independents', followed by the Mouvement Populaire took most of them.[119] In 1978, to seal the victory, the king encouraged the independents to form a political

116 Santucci, *Chroniques*, 156.

117 Majid, *Les luttes*, 59, 62; Santucci, *Chroniques*, 177-8.

118 Santucci, *Chroniques*, 80, 141; Amnesty International, *Maroc. Torture, 'disparitions', emprisonnement politique* (Paris: Les Éditions Francophones d'Amnesty International, 1991), 89.

119 López García, *Procesos*, 26-7.

party, the Rassemblement Nationale des Indépendents (National Rally of Independents – RNI) Its leader was the Prime Minister, the king's brother-in-law, Ahmed Osman. In early 1979, street protests brought it down and Maâti Bouabid, who supposedly had good relations with the USFP and other left-wing parties, was asked to take over. But unionists were still locked up, newspapers still suspended, and prisoners were still tortured.[120]

A NEW SOCIETY BEYOND THE STATE?

Moroccan society was moving more quickly than the political system. Demand for change came from outside the political parties, although it was often disorganised and unfocused, sometimes contradictory. Women, for example, wanted better treatment.

Women

In theory, the Moroccan constitutions protected women: 'Men and women shall enjoy equal political rights. Any citizen of age enjoying his or her civil and political rights shall be eligible to vote.'[121] Since parliament was powerless, that was a promise of small value. Just like their husbands and brothers, women were kept away from political, or social or economic power, even in the royal family. Women of Fatima Mernissi's generation had taken Princess Lalla Aïcha as a role model, but after the triple marriage ceremony in 1961, she and her sisters largely withdrew from public life inside Morocco. Lalla Aïcha spent much of the 1960s as ambassador first to the United Kingdom and then to Italy and Greece; Lalla Malika's husband was the Ambassador to France. Only Lalla Fatima Zohra had a public role; in 1969 she became executive president of the newly-founded Union des Femmes Marocaines, a social work organisation, not a campaigning one.[122]

Few women had a political role in the 1960s and 1970s. Left-wing parties – the neo-communist PPS and the social-democrat USFP – considered women's issues to be secondary to the class struggle, and Istiqlal made the traditional family the symbol of Moroccan identity.[123] In the mid 1970s three of the sixty members of the central committee of the Istiqlal were women, there were no women

120 Santucci, *Chroniques*, 179-80.

121 Article 8, Constitution of 1996. Earlier constitutions were much the same.

122 Daoud, *Féminisme et politique*, 263, 277; Waterbury, *Commander*, 125.

123 Daoud, *Féminisme*, 286-8, 315.

parliamentarians and only ten municipal councellors in the whole country.[124]

Laws were made by largely conservative men, so legal changes in women's status came slowly. The code of family law (*Moudawana*) that had been promulgated between 1957 and 1959 was a moderately liberal statement of Islamic law: it allowed polygamy, provided that the first wife had not stipulated in the marriage contract that her husband could not take a second. It made divorce possible for women, but it remained very difficult; for men it was easy. It set the minimum age of marriage at fifteen for women and eighteen for men, but imposed no sanctions on men who married girls as young as ten. A woman could join a union or a political party, or work, with the permission of her husband.[125] In 1979 bills were presented to parliament that would have made divorce conditional on mutual consent and allowed women to institute proceedings, banned polygamy and allowed a woman to work freely. They were rejected after a welter of attacks by conservative '*ulama*.[126]

This was quite out of step with reality. Even in 1957 a fifth of wage earners had been women, although men and women did not earn wages in the countryside. By 1971 the figure was 30%, and the permission of their husbands was beside the point: women worked because they had to and many women did not have husbands anyway. More than 45% of paid women workers were widows and just under a quarter were divorced.[127] Young girls worked at weaving, or making carpets. Fatima Mernissi interviewed several who had grown up in the 1960s and worked from the age of twelve or even nine paid by piece work and confined to workshops that were unheated in winter.[128] At the end of the 1970s the Anti-Slavery Society, a British charity, listed numerous factories where more than a third of the employees were less than twelve, some of them only eight or nine, undernourished and shut up in badly lit and unhealthy workshops.[129] They were paid exceptionally low wages and since this undercut male rates, it confirmed conservative men's dislike of women working. A survey

124 *Ibid.*, 288-9.

125 *Ibid.*, 259-60.

126 *Ibid.*, 299-302.

127 *Ibid.*, 268, 279-280.

128 Fatima Mernissi, *Doing Daily Battle: Interviews with Moroccan Women* (London: Women's Press, 1986), 106-21.

129 Anti-Slavery Society, *Child Labour in Morocco's Carpet Industry* (London: Anti-Slavery Society, 1978), 9.

of young men in a Moroccan magazine in the mid-1960s linked a desire for women not to work with the desire for a virgin bride.[130]

Women's wants were rather different. Even in the early 1960s in remote parts of the Rif mountains, women who had never even met a foreigner longed for the better life that they believed existed overseas, to the disgust of their menfolk. One man complained to an American sociologist about his sister: 'According to Muhand she is discontented with her lot as a Rifi woman. Her husband has worked in France and she has heard him telling Muhand about our ways of life and the freedom of Western women with none of the hard work, such as fetching water, cutting grass or milling barley. Now she is pestering him to take her to France.'[131] By the end of the 1970s Rifi men were doing just that. It was cheaper, because in countries like France and the Netherlands Holland, health and education were free.[132]

Whether they emigrated or stayed behind, women were becoming more powerful in their own families. If they were left behind, they managed the entire household. If they accompanied their husbands, Muhand the Rifi's worst fears were realised. Women whom Fatima Mernissi interviewed in the mid 1970s were clear about what sort of husband they wanted for themselves and their daughters: education and sobriety were the ideals:[133] 'Someone who was a drunkard or didn't behave well would not be suitable... Am I going to see her marry someone who is not educated? He should be even more educated than her.'[134]

Women also wanted a relationship based on affection: no second wife and no violence. One woman, an illiterate Berber who moved to Rabat in the early 1960s when still a child, described her ideal man: 'What I want is someone who loves me and can be responsible for a household, not someone who at any moment might have to steal to survive or who would abandon me, leaving me with the responsibility for the children. I am not looking for wealth; I would even pass up a dowry. But I need to have someone I

130 Daoud, *Féminisme*, 265.

131 Hart, *Courtyard Door*, 28.

132 Paolo de Mas, 'Dynamique récente de la migration marocaine vers les Pay-Bas: specificité régionale et réseau rifain' in *Le Maroc et la Hollande, une approche comparative des grands intérêts communs* (Rabat: Université Mohammed V, Faculté des Lettres, 1995), 223-4.

133 Mernissi, *Battle*, 54, 122.

134 *Ibid.*, 78-9.

can count on in the long term.'[135] She, too, wanted an educated husband for her daughters. Others valued education for their own personal fulfilment. A doctor's wife, who trained as a teacher to eke out his meagre salary as an intern, continued working after he had qualified

> '[...] because I am a very proud woman. I never asked my husband to buy me anything at all. I wanted my work to allow me to buy what I needed, to not depend on my husband. I preferred to keep a certain independence. Sometimes my husband would complain: "You have assumed too much independence. I know where it's from. It's from your work, from your car. I'll have to take them both away from you." But I know how to handle him. I told him that I would hand in my resignation the next day if he was ready to take over supplying my needs. Sometimes I went as far as writing out my resignation and asking him to hand it in himself. Deep down he wasn't very keen on my resigning. It was a situation that suited him.'[136]

Mernissi's sample was quite small, but it spanned the relatively well-off and the very poor, the literate and the illiterate, and those who were both Arabic-speaking and Berber-speaking in origin. Moreover the values that they attached to education, meaningful emotional relationships in marriage, a sober and kind husband and a standard of living achieved through their own work, were ones that would be repeated in wider scale social surveys in the 1980s and early 1990s.[137] These women also sought to reshape their personal relationships and living conditions on their own terms: they did not look to the state.

An informal society with informal politics

By the end of the 1970s the state had abandoned large areas of responsibility. When Morocco became independent, 80% of the population lived in the countryside; by 1980 the figure was 56%. By the beginning of the 1980s, Casablanca's population was more than 3 million; nearly two-thirds of the population were

135 *Ibid.*, 182-3.

136 *Ibid.*, 50.

137 Soumaya Naamane-Guessous, *Au-delà de toute pudeur. La sexualité féminine au Maroc: conclusion d'une enquête sociologique menée de 1981 à 1984 à Casablanca* (Casablanca: Editions Eddif, 1991); Mounia Bennani-Chraïbi, *Soumis et rebelles: les jeunes au Maroc* (Casablanca: Editions le Fennec, 1994). See also Daoud, *Féminisme*, 319-20.

under the age of twenty. The government was quite unable to cope. In 1980, when the King laid the foundation stone of a housing scheme to rehouse 6,000 families from one of the most notorious *bidonvilles* of Casablanca, that same *bidonville* had a population of 34,000.[138] In no way could the *bidonvilles* be prevented from spreading: they alone provided housing. The government could only acquiesce in a *fait accompli*.[139]

Neither could the formal economy provide jobs. In 1980 over a quarter of people in Casablanca aged between twenty and twenty-four were unemployed.[140] In the early 1980s it was estimated that 76% of the labour force depended on the informal economy, and the informal labour force was estimated to be growing at 6% a year. That was twice that of the modern sector, though statistics were little more than guesses.[141] Nor could the government provide education: only 30% of the population of Casablanca under the age of twenty had been to secondary school.[142]

People were housing themselves, and living from day to day, and the formal economy and the state provided no hope of relief; the rich and powerful seemed to care little for them. Some, in consequence, sought alternative ways to think and act.

The Islamists

El-Faqih el-Zamzami, who died in 1989, was one of several Islamist teachers who emerged in the political vacuum that followed the failed coups. His was a very personal Islam: he focused on individual behaviour, on how Muslims should dress and pray but his attacks on the rich, for their corruption and their impiety, won him much support among the poor of his native Tangier. But he did not criticise the king: it was his servants that had failed: his was a thoroughly traditional message, not a call for the overthrow of the government.[143]

Abd al-Karim Muti', a former official of the Education Ministry, founded a more radical youth movement, *al-Shabiba al-Islamiyya* (Islamic Youth), in the early 1970s that did attack the king. In the early 1980s it sent him an open letter that contained some

138 Santucci, *Chroniques*, 204.

139 Salahdine, 'Informal Sector', 23-33.

140 Santucci, *Chroniques*, 222.

141 Salahdine, *Petits Métiers*, 34-7.

142 Santucci, *Chroniques*, 222.

143 Munson, *Religion and Power*, 153-8.

incendiary advice: 'We say to you: Fear God in his religion and the religion of the Prophet before he turns you into a monkey, after having changed you into a drunkard and an opium addict.'[144]

Al-Shabiba's propaganda was tinged with nationalism and complained about American imperialism and international Zionism, but like many radical student movements, it split in the mid-1970s, after Muti' fled abroad. The government had accused him of planning the assassination of a left-wing journalist, Omar Benjelloun – though he replied that it was the government that had eliminated its left-wing critic and then put the blame on a radical Islamic spokesman.[145]

The most important Islamic voice was that of another former official in the Education Ministry, Abd al-Salam Yasin. He had published two books, in 1972 and 1973, that called for an Islamic state in Morocco, led by a moral leader inspired by the Prophet. What made him famous was an open letter to the King in 1974 entitled 'Islam or the Deluge'.[146] In it, he blamed the coups on King Hassan's failures as a ruler, saying that he was corrupt, that he advocated liberal western values and that he was indebted to foreign, particularly Zionist, capital. Yasin questioned whether the King was a Muslim at all. King Hassan, he wrote, should abandon the ways of wickedness. Yet Yasin was neither a Salafi modernist – he was a Sufi – nor was he a democrat; he wanted a just Islamic society, ruled by a just, Islamic absolute monarch who should be descended from the Prophet. His ideas echoed those of the Kittanis at the very beginning of the century. Since this was 1974, not 1909, Shaykh Yasin was not flogged; instead, he was shut up for three years in a mental hospital.[147]

Perhaps Shaykh Yasin was treated relatively gently to avoid turning him into a martyr, but perhaps also, because he was a traditionalist who favoured rule by a descendant of the Prophet, the king hoped to use him as a tool against the left. The early fundamentalist groups had been tolerated for that very reason.[148] When Yasin emerged from his mental hospital in 1979, tolerance had been abandoned. The Iranian revolution demonstrated so very graphically the power of political Islam. King Hassan briefly

144 *Ibid.*, 159.

145 Mohammed Tozy, 'Islam and the State', in Zartman, *Political Economy*, 113.

146 Muhammad Darif, *Jama'at al-'Adl wa-Ihsan: qara't fi al-Masarat* (Rabat: Manshurat al-Majallat al-Maghribiyya l-'ilm al-ijtima' al-siyyasi: 1995), 11-14.

147 Munson, *Religion and Power*, 162-7.

148 Tozy, 'Islam', 111.

gave the deposed Shah of Iran refuge but there were many protests and the Shah was soon on his way.[149] Those protests pointed out the alternative way to make the voice of the streets heard: by riot and demonstration.

The rebellion in Casablanca

In 1980 inflation reached 15% a year and the dirham began to collapse. The government's attempts to deal with the crisis were very piecemeal. Political prisoners from the USFP, but not from far-left groups like *Ila al-Amam*, were amnestied. There was yet another constitution, although all it changed was the age of majority of any future king (reduced from eighteen to sixteen) and the term of office of parliamentary deputies (lengthened from four to six years). It was only important because the referendum that approved it did so with over 95% voting in favour (100% in the Saharan provinces), an apparent symbol of national unity. More practically, the King inaugurated housing projects for the bidonvilles and promised to increase the opportunities for students to go to universities. The budget created nearly 37,000 new jobs in the public sector, and raised the salaries of civil servants.[150]

But the rains in the winter of 1980-1 were nowhere near enough, the land was parched, and the government could not afford to subsidise food. At the end of May 1981 it announced price rises. Although the opposition parties protested and the unions called strikes, they could not agree on a common tactic. Opposition to the price rises was taken out of their hands and onto the streets of Morocco's largest city.

Casablanca was the heart of the modern sector of the Moroccan economy. It accounted for 60% of industrial activity, 72% of salaries and 70% of bank accounts. But it was also the heart of its poverty: out of the population of 3.2 million 1.9 million were less than nineteen years old, 30% of adults between twenty and twenty-four years old were unemployed. Over a quarter of the population lived in the shanty-towns in conditions of extreme poverty. There was no reason why such people should put much hope in political parties or trade unions. This was an urban riot by the disinherited, the unemployed and the young, who attacked not only the forces of law but the rich. Banks and cars were burned. According to official figures sixty-six people were killed; Moroccan exile organisa-

149 Hassan II, *La Mémoire*, 223.

150 *Ibid.*; Santucci, *Chroniques*, 195-203.

tions in France estimated that the true figure was between 600 and 1,000.[151]

The need for a new consensus

The riots of 1981 shook the government. King Hassan had been in power for nearly twenty years, and in the first part of his reign he had occupied the centre of the stage quite openly. By doing so, he had strengthened his authority in the short term, but weakened it in the long term: first, it was impossible to stand above the political system and at the same time intervene between political groups; and second, he could not instigate land reform and so produce more food because he was so reliant on the support of the rural elite.[152] The consequence was economic reliance on trade with Europe to generate enough money to feed the cities, whose populations were growing because of rural poverty. It was this equation that could not be solved and it led to the attempted coups of 1971 and 1972.

In order to remake a consensus, and to withdraw himself from direct participation in the political arena, the King reactivated a multi-party system and adopted the recuperation of the Sahara as a national objective. To an extent this was successful, in that it allowed the parties to operate and support the monarchy, and so took the immediate heat out of the political struggle. As a result, the level of state violence dropped, and the repression eased, although it did not disappear. But it did not solve the essential economic problems: rural and urban poverty and an agricultural base that could not feed the country. Even worse, it undermined those who might have acted as representatives of the poor and the deprived: the political parties, having been incorporated into the system, were weakened as a result.[153]

The Iranian revolution demonstrated a new alternative, showing that religion could offer a different political structure and an alternative ideal. The time had come to move from kingship to democracy and from poverty to wealth. If change did not come, the regime would be at risk.

151 Hassan II, *La Mémoire*; Santucci, *Chroniques*, 221-22.

152 Hammoudi, *Master and Disciple*, 34.

153 *Ibid.*, 34.

10

ADJUSTMENTS

In 1980, the year before the Casablanca riots, a woman named Rachida Yacoubi got divorced. She had married in 1962 aged fourteen, and had four children. Her husband, an accountant, was a heavy drinker. None of this was unusual. In 1973 the average age for women to marry for the time was fifteen and a half, and it was estimated that 30% of married women had been married before,[1] although divorce was rather less frequent among middle-class women like Madame Yacoubi because of its awful financial and social consequences. In two things only was she exceptional: it was she who insisted on the divorce, and she wrote a book about her experiences.[2] When *Ma vie, mon cri* was published at the end of 1994, it caused a sensation, and sold more copies in a year than any book by a Moroccan author had ever done before. Her riches-to-rags story recounted, in vivid and graphic detail, the corruption of both official and personal life, the degrading treatment of women and conditions in the *bidonville* where for a time she had to live. It was also a story of great personal courage, of the power of personal religious faith, and of her own efforts to rebuild her life.

Although her book was completely apolitical (she did not even mention the Casablanca riots, her personal story mirrored that of the country as a whole, not least in her economic trajectory. Although she was (unexpectedly) poor in 1980, over the next few years she slowly regained a sort of limited prosperity. That was true of many Moroccans, for whom she stands as an exemplar, just as her experiences in the shanty-towns mirrored those of their many inhabitants.

The economic crisis

The riots in Casablanca in 1981 shocked both the Moroccan government and its allies in the United States and Western Europe.

[1] Daoud, *Féminisme*, 279.

[2] Rachida Yacoubi, *Ma vie, mon cri* (Casablanca: Eddif, 1995), especially 225.

Foreign aid, already substantial, quickly increased. Between 1980 and 1993 the International Monetary Fund made no fewer than nine 'arrangements', extensions of credit totalling 3,040 million SDRs (Standard Drawing Rights). There were also six reschedulings of debt to official lenders, three commercial bank reschedulings, and very large aid programs.[3]

This did not come without strings. The IMF required the Moroccan government to undertake a structural adjustment policy of economic austerity and fiscal conservatism. One really pressing problem was the size of the government deficit, equivalent to fourteen per cent of GDP in 1981. Yet it was hard reduce this through fiscal measures because the government was required to reduce taxes on trade at the same time. Consequently, between 1981 and 1985, the main burden fell on capital expenditure, which was cut, and the wages of state employees virtually frozen. Instead, investment was directed to export industries, the dirham was devalued, and the state was required to privatise nationalised industries and raise taxes. In practice, the change in tax structure away from taxes on trade to those on income and sales took longer to get under way, and privatisation did not begin until well into the 1990s.[4]

This was a difficult road to travel, and in the early 1980s, the balance of trade got worse, inflation stayed high (6%, in 1983, was the lowest) and the external debt went up in the early 1980s. But after 1985, external debt and the trade deficit began to fall, and *per capita* GDP began to climb, at least in years when harvests were good. (See table p. 364). External debt went down from more than 125% of the equivalent of GDP in 1985 to less than 80% in 1993. Changes in the tax system, particularly corporate taxation, increased government revenue in the late 1980s.

Most importantly, agriculture flourished, because of greater investment in rainfed agriculture, livestock and forestry. The government continued to invest in irrigation. In 1984, after three years of drought, the King abolished agricultural taxes for the rest of the century. Since the tax had raised less than it cost to levy, this encouraged agriculture and saved money. Good rainfall produced good harvests for the second half of the decade, and vegetables and cut flowers found new markets outside the EEC,

[3] Nsouli *et al.*, *Resilience and Growth*, 8ff.

[4] *Ibid.*, 161-17; Ahmed Rhazaoui, 'Recent Economic Trends: Managing the Indebtedness' in Zartman *Political Economy*, 141-58. 153-5.

in Canada and Scandinavia.[5] Even more dramatic was the emergence of the Moroccan fishing industry: exports nearly trebled between 1980 and 1991 to more than 200 million tons.[6]

The EEC remained the major trading partner, although after Spain and Portugal joined the community in 1986, restrictive tariffs were put on olive oil, wine and citrus fruit. King Hassan's response was innovative: in July 1987 the Moroccan government applied to join the EC. The application was rejected, on the unsurprising grounds that Morocco is not in Europe, but new trade preferences were negotiated that substantially reduced restraints on trade with the European bloc. By the end of 1993 only one restraint on trade remained: on trousers.[7]

Europe was also a major source of tourists: between 1-1.5 million of them came every year during the second half of the 1980s and the early 1990s. Most were French or Spanish but there were also around 100,000 each from Britain, the Netherlands and Germany. This mass tourism centred on huge beach resorts along the Atlantic coast, especially in the rebuilt city of Agadir, and it made a welcome contribution to the Moroccan trade balance. Another big spending group came in the form of a steady influx of Saudis, around 20,000 arrivals a year, who tended to buy holiday homes rather than stay in beach hotels.[8]

Self-discipline was touted as having brought results. In 1986 the influential *Economist Intelligence Unit* in London published a report on Morocco, subtitled *Growth against the Odds*.[9] Nearly ten years later, in 1995, the IMF's report on Morocco was entitled *Resilience and Growth through Sustained Adjustment*. Yet the economy was not in uniformly good health. It was still as much a prisoner of the weather in 1990 as it had been in 1830. In 1986 the harvests were good and growth was high; but they failed in 1992, and the economy shrank. Tourism was also a risky business: receipts fell by 16.5% in 1990, the year of the Gulf War.[10]

5 Santucci, *Chroniques*, 254; Rhazaoui, 'Trends', 149; *Financial Times*, 3 November 1993, 'Survey of Morocco (4)'.

6 EIU, *Growth*, 63; Nsouli *et al.*, *Resilience and Growth*, 68.

7 Bahaijoub, 'Morocco's Argument', *passim*; EIU, *Growth*, 14-28; Pomfret, 'International Relations', 174-6, 180-3; El Malki, *Trente Ans*, 115, 150-1.

8 Nsouli *et al.*, *Resilience and Growth*, 77; Statistical, Economic and Social Research and Training Centre for Islamic Countries (SESRTCIC) (a subsidiary organ of the Organisation of the Islamic Conference (OIC). The statistics quoted here come from their web page at http://www.sesrtcic.org.

9 EIU, *Growth*.

10 Nsouli *et al.*, *Resilience and Growth*, 77; SESRTCIC.

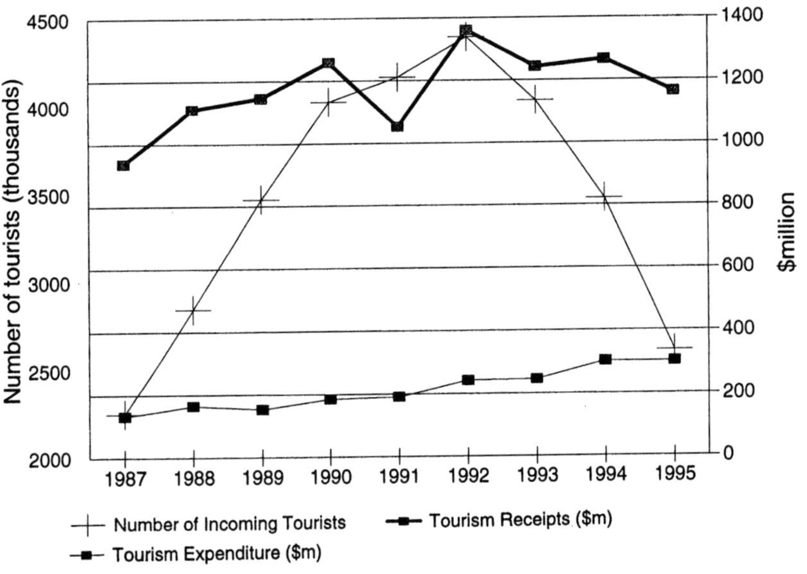

MOROCCAN TOURISM IN THE ECONOMY

The middle and lower income earners and the poor did not *feel* any richer, nor were they in the short term. Inflation ran between 5% and 9% a year, and the official unemployment rate went up from 14% to 16%. Between 60% and 90% of rural housing was officially considered insanitary, and those officially classified as poor made up 13% of the population in 1992 (and the Moroccan poverty-line was drawn very low). But this figure was half what it had been in 1980, and only 20% of urban housing was classified as insanitary. Morocco was becoming an urban, rather than a rural country: fewer than 60% of the population lived in the countryside in 1982 (it had been 70% in 1970), and by 1992 the figure had fallen to 50%. In the long term, even though education and health budgets were cut, more people were educated and lived longer. Between 1980 and 1992 the death rate nearly halved (13 to 7.3 per 1,000), life expectancy increased from fifty-six to sixty-three years and the literacy rate rose from 28% of the population to more than 40%.[11]

That was certainly a low literacy rate, but it was the basis for the rapid expansion of the Moroccan middle class, and class

11 SESRTCIC.

divisions were widening. While the commanding positions in the commercial and banking sectors were held by members of the old elites – drawn from such families as the Bargach, Benjelloun and Guessus – as the commercial sector expanded it required educated workers, and secondary and tertiary education grew quite quickly. The liberal professions expanded dramatically; one example was doctors: there were 126,000 people for each physician in 1971, 11,000 in 1980 and just under 5,000 in 1990.[12] By 1985 the top 6% of the population were responsible for nearly 22% of spending, and the top 20% spent nearly 40%. Many of the economically active new middle class were women: 34% of judges, 32% of doctors, 33% of primary teachers and 35% of tertiary level teachers.[13]

In the *bidonvilles* it was a struggle to survive. After the divorce that forced them to leave their comfortable middle-class house, Rachida Yacoubi and her children ended up in a Casablanca shanty-town, occupying a shack for which they paid 300 dirhams a month. It was filthy and infested with flies and rats, although it did share a functioning toilet with several other families (the door did not lock), and because her family was small she was less crowded than her neighbours. On one side was a family of two adults and five children in a single room; on another a woman and six children. But there was more of a sense of community here than among her former middle-class friends.

> During the day our bidonville turned itself into 'clothville'. There were lines and lines of washing everywhere, and spread out on the walls, the roofs, and carefully positioned on the ground. One had to be a real gymnast to get around. It gave the feeling of being strangled by the web of a huge spider. The special smell of the urine of children who were fed only on bread and mint tea was all around us.
>
> We were seven tenants with about thirty children, who behaved quite well. If I went away, my neighbours kept an eye on my children. One of them, Rkia, took special care of Yasmine, who was immobilised with a broken leg.[14]

Like many inhabitants of the *bidonvilles*. Rachida Yacoubi made her living in the informal market. Unlike her neighbours she could sell some of her possessions (her best coat went to buy medicines for one of her children). She had also rescued her sewing-machine

12 Benhaddou, *Elites*, 73-5; Nsouli *et al.*, *Resilience and Growth*, 19.

13 Daoud, *Féminisme*, 329-30.

14 Yacoubi, *Ma vie*, 89.

from her old house and used it to make clothes. She then sold clothes from door to door until she had saved or borrowed enough to rent a small shop. Eventually she set up a small workshop making clothes and employed a few other women. Gradually she brought herself back into the formal economy.

The real danger to the regime came not from the very poor, but from the young unemployed, some of whom were quite well educated. For most of the 1980s the youth unemployment rate was around 30%.[15] The unemployed youth led numerous riots, even in medium sized towns like Marrakesh and Tetuan in the winter of 1984,[16] but while these were serious, their profound political alienation was worse.

Alienation from the political process

In 1980 there were more than 2 million students in primary school and nearly 800,000 in secondary school, but there were no jobs for them when they left. By 1991 a government survey showed that 21% of degree holders were looking for employment and of those 38% had been trying for more than three years to find work. They even included medical doctors.[17]

This encouraged cynicism and alienation rather than political activism. Between 1989 and 1990 a sociologist, Mounia Bennani-Chraïbi, interviewed numerous young unemployed men and women. Many told her that they wanted nothing to do with politics. Politics, one said, had destroyed all law and 'put it in prison'. Another said: 'I belong to no party, I have my own system... It's my personal party. I tell myself what to do, and I do only what I decide to do.'[18] The speaker was a twenty-year-old student in Marrakesh, for whom the mainstream political leaders were part of an alien and self-serving elite. Yet few of these young people criticised the King, sometimes out of caution of course but also because many placed him above politics; they rebelled against the government and excoriated its leaders, but they respected the King, a sort of late-twentieth-century *siba.* A twenty-year-old

15 Nsouli *et al.*, *Resilience and Growth*, 18-19.

16 John Damis, 'The Impact of the Saharan Dispute on Moroccan Domestic and Foreign Policy' in Zartman, *Political Economy*, 209; Dale Eickelman, 'Religion Polity and Society,' in *ibid.*, 91-3. Zartman, 'King Hassan's New Morocco', 22, 27; Rhazaoui, 'Trends', 151-2.

17 Mounia Bennani-Chraïbi, *Soumis et rebelles. Les jeunes au Maroc* (Casablanca: Editions le Fennec, 1994), 16-18.

18 Bennani-Chraibi, *Soumis*, 207.

from Tangier declared: 'I am not a party man, I am a Moroccan, I live under a red flag with a green star. Long live Hassan II...I belong to no party, I don't like the party system, I am free. Only God should be adored, you can't adore a party'.[19] This man was a hashish-trafficker.

Whatever the views of the young, little changed at the top. To be sure, the government that had been appointed in 1979 was reshuffled and some younger ministers were brought into more junior posts. Cabinet members identified their parties more clearly. But the senior ministers hardly changed and the prime minister was Maâti Bouabid, a Moroccan political archetype, who had started out in Istiqlal and passed through the UNFP before identifying himself as an 'independent'. In 1983, when a more definite party identification was needed, he formed the Union Constitutionelle. It claimed to be a 'liberal' party, but in reality was populist, careful to incorporate moderate Islamist ideas, and masterful at using television and video. The UC did remarkably well in local and national elections in 1983 and 1984, partly, the opposition parties complained, because the elections were a travesty,[20] but partly because the UC was better at talking to an ill-educated electorate. At one election meeting a USFP candidate dismissed the UC as 'middle class' and 'capitalist', and went on to talk about classes and bourgeoisies, ideas that made little sense to rural voters; his UC opponent mocked him in the earthiest of terms. Some on the left, women prominent among them, recognised the dangers of elitism and left the USFP and the PPS to form a new left wing party, the *Organization de l'Action Démocratique et Populaire* (OADP).[21]

The Islamic movement

Opposition from outside Parliament was more dangerous. The Iranian revolution in 1979, and the reaction to the fugitive Shah seeking refuge in Morocco awakened the King to the danger of Islamic revolution. King Hassan later told Eric Laurent that the Shah's own behaviour, publicly drinking champagne, allowing the Empress Farah to visit mosques in a revealing dress and other disgraceful acts, had infuriated devout Muslims; to an extent he had himself to blame. King Hassan fought the Islamists on their

19 *Ibid.*, 206.

20 Eickelman, 'Religion', 94-5; Rkia El-Mossadeq, 'Political Parties and Power Sharing' in Zartman, *Political Economy*, 77-9; Daoud Féminisme, 306-7.

21 Santucci, *Chroniques*, 236; Kevin Dwyer, *Arab Voices: The Human Rights Debate in the Middle East* (Berkeley: University of California Press, 1991), 104.

own ground.[22] In 1980 the '*ulama* issued a religious decree (*fatwa*) declaring that Khomeini's views were unIslamic because they offended against the unity of God. The King set up a new High Council of '*ulama*, assumed its presidency and started building the third largest mosque in the world, in Casablanca, naming it after himself.[23]

At the same time, the government repressed the Islamic movement. Shaykh Yasin's Justice and Charity Society (*al-adlwal-Ihsan*) was reorganised in 1983 with a cell structure, but that provided no protection. In December that year, after Yasin's Islamist magazine was banned, the shaykh was imprisoned and then put under house arrest. Many of his supporters were imprisoned in 1984 and became 'living martyrs' as followers of the cause called them. Yet, until the restrictions were tightened in 1989, Yasin had an effective spokeswoman in his daughter Nadia, a law graduate who spoke excellent French.[24]

Yasin's supporters were generally students or the well-educated young. The poor preferred el-Fqih el-Zamzami's more generalised attacks on the rich. His sermons were distributed, Khomeini-style, on cassettes, but because he avoided direct attacks on the government, he was generally left alone, albeit under tight surveillance. El-Zamzami died in 1989.[25]

The most severe repression was reserved for the fragmented offshoots of Abd al-Karim Muti's Islamic Youth (*al-Shabiba al-Islamiyya*). Muti was in exile, but his supporters in high schools and universities turned to violence. In 1984 seventy-one were arrested and tried, and some were sentenced to death.[26]

The Islamic movement did not take off in Morocco in the 1980s, partly because it was so fragmented. Yasin, for example, used Sufi ideas that members of other Islamist groups loathed but which the poor respected. When Islamists attacked marabouts and described the brotherhoods as heretical and polytheistic, they did not win converts to their cause.[27]

22 Hassan II, *La Mémoire*, 219-20.

23 Jamal Benomar, 'The Monarchy, the Islamist Movement and Religious Discourse in Morocco', *Third World Quarterly*, 10, no. 2 (1988): 52-4.

24 Henry Munson, 'The Political Role of Islam in Morocco' in Joffe (ed.), *North Africa*, 190-1.

25 Munson, *Religion and Power*, 153-8.

26 Munson, 'Political Role', 198-9; Munson, *Religion and Power*, 159-61.

27 Henry Munson, 'The Social Base of Islamic Militancy in Morocco', *Middle East Journal*, 40, no. 2 (1985): 267-84; Mohamed Chtatou, 'Saints and Spirits and their Significance in Moroccan Cultural Beliefs and Practices: an Analysis of Westermarck's

Indeed, there was a Sufi revival in Morocco in the 1980s, and of religion more generally.[28] Most of the young people interviewed by Mounia Bennani-Chraïbi prayed regularly, and explained that religion was a personal anchor when other symbols of identity were under strain. In the 1980s more women started to wear the veil, some, certainly, under pressure from fathers and brothers who wanted 'respectability' in their womenfolk, but many young women adopted it willingly. Bennani-Chraïbi found that many working women equated the veil with personal freedom: they expressed their religious identity by wearing Islamic dress and emphasised their personal identity by working.[29]

Other women did not put on Islamic dress at all. Rachida Yacoubi rushed around town on a moped dressed in jeans, selling clothes. Yet she relied very heavily on her faith; in her most despairing moments: 'I put confidence in my Creator. How could I fail in his presence? He was the sole witness of my tears, my misery, and the only judge of what I did. I had certainly not been abandoned, as male society slyly believed'.[30]

Women and power

Whatever men believed, Madame Yacoubi could take care of herself, like most other Moroccan women. They had no choice, anyway. In the early 1980s, women were the heads of 17% of all Moroccan families and 21% of families in the towns, the result of emigration and the high rates of divorce.[31] By the end of the decade, women made up about 35% of the urban workforce, and men were happy enough to employ them, because they were cheap and uncomplaining. The managing director of one factory explained in a self-satisfied fashion: 'Seventy per cent of my employees are women. They are better at carrying out repetitive tasks. They adapt better than men to the process of assembling electric and electronic parts.'[32] Women remained much worse educated than men. A UNESCO report in 1984 estimated that 66.4% of men and 90.2% of women were illiterate.[33]

Work', *Morocco* (n.s.) 1 (1996): 77-8.

28 Munson, *Religion and Power*, 168.

29 Bennani-Chraibi, *Soumis*, 89-100.

30 Yacoubi, *Ma vie*, 91.

31 Daoud, *Féminisme*, 320, 325.

32 Quoted in Benhaddou, *Maroc*, 107; Daoud, *Féminisme*, 328-9, 325.

33 Daoud, *Féminisme*, 329.

Some discrimination was deeply personal. Those sly men assumed that because Rachida Yacoubi was alone and without a protector, she was sexually available. Within weeks of leaving her own husband, the husband of a good friend had propositioned her on his own doorstep.[34] Sexual harassment was all too general and the agents of the state were just as corrupt as her private acquaintances. A minor local official refused to supply her with a new identity card after she refused his implicit demand for sexual favours. There was nothing to stop him: without hesitating, he explained his refusal saying: 'It's quite simple: I don't want to'. A judge rejected her complaint that she had been attacked when he heard she was divorced. While not every official was corrupt, and not every judge unjust, the word 'justice' continued to make her shiver with anxiety a decade later.[35]

The corruption of the legal system was a major issue in the human rights movement that developed in Morocco in the 1980s. Women were particularly active in the creation of the Organisation Marocaine des Droits de l'Homme (OMDH) which was finally authorised in 1988 after several attempts.[36]

Human rights

Throughout the decade the government tried to silence dissent. Newspaper editors were jailed for defaming the public authorities, maligning the courts and libel. In 1981 members of the USFP were imprisoned for a year for 'perturbing public opinion' by questioning the government's commitment to the Saharan War. Using a dahir dating back to 1935 the government detained demonstrators and arrested activists from the far left (*Ila al-Amam*) or from Shaykh Yacsin's *al-Adl wal-Ihsan* for conspiring to disrupt state security.[37] Not everyone was even charged: some simply disappeared. There were secret prisons in remote parts of Morocco, often on the Saharan fringes. Conditions in the castle at Tazmamart in the High Atlas, were particularly frightful: those who took part in the Skhirat coup of 1971 were confined there.[38] The family of General Oufkir were locked up until 1987, when four of his

34 Yacoubi, *Ma vie*, 18.

35 *Ibid.*, 120, 196, 118.

36 Daoud, *Féminisme*, 313-17.

37 Bennani and Eloualladi, *Liberté de presse*, 177-9; Amnesty International, *Maroc*, 71-9, 89.

38 Amnesty International, *Maroc*, 68-9.

children, now adults, escaped and contacted a French lawyer. They were rearrested but pressure from the French government got them released in 1991 and they went to France in 1996.[39]

International presure from Amnesty International and from individuals like Danièlle Mitterrand, wife of the French President, was helpful, but the brunt was born by brave and dedicated Moroccans: members of the Bar Association who defended political offenders, and activists in the Ligue Marocaine de Défense des Droits de l'Homme (founded in 1972), the Association Marocaine des Droits de l'Homme (founded in 1979) and the OMDH who campaigned against torture and restrictions on press freedom and in favour of women's rights.[40]

State officials routinely ignored laws that determined how people should be treated. King Hassan admitted that he had no idea how bad conditions were in Tazmamart, and when he *had* found out, he said, he had put them right.[41] The most savage repression was directed against those who opposed the Saharan war, for whom the King made no allowances. He told Eric Laurent: 'I have always said that, in this country, the rights of man stopped at the question of the Sahara. Anyone who said that the Sahara was not Moroccan could not benefit from the rights of man.'[42] The Saharan question had become central to the survival of the state.

Arab allies and the Saharan war

In March 1980 Polisario comprehensively beat the Royal Armed Forces in the Jbel Ouarkziz region, so a new military strategy was adopted. Over the next two years, the army built a vast defensive wall of sand across the desert, 480 km. long, over 2 meters high, and protected by barbed wire and radar. By 1982 it had shut Polisario out of the 'useful Sahara': Laâyoune, Es-Samara and the phosphate mines. Once that perimeter had been secured, new walls were built further out, so that by 1985 Polisario guerrillas had been excluded from most of the former Spanish colony. This

39 Hassan II, *La Mémoire*, 294; *The Times*, 26 February 1996; *Al-munazima al-Maghribiyya li-huquq al- insan min khillal bilaghatiha wa-tasrihatiha, dijinbar 1992-mayu 1994* (Rabat: Organisation Marocaine de Droits de l'Homme), 130-4; Amnesty International, *Maroc*, 65; Daure-Serfaty, *Rencontres*, 185.

40 Bennani and Eloualladi, *Liberté de presse*, 265-75.

41 Hassan II, *La Mémoire*, 294-6.

42 Ibid., 293.

strategy was extremely expensive and it needed sophisticated weapons to back it up.[43]

The Saudi Arabian government underwrote the Moroccan budget. The exact figures were secret but in the late 1970s it was estimated that Saudi financial aid amounted to between $500 million and $1 billion a year. In 1984 the Saudi government gave oil to the value of $800 million, $500 million and $1 billion.[44]

This was a more useful form of Arab unity than anything the Maghrib states could offer, and Moroccan foreign policy was aligned accordingly. Since there was already popular sympathy for the Palestinian cause in Morocco, the King could satisfy that, his own inclinations, and his allies in the Gulf by becoming actively involved. In 1979 he had become chairman of a new Committee for the Liberation of Jerusalem that the Organisation of the Islamic Conference set up. In 1982, at an Arab League summit in Fez, he proposed a radical plan to dismantle Israeli occupation on the West Bank and create a Palestinian state. The Fez plan offered an implied recognition of the existence of Israel which was not enough for the Israeli government, but it did help to patch up differences between Arab governments.[45]

The King needed Arab diplomatic support because so many countries had recognised Polisario's paper republic: by 1984 these numbered seventy-three and SADR was a full member of the Organisation of African Unity. The Moroccan government left the OAU and started to fight back. First, it drew Colonel Qathafi's sting. Qadhafi agreed to abandon Polisario if the Rabat authorities said nothing about the Libyan invasion of Chad in 1980 and 1981. In 1984, enthused by his dreams of Arab unity, he quickly accepted the King's suggestion that the two countries unite, and on 13 August 1984 the two leaders singed a treaty at Oujda. Later King Hassan explained that this was a ruse 'to neutralise Qathafi who promised me not to give any more help to my enemies and to Polisario.'[46] A second advantage was that it left Polisario wholly

43 David Seddon, 'Morocco at War' in Richard Lawless and Laila Monahan (eds), *War and Refugees: The Western Sahara Conflict,* (London: Pinter, 1987), 105-11; Bruce Maddy-Weitzmann, 'Conflict and Conflict Management in the Western Sahara: Is the Endgame Near?', *Middle East Journal* 45, no.4 (1991): 597-8; Damis, *Conflict,* 99; Anthony G. Pazzanita, 'Morocco versus Polisario: a Political Interpretation', *Journal of Modern African Studies,* 32, no.2 (1994), 272-3; Hernando de Larremendi, *La política,* 330-1.

44 Damis, *Conflict,* 122; Damis 'Impact', 199.

45 Hernando de Larremendi, *La política,* 319; Hassan II, *La Mémoire,* 275-7.

46 Hassan II, *La Mémoire,* 148-9; John Damis, 'Morocco, Libya and the Treaty of

dependent on the Algerian government, which was also susceptible to Saudi pressure because it was running out of money.[47]

The diplomatic and military turnaround, and financial necessity, opened the road to a sort of peace. In 1988 Javier Pérez de Cuéllar, the UN Secretary-General, proposed that the UN should supervise the reduction of troops in the Sahara and organise a referendum. Who would be allowed to vote was deliberately kept vague so that the Moroccan government could accept the suggestion. The Algerian government, faced with an oil glut and a shortage of money, pressed Polisario to agree and repaired its relations with Rabat. In February 1989 the governments of all five countries in North Africa (Morocco, Algeria, Tunisia, Libya and Mauritania) agreed to set up an Arab Maghreb Union, whose declared purpose was to promote political and economic cooperation. Its main result was to isolate Polisario completely.[48]

The alliance with the West and with Israel

While diplomats walled in the Polisario with Arab alliances, the army fought Polisario with French and American weapons: Mirage F-1s, Northrop F-5Es, Hughes helicopter gunships, and cluster bombs. In 1985 President Reagan told Congress that American military aid 'helps to maintain the stability of a pro-Western country', that had played 'a moderating role' in the Arab-Israeli conflict.[49]

This was the personal diplomacy of King Hassan. He had good contacts with the leadership of the Israeli Labour Party through two Moroccan Jews: David Amar in Morocco and Rafi Edri, a flamboyant Member of the Knesset from the Peres faction. In January 1983 King Hassan invited 'any Israeli element wishing to open a dialogue with the PLO' to do so in Morocco, and over the next few months Amar and others tried to make this happen.[50] A delegation of Knesset members attended the first Congress of Moroccan Jews in May 1984 but only in July 1986, after intensive shuttle diplomacy by Amar and Edri, did Peres himself come. Edri subsequently became close enough to King Hassan to be

Union', *American-Arab Affairs* 13 (1995): 44-55; Hernando de Larremendi, *La política*, 332-3;

47 Damis 'Morocco, Libya', 47, 50.

48 Maddy-Weitzmann, 'Conflict', 598-9.

49 Seddon, 'Morocco at War', 106.

50 FBIS, 26 January 1983, Israel, quoting Jerusalem Radio (Domestic) 25 January 1983; *Ma'riv* 2 April 1983, 24 August 1984; *Ha'aretz*, 27 April 1984.

invited to the royal birthday party in 1989.[51] There were other links to Israel through the Moroccan Jewish community in Canada. In July 1989 Simone Bitton, who had emigrated there years before, organised a meeting in Toledo, in Spain, attended by André Azoulay, Serge Berdugo (later the Moroccan Minister of Tourism) more than forty Israelis of Arab origin, and Mahmoud Abbas, who would be the senior negotiator at the Israeli-Palestinian negotiations in Oslo.[52]

King Hassan had no influence on the negotiations in Oslo, Madrid and Washington, but his efforts at maintaining contacts brought him rich rewards. The US government supplied weapons and in 1984 there were reports in Israel that tanks and armoured personnel carriers had been sold to the Moroccan army, which the Moroccan government denied.[53] When he visited in 1986, Peres promised assistance with arid agriculture, dairy and poultry farming, and delegations and experts moved back and forth.[54]

Most Moroccans knew little about these contacts with the Israeli, American and French governments. For them, France was a place to work. Several people suggested to Rachida Yacoubi that she migrate there. She refused to leave her children, but plenty of Moroccans did go. In 1986 there were more than a million Moroccans living abroad, more than 950,000 of them in Europe. There were also large Moroccan communities in Libya and Saudi Arabia.[55] Directly, or through relatives, very many Moroccans had now experienced Europe or the rich Arab states. They also met the tourists who came to Morocco and watched European, American and Arab films. A complex picture of 'abroad' had developed.

Young Moroccans' feelings about foreigners swung between fascination and disgust. Europe and North America were, on the one hand, a consumers' paradise, lands of political and social freedom, removed from the pressure of parents, relatives and elders. On the other hand these were lands of sexual danger, the birthplace of Aids, where people made love, supposedly, in the open air. Moroccan workers in France encountered racism and exploitation,

51 FBIS, 27 November 1985, quoting Jerusalem radio (Arabic) 22 July 1986; *Ha'aretz*, 12 December 1985.

52 Mahmoud Abbas, *Through Secret Channels* (London: Garnet, 1995), 17.

53 *Jerusalem Post*, 5 April 1984; FBIS, 24 September 1986, North Africa Q6, quoting Algiers radio (domestic) 23 September 1986.

54 FBIS, 2 March 1987, quoting Jerusalem Radio (domestic) 27 February 1987 and 1 March 1987; *Ha'aretz*, 2 May 1993.

55 EIU, *Growth*, 81; Serge Leymarie and Jean Tripier, *Maroc. Le prochain Dragon? De nouvelles idées pour le développement* (Casablanca: Eddif, 1992), 219

but they earned money to send to their families and educated their children without cost in European schools. Jean-Marie Le Pen, the right-wing French politician, was all too familiar to Moroccans. Yet Moroccan feelings about Saudis and people from the Gulf were equally ambivalent. For some, the Arab east was the cradle of language and religion; Arabs were brothers in the struggle with Israel; Egypt was the source of Arab popular culture: films, television series, music. Yet the Saudi men whom Moroccans encountered were unedifying. They visited bars and nightclubs, and they were often fat: young Moroccans had absorbed the European aesthetic of slimness. Above all they were believed to be sexually depraved, debauchers of Moroccan women. Madame Yacoubi was often accused of prostituting herself to Saudis and Kuwaitis, and respectable acquaintances would not let her into their houses. Her son was bullied because she was presumed to be a 'Saudi whore'.[56]

MOROCCANS LIVING ABROAD, 1986

European Community, of which	1,045,152
France	605,622
Belgium	123,000
Netherlands	120,000
West Germany	43,000
Libya	23,000
Saudi Arabia	11,000

Source: EIU, *Morocco to 1992*, 81.

Not only were the pillars of the state, the administration and the judicial system corrupt but so, in popular belief, were the government's closest allies. When an international crisis forced itself upon the general consciousness, these ambivalent feelings burst forth.

The Gulf War

In August 1990 King Hassan sent about 1,200 Moroccan troops to Saudi Arabia to help hold the line against Iraq. This was not a militarily effective force but a gesture to support Western and Arab allies. It was unpopular with the Moroccan public. On 14 December 1990 riots occurred on the streets of nearly every city. The occasion was a strike that the unions had called to protest

[56] Bennani-Chraibi, *Soumis*, 69-82; Yacoubi, *Ma vie* 35-44, 109, 155.

about salaries, social security and retirement benefits, but the rioters were not workers. They were students and the unemployed, mainly men and nearly all young.[57] Their slogans were not about economic conditions, but rather the political diplomatic and religious orientation of the government: 'Reactionary regime: bring the Moroccan army home'; 'God is great, what a storm will destroy the Jews'; 'There is no God but God and George Bush is the enemy of God'; 'Culture for everyone, University for all'; 'Here are the youths who are unemployed, but the government still does nothing'; 'Where are the Islamist prisoners?'; 'In Iraq they have Scud, here they have "Be Quiet" ('Scud' and 'Be quiet' sound much the same in Arabic.)[58]

The United States, France, Britian and Saudi Arabia were denigrated and King Fahd, guardian of Mecca and Medina, was roundly mocked. Demonstrators shouted support for Iraq and pointed a paper model of a SCUD missile at the national assembly building in Rabat. Yet although a general strike on 28 January 1991 began with the recitation of the *Fatiha*, the opening verses of the Quran, and a call to fast, what the crowds demanded was a real election, not an Islamic regime. A political joke told how the Moroccan government changed sides and launched its own SCUD attack on Paris. The missile would not lift off the launch pad, and when the engineers investigated they found 10,000 Moroccans clutching the rocket, hoping to get to France without a passport.[59] Motivations were decidedly mixed.

The demonstrations continued through the summer. In Salé more than 300 people occupied a '*complexe artisanale*' and organised hunger strikes. These were not all youths: more than a third were over thirty and the average age was 28-29; more than half were women. They were certainly poor, with half from families where the father was unemployed, and the rest children of artisans, shopkeepers and lower-level civil servants. However, they were not uneducated: more than a third had degrees, and another third had the *baccalauréat* certificate needed to enter university. A fifth had been unemployed for more than five years. Above all, they were political neophytes, not student militants or members of political parties or Islamic movements; this was the first political action most of them had ever undertaken.[60]

57 Bennani-Chraïbi, *Soumis*, 238-57.

58 *Ibid.*, 345-49.

59 *Ibid.*, 339.

60 *Ibid.*, 287-96.

Rebuilding

The riots shook the regime. The King was growing old and gradually he began to prepare the ground for his son, Sidi Mohammed to succeed him. The crown prince had carried out his first official mission as long ago as 1974, when he attended the memorial service in Paris for President Pompidou. But he spent most of the 1980s studying law, first in Rabat, at the law school of Mohammed V University, then in France at the University of Nice, where he received a doctorate in 1993. Law had been his father's subject too, but Sidi Mohammed's specialisation was a clear sign of the path that he expected Morocco to follow in the twenty-first century: it concerned cooperation between the European Union and Maghreb states. To research it, he spent a period working in the private office of Jacques Delors, the President of the European Commission.[61] Once the Crown Prince's legal training was completed, and his intellectual credentials were assured, he and his father turned to his political standing: in 1994 he was given the rank of *Général de Division* (major-general), which theoretically made him the second-in-command of the Moroccan army. The law and the army: seemingly the prince was following closely in his father's footsteps, but the military rank carried with it no field command.[62]

The King knew that Sidi Mohammed needed more than a formal training in the use of power: if the dynasty was to survive he would have to inherit an ordered kingdom, a country at peace, and a sound economy. The politicians had to be brought back in, both the left-wing nationalists, and some of the Islamicist opposition. The palace could no longer rely on outside support, now that the Soviet Union had collapsed. The triumphant liberal democracies were less anxious to support illiberal regimes. The American government and the European Community demanded political democracy and economic liberalism. Fair elections and a dash for economic growth were King Hassan's answers to the political crisis.

So, in 1992 the constitution was changed again. Members of parliament were given more power to set up commissions of enquiry and to oblige ministers to answer questions. The Prime Minister won more control over the cabinet, and there was a specific guarantee of human rights. As usual, it was approved by an overwhelming

[61] The doctoral dissertation was published as Mohamed Ben El Hassan Alaoui, *La coopération entre l'Union Européenne et les pays du Maghreb* (Paris: Nathan, 1994).

[62] The biographical details of Sidi Mohammed are taken from Moroccan government, and semi-official sources, particularly

majority in a referendum. But when the centre parties won the elections that followed, the leader of the USFP, Abderrahmane Youssoufi declared they were fraudulent and left for voluntary exile.

Respect for human rights did improve, and many prisoners were released, though torture continued on a reduced scale. In February 1996 the Moroccan Human Rights Association [AMDH] said that thirteen people had died in detention in 1995 and estimated that there were still fifty political prisoners. But it made the claims openly in the Moroccan media, and the following month the Ministry of Human Rights admitted to one hundred prisoners, sixty of them Islamists.[63]

Islamists were now the major ideological threat to the regime, and there were fears that the civil war in Algeria might spread to Morocco.[64] This did not happen, even though, in late 1994, three alleged Algerian Islamists attacked a hotel in Marrakesh and killed two Spanish tourists. The Moroccan government accused Algerian security forces of training them and imposed visas on Algerians; the Algerian government promptly closed the frontier. But the Islamist leaders in Morocco bluntly distanced themselves from the extremes of the violence in Algeria.[65]

Liberalising the economy

This very tame political opening was accompanied by a rather more radical restructuring of the Moroccan economy. Privatisation really got under way in 1993 and by October 1997 thirty-four state owned companies had been sold off, including banks and financial institutions such as insurance companies, manufacturing concerns, transport, mining and distribution companies as well as eighteen hotels. The value came to more than 15 billion dirhams. At the end of 1998, preparations were being made to sell off the telecommunications conglomerate, Itisalat, which had a turnover of more than 7 billion dirhams and 14,000 employees.[66]

63 Reuters, Rabat, 21 March 1996, 'Morocco: US Rights Report on Morocco Lists Some Abuses'.

64 Munson, *Religion and Power*, 174-5.

65 Reuters, Rabat, 24 August 1994, 'Gunmen Kill Two Spanish Tourists in Moroccan Hotel'.

66 Royaume Du Maroc Ministère Du Secteur Public et de la privatisation, 'Itisalat Al Maghrib (IAM), Fiche d'information' (1998); This and other figures quoted here are taken from the Ministry of Privatisation's website at www.minpriv.gov.ma/français/indexfr.htm

Many of these privatised firms were bought by Moroccan investors and companies, and the share market on the Casablanca Bourse boomed in the 1990s. This was yet more fuel to stoke the expansion of the Moroccan middle class. The number of shareholders grew from 10,000 in 1993 to 180,000 two years later,[67] But a great deal of foreign investment poured in too, reaching nearly 4,000,000,000 dirhams in 1995. Only 9% came from the rich countries of the Arab East, and just of 10% from the USA, but a little less than 50% of came from European Union Countries.[68] Morocco remained very integrated into the European economy.

There were repeated claims in the early 1990s that the economy was about to take off, East Asian style, and a book published in Casablanca in 1992 had the optimistic title *Maroc: le prochain dragon* (Morocco, the next dragon). In some years the growth rates were indeed spectacular – 12% in 1994 – but the weather still ruled. During a drought in 1995 the economy contracted.

In the Sahara, the war died down. In September 1991 the United Nations brokered a cease-fire and a monitoring force, the UN Mission for a Referendum in Western Sahara (MINURSO) was set up to oversee a referendum delayed because neither Polisario nor the Moroccan government could agree on precisely whom to poll. MINURSO's 'Identification Commission', whose job was to determine precisely that, did not begin work until December 1993 and by early 1995 it had only registered 20,000 voters, fewer than a tenth of those who had applied. POLISARIO accused the Moroccan government of trying to pack the rolls with supporters who had tenuous links with the territory, and the Moroccan government said POLISARIO was delaying the referendum, for fear it would lose.[69]

Transition

It was all too slow. The system was founded on the personal power of the king, and a small group of trusted men, an inner court that included ministers like Driss Basri, the minister of the interior, and the members of the unelected Council of the Throne, who advised the king privately. It all depended on a single man.

67 *Euroweek*, 4 April 1996: 4.

68 Maroc, Ministère de l'Information, 1998.

69 Reuters, Laâyoue, 4 August 1995, 'Western Sahara Morocco to speed up W. Sahara voter registration', and Strasbourg, 15 March 1995, 'France Polisario warns of war if vote delayed'.

In November 1995, Hassan II was admitted to hospital in New York for treatment for bronchial pneumonia. Sidi Mohammed stood in for him and gave his speech to the UN General Assembly. From then on, rumours about the King's health circulated freely, despite heated denials by the Moroccan authorities that anything was wrong.[70] Less than four years later, the King was dead.

King Hassan's funeral, on 25 July 1999, two days after he died, was presided over by his son, Sidi Mohammed. It was only to be expected that the new king would emphasise the continuity between his father's reign and his own, just as Hassan had done thirty-eight years before. He even styled himself in the earliest pronouncements as King Mohammed bin Hassan, rather than the more simple Mohammed VI.

The ceremonies of enthronement and burial bore a superficial resemblance to those of his father and grandfather: the new King received the formal *bay'a*, first of his family, then of the military, then of senior politicians. The *bay'a* itself could not have been more traditional in its language and content: the old idea of contract still linked obedience to the ruler with the rights of the ruled, if in the most general terms. It declared that

> rightful allegiance is the legal duty of all Moroccans. [...] allegiance is the sacred bond between the faithful and their commander and ... a bond between Muslims and their Imam and ... allegiance is a security for the rights of the ruler and the ruled and a safeguard for trust and duty.[71]

There were even rumours that, like his father, the new King had married as soon as he acceded to the throne. Yet such stories were quickly denied: for all the apparent similarities, there were some striking differences as well.

The first was the personality of King Mohammed. When Hassan II came to the throne, he had already been chief of staff of the army and crushed two armed revolts, and served as deputy Prime Minister and Minister of Defence. Sidi Mohammed, even in the last four years of his father's life, had never held an executive role: he had welcomed visiting dignitaries, headed missions to NATO. When, in September 1995 he had taken part in talks with

70 Reuters, Rabat, 25 October 1995, 'Morocco: Moroccan king to receive treatment in NY hospital', Rabat, 25 January 1996, 'Morocco: Moroccan king's grip on power seen slackening', by Kate Dourian.

71 BBC Monitoring Service: Middle East, 26 July 1999, transciption of RTM TV, Rabat, in Arabic, 23:24 gmt, 23 July 1999.

a Polisario delegation, he was accompanied by the ever-present Driss Basri.[72]

The dignitaries who came to the funeral also showed how much Morocco had changed, not just during the long reign of King Hassan, but over the last four years. There, in the first rank was a prime minister, Abderrahmane Youssoufi, who came, not from among the men of the palace, but from the opposition, from the USFP.

In the spring of 1995 King Hassan had initiated a new wave of liberalisation, which had been a hesitant thing at first. The new government was formed mainly of elected party politicians from the right and centre, rather than personal appointments of the palace, but the Prime Minister was Abdellatif Filali, whose son was married to one of the king's daughters, and the Interior Ministry remained in the hands of Driss Basri. Even so, the new government changed the political atmosphere. Abderrahmane Youssoufi returned from voluntary exile in April 1995; in June, it was the turn of the aged Mohammed "*al-Faqih*" Basri, founder of the Organisation Secrète, after nearly three decades of involuntary exile during which time he had received three death sentences in his absence.

The opposition parties concluded that they might at last be allowed to win power, because the King was so anxious to reintegrate the left into the political system. So, in 1996, they supported yet another change in the constitution. A two chamber parliament was set up with the Chamber of Deputies elected by universal adult suffrage; the House of Counsellors would be partly indirectly elected and partly appointed by the King. In the parliamentary elections the nationalist *Kutla* coalition became the largest group, although the chamber was split three ways, and a small and moderate Islamist group entered parliament. Finally, in March 1998 Youssoufi formed a coalition government, most of whose members came from his party, the USFP, and from Istiqlal, although it also included several smaller parties like the neo-Communist PPS. But the key posts of the interior ministry remained, as always, in the hands of Driss Basri. Despite talk of a government or *alternance,* things changed quite slowly. The government's job, it seemed, was to deal with the economic problems, while state security remained a preserve of the palace. This was a government of centre-left technocrats.

72 Reuters, Rabat, 29 February 1996, 'Morocco: Morocco's King Hassan, marks 35 years on throne', by Kate Dourian; Reuters, Rabat, 17 September 1996, 'Morocco: Algeria happy with Polisario talks'.

Even many of the levers of economic power seemed to be out of reach, because Morocco had become so integrated into the global economy. At a conference in Barcelona in November 1995, the European Union agreed with governments from the southern shore of the Mediterranean to set up bilateral industrial free trade areas between the Union and individual countries. This was to develop, by 2015, into a Mediterranean free trade area. It was rather one-sided. In exchange for removing trade barriers and entering into unfettered competition with Europe, the North African governments would be given a massive increase in aid to offset the economic pain. But the EU's aid would depend on yet more economic restructuring and, particularly, the privatization of public enterprises. In February 1996 Morocco and the European Union finalised the deal with a new Association Agreement that would permit the free flow of capital, the liberalisation of competition, and, eventually, a free trade area. There was also an agreement that guaranteed that European trawlers would be banned from Moroccan waters after 1999, and provided massine aid (nearly 500 million ECUS) to the Moroccan fishing industry. Yet it soon became clear that the sacrifices were almost all Moroccan, for despite an estimate that 60 per cent of the Moroccan industrial sector might collapse without aid to cover the transition costs, European Union assistance was nowhere near the $5.4 billion that were needed. The agreement also specifically excluded agricultural produce and strictly limited migration.[73]

Nothing, it seemed, could stop Moroccans from trying to enter Europe illegally, despite intensive Spanish and Moroccan naval patrols of the Strait of Gibraltar. The bodies of those who failed floated onto Spanish beaches.[74] The risks that the poor were prepared to run were a vivid reminder that the globalisation of the Moroccan economy was the globalisation of the elite, just as the political opening of the new Morocco was a political opening to a section of the elite.

For the mass of the population there was no transition. The per capita GDP figures remained obstinately around the $US1200-1300 mark, indeed they fell (from $1365 to $1227) between 1996 and 1997. And those figures obscured an enormous gulf between the rich and the poor. In 1997 the government estimated that

73 George Joffé, 'The Euro-Mediterranean Partnership: Two Years after Barcelona, London,' *Briefing No. 44* (London: The Royal Institute of International Affairs, 1998); Reuters, 3 April 1996, 'EU: Signing of Euro-Mediterranean Association Agreement Between European Communities and Morocco'.

74 Bechir Znagie, 'The Voyage Perilous', *Index on Censorship* 3 (1994): 19-20.

47% of the population lived on less that $1 a day, more than 50% of the population was illiterate, and 17% unemployed (a figure widely suspected to be much too low).[75] The contrast with the golf-playing elite could not have been more stark.

Despite this, it was poor people who provided the most emotional scenes at King Hassan's funeral. The King's body was laid to rest in his father's mausoleum, in dignified and orderly ceremonies that emphasised his religious role, but press photographs also showed dramatic pictures of distraught Moroccans from poorer parts of the country who had travelled long distances to be present, even though public transport had shut down. The Commander of the Faithful still enjoyed much religious and emotional charisma, although not everyone was affected. Nadia Yasin, speaking for her father Abd al-Salam, the leader of the Islamicist group *Al-Adl-wal-Ihsan*, told a French news agency that while she was saddened by the death of any human being, any Muslim,

> For us this is politically a non-event. [...] The system does not die with the man. A man has died, but the system has not. We should have preferred that Hassan II live and the system die off.[76]

The new King also knew that an emotional appeal was not enough. In his first speech from the throne, a week after his father's death, he made a point of emphasising how great were the social and economic problems of the poor. The crowd was still dangerous, and it even gave a salutary shock at the funeral itself when emotional mourners broke through the security barriers and got too close for the comfort of the international dignitaries who were walking in the procession.

These foreigners provided yet another insight into a transition that was taking place not only within Morocco, but outside its borders. Presidents Chirac and Clinton and Charles, Prince of Wales walked in the procession as testimony of western support for the Moroccan system, a support of long standing. Other heads of state were evidence of how the international environment was changing. King Abdullah of Jordan and the Emir of Bahrein, Hamid bin Isa al-Khalifa, had succeeded to their own thrones only months

75 Reuters, Rabat Newsroom 'Morocco: Indicators – Morocco', updated July 13 1999; AFP Rabat 28 July 1999, 'Les Marocains impatients de connaître les orientations du nouveau roi', quoting official sources.

76 AFP, Rabat, 24 July 1999, 'Les islamistes marocains divisés face à la mort de Hassan II'.

before. A new generation of Arab leaders was coming to power, and there was a general feeling that the old Arab order was beginning to crumble away. Monarchies like Morocco, Jordan and Bahrein had the initial advantage that the succession was clear: the rulers of Egypt, Syria and Libya were also ageing, and it was less certain who would replace them.

Elections had recently brought about transitions in other Arab and Middle Eastern countries. The new prime minister of Israel, Ehud Barak attended, along with King Hassan's old interlocutor, Shimon Peres. When Yitzhak Rabin was shot dead in 1995 and Binyamin Netanyahu became Prime Minister of Israel the following year, negotiations between the Israeli government and the Palestine Authority had stalled. King Hassan had also scaled down his own diplomatic contacts. Now the political leadership in Israel had changed again, Morocco could once more provide a meeting place. In the open air, in front of television cameras, Barak met and exchanged pleasantries with the new President of Algeria, Abdulaziz Bouteflika, who had been elected in rather suspect elections the previous April. Bouteflika had already begun talking about re-opening the land-borders with Morocco, and, he asserted, the dispute over the Sahara could also be resolved.

Polisario, of course, did not send a delegation to the funeral but its foreign relations spokesman did send a letter of condolence, in quite fulsome terms, hoping that the referendum might finally take place. The whole process had been stalled since May 1996, when the Security Council postponed the whole identification procedure, after both sides refused to cooperate with the other. Yet, although Polisario had threatened to return to armed struggle, the peace held: the Algerian government was far too distracted by its own civil war to give anything beyond verbal support, and Moroccan troops now controlled four-fifths of the territory.[77] For several years, in any case, the Moroccan government had behaved as though the Saharan provinces were fully integrated. When Saharans voted in the constitutional referendum in September 1996, Rabat claimed that they had given clear evidence of their allegiance.[78]

The funeral in Rabat in July 1999 was in many ways a summation of the political history of Morocco over the previous two centuries. An Alaoui was enthroned, and another was buried in deliberately

77 Reuters, Rabat, 3 March 1996, 'Morocco: Moroccan King Criticises Algeria on W. Sahara'.

78 Reuters, Rabat, August 22 1996, 'Morocco: Moroccan Envoy to Visit Western Sahara for Talks'.

traditional ways. But the surrounding events, and the rhetoric were more modern. The official guests, Moroccan and foreign, were a demonstration of the results of limited popular participation and the virtual fulfilment of objectives of Moroccan nationalists in the 1950s; the crowds on the streets were evidence of the less successful results of the incorporation of Morocco into the global market.

Yet the funeral was only a moment in time. Certainly it brought changes of emphasis (greater concern for the poor), of style (the new King surrounded himself with young men), and even of policy (Driss Basri was removed as interior minister in November 1999). Yet despite these and other discontinuities, the state still emphasises its continuity with the past, *in terms of territorym identitym king and culture.* To illuminate the contrast between the Morocco of 1830 and the Morocco of today it is intriguing to imagine that at the beginning of the new millennium Consul-General Drummond-Hay and Ahmad bin Tuwayr al-Janna, the Mauritanian scholar-pilgrim, returned. Such a speculation might throw some light on the way in which the society, economy and political culture have changed and, perhaps, the nature of that change.

THE RETURN OF THE TRAVELLERS?

The shape of the land

In the 1990s Drummond-Hay could not even have dreamt of hunting Barbary Lion, for the species was considered extinct in the 1930s. Many of his hunting grounds would have disappeared, for the shape of the land has changed.

In 1995 Morocco's population was growing by more than 2% a year. Although many people moved to the cities, the rural population was also increasing: among the Ait Arfa of the Middle Atlas it grew threefold between 1941 and 1991.[79] Semi-nomad or transhumant herders turned to settled agriculture, even on the edges of the deserts and in the forests, which were cut down to make room for them. Loggers and charcoal burners, and overgrazing that killed off saplings, destroyed trees too. In the late 1970s forests were shrinking by 14,000 hectares a year.[80]

79 Douglas Johnson, 'Development trends and Environmental Deterioration in the Agropastoral Systems of the Central Middle Atlas, Morocco', in W Swearingen and Abdellatif Bencherifa *The North African Environment at Risk*, ed. (Boulder, CO: Westview, 1996), 47.

80 McNeill, *Mountains*, 182, 310.

Between 1956 and 1971 the Rif lost almost all the 100,000 hectares of forest that remained after the colonial depredations.[81] Instead Rifis turned to hashish or *kif*, grown for illegal consumption in Europe. One hectare can produce 2000 kilos of *kif* and no other crop can compete with it in productivity or price. But it needs a lot of weeding and care in its growing season, and a great deal of fertiliser. This was provided by manure from goats, enthusiastic eaters of almost everything, and that caused further overgrazing.[82]

The greatest environmental change took place on the coast, one of the most ecologically fragile regions. In the 1990s, 67% of overnight tourist stays were concentrated there, but from the mid 1970s on, middle-class Moroccans began buying second homes and the coast between Casablanca and Rabat was parcelled up; by the end of the 1980s this process had spread to the Mediterranean coast. In a strange echo of the *bidonvilles* in the towns, much coastal development was illegal and uncontrolled. Because local authorities could not cope with the waste, the Mediterranean coast became badly polluted.[83] Equally severe pollution was caused by disorganised dumping of rubbish. On the edge of many towns there are huge open tips, from where plastic bags blow across the countryside. Industrial development in rural areas is another polluter: wood processing is dirty and produces offensive-smelling fumes. Opposition to these new sources of pollution was muted: a small environmentalist party, (Parti des Verts pour le Développement) founded by a woman journalist, Fatima Alaoui, presented candidates in the 1993 elections,[84] but it won no seats. Political attention was concentrated on growth.

To a considerable extent, the countryside has been civilised, in the sense that it has been brought under control. Although the level of education in rural areas is much lower than in the

81 *Ibid.*, 307.

82 Abdelmalek Benabid, 'Forest Degradation in Morocco', in *The North African Environment at Risk*, Swearingen and Bencherifa (Boulder, CO: Westview, 1996), 175-90; Abdellatif Bencherifa, 'Is Sedentarization of Pastoral Nomads Causing Desertification? the Case of the Benu Guil of Eastern Morocco', in *Ibid.*, 117-30.; Johnson 'Development trends' McNeill, *Mountains*, 257-259.

83 Mohamed Berriane, 'Le tourisme sur' la côte méditerranéene. Aménagement touristique ou promotion immobilière?," in *Le Maroc Méditerranéen, la troisième dimension*, ed. El Malki Habib (Casablanca: Editions le Fennec, 1992); Mohammed Berianne, 'Environmental Impacts of Tourism along the Moroccan Coast', in Swearingen and Bencherifa, *The North African Environment at Risk.*

84 Fatima Alaoui, *Parties de rien arrivées à zéro* (Rabat: L'Ere Nouvelle, 1996), passim.

urban centres, particularly among women (in 1986-87 31% of rural girls aged between seven and fourteen years were working when they should have been studying),[85] it is now available in the countryside in regular schools rather than scattered zawiyas. Neither a modern Drummond-Hay nor a returned Ahmad bin Tuwayr would need to worry about large-scale banditry, although there is rural crime and, in the border regions of the north coast in particular there is a great deal of smuggling: electrical goods are brought in and hashish is taken out, and much of the economy of the Rif is linked to this phenomenon.[86]

Yet some of Drummond-Hay's landscapes remain. The plains north-west of Marrakesh are still wild and bleak, and from the coastal motorway between Rabat and Casablanca, rivers can be glimpsed just as he described them, flowing between wooded banks before diving into the sand a few yards from the sea. But urban life would have amazed both travellers, with its scenes of a mass culture, of extraordinary variety.

A mosaic of cultural choices

In 1830 Morocco was a land of sharp distinctions. The walls of Marrakesh divided the city from empty space and even the language of the countryside and mountains was quite distinct from that of the tiny educated elite.

Statistics repeatedly state that about 40% of Moroccans still speak Berber, but that they are rapidly being Arabised.[87] In fact most of those who speak Berber also speak Arabic (between 75 and 90% of the population), although their Arabic varies remarkably. At one extreme, a very informal vernacular Arabic, mixed with Berber, French and Spanish words, used at home and in the markets. At the other, a high literary Arabic, the spoken version of the written language, is used on formal occasions and with Arabs from other countries. Between the two lies a middle Arabic, an adaptation of the literary language, which is spoken between strangers, used by officials in the schools and on television. The

85 Daouad, *Féminisme*, 328.

86 Fouad Zaïm, 'Les enclaves espagnoles et l'économie du Maroc méditerranéan: effets et étendue d'une domination commerciale', in Habib El Malki (ed.), *Le Maroc méditerranéan: la troisième dimension*, (Casablanca: Le Fennec, 1992), 37-85; John Robert McNeill, *The Mountains of the Mediterranean World : an Environmental History, Studies in Environment and History* (Cambridge University Press, 1992).

87 Bennani-Chraïbi, *Soumis*, 29; Abderrahim Youssi, 'The Moroccan Triglossia: Facts and Implications', *International Journal of the Sociology of Language* 112 (1995): 29-43, reference to 31; Boukous, 10.

boundaries are not fixed: almost everyone understands the vernacular dialect, most people the middle form, but far fewer, maybe less than a quarter, can correctly use the literary form.[88]

Arabic spread in the 1960s and '70s as more people migrated to the towns, listened to radio and television and went to school. The nationalists had made Arabisation one of their watchwords, and Thierry de Beaucé, a visiting French cultural official, provoked a storm in September 1988 when he reaffirmed the importance of *Francophonie* in Morocco. He declared that 'French language and culture are part of the Moroccan identity,' and was rewarded for his rudeness with outrage in the nationalist press. The Istiqlali paper *al-Alam* complained of a 'colonial cultural invasion' and 'a secret war against Arabic, the language of the Quran.' *L'Opinion* declared: 'Our identity is not a French identity, our language is not the French language, and our culture is not French culture.'[89] But it made the declaration in French. Nadia Yasin, the chief spokeswoman for her father, Abd al-Salam during his years of house arrest, spoke excellent French although her father emphasised the religious quality of Arabic:

> Although I am of Berber descent, I am an Arab, I speak Arabic and I am an Arab in my heart, in my soul and in my language.[90]

The Moroccan elite has generally been reluctant to abandon French. In 1988 King Hassan, who spoke it fluently, dismissed the all-or-nothing Arabisers as suffering from an inferiority complex. Bilingualism, he said, was not an abandonment of Arabic culture, but an addition to it.[91] But for many Moroccans bilingualism is not enough. Since 1980 more and more of the elite have studied English, which they can do without leaving the country. In 1995, a new university, Al-Akhawayn, opened at the mountain resort of Ifrane in the Middle Atlas. It models its curriculum and methods on the American university system and teaches in English, concentrating on science, engineering and business.

Many of the poorer classes were quadrilingual. Migrant workers, who learned French or Spanish, Dutch or German, or English, often spoke Arabic and French, but came from Berber-speaking

88 Youssi, 'Triglossia,' 29-30.

89 Ouafae Mouhssine, 'Ambivalence du discours sur l'arabisation', *International Journal of the Sociology of Language*, 112 (1995): 45-61, reference to 47-8.

90 *Ibid.*, 50; Valenzuela and Masegosa, *La última frontera*, 157.

91 Mouhsinne, 'Ambivalence', 48-9.

areas.[92] Indeed migration helped to revive Berber too. In the mid-1970s a Berber political movement began in Paris, initially among Algerians. This encouraged interest in lexicography and grammar and some activists tried to revive Tifinagh, a pre-Islamic script that barely survived among the Tuaregs in the depths of the Sahara. In the 1990s a Rifi living in Holland, Said Essanoussi, developed a Tifinagh word-processing program for computers. Typically, Essanoussi spoke Dutch and English and made his living selling and servicing Arabic-language computer applications.[93]

The Berber revival spread to Morocco. In the early 1980s an annual Summer University in Agadir began teaching Berber language and culture and in 1991 it produced a manifesto calling for legal recognition of the language. Berber magazines and books appeared openly: there was even a translation of Shakespeare's *Romeo and Juliet.*[94] The market for such a translation was minute, but it symbolised a new openness. Anxious not to be left behind, the government participated. A radio station had broadcast in the three main dialects of Berber for many years, and in 1994 the national television channel began broadcasting a short Berber news bulletin. The king also announced that Berber would be taught in schools; it had to be safeguarded, he said, 'because the West has invaded our homes.'[95] So far that has not been put into effect.

Public mass culture

For Drummond-Hay, Moroccan culture was mere 'fanaticism.' This was prejudice, but it was true that information and knowledge were confined to a tiny elite; there could be no mass culture while the tribe was the basis of society.

There is certainly a mass culture now, one that the state has found increasingly hard to control. Television began in March 1963 with the King's yearly speech from the throne and for nearly a generation as the government prized it as a way to reach the mainly illiterate population. More money was invested in extending

92 Ahmed Berkous, 'La langue berbère: maintien et changement,' *International Journal of the Sociology of Language* 112 (1995): 9-28, reference to 12; Youssi, 'Triglossia', 30.

93 Berkous, 'La langue berbère', 12-13.

94 *Ibid.*, 12-13; William Shakespeare, *Romeo d Juliet*, trans. Adghirni, Ahmed (Rabat: Matabia Takatoul Al Watani, 1995).

95 Youssi, 'Triglossia', 39; Reuter, Rabat, 28 February 1996, 'Morocco: Moroccan Groups Want Berber As Official Language'.

the coverage of the network than in producing programs, and by the early 1990s 89% of the population had a television set, although the programs were extremely dull.[96]

Video recorders provided a greater choice. Prices were low because the equipment and the tapes were smuggled in, often through Ceuta and Melilla; by 1988 20% of houses had a video recorder. In the mid-1980s the first sattellite dishes appeared on the roofs of smart hotels, then the rich bought them: one was installed on the Royal Palace in 1986. Then they spread throughout the cities and into the countryside. Finally, the government gave way. In 1980 it had allowed a private radio station, Radio Mediterranée Internationale, to start broadcasting and in 1989 a private television company, 2M, was set up. Even so, a large share in 2M was held by Omnium Nord-Africain, whose managing director, Fouad Filali, was the son of the prime minister, and son-in-law of the King. So many people pirated the special decoder they should have purchased, that the company nearly collapsed and it was taken into state control.[97]

The problems with 2M's decoders illustrated how Moroccan culture slipped from official control. Smuggled recorders played smuggled American, French and Arabic videos, hired from unofficial video shops. Smuggled sattellite dishes picked up uncontrolled broadcasts from Europe, America and the Arab world. In the mid 1990s Moroccans got access to the Internet and the World Wide Web, and joined in with enthusiasm. Again official Morocco went with the flow – the Union Consītutionelle and the USFP opened web pages and government ministries' home pages (in French and English, but not Arabic) were extremely generous with statistical information and in depth reports.

There has not been a wholesale westernisation. Some of the young people interviewed by Bennani-Chraïbi in the late 1980s resented American and French cultural imperialism. Many others watched both American and Egyptian soap operas, but felt uneasy when they viewed films with 'shameful', that is a sexual, content when older relatives were present. But margins blurred: literate and illiterate watched the same films, and foreign culture, both Arab and European, was being domesticated.[98]

Musical tastes were equally eclectic. Radio Mediterranée Internationale mixed Umm Kalthoum, the Egyptian woman singer, with

96 Bennani-Chraïbi, *Soumis*, 36-40, OMDH *Liberté de Presse*, 43-56.

97 Bennani and Eloualladi, *Liberté de presse*, 70-3.

98 Bennani-Chraïbi, *Soumis*, 45-6.

Samantha Fox, a Briton. There were stations for classical Andalusian music, modern Moroccan pop, Algerian *Raï* or British punk. A Moroccan punk band named 'Ahlam' recorded an album named (in English) *Revolt against Civilisation*; it was strongly influenced by Arabic musical themes. So much Egyptian and Lebanese music was available that Abdel-Halim Hafez and Fairuz became Moroccan favourites.[99]

The mass culture of sport

For Edward Drummond-Hay, and for many Britons of his class, 'sport' meant hunting, an individualist activity that the Moroccan elite enjoyed as well. The Moroccan rich still hunt, but a mass society has produced a mass-sport, football. Any boy can dream of becoming a star, and several have done so because foreign clubs buy talent. Fifteen of the 22 players in the 1998 World Cup squad were employed by European clubs in France, Spain Belgium, Germany or Portugal. In 1970, the Moroccan team was the first in Africa to take part in the World Cup, although it did not get beyond the first round until 1986, and failed to do so in 1998. Yet although any boy *could* kick a ball around a street, very few went any further. In 1980 it was estimated that only 0.4% of the population were taking part in organised sport. In 1994, the Moroccan football authorities applied to host the World Cup, but FIFA quickly turned them down partly because there was not a single suitable stadium in the country. Quite reasonably, FIFA concluded that the Moroccans did not have the money.[100] In 1996 the Moroccan football federation could not afford to pay its own officials for four months of the year.[101] Financial crises also afflicted domestic teams. Widad Athletic Club, which could be said to have started Moroccan football, was overtaken in the league tables by the armed forces' team – FAR Rabat. By the end of 1995 it was bankrupt, because of bad management, and because it could not afford good players. At the last moment, it was rescued.

King Hassan helped to fund the men's national game, presented league cups and in 1996 set up an international cup, named after himself. His own favourite sport was golf. Several fine courses were built, and international stars were attracted to play on them.

99 *Ibid.*, 47-49.

100 Wladimir Andreff, 'Le Tiers Monde Vassalisé' in *Manière de Vie, 30* (Paris: Le Monde Diplomatique, 1996).

101 Najib Salmi, 'Première année depuis 1984 sans medaille d'or olympique', *La Vie Economique*, 3-9 Janvier 1997, 39.

In 1995 the king sent a personal jet to fly Nick Price from America for the 24th King Hassan Cup whose prize money was £60,000. The following year, Price and Severiano Ballesteros played in the Morocco Open, at the immaculate Royal Dar Es Salam course in Rabat. This brought the king the sort of prestige abroad that support for football won him at home. The Morocco Open became part of international golf's 'European Tour', a symbol of the country's modern western face.[102]

Athletics also helped to build national identity. In 1984, at the Los Angeles Olympics, Saïd Aouita won the 5000 metres race, and Nawal Al Moutaouakkil the women's 400-metre hurdles. She was the first Moroccan to win any Olympic medal, and the first Arab woman to win a gold so she became a popular heroine. In 1997 she joined the government as a junior minister in charge of Youth and Sports. As a woman she was an obvious symbol of the regime's liberalism, something that the Ministry of Youth and Sports had been emphasising for years. In a report that the ministry published in 1959 there were photographs of girls taking part in basketball, archery and skiing (neither of the last two were exactly mass-participation sports). Boys were shown playing football (as well as flying and yachting).[103]

A society with women

The emergence of women into the public space would have astonished Ahmad bin Tuwayr. Nowhere in his account of Morocco does he even mention women. His was a world of scholars and rulers. He travelled with his sons. The only women that Drummond-Hay saw were the very poor.

Today the streets, shops and offices are thronged with women. There are women judges doctors and scientists. Fatima Mernissi is an internationally known sociologist. There are women diplomats at the UN, and there are women in the police force and in the army in the Sahara.[104] There are also women bus drivers and street sellers. In 1993 the first two women were elected to parliament; the 1997 government included four women Ministers of State (junior ministers) in Youth and Sports, Education, Mining, and Social Affairs. The 1998 government had only two women Ministers of State, both of them from the USFP.

102 Michael Britten, 'Morocco: Sport in Brief', 9-11 March 1996.

103 'Division de la Jeunesse et des Sports', (Rabat: Royaume du Maroc Ministère de l'Eucation Nationale, 1959).

104 Daoud, *Féminisme*, 331.

Not all conservative men approved. During Ramadan in 1990 and again in 1991, the Minister for Religious Endowments declared that Islamic law did not allow a woman to exercise political power.[105] The women's organisations ignored him. At the end of 1991, left-wing women's groups collected a million signatures on a petition asking for changes to the *Moudawana* family code. They wanted equal rights for women to divorce; all divorces should be enacted through the courts and not by simple repudiation; and polygamy should be finally abolished. The main parties added their voices, and in August 1992, quoting the Traditions of the Prophet in favour of justice for women, the King set up a committee to revise the code. The revision did allow greater freedom for women to chose their husbands; it restricted polygamy, but did not forbid it entirely; repudiation was made more difficult, but not abolished. In March 1996 the women's groups announced that they would carry on the campaign to reform the *Moudawana* code.[106]

Not all politically active women, nor all publicly active ones, were on the secular left. This was the first generation in Moroccan history in which there was a widespread stress on religious instruction and activism for women as well as men. Nadia Yasin was exceptional as her father's chief spokeswoman but plenty of other young women put on Islamic dress, as personal and individual choice, even while they aspired to middle-class careers in the public service as judges or doctors. This was rather a different Islam from that of the conservatives, and either openly or by implication it challenged the patriarchal assumptions that underpinned the regime.

From Sultan to King

The Moroccan constitution, in all its different versions was clear about the relationship between religion, legitimacy and masculinty. The King is *amir al-Muminin* (Commander of the Faithful) and he must be a man.[107] A woman like Nadia Yasin (and her sisters) posed a double challenge to King Hassan's regime: her Islam was

105 Daoud, *Féminisme*, 321-2.

106 Daoud, *Féminisme*, 336-45; François-Paul Blanc and Rabha Zeidguy, *Moudawana: code de statut personnel et des successions. Édition synoptique franco-arabe* ([n.p]: Sochepresse-Université, 1994), 39-24 (the French section is numbered in reverse); Reuters, 7 March 1996, Rabat, 'Morocco: Moroccan Women Want Moslem Divorce Law Amended.'

107 Moroccan Constitution, adopted September 13, 1996, Chapter 2, 'Monarchy', articles 19 and 20.

not his. The king, clad in his jellaba, may lead the 'Id ceremonies of the whole country, or preside over the Hassanian lectures given by officially approved ulama, which are state-religious activities; or he may parade in a military uniform or wears a suit to distribute the trophies at a golf tournament, which are strictly secular moments. But on none of these occasions do women play much of a role at all.

Patriarchy is part of the hierarchical structure of Moroccan society. It is certainly one that Ahmad bin Tuwayr would recognise, as he begged to be allowed to swear his allegiance to Moulay Abderahmane in the spring of 1830. The man he visited was both a scholar and sultan, who surrounded himself with scholars and learned men, and secluded himself from general view. The sultan Drummond-Hay visited was remote and distant to Europeans as well.

Drummond-Hay's modern diplomatic counterparts are received personally by the king, and he speaks directly to them. His subjects see much more of him than did those of Moulay Abderrahmane. The King still travels around Morocco, but his modern *mahalla* moves in trains and cars and does not lay the countryside waste. He is seen on television presiding over cabinet meetings, opening conferences, and travelling abroad. There is an impression of intimacy that did not exist in the early nineteenth century. King Hassan's photograph was everywhere, and apart from his wife, who was rarely seen in public, his family was also very visible. Family ceremonies are celebrated on a national scale. In 1987 when Princess Lalla Asma was married in Marrakech, the preparations allegedly cost 80 million francs.[108] Lalla Soukaïna, his granddaughter, was photographed in the King's arms at a birthday party.[109]

Side by side with this impression of intimacy is the idea that the ruler of Morocco is now a King, a constitutional monarch presiding over a legally responsible government. Yet he is still an Alaoui, and he continues to play the role of Commander of the Faithful. On 1 January 1997, the semi-official newspaper, *Le Matin,* published a chronology of the King Hassan's activities during the previous year. He had public engagements on 112 days, on 24 of which he was specifically referred to as *Amir el Mouminine.*[110]

108 Diouri, *A qui,* 224.

109 Lucette Valensi, 'Le roi chronophage. La construction d'une conscience historique dans le Maroc postcolonial', *Cahiers d'études africaines* 30, no. 3 (1990): 279-9, reference to 293.

110 *Le Matin,* 1 January 1997, 3-7.

This religious and traditional legitimacy is one of the bases on which the regime rests. It places the King above politics, outside the debate of ordinary political activity, but able to intervene in politics through the network of patronage over which he presides.

Of the elite around the King, Drummond-Hay might recognise some names. Old sharifian families remain important. Three Alaouis were ministers in the government appointed in August 1997, although none were close relatives of the King. Abdellatif Filali was Prime Minister of the 1977 government, and foreign minister in the Youssoufi government in March 1998; his son married the King's daughter.[111] Old Makhzan families like the Benjellouns are prominent. In the mid 1990s, Othman Benjelloun, president of Citbank-Maghreb was also President of the National Bank of Morocco and a major shareholder in several very large companies. When Hajj Mohamed Benjelloun died in 1997 he had been Moroccan member of the International Olympic Committee for thirty-six years. His son, Mfadel succeeded him as president of Widad Athletic Club, the football team he founded before the Second World War, and was also president of the tennis federation. His nephew, Mohamed was president of the association of merchants of electrical equipment.[112] The pattern is repeated throughout the law, the administration, the universities.

These are not place-servers. The old families could be expected to be loyal, but their sons, and sometimes their daughters, have become highly qualified technocrats, educated at the higher institutes in France. Technical skills are highly prized, and not all the state's servants are from the old Makhzan. Driss Basri, Minister of the Interior without break since 1979, and often Minister of Information as well, was the son of a prison governor in Settat.[113] Ability as well as loyalty has been the key.

Throughout the King's reign these technocratic ministers have taken charge of the modernisation of the Moroccan economy and society in a way that protects them from much criticism from a parliamentary opposition.[114] When the *Kutla* did finally take power in 1998, it was as part of a coalition so that the mixture of royal patronage and the king's role as arbitrator in political conflicts were unchanged.

111 Benhaddou, *Maroc*, 32.

112 Reuters, 2 September 1996; Benhaddou, *Maroc*, 75, 148.

113 Javier Valenzuela and Alberto Masegosa, *La última frontera: Marruecos, el vecino inquietante* (Madrid: Temas de Hoy, 1996), 219.

114 Hammoudi, *Master and Disciple*, 22.

Yet while the King identified himself with technocracy and modernism in government he patronised the notability in the countryside. This gave him a line of authority beside, or perhaps beyond, parliament and the formal ministries of government like other mechanisms of cooption and control: the creation of a political consensus around the Saharan issue, and the use of direct coercion through the security services. In this, the King has been helped considerably by his alliance with European and western interests. Throughout the period of the cold war he was able to use the duality of world politics to win economic and military aid. The king was careful to incline towards the western side, but not enough to make contacts with the Soviet Union impractical.

That policy only worked when there was a Soviet Union to fraternise with. After 1990 that option no longer existed and the political choices that faced Morocco were rather different: capitalist liberalism, or some form of Islamic revolution. The King handled this choice deftly as well, clearly identifying his regime with western interests and encouraging Palestinian negotiations with Israel while championing the cause of Jerusalem.

King Hassan used the monarchy as a way of bridging the segments of Moroccan society, turning that diversity into a strength of his regime, and allowing him to face down the challenges from the victims of the modern economy inside Morocco, and his Arab rivals internationally. The monarchy's great flexibility, the ability to mobilise and manipulate different lines of authority, patronage and power, helped it to adapt itself to external pressures brought to bear by forces that were stronger than itself. The diversity was used by his subjects as well, as they moved between cultures in order to find employment as well as recreation and it allowed space to those who were forced to by circumstances to seek a personal autonomy: economic in the informal economy, and political in movements that the security forces could not always control. When the effects of government policy and international pressures grew too hard to bear, the urban crowd flowed out onto the streets of the cities and challenged the power and authority of the state.

Had the pilgrim and the consul returned they might have recognised, beyond the modern European-looking cities and the unveiled women in their streets and banks and offices, a country that still depends on agriculture and the weather, still looks towards Europe for its trade, is still ruled by an Alaoui king, who anxiously watches its urban crowds while wars, Moroccan and Algerian, still lap at its frontiers.

APPENDIX

SULTANS AND KINGS OF MOROCCO

Moulay Abderrahmane (1822-59)
Sidi Mohammed IV (1859-73)
Moulay Hassan I (1873-94)
Moulay Abdelaziz (1894-1908)
Moulay Abdelhafid (1908-1912)
Moulay Youssef (1912-27)
Sidi Mohammed V (1912-62)
Hassan II (1962-99)
Mohammed VI (1999-)

FRENCH RESIDENTS-GENERAL

Louis-Hubert-Gonzales Lyautey (1912-25)
Jules-Joseph-Théodore Steeg (1925-8)
Lucien Saint (1928-33)
Henri Ponsot (1933-6)
Bernard-Marcel Peryrouton (1936)
Augustin-Paul-Charles Noguès (1936-43)
Gabriel Puaux (1943-6)
Erik Labonne (1946-7)
Alphonse-Pierre Juin (1947-51)
Augustin-Léon Guillaume (1951-4)
François Lacoste (1954-5)
Gilbert-Yves-Edmond Grandval (1955)
Pierre-Georges-Jacques-Marie Boyer de la Tour du Moulin (1955)
André-Louis Dubois (1955-6)

HIGH COMMISSIONERS OF THE SPANISH PROTECTORATE

Gen. Felipe Alfau Mendoza (1913)
Gen. José Marina (1913-15)
Gen. Francisco Gómez Jordana (1915-18)
Gen. Dámaso Berenguer y Fuste (1919-22)

Gen. Ricardo Burguete Lana (1922-3)
Luís Silvela y Casado (1923)
Gen. Luis Aizpuru (1923-4)
Gen. Miguel Primo de Rivera y Orbaneja (1924-5)
Gen. José Sanjurjo Sacanell Buenrostro y Desojo, Marques de Malmusi (1925, 1931)
Gen. Francisco Gomez-Jordana y Souza, Conde de Jordana (1928-31)
Luciano López Ferrer (1931-3)
Juan Moles (1933-4)
Manuel Rico Avello (1934-6)
Juan Moles (1936)
Alvarez Buylia (1936)
Gen. Saez de Buruaga (1936)
Gen. Francisco Franco (1936)
Gen. Orgaz (1936)
Juan Beigbeder y Atienza (1936-9)
Gen. Carlos Asensio (1939-41)
Gen. Luis Orgaz y Yoldi (1941-5)
Gen. José Enrique Varela Iglesias (1945-51), appointed March 1945, died 1951
Gen. Rafael García-valiño y Marcen (1951-56)

Source: David Henige, *Colonial Governors from the Fifteenth Century to the Present* (Madison: University of Wisconsin Press, 1970), 309.

BIBLIOGRAPHY

Manuscript sources

Bodleian Library, Oxford, MS Eng. hist. e. 346-349. Diaries of Edward Drummond-Hay.

Archives du Palais Royale, Rabat, Morocco, Papers of Moulay Abderrahmane.

Public Record Office, London.

Gibraltar Government Archives.

Royal Naval Hydrographic Archive, Taunton, OD. AP.I/1, 'Extracts from Remark Books of Capt. Boteler on the Barbary Coast between August 18th and September 20th 1828, p. 1; S.L. 4 Boteler 1828-9 Captain's letters, H.M. Sloop *Hecla* at Santa Cruz de Tenerife 30 October 1828'.

Newspapers

La Vie Économique (Casablanca)
Le Matin (Casablanca)
Le Petit Marocain
Reuter's News Agency reports
Foreign Broadcating Intelligence Service (FBIS)
The Guardian (London)
The Times (London)
Le Monde Diplomatique

Official and semi-official reports and publications

Al-munazzama al-Maghribiyya li-huquq al-insan min khillal bilaghatiha wa-tasrihatiha, dijinbar 1992-mayu 1994, Rabat: Organisation Marocaine de Droits de l'Homme.

Division de la Jeunesse et des Sports, Rabat: Royaume du Maroc Ministère de l'Eucation Nationale, 1959.

Hassanian Lectures, Lectures on Topics Related to the Exegisis of the Quran and the Tradition and Delivered before HM King Hassan II over the Holy Month of Ramadan of 1407 AH (1987), [Rabat]: Ministry of Waqfs and Islamic Affairs, 1408/1988.

Historial de la harka Melilla, Melilla: Tipografía la Hispana, [n.d.].

'*Majallat al-Maghrib*'.

Books and Articles

Abbas, Mahmoud, *Through Secret Channels*, London: Garnet, 1995.

Abu Lughod, Janet L., *Rabat: Urban Apartheid in Morocco*, Princeton University Press, 1980.

Adam, André, *Casablanca: essai sur la transformation de la societé marocaine au contact de l'Occident*, 2 vols, Paris: Centre national de la recherche scientifique, 1968.

Afa, 'Umar, *Mas'alat al-nuqud fi tarikh al-Maghrib fi al-qarn al-tasi' 'ashar: (Sus, 1822-1906)*. [Agadir]: Jami'at al-Qadi 'Iyad, Kulliyat al-Adab wa-al-'Ulum al-Insaniyah bi-Agadir, 1988.

Ageron, Charles-Robert. *Politiques coloniales au Maghreb*, Paris: Presses Universitaires de France, 1972.

——— *Modern Algeria: a History from 1830 to the Present*, trans. Michael Brett, London: Hurst, 1991.

Agnouche, Abdelatif, *Histoire politique du Maroc: pouvoir – lègitimités – institutions*, Casablanca: Afrique Orient, 1987.

Ahmad ibn Tuwayr al-Jannah, *The Pilgrimage of Ahmad, Son of the Little Bird of Paradise: an Account of a 19th Century Pilgrimage from Mauritania to Mecca*, trans. H.T. Norris, Warminster: Aris & Phillips, 1977.

Akharbach, Latifa and Narjis Rerhaye, *Femmes et politique*, Casablanca: Le Fennec, 1992.

El Alami, Mohamed, *Mohammed V. Histoire de l'indépendance du Maroc*, Rabat: Les Éditions A.P.I., 1980.

Alaoui, Fatima, *Parties de rien arrivées à zéro*, Rabat: L'Ere Nouvelle, 1996.

Alaoui, Moulay Abdelhadi, *Le Maroc du traité de Fès à la libération 1912-1956*, Rabat: La Porte, 1994.

'Ali Bey': *see* Badía y Leblich, Domingo.

Al khalloufe, Mohammed Essaghir, Bouhmara: dujihad à la compromission, Rabat, 1993.

Allain, Jean-Claude, *Agadir, 1911*, Paris: Publications de la Sorbonne, 1976.

——— 'Les Chemins de fer marocains du protectorat français pendant l'entre-deux- guerres', *Revue d'Histoire Moderne et Contemporaine*, July-Sept (1987): 427-52.

Alvarez, José E., 'Between Gallipoli and D-Day: Alhucemas, 1925', *Journal of Military History*, 63, no.1 (1999): 75-98.

Amnesty International, *Maroc: torture, 'disparitions', emprisonnement politique*, Paris: Les Éditions Francophones d'Amnesty International, 1991.

Anderson, Lisa, *The State and Social Transformation in Tunisia and Libya, 1830-1980*, Princeton University Press, 1986.

Anti-Slavery, Society, *Child labour in Morocco's Carpet Industry*, London: Anti-Slavery Society, 1978.

Arnaud, Louis, *Au temps des mehallas au Maroc ou le Maroc de 1860 à 1912*, Casablanca: Atlantides, 1952.

Al-Asfi, Muhammad al-Wadi, *Al-salafi al-munadil: al-shaykh Muhammad bin al-'Arabi al-'Alawi*, al-Dar al-Baida: Dar al-Nashr al-'Arabi, 1986.

Ashford, Douglas E., *Political Change in Morocco*, Princeton University Press, 1961.

Ashmead-Bartlett, Ellis, *The Passing of the Shereefian Empire*, Edinburgh: Blackwood, 1910.

Augarde, Jacques, 'Les forces supplétives pendant les campagnes du Maroc et la libération de la France', *Maroc-Europe*, 7 (1994): 197-207.

Ayache, Albert, *Le mouvement syndical au Maroc*, 3 vols, Paris: L'Harmattan, 1982.

——— 'Les grèves de juin 1936 au Maroc', *Annales Economies Sociétés Civilisations*, 12, no. 3 (1957): 418-29.

Ayache, Germain, 'Aspects de la crise financière au Maroc après l'éxpedition espagnole de 1860' in *Études d'histoire marocaine*, Rabat: SMER, 1979, 97-138.

——— 'La crise des relations germano-marocaines (1894-1897)' in *Études d'histoire marocaine*, Rabat: SMER, 1979, 249-92.

——— 'La fonction d'arbitrage du Makhzen' in *Études d'histoire marocaine*, Rabat: SMER, 1979, 159-76.

——— *La guerre du Rif*, Paris: L'Harmattan, 1996.

——— 'L'apparition de l'imprimerie au Maroc' in *Études d'histoire marocaine*, Rabat: SMER, 1979, 139-58.

Azam, Jean-Paul, and Christian Morrisson, *The Political Feasibility of Adjustment in Côte d'Ivoire and Morocco*, Paris: OECD, 1994.

Aziza, Mimovn, 'La década trágica de Rif: el hambre y sus consecuencias sociales en los años cuarenta', *El vigía de Tierra* 2/3 (1996/7): 237-44.

Badi', Laila Khalil, *Adawa wa-malamih min al-Saqiyya al-Hamra wa-Wadi al-Dhahab (al-Sahara al-Gharbiyya)*, Beirut: Dar al-Masira, 1976.

Badía y Leblich, Domingo, *Travels of Ali Bey: in Morocco, Tripoli, Cyprus, Egypt, Arabia, Syria and Turkey: Between the Years 1803 and 1807 Written by Himself*, 2 vols, London: Longman, Hurst, Rees, Orme and Brown, 1816.

Bahaijoub, Ali, 'Morocco's Argument to Join the EEC' in George Joffe (ed), *North Africa: Nation, State, and Region*, London: Routledge, 1993, 235-46.

Baita, Abdeslam. ' "Reversion to Tradition" ' in State Structures in 19th century Morocco' in Abdelali Doumou (ed.), *The Moroccan State in Historical Perspective*, Dakar: CODESIRA, 1990, 29-61.

Barbari, Mouslim, *Tempête sur le Maroc ou les erreurs d'une 'politique berbère'*, Paris, 1931.

Baroudi, Abdallah, *Maroc, impérialisme et émigration.*, Rotterdam: Editions Hiwar, 1989.

Bartels, Albert, *Fighting the French in Morocco*, trans. H. J. Stenning, London: A. Rivers, 1932.

Beauclerk, Captain, G[eorge], *A Journey to Morocco, in 1826*, London: printed for Poole and Edwards ... and William Harrison Ainsworth ..., 1828.

Belguendouz, Abdelkrim, 'La colonisation agraire au Maroc et ses méthodes de pénétration', *Revue juridique politique économique du Maroc*, 4 (1978): 115-51.

Ben Srhir, Khalid and Mohamed Ennaji, 'La Grande Bretagne et l'esclavage au Maroc au XIXè siècle', *Hespéris-Tamuda*, 29 (1991): 249-82.

Benabid, Abdelmalek, 'Forest Degradation in Morocco' in W. Swearingen and Abdellatif Bencherifa (eds), *The North African Environment at Risk*, Boulder, CO: Westview Press, 1996.

Ben-Ari, Eyal and Yoram Bilu, 'Saints' sanctuaries in Israeli development towns: on a mechanism of urban transformation', *Urban Anthropology* 16, no. 2 (1987): 252-72.

Bencherifa, Abdellatif, 'Is Sedentarization of Pastoral Nomads Causing Desertification? the Case of the Benu Guil of Eastern Morocco' in W. Swearingen and Abdellatif Bencherifa (eds), *The North African Environment at Risk*, Boulder, CO: Westview Press, 1996, 117-30.

Benhaddou, Ali, *Maroc: les élites du royaume: essai sur l'organisation du pouvoir au Maroc*, Paris: L'Harmattan, 1997.

Benjamin, Roger (ed.), *Orientalism – Delacroix to Klee*, Sydney: Art Gallery of New South Wales, 1997.

Benjelloun, Abdelmajid, *Approches du colonialisme espagnol et du mouvement nationaliste marocain dans l'ex-Maroc khalifien*, Rabat: Okad, 1988.

——— *Fragments d'histoire du Rif oriental, et notamment des Beni Said, dans la deuxième moitié du xixè siècle, d'après les documents de Mr Hassan Ouchen*, [Rabat]: Textes à l'Appui, 1995.

——— 'La deuxième guerre mondiale, les nationalistes marocains de la zone espagnole du Protectorat et les possibilités de libération du Maroc' in *Approches du colonialisme espagnol et du mouvement nationaliste marocain dans l'ex-Maroc khalifien*, Rabat: Okad, 1988, 215-27.

——— 'La part prise par le mouvement nationaliste marocain de la zone d'influence espagnole dans le processus de libération du Maroc', *Revue d'Histoire Maghrébine*, 13, no. 43-4 (1986): 5-42.

——— 'L'enrôlement des marocains dans le rangs franquistes', *Revue Maroc-Europe*, 7 (1994): 219-34.

——— 'Les developpements du mouvement nationaliste marocain dans la zone nord sur le plan international', *Revue d'Histoire Maghrébine*, 14, no. 45-6 (1987): 31-74.

Bennani, Abdelaziz and Abdellah Eloualladi, *Liberté de presse et de l'information au Maroc – limites et perspectives*, Rabat: Organisation Marocaine des Droits de l'Homme, 1995.

Bennani-Chraïbi, Mounia, *Soumis et rebelles: les jeunes au Maroc.*, Casablanca: Editions le Fennec, 1994.

Benomar, Jamal, 'The Monarchy, the Islamist Movement and Religious Discourse in Morocco', *Third World Quarterly*, 10, no. 2 (1988): 539-55.

Benomar, Jamal Eddine, 'Working Class, Trade Unionism and Nationalism in Colonial Morocco', Ph.D. diss., Birkbeck College, University of London, 1992.

Benseddik, Fouad, *Syndicalisme et politique au Maroc*, Paris: L'Harmattan, 1990.

Bensimon, Agnès, *Hassan II et les juifs: histoire d'une emigration secrète*, Paris: Seuil, 1991.

Berges, Patrick, 'D'une guerre à l'autre: Le maroc espagnole dans la tourmente (17 juillet 1936-septembre 1940)', *Revue Maroc-Europe* 1 (1991): 107-33.

Berianne, Mohammed, 'Environmental Impacts of Tourism along the Moroccan Coast' in W. Swearingen and Abdellatif Bencherifa (eds), *The North African Environment at Risk*, Boulder CO: Westview Press, 1996, 241-53.

Berkous, Ahmed, 'La langue berbère: maintien et changement', *International Journal of the Sociology of Language* 112, (1995): 9-28.

Bernard, Stéphane, *The Franco-Moroccan Conflict 1943-1956*, trans. Marianna Oliver *et al.*, New Haven, CT: Yale University Press, 1968.

Berque, Jacques, *French North Africa: the Maghrib between Two World Wars*, trans. Jean Stewart, London: Faber, 1967.

——— 'Qu'est-ce qu'une "tribu" nord-africaine?' in *Maghreb: histoire et sociétés*, Gembloux: Duculot, 1974.

Berriane, Mohamed, 'Le tourisme sur la côte méditerranéene. Aménagement touristique ou promotion immobilière?' in El Malki Habib (ed.), *Le Maroc Méditerranéen, la troisième dimension*, Casbalanca: Editions le Fennec, 1992.

Bessis, Juliette, 'Chekib Arslan et les mouvements nationalistes au Maghreb', *Revue Historique*, 259 (1976): 467-89.

Beyen, Johan, *et al.*, *The Economic Development of Morocco: Report of a Mission Organized by the International Bank for Reconstruction and Development at the Request of the Government of Morocco.* Baltimore, MD: Johns Hopkins University Press, 1966.

Bidwell, Robin, *Morocco under Colonial Rule: French Administration of Tribal Rule 1915-1956*, London: Cass, 1973.

Bilu, Yoram and Eyal Ben-Ari, 'The Making of Modern Saints: Manufactured Charisma and the Abu Hatseiras of Israel', *American Ethnologist*, 19, no. 4 (1992): 672-87.

Bin Saghir, Khalid, *Al-Maghrib wa-Britaniya al-'Uzma fi-l-qarn al-tasi' 'ashr*, Al-Dar al-Baida: al-Walada, 1990.

Blair, Leon Borden, *Western Window in the Arab World*, Austin: University of Texas Press, 1970.

Blanc, François-Paul and Rabha Zeidguy, *Moudawana: code de statut personnel et des successions. Édition synoptique franco-arabe*, [n.p]: Sochepresse-Université, 1994.

Bois, Charles, 'Années de disette, années d'abondance, sécheresse et pluies au Maroc', *Revue pour l'Étude de Calamités*, 26-7 (1949): 1-31.

Borrow, George, *The Bible in Spain*, London: Dent/Everyman, 1947.

Bouarfa, Mohammed, *Le Rial et le Franc*, Rabat: INMA, 1988.

Bowie, Leland, *The Impact of the Protégé System in Morocco, 1880-1912, Papers in International Studies. Africa series no. 11*, Athens, OH: Ohio University, Center for International Studies, 1970.

Bravo Nieto, Antonio, *La construcción de una ciudad europea en el contexto norteafricano: arquitectos e ingenieros en la Melilla contemporánea*, Melilla: Ciudad Autónoma de Melilla, 1996.

——— 'L'architecture coloniale espagnole du xxème siècle au Maroc', *Revue Maroc-Europe*, 5 (1993): 159-76.

Brett , Michael, 'Don Roberto and the Tourmaline Affair: British Filibusters in the Canaries and Southern Morocco, 1875-1900 and the Creation of the Moroccan Protectorate, 1912' in Victor Morales Lezcano (ed.), *II Aula Canarias y el Noroeste de Africa*, 413-21, Las Palmas de Gran Canaria: Cabildo Insular, 1988.

Britten, Michael, 'Morocco: Sport in Brief', 9-11 March 1996.

Brown, K. and A. Lakhsassi, 'Every Man's Disaster – the Earthquake of Agadir: a Berber (Tashelhit) Poem', *Maghreb Review*, 5, no. 5-6 (1980): 125-33.

Brown, Kenneth L., *People of Salé: Tradition and Change in a Moroccan City 1830-1930*, Manchester University Press, 1976.

Burke, Edmund. 'The Image of the Moroccan State in French Ethnological Literature: a New Look at the Origins of Lyautey's Berber Policy' in Ernest Gellner and Charles Micaud (eds), *Arabs and Berbers: From Tribe to Nation in North Africa*, 175-99, London: Duckworth, 1972.

——— 'La Mission Scientifique au Maroc', *Bulletin Economque et Sociale du maroc*, 138-9 (1979): 37-56.

'Moroccan Resistance, Pan-Islam and German War Strategies 1914-1918', *Francia*, 3 (1975): 434-64.

——— *Prelude to Protectorate in Morocco*, University of Chicago Press, 1976.

——— 'Tribalism and Moroccan Resistance, 1890-1914: the Role of the Aith Ndhir' in E.G.H. Joffe and C.R. Pennell (eds), *Tribe and State: Essays in Honour of David Montgomery Hart*, 119-44, Wisbech: Menas Press, 1991.

Cagne, Jacques, *Nation et nationalisme au Maroc: aux racines de la nation marocaine*, Rabat: Dar Nashr al-Ma'rifa, 1988.

Casas de la Vega, Rafael, *La Ultima Guerra de Africa (Campaña de Ifni-Sáhara)*, Madrid: Servicio de Publicaciones del Estado Mayor del Ejército, 1985.

Célérier, J., 'Les conditions géographiques de la pacification de l'Atlas central', *Héspéris* 35 (1948): 359-82.

Chtatou, Mohamed, 'Bin 'Abd al-Karim in the Rifi Oral Tradition of Gzenneya' in E.G.H. Joffe and C.R. Pennell (eds), *Tribe and State: Essays in Honour of David Montgomery Hart*, 182-212, Wisbech: Menas Press, 1991.

——— 'Saints and Spirits and their Significance in Moroccan Cultural Beliefs and Practices: an Analysis of Westermarck's Work', *Morocco* (n.s) 1 (1996): 62-84.

Cigar, Norman, 'Socio-economic Structures and the Development of an Urban Bourgeoisie in Pre-Colonial Morocco', *Maghreb Review*, 6, no. 3-4 (981): 55-76.

Clément, Claude, *Oufkir*, Paris: Editions Jean Dullis, 1974.

Cohen, David, 'Lyautey et le sionisme', *Revue française d'histoire d'outre-mer* 67 (1980): 269-99.

Cook, Weston F., *The Hundred Years War for Morocco: Gunpowder and the Military Revolution in the Early Modern Muslim World* (Boulder, CO: Westview Press, 1994).

Coombs-Schilling, M. E., *Sacred Performances: Islam, Sexuality, and Sacrifice*, New York: Columbia University Press, 1989.

Cordero Torres, José María, *Organización del Protectorado Español en Marruecos*, 2 vols. Madrid: Editora Nacional, 1942.

de Cossé-Brissac, Phillipe, 'Les Rapports de la France et du Maroc pendant la guerre de l'Algérie (1930-1947)', *Hésperis*, 13 (1931): 35-203.

Coufourier, L., 'Chronique de la vie de Moulay el-Hassan', *Archives Marocaines*, 7 (1906): 330-96.

Cour Internationale de Justice, 'Sahara Occidental: requête pour avis consultatif, ordonnance du 3 janvier 1975', *Receuil des arrêts, avis consultatifs et ordennances* (1975).

Cunninghame-Graham, R.B., *Moghreb-el-Acksa*, new edn [first published London: Heinemann, 1898], London: Century, 1988.

Damis, John, *Conflict in Northwest Africa: The Western Sahara Dispute*, Stanford, CA: Hoover Institution Press, 1983.

——— 'The Impact of the Saharan Dispute on Moroccan Domestic and Foreign Policy', in I. William Zartman (ed.), *The Political Economy of Morocco*, New York: Praeger, 1987, 188-211.

——— 'Morocco, Libya and the Treaty of Union', *American-Arab Affairs* 13 (1995): 44-55.

Danziger, Raphael, *Abd al-Qadir and the Algerians: Resistance to the French and Internal Consolidation*, New York: Holmes & Meier, 1977.

Daoud, Zakya, *Féminisme et politique au Maghreb*, Casablanca: Eddif, 1993.

——— and Maâti Monjib, *Ben Barka*, Paris: Editions Michalon, 1996.

Darif, Muhammad, *al-Ahzab al-siyasiyya al-maghribiyya*, al-Dar al-Baida: Ifriqiya al-Sharq, 1988.

——— *Jama'at al-'Adl wa-Ihsan: qara't fi al-Masarat*, Rabat Manshurat al-Majallat al-Maghribiyya l-'ilm al-ijtima' al-siyyasi, 1995.

Daud, Muhammad, *Tarikh Titwan*, 5 vols, Titwan: M'ahad Mawlay al-Hasan, 1965.

Daure-Serfaty, Christine, *Rencontres avec le Maroc*, Paris: La Découverte, 1993.

Dayan, Moshe, *Breakthrough, a Personal Account of the Egypt-Israel Peace Negotiations*, London: Weidenfeld & Nicolson, 1981.

De Mas, Paolo, 'Dynamique récente de la migration marocaine vers les Pay-Bas. Specificité régionale et réseau rifain' in *Le Maroc et la Hollande. Une approche comparative des grands intérêts communs*, Rabat: Université Mohammed V, Faculté des Lettres, 1995.

Delanoè, Guy, *Lyautey, Juin, Mohammed V, fin d'un protectorat*, Casablanca: Eddif, 1993.

Diez Sánchez, Juán, 'Fin del protectorado de España en Marruecos: repliegue a Melilla de las Fuerzas del Tercio Gran Capitán, Iº De La Legión', *Trápana*, Número Extraordinario (1995).

Diouri, Moumen, *A qui appartient le Maroc?*, Paris: L'Harmattan, 1992.

Donoso-Cortés, Ricardo, *Estudio geográfico político-militar sobre las zonas españolas del norte y sur de Marruecos*, Madrid: Libería Gutenberg, 1913.

Driessen, Henk, *On the Spanish-Moroccan Frontier: a Study in Ritual, Power and Ethnicity*, Oxford: Berg, 1992.

Drummond-Hay, John, *Journal of an Expedition to the Court of Marocco in the Year 1846*, Cambridge: printed by Metcalfe and Palmer, 1848.

Drummond-Hay, John, Sir, *A Memoir of Sir John Drummond-Hay: Sometime Minister at the Court of Morocco, Based on his Journals and Correspondence*, London: John Murray, 1896.

Dunn, Ross E, 'Berber Imperialism: The Ait Atta Expansion in Southeast Morocco' in Ernest Gellner and Charles Micaud (eds), *Arabs and Berbers: From Tribe to Nation* in North Africa, London: Duckworth, 1972, 85-107.

——— 'The Bu Himara Rebellion in Northeast Morocco: Phase 1', *Middle Eastern Studies*, 17 (1981): 31-48.

——— 'France, Spain and the Bu Himara Rebellion' in E.G.H. Joffe and C.R. Pennell (eds), *Tribe and State: Essays in Honour of David Montgomery Hart*, 145-58. Wisbech: Menas Press, 1991.

——— *Resistance in the Desert : Moroccan Responses to French Imperialism 1881-1912*, London: Croom Helm, 1977.

Dwyer, Kevin, *Arab Voices: The Human Rights Debate in the Middle East*, Berkeley, CA: University of California Press, 1991.

Eickelman, Dale, *Knowledge and Power in Morocco*, Princeton University Press, 1985.

——— 'Religion in Polity and Society' in I. William Zartman (ed.), *The Political Economy of Morocco*, New York: Praeger, 1987, 84-96.

EIU (Economist Intelligence Unit), *Morocco to 1992: Growth against the Odds*, London: Economist, 1987.

Elboudrari, Hassan, 'L'exotisme à l'envers: Les premiers voyageurs marocains en orient (Espagne, XVIIème -XVIIIème siècles) et leur expérience de l'altérité' in J-C. Vatin (ed.), *D'un orient l'autre: les métamorphoses successives des perceptions et connaissances*, Paris: Editions du CNRS, 1991, 377-401.

El-Mossadeq, Rkia, 'Political Parties and Power-Sharing' in I. William Zartman (ed.), *The Political Economy of Morocco*, 59-83, New York: Praeger, 1987.

Ennaji, Mohamed and Paul Pascon, *Le Makhzen el le Sous al-Aqsa. la correspondance politique de la maison d'Iligh (1821-1894)*, Casablanca: Toubkal, 1988.

Ennaji, Mohammed, *Soldats, domestiques et concubines. L'esclavage au Maroc au xixè siècle*, Casablanca: Eddif, 1994

Espadas Burgos, Manuel and José De Urquijo Goitia, *Guerra de independencia y época constitutcional (1808-1898)*, vol. 11 of *Historia de España*, Madrid: Gredos, 1990.

Etienne, Bruno, *Abdelkader: isthme des isthmes (Barzakh al-barazikh)*, Paris: Hachette, 1994.

Al-Fasi, 'Allal, *Al-harakat al-istiqlaliyya fi-l-Maghrib al-'Arabi*, Tangier: Abd al-Salam Gassus, [n.d.].

Finlayson, Iain, *Tangier: City of the Dream*, London: Flamingo, 1993.

Flournoy, Francis Roseboro, *British Policy Towards Morocco in the Age of Palmerston*, London: P.S. King, 1935.

De Foucauld, Charles, *Reconnaissance au Maroc: journal de route conforme à l'édition de 1888 et augmenté de fragments inédits rédigés par l'auteur etc.*, Paris: Société d'Éditions Géographiques, Maritimes et Coloniales, 1939.

Forbes, Rosita, *El Raisuni, the Sultan of the Mountains*, London: Thornton Butterworth, 1924.

Gallissot, René, *Le patronat européen au Maroc: action sociale, action politique, 1931-1942*, Casablanca: Eddif, 1990.

Ganiage, Jean, *Les origines du protectorat français en Tunisie (1861-1881)*, Tunis: Maison Tunisienne de l'Edition, 1969.

García Figueras, Tomás, *La acción africana de España en torno al 98 (1860-1912)*, Madrid: CSIC, 1966.

Gellner, Ernest, *Saints of the Atlas*, University of Chicago Press, 1969.

——— 'The Struggle for Morocco's Past', *Middle East Journal*, 15 (1961): 79-90.

———, and Charles Micaud (eds), *Arabs and Berbers: From Tribe to Nation in North Africa*, London: Duckworth, 1972.

Godfrey, John Brendan, 'Overseas trade and rural change in nineteenth century Morocco: the social region and agrarian order of the Shawiya', Ph.D. diss., Johns Hopkins University, 1985.

Gouvion Saint-Cyr, Marthe and Edmond Gouvion Saint-Cyr, *Kitab aayane al-Marhrib 'l-akca: esquisse générale des moghrebs de la genèse à nos jours et livre des grands du Maroc*, Paris: Paul Geuthner, 1939.

Great Britain, Department of Overseas Trade, *Survey of Economic Conditions in Morocco 1928-1929*, London: HMSO, 1930.

Guillaume, A., *Les Berbères marocains et la pacification de l'Atlas Central 1912-1933*, Paris: René Julliard, 1946.

Hajji, Muhammad (ed.), *Mu'allamat al-Maghrib*, Salé: Matabi' Sala, 1989.

Hall, Luella, *The United States and Morocco*, Metuchen, NJ: Scarecrow Press, 1971.

Halliday, Fred, 'The *millet* of Manchester: Arab Merchants and Cotton Trade', *British Journal of Middle Eastern Studies*, 19, no. 2 (1992): 159-76.

Halstead, John P., *Rebirth of a Nation: the Origins and Rise of Moroccan Nationalism 1912-1944*, Cambridge, MA: Harvard University Centre for Middle Eastern Studies, 1969.

Hammoudi, Abdellah, *Master and Disciple: the Cultural Foundations of Moroccan Authoritarianism*, University of Chicago Press, 1997.

Harris, Lawrence, *With Mulai Hafid at Fez*, London: Smith, Elder, 1909.

Harris, Walter, *Morocco that Was*, Edinburgh: Blackwood, 1921.

Hart, David M., *The Ait 'Atta of Southern Morocco: Daily Life and Recent History*, Wisbech: Menas Press, 1984.

——— 'Clan, Lineage, Local Community and the Feud in a Rifian Tribe' in Louise E. Sweet (ed.), *Peoples and Cultures of the Middle East: An Anthropological Reader*, New York: Natural History Press, 1970, 3-75.

——— *Emilio Blanco Izaga, Colonel in the Rif*, 2 vols, New Haven: Human Relations Area Files, 1975.

——— *The Aith Waryaghar of the Moroccan Rif, an Ethnography and History*, Tucson: University of Arizona Press, 1976.

——— *Dadda 'Atta and his Forty Grandsons: the Socio-political Organisation of the Ait 'Atta of Southern Morocco*, Wisbech: Menas Press, 1981.

Hart, Ursula, *Behind the Courtyard Door: The Daily Life of Tribeswomen in Northern Morocco*, Ipswich Press, 1994.

Hassan II, *The Challenge*, trans. Anthony Rhodes, London: Macmillan, 1978.

——— *La Mémoire d'un roi: entretiens avec Eric Laurent*, Paris: Plon, 1993.

——— *Le défi*, Paris: Albin Michel, 1976.

Heinemeijer, W.F, *et al.*, *Partir pour rester: incidences de l'emigration ouvrière à la campagne marocaine*, Amsterdam: Université d'Amsterdam: Institut Socio-Géographique, 1977.

Hernando de Larremendi, Miguel, *La política exterior de Marruecos*, Madrid: MAPFRE, 1997.

Hirschberg, H.Z., *A History of the Jews in North Africa*, 2 vols, Leiden: E. J. Brill, 1981.

Hodges, Tony, *Western Sahara: the Roots of a Desert War*, Westport, CT: Lawrence Hill, 1983.

Hoffherr, René, *L'Économie marocaine*, Paris: Sirey, 1932.

Hoffman, Bernard, *The Structure of Traditional Moroccan Rural Society*, The Hague: Mouton, 1967.

Hoisington, William A., *The Casablanca Connection: French Colonial Policy 1936-1943*, Chapel Hill: University of North Carolina Press, 1984.

——— *Lyautey and the French Conquest of Morocco*, Basingstoke: Macmillan, 1995.

Horne, Alistair, *A Savage War of Peace: Algeria 1954-1962*, London: Macmillan, 1977.

Hourani, Albert, *Arabic Thought in the Liberal Age*, Oxford University Press, 1970.

Houroro, Faouzi M., *Sociologie politique coloniale au Maroc: cas de Michaux Bellaire*, Casablanca: Afrique Orient, 1988.

Joffe, E.G.H., 'The Moroccan Nationalist Movement: Istiqlal, the Sultan and the Country, *Journal of African History* 26 (1985): 289-307.

——— and C.R. Pennell (eds), *Tribe and State: Essays in Honour of David Montgomery Hart*, Wisbech: Menas Press, 1991.

Joffe, George, 'Khattara and Other Forms of Gravity-fed Irrigation in Morocco', in Peter Beaumont, Michael Bonine and Keith McLachlan (eds), *Qanat , Kariz and Khattara: Traditional Water Systems in the Middle East and North Africa*, Wisbech: Menas Press, 1989, 195-210.

——— 'The Zawiya of Wazzan: Relations between Shurafa and Tribe up to 1860', in E.G.H. Joffe and C.R. Pennell (eds), *Tribe and State: Essays in Honour of David Montgomery Hart*, Wisbech: Menas Press, 1991, 84-118.

——— 'The Euro-Mediterranean Partnership: Two Years after Barcelona, London' in *Briefing No. 44*, London: The Royal Institute of International Affairs, 1998.

Johnson, Douglas. 'Development Trends and Environmental Deterioration in the Agropastoral Systems of the Central Middle Atlas, Morocco' in Swearingen and Bencherifa (eds), *The North African Environment at Risk*, Boulder, CO: Westview, 1996.

Julien, Charles-André, *Le Maroc face aux impérialismes, 1415-1956*, Paris: Éditions Jeune-Afrique, 1978.

Kenbib, Mohamed, 'Changing aspects of State and Society in 19th century Morocco' in Abdelali Doumou (ed.), *The Moroccan State in Historical Perspective 1850-1985*, Dakar: CODESIRA, 1990, 11-27.

Kenbib, Mohammed, 'European Protections in Morocco, 1904-1939' in George Joffe(ed.), *Morocco and Europe*, London: School of Oriental and African Studies, University of London, 1989, 47-53.

——— 'Protégés et brigands dans le Maroc du XIXe siècle et début du Xxe', *Hésperis-Tamuda*, 29 (1991): 227-48.

Khallougi, Mohammed Essaghir Al, *Bouhmara: Du jihad à la compromission* Rabat: [n.p], 1993.

Kiernan, V.G., *European Empires from Conquest to Collapse, 1815-1960*, Leicester University Press, 1982.

Lacouture, Jean, *De Gaulle, the Ruler 1945-1970*, New York: W.W. Norton, 1992.

Lacroix-Riz, Annie, *Les protectorats de l'Afrique du Nord entre la France et Washington*, Paris: L'Harmattan, 1988.

Lahbabi, Mohamed, *Le Gouvernement marocain à l'aube du vingtième siècle*, 2nd edn. Rabat: Les Éditions Maghrébines, 1975.

Lahlou, Abdelmalek, *Casablanca à l'heure de l'opération Torch et de la Conférence d'Anfa*, Casablanca: [n.p.], 1993.

Lane, Edward William, *An Arabic-English Lexicon, Derived from the Very Best Sources* ... 2 vols, London: Williams and Norgate, 1877.

Laroui, Abdallah, *Esquisses historiques*, Casablanca: Centre Culturel Arabe, 1992.

——— *Les origines sociales et culturelles du nationalisme Marocain*, Paris: Maspéro, 1977.

Laskier, Michael M., *The Alliance Israélite Universelle and the Jewish Communities of Morocco, 1862-1962*, Albany: State University of New York Press, 1983.

——— *North African Jewry in the Twentieth Century: The Jews of Morocco, Tunisia, and Algeria*, New York University Press, 1994.

Le Coz, Jean, *Le Rharb, fellahs et colons: étude de géographie régionale*, 2 vols, Rabat: Ministère de l'Education Nationale, 1964.

Le Tourneau, Roger, *Fès avant le Protectorat: étude économique d'une ville de l'occident musulman*, Casablanca: Éditions la Porte, 1949.

Legrand, Jean-Charles, *Justice, patrie de l'homme: défenses devant les Tribunaoux militaires du Protectorat, 1953-1955*, Casablanca: Editions Maroc, [n.d.].

Leveau, Rémy, *Le fellah marocain – défenseur du trône*, 2nd edn, Paris: Presses de la Fondation Nationale des Sciences Politiques, 1985.

Levisse-Touze, Christine, 'La contribution du Maroc pendant la seconde guerre mondiale (1940-1945)', *Maroc-Europe*, 7 (1994): 209-17.

Lévy, Armand, *Il'était une fois les juifs marocains*, Paris: L'Harmattan, 1995.

Leymarie, Serge and Jean Tripier, *Maroc, le prochain Dragon? De nouvelles idées pour le développement*, Casablanca: Eddif, 1992.

López-García, Bernabé, *Procesos electorales en Marruecos (1960-1977)*, Madrid: CSIC, 1979.

Lorcin, Patricia M. E., *Imperial Identities: Stereotyping, Prejudice and Race in Colonial Algeria*, London: I.B. Tauris, 1995.

Luccioni, Joseph, 'L'avènement de Sidi Mohammed ben Youssef au trône du Maroc, 1927', *Revue de l'Occident Musulman* (1972): 123-9.

——— 'L'élaboration du dahir berbère du 16 Mai 1930', *Revue du Monde Musulman et de la Méditerranée* 38 (1984): 75-81.

Mackenzie, Donald, *The Flooding of the Sahara: an Account of the Proposed Plan for Opening Central Africa to Commerce and Civilization From the North-west Coast, with a Description of Soudan and Western Sahara, and Notes of Ancient Manuscripts, &c*, London: Sampson Low, 1877.

——— *The Khalifate of the West, being a General Description of Morocco*, London: Simpkin Marshall, 1911.

Madariaga, María Rosa de, 'The Intervention of Moroccan Troops in the Spanish Civil War: a Reconsideration', *European History Quarterly*, 22, no. 1 (1992): 67-97.

Maddy-Weitzmann, Bruce, 'Conflict and Conflict Management in the Western Sahara: Is the Endgame Near?', *Middle East Journal*, 45, no. 4 (1991): 594-605.

Maghraoui, Driss, 'Moroccan Colonial Soldiers: between Selective Memory and Collective memory', *Arab Studies Quarterly*, 20, no. 2 (1998): 21-42.

Majid, Majdi, *Les luttes de classes au Maroc depuis l'Indépendance*, Rotterdam: Hiwar, 1987.

Maldonado, Eduardo, *El Rogui*, Tetuan: Instituto General Franco para la Investigación Hispano-Árabe, [1949].

El Malki, Habib, *Trente Ans d'Economie Marocaine, 1960-1990*, Paris: CNRS, 1990.

El Mansour, Mohamed, 'Moroccan Perceptions of European Civilisation in the Nineteenth Century' in George Joffe (ed.), *Morocco and Europe*, London: Centre of Near and Middle Eastern Studies, School of Oriental and African Studies, 1989, 37-45.

——— *Morocco in the Reign of Mawlay Sulayman*, Wisbech: Menas Press, 1990.

Manuni, Muhammad, *Mazahir yaqzat al-Maghrib al-hadith*, 2 vols, Rabat: Manshurat wizarat al-awqaf wa-l-shu'un al-Islamiyya wa-l-thaqafa, 1973.

Marais, Octave, 'La classe dirigeante au Maroc', *Revue Française de Science Politique*, 14 (1964): 709-37.

Marquina Barrio, Antonio, 'El Plan Backbone: España, bajo dos amenazas de invasión', *Historia 16*, no. 79 (1992): 11-22.

Martin, A.-G.-P., *Quatre siècles d'histoire marocaine: au Sahara de 1504 à 1902, au Maroc de 1894 à 1912*, 2nd edn. Rabat: Éditions La Porte, 1994.

Martin, Bradford G., 'Ma' al-'Aynayn al-Qalqami, Mauritanian Mystic and Politician' in *Muslim Brotherhoods in Nineteenth-Century Africa*, 125-51, Cambridge University Press, 1976.

Martínez de Campos, Carlos, *España bélica el siglo XX Marruecos*, Madrid: Aguilar, 1969.

Maxwell, Gavin, *Lords of the Atlas: the Rise and Fall of the House of Glaoua 1893-1956*, London: Longmans, Green, 1966.

M'Barek, Zaki, 'La désertion des soldats marocains de l'armée française à l'Armée de Libération du Maghreb (A.L.M.): Rôle militaire, impact psycho-politique (1955-1956)', *Maroc-Europe*, 7, (1994): 235-71.

——— *Résistance et Armée de Libération: Portée, politique, liquidation*, Tangier: [n.p.], 1986.

McNeill, John Robert, *The Mountains of the Mediterranean World : an Environmental History*, Cambridge University Press, 1992.

Meakin, Budgett, *The Land of the Moors, a Comprehensive Description*, London: Swann Sonnenschein, 1901.

Mercer, John, *Spanish Sahara*, London: Geo. Allen & Unwin, 1976.

Mernissi, Fatima, *Doing Daily Battle: Interviews with Moroccan Women*, London: Women's Press, 1986.

——— *The Harem Within: Tales of a Moroccan Girlhood*, London: Bantam, 1995.

Meyers, Allan Richard, 'The 'Abid 'l-Buhari: Slave Soldiers and Statecraft in Morocco, 1672-1790', Ph.D. diss., Cornell University, 1974.

Michel, Nicholas, 'L'approvisionnement de la mhalla au Maroc au XIXe siècle', *Hésperis-Tamuda*, 29, no. 2 (1991): 313-40.

Miege, Jean-Louis, *Le Maroc et L'Europe (1830-1894)*, 4 vols, Paris: Presses Universitaires de France, 1961.

——— 'La Marine marocaine au XIXè siècle', *Bulletin du comité marocain de documentation historique de la marine*, no. 2 (1956): 2-4.

Miller, Susan, 'The Colonial Hunt in Nineteenth-Century Tangier' in A. Bendaoud and M. Maniar (eds), *Tanger 1800-1956, Contribution à l'histoire récente du Maroc*, 191-203, Rabat: Editions Arabo-Africaines, 1991.

——— and Amal Rassam, 'The View from the Court: Moroccan Reactions to European Penetration in the Late Nineteenth Century', *International Journal of African Historical Studies*, 16, no. 1 (1983): 25-38.

Milliot, Louis, 'L'exode saisonnier des riffains vers l'Algérie', *Bulletin Economique du Maroc*, 1, no. 5 (1934): 313-21.

Mohammed V, 'The First Anniversary of the King's Return to Morocco' [Speech of November 18, 1956]' in I. William Zartman (ed.), *Man, State, and Society in the Contemporary Maghreb*, London: Pall Mall Press, 1973, 113-17.

Montagne, Robert, *Les Berbères et le Makhzen au sud du Maroc*, Paris: Félix Alcan, 1930.

——— *Révolution au Maroc*, Paris: France-Empire, 1951.

Moore, Clement Henry, *Politics in North Africa: Algeria, Morocco and Tunisia*, Boston: Little, Brown, 1970.

Morales Lezcano, Víctor, *El colonialismo hispano-francés en Marruecos*, Madrid: Siglo XXI, 1976.

——— *España y el norte de África: el protectorado en Marruecos (1912-1956)*, Madrid: UNED, 1984.

Morillas, Javier, *Sahara Occidental: desarollo y subdesarollo*, Madrid: El Dorado, 1990.

Morsy, Magali, 'El Hajj Thami el Glaouï, un grand caïd contre le sultan et l'indépendance marocaine' in Charles-André Julien (ed.), *Les Africains*, Paris: Éditions J.A, 1976, 65-99.

Mouhssine, Ouafae, 'Ambivalence du discours sur l'arabisation', *International Journal of the Sociology of Language*, 112 (1995): 45-61.

M'rabet, Mohammed, 'Un millénaire de lutte contre le mort au Maroc, appreciation d'une thèse', *Revue Dar al-Niaba*, no. 36-27 (1990): 11- 12.

Munson, Henry, 'On the Relevance of the Segmentary Lineage Model in the Moroccan Rif', *American Anthropologist*, 91 (1989): 386-400.

——— 'The Political Role of Islam in Morocco' in George Joffe (ed.), *North Africa: nation, state, and region*, 187-202, London: Routledge, 1993.

——— *Religion and Power in Morocco*, New Haven: Yale University Press, 1993.

——— 'The Social Base of Islamic Militancy in Morocco', *Middle East Journal*, 40, no. 2 (1985): 267-84.

Naamane-Guessous, Soumaya, *Au-delà de toute pudeur. La sexualité féminine au Maroc: conclusion d'une enquête sociologique menée de 1981 à 1984 à Casablanca,* Casablanca: Editions Eddif, 1991.

Naciri, M., 'Quelques exemples d'évolution des douars à la périphérie urbaine de Salé', *Revue de Géographie du Maroc,* 8 (1965): 133-147.

Naimi, Mustapha, 'The Evolution of the Tekna Confederation: Caught between the Coastal Commerce and Trans-Saharan Trade' in E.G.H. Joffe and C.R. Pennell (eds), *Tribe and State: Essays in Honour of David Montgomery Hart,* Wisbech: Menas Press, 1991, 213-38.

Nasiri, Abu al-'Abbas Ahmad bin Khalid al-, *Kitab al-istiqsa l-akhbar duwwal al-Magrib al-Aqsa,* 9 vols, Rabat: Dar al-Kitab, 1956.

Nordman, Daniel, 'Les expéditions de Moulay Hassan: Essai Statistique', *Héspéris-Tamuda,* 19 (1990-1): 123-52.

Nsouli, Saleh M. and Saleh M. Eken, *Resilience and Growth through Sustained Adjustment: The Moroccan Experience,* vol. 115-116, Washington, DC: International Monetary Fund, 1995.

Orwell, George, *The Collected Essays, Journalism and Letters of George Orwell,* 4 vols, Harmondsworth: Penguin, 1970.

Ouardighi, Abderrahim, *La grande crise Franco-Marocaine 1952-1956,* Rabat: [n.p], 1976.

Ouazzani, Mohamed Hassan, *Combats d'un nationaliste marocain,* 2 vols, Fès: Fondation Mohamed Hassan Ouazzani, 1989.

Oved, Georges, *La Gauche française et le nationalisme marocain 1905-1955,* 2 vols. Paris: L'Harmattan, 1984.

Pallez, G., 'Les Marchands Fassis', *Bulletin Economique et Sociale du Maroc,* no. 51 (1951): 568-72.

Panet, Léopolde, *Première exploration du Sahara Occidental. Relation d'un voyage du Sénégal au Maroc, 1850,* Paris: Le Livre Africain, 1968.

Park, Thomas Kerlin, 'Administration and the Economy : Morocco 1880 to 1980: the Case of Essaouira', Ph.D diss. University of Madison-Wisconsin, 1983.

Parry, Clive (ed.), *The Consolidated Treaty Series,* 231 vols, Dobbs Ferry, NY: Oceana, 1969-81.

Parsons, F.V., *The Origins of the Morocco Question, 1880-1900,* London: Duckworth, 1976.

Pascon, Paul, *La Maison d'Iligh et l'histoire sociale de Tazerwalt,* Rabat: SMER, 1984.

——— *Le Haouz de Marrakech,* 2 vols, Rabat: Centre Universitaire de la Recherche Scientifique, 1983. English translation: *Capitalism and Agriculture in the Haouz of Marrkesh,* trans. C. Edwin Vaughan and Veronique Ingman (London: Kegan Paul International, 1986).

——— and Herman van der Wusten, *Les Beni Boufrah: Essai d'écologie sociale d'une vallée rifaine (Maroc),* Rabat: Institut Agronomique et Vétérinaire Hassan II, 1983.

Paul, Jim, 'Medicine and Imperialism in Morocco', *MERIP Reports,* 60 (1977): 3-12.

Payne, Rhys, 'Food Deficits and Political Legitimacy: the Case of Morocco' in Stephen K. Commins, Michael F. Lofchie and Rhys Payne (eds),

Africa's Agrarian crisis: the Roots of Famine, Boulder, CO: Lynne Rienner, 1986, 153-72.

Pazzanita, Anthony, G., 'Morocco versus Polisario: a Political Interpretation', *Journal of Modern African Studies*, 32, no. 2 (1994): 265-78.

Pennell, C.R., *A Country with a Government and a Flag: The Rif War in Morocco, 1921-1926*, Wisbech: Menas Press, 1986.

——— 'Dealing with Pirates: British French and Moroccans 1834-1856', *Journal of Imperial and Commonwealth History* 21, no. 1 (1994): 54-83.

——— 'The Geography of Piracy: Northern Morocco in the Nineteenth Century', *Journal of Historical Geography* 20, no. 3 (1994): 272-82.

——— 'The Interpenetration of European and Islamic Law in the Western Mediterranean in the Early Nineteenth Century', *British Journal of Middle Eastern Studies* 21 (1994): 159-89.

——— 'John Drummond-Hay: Tangier as the Centre of a Spider's web', in A. Bendaoud and M. Maniar (eds), *Tanger 1800-1956. Contribution à l'histoire récente du Maroc*, Rabat: Editions Arabo-Africaines, 1991, 107-34.

———'Law, Order and the Formation of an Islamic Resistance to Colonialism: the Rif 1921-1926', *Revue d'Histoire Maghrébine*, 21-2 (1981): 23-39.

——— 'Makhzan and Siba in Morocco: an Examination of Early Modern Attitudes', in E.G.H. Joffe and C.R. Pennell (eds), *Tribe and State: Essays in Honour of David Montgomery Hart*, Wisbech: Menas Press, 1991.

——— 'The Maritime Trade on the Northern Morocco Coast in the Early Nineteenth Century', *Morocco* (n.s), 1 (1996): 85-96.

——— 'The Moroccan Discovery of the Mediterranean Coast', *British Journal of Middle Eastern Studies*, 20, no. 2 (1993): 226-36.

——— 'The Responsibility for Anual: the Failure of Spanish Policy in the Moroccan Protectorate 1912-21', *European Studies Review*, 12 (1982): 67-86.

——— 'Tyranny, Just Rule and Moroccan Political Thought', *Morocco Occasional Papers*, 1 (1994): 13-42.

——— 'Women and Resistance to Colonialism in Morocco: the Rif 1916-1926', *Journal of African History*, 28 (1987): 107-18.

Perrault, Gilles, *Notre ami le roi*, Paris: Gallimard, 1990.

Pomfret, Richard, 'Morocco's International Economic Relations' in I. William Zartman (ed.), *The Political Economy of Morocco*, New York: Praeger, 1987, 173-87.

Porch, Douglas, *The Conquest of Morocco*, New York: Alfred A. Knopf, 1983.

Preston, Paul, *Franco, a Biography*, London: HarperCollins, 1993.

Pujo, Bernard, *Juin, Maréchal de France*, Paris: Albin Michel, 1988.

Rahmouni, Hassan (ed.), *La grande encyclopédie du Maroc*, Rabat: GEI, 1987.

Rejali, Darius, *Torture and Modernity: Self, Society and State in Modern Iran*, Boulder, CO: Westview Press, 1994.

Rhazaoui, Ahmed, 'Recent Economic Trends: Managing the Indebtedness' in I. William Zartman (ed.), *The Political Economy of Morocco*, New York: Praeger, 1987, 141-58.

R'honi, Ahmed, *Historia de Tetuán*, Tetuán: Marroquí, 1953.

Rivet, Daniel, 'La recrudescence des epidémies au Maroc durant la deuxième guerre mondiale: essai de mésure et d'interprétation', *Héspéris-Tamuda*, 30, no. 1 (1992): 93-109.

——— *Lyautey et l'institution du protectorat français au Maroc, 1912-1926*, 3 vols, Paris: L'Harmattan, 1988.

Roberts, Priscilla, 'Nineteenth-century Tangier: its American visitors – Who they Were, Why they Came, What they Wrote' in A. Bendaoud and M. Maniar (eds), *Tanger 1800-1956, Contribution à l'histoire récente du Maroc*, Rabat: Editions Arabo-Africaines, 1991, 135-65.

Robinson, R. E. and J. Gallagher, 'The Imperialism of Free Trade', *Economic History Review*, 52nd series 6 (1957): 1-15.

Rogers, P.G., *A History of Anglo-Moroccan Relations to 1900*, London: Foreign and Commonwealth Office, n.d.

Rollman, Wilfrid J., 'The "New Order" in a Pre-colonial Muslim Society: Military Reform in Morocco, 1844-1904', Ph.D. diss., University of Michigan, 1983.

Román, Juan, *Fragmentos de una conversación sobre Alhucemas*, Melilla: Ayuntamiento de Melilla, 1994.

Ruiz Bravo-Villasante, Carmen and Amin al-Rihani, *Un testigo árabe del siglo XX, Amin al-Rihani en Marruecos y en España (1939)*, 2 vols, Madrid: Cantarabia, 1993.

Ruiz Miguel, Carlos, *El Sahara Occidental y España: historia, política y derecho – análisis crítico de la política exterior española*, Madrid: Dykinson, 1995.

Al-Saffar, Muhammad, *Disorienting Encounters: Travels of a Moroccan Scholar in France in 1845-1846: the Voyage of Muhammad as-Saffar*, trans. Susan Gilson, Miller, Berkeley: University of California Press, 1992.

Salahdine, Mohamed, 'The Informal System in Morocco: The Failure of Legal Systems' in A. Lawrence Chickering and Mohamed Salahdine (eds), *The Silent Revolution: The Informal Sector in Five Asian and Near Eastern Countries*, San Francisco: ICS Press, 1991, 15-38.

——— *Les petits métiers clandestins 'le business populaire'*, Casablanca: Eddif, 1988.

——— *Maroc: tribus, makhzen et colons, essai d'histoire économique et sociale*, Paris: L'Harmattan, 1986.

Salmi, Najib, 'Première année depuis 1984 sans medaille d'or olympique', *La Vie Economique*, 3-9 Jan. 1997, 39.

Santucci, J-C., *Chroniques politiques marocaines (1971-1982)*, Paris: Editions du CNRS, 1985.

Scham, Alan, *Lyautey in Morocco: Protectorate Administration, 1912-1925*, Berkeley: University of California Press, 1970.

Schroeter, Daniel, *Merchants of Essaouira: Urban Society and Imperialism in South-western Morocco 1844-1886*, New York: Cambridge University Press, 1988.

——— 'Slave Markets and Slavery in Moroccan Urban Society', *Slavery and Abolition*, 13, no. 1 (1992): 185-213.

Seddon, David, 'Labour Migration and Agricultural Development in North-east Morocco: 1870-1970', *Maghreb Review*, 4, no. 3 (1979): 69-77.

——— *Moroccan Peasants, a Century of Change in the Eastern Rif, 1870-1970*. Folkestone: Dawson, 1981.

Seddon, David. 'Morocco at War' in Richard Lawless and Laila Monahan (eds), *War and Refugees: The Western Sahara Conflict*, London: Pinter, 1987, 98-138.

Serels, M. Mitchell, *A History of the Jews of Tangier in the Nineteenth and Twentieth Centuries*, New York: Sepher-Hermon Press, 1991.

Al-Shabi, Mustafa, *al-Nukhbat al-makhzaniyya fi Maghrib al-qarn al-tasi' 'ashar*, Jami'at Muhammad al-Khamis, Manshurat Kuliyyat al-Adab wa-'ulum al-Insaniyya, Rabat: 1995.

Shakespeare, William, *Romeo d Juliet*, Trans. by Adghirni, Ahmed, Rabat: Matabia Takatoul Al Watani, 1995.

Sinclair-Loutit, K., 'The Bishopric of Fes', *Morocco* (new series) 1 (1996): 116-28.

Smith, Charles D., *Palestine and the Arab-Israeli Conflict*, 2nd edn, New York: St. Martin's Press, 1992.

Spencer, Claire Catherine, 'The Zone of International Administration of Tangier (1923-35)', Ph.D diss., School of Oriental and African Studies, University of London, 1993.

Stewart, Charles F., *The Economy of Morocco 1912-1962*, Cambridge, MA: Harvard Centre for Middle Eastern Studies, 1967.

Stuart, Graham H., *The International City of Tangier*, 2nd edn, Stanford University Press, 1955.

Swearingen, W. and Abdellatif Bencherifa (eds), *The North African Environment at Risk*, Boulder, CO: Westview Press, 1996.

Swearingen, Will D, *Moroccan Mirages: Agrarian Dreams and Deceptions, 1912-1986*, London: I.B. Tauris, 1988.

Temimi, Abdeljelil, *Le Beylik de Constantine et Hajd Ahmed Bey (1830-1837)*, Tunis: Publications de la Revue d'Histoire Maghrébine, 1978.

Thomas, Hugh, *The Spanish Civil War*, 3rd edn, Harmondsworth: Penguin, 1977.

Tozy, Mohammed, 'Islam and the State' in I. William Zartman (ed.), *The Political Economy of Morocco*, New York: Praeger, 1987, 102-22.

Trout, Frank E., *Morocco's Southern Frontiers*, Geneva: Droz, 1969.

United States Department of State *Foreign Relations of the United States*, Washington, DC: United States Government Printing Office, 1972.

Usborne, C.V., *The Conquest of Morocco*, London: Stanley Paul, 1936.

Valensi, Lucette, 'Le roi chronophage. La construction d'une conscience historique dans le Maroc postcolonial', *Cahiers d'études africaines*, 30, no. 3 (1990): 279-99.

Valenzuela, Javier and Alberto Masegosa, *La última frontera. Marruecos, el vecino inquietante*, Madrid: Temas de Hoy, 1996.

Waterbury, John, *Commander of the Faithful*, New York: Columbia University Press, 1970.

——— 'The Coup Manqué', Hanover, NH: American Universities Field Staff, Africa, 1971.

——— 'Endemic and Planned Corruption in a Monarchical Regime', *World Politics*, 25 (1973): 533-55.

Wazan, Emily Keene, Shareefa of, *My Life Story*, London: Edward Arnold, 1912.

Weisgerber, F., *Au seuil du Maroc moderne,* Rabat: Éditions la Porte, 1947.

Werth, Alexander, *The Strange History of Pierre Mendès-France and the Great Conflict over French North Africa,* London: Barrie, 1957.

Wladimir Andreff, 'Le Tiers Monde Vassalisé' in *Manière de Vie,* 30. Paris: Le Monde Diplomatique, 1996.

Wolf, Jean, *Les secrets du Maroc espagnol, L'épopée d'Abd-el-Khaleq Torrès,* Casablanca: Eddif, 1994.

World-Bank, *World Development Report 1983,* [New York]: Oxford University Press, 1983.

Wright, John, *Libya a Modern History,* London: Croom Helm, 1981.

Yacoubi, Rachida, *Ma vie, mon cri,* Casablanca: Eddif, 1995.

Yahya, Dahiru, *Morocco in the Sixteenth Century: Problems and Patterns in African Foreign Policy,* Atlantic Highlands, NJ: Humanities Press, 1981.

Yehuda, Zvi, 'Zionist Activity in Southern Morocco, 1919-1923', *Revue des Etudes juives,* 144, no. 4 (1985): 363-8.

Youssi, Abderrahim, 'The Moroccan Triglossia: Facts and Implications', *International Journal of the Sociology of Language,* 112 (1995): 29-43.

Zartman, I. William *Morocco: Problems of New Power,* New York: Atherton Press, 1964.

——— (ed.), *Man, State, and Society in the Contemporary Maghreb,* London: Pall Mall Press, 1973.

——— (ed), *The Political Economy of Morocco,* New York: Praeger, 1987.

——— 'King Hassan's New Morocco' in *The Political Economy of Morocco,* (above), 1-33.

Znagie, Bechir, 'The Voyage Perilous', *Index on Censorship* 3 (1994): 19-20.

INDEX

Ababou, Thami: appointed *hajib*, 161; role in accession of M. Youssef, 208
Abbas, Mahmoud, 369
Abd al-Karim bin Sulayman: as foreign minister, 117, 122; financial dealings of, 123; disliked by radical *ulama*, 131
Abd al-Malik bin Muhyi al-Din: and Abu Himara, 181; activities in Rif in First World War, 181-2
Abd al-Qadir bin Muhyi al-Din: proclamation as leader in Algeria, 1832, 43; supply of armaments to, 44; al-Nasiri on, 49; *nizam* army of, 50; French attack on, 1840, 48; relations with Makhzan, 48-4; defeat of Moroccan army 1847, 51
Abd al-Salam bin al -Arbi, al-Hajj: *see* Ouezzane, Sharif of
Abd al-Salam bin Mashish (d. 1227): tomb in Jbel Alam, 11; in lineage of El Raisuni, 127
Abda, 137; rebellion under M. Slimane, 26-7; rebellion of 1893, 112; and *tariqas* in 1930s, 127
Abdallah b. Ismaïl, M.: *bay'a* of, 15
Abdelaziz, Moulay (Sultan 1894-1908): early life, 92; proclamation as sultan, 108; relationship with Ba Ahmad, 111; takes full power, 1900, 121; personality, 122; attempted reforms, 122, 124; and El Raisuni, 127; public attitudes towards, 128; relations with *ulama*, 130-1; seeks refuge with French (Sept. 1907), 137; abdication of, 139; and Abdallah bin Idris al-Sanusi, 142, and Muhammad bin Jafar al-Kittani, 142; policies of, 153; Abdelhafid, Moulay (Sultan 1908-13), as governor of Tiznit and *khalifa* of Marrakesh, 112; links with Chaouïa, 134; personality, 134, 137, and Si Madani El Glaoui, 134; marriage links of, 137; proclamation by El Glaoui, 136; as Sultan of Morocco, 136-52; *bay'a* of, 1908, 137, 139, 153; relations with Muhammad bin Abdalkabir al-Kittani, 137; and El Raisuni,, 139; financial policies of, 139, 146-7; flogs Muhammad bin Abdalkabir al-Kittani to death, 140; recognised as Sultan by European powers, Jan. 1909, 140; destruction of Abu Himara, 141; calls for French help, 149; as Sultan under French, 155-7; Lyautey and, 157; abdication of, 157
Abdeljalil, Omar, 208; education of, 205; in Zawiya, 227; and *Maghreb* magazine, 229; Minister of Agriculture, 306; and Plan de Réformes, 232; visit to Spanish Protectorate (1930), 234; visit to Paris (1936), 245, and *Hizb al-Watani* (1937), 246; drafts Istiqlal manifesto, 264
Abderrahmane, Moulay (Sultan 1822-59): lineage of, 12; meeting with Edward Drummond-Hay, 12-13; meeting with Ahmad ibn Tuwayr, 13, 14-15; *bay'a* of, 15; as governor of Essaouira, 19; succession as Sultan (1822), 18-19; attitude to European commerce, 24, 26, 43, 46, 60; political attitudes of, 27, 40, 54; attitude to French invasion of Algeria, 4; and Abd al-Qadir in Algeria, 42-3, 48-9; death, 1859, 65
Abdi, Aissa ibn Umar al-, 137
Abdi, Salem el-, 72, 73, 74, 97, 137
Abduh, Muhammad, 141
Abdullah, King of Jordan, 378
Abensur, Isaac, 35
Abid al-Bukhari, see army,
Abu Himara: origins of, 127; impersonates M. Mahammad, 128; rebellion of, 127-9; at Selouane, 129; collapse of rebellion, 140-1; death of, 141; impersonated by another rebel (1912), 168, and Abd al-Malik b. Muhyi al-Din, 181
Abu-Hatseira, Israel, 344
Action du Peuple (newspaper): founded, 230; and Fête du Trône, 231,
Al-Adl-wal-Ihsan, 363, 365, 378

Addi ou Bihi, 304
Adowa, 118
Afailal family, 20, 93
Afrique Occidentale Française, 187
Agadir, 283; in 1801, 38; industrial conditions in (1920s), 222; earthquake (1960), 315; tourism in, 358; Conference, 337; Summer University and teaching of Berber, 384,
Agadir Crisis (1911), 150-5
Agdal, 329
agriculture in pre-colonial Morocco, 3, 4, 7; agricultural policies, 75; cattle and sheep, 4-5, 43-4, 119, 148; fruits, 5; cereals, 5, 7, 23, 43, 59, 62, 148; in colonial Morocco: colon or capitalist agriculture, 182, 186, 199, 200, 201, 224; Moroccan sector, 201,209, 269; citrus fruits, 224, 239,269,273; cereals, 201, 219, 224, 239, 259, 267; Moroccan nationalists' policies towards, 232; wine and vineyards, 201, 240, 269, 273; in independent Morocco, 306, 325, 326, 329, 346 357, 369, 380; modern sector, 325; traditional sector, 269, 325, wine and vineyards, 325; see also irrigation, Secteurs de Modernisation du Paysannat, Opération Labour
Aherdane, Mahjoubi: breaks with French, 284; and Liberation Army, 289; and loyalty to Mohammed V, 301; founds Mouvement Populaire, 303
Ahlam (pop group), 386
Ahmad Bey (Constantine), 50
Ahmad bin Mubarak, family, 92; death of principal members, 121; Idris, 112, 121; Mahammad, 112; Saïd, 112, 121; *see also* Ba Ahmad
Ahmad Haybat Allah, see El Hiba
Ahmad ibn Tuwayr: origins, 1, 20; meeting with M. Abderrahmane, 13-16; on slavery, 28; attitudes, 3,7
Ahmed el Mansour, 11
Ain Sefra, 130
Aisawiyya, 96, 215
Aissa u-Ba Slam, 217
Ait Atta, 6, 54, 188, 217
Ait Ndhir: and Muhammad bin Abdalkabir al-Kittani, 140; rebellion 1911, 149; rebellion 1901, 125; resistance to French, 169
Ait Yafalman, 27
Aix-les-Bains Conference (1956), 288, 289
Ajdir, 191
Al Hoceima, 5, 12, 219; Spanish garrison at, 103, 126; guard posts at, 126; Spanish landings at 1925, 191; colonial town, 191, 226, 293; in rebellion of 1958, 311
Alam al- (newspaper), 270, 275, 383, 302
Alaoui dynasty: origins and genealogical descent, 12; legitimacy of, 17; marriage links, 92; minor members of: Abdallah, 331; Abd al-Kabir b. M. Abderrahmane bin M. Slimane, 94; Abderahman al-Kbir, 128, 199; Abderrahmane bin M. Sliman, 94; Ali, 92; Amin b. Mohammed IV, 91; Amine bin Hassan I, 317; Arafa, 92; Bilghith, 92, 112; Hassan (brother of Mohammed V), 263; Idris b. Youssef, 208; Idris bin Hassan,, 334;, Mehedi ben Ismail, Khalifa of Spanish zone, 167, 169; Muhammad bin al-Rashid, 137; Muhammad bin al-Tayyib, 47; Rashid, Kahlifa of Tafilalt, 92, 100, 115; Umar, 91; Uthman b Mohammed IV, 92; Uthman bin Hassan, 317; Zein, 149, 151, 163; *see also* Mahammad (Moulay), names of individual Sultans, Lalla Asma, Lalla Aïcha, Lalla Fatima Zohra, Lalla Malika, Lalla Soukaïna
Alaoui, Mohammed bel-Arabi el-: education, 186; in Free School movement, 186; establishes nationalist groups (1920s), 205-6; attitude towards French, 215; tutor to Lalla Aïcha, 264-5; exiled to Tafilalt, 266; attitude to Istiqlal, 266; imprisoned, 283; on Muhammad ben Arafa, 283; Minister for Throne in Bekkaï government, 291; attitude to 1962 constitution, 322
Alcalá Zamora, President Nicolás, 234
Alfau, General Felipe, 169
Algeciras, Act of, 132, 133, 140
Algeciras, Conference of, 1906, 132, 134
Algeria: revolt (1871), 70; influence of French colonial experience in on French Moroccan policy, 159, 160; emigration to, 62, 223, 304; nationalism in, 264; revolution begins, 287; FLN and Morocco, 302, 307, 312; FLN

supplies Moroccan Liberation Army, 292; war of independence, 311, 312; civil war in (1960s), 311, 333; frontier with, 187, 188, 311; independence of, and Morocco, 311, 312, 333, 334; Moroccan nationalist claims on Algerian territory, 302, 333; war with, 333; Ben Barka and, 264, 311, 302, 307, 333; and Polisario, 336, 338, 340, 343, 368, 379; Moroccan-Algerian relations, 325, 336-8, 344, 368, 373, 379; trade with, 133; civil war in (1990s), 373; and Berber nationalist movement, 384; and Arab Maghreb Union, 368; Algerian popular music, 386; *see also* Abd al-Qadir

Algiers: capture by French (1830), 1, 39, 40, 41; French war with, 1827, 39; during Second World War, 255

Ali Bey, *see* Badía y Leblich

Ali bin Sulayman, 42

Alliance Israélite Universelle: foundation, 83; and French government in nineteenth century, 83-4; establishment in Morocco, 83; at Madrid Conference (1876), 86; relations with French Protectorate administration, 177, 203, 204, 250; relations with Zionists, 204; schools and education policy, 83, 84, 250; in Spanish Zone, 250; during Second World War, 262; and independent Morocco, 345

Amar, David, 310, 344, 368

Amgala, 340

Amin, Qasim, 206, 230

Amir (tribe), 318

Amir al-Mu'minin (Commander of the Faithful), 54; title explained, 14; Abd al-Qadir as, 43; M. Yussuf as, 161; Mohammed V as, 299; in Moroccan constitution, 318, 388; Hassan II as, 389

Amjot, 10, 194

Amma, 32

Amnesty International, 366

Amziyyan, Muhammad, 145

Andalusians, 32

Anfa, 329

Anjra, 54

Annoual: Spanish defeat at, 190; political effects of, 234

Anti-Slavery Society, 349

Aouita, Said, 387

Arab League: Nationalist relations with, 271, 276; Spain and, 271; Mohammed V and, 272; Morocco joins, 310; Fez Summit (1982), 367

Arab Maghreb Union, 368

Arabic: use in pre-colonial-Morocco, 7,17, 29, 35, 81; translations into, in pre-colonial period, 52; press in pre-colonial Morocco, 143; use during protectorate period, 177, 183, 186, 196, 229, 246; press during protectorate period, 206, 230, 236, 246; language as part of nationalist project, 186, 206, 213, 246, 249, 272, 275; language use in independent Morocco, 304, 336, 382, 383; as political issue in independent Morocco, 383; music, 386

Araj, Hassan el, 301

Araucania-Patagonia, 90

Arba Taourirt, 226

architecture: French colonial, 172, 179; Spanish colonial, 226

Archives Marocaines, 159

Armée de la Libération du Maghreb Arabe *see* Liberation Army

army: under M. Ismaïl, 12; *Abid al-Bukhari*, 21, 22, 34, 72; *Jaysh*, 21, 22, 51, 136; *Naiba*, 22, 51, 164; under M. Abderrahmane, 18, 19, 21-2, 46, 47, 48; Oudaia, 20, 21, 47; defeat at Isly, 49; attempted reform of under Mohammed IV and Hassan, 51-53, 66, 71-4; *Nizam* army, 51, 72, 73, 106, 168; expedition to Tafilalt (1893), 105; under M. Abdelaziz, 112, 126, 129; Moroccan troops in Spanish colonial army, 236, 249, 250; Moroccan troops in Spanish civil war, 249, 250; Moroccan army set up by French, 1912, 146, 148, 152, 155, 168, 174, 187, 217, 267; Moroccans in French army during First World War, 174-5; Moroccans in French army during Second World War, 255, 267, 284, 290, 291; Moroccan colonial troops defect to Liberation Army, 290; Royal Armed Forces formation, 300; Hassan II and, 301, 305, 319; control of, 308; on Algerian frontier, 312, 333; in Golan (1973), 337; in Western Sahara, 340, 342, 366, 368; sources of military equipment for, 343, 368, 369; in Gulf

War, 371;
Army for the Liberation of the Sahara: origins, 301; attacks on Ifni, Tarfaya and the Western Sahara, and Algeria, 301-2; collapse of, 302
Arslan, Shakib, 230, 233
Ashash: family, 93; Abd al-Qadir, 49, 52
Ashmead-Bartlett, Ellis, 135-6, 145
Asif Melloul, 216
Asilah, 170; El Raisuni's palace at, 139; Mohammed V's reception in, 271
Association des Étudiants Musulmans du Nord de l'Afrique, 205
Association Marocaine des Droits de l'Homme, 366
Asturias, 248
Atlantic Charter, 263, 265
Auriol, President Vincent, 274, 278, 279
Australia, 147
Austria and Austrians: attack on Larache (1829), 24, 39; as supplier of armaments in nineteenth century, 73; diplomatic representation in nineteenth century Morocco, 81
Azemmour, 4, 29, 146
Azoulay, André, 369
Azoulay, David, 309
Azoulay, Salomon, 310
Azrou Berber College, 183, 319
Azzam Pasha, 271

Ba Ahmad: takes power on death of M Hassan, 108, 109; as ruler of Morocco, 111, 121; death, 121; *see also* Ahmad bin Mubarak family
Badis, 47, 126
Badía y Leblich, Domingo, 13
Baghdadi, Buchta el-: as army commander under M. Abdelaziz, 113, 137; as Pasha of Fez, 162, 213
Banditry, 27, 34, 53, 54, 98
Bank Misr, 185
Banque d'État, 139, 140, 198
Banque de Paris et des Pays Bas, 130, 198
Banu Bu Ifrur, 140, 145
Banu Bu Yahyi, 146
Banu Hassan, 47
Banu Mgild, 97
Banu Mtir, 97
Banu Sa'id, 45
Banu Waryaghal, 103, 146, 170; defeat of Abu Himara by, 141; role in Rif War, 190ff.
Barak, Ehud, 379
Baraka (concept explained), 9
Barcelona, Semana Trágica (1909), 145
Bargach family, 87, 320, 360: Muhammad Bargash, 93
Bartels, Albert, 182
Basri, Driss, 374, 376, 390
Basri, Mohamad, *al-faqih*: as head of *al-munazzama al-siriyya,* 289; and Ben Barka, 289; and Liberation Army, 292; and Istiqlal, 301; joins UNFP, 309; sentenced to death 1964, 323; return from exile, 376
Bassiri, Mohammed, 336
Bay'a, 15, 96; concept explained, 15; of Muhammad ibn Abd al-Karim al-Khattabi, 193; of M. Abdallah b. Ismaïl, 15; of Hassan II, 317; in independent Morocco, 318; of Muhammad VI, 375
Bayruk, Shaykh, 46; attitude to commerce, 59; European commerce, 26, 45; trading links of, 45; death of, 100; relationship with Makhzan, 46, 101
Bayruk, Mahammad: relations with Mackenzie, 100, 101
Beauclerk, Capt. G., 7
Béchar, 130
Beigbeder, Lieut.-Col. Juan, 248-9
Beijing, 69
Bekkaï, Si M'Barek: breaks with French, 284; in Council of Throne, 290; forms government, 291; resigns, 304
Bel-Qasim n-Gadi, 217
Belafrej, Ahmed: education of, 205, 227; in Zawiya, 227; editor of *Maghreb*, 229; visit to Spanish Protectorate (1930), 234; in Hizb al-Watani, 246; exiled 1937, 247; drafts Istiqlal manifesto, 264; Prime Minister, 304, 307-8, 312
Belgium: as arms supplier, 73; and trade in nineteenth century, 69, 116, 117; and administrarion of Tangier, 196; emigration to, 328; football clubs, 386
Ben Aaron, Joseph, 81
Ben Barka, Mehdi: education of, 228; as actor, 238; appointed tutor to Prince Hassan, 264; signs Istiqlal manifesto, 265; imprisoned 1944, 266; administrative secretary of Istiqlal, 270; marriage arrangements, 275; and cold war, 276; and Arab League, 276; exiled, 278; imprisonment and

release 1954, 286; and return of Mohammed V to Morocco, 291; and Liberation Army, 289, 292; on constitutional monarchy, 297; attempts to form police force, 300; on Saharan frontiers, 302; president of National Consultative Assembly, 303, 307; and Route de l'Unité, 303; accused of murder of Abbès Messaâdi, 304; international contacts of, 307; and Algerian war of independence, 311; popular support for, 321; splits with Istiqlal, 308; exile (1960), 314; return from exile 1962, 321; sentenced to death in absentia 1964, 323; on war with Algeria, 333; kidnap and murder, 330

Ben Bella, Ahmed: French hijack plane, 311; as president of Algeria, 333; attack on Moroccan monarchy, 333

Ben Ghabrit, Si Kaddour, 161

Ben Mizian, Mohamed: education of, 146; service in Spanish civil war, 249; in Royal Armed Forces, 301, 302

Ben Seddik, Mahjoub, 280

Ben Sliman family, 320

Benazeraf, Sam, 344

Benbarek, Larbi, 237

Beni Mtir, 164

Beni Ouarain resistance of, 187

Beni Zeroual, 166

Benjelloun: family, 91, 92, 265, 320, 360, 390; Abdelkader Benjelloun, 205; Hajj Mohamed Benjelloun, 390; Mfadel, 390; Othman Benjelloun, 390; Benjelloun, Omar: sentenced to death 1964, 323; assassination of, 353; *see also* Bin Jallun, Talib

Bennani-Chraïbi, Mounia, 361

Bennis, Muhammad bin al-Madani, 44, 75, 96

Bennouna, Muhammad, 42

Bennuna, Abdussalam, 185, 205, 233; as Minister of Finance in Spanish zone, 167; visit to Madrid 1931, 234; death 1935, 235

Bensimhon, Charles, 310

Benzaquen, Léon, 310; qualifies as doctor, 251; Minister for Posts and Telegraphs in Bekkaï government, 291

Berber language, 21, 28, 29, 35; in independent Morocco, 351, 382-4; revival of language, 384

Berber, Berbers: Makhzan attitudes to in pre-colonial Morocco, 38, 97, 107; in M. Zein revolt 1911, 149; French colonial views on, 159-60, 274; dahir of 1914, 164; dahir of 1916, 176; French policy towards, 164, 166, 173, 176,183; rumoured attempts at Christian proselytization, 209; El Glaoui and, 278, 286; nationalist attitudes towards, 214, 246, 247; in nationalist struggle, 288, 290; in post-independence administrations, 310,319; in post independence army, 301, 332; in post independence political movements, 303, 304; see also migration, Berber Dahir (1930)

Berber Dahir 1930, 212, 215; effects on Spanish protectorate, 233, 235, 249; long term implications of, 227; Ouazanni's book on, 229;

Berdugo, Serge, 369

Berenguer, General Dámaso, 188, 234

Bidault, Georges, 273, 281

Bidonvilles, 202, 223, 352; term explained, 179; in late 1930s, 223 240; in 1980s, 360; political dangers from, 329

Bilad al-Makhzan, 97; concept explained, 28

Bilad al-Siba, 96, 97; concept explained, 28; and European theories of Moroccan society, 97; Moroccan ideas about, 97; French theories on, 160; in Saharan judgement, 339

Bin Abu, Muhammad bin Abd al-Malik: as guard commander for Drummond-Hay, 22; expedition to Rif, 1856, 55; governor of Tangier, 53; relations with British and French consuls, 55; relations with Drummond-Hay, 61

Bin Idris, Sidi Muhammad: position in Makhzan of M. Abderrahmane, 19; as merchant, 24-5; meeting with Drummond-Hay, 25; opinions on commerce with Europe, 26; on rebellions, 30

Bin Jallun, Talib: position in Makhzan of M. Abderrahmane, 19; as merchant, 24-5; role in Fez rebellion 1820 and appointment as wazir, 24; and Abd al-Qadir, 44

Bin Qarrish, Sidi Abd al-Karim bin Abd al-Salam, 20

Bin Sliman, Fatmi, 290
Bin Suda, Muhammad al-Mahdi, 72
Binani family, 91
Bismarck, Otto von, 71
Bitton, Shimon, 369
Black Crescent, 292, 300
Black Hand, 284, 286
Blanco del Valle, Juan, 65
Blanco Izaga, Emilio: as administrator and anthropologist, 236; as architect, 226
Board of Deputies of British Jews, 84
Boniface, Philippe, 270, 279, 281 287
Bouabid, Abderrahman, 265,286
Bouabid, Maâti: Prime minister 1981, 348; founder, Union Constitutionelle, 362
Boucetta family, 320
Boucetta, M'hammed, 334
Boujad, 10
Boujibar family, 320
Boumeddienne, Houari, 289, 311
Bourée, Prosper, 57
Boyer de la Tour du Moulin, General Pierre-Georges-Jacques-Marie, 289-91
Brazil, 118
Brisha family, 93
Brisha, Hajj Abd al-Salam, 167
British North African Company, 118
Brunot, Louis, 205
Bu Ajiba, battle of (1908), 139
Bu Amama, 100
Bu Azza al-Habri, 97
Bu Craa, 335
Buceta, Manuel, 65
Buqquya, 113
Burgos, 248
Busilham bin Ali Aztut: as foreign minister, 52-53; attitude to European commerce, 58

Cadima, 310
Caid, see qaid
Cairo: as educational centre, 11, 143, 205, 249; as political centre, 232-33, 249, 276, 284, 292;
Caliph, title explained, 15
Capaz, General Osvaldo, 218
Cape Juby, 88, 118
Cape Spartel lighthouse, 78, 81
carpets, 186; manufacture of, 62, 95, 308, 349
Carrazu, Muhammad, 20
Carter, President James, 343
Casablanca: port, 77, 133, 222, 305; Jews in, 83, 84, 203, 251, 261, 277, 344; population, 95(1860/80), 95; (1907) 135; (1912) 179; (1971) 329; (1984), 354; in nineteenth century, 93, 119, 139, 148, 156, 157; at time of M. Abderrahmane, 4, 5, 44; opened for trade, 43; growth of in nineteenth century, 95; economic conditions in nineteenth century, 57, 62, 75, 77, 116, 119, 134; crisis of 1907, 135-38; under French Protectorate (mentioned), 162, 172, 177, 184, 201, 202, 207, 234, 270, 279, 288; construction of, 172; economic conditions in, 222, 224, 239, 241, 259; growth of, 135, 171, 172, 179, 329; Moroccan nationalist and trade union activity in, 186, 203, 213, 227, 242, 245, 266; sport in, 237; American landings 1942, 260-2; in independent Morocco, 320, 336, 352; political developments, riots strikes etc in, 300, 308, 314, 323, 347, 354-5; economic development of, 305, 352, 354, 360, 374, 381; King Hassan II Mosque, 363
Casablanca Conference 1943, 262
Casablanca Exhibition, 1915, 175
Casablanca, US airbase, 264, 276
Celle-Saint-Cloud, 290
Cerdan, Marcel, 237
Ceuta, 12, 65, 236; border question (nineteenth century), 47, 56, 66; free port in (nineteenth century), 102; remains Spanish after Moroccan independence, 293; as smuggling centre, 385; expansion of, 66
Chafarinas Islands, 102
Chaouèn: Spanish occupation of (1920), 188; Spanish abandonment of (1924), 191
Chaouïa, 6, 19, 44, 134, 137; economic conditions in, 116, 119, 135, 199, 223; rebellions in, 26, 112, 125, 136; French occupation of (1907 onwards), 146-8
Chauzy, Governor -General of Algeria, 71
Cheraga, 21
Cherarda, 30, 174; origins, 21; rebellion 1841, 47; zawiya, 30
Chiadma (rebellions and political dissi-

dence), 8, 49, 54, 112
child labour, 350
Christianity: attitudes of Moroccans towards, 38, 50, 64; missionaries and rumoured attempts at proselytisation, 66, 183, 208
Churchill, Winston: and El Glaoui, 236, 282; at Casablanca Conference, 262-3; and Moroccan independence, 264; relations with de Gaulle, 267
Cinema, 237, 238
Clauzel, General, 41
climate and weather, 3, 4, 58, 67, 222, 224, 239, 268, 302, 306, 358, 374; political consequences of, 222, 324; *see also* drought
clothing, 233, 239; of Lalla Aïcha, 272, 275; of Jews, 250; politics of, 207; of women, 364, 388
Coca-Cola, 260
Cohen, Rabbi Pinhas, 204
Collèges Musulmans, 177, 179, 183, 205, 228
colons: immigration of, 171, 182, 199, 226, 272; attitude of Lyautey towards, 171, 199; attitude of Steeg towards, 199; relations with Puaux, 265; relations with Labonne, 268; relations with Noguès, 242; relations with Juin, 272; and irrigation/agricultural development, 199, 200, 201, 209, 219, 224, 272-3; and world crisis of 1930s, 224-5 attitudes towards Arabs, 207, 226; attitudes towards Jews, 251, 261; political activities of, 199, 224, 241, 268-9, 270, 272-3, 279, 280; social life of 226, 237; campaign against Mohammed V, 279; murder of many colons at Oued Zem, 288; colon riots in Casablanca, 288
Colonisation companies, 199, 200, 209
Commander of the Faithful *see Amir al-Muminin*
Committee for the Liberation of Jerusalem, 367
Committee for the Liberation of North Africa, 276
Communes, financing of, 319
Communist Party: legalised 1936, 242; banned, (1952) 281; (1959) 313; Ali Yata as Secretary-general, 270; and Moroccan nationalists, 227, 280, 292; and Black Crescent, 292; attitude of Istiqlal towards, 276; attitude of Hassan II towards, 315, 336; relaunched as Parti du Progrès et du Socialisme (1974), 34; *see also* Parti du Progrès et du Socialisme
Compagnie Marocaine *see* Schneider Company
Compagnie Marocaine d'Exploitation Fermière Agricole, 199
Compañía Agrícola del Lucus, 200
Compañía Colonizadora, 219
Compañía Española de Minas del Rif, 219
Compañía Norte Africano, 133, 140
Confederation of Brotherhoods in Eastern Morocco, 281
Conféderation Générale du Travail, 347
Confins Algéro-Marocains *see* Frontiers, 216
Conseil de Communautés Juives du Maroc, 310
Conseil Supérieur de Habous, 178
Constitutions: Moroccan proposed 1906, 144; Moroccan proposed 1910, 144; of 1962, 321, 322, 323; of 1970, 330, 331; of 1972, 332; of 1980, 354; of 1992, 372; amended 1996, 376; and role of women, 348; Constitutions and Constitutionalism, 143-145; Iranian, 1906, 143; Japanese, 143; Ottoman, of 1876 and 1908, 143
consumerism, 238, 260, 261
Contrôleurs Civiles, 162
Convention Béclard, 85
Cook, Thomas and Co., 121
Cooper, David, murdered, 128
Corcos family, 44
Corcos, Abraham, 81
cork exports, environmental effects of, 63, 219
corruption: in nineteenth century, 123, 129; in independent Morocco, 279, 306, 327, 331, 356, 365; denounced by political opposition, 321, 323, 352
corsairing: abandonment of, 14; attempted revival under M. Abderrahmane, 1828, 24; and coastguard ships, 46
COSUMA, 242
cotton: imports, 62, 76, 89, 102; exports, 69, 70; Mohammed IV's attempts at industrialising, 76-7; see also textiles
Council of Government, 182, 199, 241

Council of the Throne, 286, 374, 290-1
coups, attempted: of 1971 (Skhirat), 331, 332, 365; of 1972, 332, 333; of 1973 left-wing plot, 333
Crémieux, Alphonse, 83
Crimean War, 59
Cromer, Lord, 70
Cunninghame-Graham, R.B., 82
currency and coinage: collapse in nineteenth century, (1845-53) 57; (1855-7), 62; 67, 115, 123; attempts to reform and restructure, (1862), 79; (1869), 80; 123; (1906), 133; 115; foreign currency in nineteenth-century Morocco, 80, 115; colonial restructuring of, 197; tied to French Franch, 197-80, 240; dirham collapse, 354; devaluation, 357
customs: customs houses as job opportunity in nineteenth Makhzan, 24, 35, 93-5; Spanish officials in, 78, 96; French officials in, 133-4, 146, 148; importance as revenue, 57, 68, 80, 101, 115, 130, 139, 146; under Protectorate, 198, 244; in independent Morocco, 326

Dahar Abarran, 190
Dakhla, 88, 342; *see also* Villa Cisneros
Daoud, Mohammed, 206, 233
Dar al-Islam, 14
Dar al-Niaba, term explained, 53
Darqawiyya, 10, 169; during Rif War, 194
Davidson, John, 45
Dayan, Moshe, 345
de Beaucé, Thierry, 383
de Chasteau, Edmonde, 56, 57
de Foucauld, Charles, 97
de Gaulle, General Charles: supporters in Morocco during Second World War, 255; and Moroccan nationalist movement, 264-5; relations with Mohammed V, 267-8; President of France after Algiers coup, 312; and Ben Barka affair, 330
de los Rios, Fernando, 229
de Redcliffe, Sir Stratford, 61
de Saint-Aulaire, Comte Auguste, 156
Debrett's Peerage, 135
debt: personal (of Moroccans) 119, 198, 244; personal (of colons), 224; public in nineteenth century, 68, 115, 130, 140, 146; public in independent Morocco, 327, 346, 353, 357; rescheduling, 357
Delaporte, Jacques, 45
Demnate, 184; Jews in, 87
Diên Biên Phû, 286
Diouri, Mohammed, 227; and Plan de Reformes, 232
Diouri, Moumen, 323
Direction des Affaires Civiles, 176
Direction des Affaires Indigènes, 176, 182
disease and epidemics, 76, 268; cholera, 65, 75; typhus, 178, 239, 259; typhoid, 75; plague, 12, 30, 259
divorce: laws on and campaigns for changes, 275, 349, 388; effects of, 202, 360, 365; rates of, 349, 356, 364
Doukkala, 4, 22; rebellion 1893, 112
Drâa valley: agriculture in, 6; *tariqas* in, 10; banditry in, 28; as frontier, 188, 336
drought: in nineteenth century (early nineteenth century), 7; (1857), 62; (1860s and 1870s), 75-6, 88; in twentieth century, 95(1929), 211; (1943), 269; (1957), 302; (1980s), 357; (1995), 374; prayer in time of (*ya latif*), 213
Drummond-Hay, Edward William Auriol: appointment as British consul, 1829, 1; background, 1,3; as huntsman, 3; on agriculture, 3, 4, 5; on religion, 9, 30; on army, 22, 29; on commerce, 25; on Berbers, 29; on women, 34; on Jews, 34-5, 36; sources of information, 8, 25, 35; meeting with M. Abderrahmane, 12-13; presents to officials, 19-20; meeting with ibn Idris, 25; death, 56
Drummond-Hay, Sir John: early life, 61; as acting British consul, 56; and commercial economic affairs, 56, 57, 58, 75, 76; as proponent of 'reform', 71, 77, 78; mediates with foreign governments, 51-8, 85, 86; negotiates 1856 treaty, 59-61; relations with French consulate, 56, 59; relations with Mohammed IV, 80; relations with Moroccan notables, 6; role in Moroccan-Spanish War, 1859-60, 65, 66; at Madrid Conference, 85-6; on Jews, 86; on British residents, 90; as consul for other powers, 81; retirement and

death, 89
Dubois, André-Louis, 291
Dukkali, Mustafa al-, 58
Dukkali, Abu Shuayb al-, 143

economy; economic conditions: in 1980s, 357, 359; in late 1990s, 377; economic plans: 1960-4 Five Year Plan, 326; Three Year Plan 1964-7, 326; 1968-72 Five Year, 326; 1973-7 Five Year Plan, 345; stabilisation plan 1978, 346; *see also* IMF
Economist Intelligence Unit, 358
Edri, Rafi, 368
education: in pre-colonial period, 17, 20; in reform and modernisation projects, 50, 52, 144; French policy on, 154, 162 177, 205, 274; Écoles des Fils de Notables , 177, 205, 228; École Moulay Hassan, 320; Écoles Franco-Israélites, 177; of Berbers, 183; during Rif War, 194; of nationalist leaders, 227, 228; nationalist policies on, 185-6, 194, 206, 228, 230, 232, 237, 246, 264, 267; in Plan de Réformes, 232; of girls, 228, 230, 232, 233 236, 237, 246, 264, 266, 267, 274, 296, 350-1, 364; Mohammed V's ideas on, 264, 265, 274; provision after independence, 305, 308, 323, 326, 352, 359, 360, 381; of Moroccan elite, 320; school numbers in 1970s, 352; *see also* Jews, Alliance Israélite Universelle
Egypt: as exemplar in nineteenth century, 40, 50, 52, 56, 76, 77; debts, 68; British occupation of, 1881, 70, 125, 130, 152, 159; Franco-British agreement on, 125; as export market, 94; influence on Moroccan nationalism, 141, 143, 185, 194; as cultural influence after Moroccan independence, 238
elections: 1960 (local), 314; 1963, 322, 323; 1970, 330; 1977, 347; 1983 (local), 362; 1984, 362; 1993, 373; 1997, 376
elite: in independent Morocco, 320; housing patterns, 329
employment: in nineteenth century, 62, 95; under protectorate regime in 1920s, 201, 203; in 1930s, 222-3, 225, 240; in independent Morocco, 354; in 1970s, 328, 331, 352, 355, 359; in 1980s, 361; in cities, 352; *see also* informal economy, women, wages, unemployment
energy supplies: firewood, 62-3; oil, 273, 334, 343, 346, 368
English: extent of use of language in 1990s, 383
Entente Cordiale, 125, 132
environment and environmental degradation: in nineteenth century, 6, 62-3, 67; in colonial period, 219; in independent Morocco, 380, 382
environmental politics, 381
Erckman, Jules, 74
Es-Semara: construction of by Ma al-Aynayn, 114; burned by French (1913), 163; occupied by Spanish (1934), 218; in Moroccan-Polisario conflict, 342, 366
Essanoussi, Said, 384
Essaouira (formerly known as Mogador), 54, 62, 82 160; construction of, 24, 35; Jews in, 24, 35, 44, 81, 83, 84, 91, 101, 203; in nineteenth century, 90, 93, 99; M. Abderrahmane as governor, 19, 24; commerce of in nineteenth century, 24, 26, 58, 89; bombarded by French fleet, 49, 54; visited by European naval squadrons, 85; growth and development, 62, 77, 95, 116; public order questions, 96, 98, 127;
Etoile Nord-Africaine, 227
Euan Smith, Sir Charles, 89
Europe and Europeans: nineteenth-century Moroccan attitudes towards, 38-9, 63-4, 68, 109; late twentieth-century attitudes towards, 328, 350, 369-71
European Union, EEC, European Community, European Common Market: 1969 association agreement, 326; trade restrictions in late 1970s, 346; Moroccan application to join, 358; relations with Morocco in 1980s, 358; as major foreign investor in 1990s, 374; Association Agreement 1996, 377; economic assistance, 377
exports, see trade

Fajr al- (newspaper), 143;
Fassi, Allal El: in Free School movement, 186; on Rif war, 194; establishes nationalist groups in 1920s, 205; founds

Umm al-Banin, 206; arrest over Berber Dahir protests, 213; education of, 227; activities in Zawiya: 228; exiled, 228; and Mohammed V, 231; takes *Plan de Réformes* to Residency, 232; and *Kutla*, 245; relations with Ouazzani, 245, 246; arrested (1936), 245; President of *Hizb al-Watan*, 246; exile in Gabon, 247, 265; return from exile in Gabon, 270; and American bases, 276; and Arab League, 276; wife's protests over founding of state of Israel, 277; and terrorism, 284; and Liberation Army, 292; meeting with Torrès to discuss nationalism in Spanish zone, 293; personal popularity of, 299; idea of 'Greater Morocco', 302 and split in Istiqlal, 308; death, 347

Fassi, Mohammed El-: education, 205; meets Shakib Arslan, 234; in *Hizb al-watani*, 246; helps draft Istiqlal manifesto, 264; tutor to Prince Hassan, 266

Fassi, Malika El-: and education for girls, 230; marriage to Mohammed El-Fassi, 230; in *Hizb al-watani*, 246; as nationalist organiser, 266

Fez, 19, 42, 99, 103, 104, 105, 113-15, 137, 138, 146, 169, 256; foundation, 11; as educational centre, 17, 18, 20, 42, 48, 93, 144, 173, 177; government of, 24, 91, 92, 94, 148, 157, 162, 283; name synonymous with Morocco, 31; Andalusians in, 31; economy and industry of, 32, 44, 77, 80, 62, 63, 95, 106, 201, 240, 241, 273; Jews in, 83, 203, 204; tourism, 121; health, 126; *Makina* arms factory, 73; pre-colonial political disorder, (1820), 23, 32; (1832), 47-8; (1873), 96, 98, 111; (1901), 125; (1911), 149-50; murder of Mr Cooper, 128; M. Abdelhafid in, 137-9; *bay'a* of M. Abdelhafid, 144; occupied by French, 149-51; rising, 1913, 155-7; dropped as capital, 172; European quarter in, 172; Nationalist activity in, 186, 206-7, 213-14, 227, 231, 238, 245, 266, 275, 279, 282, 286, 292; during Rif war, 191, 195; Mohammed V visits, 231; proposed bishopric, 265; El Glaoui besieges, 278; political activity in independent Morocco, 300, 314, 322; Arab League summit in and Fez plan (1982), 367; Treaty of Fez, *see* treaties

Figaro Le, 279;

Figuig : government of, 100; French attack on (1903), 126; frontier questions, 311, 333

Filali, Abdelatif, 376, 390

Filali, Fouad, 376, 385

Fishtala, 168

Franco, Gen. Francisco: and occupation of Spanish protectorate, 191; as defence counsel of Dámaso Berenguer, 234; uses Moroccan troops in Asturias (1934), 236; in Spanish Civil War, 248, 249, 250; and Jews, 250; as dictator of Spain, 254; policy during Second World War, 256-7; and relations with Arab states after Second World War, 271; and relations with Moroccan nationalists, 271, 285; attitude towards Moroccan independence, 292-4; attitude towards Western Saharan question, 335-6, 338; death 339-40

frontiers: with Algeria (nineteenth century), 42-3, 48-9, 87, 93, 97, 103, 118; with Algeria (twentieth century), 304, 311, 340, 373, 379; with Ceuta and Melilla, 47, 64, 102-3, 129-30, 133, 146, 153, 162, 169; southern, 187, 188, 216, 218; nationalist claims to, 302

Free Schools Movement, 186, 205, 211, 226, 233

Gaillard, Henri, 149, 151

Gao, 11

García Valiño, Rafael: attitude to ben Arafa, 285; finance for Liberation Army, 289; last attempts to preserve Spanish control, 292

Garet plain, 190

Geneva, 230, 233

Germany, German: trade, 88, 89, 101, 116, 117; Franco-Prussian war, 70; as arms supplier in nineteenth century, 71, 73, 74; policies towards Morocco in pre-colonial period, 70, 71, 87, 88, 89, 112, 118, 124, 132, 140, 148 151; involvement in southern Morocco in early twentieth century, 101, 116, 150-5; protégés, 118-19; and Algeciras conference, 132; and Morocco in First World War, 180-2; and Morocco in Second World War, 254-60, 262-4; Moroccan troops in Germany, 267; as

migration destination, 328, 383; tourists in Morocco, 358; and Moroccan football players, 386; see also Agadir
Ghanjawi, Abu Bakr bin al-Hajj al-Bashir al-, 82-3
Gharnit, Si Feddoul, 122
Ghazi, Mohamed: education, 186, 225; establishes nationalist group 1925, 205; and Zawiya, 227; and Plan de Réformes, 232; signs Istiqlal manifesto, 265
Gibraltar, 35, 71; and training of Moroccan officers, 73; as bargaining chip between Spain and Nazi Germany, 256; trade with, 44, 60
Giscard d'Estaing, President Valéry, 343
Glaoui family : origins of power of, 99; land ownership, 119; Muhammad, 99; Hammu, 184
Glaoui, Madani El: southward expansion of, 114, 126; and El Menebhi, 112; relations with M. Abdelhafid, 134-7; proclamation of M. Abdelhafid, 136; as *wazir* of M. Abdelhafid, 148; removed as *wazir*, 151; attitude to French, 148-49, 163, 175-7; death, 183
Glaoui, Thami El: as huntsman, 126; military support for French conquest, 184; visit to Paris 1921, 184; employs forced labour, 202; wealth of, 184, 201, 241, 273; liking for golf, 236; and Churchill, 236, 282; as trade union leader, 243; Pasha of Marrakesh, 163, 183, 184; relations with French, 163; wealth of, 201, 202, 241; nationalists' dislike of, 246; and workers' organisations, 246; and SOE, 257, 259, 263; relations with US representatives during Second World War, 263; death of son at Monte Cassino, 267; relations with French after Second World War, 273, 278-9, 281-2; argument with Mohammed V, 278; use of tribes, 278, 283, 286; attempted assassination of, 285; petitions to remove Mohammed V, 281-2; at Académie Française, 279; and coronation of Elizabeth II, 282; represented at Aix conference, 289; agrees to return of Mohammed V, 290; death, 290-1 292; confiscation of property, 300, 306, 307
Goebbels, Josef, 256
Gómez Jordana, General Francisco, 180
Goundafa tribe, 99
Goundafi caïds: origins of family, 98, 99
Goundafi, Muhammad bin al-Hajj Ahmad El, 99
Goundafi, Taïeb El, 99, 114, 126; military support for French occupation, 163, 176; governor of Sous, 176; death (1928), 183; biography published, 273
Goums, 149, 155, 168, 175; term explained and origin of, 146; Moroccan troops in French colonial army, 217; during Second World War, 255
Gouraud, General, 156, 175
Grandval, Gilbert, 288
Greater Mauritania, 336
'Greater Morocco', 11, 333, 334; according to Allal El Fassi, 302
Green March, 339, 340
Guebbas, Mohammed , 129, 131, 161
Guédira, Ahmed Réda: education, 205; pro-US journalism and membership of Roosevelt Club, 263; in first independent government, 29; minister for defence, 301; out of office 1958, 304; pro-American attitudes during Cold War, 312; role in Moroccan politics in 1960s, 313; minister of interior, 321; and 1963 election, 322
Guelaya: 'piracy' from, 55; Makhzan expedition to 1880, 91; relationship with Makhzan, 102; migration from, 103; occupation by Spanish army 1909, 145
Guelmim, 6, 26, 45, 59
Guessous family, 91, 320, 360
Guest, Keen and Nettlefolds, 133
Guillaume, General Augustin: on final stages of conquest of High Atlas, 217; appointed Resident General, 279; attitude to nationalists, 279; relations with Paris, 281; attempted assassination of, 286; replaced as Resident General, 286
Guiot, Gaston, 148
Gulf War, 370, 371

Hached, Ferhat, 281
Hadary, Sidi Muhammad al-, 45-6
Hadawiyya, 169
Haganah, 277
Haha, 47
Hajjami, Sidi Muhammad al-, 155, 156
Hajoui, Mohamed; as minister for jus-

tice, 162; as minister for education, 185, 230; and *nizam*, 194
Hamadsha, 96, 215
Haouz: irrigation in, 5, 201; rebellions in (1894), 112; (1907), 136; landholdings of Glaoui family in, 119, 241, 273; landholdings of colons in, 171, 272;
Harakat Tahrir Saqia al-Hamra wa Wad -al-Dhahab (Movement for the Liberation of Saguia el-Hamra and Oued ed-Dahab), 336
Harb, Tal'at, 185
Harris, Walter, 149; relations with M. Abdelaziz, 122; kidnapped by El Raisuni, 127; on administration of Tangier, 196
Hashish (*kif*), cultivation of, 381
Hassan I, Moulay: personality, 104, 106-7; becomes Sultan, 73, 96; relations with European powers, 73-4, 81, 87; economic policy, 75, 77, 101-2, 106; administrative reforms, 789-80; family relationships, 91-2, 94;
Makhzan of, 92-3; rebellions against, 94, 96-8, 101, 103, 105; expedition to Sous (1882), 104; expedition to Tafilalt (1893), 105; death of, 108
Hassan II, Prince then King: and scouting movement, 228; at Casablanca Conference (1943), 262; speech in Tangier 1947, 272; education, 264, 266; chief of staff of Moroccan army, 301; crushes Rif rebellion 1958, 304; crushes Tafilalt rebellion 1958, 304-5; on French, 305, 383; as Defence Minister, 314; at Agadir earthquake, 314; succession of, 317; as Prime Minister, 319-24; rules by decree 1965, 324; and coups d'état, 331-2; and Oufkir, 290, 330, 331-2, 366; and Franco, 336; and Giscard d'Estaing, 343; and Shah of Iran, 362; and Qathafi, 367; attitude to USA, 312-13, 315, 329; attitude to USSR, 315, 343; on Algeria, 312, 333; on Sahara, 335, 338-9; on Jews, 344; and Arab-Israeli question, 345, 368-9, 379; and EEC, 358; and Gulf War, 370; Moroccans' views of, 353, 362, 378; religious role of, 310, 318, 388-9; illness in 1995, 375; death, 375; funeral, 378-80
Hassanian Lectures, 317
Hassar family, 320
Hayat al-(newspaper), 235;
Henrys, General, 164
Hiba El : jihad of, 157-8; pursuit of into the Sahara, 163-4, 176
High Council of Ulama, 363
Hisham, Sharif of Iligh, 26
Hizb al-'Amal al-Watani, 246
Hizb al-Islah al-Watani, 247-48
Hizb al-Wahda, 248
Hizb al-Watani l-Tahqiq al-Matalib, 246-47
Ho Chi Minh, 275
Hoare, Sir Samuel, 257
Howard League for Penal reform, 120
Hull, Cordell, 264
human rights: in 1980s and 1990s, 365, 366; in late 1990s, 373; Ministry of Human Rights, 373; repression of Islamic movements, 363; *see also* Ligue Marocaine de Défense des Droits de l'Homme and Organisation Marocaine des Droits de l'Homme, 365
Humanité, L' (newspaper), 279;
hunting, 3, 61, 120
Husayn bin Hisham, Sharif of Iligh: trade with Europeans, 45, 101; relations with Makhzan, 33, 46, 55
Husayn, Demnati, 241
Hutton, Barbara, 268
Hyatt, Thomas, US Consul, 58

Ibn al-Hami, 43
Ibn Ghazi, 19
Ibn Mashish, *see* Abd al-Salam bin Mashish
Ibn Suda family, 20
Ibrahim, Abdallah: signs Istiqlal manifesto, 265; and Liberation Army, 292; joins UNFP, 309; Prime minister, 308; land policies, 306; removed as PM, 314
'Id al-Kabir, celebration of, 160, 318
Idris al-Jarari, 43
Idris I, 11
Idris II, 11
Ifni (formerly Santa Cruz de Mar Pequeña), 166, 257, 301; designated as Spanish, 1860, 66; exploratory expedition (1879), 71; occupied by Spanish troops 1934, 218; remains Spanish after Moroccan independence, 294; beseiged by Army for Liberation of Sahara, 301-2; liberation

proposed by UNGA, 335; returned to Morocco (1969), 336
Ila al-Amam, 347, 354, 365
Iligh, 10, 26, 45, 46, 55; *see also* Husayn bin Hisham, Sharif of Iligh; Hisham, Sharif of Iligh, Muhammad bin Husayn
In Salah, 115
independent (non-party) politicians: membership in Bekkaï government, 291; in 1960 government, 314; in King Hassan's first cabinet, 321; in 1970 elections, 330; in 1977 election, 347-8
informal economy, 329, 351-2, 360, 391
International Court of Justice, Sahara Judgement, 337, 339
International Monetary Fund: financial 'arrangements', 357; 1995 report on Morocco, 358
International Olympic Committee, 390
Internet, 385
Iran: constitution of 1906, 143, 144; revolution 1979, 353, 355, 362, 363
irrigation, 4, 6, 7; in Haouz plain, 5; in Rif, 5, 6; in Tazeroualt, 10; manpower used for construction, 33, 77; policy in First World War, 178; use by European farmers, 201, 209; attempts to help Moroccan farmers, 244, 270, 273
French legacy of irrigated land, 305; *politique des barrages* after independence, 325, 327, 345; advantages for big landowners, 346, 357; policy in 1980s, 357; irrigable area in 1980s, 346; dams, 7, 200-1, 273, 305, 325, 346; *khattara*, 5, 200
Islam, French 'protection' of, 173
Islamic Conference Organisation, 367
Islamic movements, 352, 362, 364, 378; attitudes to women, 388; in parliament, 376; King Hassan's attitude towards, 362; rejection of Algerian civil war, 373; repression of, 373
Islamic Society of Fez, 214
Isly, 49-50
Ismaïl, Moulay (1672-1727), 12, 15; al-Yusi's letter to, 16; and *abid al-bukhari*, 17; civil war following death, 21
Israel, 309, 311, 368, 369; and Moroccan nationalist opinion, 277, 370, 371; migration to, 277, 310, 311, 344; wars of 1948, 277; Suez war (1956), 309; June War (1967), 343; October War (1973), 337, 343; Moroccan relations with, 345, 369; King Hassan's personal links with, 345; Morocco as intermediary between Israel andArab states, 345, 368-9, 379, 391; and Arab states, 343, 367; as factor in relationship with USA, 295-6, 311, 343-5; *see also* Palestine, Mossad, Cadima, Fez Plan, Amar (David)
Israeli Labour Party, 368
Istiqlal manifesto, 264, 265
Istiqlal party: formation, 264-5; Mohammed V and, 266, 274, 278, 286, 300; Labonne and, 270; and trade unions, 270; banned (1952), 281; and murder of Ferhat Hached, 281; and terrorism, 284-9; and Liberation Army, 290, 292, 300-2, 304; and Aix-les-Bains conference, 286-9; rivalry with Parti Démocratique de l'Indépendence, 295, 303-4; split (1958), 308; role in governments: Bekkaï (1956), 291, 303; Belafrej (1958), 304; Mohammed V (1960) 314; Hassan II, 321; Youssouffi (1998), 376; in 1960 elections (local), 314; in 1963 elections, 322, 323; attitude to 1962 constitution, 321-2; bel-Arabi on (characterisation as 'cowardly fox'), 322; boycott of constitutional referendum (1970), 330; conference (1974), 347; and women, 275, 290, 348; youth organisation, 300; militias, 291, 300; and Israel, 277, 309, 343; territorial ambitions of, 302, 334; and Algerian war of independence, 311, 312; position of in Cold War, 276, 277; in government 1998, 376; *see also* Ben Barka, *Al-Alam*, El Fassi (Allal)
Italy, Italian: policy in Morocco in nineteenth and early twentieth century, 87, 88, 118, 124; protégés, 82, 118; trade in nineteenth century, 116; and *Makina* in Fez, 73, 74; consuls, 81,86; navy off Essaouira, 1869, 85; navy off Tangier, 1928, 196; and Tangier, 195; during Second World War, 256, 257, 267, 272

Jagerschmidt, Charles: appointment to French consulate in Tangier, 57; relations with John Drummond-Hay, 59

jemaas: establishment as part of French administrative system, 164, 176; easily dominated by qaids, 183
jemaas judiciares, establishment of, 176; reorganisation of as part of Berber Dahir, 212
Jama'i family: origin of, 2; rivalry with bin Mubarak family, 20, 92; position in Makhzan of M. Abderrahmane, 19; marriage links with Alaoui family, 92; Mukhtar bin Abd al-Malik al-Jama'i, 19, 58; al-Ma'ti, 92; Muhammad bin al-Arbi al-Jama'i, 92; Muhammad al-Saghir, 92, 108; destruction of family by Ba Ahmad, 108, 112; in nationalist movement, 265
Japan: as constitutional exemplar, 143; war with Russia (1905), 143; imports from, 222, 239, 245
Jaysh see army
Jazulot, Jules, 90
Jbel Alam, 11, 127
Jbel Sarhro, 6, 27, 217
Jbel Zerhoun 11, *see also* Moulay Idris
Jews: 83-5, 91, 250-2, 309, 310, 344, 345; languages spoken by, 35, 116, 230; Moroccans' attitudes to, 37, 84, 90, 91, 277, 315, 371; attacks on, 36; (Fez, 1907), 137 (Fez, 1912), 155; (Oujda, 1948), 277; in pre-colonial Morocco: Andalusian, 35; at time of M. Abderrahmane, 34, 44; religious status of, 36; *jizya,* 91; relations with pre-colonial Makhzan, 34-6, 83, 93; relations with rich Muslims, 44, 45, 75, 91; rural, 9; in Essaouira, 24, 35; in Settat, 35; in Rabat, 34; in High Atlas, 35; in Gibraltar, 44; in Manchester, 9; as *tujjar al-sultan,* 24, 44; corporal punishment of, 84; social conditions of in nineteenth century, 34, 91; trading links of, 35, 44, 83, 90; and 'Abd al-Qadir, 44; appointment to consular posts, 36, 44, 81, 93; as protégés, 36, 44, 81, 83, 65, 118; and Conference at Madrid, 1880, 86; as smugglers, 90; attitudes towards Alliance Israélite Universelle, 83; relations with British Jewish community, 84, 87; in colonial Morocco: in French Protectorate, 177, 203; in municipalities, 167; and French citizenship, 204, 251; French anti-Semitism, 204, 251, 252, 261, 277; in Spanish Protectorate, 203, 250; in Tangier, 167, 196, 203; during First World War, 177; in 1920s, 203, 204; employment of, 251; 'modernisation' of, 250-51; in trade unions, 203; Orwell on, 251; during Spanish civil war, 250; during Second World War, 250, 261, 262; protected by Mohammed V, 262; and US occupation, 251; nationalist attitudes towards, 214, 277, 309-10; during Mohammed V's visit to Tangier, 1947, 272; Juin's attitude towards, 277; in independent Morocco: in government and government service, 252, 309-10, 344; relations with Palace, 262, 272, 310; numbers, 311; migration to Palestine, 204, 252; migration to Israel, 277, 310, 311, 344; Moroccan Jews in Israel, 344-5, 368; migration to France, USA and Canada, 311; limited return of Jews to Morocco in 1970s, 344; and Arab-Israeli conflict, 309-10 and diplomatic contacts with Israel, 341; Congress of Moroccan Jews (1984), 368
jihad, 14, 107, 140, 155; ibn Abd al-Karim on, 192; in Ouerrha (1913), 168; in Rharb (1912), 168; localised, 126 in Tafilalt (1907), 146; Salafi views on, 143;
Jilani bin Idris see Abu Himara
Jilani al-, 96
jizya, 83, 91; term explained, 36; as a cause of rebellion, 95, 98; at time of M. Abderrahmane, 22; attitude of ulama towards, 95 *see also* taxation
Jordana, General Francisco, 188
Juin, General Alphonse-Pierre: appointed Resident General, 272; relations with settlers, 272-3; views of Moroccan society, 273-4; quarrel with Mohammed V, 274; views on Jewish emigration, 277; cooperation with El Glaoui to remove Mohammed V, 278; replaced as Resident General and appointed NATO commander, 279; as member of French Academy, 279
Justice and Charity *see al-Adl wal-Ihsan*
Justinard, Col., 176

Karaouiyne *see* Qarawiyyin
Keene, Emily, 90

Kénitra: French use as base to invade Fez, 149; renamed Port Lyautey, 179; development of, 179, 273; nationalist and labour agitation at, 186, 203, 227, 279, 286; American landings at, 260; US base at, 264, 278, 313
Kettani, General ben Hamou, 301
Khalifa, Hamid bin Isa al-, Emir of Bahrein, 378
Khalifa of Spanish zone, 166, 167,
khassa, term explained, 31
Khatib family, 320
Khatib, Dr Abdelkrim El: joins opposition to French. 284; and Liberation Army, 289; and loyalty to Mohammed V, 301; founds Mouvement Populaire, 303
Khatib, Hajj Muhammad al-, 53, 60
Khattabi, Abd al-Karim al-: appointed as qaid of Banu Waryaghal, 103; relations with the Spanish, 146; Spanish pensioner, 170; breaks relations with Spanish, 190
Khattabi, Mahammad bin Abd al-Karim al-: return to Rif from Spain, 190; in Rifi government, 193; al-Khattabi, Muhammad bin Abd al-Karim (ibn Abd al-Karim): education and connection to Salafiyya, 142; as qadi of Melilla, 146; honoured by Spanish, 170; and Germany in First World War, 18; return to Rif in 1919, 190; takes control of Rif 1921, 190; proclaimed Amir, 190; victory at Chaouèn, 1921, 191; *bay'a* of, 193; surrender 1926, 192; exile in Réunion, 192; policies and intentions of, 192, 194; escape to Cairo, 276; as symbol of 1958 Rif rebellion, 304; family, 320
Khénifra, 175
Khomeini, Ayatollah, 363
Khouribga: growth of, 240; phosphate mines at, 242; labour agitation at, 203, 243
king: as title, 231and constitutional monarchy, 297, 299, 321;
Kirby Green, Sir William: as British Consul-General, 89; and North West African Company, 105
Kitaniyya, 131, 143, 164, 215, 278
Kittani, Abdelhay El: hatred of Salafiyya, 164, 207, 215; nationalist dislike for, 207; relations with Juin, 278; relations with Guillaume and El Glaoui, 279; and Conference of Religious Orders of North Africa, 281; and Aix-les-Bains conference, 289; property confiscated, 307
Kittani, Ibrahim al-, 275
Kittani, Muhammad bin Abdalkabir al-: on the drinking of tea, 106; relations with M. Abdelaziz, 13; views on Europeans, 131; calls for *jihad*, 13; and bay'a of M. Abdelhafid, 137, 138; flogged to death, 140, 149;
Kittani, Muhammad bin Jafar al-, 143, 185: *Nasihat ahl al-Islam*, 142, 194
Krupp, 133; and fortifications of Rabat, 74; cannon for El Glaoui, 99, 114
Ksar-el-Kebir: Spanish occupation of, 150
Kutla al-Wataniya al: formation, 1970, 330; boycotts 1972 referendum, 332; in 1997 elections, 376
Kutla al-Amal al-Wattani al-: formation, 227; first conference in Rabat 1936, 245; Second conference in Casablanca 1936, 245; reorganised as political party 1937, 246

Laâyoune, 335; attacked by Polisario, 342; Polisario excluded from, 366
Labonne, Eric: appointed Resident General, 268; economic policies of, 269; relations with colons, 268, 270; sacked, 272
Lac Tislit (Isly), 216, 217
Lacoste, Francis: appointed Resident General, 286; replaced as Resident General, 288
Laghzaoui, Mohamed: director of Sûreté National, 300; director of the Office Chérifien des Phosphates, 310
Lahbabi, Mohamed: on constitutional monarchy, 297, 298
Lalla Asma, 389
Lalla Aïcha: education, 264; speech in Tangier 1947, 272; as role model for women, 272, 275; marriage, 318; ambassador, 348;
Lalla Fatima Zohra, 317-18, 348
Lalla Malika, 317-18, 348
Lalla Soukaïna, 389
land ownership: development of, 119; European ownership of in early twentieth century, 134, 148; in French

Protectorate, 171, 244; registration, 171; during First World War, 178; privatisation of collective land, 199; in Spanish zone, 200; at independence, 305; in independent Morocco, 327, 345
Lane, Edward, 23
Language policy, 304
Larache: Austrian naval attack on (1829), 24, 39; Spain threat to occupy 1881, 87; Spanish occupation of, 150
Latif prayer, 213
Laurent, Eric, 324
law: international and Morocco in pre-colonial period, 38; use of international law against protectorate, 214-15 use of international law by independent Morocco at International court, 339; Moroccan views of European law in pre-colonial period, 50; Moroccan views of law in independent period, 361, 366; Sir John Drummond-Hay on Moroccan law, 87; in proposed 1910 constitution, 144; customary, 164, 166, 173, 176; conflict between customary law and *shari'a* used to deprive Moroccans of land, 200; French theories about customary law, 159, 160; in Tangier, 197; consular courts, abolition of, 173; civil and commercial, administration under French protectorate, 173, 213; criminal, administration under French protectorate, 176, 212; as subject of study for Moroccans, 205, 233, 251, 337, 363; labour laws under protectorate, 225; laws on landownership under protectorate, 244; Ben Barka uses 'the laws of the underground struggle' to justify assassination, 304; in Moroccan constitution, 381; elite domination of legal system, 390 see also *shari'a*
laws: *dahir* (1861) on administration, 78; *dahir* (1864) ending corporal punishment for Jews, 84; *dahir* on Berber law (1914), 164; *dahir* on land ownership (1913), 171; *dahir* on organisation of justice (1913), 173; *dahir* laying down building regulations (1914), 172; *dahir* setting up *jemaas* (1916), 176; *dahir* on privatisation of collective land (1919), 199; *dahir* on freedom of association in Spanish zone (1936), 235; Berber Decree (1914), 164; on Moroccan membership of Trade Unions (1938), 243; on Trade Unions 1936, 243; *dahir* setting up schools for Muslim girls (1944), 266; *dahir* appointing new *qaids* (1961), 317; *see also* Berber Dahir 1930
Le Corbusier, 226
Le Pen, Jean-Marie, 370
Lebanon, independence of, 264
Lecomte, Jean, 270,
Legrand, Jean-Charles: defends Black Hand members, 286; attempted murder of, 288
Lemaigre-Debreuil, Jacques, murder of, 287
Liberal party, 248
Liberation Army (Armée de la Liberation du Maghreb Arabe): foundation and first campaigns, 289- 290; Spanish finance for, 289; relations with Istiqlal, 289; primary loyalty to Mohammed V, 289, 292, 295; propaganda, 290; break with Spain, 294; Istiqlal failure to control after independence, 292, 295; war on 'collaborators', 292; partial demobilisation and incorporation in Royal Armed Forces, 301; section becomes Army for the Liberation of the Sahara, 301
Libya: Franco-Italian agreement over, 124; Italian conquest of, 230; invasion of Chad (1980), 367; Qathafi's coup, 1969, 336; proposed Moroccan union with, 367; as member of Arab Maghrib Union, 368; Moroccan workers in, 369
Ligue Marocaine de Défense des Droits de l'Homme, 366
Lions of the Liberation, 285
Lisan al-Maghrib, 143, 144
literacy: nationalist campaign in Spanish zone (1938), 249; rate in Spanish Sahara, 1974, 335; in 1970s and 1980s, 359; in late 1990s, 378
locust plagues: 1799, 1813-15, 1820, 7; 1867-6, 75; 1885, 75; 1896, 116; 1905-6, 134; 1929-30, 211; control of, 120
Longuet, Jean, 229
Longuet, Robert, 229
López Ferrer, Luciano, 234

Loti, Pierre, 104
Lyautey, General Louis-Hubert Gonçalves: as commander at Ain Sefra 1903, 130; ideas on military conquest, 130, 146, 156, 158, 168; British and Dutch models for ideas, 159; on Berbers, 160; occupation of Oujda, 1907, 135; arrival in Fez 1912, 156; removal of M. Abdelhafid, 157; relations with M. Youssef, 160; opinion of El Mokri, 161; and big qaids, 163; military strategy, 169, 187; relations with colons, 171; and design of new cities, 172; as War minister, 175; role during First World War, 174-75; educational policy of, 177, 183; on conversion of Berbers, 183; promoted Marshall of France, 187; resignation, 191; attitude to Jews, 204
Lyazidi, Mohammed, 227, 245; and Plan de Réformes, 232; arrested 1936, 245; exiled to Sahara, 1937, 247

Ma al-Aynayn: origin of, 102; and M. Hassan, 102; and Ba Ahmad, 114; construction of Es-Semara, 114 and Moulay Abdelaziz, 114, 126; as teacher of M. Abdelhafid, 134; *see also* El Hiba
Mamura, 27
Mackenzie, Donald, 101, 105, 118
Maclean, Kaid Sir Harry Aubrey de Vere: trains army, 74; and death of M. Hassan, 117; relations with Ba Ahmad, 117; financial chicanery of, 123; kidnapping by El Raisuni, 136
Madagascar, Mohammed V in, 283, 286
Madrasat al-Muhandisin (School of Engineers)., 52
Maghreb (newspaper), 229
Mahalla: term and functions explained, 22, 79, 103-5; organisation of, 79, 104; to Sous (1882 and 1886), 104, 105; to Oujda (1876), 104; to Guelaya (1880), 91; to Banu Snassen (1875), 92; to Taroudannt (1893), 94; to Mtougga (1886), 99; to Zaër (1890), 104; to Tafilalt (1893), 104, 105, 108; to Tanger and Tetuan (1889), 104; from Marakesh to Fez (1902), 125
Mahammad, Moulay: early life and imprisonment under M. Hassan, 94; attempts to proclaim him at beginning of reign of M Abdelaziz, 111-12; imprisonment in Meknès, 114; impersonated by Abu Himara, 127-29; proclaimed by Zaër, 1908, 140; death, 140
Mahbès, 342
Mahdis, 27
Majallat al-Maghrib (newspaper): founded, 230; and Fête du Trône, 230; contents, 230; advertisements in, 238
Maks: term explained, 23; attitude of ulama towards, 23; al-Simlali's defence of, 93; Hassan I's attempt to raise and subsequent abolition, 96; condemned in *bay'a* of M. Abdelhafid, 137, imposed by M. Abdelhafid, 139; condemned by El Hiba, 157
Maroc Socialiste (newspaper), 243
Matin Le (newspaper), 389
Mantenution Marocaine, 222
Majlis al-ayan, 131, 132
Makhzan: term explained, 12; political thinking of Makhzan members in nineteenth century , 53, 59, 64, 71-2, 84, 96, 97, 106-9; difficulty of reforming in nineteenth century, 40, 52, 78; organisation under M. Abderahman, 18-20, 31, 34, 44; organisation under Mohammed IV and Hassan I, 75, 91-93; organisation under Ba Ahmad, 111-12; organisation under M Abdelaziz, 122-3; organisation under M Abdelhafid, 137, 148; organisation under French protectorate, 151-2, 160, 161-2; *see also bilad al-makhzan*
Makina, Fez (arms factory), 73, 74
Mammeri, Azouaou, 173
Mammeri, Si Mohammed, 161
Mamora, 63
Manar al- (journal), 141, 194
Manchester, 62; Moroccan community in, 91
Mangin, Charles, 164, 169, 174
Mangin, Emile, 148, 152
Marabouts: concept explained, 9-10; M. Slimane's dislike of, 20; Wahhabis' dislike of, 21; political influence of, 26, 32, 45, 99, 107, 126, 194 Salafis' dislike of, 142; Islamic movement's dislike of, 363
Marina, General, 180
Marrakesh: at time of M. Abderrahmane, 30; commercial activities, 26;

US airbase, 264; economy of, 4, 5, 26, 31, 73, 77, 80; European trade with, 82; education in, 17, 177; government of in nineteenth century, 18, 92-4; proclamation of Hassan I in, 96; as capital, 24, 30-1, 56, 104, 116; famine 1850, 57; name synonymous with country, 31; Jews in, 34; Ma al-Aynayn in, 102, 114; M. Abdelhafid as governor of, 112, 134; seige of 1896, 113; murder of Mauchamp, 135; support for M Abdelhafid in, 137; Thami El Glaoui as Pasha of, 151, 163, 184, 236, 278; El Hiba in, 157-8; European quarters in, 172; nationalist activity in, 186, 227, 247, 283, 285; Zionists in, 204; George Orwell on, 251; US base at, 264; Mohammed V's visit to, 267; post-independence political activity in, 308, 361, 373
Marx, Karl, 229
Misfioua, 29, 113
Matches, 117
Mathews, Felix (US Consul), 81, 82
Matin Le (newspaper), 389
Mauboussin, Victor (French Consul), 56
Mauchamp, Emile: murder of, 135
Mauriac, François 279
Mauritania: basis of Moroccan claims to, 102; Moroccan involvement in nineteenth century, 102, 126, 127; and guerrilla warfare, 342; coups of 1978 and 1979, 342; Protectorate involvement in, 163, 218; Army for Liberation of Sahara and, 301; Moroccan claims on, 302; independence of, and Morocco, 333, 334; claim to Western Sahara, 336; at International Court, 338-9; secret agreement with to divide Western Sahara, 338; splits Western Sahara with Morocco, 340; abandonment of claim, 342; membership of Arab Maghrib Union, 368
Meakin, Edward Budgett, 89, 121
Medboh, General, 331
Meissa, Muhammad Salah, 230
Meknès, 19, 114, 139; anti-Jewish riots in, 36; siege of 1901, 125; proclamation of M Zein in, 149; occupation by French, 150; European quarter in, 172; Jews in, 204; nationalist agitation in, 213, 247, 279; *bay'a* of ben Arafa in, 283; political activity in after independence, 314
Mekouar, Ahmed, 227, 247
Melilla: as Spanish garrison, 12, 38; as point of contact with Rifis, 46; piracy near, 55; war of 1860, 65; expansion of, 66; free port in, 102, 103; labour migration through, 103; war of 1893, 105, 115; guard posts at, 126; land ownership near, 119; mineral railway to, 140; Muhammd bin Abd al-Karim as *qadi* of, 146, 170, 181, 190; population density during Protectorate, 223; colonial architecture in, 226; during Spanish Civil War, 236, 248; remains Spanish after Moroccan independence, 293; as smuggling centre, 385
Mendès-France, Pierre, 286, 287
Mennebhi, Si Mehdi el; as military commander under Ba Ahmad, 112; as minister of war, 121; relations with M. Abdelaziz, 122; financial dealings of, 123; intercedes for El Raisuni, 127; defeat of Abu Himara, 129; loss of post of war minister, 129; supports proclamation of M. Abdelhafid, 139
Mernissi family, 241, 260
Mernissi, Fatima, 387; childhood, 260; education of, 275; interviews with Moroccan women, 348-9
Mesali Hadj, 227
Messaâdi, Abbès: as commander in Liberation Army, 290; murder, 304
Michaux-Bellaire, Édouard, 159
migration: in 1840s and 1850s, 62; from Rif, 103, 223, 328; rural-urban, 202, 329; during Second World War, 258; economic effects of, 328; effects of on language use, 384; from Sous, 328; in 1980s and 1990s, 369, 377; of women, 350; to Europe, 328, 369; to Libya and Saudi Arabia, 369; see also Palestine, Jews.
Military missions (European), 75
Millah, *see* Jews
MINURSO, 374
Misfioua, 29, 113
Mission Scientifique du Maroc, 159
Mitterrand, Danielle, 366
Mohamed ben Arafa: proclamation as sultan, 282; *bay'a* of, 283; as Sultan, 283-9; resistance to, 283; attempted assassination of, 284; proposed resignation 1955, 288; resignation, 289

Mohammed III (1757-90): military policy, 21; construction of Essaouira, 24; death of, 18
Mohammed IV: defeat at Isly, 49; as army commander, 52, 55; as proponent of education, 52; as proponent of reform, 52, 71, 76-80; becomes sultan, 1859, 65; personality, 72; economic policy, 23, 76-80, 95; and protection problem, 85; attitude to rebellion, 98; and big caids, 99; death of, 73
Mohammed V, Sultan and King, 316; education of, 161; accession, 208; early political actions of, 208; attitude to Berber Dahir, 213; and early nationalists, 214, 231; and Fête du Trône, 231; attitude to *Plan de Réformes*, 235; support for French during Second World War, 254, 256; attitude towards USA, 260, 309, 312, 315; calls for no resistance to Operation Torch, 260; and Roosevelt, 262; assistance to Jews during Second World War, 262; and Istiqlal manifesto, 264; seeks US and British support, 263; ideas about education, 264, 267; visit to Marrakesh, 1945, 267; at victory parade in Paris, 267; trip to Tangier, 1947, 270-3; libellous French attacks on, 274; and Juin's decrees, 274, 278; attitude to Israel, 277; Juin threatens to depose, 278; political memorandum to Guillaume 1951, 280; speech from throne 1951, 280; deposition of, 283; in Madagascar, 283; popular fantasies about, 284; and Aix-les-Bains conference, 289; leaves Madagascar, 290; return to Morocco, 291; trip to Madrid to secure independence, 293; speech from Throne 1956, 296; and constitutional monarchy, 299; as his own prime minister, 314; death, 315
Mohammed VI: education of, 372; at European Union, 372; military career, 372; UN Speech of, 375; accession of, 375; *bay'a* of, 375
Moinier, General, 149, 150, 151, 155
Mokri family, 143, 148, 320
Mokri, Ahmad El, 148
Mokri, Mohammed El: and Egyptian nationalism, 143; as minister of finance, 148; negotiations for loan of 1913, 150; appointed as wazir by M. Abdelhafid, 151; Grand Vizir in Protectorate, 161; rivalry with Thami Ababou, 161; Lyautey's views on, 161; property of, 171; suggestions about education of qaids, 183; role in accession of Mohammed V, 208; attitude to Berber Dahir, 213; and attempted deposition of Sultan, 282; role in dethroning Mohammed V, 283; proposed as chairman of regency council, 288; in Council of Throne, 290; loses last public office, 291; death and confiscation of his property, 307; palace used as torture centre, 321
Mokri, El Taïeb El, 148, 155, 161
Mokri, Mukhtar El, 148, 161
Monde Le (newspaper), 279, 302
Monnet, Georges, 229
Montefiore, Sir Moses, 84
Morocco, name of country, 31
Moudawana (family legal code); attempted modification of 1991, 388; promulgation, 349; proposals to revise 1979, 349
Moulay, title explained, 11
Moulay Idris, 128, 173
Moulouya River, 103, 166
Mouslim Barbari, pseudonym of Ouazanni, 229, 230
Moutaouakkil, Nawal Al, 387
Mouvement Populaire: founded, 303; leaders arrested, 304; legally resgistered, 308; as factor in splitting opposition, 313; in 1960 elections (local), 314; position in elite, 320; attitude to 1962 constitution, 321; in 1977 election, 347
Movement for the Liberation for Saguia el-Hamra and Oued ed-Dah, 336
Mrebbi Rebbo, 158
Mtouggi caïds: emergence of, 99; Hajj Umar, 99; Al-Hajj Misa'ud, 99;
Mtouggi, Abd al-Malik El, 100, 126, 137; joins El Hiba, 157; during First World War, 176; death, 183
Muha U Hammu, 164, 169, 175
Muhammad Ali (of Egypt), 50
Muhammad al-Arabi al-Madaghri, 107
Muhammad bin Husayn, ruler of Iligh, 90, 91
Munazzama al-Sirriyya (Secret Organisation), 285, 289, 308
Murphy, Robert, 259, 264

music: Arab, 385; classical Andalusian orchestras, 238; Punk, 386; Western, 386
Muti', Abd al-Karim, 352; death, 363

Nablus, 205, 207, 233
Naciri, Mekki: education of, 205; joins *Hizb al-Islah al-Watani* (Party of National Reform), 247-8; founds *Hizb al-Wahda* (Party of Unity), 248; British agent during Second World War, 257; draws up independence manifesto in Spanish zone, 1943, 263; and Roosevelt, 263
Nador: growth of, 240, 329; during Spanish civil war, 248; and Liberation Army, 289
Naiba see army
Napier, Admiral, 57
Nasiri, Ahmad al-: on Abd al-Qadir, 49; on Jews, 84; education of, 93; on *maks* taxes, 96; on rebels, 96-7; on relations with Europe, 106-7; on European penetration of Morocco, 108
Nasiriyya, 10, 215; relations with M. Abdelhafid, 134; resistance to French by, 169; relations with French Protectorate authorities, 215;
National Action Bloc *see Kutlat al-Amal al-Wattani*
Navarro, General Felipe, 190
Navy, Moroccan, disintegration of, 46
Nemour, Arthur and Faraj-Allah, 143
Newspapers, journals and magazines: for individual titles *see al-Alam, Al-Fajr, Le Figaro, al-Hayat, L'Humanité, Maghreb, Majallat al-Maghrib, Le Matin, Le Monde, Al-Manar, Maroc Socialiste, L'Opinion, Revue du Monde Musulman., Umm al-Banin, Urwa al-Wuthqa, La Voix Nationale, al-Widad; see also* Press
Nfiss valley, 98
Nieto, Enrique, 226
Nizam: term explained, 50; in Turkey, Egypt and Abd al-Qadir's Algeria, 50; as concept, 72; in Rif under Muhammad ibn Abd al-Karim, 194
Noguès, General Charles: as head of Affaires Indigènes, 212; attitude to Berber Dahir, 212; appointed Resident General, 242; military career, 242; relations with colons, 242; and trade union question, 242-3; economic policies, 244-5; suppression of nationalist movement, 245-6; as Vichy supporter in Second World War, 251, 261; relations with Mohammed V in Second World War, 256; refuses to cooperate with USA, 259; surrender to USA, 260; replaced, 265
North West Africa Company: relationship with Bayruk family, 101; evacuation of Tarfaya, 105
Nouasseur, military base, 276

O'Donnell, General Leopoldo, 64
Office Chérifien de Contrôle et d'Exportation, 224
Office Chérifien des Phosphates: establishment of, 198; as employer of forced labour, 202;sacks Moroccan staff in 1930s, 222; Mohamed Laghzaoui as director of, 310; *see also* phosphates
Office Nationale de Transport, 327
Office of the Arab Maghrib, 276, 289
Oil *see* energy
Omnium Nord-Africain, 385
OPEC, 327
Opération Labour *see* Operation Plough
Operation Plough, 306, 325
Operation Torch, 259, 260
Opinion l' (newspaper), 383
Ordega, Ladislas, 89
Organisation de l'Action Démocratique et Populaire, 362
Organisation Marocaine des Droits de l'Homme, 365-6
Organisation of African Unity, 333, 343
Orwell, George, 251
Oslo peace negotiations, 369
Osman, Ahmad, Prime Minister, 348
Ottoman Empire, 1, 11, 39, 40, 41; name for Morocco, 31; boundary with, 15, 42; and 'Eastern Question', 70; collapse in Algeria, 1, 11, 40-3, 59; debts, 68; *nizam* in, 940, 50, 51, 61; as exemplar in nineteenth century, 50, 144; constitution, 143-4; Committee of Union and Progress, 144; military mission to Morocco, 144
Ouali Mustapha Sayed El-, 337
Ouazzani, Mohamed Hassan: education of, 205; early political positions of, 206; arrested and flogged during Berber Dahir protests, 213; and foundation of Zawiya, 227; contributor to *Maghreb*, 229; uses pseudonym of

'Mouslim Barbari', 229; secretary to Shakib Arslan, 229-30; founds newspaper *L'Action du Peuple*, 230; and *Plan de Réformes*, 232; visit to Paris, 1936, 245; secretary of *Kutla* 1936, 245; arrested, 245; split from *Hizb al-Watani* and *forms Hizb al-Amal al-Watani*, 246; exiled to Sahara, 1937, 247; founds *Parti Démocratique de l'Indépendance*, 270; protected by Oufkir, 281; and return of Mohammed V 1956, 291; quarrel with Istiqlal, 300, 303; antipathy to Istiqlal, 303; attitude to Algerian war, 311

Oudaia see army

Oued Zem massacre, 288

Oued Beth and Nfis, 201

Ouezzane, Sharif of, Abd al-Salam bin al -Arbi: protégé of France, 90; marriage to Emily Keene, 90; and execution of Bu Azza, 97; land ownership, 90, 119

Oufkir, Mohammed: origins of, 146; service during Second World War, 267; protects PDI, 28; attitude to ben Arafa, 284; as confident of Grandval, 288; aide-de-camp to Boyer de la Tour, 289; interpreter to Mohammed V, 290; relations with Prince Hassan, 290; and return of Mohammed V to Morocco, 291; in Royal Armed Forces, 301; arrives late for hand-over of Tarfaya, 1958, 302; chief of police, 321; minister of the interior, 323; repression of 1965 riots, 323; involvement in death of Ben Barka, 330; attampts to control King Hassan, 330; during Skhirat coup, 331-2; Minister of Defence, 332; death and disgrace, 332; imprisonment of family, 365

Oujda, 42, 43, 49, 97, 139; as Moroccan border town, 11, 312; occupied by France (1844), 48; returned to Morocco, 49; *mahalla* to (1876), 104; famine in, 116; occupation of 1907, 135; riots in, (1937), 245; (1951), 279-80, 282; Spanish demand for, during Second World War, 256; attacks on Jews, 1948, 277; Treaty of Oujda (with Libya, 1984), 367

Ould Dada, Mokhtar, 336

Palestine: Jewish migration to under Mandate, 204; Arab campaigns against British Mandate, 205, 252; as education centre for Moroccan nationalists, 205; nationalist views on, 246; in Zionist propaganda, 252; Palestine Liberation Organisation, 339, 340; Palestine Authority, 379; see also Israel, Zionism

Palmerston, Lord, 56

Panther, 150

Parastatal companies, 326

Parientes family, 35

Parti Démocratique de l'Indépendance (PDI): foundation, 270; protected by Oufkir, 281; and Aix-les-Bains conference, 289; membership in Bekkaï government, 291; and Black Crescent, 292; terrorist attacks on, 300; rivalry with Istiqlal, 303; suppression of, 304; and Algerian war of independence, 311; and US bases, 312; in King Hassan's first cabinet, 321

Parti des Verts pour le Développement, 381

Parti du Progrès et du Socialisme: founded, 347; in 1977 election, 347; position on women's issues, 348; split, 362; in government 1998, 376; *see also* Communist Party

Patton, General George, 262

Penet, Paul, 178

Penon de Vélez, 47, 12, 293

Perdicaris, Ion, 184; kidnapped by el-Raisuni, 127

Peres, Shimon: visit to Morocco, 1986, 368-9, 379

Pérez de Cuéllar, Javier, 368

Pétain, Marshal Philiippe: military commander in Morocco, 191; President of France, 255

Peyrouton, Bernard-Marcel: appointed High Commissioner, 241; relations with colons, 242

phosphates, 258, 273; production, (1920s), 198; (1930s), 219, 239, 240; (Second World War), 258; (1950s), 273), 305; (1970s), 327, 346; mines at Khouribga, 242; mines at Louis Gentil (Youssoufia), 243; in Sahara, 334, 337, 366; and trade agreement with USSR, 334; *see also* Office Chérifien des Phosphates

Picciato, Moses, 84

Pinto family, 35
piracy: difficulties of controlling on Rif coast, 28; in Guelaya peninsula and suppression, 55; diplomatic consequences of, 57, 61; in Rif in 1890s, 113-14; *see also* corsairing
Pisces incident, 311
Plan de Réformes, 232, 233, 235
PLO see Palestine Liberation Organisation
police force: establishment of Sûreté Nationale, 300; under Oufkir, 321
Polisario: foundation, 337; and UN mission 1975, 338; attack on Bu Craa conveyor belt, 337; US attitude towards, 339; diplomatic support among Arab states, 340; proclaims SADR, 340; sole legitimate representative of the Saharaui people, 340, 342; relations with Algeria, 338, 343, 367, 368; relations with Libya, 367; and Saharan referendum, 374; use of Soviet military equipment, 342; cease-fire with Mauritania, 342; military successes against Moroccan army, 340 342, 366; containment behind sand barriers, 366; diplomatic activity, 367; conflict in 1980s, 366, 368; cease-fire 1991, 374; and death of King Hassan, 379;
political parties: *see* Hizb al-'Amal al-Watani, Hizb al-Islah al-Watani, Hizb al-Wahda, Hizb al-Watani l-tahqiq al-matalib, Independent (non-party) politicians, Istiqlal party, Liberal party, Organisation de l'Action Démocratique et Populaire, Parti Démocratique de l'Indépendance (PDI), Parti des Verts pour le Développement, Communist Party; Parti du Progrès et du Socialisme, Rassemblement Nationale des Indépendents,
polygamy, 275, 349, 388
Ponsot, Henri: as Resident-General, 225; and colon lobby, 225, 241; and *Plan de Réformes*, 233
population: European (nineteenth century), 80, 89, 119; French zone, 1936 census, 223; Spanish zone (1930s), 223; Casablanca (late nineteenth century), 95; (early twentieth century) 135, 179; (1970s), 329 (1980s); 351, 354; Tangier (inter-war), 196; Laâyoune, 335; other cities, 179, 222, 329; growth (nineteenth century), 95 (1920s and 1930s), 223; (1980s), 355 (1990s), 380
Port Lyautey *see* Kénitra
Post Offices: foreign, 78; foreign, in Tangier, 196; foreign, as nationalist conduit, 206
Présence Française, 281, 290
Press: European language, 120; in Spanish zone, 235; in nationalist policy, 206; in Spanish zone, 235; nationalist attitudes towards, 229, 231; liberal press in colonial Morocco, 287; liberalisation, 246; censorship in independent Morocco, 313, 366: *see also* 'newspapers'
Primo de Rivera, Gen. Miguel, 191
printing, 77
privatisation, 357, 373
Prost, Henri: aesthetic ideas of, 172; recruitment by Lyautey, 172; attitude to *bidonvilles*, 179, 223
protection and protégés: origins of propblem, 45; growth of problem in nineteenth century, 80, 83, 119; Madrid Conference on, 85-7; Jewish, 83, 86, 91; political advantages of, for Sharif of Ouezanne, 90; opinions of *ulama* regarding, 107, 137; effects of in 1890s, 119; and taxation, 123; as landowners, 134, 136; Thami El Glaoui as protégé, 151; British during protectorate period, 195, 206, 245; French attempts to abolish under Protectorate, 173
Puaux, Gabriel: appointed Resident General, 265; relations with colons, 265; proposes reform plan, 266; replaced, 268
punishment: physical torment as, 113, 140, 141; public violence, 30, 48, 141, 28; pillage, 30, 104; European attitudes towards, 119, 141, 170; El Raisuni on, 170; corporal, of Jews, 84; corporal, of Muslims, 232, 287; during Protectorate period, 197, 214, 266, 286, 287; during Rif War, 193; flogging of nationalists in Rif in 1950s, 271; nationalist views of, 232; torture and mistreatment of prisoners in independent Morocco, 321, 323, 347, 373; campaigns against, 366

Qabila see tribe
Qathafi, Col Muammar: attitude to Morocco, 336; blamed for Skhirat coup, 332; relations with, 367, 368; support for Mauritania, 336
qadi : title explained, 17; functions of under French protectorate, 163
Qadiriyya, 43
Qaids: in pre-colonial Morocco, 27, 32, 55, 100, 103, 149; big qaids, 98-100, 110-11, 114-15, 126-7, 137, 157-8, 163-4, 166, 171, 175-6, 181, 183-4; as French agents, 161, 162, 176, 182, 183, 198, 202, 209, 210, 215, 282, 287, 296; in Spanish protectorate, 226, 236; in Rif during Rif War, 190, 191; in independent Morocco, 301, 307, 317, 319
Qarawiyyin, 127, 143, 146, 164; as educational centre in pre-colonial North Africa, 11, 17; as centre of support for M Abdelhafid, 137; Muhammad bin Abd al-Karim and, 142; organisation etc under French protectorate, 177, 185; as educational origin of nationalists, 186, 227, 265; political controversy in, 207, 215, 228, 231, 244; attempt to modernise, 185
Qsars, 7
Quiepo de Llano, General, 248

R'honi, Ahmed, 185
Rabat: irrigation at, 5; Jews in, 34, 36, 203, 251; bombarded by French fleet 1851, 57; commerce industry and trade in, 58, 62, 94, 116; growth of, 62, 223, 329; fortifications of, 21, 74; administration of in nineteenth century, 78; as capital, 104, 157, 160, 172; occupied by French troops, 150; European town and architecture in, 172, 179, 226; education in, 177; population, (1912), 179; (1930s), 223; (1960s), 329; nationalist and labour activity in, 186, 203, 206, 227, 238, 245, 266, 274, 280; bishop of, 208; reactionary pasha of, 233; epidemics in Second World War, 259; political activity in after independence, 308, 314; smart housing for the elite, 329, 381; Arab summit, 1974, 340; funeral of Hassan II, 379;
Rabin, Yitzhak, 345
Rachid, Moulay, (1664-72), 12
Rahu, Sidi, 155, 15, 157
rainfall: general patterns, 4; poor rains: (1820s), 24; (1902-03), 123; (1930s), 222; (1940s), 268; (1950s), 304; (1970s), 346); effects on GDP, 325 *see also* climate
railways: Hassan I's refusal to permit, 77; trans- Saharan railway as motive for occupying Touat, 124; and armed revolt in Casablanca, 135; and armed resistance in Guelaya, 145; expansion in First World War, 179; French companies and, 198; as employer of labour, 202; as focus of labour militancy, 203, 227, 243, 347; extent of French legacy, 305; Polisario attacks on Mauitanian iron railway, 334
Raisuni, Moulay Ahmad El: origins of, 127; imprisoned by M. Hassan, 127; helped by el-Mennebhi, 127; kidnaps Ion Perdicaris, 127; Pasha of Tangier, 127; kidnapping of Maclean, 136; as British protégé, 136; proclaims M Abdelhafid, 139; as Pasha of Asilah, 139; opinion of M. Abdelhafid, 139; relations with Spanish 1913, 170; argument with Silvestre over prison conditions, 170; 'sultan of the jihad', 171; and Germany in First World War, 181; and Spain in First World War, 181; and Turkey in First World War, 181; attacked by Spanish 1919, 188; defeat by Spanish 1922, 191; dictates biography to Rosita Forbes, 191; captured by Rifis, 191; attitude during Rif War, 194; death, 191
Raisuni, Khalid El: forms Liberal Party, 248; property confiscated, 307
Rassemblement Nationale des Indépendents, 348
Razini family, 93
Razini, Hajj Muhammad al-, 60
Reagan, President Ronald, 368
referendums: 1962 constitution, 322; 1970 constitution, 330; 1972 constitution, 332; 1980 constitution, 354; 1996 constitution, 379; proposed concerning Sahara dispute, 338, 368 374, 379
Regnault, Eugène, 199
Regnault, Henri, 152
Reguibat, 188
Regulares regiments, 236

Rehamna: rebellion 1893, 112; rebellion 1907, 136
Revue du Monde Musulman. (journal), 159
Rharb plain; in 1830s, 3, 4, 6; Wazaniyya tariqa estates in, 10; Glaoui estates in, 119; local jihad in, 168; estates owned by colonisation companies, 199; irrigation in, 201; politics in, 215; colonisation in, 272; floods in (1963), 325
Rida, Rashid, 141, 194
Rif: agriculture and climate, 4-5; emigration, 62, 223, 328, 350; environmental degradation, 63, 380-1; relations with pre-colonial Makhzan, 27, 28, 29; trading links of, 45; gun trade in, 103; control of, 47; *ripublik* or *réfoubliqué* period, 126; during First World War, 181; Rif War, 188, 190, 195; Spanish colonial policy in, 226, 236, and troops for Spanish civil war, 249-50; in Second World War, 268; suppression of nationalism in Rif, 271; miraculous accounts of Moroccan independence, 293; rebellion 1958, 304; smuggling, 382; computer system for Rifi Berber, 384; *see also* piracy
Rimayya, 134
Rio de Oro *see* Saquïa al-Hamra
Rissani, 217
Roches, Léon, 56, 57
Roosevelt Club, 272, 291, 300, 312; establishment and membership, 263;
Roosevelt, President Franklin; and Moroccan nationalist movement, 263; at Casablanca Conference, 262, 263; relations with Mohammed V, 262
Roosevelt, President Theodore: threat to declare war on Morocco, 127
Route de l'Unité, 303
Royal Armed Forces see army
Royal Navy (British) hydrographic survey of Moroccan coast, 25, 39
Rumat: term explained, 23; as rebels, 23, 96

Saadi dynasty: origins, 6, 11; collapse, 12
Sadat, President Anwar, 345
Saharan Arab Democratic Republic *see* Polisario
Saffar, Muhammad al-: embassy to France, 49, 50; views of French legal system, 53; attitude to commerce, 59; negotiations for 1856 treaty, 59, 63; as wazir, 59; on environment, 62; on Christianity, 64
Safi, 133
Sahara: conquest by Ahmad al-Mansur, 11; trans-Saharan trade, 44, 88; Makhzan presence in nineteenth century, 100,114, 115, 102; Moroccan claims to coast of, 1895, 118, 124; Ma al-Aynayn and Moroccan claims to, 126
Spanish claim to in nineteenth century, 88, 124, 125, 187; French occupation, 115, 124; Spanish claims in Second World War, 256; *see also* Polisario, Touat, Spanish Sahara, Western Sahara
Saint, Lucien, 212
Saint-René-Taillandier, Georges: embassy to Morocco 1905, 130; meeting with M. Abdelaziz, 131
Salafiyya: origins of in Morocco, 141,143; attacks on by conservative Abd al-Hayy al-Kittani, 164, 207; and Free School movement, 186, 233, 295; during Rif War, 194, 195
Salé: military forces of in 1829/30, 22; industry and trade and commerce, 32, 62, 94, 95, 202, 222; growth of in nineteenth century, 62; Jews in, 91, 207; as city of culture, 93; bombardment (1851), 57; attacked by neighbouring tribes 1867, 97; government of under Protectorate, 162; nationalist activity in, 168, 186, 206, 207, 212, 213, 227, 231, 245, 266, 290; political activity after independence, 371
Salisbury, Lord, 87
Sanhaji, Abdallah: and loyalty to Mohammed V, 301; in Liberation Army, 290
Santa Cruz de Mar Pequeña see Ifni
Sanusi, Abdallah bin Idris al-, 142
Saquïa al-Hamra *see* Spanish Sahara
Satow, Sir Ernest, 118
Saudi Arabia, Saudis: Moroccan migration to, 369; Moroccan opinions concerning, 369, 370, 371; as tourists, 358; relations with, 342, 342, 367, 370
Sbihi, Batoul, 289
Schneider Company, 123, 130, 133
Schumann, Robert, 279
Scout movement: establishment and

connection with royal family, 228; Ben Barka and, 270, 275; in Spanish zone, 235
Sebti family, 258
secret organisation, *see Munazzama al-sirriyya*
Secteurs de Modernisation du Paysannat, 269, 270
Sefrou, 149
Segangane, 329
Selouane: 102, 103, 105; as base of Abu Himara, 129; fort at, 102
Serfaty, Abraham: at Office Chérifien des Phosphates, 310; arrest and torture, 347
Serrano Suñer, Ramón, 256
Shabiba al-Islamiyya al-, 352, 353, 363
Shadhili, Abu al-Hasan al-, 11
Shah of Iran: stay in Morocco 1979, 354; opinion of Hassan II regarding, 362
Shari'a: concept explained, 14; and leadership of state, 15, 16; and taxation, 22; and trade, 23; and rural tribes, 29; and Jews, 36; and coinage, 80; as political rallying cry, 142, 143, 144, 157, 193, 214, 215; El Raisuni on shari'a and punishment, 170; Europeans not to be exposed to, 173; during Rif war, 193; and irrigation, 200; and Moudawana family code, 349; and women, 388
Sharifs: concept explained, 11
Sharqawiyya, 10
Sheean, Vincent, 192
Shinqiti al-, 169
Sidi al-Makki, 216-17
Sidi Ifni, 302
Sidi Kacem, 240
Sidi Slimane, 276
Sijilmasa, 6
Simlali, Ali bin Muhammad al-: education and career, 93; defence of *maks* taxes, 93; on jihad, 107; opinions of Europe, 106, 107
Simsars: term explained, 81
slaves: in army, 21, 34; status of in nineteenth century, 32-4; trade, 26, 88, 120; see also *abid al-bukhari,* Anti-Slavery Society
Slawi, Muhammad bin 'Abd al-Salam al, 38
Slimane, Moulay: attitude to Europe, 14, 23; education, 17; attitude to Wahhabis, 21; attitude to *tariqas*, 20; rebellions against, 18, 19; Makhzan of, 20; army of, 21, 22; attitude to *maks*, 23; attitude to *amma*, 32; attitude to Jews, 36
smuggling: Melilla, 103, 382; in nineteenth century, 46, 47, 85, 90 102, 103
Sobeïhi, Hajj el-Taïeb al-, 162
Sociedad Española de Minas del Rif, 133
Sociétés Indigènes de Prévoyance, 201, 244
Solal family, 35
Souk El Arbaâ, 240
Sous and Sousis: river, 6; and Saadis, 11; revolts, 47, 100, 157-8; Jews, 91; commercial activities, 26; relationship with Makhzan, 55,100, 101, 103; *mahalla* to, 104-5; famine (1899), 116; (1929), 211; plague (1940), 259; employment in cities, 135, 238; migration from, 328; German interests, 151, 181
Soviet Union *see* USSR
Spanish Sahara: Spanish Sahara colony, 334, 339; remains Spanish after Moroccan independence, 294; economy of, 334, 335; nationalism in, 336, 339; political structures in, 335; social development of, 335; Spanish rule ends, 339, 340; United Nations and decolonisation of, 335, 336; Green March, 334; *see also* Sahara, Polisario, Western Sahara
Special Operations Executive, 257
sport: 236-8, 386, 387; golf, 236, 282, 344, 378, 386-87, 389; and nationalism, 275, 279; athletics, 387; boxing, 237; football, 237-8, 252, 275, 279, 386-7, 390; for girls and women, 237, 387; golf, 386; hunting, 3, 5, 25, 61, 63, 120, 126, 136, 236, 386; Olympics, 387, 390; swimming, 237
Sraghna, 30
St-Réné Taillandier, 200
Steeg, Théodore: appointed Resident-General, 199; water policy of, 200; financial policy, 200; attitude to Zionism, 204; relations with Moulay Youssef, 207; unaware of sultan's illness, 208; report on 1937 famine, 239; relations with colons, 241
Sufi, Sufism: concept explained, 9; historical origins in Morocco, 11,127;

attitude of M. Abderrahman towards, 13; Ma al-Aynayn and sufism, 102; ambivalent Salafi attitudes towards, 142, 215; attitude of M. Abdelhafid towards, 143; attitude of Islamists towards, 363; revival in 1980s, 364; *see also tariqas*
Sumbel family, 36
Sûreté Nationale, see police

Tafilalt: early history, 6; origin of Alaoui family, 12; rebellion 1841, 47-8; M. al-Rashid as khalifa, 92, 100, 115; M. Abdelaziz's trip to 1893, 92; Hassan I's *mahalla* to 1893, 99, 104, 105, 10; opposition to Europeans in, 107, 126, 146; occupied by French, 217; undefined frontier at, 218; French agricultural schemes in, 244; exile of Mohammed bel-Arabi to, 266; rebellion 1957, 304
Taifa (nationalist organisation), 227
Tamgrout, 10
Tangier: nationalist activities in, 143, 213, 227, 231, 233, 293; Jews in, 35, 167, 203; in pre-colonial period: administration of, 19, 24, 35, 48, 53, 61,120, 148; as diplomatic centre, 45, 53, 55, 59, 60, 65, 93; British determination to prevent European colonisation of, 65; rapid change of French consuls in, 61; bombarded by French fleet 1844, 49; public order, 54; trade commerce and economy, 58, 62; environmental problems, 62; famine and epidemic 1878, 75; US naval visit to (1848), 58; port works, 77; Spanish threat to occupy (1881), 8; as tourist centre, 120; golf course in, 236; trade of, 197; visit of Kaiser Wilhelm II to (1905), 132; European community in, 118, 120 134; European consuls control health committee, 120; Tangier Tent Club, 120; M. Abdelaziz retires to, 139; proclamation of M Abdelhafid in, 139; M. Abdelhafid retires to, 157; Tangier International Zone: first proposals, 167-68; during First World War, 174, 181; Glaoui property holdings in, 184; economy of, 197, 219; Statute of Tangier, 1924, 195; administration of, 195-97; Belgian role in, 196; Mussolini and, 196; Spanish occupation of, 256, 257; spies in, during Second World War, 257-58; international relief for famine, 1945, 268; Mohammed V's trip to (1947), 270-272; M. Ben Arafa retires to, 289; International Zone abolished, 293; political activities in independent Morocco, 352, 361
Tarfaya: occupied by North West Africa Company, 101, 105; Spanish claim to, 125; included in Spanish protectorate zone, 166; borders of, 187, 218, 311; Spanish refusal to return after Moroccan independence, 294; Liberation Army attacks on, 301; returned to Morocco, 302
Tariqas: term explained, 9-10, attitude of M. Slimane towards, 20; relations with pre-colonial Makhzan, 37; and deposition on Mohammed V, 281; attitude towards French, 164, 169, 209, 215, 281; Muhammad bin Abd al-Karim's attitude to, 194; Salafi opinions of, 194, 215, 247; *see also* Aisawiyya, Darqawiyya, Hadawiyya, Hamadsha, Kitaniyya, Nasiriyya Qadiriyya, Rimayya, Sharqawiyya, Tijaniyya, Wazzaniyya
Taroudannt, 6, 20, 94, 125
Tartib, 146; term explained, 123; opposition to from *ulama*, 136; imposition of, 150; under protectorate, 178, 198, 201
taxation: and definition of Makhzan, 12; exemption of tribes in exchange for military service, 22; legal taxes under *shari'a*, 22; on exports, 43, 132; taxing of remote areas in pre-colonial period, 47, 55; tax farming, 58; and currency question, 80; and protégés, 83, 85, 86; and makhzan sovereignty, 100, 105, 107, 114; collapse of tax system under M. Abdelaziz, 123-4, 125; tax system under protectorates, 178, 182, 197, 198, 212, 244; in nationalist thinking, 232, 263; in independent Morocco, 346, 357; *see also tartib, jizya, maks*
Taza: trade, 102; capture by Abu Himara, 128-9; French occupation of, 169; European quarter of, 172; Tache de Taza, 187; nationalist agitation in, 245

Tazeroualt: agriculture, 6, 10; zawiya at Iligh, 10, 26
Tazi family: rise of, 129; El Hadj Omar Tazi,, 162; Muhammad al-Tazi, 93; Si Abdessalam el-Tazi, 112
Tazmamart, 365-66
Tazrut, 127, 170, 188
tea: imports of, 76, 89, 102, 116; as irreligious drink, 106; price of 267
Tekna, 7
telegraph, Hassan I's refusal to permit, 77
Telouèt, 99, 114, 126, 151, 184
terrorism and terrorist groups, 284, 288 *see also* Black Crescent, Black Hand, Lions of the Liberation, Secret Organisation
Testa, Charles, 89
Tetuan: pre-colonial elite of, 20, 31, 93, 94; trade, industry and economy, 45, 58; public order in, 54; occupation by Spanish troops, 1860, 65-6, 68, 69; Jews in, 83-4; *mahalla* to, 1889, 104; proclamation of M. Yussef in, 160; as capital of Spanish protectorate, 166; government in, during Spanish protectorate, 167, 205; Spanish occupation of, 169; modernisation of, 185; nationalist activities in, 185, 186, 206, 227, 233-5, 247, 249, 257, 271, 285, 287, 289, 290, 292, 293; and Mohammed V's visit to Tangier, 272; political activity in independent Morocco, 361
Thaâlibi, Abdelaziz, 206
Tifinagh, 384
Tijaniyya, 10, 215
Timbuktu, 11, 44, 45
Tindouf, 188, 218; attacks on French positions by Army for Liberation of Sahara, 302; Moroccan army occupies, 333; Polisario camps at, 343
Tinmel, 99
Tirailleurs Sénégalais, 135, 243, 247 266, 270
Tiznit, 105
Tlemcen, 11; bay'a to M. Abderrahmane, 42; evacuation of, 43; Fasi interests in, 42; occupation of, 42
Toledano family, 35
Torrès, Abdelkhalek: early activities of, 233, 235, 236; forms *Hizb al-Islah al-Watani*, 247-8; relations with Mekki Naciri, 248-9, 257; and Spanish civil war, 248, 249; views on democracy, 249; and Spanish occupation of Tangier, 257; visit to Berlin 1941, 257; becomes pro-American, 263; Madrid trip 1945, 271; relations with Spanish in final stages of protectorate, 285; minister of justice, 285, 292; breaks with Spanish, 292; meeting with Allal El Fassi, 293; in 1963 elections, 322
Torres, Hajj Ahmad, 167
torture *see* punishment
Touat, 100, 124, 188
tourism, 121, 345; development of, 120, 358; environmental effects of, 381; receipts from, 358
Toussaint, Réné, 280
trade: opinion of ulama regarding, 105; trans-Saharan, 19, 26, 33, 44, 88, 101, 105; at time of M. Slimane and M. Abderrahmane, 23-24, 43; British ideology of trade, 24-5, 56, 58-9, 75, 77, 88-9, 93, 110, 125; French on benefits of free trade, 69-70, 125, 134; Moroccan ideology and trade, 24-5, 43-4, 53, 58, 60, 62, 105-6; European trade treaties in 1820s, 24; trade and rebellion, 26, 45; trade in 1840s, 57; trade in 1850s, 62
trade balance and major trading partners, 1870s and 1880s, 76; in 1880s and 1890s, 88, 89; under Ba Ahmad, 116; under M. Abdelaziz, 133; under M. Abdelhafid, 147; in 1920s, 197, 198; in 1930s, 219, 245; in 1960s, 326; in 1980s, 357, 358; free trade in 1990s, 377
trade unions: European membership of, 203; attitude to Moroccan workers, 225; in France, 227; in Spanish zone, 235; involvement of Moroccans in, 203, 242; Moroccans forbidden to join, 243, 244; Istiqlal and, 270 growth of, 275; Union des Syndicats du Maroc, 270; French suppresssion of, 280; Moroccanisation of, 287; Trade unions in independent Morocco, 303, 308, 347, 354; *see also* Conféderation Générale du Travail; Union Marocain du Travail
treaties: Belgium (1862), 69; Britain (1824), 24; (1856), 59-61, 66, 75, 245; (1938), 245; France (1825), 24; (1863), 69; Libya (Oujda 1984), 367;

Portugal (1823), 24; Sardinia (1825), 24; Spain (1799), 28, 29; (1861), 81; (Tangier, 1844), 49; (Ouad Ras, 1860), 66, 67, 105, 18; (Madrid, 1861), 69, 81; United States (1786), 14; Spartel Convention 1869, 79; Fez, 1912 (Protectorate treaty) 152, 154, 158, 167, 173, 214, 231, 232, 252, 279, 280, 294, 298; Madrid (Spanish protectorate treaty) 1912, 166; Statute of Tangier 1924 (international zone), 195; Treaty of Oujda (with Libya, 1984), 367; Franco Spanish Convention on delimitation of possessions in East Africa, June 1900, 124; France-Spain, 1902, 124; Mauritania Polisario treaty (April 1979) 342;

tribes: tribal structures, 7- 8; and allegiance to Makhzan, 15, 18, 27, 97, 104, 131, 136, 146; in early constitutional thinking, 144; as basis of personal political power, 26, 99; inter-tribal rivalry, 27, 115; relations with cities, 32; abandonment of tribes by women, 34; Makhzan servants' contemptuous references to tribes, 49, 107-8; as basis of French rural administration, 176, 182, 183; as basis of Muhammad bin Abd al-Karim's administration, 190, 193; tribal structures and migration, 224; *see also* army (jaysh), Berber

Tuhami, Hassan al-, 345

Tujjar al-sultan, term explained, 24

Tunisia: debts, 68; occupation by France, 70, 87; Destour Party, 206; Néo-Destour party, 307; Moroccan troops in duing Second World War, 255; independence of, 287

Turkey, 239; see also Ottoman Empire

Times of Morocco, 89

Times, The (London), 122, 127, 196

Torture *see* punishment

Ubbi al-, 42

Ulama: role, training and organisation of, 16-18; and proclamation of new sultans, 18, 96, 137-8, 141, 149, 160; relations with Makhzan, 20; views about reformist Islam and modernisation, 21, 142, 233, 244, 264; and political opposition, 23; and resistance to French in Algeria, 42, 48; as providers of *fatwas*, 42, 62, 72, 95, 106, 130; attitude towards military reform, 72; attitude towards taxation, 23, 95, 124,; social attitudes, 91; attitude of ulama towards foreigners, 103, 130, 131, 136; relations with French under protectorate, 156

Umar al-Mukhtar, 230

Umm al-Banin (journal), 206

Umm Kalthoum, 237, 385

unemployment: in 1930s, 223; in Second World War, 269; in 1970s, 328, 331, 335; in 1980s, 359, 361; in late 1990s, 378

Union Consitutionelle: formation 1983, 362; website, 385

Union des Femmes Marocaines, 348

Union des Mines Marocaines, 133

Union Marocain du Travail, 287, 308, 311

Union Nationale des Forces Populaires (UNFP): established, 308, 309; relationship with Mohammed V, 313; in 1960 elections (local), 314; attitude to 1962 constitution, 321-2; in 1963 elections, 322-3; repression of UNFP after 1963 elections, 323; boycott of constitutional referendum 1970, 330; repression of UNFP in 1970s, 333; attitude to Mauritanian question, 334; split 1974, 347 *see also* Union Socialiste des Forces Populaires

Union Socialiste des Forces Populaires (USFP): formation, 347; and street-protests, 1978, 348; on women's issues, 348, 387; amnesty for USFP political prisoners, 354; in 1984 elections, 362; members arrested 1981, 365; in 1992 election, 373; in government 1998, 376; website, 385 *see also* Union Nationale des Forces Populaires

United Nations: and Spain, 285; Moroccan membership of, 310; and dispute over Mauritania, 334; Moroccan complaint about Spanish Sahara 1965, 335; and Sahara dispute, 338, 343, 368; mission to Spanish Sahara 1974, 338-39; attempts to organise a referendum, 368, 374, 379; UN brokered cease-fire in Sahara 1991, 374

United States: first foreign treaty with Morocco, 14; trade relations with Makhzan, 58; and legal system in nineteenth century, 63-4; American Civil War, effects of, 62, 75; arms supplies, 73; corrupt consul, 81; Spanish American war (1898) and Morocco, 118; and protégés, 119, 173, 195; tourism, 120; US threat to declare war on Morocco over Perdicaris affair, 127; and internationalisation of Tangier, 167; as model for Moroccan irrigation policy, 224; and popular culture in Morocco, 237-38, 260-1, 369; 'free' trade with, 245; espionage activities in Morocco during Second World War, 257, 259; policy in Morocco during Second World War, 259-60, 262,264, 268; Moroccan attitudes towards, 260, 264; military bases, 264, 276, 304, 307, 312, 314, 315; emergency aid, 1945, 268; Mohammed V's views of USA, 272, 309, 312, 315; US government's attitude to Moroccan independence, 276; and Arab-Israeli question, 295, 296, 309, 311, 343, 344, 345; and Agadir earthquake, 314; aid package (1967), 329; attitude to Green March, 339; military aid from, 343, 368; antipathetic public opinion towards, 353, 385; Moroccan public opinion of US during Gulf War, 371

Urwa al-Wuthqa (journal), 141

ushur, term explained, 22

USSR (Soviet Union): Moroccan left and, 276, 296; aid from, 315, 344; collapse of, 372; military supplies, 315, 342; Moroccan relations with, 312, 313, 343, 391

Varela Iglesias, General José Enrique: as Spanish High Commissioner, 271

Vietnam, 130, 278, 286, 289

Villa Cisneros: occupied by Spain 1884, 87, 102, 335; see also Dakhla

Villa Sanjurjo: construction of, 226; name changes to Al Hoceima, 293; *see also* Al Hoceima

Vizir *see* wazir

Voix Nationale La (newspaper), 263

wages and salaries:, 78, 123; under French, 156; for migrant labourers, 202; decline of in late nineteenth century, 95; in 1930s, 222, 223, 225, 227, 240, 241, 242, 243; in 1920s, 202; in 1940s, 273; in 1960s and 1970s, 330, 351; in 1980s, 354, 357, 371; of women, 240, 273, 349

Wahhabis, 21

Walata, 102

water *see* irrigation

Wazzaniyya tariqa, 10, 90, 215

Wazir: role of, 19, 26; appointment of, 24; role of *wazir al-azam*, Grand Vizir, 79, 161, 208, 213; foreign minister, *wazir al-bahar*, 38, 79; *wazir al-harb* (war minister), 79; *wazir al-shikayat*, term explained, 79; in Hassan I's makhzan, 108; in M. Abdelhafid's makhzan, 137; post changed to 'minister of justice', 162

Weather see climate

Weisgerber, Félix, 112, 121, 125, 151

Western Sahara: division with Mauritania proposed, 338; occupied by Morocco and Mauritania, 340; entirely claimed by Morocco, 342; *see also* Sahara, Spanish Sahara, Polisario

Weygand, General Maxime, 255

Widad al- (newspaper), 206

Wifaq group, 309

Wilhelm II, Emperor German, 132

women: slaves in nineteenth century Morocco, 33, 34; relations with men in nineteenth century Morocco, 34; Moroccan views of European women, 38, 59, 350; agricultural labour of 103; employment of, 95, 202, 203, 222, 240, 349, 360, 361, 364, 387; education of, 206, 230, 246, 264, 274, 291, 292, 305, 364, 381; Qasim Amin's ideas about, 206; nationalist ideas about, 230, 246, 277, 296, 348; conservative male ideas about, 233, 261, 348-50; during Rif War, 193, 194; during Second World War, 260, 261; clothing of, 364, 388; conservative male views of, 388; legal and constitutional rights of, 318, 348, 349; in nationalist movement, 266, 275, 277, 286, 289, 290, 296; in politics of independent Morocco, 320, 348, 349, 362, 371, 387, 388; and Islamic movement, 364, 388; and migration, 350; aspirations of, 350, 351; marriage ages, 356; sexual harassment and violence, 281, 365, 370; sport, 237; campaigns for women's rights, 360, 388; divorce, 202, 349,

356; views of Lalla Aïcha, 272
wool, 43, 44, 45, 59, 62, 70, 75, 76, 88, 94, 95, 116, 259
World Bank, 325
World Cup, 386
World Jewish Council, 310
First World War, 174-82
Second World War, 254-68

Yacoubi, Rachida, 356-70
Yasin, Abd al-Salam, 353, 365; imprisoned, 363; and *al-Adl wal-Ihsan,* 363
Yasin, Nadia, 363, 378, 383, 388
Yata, Ali: Secretary General of Communist party, 270; trip to Moscow (1974), 344;
Yazid, Moulay, 18
Yemaa (in Spanish Sahara), 335, 338, 340
Youssef, Moulay: *Khalifa* in Fez, 157; proclamation of, 157, 158 160; personality of, 160, 161; attitude during First World War, 174; Muhammad bin Abd al-Karim and, 193; relations with Steeg, 207; death, 208
Youssoufi, Abderrahmane:signs Istiqlal manifesto, 265; imprisoned 1964, 323; voluntary exile 1993, 373; return from exile, 376; as Prime Minister, 376
Youssoufia (formerly Louis-Gentil), 240
Yusi, Hasan al-, 16
Yusufiyya (mosque in Marrakesh), 177

Zaër, 27, 47, 54, 104, 140
Zaghlul, Sa'ad, 206
Zagora, 216
Zaïane, 137, 169, 187
Zaio, 319
Zakkat, 22
Zamzami, al-Faqih, 352, 363
Zawiyas: function of, 10; authority in, 11; Makhzan subsidies to, 102, 114; Makhzan suppression of, 30, 140; as sanctuaries, 10, 34, 122-3; economic role of, 10, 119; opposition of Wahhabis to, 21; political role of, 12, 21, 26, 30, 31, 281
Zawiya (nationalist group in 1930s), 227, 228, 232, 234
Zemmour, 19
Zionism and Zionists: activity in Morocco in 1920s, 203-4; and Alliance Israélite Universelle, 204; in late 1930s, 252; in 1940s, 277; 'international Zionism' and Islamist propaganda, 353; see also Palestine, Jews, Israel
Zouerate iron mines, 302